# An Introduction to Persons with Moderate and Severe Disabilities

## Educational and Social Issues

### SECOND EDITION

**John J. McDonnell**

*University of Utah*

**Michael L. Hardman**

*University of Utah*

**Andrea P. McDonnell**

*University of Utah*

Boston   New York   San Francisco
Mexico City   Montreal   Toronto   London   Madrid   Munich   Paris
Hong Kong   Singapore   Tokyo   Cape Town   Sydney

**Executive Editor:**  *Virginia Lanigan*
**Editorial Assistant:**  *Robert Champagne*
**Marketing Manager:**  *Amy Cronin*
**Editorial-Production Service:**  *Omegatype Typography, Inc.*
**Manufacturing Buyer:**  *JoAnne Sweeney*
**Cover Administrator:**  *Kristina Mose-Libon*
**Electronic Composition:**  *Omegatype Typography, Inc.*

For related titles and support materials, visit our online catalog at www.ablongman.com

Between the time Website information is gathered and published, some sites may have closed. Also, the transcription of URLs can result in typographical errors. The publisher would appreciate notification where these occur so that they may be corrected in subsequent editions.

**Library of Congress Cataloging-in-Publication Data**

McDonnell, John J. (John Joseph)
    An introduction to persons with moderate and severe disabilities: educational and
social issues.–2nd ed. / John J. McDonnell, Michael L. Hardman, Andrea P. McDonnell.
      p.  cm.
    Rev. ed. of: An introduction to persons with severe disabilities / John J. McDonnell…
[et al.]. c 1995.
    Includes bibliographical references and indexes.
    ISBN 0-205-33569-1 (alk. paper)
    1. Handicapped–Services for–United States.   2. Handicapped–Education–United
States.   I. Hardman, Michael L.   II. McDonnell, Andrea P.   III. Introduction to persons
with severe disabilities.   IV. Title.

HV1553 .I59 2003
362.4'048'0973–dc21                                   2002025350

Printed in the United States of America

10  9  8  7  6     12  11  10  09  08

Credits: Page 1, © Ellen Senisi/The Image Works; 23, © Richard Hutchings/PhotoEdit; 40, © Elizabeth Crews/ The Image Works; 71, © Jonathon Nourok/PhotoEdit; 94, © Michael Newman/PhotoEdit; 138, © Amy Etra/ PhotoEdit; 160, © Elizabeth Crews; 185, © Richard Hutchings/PhotoEdit; 226, © Jeff Greenberg/The Image Works; 272, © Paul Conklin/PhotoEdit, 307, © Paul Conklin/PhotoEdit; 331, © Bob Daemmrich/The Image Works; 351, © Jack Kurtz/The Image Works.

# Contents

**9**    *Programs for Preschool Children*    **226**

## 12    *Employment and Residential Programs for Adults     331*

## 13    *Programs for Older Adults     351*

# *Preface*

Society's perceptions of people with moderate and severe disabilities have changed dramatically in the last three decades. Historically, "difference" or "deviance" was something to be shunned. People's differences were often used as a rationale for denying them their basic civil rights and segregating them from the "mainstream" of society (Minnow, 1990). Many groups have suffered as a result of this oppressive social policy, including ethnic minorities, women, and people with disabilities. Although such discrimination continues to occur in many communities, public policy regarding people who are "different" has gone through a subtle but important transformation (Minnow, 1990). At least at the institutional level, we have come to realize that one thing that human beings have in common is that we are all different from one another. Equally important, the extent to which someone is different from you depends on your perspective. If you are seven feet tall, nearly everyone is shorter than you; if you are five feet tall, then only some people are shorter than you. Furthermore, whether these differences are important depends entirely on the context. For example, being seven feet tall is an advantage if you want to play basketball for a living; it is a disadvantage if you own a compact car.

Our society's increasing openness to differences between people has created the conditions necessary to improve the quality of life of people with moderate and severe disabilities. Less than thirty years ago these individuals were routinely placed in large institutions. Today, most attend public schools, work in local businesses, and live in the community. Society's changing attitudes have occurred simultaneously with dramatic improvements in the effectiveness of educational and community service programs. Our understanding of how to support people in school, home, and community settings has grown at a rapid pace. The research literature is replete with demonstrations showing that they can learn activities and skills that would have been dismissed as impossible just ten years ago. Advances in our technology and instructional procedures have revolutionized the way that advocates, researchers, and policy makers think about service programs for this group of people.

However, in spite of these advancements, people with moderate and severe disabilities still face significant challenges in becoming part of our communities. This book is designed as an introduction to some of the crucial educational and social issues that still confront them on their path to full community membership. It is written using a life-span approach so that professionals can develop an understanding of the needs of people with moderate and severe disabilities from birth through old age. Chapter 1 explores the various definitions of moderate and severe disabilities and describes the influence that each of these definitions has on the design of educational and community service programs. Chapter 2 reviews the history of service programs in this century and outlines the emerging values and principles undergirding the development of current programs. Chapter 3 discusses the role of families, friends, and society in supporting these individuals in our communities. It emphasizes the need for service programs to supplement rather than supplant the natural supports that people have available to them. Chapter 4 examines some of the most critical ethical issues facing society in the treatment of this group of people. It provides an ethical framework for exploring topics such as genetic screening, abortion, and withholding of medical treatment. Chapter 5 examines how the cultural and linguistic backgrounds of these individuals influence the design of educational and community service programs. Chapters 6 through 13 describe recommended practices and emerging service models for people at all age levels.

## Acknowledgments

We would like to thank our families, friends, and colleagues for their continuing support, and the reviewers of this edition: Rhoda Cummings, University of Nevada, Reno; Joseph D. George, Columbus State University; and Craig Miner, California State University, Fresno.

J. M.

## Reference

Minnow, M. (1990). *Making all the difference: Inclusion, exclusion, and American law.* New York: Cornell University Press.

# 1

# *Understanding People with Severe Disabilities*

*Parents, advocates, and professionals should use people first language. For example, one would say "individuals with disabilities" rather than "the severely disabled." Traditional disability labels can promote stereotyping, discrimination, and exclusion from the community.*

## WINDOW 1.1 • *Anita*

Anita is 9 years old, and lives with her mother and two brothers in a small town on the western plains of Nebraska. She attends Edgemont Elementary School with her younger brother, John, and friends from the neighborhood. Each morning at 7:00 A.M., John and Anita's mother help her into the family van, and along with her wheelchair, drive to a street corner a mile away to wait for the school bus. After a 45-minute ride, Anita settles in for a day at school with her fourth-grade classmates, her teacher, and the special education support team.

Anita is in a setting with "typical" students, all bringing their own individual needs and experiences to the class and school. She is one of twenty-six kids, with her own unique personality, a beautiful smile, and a somewhat short temper when it comes to wanting something she can't

have. Did we also mention that Anita has mental retardation, is blind, and is unable to walk?

So, what is Anita, a child with severe disabilities, doing in a regular education setting? No, the instructional goals and strategies used to foster her learning are not necessarily the same as her twenty-five "typical" classmates, but the overall intended outcomes are very much the same: access to, and participation in, a complex and often ambivalent society.

Throughout her school day, the classroom teacher, special education support team, and her peers work with Anita on individualized goals that range from increasing her communication skills to learning how to be more independent when eating. This takes place in the context of the general education school and classroom using strategies that promote learning for all children.

This book is about *people* with severe disabilities. Although these individuals are often defined and characterized by their disability, they bring a unique set of needs, characteristics, and life experiences to this world. As we begin our discussion of the various definitions and characteristics associated with severe disabilities, we hope to maintain a clear separation of the person, as an individual, and the "disability" label. Anita, in our opening window, is a 9-year-old child, who also happens to have severe disabilities. Instead of initially describing Anita as a child with green eyes and a beautiful smile who loves to listen to Bon Jovi with her brothers, she may be described solely by her deficits: severely multiply disabled with profound retardation, blindness, and physical impairments.

The failure to separate a person from the label can be taken even further when people's names are actually replaced by "disability" labels. Anita, Devyn, and Thomas may be grouped together as "the severely disabled," or "the retarded." In this book, regardless of whether we are talking about definitions, characteristics, or causation, the language will be "people first." As in our opening window, the focus is on Anita, *a child with severe disabilities.*

## Defining Severe Disabilities

When the term *severe disabilities* is broken down into its two component parts, there is a stark revelation about what labels communicate. *Severe* is defined in the dictionary as extreme, bleak, harsh, inflexible, and uncompromising. *Disability* is described as lacking ability, debilitated, incapacitated, mutilated, or crippled. To say the least, these are omi-

**POINT OF INTEREST 1.1** • *Definitions Tell Us Very Little about People with Severe Disabilities*

If you have a severe disability, the very first thing that others would most likely be told about you would be a summary of your "deficits." Chances are, whatever they were, there would be a file containing a lengthy description of your intellectual shortcomings, your physical impairments, and your behavior problems, Even the most rudimentary personal information included on a driver's license—your eye color, hair color, height, and weight—would remain a mystery throughout hundreds of pages of written records. Nowhere would someone learn that you had a lovely smile, a strong sense of identity, and a family that cared about you. Instead, we might read about your "inappropriate affect," your "non-compliance," and the "overprotectiveness" of your "difficult" parents. And although you might like to think of yourself as an active teenager interested in the "top 40" hits and the latest fashion in dress, hairstyle, and make-up, you may find yourself listening to nursery rhymes, dressed in a shapeless sweatsuit, your hair cropped short and straight, and with no access to even acne medication much less makeup. Why? Because an assumption has been made that your *disability* tells all there is to know about you, and from the moment you were diagnosed (or even *dually* diagnosed), you ceased being regarded as a person and became a "subject," a "client," or—worse yet—a "case." Your personality, your identity, and your lifestyle have become minor and even hidden details in a clinical history that tells the world about your weaknesses, faults, and deficits.

*Source:* From Meyer, L. H., Peck, C. A., & Brown, L. (1991). Definitions and diagnoses. In L. H. Meyer, C. A. Peck, and L. Brown (Eds.), *Critical issues in the lives of people with disabilities* (p. 17). Baltimore: Paul H. Brookes.

nous descriptors with a foreboding sense of hopelessness and despair. Possible combinations of dictionary terms for severe disability could then include: extremely debilitating, inflexibly incapacitated, or uncompromisingly crippled. This sense of hopelessness is often reflected in historical definitions of severe disabilities. (See Point of Interest 1.1.)

## *Historical Definitions*

> *Focus 1*
> Distinguish between definitions of severe disabilities that are based on negative descriptors and those emphasizing the person's needs and abilities.

Abt Associates (1974) described the "severely handicapped[1] individual" as mentally retarded, emotionally disturbed, deaf-blind, or multiply handicapped. They are unable "to attend to even the most pronounced social stimuli, including failure to respond to invitations from peers or adults, or loss of contact with reality" (p. v). This definition uses such terms as *self-mutilation* (head banging, body scratching, hair pulling), *ritualistic behaviors*

---

[1]The terms *handicapped* and *disability* are often used interchangeably in definitions. The authors use the term *disability* throughout this book except when citing directly from a source where *handicapped* is part of a quotation.

(rocking, pacing), and self-stimulation (masturbation, stroking, patting) as descriptors of behavior exhibited by individuals with severe disabilities. The focus is on the individual's deficits. All the possible conditions that could be considered a severe disability are listed first, and then the accompanying characteristics are described.

Justen (1976) proposed a definition that described individuals with severe disabilities as having a developmental disability with learning and behavior problems that required extensive modification in their instructional program:

> The "severely handicapped" refers to those individuals age 21 and younger who are functioning at a general development level of half or less than the level which would be expected on the basis of chronological age and who manifest learning and/or behavior problems of such magnitude and significance that they require extensive structure in learning situations if their education needs are to be well served. (p. 5)

The Justen definition defines severe disabilities on the basis of the discrepancy between what is "normal" development for a child at a specific chronological age, and the manifestation of significant learning and behavior problems that require extensive modifications in educational services. Both criteria must be met for the individual to be considered severely disabled. First, a child with a severe disability would have to be at one-half the developmental level of his or her peers who are not disabled. For example, a 10-year old child would have to have an intelligence quotient (IQ) of 50 or less where 100 is the average, or a language age of less than 5 years. In addition, such children would also require intensive specialized instruction due to the nature and extent of their learning and behavior differences.

Sailor and Haring (1977) abandoned Justen's emphasis on establishing a discrepancy between normal and atypical development, and proposed a definition that was oriented solely to the instructional needs of the child:

> A child should be assigned to a program for the severely/multiply handicapped according to whether the primary service needs of the child are basic or academic.... If the diagnosis and assessment process determines that a child with multiple handicaps needs academic instruction, the child should not be referred to the severely handicapped program. If the child's service need is basic skill development, the referral to the severely/multiply handicapped program is appropriate. (p. 68)

Sailor and Haring do not include any behavioral descriptors in their definition, developmental or otherwise, but focus solely on the differences in educational need (basic or academic). Furthermore, the children are defined by the program they would attend, rather than the nature of their disability.

Snell (1991) went one step further, suggesting that the definition of severe disabilities emphasize the importance of meeting each individual's needs in an inclusive education program. Westling and Fox (2000) focused on independence in "typical life environments" and the need for a "nondisabled support network":

> The general ability to demonstrate skills necessary to maintain oneself independently in typical life environments is reduced for persons with severe disabilities; and often the condition requires assistance and ongoing support from individuals without disabilities, including family members, friends, and other professionals. (p. 3)

For Anita of our opening window, this would mean structuring an educational program that is intended to decrease her dependence on others and create opportunities for her to be included in home, school, and neighborhood settings. In defining severe disabilities, the emphasis moves to developing skills that promote independence, rather than identifying a set of general characteristics that attempt to describe individuals on the basis of what they cannot do. The identification of the supports necessary to promote access and opportunity in inclusive settings is at the foundation of the TASH definition of severe disabilities.

## *The TASH Definition*

> *Focus 2*
> Identify the three components of the TASH definition of severe disabilities.

The Association for Persons with Severe Handicaps (TASH) proposes a definition of severe disabilities that emphasizes the need for extensive ongoing support in inclusive settings across the life span of the individual. People with severe disabilities:

> ...include individuals with disabilities of all ages, races, creeds, national origins, genders and sexual orientation who require ongoing support in one or more major life activities in order to participate in an integrated community and enjoy a quality of life similar to that available to all citizens. Support may be required for life activities such as mobility, communication, self-care, and learning as necessary for community living, employment, and self-sufficiency. (TASH, 2000)

TASH defines severe disabilities in terms of an adaptive fit between the individual and the environment. *Adaptive fit* is the degree to which an individual is able to cope with the requirements of a family, school, or community environment, and the extent to which the environment recognizes and accommodates individual diversity. The process of creating an adaptive fit is always dynamic, with continuous adjustments between the individual and the environment in order to foster a mutually supportive coexistence. The TASH definition suggests that to create an adaptive fit for persons with severe disabilities, there is a need to develop "extensive ongoing support" in a variety of life activities that include getting around from place to place, interacting with people who are not disabled, taking care of one's own needs, and learning about lifestyle choices and economic self-sufficiency.

## *Definitions by Category of Disability*

The evolution of definitions associated with severe disabilities has been primarily multicategorical. The multicategorical approach has run parallel to definitions based on specific categories of disability (such as mental retardation and hearing impairments). Definitions based on specific categories use criteria such as intelligence, adaptive behavior, achievement, or physical characteristics to separate one condition from another. Once the criteria have been established for a specific category, people within that category can be classified according to the severity of the condition. For example, a person with mental retardation may be described as having significant intellectual and adaptive behavior limitations that can be classified as mild to severe in nature. A person with a hearing impairment may be described as having a hearing loss that is mild (hard-of-hearing) or severe (deaf). In this section we will examine some of the individual disability categories and classification systems that are based on severity of the condition. It is important to note that mental retardation is often the primary condition associated with severe disabilities, in addition to one or more other disability conditions. Table 1.1 provides a summary of disability categories and classification systems.

---

**Focus 3**
How is severity described in the disability categories of mental retardation, serious emotional disturbance, autism, sensory impairments, traumatic brain injury, and physical and health impairments?

---

***Mental Retardation.***    According to the American Association on Mental Retardation (AAMR) mental retardation (also known as intellectual disabilities) is a condition characterized by:

> ...significantly subaverage intellectual functioning, existing concurrently with related limitations in two or more of the following applicable adaptive skill areas: communication, self-care, home living, social skills, community use, self-direction, health and safety, functional academics, leisure and work. Mental retardation manifests before age 18. (Luckasson et al., 1992)

Mental retardation has historically been associated with classification by *severity* of the condition. The extent to which intellectual functioning and adaptive skills deviate from the average can be described in terms of mild, moderate, severe, and profound mental retardation. Many state education systems use a symptom severity approach to classify students with mental retardation on the basis of intelligence quotient (IQ) and adaptive skills. IQ levels include mild (IQ 55–70), moderate (IQ 40–55), severe (IQ 25–40), and profound (IQ 25 or lower). In the school setting, adaptive skills can be described in terms of how well the student applies what has been learned in a classroom setting to home and community environments. Adaptive skill deficits are described in terms of the degree to which an individual's behavior differs from what is expected according to his or her chronological age. These differences can be described in terms of either severity or educational expectations. Severity descriptors include mild, moderate, severe, and profound adaptive skill deficits. Educability classification descriptors include educable, trainable, and custodial retardation. Severity and educational classification approaches to mental retardation according to IQ level may be found in Table 1.2.

The current AAMR definition of mental retardation (Luckasson et al., 1992) has abandoned the severity approach to classification and adopted a system that concentrates on the *supports* needed for the individual to have optimal growth and development in family, school, and community settings. These supports include both human and material resources. Human supports can be both natural (family, friends, neighbors, co-workers) and

**TABLE 1.1**   *Disability Categories and Classification by Severity*

| Disability Category | Description | Severity Classification |
|---|---|---|
| Mental retardation | Intellectual functioning (IQ) is below 70–75<br><br>Significant disabilities in two or more adaptive skill areas | Based on IQ and level of support:<br><br>• *Severe* mental retardation includes individuals with IQs of 25–40 and adaptive skill deficits, which may include fine and gross motor difficulties, speech and language delays, difficulty taking care of personal needs and developing interpersonal relationships<br>• Individual requires *extensive or pervasive* support in environmental settings |
| Serious emotional disturbance | The following characteristics are exhibited over a long period of time and to a marked degree:<br><br>• Inability to have satisfactory relationships<br>• Inappropriate behaviors or feelings under normal circumstances<br>• Pervasive mood of unhappiness or depression<br>• Develops physical symptoms or fears associated with personal or school problems | Based on frequency and extent of behavior exhibited<br><br>Terminology associated with severe behavior problems may include:<br><br>• Severe emotional disturbance<br>• Psychosis<br><br>Behavior exhibited may include:<br><br>• Lack of contact with reality (such as withdrawal)<br>• Behavior excesses (aggression; vandalism)<br>• Low achievement in school<br>• Hyperactivity and impulsivity |
| Autism | Significant difficulties with verbal and nonverbal communication, as well as social interactions | Although extent of communication difficulties vary from person to person, autism is generally considered a *severe* disability<br><br>Behavior exhibited may include:<br><br>• Irregular and impaired communication<br>• Repetitive activities and stereotypical movements<br>• Resistance to change in daily routines or environmental conditions<br>• Unusual responses to sensory experiences |

*(continued)*

**TABLE 1.1** *Continued*

| Disability Category | Description | Severity Classification |
|---|---|---|
| Hearing impairments | Includes hearing losses ranging from the ability to process information from sound with an aid to losses so severe that hearing cannot be used as a means to acquire information | Classification by severity of loss includes hard-of-hearing and deaf<br><br>• Hard of hearing: Generally described as a milder hearing loss in which residual hearing is sufficient to process information from sound with an aid<br>• Deaf: *Severe hearing loss* of 90 db or more. Even with aids, the individual is unable to use hearing as primary way to acquire information |
| Visual impairments | Includes visual losses ranging from the ability to process information through sight with an aid to losses so severe that sight cannot be used as a means to acquire information | Classification by severity includes partially sighted and blind<br><br>• Partially sighted: Having enough vision with an aid to acquire information through the eyes<br>• Blind: Unable to use sight, and must rely on other senses to acquire information |
| Traumatic brain injury | Injury to the brain caused by an external force, resulting in total or partial functional disability or psychosocial impairment<br><br>Disabilities may occur in such areas as intelligence, language, memory, attention reasoning, abstract thinking, judgment, problem solving, sensory, perceptual and motor abilities, behavior, physical functioning, information processing, and speech | Traumatic brain injuries are not generally classified by severity, although the nature and extent of the trauma can result in mild through severe conditions |
| Physical and health disorders | Physical disorders: Interfere with mobility and coordination, and may also have secondary effect on communication, learning, and emotional adjustment<br><br>Health disorders: Chronic or acute health problems that result in limited strength, vitality, and alertness, and may also adversely affect school performance | Physical and health disorders are not generally classified by severity, although various conditions can result in mild through severe conditions (such as cerebral palsy, seizure disorders, or AIDS) |

**TABLE 1.2** *Severity and Educability Classification Approaches in Mental Retardation According to IQ Level*

| IQ Level | Severity of Condition | Educability | Expectation |
|---|---|---|---|
| 55–70 | Mild | Educable | Achievement in school may range from second- to fifth-grade level; may achieve total or partial independence in the community, including competitive employment |
| 40–55 | Moderate | Trainable | Learning primarily in functional skill areas (such as self-help); may acquire some primary academic skills in reading and math; may achieve partial independence in the community, including competitive employment with support |
| 25–40 | Severe | Custodial | Individual may need extensive and ongoing support (social, educational, and medical) to adapt to home and community living |
| Below 25 | Profound | Custodial | |

formalized (teachers, job coaches, physicians). Material supports may range from access to barrier-free buildings for people who are in wheelchairs to the use of electronic devices to assist communication.

AAMR has developed a set of steps to identify appropriate supports for each individual:

1. Describe the person's strengths and weaknesses in reference to psychological/ emotional considerations.
2. Describe the person's overall physical health and indicate the condition's cause.
3. Describe the person's current environmental placement and the optimal environment that would facilitate the person's growth and development (Luckasson et al., 1992).

Once the description of a person's *adaptive fit* with the environment has been completed, the next step is to identify the level of support required to facilitate optimal growth and development. AAMR breaks down these supports into four levels: intermittent, limited, extensive, and pervasive. See Table 1.3.

***Serious Emotional Disturbance.*** People with serious emotional disturbance experience problems relating to others in a variety of ways and across multiple environments. One of the more widely adopted definitions of serious emotional disturbance is included in the *Individuals with Disabilities Education Act* (IDEA).[2] It relies heavily on negative behavior descriptors:

[2]See Chapter 3 for an in-depth explanation of the major provisions of the IDEA.

**TABLE 1.3**  *AAMR Levels of Support for People with Mental Retardation*

| Level | Intensity |
|---|---|
| Intermittent | Supports are provided as needed and may be episodic (supports not always necessary) or short-term (job loss or medical crisis). Intermittent supports may be high or low intensity. |
| Limited | Supports are characterized by consistency. Time may be limited but is not intermittent. In comparison to more intensive supports, fewer staff may be required and costs may be lower (for example, time-limited employment training or transitional supports from school to adult life). |
| Extensive | Supports are characterized by regular involvement (such as daily) in some environments, but are not time-limited (for example, long-term job and home-living support). |
| Pervasive | Supports are characterized by constancy and high intensity across all environments; may be potentially life-sustaining in nature. Pervasive supports typically involve more staff and are more intrusive than extensive or time-limited supports. |

*Source:* Luckasson, R., Coulter, D., Polloway E., Reiss, S., Schalock, R., Snell, M., Spitalnik, D., & Stark, J. (1992). *Mental retardation: Definitions, classification, and systems of supports* (9th ed.). Washington, DC: American Association on Mental Retardation.

   (i)   The term means a condition exhibiting one or more of the following characteristics over a long period of time and to a marked degree, which adversely affects educational performance:

      (A)  An inability to learn which cannot be explained by intellectual, sensory or health factors;

      (B)  An inability to build or maintain satisfactory interpersonal relationships with peers and teachers;

      (C)  Inappropriate types of behavior or feelings under normal circumstances;

      (D)  A general pervasive mood of unhappiness or depression;

      (E)  A tendency to develop physical symptoms or fears associated with personal or school problems.

  (ii)  The term includes children who are schizophrenic. The term does not include children who are socially maladjusted, unless it is determined that they are seriously emotionally disturbed. (IDEA, 34 C.F.R. 300.5[b][8] [1990])

Although this definition includes multiple behavioral descriptors, the most important determinants of the condition are that the behaviors are significant in nature (to a marked degree) and occur over a long period of time. The condition is characterized by poor interpersonal relationships, inappropriate behavior, a pervasive sense of unhappiness, and physical symptoms associated with the problems. Hardman, Drew, and Egan (2002) suggest that serious emotional disturbance in its most severe form may be characterized by one or more of the following: significant deficits in academic skills; avoidance of social relationships; major problems in everyday living skills and caring for oneself; consistent and frequent violent, assaultive, destructive, or self-injurious behavior; bizarre language and poor communication skills; fantasizing and hallucinations; depression; and eating disorders.

***Autism.*** Autism has traditionally been characterized as a condition associated with serious emotional disturbance. When first identified (Kanner, 1943), autism was thought to be the result of parental rejection and hostility toward the child. Today, autism is described as a severe language disorder resulting from brain dysfunction. The condition is one of twelve disability categories identified in the IDEA.

> Autism means a developmental disability significantly affecting verbal and nonverbal communication and social interaction, generally evident before age three, that adversely affects educational performance. Characteristics of autism include irregularities and impairments in communication, engagement in repetitive activities and stereotyped movements, resistance to environmental change or change in daily routines, and unusual responses to sensory experiences. (IDEA, 34 C.F.R. 300.7[b][1] [1992])

The American Psychiatric Association (1994) has developed criteria for diagnosing autism based on time of onset and manifestation of behaviors that are atypical for a child's developmental level and chronological age. A summary of these diagnostic criteria is presented in Window 1.2.

***Sensory Impairments.*** Hearing and visual impairments are defined by the type and degree of sensory loss. The terms describe the entire range of auditory and visual loss, from mild through severe conditions. People with hearing impairments are usually divided into two groups: hard-of-hearing and deaf. For the person who is hard-of-hearing, audition is deficient but the individual has enough residual hearing with an aid to acquire information through auditory channels. Deafness is typified by a hearing loss so great that, even with the use of hearing aids or other forms of amplification, the primary means for developing language and communication is through visual channels. Deafness, as defined by the Individuals with Disabilities Education Act (IDEA), means

> ...a hearing impairment which is so severe that the child is impaired in processing linguistic information through hearing, with or without amplification, which adversely affects educational performance. (IDEA, 34 C.F.R. 300.7 [1997])

People with visual impairments have losses ranging from partial to total blindness. The term *visual impairment* encompasses people who have never experienced sight; those who had normal vision before becoming partially or totally blind; those who have experienced a gradual or sudden loss of acuity across their field of vision; and those with a restricted field of vision.

Hearing and visual impairments are most often classified by the *severity* of the condition. Hard-of-hearing and partially sighted represent the milder end of the severity spectrum; deafness and blindness are both considered *severe* disabilities. Deafness is usually defined by a loss of 90 decibels (db) or greater. Even with the assistance of hearing aids or other amplification, communication skills are developed primarily through visual channels. Blindness is

**WINDOW 1.2 • *American Psychiatric Association Diagnostic Criteria for Autism***

A. A total of six (or more) items from (1), (2), and (3), with at least two from (1), and one each from (2) and (3):
1. Qualitative impairment in social interaction, as manifested by at least two of the following:
   a. Marked impairment in the use of multiple nonverbal behaviors such as eye-to-eye gaze, facial expression, body postures, and gestures to regulate social interaction.
   b. Failure to develop peer relationships appropriate to developmental level.
   c. A lack of spontaneous seeking to share enjoyment, interests, or achievements with other people (e.g., by a lack of showing, bringing, or pointing out objects of interest).
2. Qualitative impairments in communication as manifested by at least one of the following:
   a. Delay in, or total lack of, the development of spoken language (not accompanied by an attempt to compensate through alternative modes of communication such as gestures or mime).
   b. In individuals with adequate speech, marked impairment in the ability to initiate or sustain a conversation with others.
   c. Stereotyped and repetitive use of language or idiosyncratic language.
d. Lack of varied, spontaneous make believe play or social imitative play appropriate to developmental level.
3. Restricted repetitive and stereotyped patterns of behavior, interests, and activities, as manifested by at least one of the following:
   a. Encompassing preoccupation with one or more stereotypes and restricted pattern of interest that is abnormal either in intensity or focus.
   b. Apparently inflexible adherence to specific, nonfunctional routines or rituals.
   c. Stereotypic and repetitive motor mannerisms (e.g., hand or finger flapping or twisting, or complex whole body movements).
   d. Persistent preoccupations with parts of objects.

B. Delays or abnormal functioning in at least one of the following areas, with onset prior to age 3 years: (1) social interaction, (2) language as used in social communication, or (3) symbolic or imaginative play.
C. The disturbance is not better accounted for by Rett's Disorder or Childhood Disintegrative Disorder.

*Source:* American Psychiatric Association (1994). *Diagnostic and statistical manual of mental disorders* (4th ed.). (pp. 70–71). Washington, DC: Author.

the counterpart of deafness in the visual channel. A person who is blind has a visual acuity of 20/200 or worse in the best eye with correction. A person who is blind will use auditory channels as the primary avenue for acquiring information.

***Traumatic Brain Injury.***    Traumatic brain injury (TBI) results from a blow to the brain caused by an external force. The result of the injury is a total or partial loss of physical functioning and/or psychosocial impairments. Physical problems may include loss of motor abilities, intellectual deficits, as well as sensory and communication difficulties (IDEA, 34 C.F.R. 300, 301[1992]. TBI is also associated with a diminished or altered state of consciousness, which results in psychosocial impairments ranging from mild depression and social adjustment problems to psychosis.

TBI does not apply to brain injuries that are degenerative, congenital, or caused by trauma at birth (e.g., strokes, tumors, and infections of the brain). It does apply to *open head* and *closed (generalized) head injuries*. In an open head injury, there is a penetrating head wound. No penetration occurs in a closed head injury, but damage to the brain is caused by a tearing of nerve fibers, contusion in the skull, or edema (swelling) (Lehr, 1990). There are numerous causes of TBI, including gunshots, falls, assaults, auto accidents, or violent shaking.

TBI ranges in severity from mild to severe. Most cases are mild with short-term effects, such as headaches, anxiety, and blurred vision (Clark, 1996; Hux & Hacksley, 1996). For TBI to be considered a disability category under the IDEA, the injury must result in a significant influence on educational performance that requires special education. Special education services are most often needed in the areas of speech and language development, social and behavioral skills, and motor functioning (Ponsford, 1995).

***Physical and Health Impairments.*** The range of physical and health impairments is extremely diverse, and includes conditions that interfere with mobility and coordination, as well as those that limit strength, vitality, and alertness. Physical impairments, described in the IDEA as orthopedic impairments, include such conditions as traumatic brain injury, cerebral palsy, spina bifida, amputations, spinal cord injuries, and muscular dystrophy. Health impairments, which result from chronic or acute health problems, involve such conditions as AIDS, tuberculosis, heart disease, rheumatic fever, leukemia, diabetes, and lead poisoning. In order for a student with a physical or health impairment to be considered eligible for special education services under the IDEA, the condition must adversely affect educational performance.

Physical and health impairments are most often classified by the type and nature of the condition, such as problems resulting from genetic anomalies, trauma, cancer, heart disease, or virus. Although physical and health problems are not generally classified according to severity, many of these conditions result in serious impairments that not only affect an individual's educational performance and community living, but are life threatening.

---

*Focus 4*
Define the terms multiple disabilities and deafness-blindness as described in the IDEA.

---

## The IDEA Definitions of Severe and Multiple Disabilities

The IDEA does not include the term *severe disabilities* as one of the twelve categorical definitions of disability identified by federal regulation. The law does, however, describe children with severe disabilities and their need for intensive educational services:

> "Children with *severe disabilities* refers to children with disabilities who, because of the intensity of their physical, mental, or emotional problems, need highly specialized education, social, psychological, and medical services in order to maximize their full potential for

useful and meaningful participation in society and for self-fulfillment. (IDEA, 34 C.F.R. 300, 315.4[d] [1977])

The law indicates that students with severe disabilities may be subsumed under any one of the IDEA categories, such as mental retardation, autism, serious emotional disturbance, or speech and language impairments. The IDEA does include multiple disabilities and deafness-blindness as specific disability categories.

***Multiple Disabilities.***    Multiple disabilities as defined in the IDEA federal regulations means concomitant impairments (such as mental retardation and orthopedic impairments), the combination of which causes such severe educational problems that they cannot be accommodated in special education programs solely for one of the impairments. The term does not include children who are deaf-blind (IDEA, 42 C.F.R. 63, 1977, pp. 42,478–42,479).

This definition includes multiple conditions that can occur in any of several combinations. One such combination is described by the term *dual diagnosis*. Dual diagnosis involves persons who have serious emotional disturbance or present challenging behaviors in conjunction with severe mental retardation. Estimates of people with mental retardation also having serious challenging behaviors vary, ranging from 5 percent to 15 percent of those living in the community to a much higher percentage when people living in institutions are included (Beirne-Smith, Ittenbach, & Patton, 2002; Griffiths, Nugent, & Gardner, 1998). So, why do people with mental retardation and other developmental disabilities often have higher rates of challenging behaviors? Griffiths et al. (1998) indicated that "it is important to understand the challenging behaviors are not a fundamental characteristic of developmental disabilities" (p. 3). These authors further suggest that the increase is related to various risk factors. People with developmental disabilities have:

- An increased prevalence of neurological, sensory, and physical abnormalities.
- Lifestyles that frequently are characterized by restrictiveness, prejudice, limited personal independence, restricted personal control, paucity of mentally healthy experiences, and victimization.
- Skill deficits in critical functional areas. These skill deficits make it more difficult to deal appropriately with stresses in life.
- Atypical learning histories. Often, positive behaviors have not been acknowledged and negative and disruptive behaviors have attracted excessive attention. (Griffiths et al., pp. 3–4)

The term *dual diagnosis* has raised apprehension among some professional groups, particularly TASH. TASH suggests that the term may be misapplied as a rationale for the use of aversive behavioral procedures, psychotropic medications, and punishment through the judicial system. To deal with the confusion surrounding the use of this label more effectively, TASH recommends the following:

- Programs for people described as having a dual diagnosis must include individualized, personalized services and nonaversive methods.

- Additional research must be undertaken to determine the influence of environmental factors affecting the increase in behaviors associated with mental illness.
- Support and assistance must be based on individual need rather than labels. (Meyer, Peck, & Brown, 1991)

***Deafness-Blindness.***   For some people with multiple disabilities, mental retardation may not be a primary symptom. One such condition is deafness-blindness, a dual sensory impairment. The concomitant vision and hearing difficulties exhibited by people who are deaf-blind result in severe communication deficits as well as developmental and educational difficulties that require extensive support across several professional disciplines. IDEA defines deafness-blindness as:

> ...concomitant hearing and visual impairments, the combination of which causes such severe communication and other developmental and educational problems that they cannot be accommodated in special education programs solely for children who are deaf or blind. (IDEA, 42 C.F.R. 63, 1977, pp. 42,478–42,479)

The impact of both vision and hearing loss on the educational needs of the student is a matter of debate. One view of deaf-blindness is that the individuals are so severely mentally retarded that both vision and hearing are also affected. Another view is that they are average in intelligence and lost their hearing and sight after having acquired language. Intellectual functioning for persons who are deaf-blind may range from normal or gifted to severe mental retardation. All people with deaf-blindness experience challenges in learning to communicate, access information, and move comfortably through their environment. These individuals may also have physical and behavioral disabilities. However, the specific needs of each person will vary enormously according to age, onset, and type of deaf-blindness (Deafblind International, 2000).

---

**Focus 5**
What are the estimated prevalence and causes of severe disabilities?

---

# Prevalence

People with severe disabilities make up a very small percentage of the general population. Prevalence ranges from 0.1 to 1.0 percent, and about 4 in every 1,000 persons with severe disabilities have mental retardation as their primary condition. The U.S. Department of Education (2000) estimated that about 107,763 students between the ages of 6 and 21 were served in the public schools under the label multiple disabilities during the 1998–1999 school year. These students account for 2 percent of the over six million students considered eligible for services under the IDEA. The Department of Education also reported that

1,609 students between the ages of 6 and 21 were identified as deaf-blind. These students account for 0.0002 percent of students with disabilities served under the IDEA.

There is some disagreement regarding the prevalence of severe behavior disorders. The Office of Technology Assessment and the National Institute of Medicine suggest that more than 3 percent of children and adolescents have severe behavior disorders. Other researchers indicate that between 3 and 8 percent of school-age children may have serious emotional disorders sufficiently severe to warrant treatment (Rosenblatt et al., 1998; Ruehl, 1998).

## Causation

People with severe disabilities are a heterogenous group, and the causes associated with their condition are equally diverse. The nature of the disability(ies) is most often present at birth, whether it be problems resulting from a genetic origin (such as chromosomal abnormalities), or difficulties that result from inadequate prenatal care, poor maternal nutrition, substance abuse, birth trauma, infectious diseases, radiation exposure, or sexually transmitted diseases. However, it is also possible for severe disabilities to occur later in life as a result of abuse and neglect, poisoning, disease, malnutrition, or trauma.

## Current Issues in Assessment and Labeling

Definitions and classification systems result from an assessment process intended to differentiate the characteristics of one person from another. Once a common set of characteristics has been established for a specific group of people, then a definition is developed, and a label applied. One fundamental purpose for definitions and labels is to determine who is eligible for services (social, medical, or educational), and who is not. For example, Anita, in our opening window, is a child with characteristics that are consistent with the definitions and labels associated with *mental retardation* or *severe multiple disabilities*. Labels evolve out of definitions, and definitions evolve from the process of assessment.

The purposes for assessment are primarily to compare one person's performance to another, or to compare performance with a desired goal. Although assessment and testing are often used synonymously, they are not the same. Testing is one element of the assessment process, which may also include observations, interviews, or behavior sampling. Testing can be either norm-referenced or informal in nature. Informal or criterion-referenced tests focus on how the person performs relative to a set objective or goal (the criterion). Norm-referenced tests compare one person to another in order to determine any given individual's extent of deviation from the average (either higher or lower). Norm-referenced tests are standardized—that is, everyone who takes the test gets the same set of questions, using the same administration procedures. The answers to these questions form "a score" for the person that is relative to everyone else who has taken the test. More than 250 million norm-referenced tests are given each year to school-age children in the United States for purposes ranging from eligibility for special education services in the public schools to establishing college entrance requirements.

## Definitions and Use of Norm-Referenced Tests

> **Focus 6**
> Why do many professionals prefer the functional approach over the use of norm-referenced tests in assessing persons with severe disabilities?

Traditionally, most definitions of disability have relied on norm-referenced tests as the means to assess whether a person's characteristics are consistent with the established criteria. The most obvious example of reliance on norm-referenced tests is the AAMR's definition of mental retardation. "Significantly subaverage intellectual functioning" is determined by an intelligence test that results in an IQ score. In order for an individual to be considered mentally retarded, the IQ score must fall below 70 to 75 where the norm (average) is 100 (Luckasson et al,, 1992). Even in the measurement of adaptive skills, where there is more opportunity for a broader assessment using observations or behavior sampling, the move has been toward the development of norm-referenced tests, such as the AAMR Adaptive Behavior Scales—Revised (Nihira, Leland, & Lambert, 1993; Lambert, Nihira, & Leland, 1993), the Vineland Social Maturity Scale—Revised (Sparrow, Balla & Cicchetti, 1984), and the Scales of Independent Behavior—Revised (Bruininks, Woodcock, Weatherman, & Hill, 1996).

The reliance on norm-referenced tests is also evident in other disability definitions. Definitions of hearing and visual impairments are based on a standard measure of sight or hearing loss. Serious emotional disturbance relies heavily on standardized behavior scales or checklists to identify characteristics consistent with the definition.

The validity of norm-referenced assessments, particularly the intelligence (IQ) test, to define and describe people with severe disabilities has been seriously questioned (Brown & Snell, 2000; Evans, 1991). Evans suggests that "IQ tests, as currently constituted, have no place in the assessment of individuals with severe intellectual disabilities" (p. 40).

## Functional Assessment

Whether it is establishing a definition, determining eligibility for services, or developing an instructional program for students with severe disabilities, the use of norm-referenced testing has been strongly criticized. One alternative is a functional assessment approach. As described by Horner, Albin, Sprague, and Todd (2000), the goal of functional assessment is to gather accurate information on the individual in order to improve the effectiveness of an individualized plan of support in natural settings. Gaylord-Ross and Browder (1991) suggest that functional assessment:

- Focuses on practical *independent living skills* that enable the person to survive and succeed in the real world
- Has an *ecological* emphasis that looks at the individual functioning in his or her surrounding environment
- Examines the *process* of learning and performance

- Suggests *intervention* techniques that may be successful
- Specifies ongoing monitoring procedures that can evaluate treatment progress (p. 45)

Functional assessments concentrate on the actual skills and supports necessary for a person to access and participate in natural settings, such as the home, school or classroom, and community at large. The *ecological* aspect of functional assessments is an important element in meeting the needs of individuals with severe disabilities. The ecological approach is concerned with creating a match between environmental demands and individual needs, experiences, and abilities. This notion of an adaptive fit between the individual and the environment is consistent with the definition of severe disabilities proposed by The Association for Persons with Severe Handicaps (TASH), discussed earlier in this chapter. The outcomes for each individual are related to an assessment process that results in the availability of the *supports* necessary for the individual to participate in natural settings. The skills taught correspond directly to actual performance demands. As such, the person learns and uses skills in the setting where the behavior is expected to occur. (See Figure 1.1.)

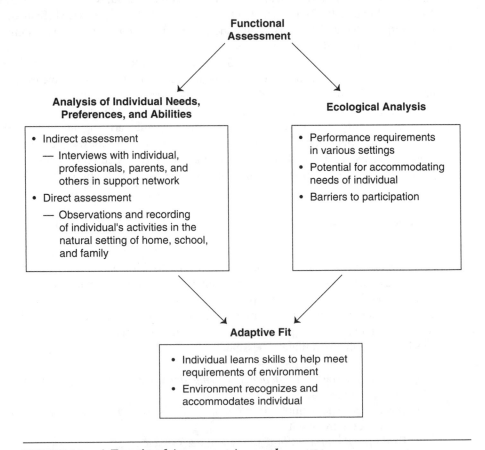

**FIGURE 1.1    A Functional Assessment Approach**

**POINT AND COUNTERPOINT 1.1 • *Norm-Referenced versus a Functional Approach to Assessment***

The debate regarding norm-referenced (standardized) versus functional approaches to assessment for people with severe disabilities is important to our understanding of the diverse needs and characteristics of these people. The following are two points of view on the use of standardized intelligence tests for people with severe disabilities.

*Point*

It is generally too expensive and inconvenient to observe people's daily behavior sufficiently in school and work to obtain a dependable measure of intelligence. One problem with observation is that it is all but impossible to standardize the conditions of everyday life to permit fair comparisons. Intelligence tests, however, do contain standardized series of tasks or work samples that provide for the efficient assessment of intelli-

gence. Such intelligence tests or scales are administered under highly controlled conditions so that an individual's score may be appropriately compared with the norms secured for other people. (Grossman, 1983)

*Counterpoint*

Traditional methods of intelligence testing are virtually useless with many children whose disabilities are [severe and] profound.... If tested such students tend to be assigned IQ scores at the extreme lower end of the continuum. Knowing that a particular student has an IQ of 25, however, is of no value in designing an appropriate educational program. Educators of students with severe and profound disabilities tend to focus on the specific skills a child needs to learn, rather than on intellectual level. (Heward, 2000)

## Conclusion

This chapter has examined the myriad definitions associated with severe disabilities. The more traditional definitions use negative behavioral descriptors and rely on norm-referenced tests to assess and describe people with severe disabilities. Concerns regarding the validity of this approach have resulted in more recent definitions (such as the TASH definition of severe disabilities and the 1992 AAMR definition of mental retardation) that concentrate on functionally assessing the relationship between the person and the demands of the environment. These definitions address the supports necessary for the individual to access and participate in inclusive school and community settings.

If the purpose of human services is to prepare and support people with severe disabilities for an inclusive lifestyle, then it follows that the definitions used to characterize these individuals should be consistent with that objective. Definitions and classification systems that are more concerned with supporting the individual in natural settings will result in social and educational programs that lead to greater independence, choice, autonomy, and economic self-sufficiency.

## Focus Review

Focus 1: Distinguish between definitions of severe disabilities that are based on negative descriptors and those emphasizing the person's needs, preferences, and abilities.

- The more traditional definitions of severe disabilities described the individual in terms of their negative behavioral characteristics. Characteristics such as self-mutilation and self-stimulation, loss of contact with reality, or failure to respond to social stimuli were included in these definitions.
- Whereas historical definitions focus on individual deficits, others emphasize skills for "typical life environments" and the need for a "nondisabled support network."

Focus 2: Identify the three components of the TASH definition of severe disabilities.

- The definition includes people with severe disabilities of all ages, races, creeds, national origins, genders, and sexual orientation.
- Ongoing support is required in one or more major life activities.
- Participation in integrated community settings is facilitated.

Focus 3: How is severity determined in the disability categories of mental retardation, serious emotional disturbance, autism, sensory impairments, traumatic brain injury, and physical and health impairments?

- Mental retardation: The severity of the condition is the extent to which intellectual functioning and adaptive skills deviate from the average. Individuals with severe mental retardation are usually described as having IQs below 40.
- Serious emotional disturbance: In its most severe form, serious emotional disturbance may be characterized by one or more of the following: significant deficits in academic skills; avoidance of social relationships; major problems in everyday living skills and caring for oneself; consistent and frequent violent, assaultive, destructive, or self-injurious behavior; bizarre language and poor communication skills; fantasizing and hallucinations; depression; and eating disorders.
- Autism: This condition is generally considered a severe disability, and includes (1) irregular and impaired communication, (2) repetitive activities and stereotypical movements, (3) resistance to change in daily routines or environmental conditions, and (4) unusual responses to sensory experiences.
- Sensory impairments: Classification by severity is based on the type and extent of hearing or visual loss. Deafness is a severe hearing loss in which, even with aids, the individual is unable to use hearing as a primary avenue to acquire information. Blindness is a severe visual loss in which the individual is unable to use sight, and must rely on other senses to acquire information.
- Traumatic brain injury: Most cases of TBI are mild with short-term effects. However, for TBI to be considered a disability category under the IDEA, the injury must result in a *significant influence* on educational performance that requires special education.
- Physical and health impairments: Although not generally classified by severity, these conditions may result in mild through severe problems.

Focus 4: Define the terms *multiple disabilities* and *deafness-blindness* as described in the IDEA.

- *Multiple disabilities* refers to concomitant impairments (such as mental retardation and physical disabilities). The combination causes educational problems so severe that they cannot be accommodated in special education programs solely for one impairment.
- *Deafness-blindness* involves concomitant hearing and visual impairments. The combination causes communication and other developmental and educational problems so severe that they cannot be accommodated in special education programs solely for children who are either deaf or blind.

Focus 5: What are the estimated prevalence and causes of severe disabilities?

- Prevalence ranges from 0.1 percent to 1.0 percent, and about 4 in every 1,000 persons with severe disabilities have mental retardation as their primary condition.
- Students with severe disabilities account for 2 percent of the more than six million students considered eligible for services under the IDEA.
- Between 3 and 8 percent of school-age children may have emotional disorders sufficiently severe to warrant treatment.
- The causes associated with severe disabilities are diverse. Severe disabilities are often present at birth, resulting from a genetic origin or inadequate prenatal care, poor maternal nutrition, substance abuse, birth trauma, infectious diseases, radiation exposure, or sexually transmitted diseases. Severe disabilities can also occur later in life as a result of abuse and neglect, poisoning, disease, malnutrition, or trauma.

Focus 6: Why do many professionals prefer the functional approach over the use of norm-referenced tests in assessing persons with severe disabilities?

- Norm-referenced tests, particularly IQ measures, may have no validity in defining severe disabilities.
- Functional assessments concentrate on the actual skills necessary for an individual to access and participate in natural settings. The functional approach is concerned with a match between environmental demands and individual needs, experiences, and abilities.

## References

Abt Associates (1974). *Assessments of selected resources for severely handicapped children and youth. Vol. I: A state-of-the-art paper.* Cambridge, MA: Author. (ERIC Document Reproduction Service No. ED 134 614.)

American Psychiatric Association (1994). *Diagnostic and statistical manual of mental disorders* (4th ed.). Washington, DC: Author.

Beirne-Smith, Ittenbach, R. F., & Patton, J. R. (2002). *Mental retardation* (6th ed.). Upper Saddle River, NJ: Merrill.

Brown, F., & Snell, M. (2000). Meaningful assessment. In M. E. Snell & F. Brown (Eds.), *Instruction of students with severe disabilities* (pp. 67–114). Upper Saddle River, NJ: Merrill.

Bruininks, R. H., Woodcock, R., Weatherman, R., & Hill, B. (1996). *Scales of independent behavior—Revised.* Chicago: Riverside.

Clark, E. (1996). Children and adolescents with traumatic brain injury: Reintegration challenges in educational settings. *Journal of Learning Disabilities, 29,* 549–560.

Deafblind International (2000). *What is deafblindness?* Available: http://www.deafblindinternational.org/whatisdb/whatisdb.htm.

Evans, I. M. (1991). Testing and diagnosis: A review and evaluation. In L. H. Meyer, C. A. Peck, & L. Brown (Eds.), *Critical issues in the lives of people with severe disabilities* (pp. 25–44). Baltimore: Paul H. Brookes.

Gaylord-Ross, R., & Browder, D. (1991). Functional assessment: Dynamic and domain properties. In L. H. Meyer, C. A. Peck, & L. Brown (Eds.), *Critical issues in the lives of people with severe disabilities* (pp. 45–66). Baltimore: Paul H. Brookes.

Griffiths, D. M., Nugent, J. A., & Gardner, W. I. (1998). Introduction. In D. M. Griffiths, W. I. Gardner, & J. A. Nugent (Eds.), *Behavioral supports: Individual centered interventions* (pp. 1–5). Kingston, NY: NADD Press.

Grossman, J. J. (Ed.) (1983). *Manual on terminology and classification in mental retardation.* Washington, DC: American Association on Mental Deficiency.

Hardman, M. L., Drew, C. J., & Egan, M. W. (2002). *Human exceptionality: Society, school, and family* (7th ed.). Boston: Allyn & Bacon.

Heward, W. L. (2000). *Exceptional children* (6th ed.). New York: Merrill/Prentice-Hall.

Horner, R. H., Albin, R. W., Sprague, J. R., & Todd, A. W. (2000). Positive behavior support. In M. E. Snell & F. Brown (Eds.), *Instruction of students with severe disabilities* (pp. 207–243). Upper Saddle River, NJ: Merrill.

Hux, K., & Hacksley, C. (1996). Mild traumatic brain injury: Facilitating school success. *Intervention in School and Clinic, 31,* 158–165.

IDEA, 34 C.F.R. 300.7 (1997).

IDEA, 34 C.F.R. 300.5(b)(8) (1990).

IDEA, 34 C.F.R. 300.7(b)(1) (1992).

IDEA, 34 C.F.R. 300, 301 (1992).

IDEA, 42 C.F.R. 63 (1977).

IDEA, 34 C.F.R. 300 315.4[d] (1977).

Justen, J. (1976). Who are the severely handicapped? A problem in definition. *AAESPH Review, 1*(5), 1–11.

Kanner, L. (1943). Autistic disturbances of affective contact. *Nervous Child, 3,* 217–250.

Lambert, N., Nihira, K., & Leland, H. (1993). *AAMR Adaptive Behavior Scale—School* (2nd ed.). Washington, DC: American Association on Mental Retardation.

Lehr, E. (1990). *Psychological management of traumatic brain injury in children and adolescents.* Rockville, MD: Aspen.

Luckasson, R., Coulter, D., Polloway, E., Reiss, S., Schalock, R., Snell, M., Spitalnik, D., & Stark, J. (1992). *Mental retardation: Definitions, classification, and systems of supports* (9th ed.). Washington, DC: American Association on Mental Retardation.

Meyer, L. H., Peck, C. A., & Brown, L. (1991). Resolution on people with mental retardation who are also diagnosed as mentally ill. In L. H. Meyer, C. A. Peck, & L. Brown (Eds.), *Critical issues in the lives of people with severe disabilities* (p. 20). Baltimore: Paul H. Brookes.

Nihira, K., Leland, H., & Lambert, N. (1993). *AAMR Adaptive Behavior Scale—Residential and Community* (2nd ed.). Washington, DC: American Association on Mental Retardation.

Ponsford, J. (1995). Mechanisms, recovery, and sequelae of traumatic brain injury: A foundation for the REAL approach. In J. Ponsford, S. Sloan, & P. Snow, *Traumatic brain injury: Rehabilitation for everyday adaptive living* (pp. 1–31). Hillsdale, NJ: Erlbaum.

Rosenblatt, J., Robertson, L., Bates, M., Wood, M., Furlong, M., & Sosna, T. (1998). Troubled or troubling? Characteristics of youth referred to a system of care without system-level referral constraints. *Journal of Emotional & Behavioral Disorders, 6*(1), 42–54.

Ruehl, M. E. (1998). Educating the child with severe behavioral problems: Entitlement, empiricism, and ethics. *Behavioral Disorders, 23*(3), 184–192.

Sailor, W., & Haring, N. (1977). Some current directions in the education of the severely/multiply handicapped. *AAESPH Review, 2,* 67–86.

Snell, M. E. (1991). Schools are for all kids: The importance of integration for students with severe disabilities and their peers. In J. Lloyd, N. N. Singh, & A. C. Repp (Eds.), *The regular education initiative: Alternative perspectives on concepts, issues, and models* (pp. 133–148). Sycamore, IL: Sycamore.

Sparrow, S., Balla, D., & Cicchetti, D. (1984). *Manual for the Vineland Adaptive Behavior Scales.* Circle Pines, MN: American Guidance Service.

TASH (2000). *TASH resolution on the people for whom TASH Advocates.* Baltimore: Author. (Definition originally adopted April 1975; revised December 1985 and March 2000.) Available: http://www.tash.org/resolutions/R21PEOPL.html

U.S. Department of Education (2000). To assure the free appropriate public education of all children with disabilities. *Twenty-second annual report to Congress on the implementation of the Individuals with Disabilities Education Act.* Washington, DC: U.S. Government Printing Office.

Westling, D., & Fox, L. (2000). *Teaching students with severe disabilities* (2nd ed.). Upper Saddle River, NJ: Merrill.

# 2

# *Valuing People with Severe Disabilities*

## *Toward Effective Education and Community Service Systems*

*The inclusion of people with severe disabilities in the community acknowledges the importance that our culture and society place on diversity.*

## WINDOW 2.1 • *Getting to Know Craig*

Craig's life is very much like yours and mine. He gets up in the morning, goes to work, cleans his apartment, does errands on the weekends, and tries to find time to have fun with his friends. These things may seem rather mundane to many of us, but for Craig they are part of a completely new life. Just over three years ago Craig was released from a large state institution. He had spent nearly twenty years of his life there. While living in the institution Craig worked on the grounds as part of a work crew. He would sometimes get very angry when someone asked him to do something, and when he got mad he would hit other people or himself. And even though he could take care of himself, he often wouldn't change his clothes or shower unless someone forced him to do it. Craig's "release" from the institution occurred because of increasing pressure by advocacy groups on the state agency that operated the institution to develop community-based

living and work alternatives for people with severe disabilities.

Craig moved out of the institution and into an apartment program with two other young men who had also been living in the institution. These three men got help in learning how to take care of their home from several people who worked for a local nonprofit agency set up to provide residential services to persons with disabilities. During the day Craig went to an employment agency, and he eventually got a job in a large hotel working as a maintenance man. He gets support from a job coach who is paid by the employment agency. Craig is learning to deal with his anger in more appropriate ways and hasn't hit anyone else or himself for over a year. He also takes a shower and puts on clean clothes every day without anyone telling him to do it.

---

Over the last century, society's view of people with disabilities has changed dramatically. In the early 1900s it was assumed that people with disabilities were incapable of becoming productive members of the community. Many local and state governments established large institutions that were intended to provide humane, long-term care and treatment to this group of people. However, in spite of the stated purposes, many institutions became little more than human warehouses that barely met the basic physical needs of the people who lived there. Many people with disabilities lived their entire lives in deplorable conditions segregated from the mainstream of community life.

During the 1960s and 1970s the public began to question some of the basic assumptions on which institutional programs were based. Research began to show that, with systematic training, persons with severe disabilities could learn a variety of complex vocational and self-care skills, and with adequate support could work and live successfully in the community (Switzky, Dudzinski, Van Acker, & Gambor, 1988). Empirical evidence also indicated that, rather than providing therapeutic environments, institutions actually limited and decreased the development of persons with disabilities (Dennis & Sayegh, 1965; Kaplan, 1943; Skeels, 1966; Sloan & Harmon, 1947). Most troubling were the frequent reports of mistreatment and abuse of people living in these settings (Blatt, Biklen, & Bogdan, 1977; Blatt & Kaplan, 1966). In all too many cases, the basic human rights of these people were simply ignored.

These issues led many advocates and policy makers to question the morality of institutionalization. Over the last several decades, the number of people living in large institutions has steadily decreased (Anderson, Lakin, Mangan, & Prouty, 1998; Prouty, Lakin, & Anderson, 2000). Alternative programs have emerged that are based on the assumption that people with disabilities have a fundamental right to live, work, and go to school in their own communities. However, in spite of the progress that has been made, people with disabilities, and especially those with the most significant disabilities, have still not been fully accepted by our society and still face a number of barriers to securing equal access to the community (Gilson, 1998; Walker, 1999).

This chapter provides an overview of the changing societal values that have driven services for persons with severe disabilities over the last century. The primary service models developed during this century will be reviewed and discussed. Finally, the emerging values that will undergird educational and community service programs for persons with severe disabilities in the future will be outlined.

# History of Educational and Community Services

Three different program models have been used to provide services to persons with disabilities during this century including: (1) the institutional model, (2) the developmental model, and (3) the ecological model. The emergence of each of these program models reflects significant changes in society's view of and assumptions about persons with disabilities.

## The Institutional Model

For the better part of the twentieth century the expected outcomes of service programs for people with disabilities focused simply on providing care and protection. The primary approach used to achieve these outcomes was to place individuals in large state institutions. The institutional model is based on three misconceptions about people with disabilities.

> **Focus 1**
> Identify the three assumptions underlying the institutional model.

• *Individuals with disabilities are "sick."* Institutions are based on a medical orientation of service delivery. This approach assumes that individuals with disabilities can be cured if they are provided effective "treatment." People who are placed in institutions are often referred to as patients, living areas are called "wards," and the staff are attendants, nurses, and physicians. Service is based on a diagnosis of the individual's pathology and a treatment regimen that is designed to return the person to a normal "healthy" state. When a "cure" cannot be expected, the prescribed treatment is long-term invalid care designed to meet the individual's basic physical needs.

• *Individuals with disabilities cannot learn.* A second assumption of the institutional model is that persons with disabilities, especially those with severe and profound mental retardation, are incapable of benefitting from education and training: "...the severely and profoundly retarded cannot be expected to profit from a program of normalization that emphasizes the traditional goals of education, nor can they be expected to take on a self directed role in society" (Burton & Hirshoren, 1979; p. 599). Proponents of institutional programs have also argued that attempts to teach persons with severe disabilities basic academic and personal care skills are not only unrealistic but could also be perceived as a particularly perverse form of mistreatment, by forcing these individuals to participate in training with no hope of mastering targeted skills. As such, comprehensive attempts at education and training are often deemed unnecessary.

• *Individuals with disabilities are a threat to society.*  While institutions are designed to provide care and protection to individuals with disabilities, they are also structured in part to protect society from persons with disabilities. In the early 1900s individuals with disabilities were held responsible for a whole host of social evils, including corruption, crime, sexual immorality, venereal diseases, and prostitution and degeneracy (Wolfensberger, 1972). Therefore, many states initiated systematic programs of compulsory commitment to institutions for people with mental retardation, with "parole" being allowed only after the person demonstrated no further threat to the community.

---

*Focus 2*
What factors prompted the deinstitutionalization movement of the late 1960s and 1970s?

---

During the 1960s and 1970s the institutional model was challenged by parents, advocates, and professionals. This challenge stemmed from the growing evidence that institutions were ineffective in "treating" persons with disabilities (Dennis & Sayegh, 1965; Kaplan, 1943; Skeels, 1966; Sloan & Harmon, 1947). Furthermore, research suggested that the structure and organization of institutions often led to significant abuse and mistreatment by staff. Questions were raised about the values of a society that allows anyone to be placed in such nontherapeutic environments:

> Our concern reflects our belief that institutions are products primarily of society, not of individuals, and that the effects of institutionalization can best be understood as originating from social rather then individual forces.... It would be easy to lay the blame for wrongdoing with the attendants who manage these wards, but that would be rather like prosecuting the soldier for firing his gun after sending him to do battle. While individuals occasionally may make institutional life intolerable, institutions are primarily the products of societies, not individuals. (Blatt et al., 1977, pp. 35–36)

Additional challenges to institutions came from the courts (Henderson & Vitello, 1991). An increasing number of judicial actions questioned the rights of states to commit individuals with disabilities to environments that (1) frequently violated their basic constitutional rights and (2) provided no consistent educational or habilitative benefit. Ultimately, the findings of the courts forced many states to initiate "deinstitutionalization" programs and develop community-based alternatives for persons with disabilities.

Although the deinstitutionalization movement did result in a significant reduction in the total number of persons with disabilities served in institutions, research suggests that there are still more than 50,000 individuals living in these settings nationally (Anderson et al., 1998; Prouty et al, 2000). In addition, although the overall population of institutions has decreased, the number of persons with severe and profound disabilities in these settings has increased. Heated debates continue in many states about the closure of institutions in spite of the overwhelming evidence that community-based service alternatives are better able to meet the needs of people with severe disabilities on a number of different measures of effectiveness. For example:

1. Individuals living in community settings make more gains in general adaptive behavior than those individuals living in institutions (Lynch, Kellow, & Willson, 1997).
2. The quality of life enjoyed by persons living in community settings is better than that of individuals living in institutional programs (Conroy & Elks, 1999).
3. Individuals who have moved into community residences have more control over their own lives than people who remain in institutions (Stancliffe & Abery, 1997).

In addition, there is evidence to suggest that nationally the average costs of providing institutional care to a person with disabilities has doubled since 1984, to nearly $100,000 per year (Anderson et al., 1998). It is also clear that the high costs of institutional programs are having a negative effect on the ability of states to meet the growing demand for community-based service programs (Lakin, 1998; Stancliffe & Hayden, 1998). Finally, there is growing evidence suggesting that the quality of services provided to people living in institutions may be declining in spite of the high costs (Stancliffe & Hayden, 1998). These factors have prompted advocacy groups for people with disabilities to call for the closure of all remaining institutions (ARC, 1995; TASH, 1986).

## The Developmental Model

The developmental model of services for persons with disabilities emerged as the need to move beyond institutional programs became more widely accepted by policy makers and the public at large. Switzky et al. (1988, p. 32) state: "The 'developmental model' conceives of handicapped persons as individuals who can benefit from training and educational instruction…and that the same principles of learning and development apply to both handicapped and nonhandicapped persons."

---

**Focus 3**
What are the primary assumptions underlying the developmental model?

---

A basic assumption underlying the developmental model is that persons with and without disabilities acquire cognitive, communication, social, motor, and self-care skills in the same way, except that persons with disabilities require more intense levels of training and support to develop these skills. This assumption led to the emergence of comprehensive developmental curricula designed to promote the acquisition of skills that would allow "normal" performance by persons with disabilities in home, school, work, and other community settings. The instructional objectives in these curricula were organized around the developmental milestones exhibited by persons without disabilities. In general, it was believed that if people with disabilities had access to these curricula and systematic instruction, they would learn the skills necessary to function independently in the community.

A second but equally important movement during this phase of program development was the articulation of the *principle of normalization* (Nirje, 1969; Wolfensberger, 1972). The principle of normalization is based on the assumption that persons with disabilities have a right to a lifestyle that is as close as possible to that of individuals without disabilities. The principle of normalization states that individuals with disabilities should participate equally in the normal routines of community life, including having a home to live in, access to school or a job, self-selected and self-directed leisure time, and the opportunity to establish social networks that include individuals without disabilities. Based on the principle of normalization, service programs were designed to promote the participation of individuals with disabilities in all aspects of community life.

These concepts provided the framework for the development of an elaborate system of community-based educational, residential, and employment programs that are still intact today. To achieve the goals of developmental learning and normalization, these service systems adopted a structure known as the *continuum of services* (Taylor, 1988). This "continuum" was conceived as a hierarchy of service programs (Figure 2.1). It is designed to teach persons with disabilities increasingly more complex skills and to move them incrementally toward a more normal lifestyle. Service programs at the first level in the continuum were designed to provide the most intense service support and focus training efforts on basic developmental milestones. As individuals learned these skills they would graduate to the next program in the continuum. It was believed that this structure would ultimately result in the entry of persons with disabilities into the mainstream of the community.

> *Focus 4*
> Identify the factors that prevented the developmental model from achieving its primary goals and objectives.

Despite the more positive view of persons with disabilities inherent in the development model and the continuum of services, they have failed to meet initial expectations for achieving the full inclusion of people with disabilities in community life (Lakin, 1998; Mank, Cioffi, & Yovanoff, 1998; Wehman, West, & Kregel, 1999; U.S. Department of Education, 2000). Many people with disabilities find themselves continually getting ready for their entry into the mainstream of the community but with little hope of ever actually achieving this outcome. This occurs because their disability often prevents them from mastering the "prerequisite developmental skills" necessary to graduate to the next level in the continuum.

For example, recent studies suggest that nationally there are between 800,000 and 1 million people with disabilities who are served in sheltered workshop or work activity centers (Mank, Buckley, Cioffi, & Dean, 1996; Wehman & Revell, 1997). Individuals with the most significant disabilities, such as severe mental retardation or multiple disabilities, are the least likely to access more inclusive employment programs (Bond, Dietzen, McGrew, & Miller, 1995; Gilmore, Schalock, Kiernan, & Butterworth, 1997; Kregel & Wehman, 1997; Revell,

## The School Continuum

**FULL-TIME REGULAR CLASS PLACEMENT**

Participation in age-appropriate grade-level or content-area classes.

↑

**REGULAR CLASS WITH RESOURCE SUPPORT**

Participation in age-appropriate grade-level or content-area classes. Students are pulled out of regular classes for instruction on specific educational goals.

↑

**PART-TIME SPECIAL CLASS PLACEMENT**

Students are served in a separate class for children with disabilities for instruction in the primary curriculum domains. They participate in regular grade-level or content-area classes for "nonacademic" or "elective" courses.

↑

**SPECIAL CLASS PLACEMENT**

Students are served in separate classes for children with disabilities for instruction on all curriculum domains.

↑

**SPECIAL SCHOOLS**

Students are served in a separate school for children with disabilities.

↑

**HOMEBOUND INSTRUCTION**

Students receive educational services at home.

↑

**RESIDENTIAL SCHOOL**

Students are placed and live in a private school structured to provide services to a specific group of children with disabilities.

↑

**PUBLIC INSTITUTION**

Students are placed and live in publically operated institution for persons with disabilities.

## The Vocational Continuum

**COMPETITIVE EMPLOYMENT**

Employed in an integrated community business.

↑

**TRANSITIONAL EMPLOYMENT SERVICES**

Individuals are provided training in a specific job in a community business. Once trained, individuals are placed in competitive employment.

↑

**SHELTERED WORKSHOPS**

Individuals are placed in a separate facility for adults with disabilities located in the community. The habilitative program is designed to provide therapeutic and tolerance activities designed to foster work readiness. Individuals must be provided remunerative work at no less than 50% of minimum wage.

↑

**WORK ACTIVITY CENTERS**

Individuals are placed in a separate facility for adults with disabilities located in the community. The program is focused on personal and social adjustment, and work readiness skills.

↑

**DAY TREATMENT CENTER**

Individuals are placed in a separate facility for adults with disabilities located in the community. The program is focused on basic academic motor communication, and self-help skills.

## The Residential Continuum

**INDEPENDENT LIVING**

Individuals live in their own home.

↑

**SEMI-INDEPENDENT LIVING**

Individuals live in a community with a small number of other persons with disabilities, the habilitative program is focused on training personal and household management skills necessary for independent living.

↑

**FOSTER CARE**

Individuals live with a nondisabled person or family. The individual or family may serve more than one person with disabilities. The program focuses primarily on care but may include some skill training.

↑

**GROUP HOMES**

Individuals live in a home with several other adults with disabilities. Paid staff provide support to the residents in meeting basic personal needs. The habilitative program focuses on personal and household management skills.

↑

**INTERMEDIATE CARE FACILITIES**

Individuals are placed in a facility with a large number of individuals with disabilities. The program is structured to provide ongoing medical services to the individuals.

↑

**PUBLIC INSTITUTION**

Individuals are placed and live in a publically operated institution for persons with disabilities.

---

**FIGURE 2.1**  *Continuums of Service*

Wehman, Kregel, West, & Rayfield, 1994). Researchers have reported similarly dismal findings in the residential (Lakin, 1998; Mangan, Blake, Prouty, & Lakin, 1994; Taylor, 1995; Walker, 1999) and educational service systems (U.S. Department of Education, 2000). These data clearly show that in spite of the promises of the developmental model, it has not led to the full inclusion of all people with severe disabilities in the community.

The failure of the developmental model to achieve its primary objectives has prompted a reevaluation of the underlying assumptions of the service programs operating today. Increasingly, people with disabilities, parents, advocates, professionals, and policy makers are recognizing the need for a system of service delivery that is not based on the assumption that persons with disabilities must "earn" access to the community. Rather, services should be redesigned to provide the support necessary to allow these individuals to be successful in home, school, work, and other community settings.

## The Ecological Model

The ecological model is also based on the assumption that people with disabilities should have the opportunity to participate in the social, economic, and recreational life of the community. The ecological model differs from the developmental model in that it assumes that achieving these outcomes will require not only developing the skills of the individual but also providing adequate support in home, school, work, and community settings. In addition, the ecological model does not require individuals with disabilities to "earn" their way into the community.

---

**Focus 5**
What are the primary assumptions underlying the ecological model?

---

As described by Schalock (1986), the model "stresses that successful adjustment to the environment depends less on individual characteristics per se and more on the match between person and environmental attributes" (p. 2). The intended outcomes of service programs are to support a person–environment fit. In order to achieve this fit, training focuses on activities that are performed in a natural setting (grocery shopping, eating in a restaurant, work, home, etc.), and the expected level of independent performance is adjusted to match the individual's capabilities. In other words, training is focused on achieving the maximum level of participation possible for the person, not necessarily on achieving "normal" performance. For some people, this may mean total independence and for others it may mean partial participation in activities. In each case, the intervention provided by the service program is tailored to the individual's needs.

The ecological model uses a three-phase process to maximize the fit between the person and the environment (Schalock, 1986). First, each person's behavioral capabilities are assessed in relationship to specific demands of the activity and environment. Second, the "goodness of fit" between the person's capabilities and the environmental demands is determined, focusing specifically on the barriers that prevent the individual's successful performance in the setting. Finally, an intervention is designed to overcome these barriers. The intervention may include skill training, adaptation of activity or physical environment, or the provision of support.

---

**Focus 6**
What current service delivery programs for persons with severe disabilities incorporate the critical features of the ecological model?

---

The ecological model has provided the basis for the development of a number of educational and community service programs for persons with disabilities. These include supported inclusive education, supported employment, and supported living (c.f. Meyer, Peck, & Brown, 1991). The primary focus of these programs is to identify life options for individuals that meet their personal needs and interests, then to provide the training and support necessary to ensure their success. In such programs, services are brought to the person and designed around their needs, rather than placing an individual in a service program.

For example, supported employment is designed to assist individuals in finding jobs that match their personal interests and needs, to promote their acquisition of necessary work and work-related skills, and to provide ongoing support in the job site to ensure their success (see Window 2.2). Research indicates that in comparison to those people served in the continuum of employment services, people enrolled in supported employment programs earn significantly higher wages, engage in more remunerative work, have more frequent social interactions with co-workers without disabilities during the work day, have more frequent social interactions with individuals without disabilities after the work day, and utilize community services to a greater extent (Gilmore et al., 1997; Mank et al., 1998; Wehman et al., 1999). Similar results have been found in both supported living (Clees, 1996; Taylor, 1995) and supported inclusive educational programs (Hunt & Goetz, 1997).

The ecological model and the notion of supported inclusive education, work, and living have opened new doors for persons with severe disabilities. Indeed, these programs have created the first real opportunities for persons with severe disabilities to become an integral part of our communities.

---

**Focus 7**
What values will drive the development of educational and community service programs for persons with severe disabilities during the next decade?

---

## Emerging Values in Service Programs

Each step in the evolution of service programs for persons with disabilities has been initiated and bolstered by changing societal values. Individuals with disabilities, parents, professionals,

## WINDOW 2.2 • *A Real Job to Go To!*

Martha is 24 years old and works at A Child's Place, a day care center for preschool-age children. She has always liked children. When she was in high school she would babysit for her younger brother and sister and would occasionally stay with the kids of some of her next-door neighbors. When she left high school she was placed in a sheltered workshop program in the community in which she lived. Although she liked the staff and the people she worked with, she was never very happy about the job that she was doing. The workshop had a contract with a national airlines to clean and package the ear phones that passengers used to listen to music or watch movies on the plane. She worked about three hours a day. The rest of the time was spent working on skills that she had learned while she was in school. She made about $25 to $30 a week. She would frequently complain to her mother and father that she really did not like her job and she felt like she spent most of her time doing nothing.

After about a year, Martha was given the opportunity to participate in the supported employment program operated by the agency. Before she got involved, the staff in the supported employment program talked with Martha and her parents about what she would like to do. The first thing that she said was that she would like to take care of kids. Both her mom and dad told the staff that she had done sitting for them and for neighbors and had done a great job. After some discussion Martha, her parents, and the staff in the supported employment program agreed to look for a job in a child care center. The staff from the supported employment program scoured the newspaper and contacted the local Job Service office to see if any positions were open. A Child's Place was advertising for a 30-hour-a-week aide. A staff person from the supported employment program contacted Marge Smith, the director of A Child's Place, and asked her if she would consider hiring a person with a disability. At first she was hesitant, but she agreed to meet with the staff person to discuss the possibility.

During the meeting the staff person explained the supported employment program to Marge and told her a little bit about Martha. Marge agreed to meet Martha and talk with her about the job. On the day of the interview Martha was nervous. She and the staff person from the supported employment program went to A Child's Place, and Martha spent about 30 minutes talking with Marge about her experience with children and what she liked to do with them. Marge told Martha and the staff persons that she wanted a day or so to think about it and she would get back to them. The next day Marge call Martha to let her know that she had gotten the job.

Before Martha went to work, staff from the supported employment program went out to A Child's Place and analyzed the steps of the job that Martha would be expected to do. They worked closely with Marge to make sure that they had accurately identified the demands of the job. Once the analysis was completed, Martha came to work with one of the staff people. The staff person worked with Martha to learn the jobs she was responsible for and to ensure that the jobs got done to Marge's satisfaction. As Martha got better at the job, the staff person began to reduce the amount of assistance she provided. She also worked with Marge and with the other aides in the program on when and how to give Martha help when she needed it. In addition, she helped Martha make arrangements to come to weekly staff meetings and to participate in the after-school social outings that the staff had every Friday. Eventually, the staff person had reduced their assistance to weekly visits. When Martha needed help, Marge or the other aides would give it to her; when she needed to learn a new task, they would help her with it. The staff person continued to follow up with Martha to make sure she was doing her job right and that Marge was satisfied with her work. Martha now earns about $180 a week after taxes. Martha has become an important part of the staff of A Child's Place. Marge has told both Martha and her parents that she is one of the best employees that she has ever had. Best of all, Martha is very happy with her new job. She recently told her Mom that she liked work because she had "a real job to go to"!

and policy makers are now beginning to articulate a new set of values that will guide the development of educational and community service programs over the next decade. These values expand upon many of the assumptions underlying the developmental and ecological models. However, they also stress the need for increased individualization of service and reliance on other community members, rather than service programs, to support the participation of people with disabilities in community life. This emerging set of values are (1) full inclusion, (2) natural supports, and (3) choice and autonomy.

## *Full Inclusion*

Since the late 1960s, service programs have sought to increase the involvement of children and adults with severe disabilities in community life. Despite the intentions of these programs, their actual success in achieving this outcome has been marginal. For many persons with severe disabilities, community life remains a protracted story of segregation. They live, work, and go to school only with other individuals who have disabilities and access community resources only when the program staff paid to serve them schedules "community activities." Although the development of supported work, living, and educational programs has the potential to open many doors for persons with severe disabilities, only a limited number of these people have access to these programs (Taylor, 1995; Wehman et al., 1999). In many states, these programs are simply "add-ons" to the existing service delivery system (Lakin, 1998; West, Revell, Kregel, & Bricout, 1999). Furthermore, they are perceived by many professionals as just one more step in the continuum of service. Just as people with severe disabilities have been traditionally required to "earn" their way into competitive employment, independent living, and the educational mainstream, they are now being required to demonstrate that they are "ready" to benefit from inclusive supported employment, living, and education programs. In this way, the current service system continues to function as a gatekeeper rather than as a promoter of inclusion for persons with severe disabilities.

Many persons with disabilities, parents, and advocates now argue that full inclusion must not be simply a philosophical ideal, but an integral component of all educational, employment, and living programs. Achieving this outcome will require two fundamental changes in the way in which service programs are designed and implemented.

First, many of the specialized services now provided to persons with disabilities exist simply because the generic services and resources available to persons without disabilities have not been structured to accommodate diversity (Taylor, 1995). If people with severe disabilities are going to be fully included in the community, then service and resource programs for people without disabilities must be restructured to meet the needs of all people. For example, the expansion of supported inclusive educational programs for students with severe disabilities has led to the idea of the "universal design" of curriculum and instruction for all students. A basic premise of universal design is that the curriculum must be:

> ...accessible and applicable to students, teachers, and parents with different backgrounds, learning styles, abilities, and disabilities in widely varied learning contexts. The "universal" in universal design does not imply one optimal solution for everyone, but rather it underscores the need for inherently flexible, customizable content, assignments, and activities. (Center for Applied Special Technology, 1999, p. 1)

Recent amendments to the Individuals with Disabilities Education Act (IDEA) have reinforced this approach by emphasizing the need for the Individualized Education Program (IEP) to address how students will be involved and progress in the general education curriculum (Section 300.347). The language of this section of the statute implies a strong preference for a single curriculum for all students and that special education services should be structured to support the participation of all students with disabilities in that curriculum.

The second fundamental change that must occur if full inclusion is to be achieved is the replacement of the current "continuum of service" with a "menu of services." Functionally, the continuum of service is designed to "plug" individuals into service programs. The result is that the living, work, and educational opportunities available to persons with severe disabilities are limited to the service programs offered by the system. In contrast, a menu of service approach would be structured to allow individuals to select the types and intensity of service they needed to be successful in home, school, work, or community settings. The mix of services actually provided to individuals would vary significantly and would be tailored to the person. The supported living, work, and educational programs of today are the initial prototypes of this kind of service structure. However, the type and intensity of services provided through these programs are also often restricted by the philosophical orientation and administrative organization of the agencies that provide these services. Furthermore, the limited availability of these programs in local communities often restricts the options available to people with severe disabilities. For example, the only supported employment program available in a small rural community may be organized to provide support to those individuals interested in employment in the agricultural industry. Obviously, in this situation the choices available to people with severe disabilities who live in this community are going to be limited by the options provided by the local service program. Ultimately, achieving full inclusion of people with disabilities in the community will require a flexible system that can not only provide specific services but also create new services as necessary to meet the needs of individuals with severe disabilities.

## Natural Supports

Individuals without disabilities derive a significant amount of support in coping with the demands of daily life from friends, family, neighbors, and co-workers. This support can range from getting a ride to the grocery store when our car is in the shop to just having someone around to listen to us when we have had a tough day at work. The support that we receive from these various people is not only critical to successful community living, it influences our quality of life. Sociologists have long recognized the interdependence of individual members of any community (Unger & Powell, 1980; Unger & Wandersman, 1985). In one way or another, each member of the community is dependent on all other members to deal successfully with day-to-day life.

Although this is a widely accepted truism for people without disabilities, it is far from reality for most people with severe disabilities. The design and structure of most educational, living, and employment programs inhibit the development of these natural sources of support for persons with disabilities. Not only are persons with severe disabilities segregated from other community members, often the only time they access community settings is when they participate in a specially organized activity. Furthermore, particularly as adults, these people are often cut off from their family because they are forced to live in communities where services are located rather than where their parents or siblings live. The bottom line is that for most people with disabilities, the primary source of support in the community comes from individuals who are paid to provide services. Notwithstanding the commitment of professionals who work in these programs, the very nature of this relationship creates conditions that will inevitably lead to the intrusion of paid staff into the lives of persons with severe disabilities. The level of community inclusion that persons with severe disabilities enjoy often evolves around the skills, resources, and values of paid staff.

Not surprisingly, individuals with severe disabilities, parents, advocates, professionals, and policy makers are calling for the development of service programs that rely more heavily on the natural supports available in schools, businesses, and neighborhoods (Mank et al., 1998; Snell & Janey, 2000; Walker, 1999). Such service programs would attempt to (1) foster support by individuals who live, work, or go to school with a person with severe disabilities and (2) reduce the frequency and intensity of support provided by paid staff.

It is unlikely that significant progress toward full inclusion of persons with severe disabilities in the community will be made until other community members acknowledge their social responsibility in supporting this group of individuals. The reliance on paid staff by educational and community service programs is likely to continue to reinforce attitudes of segregation by the community at large and reliance on specialized services for persons with disabilities.

## Choice and Autonomy

Although the values of full inclusion and natural support are critical to enhancing the quality of life of persons with severe disabilities, these concepts hold very little weight if the decisions about how they are operationalized are not driven by individual needs and preferences. There is no single answer for what constitutes an acceptable quality of life. Each of us has different hopes and dreams, different ways of thinking about work, and different ways of meeting the demands of community living. Through the long evolution of service programs for people with severe disabilities, society has made serious errors in judgment about what this group of people are capable of and what they might want or need. In our attempts to deal humanely with persons with severe disabilities we have often ignored one of the most basic human rights: the right to choose.

Supporting choice for persons with severe disabilities is a complex matter. It is often assumed that people with severe disabilities lack the cognitive and communication skills necessary to indicate choices about where they live, where they work, who they spend time with, and so on. However, for many persons with severe disabilities it is equally likely that their lack of choice simply reflects (1) the unresponsiveness of caretakers to nontraditional strategies of communication used to indicate preference, (2) a lack of training in more effective ways of communicating choices, and (3) a lack of opportunity in many educational and community service programs to make choices (Everson & Zhang, 2000; Miner & Bates, 1997; Wehmeyer, Bersani, & Gagne, 2000). Although the research base in this area is small, it is clear that nearly all persons with severe disabilities can assume some role in the decisions that are made about their lives.

Consequently, people with disabilities and their advocates are demanding that educational and community service programs adopt strategies that maximize the participation of people with severe disabilities in decisions that affect their lives. These strategies include procedures for making major life decisions such as where a person works and lives (O'Brien, 1987; Vandercook, York, & Forrest, 1989), to involving the individual in deciding the activities they complete on a day-to-day basis (Parsons & Reid, 1990; Rice & Nelson, 1988). It is unlikely that people with severe disabilities will achieve full inclusion in the community unless they are empowered to make choices for themselves and given the resources and tools necessary to act on those choices.

## Conclusion

Historically, society has not valued people with severe disabilities. These individuals were often viewed as being incapable of making a meaningful contribution to the economic and social fabric of the community and, further, as having little capacity to improve that situation. In response, society developed service delivery systems that were designed to remove people from the mainstream of society and to meet their basic physical needs. Since the 1960s and 1970s the focus on care and protection in educational and community service programs has been replaced by an emphasis on personal development, inclusion in the community, and self-determination. Although much progress has been made since then, the quality of life of individuals with and without disabilities is still extremely discrepant. However, the new set of values that is being articulated by persons with severe disabilities and their advocates will hopefully begin to shape public policy and professional practice in ways that will close this gap. The subsequent chapters in this book will describe program models at each age level that reflect this emerging set of values and will describe the roles of professionals in supporting people with severe disabilities in the community.

## Focus Review

Focus 1: Identify the three assumptions underlying the institutional model.

- Individuals with disabilities are sick.
- Individuals with disabilities cannot learn.
- Individuals with disabilities are a menace to society.

Focus 2: What factors prompted the deinstitutionalization movement of the late 1960s and 1970s?

- Research demonstrated that persons with disabilities, even persons with the most severe disabilities, could learn to function in the community.

- Research demonstrated that institutional programs often inhibited rather than promoted the development of persons with disabilities.
- There were frequent reports of mistreatment and abuse.

Focus 3: What are the primary assumptions underlying the developmental model?

- Individuals with disabilities learn in the same way as people without disabilities but require more time to master basic skills.
- Individuals with disabilities have the right to participate in the normal routines of community life and to establish a lifestyle comparable to that of persons without disabilities.

Focus 4: Identify the factors that prevented the developmental model from achieving its primary goals and objectives.

- The structure of the continuum of services required individuals with disabilities to "earn" their way into the community.
- There were poor outcomes for people with disabilities.

Focus 5: What are the primary assumptions underlying the ecological model?

- People with disabilities have the right to participate in economic and social aspects of the community.
- Service programs should be designed to provide support to people with disabilities in natural home, school, work, and community settings.

Focus 6: What current service delivery programs for persons with severe disabilities incorporate the critical features of the ecological model?

- Supported inclusive education: Providing training and support to students with disabilities in regular education settings.
- Supported work: Providing training and support to adults with disabilities in competitive employment settings.
- Supported living: Providing training and support to people with disabilities in their own homes.

Focus 7: What values will drive the development of educational and community service programs for persons with severe disabilities during the next decade?

- Full inclusion in all aspects of community life.
- Increased reliance on natural supports to promote the success of persons with disabilities in the community.
- Maximizing personal choice and autonomy.

# References

Anderson, L. L., Lakin, K. C., Mangan, T. W., & Prouty, R. W. (1998). State institutions: Thirty years of depopulation and closure. *Mental Retardation, 36,* 431–443.

ARC (1995). *Position statement XII: Where people live.* Silver Spring, MD: The Arc of the United States.

Association for Persons with Severe Handicaps (TASH) (1986). *Deinstitutionalization policy.* Washington, DC: Author.

Blatt, B., Biklen, D., & Bogdan, R. (1977). *An alternative textbook in special education: People, schools and other institutions.* Denver, CO: Love.

Blatt, B., & Kaplan, F. (1966). *Christmas in purgatory: A photographic essay in mental retardation.* Boston: Allyn & Bacon.

Bond, G. R., Dietzen, L., McGrew, J., & Miller, L. (1995). Accelerating entry into supported employment for persons with severe psychiatric disabilities. *Rehabilitation Psychology, 40,* 91–111.

Burton, T. A., & Hirshoren, A. (1979). The education of severely and profoundly retarded children: Are we sacrificing the child to the concept? *Exceptional Children, 45,* 618–623.

Center for Applied Special Technology (1999). Summary of university design concepts. Available: http://wwe.cast.org/concepts/concepts_summary.htm.

Clees, T. J. (1996). Supported living and collaborative transition. In P. McLaughlin and P. Wehman (Eds.), *Mental retardation and developmental disabilities* (pp. 339–369). Austin, TX: Pro-Ed.

Conroy, J. W., & Elks, M. A. (1999). Tracking qualities of life during deinstitutionalization: A covariance study. *Education and Training in Mental Retardation and Developmental Disabilities, 34,* 212–222.

Dennis, W., & Sayegh, Y. (1965). The effect of supplementary experiences upon the behavioral development of infants in institutions. *Child Development, 36,* 81–90.

Everson, J. M., & Zhang, D. (2000). Person-centered planning: Characteristics, inhibitors, and supports. *Education and Training in Mental Retardation and Developmental Disabilities, 35,* 36–43.

Gilmore, D. S., Schalock, R. L., Kiernan, W. E., Butterworth, J. (1997). National comparisons and critical findings in integrated employment. In W. E. Kiernan & R. L. Schalock (Eds.), *Integrated employment: Current status and future directions* (pp. 49–66). Washington, DC: American Association on Mental Retardation.

Gilson, S. F. (1998). Choice and self-advocacy: A consumer's perspective. In P. Wehman and J. Kregel (Eds.), *More than a job: Securing satisfying careers for people with disabilities* (pp. 3–24). Baltimore: Paul H. Brookes.

Henderson, R. A., & Vitello, S. J. (1988). Litigation related to community integration. In L. W. Heal, J. I. Haney, and A. R. Novak Amado (Eds.), *Integration of Developmental Disabled Individuals into the Community* (pp. 273–282). Baltimore: Paul H. Brookes.

Hunt, P., & Goetz, L. (1997). Research on inclusive educational programs, practices, and outcomes for students with severe disabilities. *Journal of Special Education, 31,* 3–29.

Kaplan, O. L. (1943). Mental decline in older morons. *American Journal of Mental Deficiency, 47,* 277–285.

Kregel, J., & Wehman, P. (1997). Supported employment: A decade of employment outcomes for individuals with significant disabilities. In W. E. Kiernan & R. L. Schalock (Eds.), *Integrated employment: Current status and future directions* (pp. 41–48). Washington, DC: American Association on Mental Retardation.

Lakin, K. C. (1998). On the outside looking in: Attending to waiting lists in systems of services for people with developmental disabilities. *Mental Retardation, 36,* 157–162.

Lynch, P. S., Kellow, T., & Willson, V. L. (1997). The impact of deinstitutionalization on the adaptive behavior of adults with mental retardation: A meta-analysis. *Education and Treatment in Mental Retardation and Developmental Disabilities, 32,* 255–261.

Mangan, T., Blake, E. M., Prouty, R. W., & Lakin, K. C. (1994). *Residential services for persons with mental retardation and related conditions: Status and trends through 1993.* Minneapolis, MN: University of Minnesota, Center on Residential Services and Community Living/Institute on Community Integration.

Mank, D., Buckley, J., Cioffi, A., & Dean, J. (1996). Do social systems really change? Retrospective interviews with state-supported employment systems-change directors. *Focus on Autism and Other Developmental Disabilities, 11,* 243–250.

Mank, D., Cioffi, A., & Yovanoff, P. (1998). Employment outcomes for people with severe disabilities: Opportunities for improvement. *Mental Retardation, 36,* 205–216.

Meyer, L. H., Peck, C. A., & Brown, L. (1991). *Critical issues in the lives of people with severe disabilities.* Baltimore: Paul H. Brookes.

Miner, C. A., & Bates, P. E. (1997). The effect of person centered planning activities on the IEP/transition planning process. *Education and Training in Mental Retardation and Developmental Disabilities, 32,* 105–112.

Nirje, B. (1969). The normalization principle and its human management implications. In R. Kugel & W. Wolfensberger (Eds.), *Changing Patterns in Residential Services for the Mentally Retarded* (pp. 231–240). Washington, DC: President's Committee on Mental Retardation.

O'Brien, J. (1987). A guide to life-style planning: Using the Activities Catalog to integrate services and a natural support systems. In B. Wilcox & G. T. Bellamy (Eds.) *A comprehensive guide to the Activities Catalog: An alternative curriculum for youth and adults with severe disabilities* (pp. 175–189). Baltimore: Paul H. Brookes.

Parsons, M. B., & Reid, D. H. (1990). Assessing food preferences among persons with profound mental retardation: Providing opportunities to make choices. *Journal of Applied Behavior Analysis, 23,* 183–195.

Prouty, R. W., Lakin, K. C., & Anderson, L. L. (2000). Five year trends in Medicaid institutional (ICF/MR) populations, home and community based services reflect major changes. *Mental Retardation, 38,* 294.

Revell, W. G., Wehman, P., Kregel, J., West, M., & Rayfield, R. (1994). Supported employment for persons with severe disabilities: Positive trends in wages, models, and funding. *Education and Training in Mental Retardation, 29,* 256–264.

Rice, M. S., & Nelson, D. L. (1988). Effect of choice-making on a self-care activity in mentally retarded adult and adolescent males. *The Occupation Therapy Journal of Research, 8,* 75–83.

Schalock, R. (1986). *Transitions from school to work.* Washington, DC: National Association of Rehabilitation Facilities.

Skeels, H. M. (1966). Adult status of children with contrasting early life experiences. *Monographs of the Society for Research in Child Development, 31*(3), 1–65.

Sloane, W., & Harmon, H. H. (1947). Constancy of IQ in mental defective. *Journal of Genetic Psychology, 71,* 177–185.

Snell, M. E., & Janney, R. (2000). *Social relationships and peer support.* Baltimore: Paul H. Brookes.

Stancliffe, R. J., & Abery, B. H. (1997). Longitudinal study of deinstitutionalization and the exercise of choice. *Mental Retardation, 35,* 159–169.

Stancliffe, R. J., & Hayden, M. F. (1998). Longitudinal study of instructional downsizing: Effects on individuals who remain in the institution. *American Journal of Mental Retardation, 102,* 500–510.

Stancliffe, R. J., & Lakin K. C. (1999). A longitudinal comparison of day program services and outcomes of people who left institutions and those who stayed. *Journal of the Association for Persons with Severe Handicaps, 24,* 44–57.

Switzky, H. N., Dudzinski, M., Van Acker, R., & Gambor, J. (1988). Historical foundations of out-of-home residential alternatives for mentally retarded persons. In L. W. Heal, J. I. Haney, & A. R. Novak Amado (Eds.), *Integration of developmental disabled individuals into the community* (pp. 19–36). Baltimore: Paul H. Brookes.

Taylor, S. J. (1988). Caught in the continuum: A critical analysis of the principle of the Least Restrictive Environment. *Journal of the Association for Persons with Severe Handicaps, 13,* 41–53.

Taylor, S. J. (1995). Living in the community: Beyond the continuum. In L. Nadel (Ed.), *Down syndrome: Living and learning in the community* (pp. 249–255). New York: Wiley-Liss.

Unger, D. G., & Powell, D. R. (1980). Supporting families under stress: The role of social networks. *Family Relations, 29,* 566–574.

Unger, D. G., & Wandersman, A. (1985). The importance of neighbors: The social, cognitive, and affective components of neighboring. *American Journal of Community Psychology, 13,* 139–169.

U.S. Department of Education (2000). *22nd annual report to Congress on the implementation of the Individuals with Disabilities Education Act.* Washington, DC: U.S. Government Printing Office.

Vandercook, T., York, J., & Forest, M. (1989). The McGill Action Planning System (MAPS): A strategy for building the vision. *Journal of the Association for Persons with Severe Handicaps, 14,* 205–215.

Walker, P. (1999). From community presence to sense of place: Community experiences of adults with developmental disabilities. *Journal of the Association for Persons with Severe Handicaps, 24,* 23–32.

Wehman, P., & Revell, G. W. (1997). Transition into supported employment for young adults with severe disabilities: Current practices and future direction. *Journal of Vocational Rehabilitation, 8,* 65–74.

Wehman, P., West, M., & Kregel, J. (1999). Supported employment program development and research needs: Looking ahead to the year 2000. *Education and Training in Mental Retardation and Developmental Disabilities, 34,* 3–19.

Wehmeyer, M., Bersani, H., & Gagne, R. (2000). Riding the third wave: Self-determination and self-advocacy in the 21st century. *Focus on Autism and Other Developmental Disabilities, 15,* 106–115.

West, M., Revell, G., Kregel, J., & Bricout, J. (1999). The Medicaid Home and Community Waiver and supported employment. *American Journal on Mental Retardation, 104,* 78–87.

Wolfensberger, W. (1972). *Normalization: The principle of normalization in human services.* Washington, DC: National Institute on Mental Retardation.

# 3

# *Family, Friends, and Society*
## *Supporting People with Severe Disabilities*

*We all rely on family, friends, neighbors, and our communities for support. Promoting the inclusion of individuals with severe disabilities in the community requires that we recognize our interconnectedness as members of that community.*

## WINDOW 3.1 • *Yvonne*

"Yvonne belongs with us!" we firmly told the psychiatrist when he insisted that we place our two-year-old daughter in an institution. To us, Yvonne's sudden regression meant that she needed us more than ever—we could not abandon her, we could not reject her. At first we struggled on our own; there were no community supports. Then, together with other parents, we advocated for appropriate supports in the community for children who were labeled "severely mentally handicapped." We believed that Yvonne, and children like her, had a right to live at home, had a right to go to school, and had a right to participate in the life of the community. Our vision was shared and supported by some service providers but other professionals opposed our view and worked against us.

*Source:* Penner, I. (1999). *The right to belong: The story of Yvonne.* Available: http://www3.nb.sympatico.ca/ipenner/.

---

**Focus 1**
Distinguish between formal and natural supports for people with severe disabilities.

The need to support and be supported is an integral part of who we are in this world. Whether it be the love of a family member, the strength of a friend, the encouragement of a teacher, or the challenges provided by an employer, everyone is part of a support network. For the young child, this network is most often the family unit, which in today's society may be constituted in many different ways. As the child grows up, supports expand to the neighborhood, the school, and eventually to a larger heterogeneous group we call "community."

Is the need for a support network of family, friends, and community any different for a person with severe disabilities? Obviously, the answer is "no," although the nature and extent of the supports may vary for individuals with severe disabilities. As suggested by the Association for Persons with Severe Handicaps (TASH) (2000) people with severe disabilities will require extensive ongoing support in more than one major life activity in order to participate in integrated community settings and to enjoy a quality of life that is available to citizens with fewer or no disabilities.

In this chapter we will examine both formal and natural support networks for people with severe disabilities. Whereas formal supports are structured through agencies and organizations, natural supports may be provided directly by the nuclear and extended family members, friends, or neighbors. We will look at the nature of the supports provided to and by family members, the importance of building friendships in community settings, and the diversity of formal societal support networks.

## Formal Support Networks

Historically, formal supports have focused on isolating people with severe disabilities in order to protect them from an uncaring society, and to protect the society from the individual.

One manifestation of this social isolation was institutions for people defined as deviant. Institutions are an example of societal support that, while attempting to provide care to a person, actually promote dependence and highlight differences between people. More recently, support for people with severe disabilities has moved away from isolating the individual in programs and services that are separate from people who are not disabled to providing both formal as well as natural supports within the home, regular school, and community.

The purpose of a formal support system is to bring together the programs and services necessary in assisting the individual with severe disabilities to participate more actively in community and family life. Formal support systems are funded through the government in areas such as income maintenance, health care, education, housing, or employment. Examples of formal government supports include Social Security, Medicaid, special education, and vocational rehabilitation.

The inclusion of people with severe disabilities into the life of a community is framed in a philosophy that recognizes and accepts the range of human differences (Hardman, Drew, & Egan, 2002). However, stating a philosophy is one thing; turning it into positive outcomes for persons with severe disabilities is quite another. As suggested by Gerry and McWhorter (1991), "persons with severe disabilities pursue the same personal goals as do persons without disabilities: a comfortable home, a meaningful job, and social network of family members and friends" (p. 509). When a philosophy of inclusion is backed up by social policies that translate words into action, people with disabilities become valuable members within the community. The question then, is, how do we establish formal support networks that will foster the inclusion of people with severe disabilities? What are the barriers to participation, and how do we break them down? We will examine these issues from several perspectives: civil rights legislation, government-supported programs, and the role of advocacy in the lives of people with severe disabilities. We begin with the provisions of the Americans with Disabilities Act.

*Focus 2*
Identify the major provisions of the Americans with Disabilities Act (ADA).

## The Americans with Disabilities Act (ADA)

The Americans with Disabilities Act of 1990 (Public Law 101-336) is a national mandate to break down the barriers of discrimination against people with disabilities in private-sector employment, all public services, and public accommodations, transportation, and telecommunications. Under the ADA, businesses that serve the public must remove architectural barriers, such as curbs on sidewalks, narrow doorways, or shelving and desks that prevent access by a person with a disability. These same businesses must provide "reasonable accommodations" to people with disabilities in hiring or promotion practices, restructuring jobs, and modifying equipment. All new public transit facilities (such as buses or train stations) must be accessible, and transportation services must be available to people with disabilities who cannot use fixed bus routes. The law also mandates against discrimination in public accommodations (restaurants, hotels, retail stores), and in state and local government agencies. Telecommunication devices for people who are deaf must be made

**POINT OF INTEREST 3.1 • *Myths and Facts about the Americans with Disabilities Act***

**MYTH: The ADA is rigid and requires businesses to spend lots of money to make their existing facilities accessible.**

FACT: The ADA is based on common sense. It recognizes that altering existing structures is more costly than making new construction accessible. The law requires only that public accommodations (e.g., stores, banks, hotels, and restaurants) remove architectural barriers in existing facilities when this is "readily achievable," that is, it can be done "without much difficulty or expense." Inexpensive, easy steps to take include ramping one step; installing a bathroom grab bar; lowering a paper towel dispenser; rearranging furniture; installing offset hinges to widen a doorway; or painting new lines to create an accessible parking space.

**MYTH: Restaurants must provide menus in Braille.**

FACT: Not true. Waiters can read the menu to blind customers.

**MYTH: The ADA requires extensive renovation of all state and local government buildings to make them accessible.**

FACT: The ADA requires all government programs, not all government buildings, to be accessible. "Program accessibility" is a very flexible requirement and does not require a local government to do anything that would result in an undue financial or administrative burden. Local governments have been subject to this requirement for many years under the Rehabilitation Act of 1973. Not every building, nor each part of every building, needs to be accessible. Structural modifications are required only when there is no alternative available for providing program access. Let's say a town library has an inaccessible second floor. No elevator is needed if it provides "program accessibility" for persons using wheelchairs by having staff retrieve books.

**MYTH: Sign language interpreters are required everywhere.**

FACT: The ADA requires only that effective communication not exclude people with disabilities—which in many situations means providing written materials or exchanging notes. The law does not require any measure that would cause an undue financial or administrative burden.

**MYTH: The ADA forces business and government to spend lots of money hiring unqualified people.**

FACT: No unqualified job applicant or employee with a disability can claim employment discrimination under the ADA. Employees must meet all the requirements of the job and perform the essential functions of the job with or without reasonable accommodation. No accommodation must be provided if it would result in an undue hardship on the employer.

**MYTH: Accommodating workers with disabilities costs too much.**

FACT: Reasonable accommodation is usually far less expensive than many people think. In most cases, an appropriate reasonable accommodation can be made without difficulty and at little or no cost. A recent study commissioned by Sears indicates that of the 436 reasonable accommodations provided by the company between 1978 and 1992, 69 percent cost nothing, 28 percent cost less than $1,000, and only 3 percent cost more than $1,000.

**MYTH: The government is no help when it comes to paying for accessibility.**

FACT: Not so. Federal tax incentives are available to help meet the cost of ADA compliance.

**MYTH: ADA suits are flooding the courts.**

FACT: The ADA has resulted in a surprisingly small number of lawsuits—only about 650 na-

*(continued)*

**POINT OF INTEREST 3.1 • *Continued***

tionwide in five years. That's tiny compared to the 6 million businesses, 666,000 public and private employers, and 80,000 units of state and local government that must comply.

**MYTH: Everyone claims to be covered under the ADA.**

FACT: The definition of "individual with a disability" is fraught with conditions and must be applied on a case-by-case basis.

**MYTH: The ADA is being misused by people with "bad backs" and "emotional problems."**

FACT: Trivial complaints do not make it through the system. And many claims filed by individuals with such conditions are not trivial. There are people with severe depression or people with a history of alcoholism who are judged by their employers, not on the basis of their abilities, but rather on stereotypes and fears that employers associate with their conditions.

*Source:* Adapted from U.S. Department of Justice (2000). Myths and Facts about the Americans with Disabilities Act. Available: http://www.usdoj.gov/crt/ada/pubs/mythfct.txt.

available by all companies that offer telephone service to the general public. (See Point of Interest 3.1)

The ADA, as social policy, is one way that government can ensure that the rights of citizens with disabilities are protected. It is an attempt to provide people with disabilities an "equal playing field" as they seek access to the same opportunities afforded those who are not disabled. Another way to assist people with disabilities is for the government actually to develop and fund programs and services to provide income, health care, adequate housing, employment, and education.

## *The Individuals with Disabilities Education Act (IDEA)*

> *Focus 3*
> Identify the major provisions of the Individuals with Disabilities Education Act.

Education is a basic American value, reflecting the view that every person should have access to schools that promote personal growth and development throughout life. School is a place to prepare students for life, as well as an environment in which one can engage in reflection and reasoning. Schools exist to promote literacy, personal autonomy, economic self-sufficiency, personal fulfillment, and citizenship. Whether the value be reason and reflection or practical knowledge for living and learning in a democratic society, the expectation is full participation for everyone, including students who have severe mental and physical disabilities.

The translation of this value into actual practice for all students with disabilities began with the landmark case of *Brown v. Topeka, Kansas, Board of Education* in 1954. Although heralded as a mandate to end racial segregation, the U.S. Supreme Court's decision that education must be made available to everyone on an equal basis also set a major precedent for students with disabilities. A unanimous Supreme Court stated: "In these days, it is doubtful that any child may reasonably be expected to succeed in life if he is denied the opportunity of an education. Such an opportunity, where the state has undertaken to provide it, is a right which must be made available to all on equal terms" (*Brown v. Topeka, Kansas Board of Education,* 1954).

Nearly twenty years later, the Pennsylvania Association for Retarded Citizens filed a class-action suit on behalf of children with mental retardation who were excluded from public education on the basis of intellectual deficiency (*Pennsylvania Association for Retarded Citizens v. Commonwealth of Pennsylvania,* 1971). The issue was whether public school programs should be required to accommodate the students with significant intellectual differences. Under a court order, schools were to provide a free public education to all children with mental retardation, ages six to twenty-one, consistent with their individual learning needs. Preschool-age children with mental retardation were also entitled to a free and appropriate public education if the local school district was providing it for other children. The *Pennsylvania* decision was expanded in the case of *Mills v. District of Columbia Board of Education* (1972) to include all children with disabilities. The *Pennsylvania* and *Mills* cases served as catalysts for several court cases, and eventually the passage of Public Law 94-142 (Part B of the Education of the Handicapped Act) in 1975. This act was renamed the Individuals with Disabilities Education Act (IDEA) in 1990.

***Basic Requirements of IDEA.***    IDEA mandates that all eligible students, regardless of the extent or type of disability, are to receive at public expense the special education services necessary to meet their individual needs. Special education means specially designed instruction provided at no cost to parents in all settings (such as the classroom, physical education facilities, the home, and hospitals or institutions). The IDEA also stipulates that students with disabilities are to receive any related services necessary to ensure that they benefit from their educational experience. In order for a student to receive the specialized services available under the IDEA, two criteria must be met. First, the student must be identified as having one of the twelve disability conditions identified in federal law or their counterparts in a state's special education law. These conditions include mental retardation, specific learning disabilities, serious emotional disturbances (behavior disorders), speech or language impairments, vision loss (including blindness), hearing loss (including deafness), orthopedic impairments, other health impairments, deafness-blindness, multiple disabilities, autism, and traumatic brain injury.

The basic provisions of the IDEA provide for (1) nondiscriminatory and multidisciplinary assessment, (2) parental involvement in the development of the student's educational program, (3) placement in the least restrictive environment (LRE), and (4) an individualized education program.

Nondiscriminatory and multidisciplinary assessment involves testing students in their native or primary language whenever possible. Evaluation procedures must be selected and administered to prevent cultural or racial discrimination. A multidisciplinary team must conduct the assessment using several pieces of information to formulate a placement decision. All assessment tools used by this team must be validated for the purpose for which they are being used.

Under the IDEA, parents have the right to:

1. Consent in writing before the child is initially evaluated
2. Consent in writing before the child is initially placed in a special education program
3. Request an independent education evaluation if they feel the school's evaluation is inappropriate
4. Request an evaluation at public expense if a due-process hearing decision is that the public agency's evaluation was inappropriate
5. Participate on the committee that considers the evaluation, placement, and programming of the child
6. Inspect and review educational records and challenge information believed to be inaccurate, misleading, or in violation of the privacy or other rights of the child
7. Request a copy of information from their child's educational record
8. Request a hearing concerning the school's proposal or refusal to initiate or change the identification, evaluation, or placement of the child, or the provision of a free appropriate public education

The least restrictive environment is as an educational setting that (1) is consistent with the academic, social, and physical needs of the student, and (2) educates students who are disabled with their nondisabled peers to the maximum extent appropriate. In order to comply with this requirement, federal regulations mandate the development of a continuum of placements, including regular classrooms with support services, resource rooms, special classes and schools, and homebound and hospital programs.

The individualized education program (IEP) is a set of goals and activities that are based on the needs of each student as determined by the multidisciplinary team. As per the 1997 amendments, the IDEA requires that each child's IEP must include:

- a statement of the child's present levels of educational performance, including how the child's disability affects involvement and progress in the general curriculum. For preschool children the statement must describe how the disability affects the child's participation in appropriate activities.
- a statement of measurable annual goals, including benchmarks or short-term objectives related to meeting the child's needs that result from the disability. The annual goals should enable the child to be involved and make progress in the general curriculum and meet each of the child's other educational needs that result from the disability.
- a statement of the special education and related services and supplementary aids or services to be provided to, or on behalf of, the child. The statement must include (1) any program modifications or supports for school personnel that will be provided for the child to advance appropriately toward attaining the annual goals, (2) how the child will be involved and progress in the general curriculum and participate in extracurricular and other nonacademic activities, (3) how the child will be educated and participate with other children with disabilities and nondisabled children, and (4) an explanation of the extent, if any, to which the child will not participate with nondisabled children in the regular [general education] class and in the activities described above.
- a statement of any individual modifications in the administration of State or district-wide assessments of student achievement that are needed in order for the child to participate in

such assessment. If the IEP Team determines that the child will not participate in a particular State or district-wide assessment of student achievement (or part of such an assessment), there must be a statement of why that assessment is not appropriate for the child and how the child will be assessed.
• the projected date for the beginning of the services and modifications, and the anticipated frequency, location, and duration of those services and modifications.
• a statement of how the child's progress toward the annual goals will be measured and how the child's parents will be regularly informed (by means such as periodic report cards), at least as often as parents are informed of their nondisabled children's progress, of their child's progress toward the annual goals. The statement should include the extent to which that progress is sufficient to enable the child to achieve the goals by the end of the year. (IDEA 97, PL 105-17, Sec. 614[d])

The IDEA also requires that beginning at age 14, and updated annually, a student's IEP must include a statement of the transition services that relate to various courses of study (such as participation in advanced placement courses or a vocational education program). Beginning at age 16 (or younger, if determined appropriate by the IEP team), an IEP should include a statement of needed transition services, including, when appropriate, a statement of the responsibilities of other agencies (such as vocational rehabilitation) or any other needed linkages. The term *transition services* means a coordinated set of activities for a student with a disability that:

• is designed within an outcome-oriented process, which promotes movement from school to post-school activities, including post-secondary education, vocational training, integrated employment (including supported employment), continuing and adult education, adult services, independent living, or community participation;
• is based upon the individual student's needs, taking into account the student's preferences and interests; and
• is includes instruction, related services, community experiences, the development of employment and other post-school adult living objectives, and, when appropriate, acquisition of daily living skills and functional vocational evaluation. (Sec. 602[30])

***Early Intervention and Preschool Services under the IDEA.*** The Education of the Handicapped Act (now IDEA 97) was amended in 1986 to include provisions for preschool-age students with disabilities. *Public Law 99-457* established a mandate to provide a free and appropriate education for all preschool-age children with disabilities (3 through 5 years), and established a new early intervention program for infants, toddlers, and their families, *The Infant and Toddlers with Disabilities Program [Part H]*. Within IDEA 97, *The Infant and Toddlers with Disabilities Program* is located in Part C.

While programs for preschool-age students were mandated under P.L. 99-457, participation in early intervention programs under Part H and Part C is a discretionary program, operated at the option of each individual state. States are eligible for federal funds if they choose to participate and agree to meet federal implementation requirements. The Part C program includes some unique requirements, not specified in the Part B preschool and school-age educational programs. These requirements are designed to recognize the unique needs of infants and toddlers and their families, and to support individualized family-centered intervention rather than creating school-like programs for younger children. For example, infants and toddlers may become eligible for early intervention services based on the presence of a developmental delay or a condition, such as Down syndrome, which has a high probability of resulting in a developmental delay. This means that it is not necessary to establish the presence of a permanent disability or a specific category of disability (e.g., mental retardation) in order to provide early intervention services. In early intervention an Individualized Family Service Plan (IFSP), rather than an IEP, is developed for every eligible child and their family. The IFSP is very important because it includes the major outcomes expected to be achieved for the child or family, the criteria, procedures, and time lines used to determine progress toward achieving those outcomes, specific early intervention services necessary to meet the unique needs of the infant or toddler and the family, and a statement of the natural environments in which early intervention services will be provided (Part C, Sec. 303.344). A more in-depth discussion of IFSPs and other requirements for Part C early intervention programs is provided in Chapter 5.

The original provisions in P.L. 99-457 represented the same breakthrough for preschool-age children and their families that the 1975 passage of P.L. 94-142 (now the IDEA) had been for school-age children. While P.L. 94-142 provided some incentives for states to establish preschool programs for children with disabilities, they were not required to do so unless they also provided educational opportunities for all typically developing 3-, 4-, and 5-year-olds. Many states did provide kindergarten for 5-year olds, but most did not routinely educate 3- and 4-year-olds. Therefore, most states were under no legal pressure to provide preschool special education services. P.L. 99-457 eliminated this "loophole" and established a full service mandate for all preschoolers eligible to receive special education and related services. Additionally, it provided the same protections and rights for these children and their families as had previously existed for school-age children. All states receiving funds under the IDEA had to assure that 3- to 5-year-old children were receiving a free appropriate public education by the 1990–1991 school year.

There are two distinctions that directly affect children and families between Part B requirements for preschool-age children, and older students eligible for special education and related services. First, as in early intervention, states have the option of identifying children as eligible for services based on a developmental delay, as defined by the individual state, rather than the presence of a specific or permanent disability classification. Part A of IDEA 97 also allows states to extend this eligibility option through age 9. Unlike early intervention, preschool-age children must be eligible for services either through developmental delay, or through meeting the state eligibility criteria for specific disability classifications such as autism, communication disorder, or mental retardation. Second, transition planning with early intervention is required (Part C, Sec. 303.148) in order to ensure a smooth transition for children who are leaving early intervention for either preschool special education or other appropriate services. Transition planning needs to include a description of how the family will be included in the transition plans and notification of the local educational agency that the child will soon be turning 3, the age of eligibility for preschool special education services. For children who may be eligible for preschool special education, and with the approval of the family of the child, preschool staff participate in planning the transition to preschool at least 90 days ahead of the child's third birthday, so that no gaps or loss of service to the child occur as a result of the transition between programs. A more in-depth discussion of other federal legislation influencing programs and services for preschool-age children may be found in Chapter 6.

---

**Focus 4**
Identify four basic assumptions of an alternate assessment system for students with severe disabilities.

---

## School Reform and Accountability for Students with Severe Disabilities

"Higher expectations for all students" is the mantra for today's schools. The call for high expectations has resulted in a standards-based approach to reform—set high standards for what should be taught and how student performance should be measured. Four common elements characterize standards-based reform in America's schools.

1. A focus on student achievement as the primary measure of school success
2. An emphasis on challenging academic standards that specify the knowledge and skills students should acquire and the levels at which they should demonstrate mastery of that knowledge
3. A desire to extend the standards to *all* students, including those for whom expectations have been traditionally low
4. Heavy reliance on achievement testing to spur the reforms and to monitor their impact (National Research Council, 1997)

To ensure higher expectations for students with disabilities, the 1997 reauthorization of the IDEA required that a student's IEP must describe how the disability affects the child's involvement and progress in the general education curriculum. In addition, the IEP goals must enable the child to access the general education curriculum when appropriate. The law requires an explanation of any individual modifications in the administration of state- or district-wide assessment of student achievement that are needed in order for the child to participate.

A major challenge for education is to demonstrate accountability for *all* students, including those with severe disabilities. IDEA 97 requires that all students with disabilities must participate in state or district-wide assessments of achievement or there must be a statement of why that assessment is not appropriate for the child. The law also requires that individual modifications in the administration of state- or district-wide assessments be provided as appropriate in order for the child to participate. Examples of student accommodations include large-print text, testing in a separate setting, or extended time. Ysseldyke, Olsen, and Thurlow (1997) estimate that about 85 percent of students with disabilities have mild or moderate disabilities and can take state or district assessments, either with or without accommodations. For many students with severe disabilities, these assessments are inappropriate and they are excluded from taking them. Schools are still accountable, however, for the progress of these students. IDEA 97 mandated that by July 2000, states must be conducting alternate assessments to ensure that all students are included in the state's accountability system. Ysseldyke and Olsen (1997) indicate that there are four assumptions that are the foundation of alternate assessments:

- Alternate assessments focus on authentic skills and on assessing experiences in community and other real-life environments.
- Alternate assessments should measure integrated skills across domains.
- If at all possible, alternate assessment systems should use continuous documentation methods.
- Alternate assessment systems should include as critical criteria the extent to which the system provides the needed supports and adaptations, and trains the student to use them.

Alternate assessments may involve either normative or absolute performance standards (Ysseldyke & Olsen, 1997). If a normative assessment is used, then a student's performance is compared to that of peers (other students of comparable age or ability participating in the alternate assessment). If an absolute standard is used, then a student's performance is compared against a set criterion—for example, the student is able to cross the street when the "walk" sign is flashing 100 percent of the time without assistance. (See Point of Interest 3.2.)

## POINT OF INTEREST 3.2 • *Alternate Assessment Strategies*

### *What is an alternate assessment?*

An alternate assessment is different from the assessment given to most students. It is best viewed as a "process" for collecting information about what a student knows and can do. Generally, when we think of assessment, we think of a test. This is because most statewide assessments consist of taking a test, although some states are also using a portfolio approach that allows for collecting samples of student work. The majority of students participate by taking the tests, some by using accommodations. Some students, however, are unable to take the test even with accommodations or modifications. For these students, there must be an alternative way of determining their learning progress.

### *What are some data collection strategies that can be used in an alternative assessment system?*

- Observing the child in the course of the school day over a specified period of time
- Interviewing parents or family members about what the child does outside of school
- Asking the child to perform a specific activity or task and noting the level of performance
- Administering a commercially developed assessment instrument (e.g., Brigance) and comparing the results with a set of state established standards
- Reviewing records that have been developed over a designated period of time

*Source:* Adapted from Massanari, C. (2000). *Alternate assessment: Questions and answers. IDEA practices.* Available: http://www.ideapractices.org/ideaquests/AlternateAssess.htm#whatisalt.

## *Other Government-Supported Programs*

> ### *Focus 5*
> How do government-supported programs provide assistance to people with severe disabilities?

The overall purposes of government-supported programs range from providing basic economic support for people with disabilities (such as income maintenance, Medicaid and Medicare) to education and training (such as vocational rehabilitation and special education services). Table 3.1 presents a summary of the key federally funded programs that are intended to support people with disabilities in community settings. Historically, federal and state government programs have sent a mixed message to people with severe disabilities and their families. While one government program, such as education, encourages people to become contributing members of society, another (Social Security) has supported their continued dependence. Government programs that provide basic economic support have sometimes been criticized as a barrier to equal opportunity for people with disabilities, because they create disincentives to work. For many years, income maintenance programs, such as Supplemental Security Income (SSI), have created a major disincentive for people with severe disabilities to seek employment. Gerry and McWhorter (1991) suggest that income maintenance programs have been completely ineffective in helping people with severe disabilities enter and stay in the competitive labor force. These authors recommended significant changes in the structure of federal programs providing support to people with severe disabilities. These changes included

1. Expansion of federal financial support for programs serving infants and toddlers
2. The passage of new federal legislation to develop and implement public schools that would serve all children, including those with severe disabilities
3. A new program in the U.S. Department of Health and Human Services that would focus on effective transition from school to adult life, expanded community employment opportunities, and support for independent living
4. Elimination of work disincentives and other inequities within the income maintenance programs

Many of the recommendations from Gerry and McWhorter have come to fruition, including increased federal funding for infants and toddlers, new initiatives for transition services under IDEA, and passage of the Ticket to Work and Work Incentives Improvement Act of 1999 (TWWIIA).

The TWWIIA is intended to improve work opportunities for people with severe disabilities by addressing the barriers that prevent employment. A major barrier has been the possible loss of the individual's publicly funded health care should he or she go to work. The act provides grants to states that provide funding for workers with disabilities who return to work and continue to receive their Medicaid benefits (Braddock, Hemp, Parish, & Rizzolo, 2000).

**TABLE 3.1** *Key Federally Funded Programs for People with Disabilities*

| Program | Federal Legislation | Purpose | Services |
|---------|---------------------|---------|----------|
| *Income Maintenance* | | | |
| Supplemental Security Income (SSI) | Social Security Amendments of 1972 (P.L. 92-603), Title XVI | Basic economic support | Direct cash payments to eligible people with disabilities |
| | Employment Opportunities for Disabled Americans Act of 1986 | Reduce disincentives to work under SSI | SSI payments reduced (but not terminated) by $1 for every $2 earned above $85 monthly income |
| Social Security disability insurance for adult disabled children (ADC) | Social Security Act of 1956, Title II | Basic economic support | Direct cash payments for disabled children 18 and over or disabled workers eligible for Social Security |
| *Health Care* | | | |
| Medicare | Social Security Act, Title XVIII | National insurance program for elderly and eligible people with disabilities | Short-term hospitalization; related care in nursing homes; home care, physician services; outpatient services; ambulance, medical supplies, and equipment |
| Medicaid | Social Security Act, Title XIX | Payments for health care services to eligible residents | Inpatient and outpatient hospital services; laboratory services; physician services; family planning; skilled nursing services; early screening; treatment and immunization; other medical services as established by states on an individual basis |
| *Residential Alternatives* | | | |
| Intermediate care facilities for the mentally retarded | Social Security Act (P.L. 92-223) as Amended in 1971, Title XIX | Fund residential living and other services to people with mental retardation needing 24-hour care | Reimbursement to states for costs of service in facilities that provide health care, rehabilitation, and active treatment to Medicaid-eligible clients |

| | | | |
|---|---|---|---|
| Home and community-based waiver | 1981 Amendments to the Social Security Act | Allow states to include community-based home care in Medicaid plans | Same services as above, but can be provided in noninstitutional settings |
| *Employment* | | | |
| Vocational rehabilitation | Vocational Rehabilitation Act of 1973 (P.L. 93-516) | To train and place people with disabilities in employment | Vocational training and placement, career guidance, reimbursement for prosthetic appliances (supported employment services added in 1986 amendments) |
| Coordinated planning and service delivery | Developmental Disabilities and Bill of Rights Act of 1970 | Incentives for states to establish coordinated planning and service activities | Planning councils to coordinate service of various government agencies; "bill of rights" that defined appropriate service in the least restrictive environment; protection and advocacy systems; university centers of excellence |
| Incentives for employment | Ticket to Work and Work Incentives Improvement Act of 1999 | To address the barriers (such as possible loss of health care benefits) that prevent people with disabilities from obtaining employment | Allows states to remove the income limit of 250 percent of poverty (about $21,000), allowing them to set higher income, unearned income, and resource limits. Allows people with disabilities to buy into Medicaid when their jobs pay more than low wages but may not have access to private health insurance. Creates the option to allow people with disabilities to retain Medicaid coverage even though their medical condition has improved as a result of medical treatment. |
| *Education* | | | |
| Special Education Services | The Individuals with Disabilities Education Act (formerly P.L. 94-142) | To provide a free and appropriate public education to all students who are disabled | Special education and support (related) services provided through an individual education program in the least restrictive environment; multidisciplinary and non-biased assessment; parent involvement and safeguards |

The TWWIIA is a major step forward in government-funded programs that facilitate access and participation in inclusive community settings for people with severe disabilities. Other community-based programs, such as family support, supported living, and personal assistance, have all expanded in the last decade. Family support, which consists of programs such as respite care, family counseling, and in-home behavioral support, are now available in forty-eight states. Supported living, now available in forty-five states, includes housing in which individuals choose where and with whom they live; someone other than a provider owns the property (such as a person with a disability, the family, or landlord); and the individual receives personalized support based on needs and preferences. Personal assistance programs, which include assistance to people living in their own homes, are available in twenty-one states (Braddock et al., 2000).

## *Advocacy Organizations*

> ### *Focus 6*
> How do advocacy organizations assist people with severe disabilities?

Advocacy is speaking for, or on behalf of someone else. Advocacy may occur in many ways for people with severe disabilities. Family members and friends may serve in advocacy roles to ensure that the rights of the individuals with severe disabilities are not ignored. There are also formal disability advocacy organizations, such as the Association for Persons with Severe Handicaps, the ARC-A National Organization on Mental Retardation (formerly the Association for Retarded Citizens), the Council for Exceptional Children, the National Society for Autistic Citizens, and United Cerebral Palsy. These organizations have successfully lobbied Congress, state, and local policy makers for the improvement of formalized support systems for people with severe disabilities. Along with "mutual aid" groups from local hospitals and schools (parent–teacher–student organizations), these disability advocacy organizations have also served as an important contact point for information and assistance to families, and have been influential with the general public in creating awareness of the needs of people with severe disabilities.

A major movement in this country is toward "self-advocacy": people with disabilities having more to say in their lives rather than having others always "do" and speak for them. At the core of the self-advocacy movement is self-determination: the power of choice. Even in some of the "best" programs and services for people with severe disabilities, these people may have little choice about who their friends are, where they live, what time they go to bed, when they eat, or what they do with their free time. As we move more toward the reality of an inclusive society, it seems inconceivable that such an ideal could ever be fully reached without people with severe disabilities being able to guide, wherever possible, the choices that affect their lives.

## *Natural Supports*

Whereas formal supports are structured through agencies and organizations, natural supports may be provided directly by the nuclear and extended family members, friends, or neighbors. Natural supports are often more effective than formal systems in assisting individuals and their family members not only to cope with the barriers imposed by a severe disability, but to learn and succeed in family, school, or community settings. Research suggests that the family may be the single most powerful force in preparing an adolescent with disabilities for the adult years (Berry & Hardman, 1998). This is evident in the area of employment, where adults with disabilities who are successfully employed after leaving school often find more jobs through their network of family and friends than through formal support systems.

## Family

The family is an evolving, dynamic system characterized by a set of unique purposes, roles, and expectations for its various members, depending on the basic organization of the unit. Traditionally, families have been defined as a group of individuals, all of whom have biological and/or emotional bonds, and live under one roof with a mother and a father. In the most traditional sense, we may think of a working father, and a mother who stays at home to take care of the children and manage the house. However, we see a much more diverse picture of this evolving social system in the twenty-first century. One in three children are born to unmarried parents; one in two preschoolers has a mother in the labor force; one in two children will live in a single-parent family at some point in childhood; one in four children lives with only one parent; one in three children will be poor at some point in childhood; and one in sixty sees his or her parents divorce in any year (Children's Defense Fund, 2000). The reality is that the traditional family consisting of a mother, father, and children all under one roof is now only one of many different family constellations that may range from single-parent households to formal family support systems (such as foster care).

The family, which is more diverse than ever and already under considerable stress in today's world, often faces an even greater challenge with the advent of a child with severe disabilities. This child may throw the family into further crisis, weakening emotional bonds and imposing severe financial problems. However, it is also possible that family members may view a child with a disability as a source of unity that brings them together and actually strengthens their relationships (Hardman et al., 2002). How the family responds to the member with severe disabilities depends on a number of internal factors, as well as the formal and natural supports available to its members (See Newsworthy 3.1.)

---

*Focus 7*
What is the purpose of family supports, and how do they prevent or delay "out-of-home" placements for children with severe disabilities?

---

***Strengthening Formal Family Supports.***    For the better part of the twentieth century, families of children with severe disabilities confronted a human services system that provided little, if any, direct family support. Many families were unable to receive medical, financial, or educational assistance unless the child was removed from the home and placed in a separate facility or hospital, usually a large institution. The national mandate to provide a free and appropriate public education to all students with disabilities did not occur until 1975, and has paralleled the deinstitutionalization movement of the past two decades.

**NEWSWORTHY 3.1 •** *Perfectly Ashlynne Is a Blessing to All Members in Family*

My parents have eight children, 54 grandchildren and, at last count, 51 great-children, with six more on the way. Great-grandchildren, that is. According to my father, they are all beautiful, talented and smart. If you want to design good-looking, gifted and brilliant human beings, just gather a few Walker genes, and you're set. Ok, he's biased.

Still, we do feel remarkably fortunate as a family. We've had comparatively few major health problems, nobody had done any serious jail time and the only mental impediment we've experienced has been an apparently inherited deficiency in the math and science chromosomes.

"SOMETIMES, I look around me and see families struggling with all kinds of disabilities, and I feel a little guilty," I confessed to a colleague not too long ago. "In more than 100 births, we've never had a handicapped child in our family."

"And what makes you think that's a blessing?" my friend asked. His question took me by surprise. I mean, that's self-evident, isn't it? I looked at my colleague for a moment, searching for tell-tale signs of teasing. There were none. "Well," I said, hesitantly "it seems like a blessing, doesn't it? To not have a disability or anything?"

He smiled. "Of course good health is a blessing," he said. "But there are other blessings that aren't as obvious. They seem like tragedies at first. Then you live through them and you discover that God was blessing you even when you thought He was looking the other way."

He told me about his nephew, Teddy, who was born with Down's syndrome. "When our family first found out that he wasn't…you know perfect, we were heartbroken," he said. "We cried. We hugged each other. We wondered why."

"THEN MY sister brought Teddy home," he continued. "Through the years we got to know him, and we found out that he is a pretty terrific kid. I love that little boy…." His voice broke. "I can't even tell you how much love he's brought into our family. We're closer, more tolerant, more forgiving, more faithful—all because of him. He hasn't been a handicap—he's been a blessing. And we don't think of him as being disabled. We just think of him as being Teddy." I've been thinking about that conversation a lot this week. Sweet little Ashlynne—great-grandchild No. 51—was born in Canada with a heart condition, an obstructed bowel and Down's syndrome. The news hit hard. But her parents, Derrick and Debbie, have already been blessed with a powerful gift of love for their baby girl. And that love has emanated to family members around the world.

Of course, we know it won't be easy for Derrick and Debbie, or for the rest of us who love Ashlynne. We'll want life to be easier for her. We'll want other children to be more kind. We'll want people to quit staring at her. We'll wish that her life could be perfect. But we'll take comfort in that God, who makes no mistakes, made Ashlynne to be precisely who she is. Therefore, she is perfect—for herself, for her family, for our family. Perfectly Ashlynne.

What a blessing!

*Source:* Walker, J. (1997, October 22). Perfectly Ashlynne is a blessing to all members of the family. *Provo Daily Herald,* 9.

With the passage of Public Law 94-142 (now the Individuals with Disabilities Education Act), and the movement of people with severe disabilities out of institutions and into community settings, the need for formalized family supports has become critical.

Family support programs are designed to assist families in meeting the needs of the child or adult with disabilities within the context of the home. Such programs attempt to prevent or at least delay "out-of-home" placements (Berry & Hardman, 1998; Dyson,

1993; Herman & Hazel, 1991; Norton & Drew, 1994). The most obvious formal supports include any one or more of government-supported programs for people with disabilities, such as special education services, health care, income maintenance, employment training and placement, or housing. Programs that are less obvious, but nevertheless important to families, include respite care, in-home assistance, family counseling, and skill training. The purpose of respite care and in-home assistance is to provide some additional relief and help for family members attempting to cope with everyday stresses that may seem over-whelming at times. In-home respite care may involve a companion or sitter spending some time with the individual with severe disabilities. Out-of-home respite care may include any one of several options. It may be provided by families who are licensed to take people with severe disabilities into their home for a limited period of time, or by parent cooperatives, day care centers, and community recreational programs. Nisbet, Clark, and Covert (1991) suggest that respite care services may "enable family members to become more socially active and in turn reduce their feelings of social isolation" (p. 135). An example of in-home assistance is help from a professional homemaker to reduce the family's time in dealing with household management tasks. (See Point of Interest 3.3.)

In addition to respite care and in-home assistance, families may also receive counsel-ing services and training to help them meet the challenges and stress associated with living with a child who is severely disabled. It is important that both counseling services and family education programs focus on the relationships and interactions between and among the members, and not just on the individual with severe disabilities. Such an approach, re-ferred to as a "family systems perspective," is based on the premise that every aspect of the family is interrelated, with unique properties that can only be understood by observing the relationships and interactions among all its members (Turnbull & Turnbull, 2001).

As described by Turnbull and Turnbull, the family systems approach has four compo-nents: family characteristics, family interaction, family functions, and family life cycle. The *family characteristics* component is concerned with identifying the basic descriptors of the family unit, such as size, cultural background, socioeconomic status, individual coping styles and skills, health, and geographic location. This information is factored in with the character-istics (type and severity) of the member who has a disability. Understanding the family's co-hesiveness and adaptability in coping with the challenges of a member with disabilities is the major element of the *family interactions* component. Essentially, the more cohesive and adaptable each family member is to living with an individual with severe disabilities, the healthier the family. *Family functions* are those activities in which the family engages to meet its needs. These functions include socialization, self-esteem, affection, daily care, recreation, economics, and educational endeavors. The *family life cycle* component analyzes the impact of the child's disability on each member of the family over time. The impact will vary, as it does for all families, during different phases and transitions of the life cycle. For example, a 3-year-old child, who has a strong need for parental attention, may express more jealousy and resentment toward his sibling with disabilities than a teen who is less concerned with parents and more oriented to peers outside the family.

Family support programs that are consistent with a systems approach pay particular at-tention to (1) facilitating positive intrafamily interactions, (2) developing skills for support-ing the child with a disability that can be used effectively by all family members, and (3) the importance of the family working together when interacting with professionals. Specific

## POINT OF INTEREST 3.3 • *Individualized and Flexible Family Support*

Family support services should be flexible, individualized, designed to meet diverse needs of families, and based on the principle of finding the best approach to support the individual and the family. They must be built on a relationship of respect and trust that recognizes that families are better able to determine their own needs than to have their needs determined by the state or a public policy.

Family support services should be service options offered to families, but not imposed on them, and should not be confined to a single program or set of services but should be a philosophy that permeates all programs and services.

Family support services may include but are not limited to:

- Respite
- Homemaker services
- Child care
- Personal assistance services
- Sitter service
- Chores
- Home repairs
- Home health care
- Adaptive equipment
- Nursing
- Home modification
- Recreation
- Utilities

- Camp
- Family counseling
- Transportation
- Family support groups
- Vehicle modification
- Health insurance
- Special diet
- Rent assistance
- Special clothing
- Evaluation/assessment
- Case management
- Behavior management
- Service coordination
- Speech therapy
- Financial assistance
- Occupational therapy
- Discretionary cash subsidy
- Physical therapy allowances
- Individual counseling vouchers
- Medical/dental reimbursement
- Skill training line-of-credit
- Nutritional services

Family supports should build on existing social networks and natural sources of support, maximize the family's control over the services and supports received, support the entire family, and encourage the integration of family members with disabilities into the community.

*Source:* Adapted from United Cerebral Palsy (1999). *Position statement on family support.* Washington, DC: Author. Available: http://www.ucp.org/ucp_generaldoc.cfm/1/8/30/30_30/263.

support programs may focus on divergent areas of need, such as coping with emotional and financial stress, locating appropriate resources in the community, effective behavioral interventions in the home, or strengthening the family's network of natural supports.

*Focus 8*
What are natural family supports, and why are they an important part of an effective support network for people with severe disabilities?

***Strengthening Natural Family Supports.***   The family support network also extends beyond the services sponsored by government programs and provided by trained professionals to an informal system of assistance: natural supports provided by extended family members, friends, and neighbors. The importance of a natural family support network cannot be overstated. It is through this network that family members may find a personal bonding with others who will listen, understand, and support them as they attempt to cope with the many challenges of a family member with severe disabilities. Berry and Hardman (1998) suggest that natural supports "hold the key to stress reduction and positive coping for families because they enhance self esteem and mastery through social support and community inclusion" (p. 91).

Lehman, Ellard, and Wortman (1986), in a study of people who had recently lost a close relative, identified the natural supports that were most helpful to families under stress. These individuals benefited from ongoing contact with others who were in similar circumstances and could relate directly to their feelings of loss. Additionally, they were able to cope more with their loss when they could express their feelings openly to others, and receive expressions of concern. Support that was least helpful included providing advice on what to do and how to cope, trying to minimize the feelings of loss, and expressing forced cheerfulness. As Singer and Irvin (1991) point out, the feelings of isolation for parents of children with disabilities may be "aggravated by well-meaning but painfully superficial statements of support from others" (p. 300).

Natural family supports may include the extended family unit, as well as close friends, colleagues, and neighbors. Extended family members are those individuals who do not necessarily live in the same household, but who have ongoing contact with the members of the nuclear family. They might include grandparents, uncles, cousins, and so on. These extended family members are often an important base of support to the family unit. For example, grandparents may be a primary source of respite care for the parents (Lian & Aloia, 1994). Extended family members may also provide in-home assistance by helping periodically with meals, cleaning the house, providing transportation, or just listening when everyone is overwhelmed. Hardman et al. (2002) suggest that grandparents and other extended family members are a critical resource network, especially if they are willing to provide assistance before the primary family unit has depleted all its emotional and financial resources in coping with a child with severe disabilities.

However, the effectiveness of extended family members as a resource will depend on their willingness to help, as well as how prepared and informed they are about the child with severe disabilities. These extended family members must be able to openly voice their questions, feelings, and concerns about the child with disabilities, and the emotional impact he or she is having on family members. In turn, parents must be willing to help extended family members to learn as much as possible by sharing their own feelings, as well as by providing written information (as suggested by professionals) on the nature and impact of the child's condition on the family unit (Hardman et al., 2002).

Many of the issues regarding whether extended family members are in a position to serve as a support network also apply to friends and neighbors. However, parents of a child with a severe disability may be less likely to reach out to friends and neighbors than to extended family members, for several reasons. They may want to keep the family's personal business private, or not burden a friend with their problems. They may fear rejection from friends or neighbors who don't understand their emotional needs and concerns. Thoits (1986) suggests that people in general are more comfortable seeking help from others who have had similar experiences, and whose reactions to difficulties are comparable to their own. Nevertheless, it is possible for friends and neighbors to be part of a natural support network for the family. The nature and type of support will be unique to the individuals involved, and will depend on a mutual level of comfort in both seeking and providing assistance. Clear communication regarding what friends or neighbors are willing to do, and how that matches the needs of the family, is essential if this support is to be meaningful to the child with a severe disability and his or her family members.

## *Friends*

> All children need to learn with and from other children.... All children need to belong and feel wanted and loved.... All children need to have fun and enjoy noise and laughter in their lives.... And fall and cry and get hurt.... All children need to be in real families and real schools and real neighborhoods. (Forest, 1991, p. 403)

Friendship is a bond between individuals—favored companions who are emotionally connected to each other by mutual affection or esteem. Friendships develop as an evolutionary process. First, there is an awareness of common values, interests, concerns, or backgrounds. Then, individuals must have the opportunity to interact with one another to discover and explore these similarities. During this exploration, friendships are more likely to develop when people are able to initiate and maintain social interaction and make competent social discriminations.

If common abilities and interests are the basis for friendship development, one might conclude that people with severe disabilities would only have friends who are also disabled. Certainly, friendships among people with disabilities do occur, and are an integral part of each person's social network (Day & Harry, 1999). However, several researchers (Green, Schlein, Mactavish, & Benepe 1995; Siperstein, Leffert, & Wenz-Gross, 1997; Staub & Hunt, 1993) suggest that although "true friendships" are often rare and society tends to promote homogeneous relationships among friends with similar abilities, it is *possible* to develop and maintain mutually rewarding, heterogeneous friendships among people with and without disabilities. There are compelling reasons why friendships between people with and without disabilities benefit everyone involved.

---

**Focus 9**
What are the mutual benefits of building friendships between people with and without disabilities?

---

***Benefits to People with Severe Disabilities.***    Friendships with people who are not disabled contribute directly to a "social, emotional, and practical" support base for people with severe disabilities that will facilitate active participation in the life of the family and community (Traustadottir, 1993). It is through these one-to-one friendships that we see the long-term changes in behavior that promote the acceptance of differences, and move us closer to an inclusive society. Rees, Spreen, and Harnadek (1991) found that direct contact between people with mental retardation and their nondisabled peers resulted in improved attitudes for university undergraduate students over time. They further suggest that shifts in public policy (such as the passage of the Americans with Disabilities Act) and the movement toward community integration have also contributed significantly to the positive change in attitudes toward people with severe disabilities.

Haring (1991) suggests five reasons why social relationships between people with and without disabilities should be considered a defining characteristic of an integrated service system:

1. Social relationships contribute substantially to quality of life.
2. Social interaction skills, ideally produced within the context of an ongoing relationship with another person, are necessary for functional participation in many critical activities.
3. Many critical skills are maintained over time by complex, remote schedules of reinforcement but are maintained on an immediate basis by the socially reinforcing aspects of interacting with people with whom you have a relationship.
4. There is a relationship between social skills use and the lessening of a need for programming based on behavioral control.
5. There is an increasing awareness that disability is more an attitude held by professionals and [people who are not disabled] than it is a property or defining characteristic of the person with disabilities. (p. 197)

The benefits of building friendships with nondisabled peers are receiving increased attention in the education of students with severe disabilities. Many educators and parents are demanding a greater emphasis on the development of socialization skills that will facilitate ongoing friendships. Hamre-Nietupski, Nieptupski, and Strathe (1992) indicate that parents are challenging the prevailing skills training approach, and are emphasizing to educators how important friendships are in supporting their children's integration into the community. In a survey of parents of children with severe and profound disabilities, these researchers found that friendship/social relationship development was considered equal in importance to functional skills (such as paying for meals in a restaurant or brushing teeth), but was significantly more important than academic skills.

***Benefits to People Who Are Not Disabled.*** Although much of the emphasis on the importance of friendships focuses on benefits to people with severe disabilities, there are some positive outcomes for people without disabilities as well. Biklen, Corrigan, and Quick (1989), in a study of students with severe disabilities and their nondisabled peers in an integrated elementary school classroom, reported that the experience had resulted in an enhanced understanding and caring about other people on the part of students who were not disabled. In a study of an inner-city high school, Peck, Donaldsen, and Pezzoli (1990) examined the perceptions of twenty-one high school-age students without disabilities to determine their perceptions on the benefits of developing relationships with students who are moderately and severely disabled. As Peck et al. reported, these high school students appeared to have benefited in a number of ways from their experiences, including "improved self-concept, social-cognitive growth, reduced fear of human differences, increased

**POINT OF INTEREST 3.4** • *The Importance of Friendships*

---

*Why are friendships between people with and without disabilities important?*
Friends are important for several reasons. They support each other emotionally, are willing to see things from the other's point of view, and provide assistance and feedback when needed. Friends choose each other and remain close through good times and times of crisis. They provide companionship for community and school activities and help each other enjoy new experiences and appreciate life more fully. Friendships between people with and without disabilities usually enrich the lives of both.

*When should friendships begin?*
If people with severe disabilities are to form friendships and be a part of society as adults, these relationships must develop during childhood. Classmates and neighbors will grow into adult co-workers and friends later in life. Therefore, inclusive classrooms and recreational activities are important. In these settings children with and without disabilities get to meet each other and form relationships. Unfortunately, many parents have found that even though their children are in inclusive schools, they have few nondisabled friends.

*What makes the development of relationships difficult?*
Many individuals with disabilities interact primarily with their family, the people who take care of or provide services to them, and others in the programs in which they participate. These relationships can clearly be significant and should be encouraged. However, beyond family members, people may have no freely given and chosen relationships. Generally, many people with disabilities face certain disadvantages in meeting and getting to know others.

• *Opportunity.* Many people with disabilities have limited opportunities to take part in activities where they can meet peers. This may be due to physical segregation or being placed in a role as "client" or "special education student."

Services may restrict people's chances to get together, through curfews, transportation restrictions, and other limitations. Whatever the reason, people with disabilities frequently become cut off and isolated from others.

• *Support.* Relationships between people with and without disabilities are not formed by simply grouping people together. Some individuals need assistance with fitting into certain settings and activities. Others may need someone to facilitate their involvement or to interpret for them. Without supports, some people with and without disabilities may never have the opportunity to know each other.

• *Continuity.* Although most people enjoy meeting new people, they are sustained by those they have known over time. The continuity of relationships over the years is an important source of security, comfort, and self-worth. Many people with disabilities do not have continuous relationships. Instead, they may leave their families, be moved from one program to another, and have to adjust to staff people who come and go.

*What are some of the ways to facilitate personal relationships between people with and without disabilities?*
It takes effort to help people establish connections. Described below are some of the ways this has been tried.

• *Bridge-building.* Facilitators who initiate, support and maintain new relationships are called bridge-builders, as they "build bridges and guide people into new relationships, new places, and new opportunities in life" (Mount, Beeman, & Ducharme, 1988). Bridge-builders involve people with disabilities in existing groups or with specific individuals.

• *Circles of friends or circles of support.* Groups of people who "meet on a regular basis to help a person with a disability accomplish certain personal visions or goals" (Perske, 1988). Circle members try to open doors to new opportunities, including establishing new relationships.

• *Citizen advocacy.* Recruited and supported by an independent citizen advocacy office, a citizen advocate voluntarily represents the interests of a person with a disability as if the interests were the advocate's own. Citizen advocates may take on one or several roles (e.g., friend, ally, mentor, protector), and some of these may last for life.

There are different ways that personal relationships between people with and without disabilities may be encouraged. Perhaps more important than the specific method is the supporting, connecting role of one or more people (family members, staff members, friends, neighbors, etc.) who can spend time and energy for this purpose.

### What can families and service providers do to enhance opportunities for friendships?

People can establish friendships with each other, but it is not possible to force friendships on others. It is possible to create opportunities for people with and without disabilities to meet and share time with each other in ways that encourage friendships to take root and flourish. Families and service providers can do different things to make such opportunities available.

Families can:

• Work for the total inclusion of their son or daughter into the regular school system. In addition to being physically present, students with disabilities need adequate supports to enable them to participate fully in classroom and school activities. Parents can also ensure that their child with a disability takes part in a variety of integrated recreation and leisure activities after school hours. A consistent physical presence in each others' lives helps lead to friendships between children with and without disabilities.

• Ensure social participation. How people with disabilities are supported within integrated settings is important. Students need to be enabled to participate as much as possible, and to do so in ways acceptable to other people. People without disabilities need the opportunity to meet their counterparts with disabilities as peers, not as objects of tutoring or volunteer service.

• Involve and trust others. All parents feel protective toward their children. Although there may be differences in how independent people can become, parents can come to believe that there are people in the community who would, if given the opportunity, enjoy and welcome a friendship with their son or daughter.

Service providers can:

• Reduce barriers to friendship. The way in which support services are provided to people with disabilities and their families can enhance or reduce the opportunities for friendships to develop. Segregated programs dramatically lessen the chances for contact between people with and without disabilities. Even in integrated settings, students with disabilities may not be able to take part in extracurricular activities (e.g., choir, clubs, sports) because of lack of transportation from school. When efforts are made to bring people with and without disabilities together, the people without disabilities are often treated as volunteers responsible to the teacher or program coordinator rather than as peers.

• Encourage people who seem to like one another to pursue friendships. Service providers can review practices, such as curfews, lack of privacy, and so on, that limit opportunities for people to meet and form friendships with each other.

• With an awareness of and commitment to facilitating friendships between people with and without disabilities, all people can have the opportunity to form relationships that will allow them to live life more fully.

*Source:* Adapted from Lutfiyya, Z. M. (1997). *The importance of friendships between people with and without mental retardation.* Syracuse, NY: Research and Training Center on Community Integration, Center on Human Policy, Division of Special Education and Rehabilitation, School of Education, Syracuse University.

tolerance of other people, development of principles of personal conduct, and enjoyment of relaxed and accepting friendships" (p. 248).

Many people express some fear about interacting with a person with a severe disability and are very cautious in their initial encounter (Green et al., 1995). However, once the barriers are broken down, people without disabilities can have valued, accepting, and caring relationships with people who have a severe disability. As a result of this relationship, nondisabled individuals are able to see the person with severe disabilities in a more positive light, thus breaking down negative stereotypes and discrimination. When this happens, a person without a disability becomes a part of a community network of friends and supporters. The mutual benefits that occur as a result of friendships among people with and without disabilities may be best summed up in the following scenario.

> On the first day of school a new student with severe disabilities arrived in one of our schools. Because of his appearance, and the fact that he was in a wheel chair, most students were reluctant to interact with him. One third-grade boy reacted quite negatively to the arrival of this student. As time passed, this boy observed how the teachers and students acted toward this student in a loving and caring manner. He noted how this student was "included," just like everyone else. One day the third grader asked to be the student's special helper during recess. As the days passed the two boys developed a real friendship. *Both students came to feel liked and important* [emphasis added]. (Stephens & Engle, 1993, p. 11)

---

**Focus 10**
Why is it important for people with severe disabilities to access "generic community services"?

---

## Community

Supporting people with severe disabilities in community settings is based on a philosophy that recognizes and accepts the range of human differences. For people with severe disabilities, successful participation in community life depends on the availability of an array of natural supports beyond family and friends. This means providing people with severe disabilities access to "generic services" within their community, and thus lessening their dependence on "disability-based programs" (e.g., sheltered employment, congregate care living, special day activity centers). "Generic" is defined as those services and supports that are readily available to people without disabilities, including adequate housing, medical and dental treatment, community employment, insurance, restaurants, theaters, recreation, shopping malls, and so on.

Successful participation in community life depends on three interrelated factors: (1) the competence of the individual with appropriate training and support to adapt to societal expectations, (2) access to the community's generic service system, and (3) the willingness of community members to serve as natural supports for people with severe disabilities. (See Chapter 1.) For example, in the area of recreation and leisure, many people with severe disabilities are unable to access community activities such as swimming lessons, scouting, skiing, or golf—activities that are generally available to others within the community. Many people with severe disabilities do little with their leisure time beyond watching television. In the area of work, both employers and co-workers must be willing to recognize and support the accommodations needed by a person with a severe disability in a community employment setting. Employers must be willing to work closely with a supported employment job coach in discussing job options and responsibilities for a person with severe disabilities; provide assistance as needed in helping the person prepare for the work day and unwind from daily activities and the stresses of work; and support opportunities to improve working conditions, provide higher pay, and provide job advancement (Walker & Racino, 1993). Co-workers must also be willing to provide support in any number of ways, such as providing verbal or physical cues to assist the person in learning his or her job duties; provide consistent feedback and instruction of job tasks; or assist the person in developing compensatory or self-management strategies to regulate his or her work performance (Inge, 1999).

## *Conclusion*

This chapter has examined both formal and natural supports for people with disabilities in the context of family, friends, and community. Formal supports may result from government-funded programs, or come through advocacy organizations. Natural supports may be provided by the nuclear family, extended family members, friends, colleagues, or neighbors. Both formal and natural supports are necessary for the person with severe disabilities to participate actively in community settings.

Formal supports may result from civil rights legislation, government-supported programs, and involvement through advocacy organizations. The Americans with Disabilities Act (ADA) is civil rights legislation that attempts to break down the barriers of discrimination against people with disabilities. The major provisions of this act ban discrimination in private-sector employment, public services, and public accommodations, transportation, and telecommunications. Government-supported programs for people with disabilities may include such services as direct financial assistance, health care, employment training and ongoing support, housing, and access to a free and appropriate public education. Advocacy organizations play an important role in lobbying Congress and other policy makers for improved and expanded programs and services for people with severe disabilities. These organizations are also an important source of information and assistance to persons with disabilities and their families.

Formal family supports, which include respite care, in-home assistance, family counseling, and skill training, are services intended to help family members meet the needs and challenges of a child or adult with severe disabilities living in the home. Natural family supports, provided by extended family members, friends, and neighbors, provide a network of assistance that develops personal bonding between individuals to help cope with everyday stress and feelings of isolation.

Friendships between people with and without disabilities can be mutually beneficial for everyone involved. For people with disabilities, friendships provide a network of support that helps facilitate their active participation in community life. These friendships often result in long-term attitude and behavioral changes toward people with disabilities. For people who are not disabled, a friendship with a person with severe disabilities may

## POINT AND COUNTERPOINT 3.1 • *Friends*

Is it really possible for a person with severe disabilities to be "friends" with someone who is not disabled? While one approach to friendships emphasizes common abilities, interests, and backgrounds as a basis for a relationship, another is more concerned with people accepting and caring about each other regardless of individual abilities. Here are two points of view on friendships between people with and without disabilities.

*Point*
Friendships between people with severe disabilities and those who are not disabled really don't make a lot of sense. People become friends because of their common intellect, background, and interests. If one person is more intellectually capable than another, then the relationship is really one that is protective or care giving. One person will be in a position of dominating the other. True friend-

ships for individuals with severe disabilities are with others who are similar in their capabilities.

*Counterpoint*
It is a very narrow viewpoint that focuses only on people being friends with "their own kind." Such a perspective disregards the individuality in each of us. We all establish friendships for many different reasons. Friendships may develop from the comfort of being with someone who accepts you for who you are, regardless of your "limitations." It may be that the person who is not disabled learns more about themselves through a friendship with a person with severe disabilities, or maybe it's just that they enjoy a relaxed and accepting relationship. Perhaps, Robert Perske says it best: "Every friendship is unique and unrepeatable. What happens in each relationship sets it apart as vividly as a fingerprint" (1988, p. 13).

improve their self-concept, reduce their fear of people who are different, increase their tolerance of other people, and help them enjoy a relaxed and accepting relationship.

Natural supports in the community focus on access to generic services and encourage less dependence on "disability-based programs." Generic services include adequate housing, medical and dental treatment, community employment, insurance, restaurants, theaters, recreation, shopping malls, and so on. These are the same services and supports that are readily available to people without disabilities.

## *Focus Review*

Focus 1: Distinguish between formal and natural supports for people with severe disabilities.

- Formal supports bring together the services necessary in assisting the individual with severe disabilities to participate more actively in community and family life.
- Formal supports may (1) be funded through the government in areas such as income maintenance, health care, education, housing, or employment, or (2) come through advocacy organizations that lobby on behalf of people with severe disabilities and provide family members a place to interact and support one another.
- Natural supports may be provided directly by nuclear and extended family members, friends, neighbors, co-workers, and other community members.

Focus 2: Identify the major provisions of the Americans with Disabilities Act (ADA).

- The ADA bans discrimination against individuals with disabilities in private-sector employment, all public services, and public accommodations, transportation, and telecommunications.

Focus 3: Identify the major provisions of the Individuals with Disabilities Education Act.

- The basic provisions of the IDEA provide for (1) nondiscriminatory and multidisciplinary assessment, (2) parental involvement in the development of the student's educational program, (3) placement in the least restrictive environment (LRE), and (4) an individualized education program.
- The IDEA also requires that, beginning at age 14, and updated annually, a student's Individualized Education Program (IEP) must include a statement of the transition services that relate to various courses of study. Beginning at age 16 (or younger, if determined appropriate by the IEP team), an IEP should include a statement of needed transition services, including, when appropriate, a statement of the responsibilities of other agencies (such as vocational rehabilitation) or any other needed linkages.
- States have the option of establishing an early intervention programs for infants and toddlers under Part C that (1) provides services to infants and toddlers with developmental delays or who have diagnosed physical or mental conditions with a high probability of resulting in developmental delay, and (2) establishes a written Individualized Family Service Plan (IFSP) for every eligible child and their family.
- States are required to meet the same requirements for preschool-age children as mandated in the IDEA for school-age children with the following exceptions: (1) eligibility may be noncategorical, under a developmental delay classification, and (2) with parental permission, participation in transition planning with early intervention agencies is instituted at least ninety days ahead of the child's third birthday to assure a smooth transition without gaps or loss in services to the child and family.

Focus 4: Identify four basic assumptions of an alternate assessment system for students with severe disabilities.

- Alternate assessments focus on authentic skills and on assessing experiences in community and other real-life environments.
- Alternate assessments should measure integrated skills across domains.
- Alternate assessment systems should use continuous documentation methods.
- Alternate assessment systems should include as critical criteria the extent to which the system provides the needed supports and adaptations, and trains the student to use them.

Focus 5: How do government-supported programs provide assistance to people with severe disabilities?

- Government-supported programs may provide direct income (financial assistance), health care, employment training and ongoing support, housing, as well as access to a free and appropriate public education for persons with severe disabilities. New legislation, the Ticket to Work and Work Incentives Act of 1999, is designed to improve work opportunities for people with severe disabilities. The act breaks down the barriers that prevent employment, specifically possible loss of the individual's publicly funded health care should he or she go to work.

Focus 6: How do advocacy organizations assist people with severe disabilities?

- Advocacy organizations may lobby Congress, state, and local policy makers for the improvement of formalized support systems for people with severe disabilities.
- Self-advocacy groups help people with disabilities speak up for themselves and make personal choices.

Focus 7: What is the purpose of family supports, and how do they prevent or delay "out-of-home" placements for children with severe disabilities?

- Formal supports assist families in meeting the needs of the child or adult who is disabled within the context of the home.
- Services, such as respite care, in-home assistance, family counseling, and skill training, are made available to the family to help members support the child with severe disabilities in a home environment.

Focus 8: What are natural family supports, and why are they an important part of an effective support network for people with severe disabilities?

- Natural family supports may include the extended family unit, as well as close friends, colleagues, and neighbors.
- Family members find a personal bonding with others who will listen, understand, and support them as they attempt to cope with the many challenges of a family member with severe disabilities.

Focus 9: What are the mutual benefits of building friendships between people with and without disabilities?

- Friendships with people who are not disabled will contribute directly to a support base for people with severe disabilities that will facilitate active participation in the life of a community.
- Friendships among people with and without disabilities result in long-term changes in behavior that promote the acceptance of differences.
- People without disabilities are challenged by the opportunity of working with people who are disabled, and have positive feelings about knowing that they are helping others.
- Friendships may result in improved self-concept, social-cognitive growth, reduced fear of human differences, increased tolerance of other people, development of principles of personal conduct, and enjoyment of relaxed and accepting friendships for people who are not disabled.

Focus 10: Why is it important for people with severe disabilities to access "generic community services"?

- Successful participation in community life depends on the availability of an array of natural supports beyond family and friends. This means providing people with severe disabilities more access to "generic services" within their community and less dependence on disability-based programs.
- Successful participation in community life depends on three interrelated factors: (1) the competence of the individual with appropriate training and support to adapt to societal expectations, (2) access to the community's generic service system, and (3) the willingness of community members to serve as natural supports for people with severe disabilities.

## *References*

Association for Persons with Severe Handicaps, The (TASH) (2000). *TASH resolution on the people for whom TASH advocates.* Baltimore: Author. Available: http://www.tash.org/resolutions/R21PEOPL. html.

Berry, J., & Hardman, M. L. (1998). *Lifespan perspectives on the family and disability.* Boston: Allyn & Bacon.

Biklen, D., Corrigan, C., & Quick, D. (1989). Beyond obligation: Students' relations with each other in integrated classes. In D. Lipsky & A. Gartner (Eds.), *Beyond special education: Quality education for all* (pp. 207–221). Baltimore: Paul H. Brookes.

Braddock, D., Hemp, R., Parish, S., & Rizzolo, M. C. (2000). *The state of the states in developmental disabilities.* Chicago: Department of Disability and Human Development at the University of Illinois at Chicago.

Brown v. Topeka, Kansas, Board of Education, 347 U.S. 483 (1954).

Children's Defense Fund (2000). *The state of America's children yearbook 2000: 25 key facts about American children.* Washington, DC: Author. Available: http://www.childrensdefense.org/keyfacts.html.

Day, M., & Harry, B. (1999). Best friends: The construction of a teenage friendship. *Mental Retardation, 37*(3), 221–231.

Dyson, L. L. (1993). Response to the presence of a child with disabilities: Parental stress and family functioning over time. *American Journal on Mental Retardation, 98,* 207–218.

Forest, M. (1991). It's about relationships. In L. H. Meyer, C. A. Peck, & L. Brown (Eds.), *Critical issues in the lives of people with severe disabilities* (pp. 399–407). Baltimore: Paul H. Brookes.

Gerry, M. H., & McWhorter, C. M. (1991). A comprehensive analysis of federal statutes and programs for persons with severe disabilities. In L. H. Meyer, C. A. Peck, & L. Brown (Eds.), *Critical issues in the lives of people with severe disabilities* (pp. 495–525). Baltimore: Paul H. Brookes.

Green, F. P., Schlein, S. J., Mactavish, J., & Benepe, S. (1995, June). Nondisabled adults' perceptions of relationships in the early stages of arranged partnerships with peers with mental retardation. *Education and Training in Mental Retardation and Developmental Disabilities,* 91–108.

Hamre-Nietupski, S., Nietupski, J., & Strathe, M. (1992). Functional life skills, academic skills, and friendship/social relationship development: What do parents of students with moderate/severe/profound disabilities value? *Journal of the Association for Persons with Severe Handicaps, 17*(1), 53–58.

Hardman, M. L., Drew, C. J., & Egan, M. W. (2002). *Human exceptionality: Society, school, and family* (7th ed.). Boston: Allyn & Bacon.

Haring, T. (1991). Social relationships. In L. H. Meyer, C. A. Peck, & L. Brown (Eds.), *Critical issues in the lives of people with severe disabilities* (pp. 195–217). Baltimore: Paul H. Brookes.

Herman, S. E., & Hazel, K. L. (1991). Evaluation of family support services: Changes in availability and accessibility. *Mental Retardation, 29*(6), 351–357.

Inge, K. (1999, Spring). Who's providing the support? Job-site training issues and strategies. *Supported Employment Consortium Newsletter* (Virginia Commonwealth University), 1–6. Available: http://www.vcu.edu/rrtcweb/sec/newsletter.html.

Lehman, D. R., Ellard, J. H., & Wortman, C. B. (1986). Social support for the bereaved: Recipients' and providers' perspectives on what is helpful. *Journal of Consulting and Clinical Psychology, 54,* 438–446.

Lian, M. J., & Aloia, G. (1994). Parental responses, roles, and responsibilities. In S. K. Alper, P. J. Schloss, & C. N. Schloss (Eds.), *Families of students with disabilities: Consultation and advocacy* (pp. 51–94). Boston: Allyn & Bacon.

Lutfiyya, Z. M. (1997). *The importance of friendships between people with and without mental retardation.* Syracuse, NY: Research and Training Center on Community Integration, Center on Human Policy, Division of Special Education and Rehabilitation, School of Education, Syracuse University.

Massanari, C. (2000). *Alternate assessment: Questions and answers. IDEA practices.* Available: http://www.ideapractices.org/ideaquests/AlternateAssess.htm#whatisalt.

*Mills v. District of Columbia Board of Education* (1972), 348 F. Supp. 866 (D. D.C.).

Mount, B., Beeman, P., & Ducharme, G. (1988). *What are we learning about bridge-building?* Manchester, CT: Communitas, Inc.

National Research Council (1997). *Educating one and all: Students with disabilities and standards-based reform.* Washington, DC: National Academy Press.

Nisbet, J., Clark, M., & Covert, S. (1991). Living it up! An analysis of research on community living. In L. H. Meyer, C. A. Peck, & L. Brown (Eds.), *Critical issues in the lives of people with severe disabilities* (pp. 115–144). Baltimore: Paul H. Brookes.

Norton, P., & Drew, C. J. (1994). Autism and potential family stressors. *American Journal of Family Therapy, 22,* 68–77.

Peck, C. A., Donaldson, J., & Pezzoli, M. (1990). Some benefits nonhandicapped adolescents perceive for themselves from their social relationships with peers who have severe handicaps. *Journal of the Association for Persons with Severe Handicaps, 15*(4), 241–249.

Penner, I. (1999). *The right to belong: The story of Yvonne.* Available: http://www3.nb.sympatico.ca/ipenner/.

*Pennsylvania Association for Retarded Citizens v. Commonwealth of Pennsylvania* (1971). 334 F. Supp. 1257 (E.D.Pa. 1971).

Perske, R. (1988). *Circles of friends.* Nashville: Abingdon.

Rees, L. M., Spreen, O., & Harnadek, M. (1991). Do attitudes towards persons with handicaps really shift over time? Comparison between 1975 and 1988. *Mental Retardation, 29*(2), 81–86.

Singer, G. H. S., & Irvin, L. K. (1991). Supporting families of persons with severe disabilities: Emerging findings, practices, and questions. In L. H. Meyer, C. A. Peck, & L. Brown (Eds.), *Critical issues in the lives of people with severe disabilities* (pp. 271–312). Baltimore: Paul H. Brookes.

Siperstein, G. N., Leffert, J. S., & Wenz-Gross, M. (1997). The quality of friendships between children with and without learning problems. *American Journal on Mental Retardation, 102*(2), 55–70.

Staub, D., & Hunt, P. (1993). The effects of social interaction training on high school peer tutors of schoolmates with severe disabilities. *Exceptional Children, 60*(1), 41–57.

Stephens, T., & Engle, S. (1993, January). Severely disabled clearly benefit from public school. *Washington County Schools Newsletter, 11.*

Thoits, P. A. (1986). Social support as coping assistance. *Journal of Consulting and Clinical Psychology, 54,* 416–423.

Traustadottir, R. (1993, January). Gender patterns in friendships. *TASH Newsletter, 8.*

Turnbull, A. P., & Turnbull, H. P. (2001). *Families, professionals, and exceptionality: Collaborating for empowerment* (4th ed). Upper Saddle River, NJ: Prentice Hall.

United Cerebral Palsy (1999). *Position Statement on Family Support.* Washington, DC: Author. Available: http://www.ucp.org/ucp_generaldoc.cfm/1/8/30/30-30/263.

U.S. Department of Justice (2000). Myths and facts about the Americans with Disabilities Act. Available: http://www.usdoj.gov/crt/ada/pubs/mythfct.txt.

Walker, J. (1997, October 22). Perfectly Ashlynne is a blessing to all members of the family. *Provo Daily Herald, 9.*

Walker, P., & Racino, J. A. (1993). Being with people: Support and support strategies. In J. A. Racino, P. Walker, S. O'Connor, & S. J. Taylor (Eds.), *Housing, support, and community* (pp. 81–106). Baltimore: Paul H. Brookes.

Ysseldyke, J. E., & Olsen, K. (1997). *Putting alternate assessments into practice: What to measure and possible sources of data. NCEO synthesis report 28.* Minneapolis: The National Center on Educational Outcomes, University of Minnesota. Available: http://www.coled.umn.edu/NCEO/OnlinePubs/Synthesis28.htm.

Ysseldyke, J. E., Olsen, K., & Thurlow, M. (1997). *Issues and considerations in alternate assessments. NCEO synthesis report 27.* Minneapolis: The National Center on Educational Outcomes, University of Minnesota. Available: http://www.coled.umn.edu/NCEO/OnlinePubs/Synthesis27.htm.

# 4

# *Biomedical Issues*

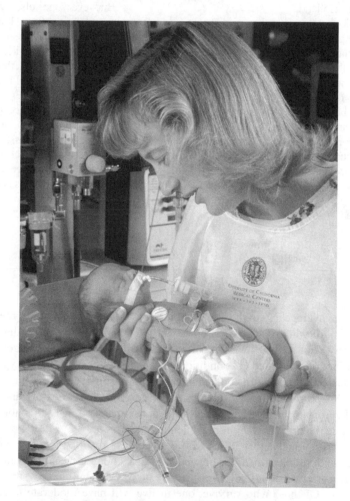

*Advances in medical science have allowed an increasing number of at-risk infants to survive far longer than what was possible a decade ago. These developments have raised a number of ethical dilemmas for society.*

## WINDOW 4.1 • *But I Wanted to Go to Italy?*

When you're going to have a baby, it's like you're planning a vacation to Italy. You are all excited. Seeing the Coliseum...the Michelangelo...the gondolas of Venice. You get a whole bunch of guidebooks. You learn a few phrases in Italian so you can order in restaurants and get around. When it comes time, you excitedly pack your bags, head for the airport and take off for Italy... only when you land, the stewardess announces "Welcome to Holland."

You look at one another in disbelief and shock saying, Holland? What are you talking about—Holland? I signed up for Italy!! But they explain that there's been a change of plans and the plane has landed in Holland—and there you must stay.

"But I don't know anything about Holland! I don't want to stay here," you say. "I never wanted to come to Holland! I don't know what to do in Holland and I don't want to learn!!" But, you do stay, you go out and buy some new guidebooks. You learn some new phrases in a whole new language and you meet people you never knew existed.

But the important thing is that you are not in a filthy, plague-infested slum full of pestilence and famine. You are simply in another place...a different place than you had planned. It's slower-paced than Italy; less flashy than Italy; but after you've been there a little while and have had a chance to catch your breath, you begin to discover that Holland has windmills...Holland has tulips ...and Holland even has Rembrandts.

But everyone else you know is busy coming and going from Italy. And they're all bragging about what a great time they had there. And for the rest of your life you will say, "Yes, that's where I was going...that's where I was supposed to go...that's what I had planned." And the pain of that will never, ever go away.

And you have to accept that pain because the loss of that dream, the loss of that plan is a very, very significant loss. But...if you spend your life mourning the fact that you didn't get to Italy, you will never be free to enjoy the very special, the very lovely things about Holland.

*Source:* E. P. Kingsley (cited in Crutcher, 1990).

On an average day in the United States, more than 10,000 babies are born (one every 8 seconds), of whom 411 have a serious birth defect. Infants with birth defects are born prematurely with low birthweight (often less than 1,500 grams), congenital disorders, and any variety of other medical conditions, such as asphyxia (lack of oxygen), hyaline membrane disease (immature lung development), chromosomal abnormalities (Down syndrome, fragile X syndrome), heart problems, underdeveloped brains, drug and alcohol syndromes, or infections (March of Dimes, 2000). Approximately 4 in 1,000 babies are severely disabled where the primary symptom is mental retardation.

Rapid advances in medical science have resulted in a growing number of these infants surviving at birth far beyond what was thought possible even a decade ago. The majority of critically ill newborns (nearly 90 percent) will survive the neonatal period (Jamal, 1999). Of those who survive, one in five will have moderate to severe disabilities (U.S. Congress, 1987). While medical science continues to decrease infant mortality and increase the average lifespan, this same technology is also raising a number of serious ethical issues regarding decisions about prevention, care, and selective nontreatment of infants with severe disabilities. When do individual rights begin? Who should live and who should die? What is personhood? Who defines quality of life? What are the rights of the individual in relationship to the obligations of a society? Who shall make these difficult decisions? As suggested by Boyle (2001),

> ...any discussion of these issues must recognize the tragedy that underlies these situations: the loss of newborn life, the short-term and long-term health problems of survivors, the disabilities that many infants will face, and the emotional cost to families and clinicians.... The decisions are often very difficult. However, we should be extremely concerned if the discussion ever becomes routine or we are comfortable with all the decisions. (p. 36)

## Bioethics

In recent years, there has been an increasing awareness and interest in what is termed "bioethical" issues, particularly as they relate to serious illness and disabilities that occur both prior to and after birth. These issues range from concerns about the purpose and use of genetic engineering (such as cloning, gene mapping, and transplants), to screening for genetic diseases, and the withholding of life-sustaining treatment. In this chapter we will address each of these issues as they relate to people with severe disabilities and their families. Our discussion begins with an overview of the principles of bioethics.

---

**Focus 1**
Distinguish between the two philosophical positions of utilitarianism and deontological theories.

---

Each of us lives by a basic set of principles derived from a personal philosophy about who we are and how we fit into this world. Although we may not give these principles much conscious consideration, they are the foundation of a code of ethics that governs our actions. In recent years ethicists have given considerable attention to two philosophical positions (ethical theories) that guide people in making decisions about what should or should not be done in any given circumstance: utilitarianism and deontological theories.

*Utilitarianism* is based on the premise that any action is "right" if it leads to the greatest good for the greatest number of people (Veatch, 2000). The utilitarian theory holds that the "end justifies the means." An individual has only those rights granted by the larger society. Whereas utilitarianism is based on consequences that lead to the greater good, *deontological theorists*[1] suggest that some acts may be wrong and others right, independent of their consequences (Beauchamp & Childress, 1994). It is not the impact on society as a whole that is paramount, but the rights of an individual. *Deontological theories* hold that an individual has basic rights that cannot be abrogated or curtailed by others in society. Individual rights supercede those of society (Veatch, 2000).

The application of either of these theories in the extreme leads to difficult and complex dilemmas for both the individual and society. A literal interpretation of utilitarianism

---

[1]Deontology is also known as formalism. *Deontology* is derived from the Greek word for duty.

results in those with power remaining in power by limiting the rights of others. A literal interpretation of deontological theories, on the other hand, means that as we enhance the rights of some, we are infringing on the rights of others. Nowhere are the issues surrounding utilitarianism and deontological theories more evident than in the current national debate over abortion rights and the Supreme Court's decision in *Roe v. Wade*. As society attempts to legislate abortion rights (utilitarianism), people take up personal philosophical positions that range from "the greater good for society" to the individual rights of the woman and the fetus. Similar issues are raised every day in the newborn intensive care units of our nation's hospitals. When a child is born with serious and significant birth defects and requires life-sustaining support, should the parents and physicians have the right to choose life or death, or should the right of the infant to life always prevail? Whose rights carry more weight? When there are conflicts, whose rights take precedence? The answers to these questions may ultimately be unanswerable to everyone's satisfaction, and will only come through reasoning and reflection on moral principles and rules (Beauchamp & Childress, 1994). Three principles, which are most often identified by ethicists as the driving forces in moral decision making, include autonomy (self-rule, free of external control), beneficence (do no harm), and justice (receiving what is deserved—fairness). Differing perspectives on the application of these principles to a fetus or infant with severe disabilities creates societal dilemmas often referred to as "competing equities." When considering the issue of abortion, who is more autonomous, the mother or the fetus? Who shall be considered first as the principle of "do no harm" is applied? What is fair?

In the following section, we examine bioethical issues as they apply to the prevention of severe disabilities. Developments in genetic engineering, organ transplantation, as well as genetic screening and counseling are addressed. The chapter concludes with a discussion of recent advances in medical care and treatment for the newborn with severe disabilities.

## Prevention

The prevention of severe disabilities, particularly mental retardation, has historically been hailed by health care professionals, disability organizations, and the general public as a laudable goal. Over the years, efforts at preventing severe disabilities have taken on many forms. Isolation (quarantining people with severe disabilities) and mandatory sterilization procedures were predominant forms of prevention in the first half of the twentieth century. They were eventually replaced by less controversial forms of prevention, such as immunizations against disease, proper nutritional habits during pregnancy, and appropriate maternal prenatal care. Immunizations protect against the contraction of serious illnesses (such as rubella) that can result in mental retardation or blindness. The failure of the mother to access appropriate prenatal care, maintain proper maternal nutritional habits, and avoid smoking and alcohol during pregnancy may contribute significantly to fetal problems. These problems include increased risk of low-weight births, premature births, as well as infant and maternal mortality (Kiely & Kogan, 1994; Perry, Zyrkowski, Clark, & Yu, 1994).

As medical science continues to progress rapidly in its understanding of human genetics and accompanying diseases, prevention has now expanded even further, into the areas of genetic engineering, organ transplantation, and biomedical screening. The importance of genetics research cannot be overstated. As the causes of these diseases are identified, more accurate diagnoses will be made and effective treatment procedures implemented.

## Genetic Engineering

> **Focus 2**
> What is the purpose of genetic engineering, and why are there concerns about its future use with human beings?

There are about 5,000 inherited genetic diseases in human beings, such as Huntington's disease, cystic fibrosis, and sickle cell anemia. Other common disorders such as heart disease and most cancers result from an interplay among multiple genes and environmental factors. Scientists believe that eventually most, if not all, of these diseases can be prevented and treated (U.S. Department of Health and Human Services, 2001). Whereas understanding the genetic structure of organisms was once thought to be forever out of reach, it is now possible that we will have a complete and accurate DNA sequence of the 100,000 or so human genomes as early as 2003. The focus is on DNA, the substance that contains all genetic instructions. By identifying the genes we inherit from our parents, scientists are making significant progress against fatal genetic diseases. In fact, major strides have already been made against sickle cell anemia, hemophilia, Huntington's disease, Tay-Sachs disease, and cystic fibrosis (CF). (See Point of Interest 4.1.)

Genetic engineering is concerned with the conquest of disease. The prevention and treatment of genetic diseases first requires the identification of the faulty gene that causes the disease (as in cystic fibrosis). The next phase is to identify the protein that the gene normally produces. Finally, there is an attempt to fix or replace the defective protein or gene through a technique known as gene therapy (cell manipulation). The purpose of gene therapy is to change the characteristics of some genes in an attempt to treat, cure, or ultimately prevent disease (Human Genome Project, 1999). "Using recombinant DNA and other techniques of molecular biology…genetic material from one organism can be inserted into an organism of a different species" (President's Commission, 1983a, p. 40). Gene therapy should not, however, be confused with cloning. Cloning is very different from gene therapy and involves creating another person with essentially the same genetic makeup.

Today, gene therapy remains experimental, with human clinical trials underway. Whereas some geneticists dismiss gene therapy as "pie in the sky," others suggest it has value and that basic research should continue (Human Genome Project, 1999). Kmiec (1999) indicates that "making gene therapy a successful endeavor will require careful research to understand why traditional approaches have not produced the hoped-for results and, in turn, to improve them, while exploring new ways to deal with genetic defects…. At its core, the notion of gene therapy or gene correction is scientifically sound" (online).

***Bioethical Issues.*** Genetic research holds considerable promise for altering human suffering in the future. As suggested by Pine (1991), "the miraculous substance that contains all our genetic instruction—DNA—is rapidly becoming a key to modern medicine. "However,

**POINT OF INTEREST 4.1** • *The Human Genome Project*

*Q. What is the Human Genome Project?*
The Human Genome Project (HGP) is an international 13-year effort formally begun in October 1990. The project was planned to last 15 years, but rapid technological advances have accelerated the expected completion date to 2003. Project goals are to discover all the approximately 100,000 human genes (the human genome) and make them accessible for further biological study and to determine the complete sequence of the 3 billion DNA subunits (bases).

   The Department of Energy's Human Genome Program and the National Institutes of Health's National Human Genome Research Institute (NHGRI) together make up the U.S. Human Genome Project. A rough draft of the human genome was completed in June 2000. Efforts are still under way to complete the finished, high-quality sequence.

*Q. What other countries are participating in the HGP?*
At least 18 countries have established human genome research programs. Some of the larger programs are in Australia, Brazil, Canada, China, Denmark, European Union, France, Germany, Israel, Italy, Japan, Korea, Mexico, Netherlands, Russia, Sweden, United Kingdom, and the United States. Some developing countries are participating through studies of molecular biology techniques for genome research and studies of organisms that are particularly interesting to their geographical regions. The Human Genome Organisation (HUGO) helps to coordinate international collaboration in the genome project.

*Q. What happens when the genome sequence is completed?*
Deriving meaningful knowledge from DNA sequence will define biological research through the coming decades and require the expertise and creativity of teams of biologists, chemists, engineers, and computational scientists, among others. A sampling follows of some research challenges in genetics—what we still won't know, even with the full human sequence in hand.

- Gene number, exact locations, and functions
- Gene regulation
- DNA sequence organization
- Chromosomal structure and organization
- Predicted versus experimentally determined gene function
- Correlation of SNPs (single-base DNA variations among individuals) with health and disease
- Disease-susceptibility prediction based on gene sequence variation
- Genes involved in complex traits and multigene diseases
- Developmental genetics, genomics

*Source:* Human Genome Program (2001). Frequently asked questions. Washington, DC: U.S. Department of Energy Office of Science. Available: http://www.ornl.gov/hgmis/faq/faqs1.html#HGP.

genetic research and engineering are not without detractors (Brock, 1994; Butchvarov, 1994; Fox, 1999; Lappe, 1993). In 1983, a Presidential Commission was organized to study the ethical problems in biomedical and behavioral research. In a report entitled *Splicing Life* (President's Commission, 1983b), the commission found that the general public had "exaggerated" fears about genetic engineering research remaking human beings into Frankenstein's monster. They did, however, acknowledge that such techniques challenge "some deeply held feelings about the meaning of being human and of family lineage" (p. 41). The commission stressed that the future of genetic engineering must be one of ameliorating genetic deficiencies, not enhancing or perfecting human beings. Fitzgerald (1998) suggests that, as proposed under the Human Genome Project, genetic engineering could have detrimental effects on people with disabilities if the value is to eliminate rather than care. "Disability is not a blemish awaiting removal, but a part of life waiting to be embraced.... We might try to construct a world without disability, but basically in doing so, we are embarking on a losing battle—for pain and pleasure are two side of the one piece of paper" (p. 163).

## *Organ Transplantation*

> **Focus 3**
> Identify two bioethical issues associated with the advancement of organ transplantation.

Advances in medical technology, such as improved surgical techniques and medications that reduce rejection, have resulted in an ever-increasing rate of success for pediatric organ transplants. Patients with congenital heart and lung problems, as well as kidney and liver disease, have much greater chances of survival and an enhanced quality of life as a result of organ transplantations (Fox, 1999; Kass, 1993; National Institute of Transplantation [NIT], 2001). The NIT reports that 92 percent of people receiving kidney transplants survive at least three years following the operation. This advancing technology does, however, have its problems—specifically, a shortage of available organs, and the necessity to often remove organs from a donor prior to the cessation of heart and breathing functions. As of February 2001, there were 74,480 on waiting lists for organ transplantation in the United States. Each day about sixty people receive an organ transplant in 261 medical institutions in the United States, but another seventeen people on the waiting list die because not enough organs are available (Transplant Patient DataSource, 2001).

The lack of available organs for transplantation results from several factors. For infants and young children the mortality rate is low, and few die from accidents to meet the need for several hundred infant hearts and livers required each year for transplantation. About 30 percent of children between the ages of 1 and 5 who need a heart transplant die each year because there are not enough matched organs available (U.S. Department of Health and Human Services, 1999). Other factors that contribute to a shortage of available organs include no available matched donor, the failure of the public to designate themselves as donors, and reluctance of family members to donate organs after the death of a loved one. Although public support for organ donation remains strong and the number of cadaveric and living donors increased 70 percent between 1989 and 1998, there is still a critical need for people to donate organs (U.S. Department of Health and Human Services, 1999).

*Bioethical Issues.*    The removal of organs from a donor prior to the cessation of heart and breathing functions is a bioethical issue. Many organs used in transplantation must be removed prior to the cessation of these circulatory actions. Therefore, normal circulation must be maintained, often by mechanical means, to preserve the organs until they are removed from the body and prepared for transplantation. Since medical life-support techniques can maintain breathing and heart actions even when the brain is no longer functioning, it is possible to "harvest" organs following "brain death." A definition of brain death, recommended by the President's Commission (1983c), was adopted into federal law in 1990 under the Uniform Determination of Death Act (UDDA).

An individual who has sustained either (1) irreversible cessation of circulatory and respiratory functions, or (2) irreversible cessation of all functions of the entire brain, including the brain stem, is dead. A determination of death must be made in accordance with accepted medical standards. (p. 2)

The UUDA recognizes two clinical situations as death: cessation of circulatory and respiratory functions or cessation of brain functions. Byrnes, Evers, and Nilges (1993) suggest, however, that the diagnosis of brain death will vary depending on which of the more than thirty sets of criteria are used to determine "irreversible cessation of all brain functions." In fact, the actual determination of brain death is a difficult legal and moral issue, particularly as applied to infants with severe disabilities. One condition that is particularly problematic is anencephaly. Anencephaly is a congenital disorder in which the cerebral cortices (centers of higher cognitive operations) are missing. The condition, which effects about 3,000 babies each year, is irreversible, and the majority of infants with this condition die in the first few days after birth. Babies with anencephaly usually die slowly and their organs atrophy, rendering them unsuitable for organ transplantation once death occurs. The difficulty is that because the organs atrophy as the baby is dying, physicians may attempt to "harvest" them before brain death occurs.

There are numerous ethical complexities associated with anencephaly and other similar conditions resulting in severe disabilities. Cohen (1990) points out that when severe disabilities are diagnosed *in utero,* "parents are faced with an agonizing dilemma. If the pregnancy is carried to term, their child will be stillborn or face almost certain death within a few days or months of birth" (p. 106). Cohen suggests that the alternatives facing parents are either selective abortion following the *in utero* diagnosis, or carrying the fetus to term and donating the organs once the child is born. This dilemma has resulted in professional and parent groups speaking out on behalf of infants born with severe neurologic disabilities. A Resolution on organ transplantation was adopted by the Association for Persons with Severe Handicaps (Meyer, Peck, & Brown, 1991). The resolution emphasizes that organ donation should occur only when the donor is legally "brain dead" and where proper consent has been obtained from the parents. Byrnes et al. (1993) argue that removing organs from an infant who is not brain dead is medically dishonest and morally reprehensible:

The infant with anencephaly is a living human being who has a congenial abnormality that usually is not associated with long-term survival. If the infant with anencephaly is dying but not yet dead, he/she is still a living person. Being inherently vulnerable, every infant—including one with anencephaly—has a greater moral claim to our care and protection than an adult who is otherwise healthy and self-sufficient. (p. 33)

## Genetic Screening

> **Focus 4**
> Identify the three major types of genetic screening.

Genetic screening is a search for certain genes that are predisposed to disease, already diseased, or may lead to disease in future generations of the same family. It involves a one-time

**POINT AND COUNTERPOINT 4.1 • *Infants with Anencephaly as Organ Donors***

Organ transplantation offers an increasing number of seriously ill children the opportunity for a healthy life. However, many organs used in transplantation must be removed prior to the cessation of circulatory actions. Therefore, normal circulation must be maintained, often by mechanical means, to preserve the organs until they are removed from the body and prepared for transplantation. Since medical life-support techniques can maintain breathing and heart actions even when the brain is no longer functioning, it is possible to "harvest" organs following "brain death." The Uniform Determination of Death Act (UDDA) indicates an individual is "brain dead" when he or she has sustained either (1) irreversible cessation of circulatory and respiratory functions, or (2) irreversible cessation of all functions of the entire brain, including the brain stem.

There is currently a severe shortage of pediatric organs. Young children rarely die in circumstances that would make them medically acceptable sources of organs. In all likelihood pediatric organs will remain a scarce medical resource. One potential source for organ transplantation is an infant with anencephaly. Anencephaly is a congenital defect in which the cranium is absent and the cerebral cortex is virtually absent. However, vital organs, such as the heart and kidneys, are often normal. About 1,000 to 2,000 live anencephalic births occur annually in the United States. Brain stem function enables many anencephalic infants to survive for hours or days and, in rare cases, for a few weeks (American Academy of Pediatrics, 1992).

*Point*

Anencephaly is a tragic condition, but nothing can be done to save the lives of these children over time. Given these circumstances, there are several compelling reasons why the organs of these infants should be made available for organ transplantation even though the child has not been diagnosed as brain dead. First, infants with anencephaly often die slowly and their organs atrophy, rendering them unsuitable for organ transplantation once brain death occurs. Because the organs

atrophy as the baby is dying, physicians must be able to "harvest" them before brain death occurs. Second, the diagnosis of brain death will vary from physician to physician depending on which of the more than thirty sets of criteria are used to determine "irreversible cessation of all brain functions." Third, the available medical evidence indicates that these infants cannot experience pain; they are permanently unconscious. Fourth, many parents of children with anencephaly have expressed their wish that some good come of their loss. These four reasons makes a compelling case for using the organs of an anencephalic infant to give life and health to other children even in circumstances where the child has not been diagnosed as brain dead.

*Counterpoint*

Removing organs from an infant who is not brain dead is medically dishonest and morally reprehensible. Even if the infant is dying but not yet dead, he or she is still a living, breathing human being. Being inherently vulnerable, the infant with anencepahly has a greater moral claim to our care and protection than a person who is otherwise healthy and self-sufficient (Byrnes et al, p. 33). The removal of organs from an infant with anencephaly prior to brain death puts society on a dangerous "slippery slope." Couldn't the case be made that other infants born with severe disabilities, or even older individuals with Alzheimer's disease, could be sacrificed in order to harvest their organs as well? Finally, the American Academy of Pediatrics indicates that there is no convincing reason for changing the law preventing organ harvesting prior to brain death. "The costs of amending the law on organ retrieval or definition of death can only be estimated. Such an amendment might produce decreased respect for human life in other areas.... It should also be noted that an amended law could trigger public fears that organs are or will be taken from other humans not fully brain dead. As a result, donations in general might fall, further reducing the overall gain in lives saved from changing the law (1992, p. 6)."

test to detect flaws in a person's underlying genetic makeup (Weaver, 1997). There are three major categories of genetic screening: prenatal, newborn, and carrier.

*Prenatal assessment* involves several techniques, among which the more common are amniocentesis, fetoscopy, and ultrasound. The purpose of amniocentesis is to access cells in the fetus when there is an increased risk of chromosomal or inborn metabolic error. Using ultrasound to determine the baby's position, the physician inserts a needle to withdraw about 1 ounce of amniotic fluid from around the fetus. During the procedure, the fetus is not touched, and the test is not usually painful to the mother. Cells are then extracted from this fluid, grown in a culture for two weeks, and then analyzed for various abnormalities. Amniocentesis is most often done when there are risk factors associated with advancing maternal age, a history of chromosomal defects in previous pregnancies, a family history of Down syndrome or other chromosomal abnormality, or a history of multiple miscarriages. Amniocentesis is a test with a low risk for maternal or fetal complications (1 in 200 risk of fetal loss through miscarriage). The procedure, which is usually conducted between the fifteenth and eighteenth weeks of pregnancy, can be used to diagnose such conditions as Down syndrome, hydrocephalus, Tay-Sachs disease, and anencephaly, to name but a few.

Fetoscopy also involves inserting a needle into the amniotic sac with a fiber optic, tubular telescope-like endoscope to observe the fetus directly. A thin needle can also be inserted alongside the endoscope to draw blood samples. The procedure is usually conducted between the fifteenth and twentieth weeks of pregnancy, and has a miscarriage rate of 3 to 5 percent (President's Commission, 1983d). Fetoscopy has been successful in the diagnosis of several genetic disorders, including spina bifida and trisomy 13 (Cohen, 1990).

Ultrasound, which is now a routine technique in prenatal care, involves the transmission of high-frequency, low-intensity sound waves through the abdomen of the pregnant woman. These sound waves pass through tissue and are then reflected back as two-dimensional visual images on a television screen. The procedure is performed at about sixteen to twenty weeks of pregnancy and is generally considered to be safe for both the fetus and the mother. There are three types of ultrasound techniques. The first, which generates two-dimensional pictures, can estimate fetal age, weight, location of the placenta, and body parts. The second can show the movements of the fetus, including heartbeat, breathing, swallowing, and the activities of the arms and legs. The third type can actually measure fetal heart rate and sound. Ultrasound has been effective in diagnosing many conditions, such as hydrocephaly, anencephaly, renal dysplasia, duodenal atresia, and mengomyelocele. Ultrasound is often used in conjunction with amniocentesis and fetoscopy to provide a more accurate diagnosis relative to the location of the fetus, to determine multiple pregnancies, and to assist in fetal surgery *in utero*.

*Newborn screening* may involve testing for "inborn errors of metabolism" and chromosomal abnormalities. Inborn errors of metabolism result from a defective gene(s) that has "abnormal or missing enzymes or other protein" (President's Commission, 1983d, p. 12). These metabolic conditions, which are usually inherited, include phenylketonuria, Tay-Sachs disease, and sickle cell anemia. Most inborn errors are now treatable if caught early in the child's life by supplying the body with the missing substance or by altering the environment to remove whatever is harmful to the individual. Since inborn errors of metabolism are inherited from an autosomal recessive gene, there is a 25 percent risk that future pregnancies will result in a child exhibiting the same symptoms.

The second type of newborn screening, chromosomal testing, attempts to identify inborn genetic errors that result from abnormalities in the configurations of chromosomes in the body. Chromosomes are the structures in the human body that contain the genes, which in turn are composed of molecules of deoxyribonucleic acid (DNA). Genetic disorders can result when genes along the chromosome mutate—become altered in some way. There are some 500 genetic disorders that are inherited, including cystic fibrosis and tuberous sclerosis (Widerstrom, Mowder, & Sandall, 1991). Genetic disorders may also result from "genetic accidents," and are therefore not inherited conditions. The most common type of Down syndrome, trisomy 21, accounts for 95 percent of all cases of the disease, and is not linked to genetic predisposition (Drew & Hardman, 2000).

*Carrier screening* is aimed at identifying people of reproductive age who carry abnormal genetic information that could be passed on to their offspring, although they may not have a genetic disease themselves. The technique, which began in the 1970s to screen for sickle cell anemia and Tay-Sachs disease prior to conception, is simple to conduct, and quite accurate. For example, prior to 1970 when the testing began, between 50 and 100 children were born with Tay-Sachs disease each year. After 1980, the number of children born with Tay-Sachs decreased to less than 15 per year (President's Commission, 1983d).

Carrier screening, like its newborn screening counterpart, has been expanded to include numerous other genetic conditions, including cystic fibrosis (CF) and phenylketonuria (PKU). As a result of carrier screening, we know that one in thirty-one Americans is an unknowing, symptomless carrier of the defective CF gene (Cystic Fibrosis Foundation, 2001). Carrier screening, now required in every state in the United States, also identifies nearly 400 PKU babies born each year. Such screening is essential, because if not identified and treated early with a special diet, PKU children often acquire severe cognitive disabilities.

**Bioethical Issues.**    As the use of genetic screening techniques becomes widespread, their continued use and expansion has become a matter of ethical debate. Cohen (1990) reviewed the literature on ethical issues associated with prenatal diagnosis, and found opposing viewpoints on the subject. Some ethicists contend that prenatal diagnosis must be restricted in its use or society will be less willing to "accept and care for abnormal children" (Ramsey, 1973, p. 148). Hauerwas (1986) suggests that "it has become common in our society to assume that certain children born with severe birth defects who also happen to be retarded should not be kept alive in order to spare them a lifetime of suffering" (p. 54).

Fletcher (1983) expressed concerns that advances in genetic screening could pressure certain groups of people who were either carriers of genetic disease, or who had the disease identified *in utero,* to be screened on a compulsory basis. The rationale would be that the cost of raising a child who is disabled far exceeds the costs of a selective abortion. Morison (1973) agrees with this utilitarian approach, suggesting that it is in society's best interest to maintain limits of both quantity and quality in human reproduction:

> Now, when a defective child may cost the society many thousands of dollars a year for a whole lifetime without returning the benefit, it would appear inevitable that society should do what it reasonably can to assure that those children who are born can lead normal and reasonably independent lives. (p. 208)

Weaver (1997) poses three concerns regarding the widespread use of genetic screening. First, the process is not completely accurate in its predictions of future genetic problems. Second, even if the tests were totally reliable and indicated a predisposition toward a certain genetic disease or condition, a tested individual may still not develop the illness. Finally, genetic screening may allow insurers and employers to discriminate on the basis of genetic defects, reducing or eliminating health benefits to identified individuals. "Effectively, these individuals will become a biologic underclass…. With genetic screening, employers will be able to avoid many costs associated with genetic illness (Weaver, 1997, p. 253)."

## Genetic Counseling

**Focus 5**
What are the responsibilities of genetic counselors, and how do they ensure their neutrality in the decision making process?

The next logical step following genetic screening is for the family members to work with a genetic counselor in order to more fully understand the test results, and their implications for the future. Resta (2001) suggests that a genetic counselor must be able to:

> (1) comprehend the medical facts, including the diagnosis, probable course of the disorder, and the available management; (2) appreciate the way heredity contributes to the disorder, and the risk of recurrence in specified relatives; (3) understand the alternatives for dealing with the risk of occurrence; (4) choose the course of action which seems to them appropriate in view of their risk, their family goals, and their ethical and religious standards, to act in accordance with that decision; and (5) to make the best possible adjustment to the disorder in an affected family member and/or the risk of recurrence of that disorder. (p. 1)

The primary role of the counselor is "information giving," although there are paradigms of genetic counseling that involve serving as a "moral advisor," or "psychotherapist." In the past, some counselors were directive, attempting to help family members make the "right" reproductive decision—a decision that was in the best interests of society as a whole. Today, however, it is widely accepted that the counselor's role is one of neutrality. This professional must be nondirective, so that the family can make an autonomous and fully informed decision.

Genetic counselors come from varied backgrounds and training. Some are physicians trained in counseling techniques; others come from outside the medical profession, bringing with them extensive backgrounds in human genetics. Beyond a background in genetics, however, these counselors must also be highly trained in communication skills, and be able to work as a member of a medical genetics team. Other team members may include physician geneticists, nurses, social workers, and laboratory technicians.

***Bioethical Issues.*** Although the neutral role of the counselor in genetic decision making has been strongly emphasized, there is still concern that the counselor must guard against becoming actively engaged in directing the family's decision for them. This is especially true given society's general reliance on physicians as family advisors and authority figures. To ensure neutrality, genetics counselors become acutely aware of what constitutes informed consent in a decision-making situation.

The American Association on Mental Retardation developed a consent handbook (Turnbull, 1977) with the expressed intent of identifying the three critical elements of informed content: capacity, information, and voluntariness. The first element, *capacity,* involves three factors to be taken into consideration: the person's age (age of majority), mental and emotional competence, and the specific situation in which the decision is to be made. With regard to genetic counseling, the question is does the family member(s) have the ability to process the information given, particularly in light of a situation that may be emotionally charged and extremely stressful?

*Information* must be presented in such a way as to ensure that within reason the possible situations and consequences have been taken into account—provide a balanced perspective on the issue at hand. As stated by Turnbull, "the focus is on 'what' information is given and 'how' it is given since it must be effectively communicated (given and received) to be acted upon" (p. 8). It is also important that the family is encouraged by the counselor to seek out other opinions on the information provided to ensure as much knowledge about the issue as possible.

*Voluntariness* is defined as placing individuals in a situation where they are able to "exercise free power of choice without the intervention of any element of force, fraud, deceit, duress, overreaching or other ulterior form of constraint or coercion" (Turnbull, p. 10). This element of consent reinforces the counselor's position as an informant, and not a moral advisor. Although the family's views may not be consonant with that of the counselor, this should not become a dilemma for the professional. As suggested by Drew and Hardman (2000), this may be particularly difficult for the counselor who has his or her own personal beliefs and feelings about what should be done.

## *Abortion*

---
**Focus 6**
What is selective abortion, and what is its relationship to genetic screening?

---

> The Court for the most part sustains this position: During the period prior to the time the fetus becomes viable, the Constitution of the United States values the convenience, whim, or caprice of the putative mother more than the life or potential of the fetus; the Constitution, therefore, guarantees the right to an abortion as against any state law or policy seeking to protect the fetus from an abortion not prompted by more compelling reasons of the mother. (*Roe v. Wade,* 1973)

Selective abortion is the process by which a woman may make the decision to terminate a pregnancy. In the past several years, laws that have attempted to limit a woman's right to abortion have been significantly modified or struck down by the courts. In general, the rights of the mother to an abortion outweigh the rights of the fetus. In recent times, the most significant decision regarding abortion rights was made by the U.S. Supreme Court in

*Roe v. Wade.* The Court upheld a mother's right to abortion until the time when the fetus becomes viable. Viability is defined by the Court as the point when the fetus is capable of meaningful life outside the uterus.

The reasons why a woman would choose selective abortion are numerous, and may include health risks to the mother or unborn child (e.g., heart complications), financial burden, emotional trauma, or the identification of metabolic or chromosomal disorders (e.g., Down syndrome) during genetic screening.

***Bioethical Issues.***    The issues surrounding a woman's right to an *abortion* have arguably created the most highly visible and volatile debate in the United States today. No other single issue polarizes people like the unborn child's right to life versus the woman's right of choice. The issues become even more complex when viewed in the context of rapidly advancing medical technology, and the identification of the unborn fetus with disabilities. The progress made in genetic screening, including the number of chromosomal and metabolic disorders that can now be identified *in utero,* have placed the parents and the physician in the most difficult of positions: deciding whether to abort a fetus. Opponents of selective abortion argue that whereas a woman has received considerable legal protection under the law, the fetus has been basically left unprotected. They argue that there is no justifiable reason for abortion. It does not matter whether the unborn child is damaged or not; the child has a right to life.

Those who favor selective abortion argue not only that the woman's rights may not be abrogated or curtailed, but that the quality of life for the child born with a severe disability may be so diminished that, if given the choice, the child would choose not to live under such circumstances (the suffering child). Silver (1981) suggests that the family may benefit from a selective abortion as well. Some families are just not able to cope with a child who is disabled, due to serious physical, emotional, and financial stress. Glover and Glover (1996) indicate that whereas public opinion is split on the issue of selective abortion, attitudes "shift dramatically when it is believed that the fetus will be born with a defect. Even pro-life advocates may make an exception in the case of a fetus with a disability" (p. 208). (See Newsworthy 4.1.)

These arguments are countered by opponents to abortion who point out that no one has the right to decide for someone else whether a life will "be happy" or "a quality experience." Furthermore, Peuschel (1991) suggests that a woman whose fetus has been diagnosed with birth defects, such as Down syndrome, may receive only negative information from a physician about the child's condition. Thus, parents are often faced with making an uninformed decision that fails to take into account major strides that have been made to enhance the quality of life for people with disabilities in many areas, including education, medical care, assistive technology, and social inclusion.

## Withholding Medical Treatment

> **Focus 7**
> Distinguish between active euthanasia and the withholding of medical treatment (passive euthanasia).

In 1982, an infant with Down syndrome was born in an Indiana hospital suffering from a tracheoesophageal fistula. This condition blocked the child's esophagus and prevented oral

# NEWSWORTHY 4.1 • *Attitudes toward Abortion*

In January of 1993 (one day after the twentieth an-
niversary of the *Roe v. Wade* decision), some
75,000 anti-abortion protesters marched on Washington, D.C. The *Washington Post* (Warden, 1993)
interviewed 742 randomly selected demonstrators
on their attitudes toward abortion, and then compared the data with (1) a random sample of 881
abortion-rights demonstrators who marched on
Washington in April of 1992, and (2) a national
random sample of 1,510 adults.

*QUESTION: Should abortion be legal under each of the following circumstances:*

| Question | Anti-Abortion Marchers | Abortion-Rights Marchers | National Sample |
|---|---|---|---|
| If the woman's life is in danger | 35% | 99% | 91% |
| If the pregnancy is the result of rape or incest | 9% | 100% | 86% |
| If the family cannot afford to have the child | 1% | 97% | 49% |
| If the parents don't want another child | 1% | 95% | 45% |
| **If there is a chance that the child will be born deformed** | 2% | 97% | 73% |

(Shown: Percentage who said "yes.")

*Source:* Warden, S. (1993, January 23). Anatomy of a march. *Washington Post*, p. A8.

feeding because food or water would go into the baby's lungs. The parents, following the
recommendation of the obstetrician, decided not to have the surgery necessary to remove
the blockage and allow the child to eat and drink. The courts upheld the parents' decision
and the baby, denied food and water, died within days. (Cited in Batshaw & Cho, 1997)

As is true with abortion, the issues surrounding withholding medical treatment, sometimes
referred to as "passive euthanasia," are extremely controversial whether the focus is on infants with disabilities, people with a terminal illness, or those who are in the later years of
their lives. Legal experts and ethicists have attempted over the years to distinguish between
two types of euthanasia: active and passive. Active euthanasia is taking a direct action (voluntary or involuntary) designed to end the individual's life. Individuals may voluntarily
carry out the act themselves (take an overdose), or have someone else do it for them. It is
also possible for active euthanasia to be involuntary, where the act is done on their behalf,
but not with their knowledge or permission (mercy killing). Passive euthanasia is more
often described as allowing the individual to die by foregoing treatment (Veatch, 2000).
Arguments have been made that there is a crucial difference between these two types of euthanasia. For example, active euthanasia may involve a doctor taking a direct action (giving a lethal injection) to bring about a patient's death; whereas in passive euthanasia, the
doctor does nothing, and the patient dies. Rachels (1982), however, argues that it is misleading to say the doctor does nothing. The doctor lets the patient die—life-sustaining
treatment is withheld.

***Bioethical Issues.***    For individuals born with disabilities, particularly those with more severe conditions, issues involving active euthanasia and the withholding of medical treatment are enormously important to understand. The frequency with which infants with disabilities were being allowed to die in newborn nurseries first came to light in the literature in the early 1970s (Duff & Campbell, 1973). In several instances, it was found that treatment, considered routine for an infant who was not disabled, was being withheld on the basis that a child had a disability. For example, in the situation in an Indiana hospital described at the opening of this section, an infant with Down syndrome was denied treatment for an intestinal obstruction even though it was clear the child would die without the treatment. The obstruction, though fully correctable in a virtually risk-free operation, was not performed *because* the child had Down syndrome. It would have been performed routinely on a child who was not disabled. It was clear that a separate standard was applied to infants with disabilities, which was not being applied to those who were not disabled. In the past twenty years, concerns regarding this separate standard have resulted in greater protections for infants with disabilities, but have not resolved some critical questions. As framed by Neal (1990), these questions are:

- Does every living newborn have the right to the treatment that is most likely to preserve life, or is it permissible to sometimes let such an infant die, or even take active steps to end the life of the infant?
- Who has the responsibility, or the right, to make decisions on these matters, either for the individual infant or for such infants in general?
- How should the care and expensive resources required for neonatal intensive care (NIC) be allocated, both at the individual and general level? (p. 92)

These questions are not easy to answer, and as would be expected, there are opposing viewpoints. The questions of "what is in the best interest" of the infant, and "who shall decide" immediately suggest that some type of criteria must be applied in the decision-making process. Among the arguments used to make the case that euthanasia is justified is the moral principle of beneficence or nonmalfeasance—do no harm. This argument focuses on the perspective that it is not always in the best interest of the infant to be kept alive at all costs. In other words, sustaining life is harming the baby by prolonging the agony. It can also be argued, however, that sustaining life is the physician's ultimate responsibility and most important role. It is not up to the physician to make moral decisions about what constitutes a quality life. However, the dilemma for the physicians is what happens when the commitment to sustain life conflicts with the duty to relieve suffering?

In the past several years, hospitals have established Infant Care Review Committees to assist physicians and family members in making the difficult decisions of treatment or nontreatment in the newborn nursery. However, these committees, which were established in law by the U.S. Congress in the Child Abuse Prevention and Treatment Act of 1984, have no authority in the decision-making process. They may only make recommendations to physicians concerning appropriate procedures in the treatment of seriously ill newborns.

Weir (1984) suggested that four criteria be used to determine who is in the best position to either assist family members and physicians, or to serve as a proxy in making difficult and complex treatment decisions. First, anyone who decides whether treatment will be withheld from a seriously ill newborn should have (1) all the medical facts in the case, (2) understand the dynamics of the family unit into which the baby has been born, and (3) be knowledgeable regarding possible alternatives for placement other than in the biological family (e.g., adoptive parents). The individual(s) must meet the fundamental moral requirement of impartiality. "To maximize the possibility of being objective, the persons making the...decision should be disinterested in the particular case and issue and dispassionate in weighing available alternatives" (p. 256). These possible proxies must also be emotionally stable and consistent from case to case. "In terms of the principle of justice, morally similar cases should be handled in similar ways" (Weir, p. 257).

Several organizations concerned with disability (i.e., the Association on Mental Retardation; The ARC-A National Organization on Mental Retardation; the Association for Persons with Severe Handicaps) have taken positions opposing withholding medical treatment when any decision is based on the person's having a disability. (See Point of Interest 4.2.) The crux of these positions is that all individuals are entitled to the right to life under the Constitution of the United States, and that it is the obligation of society to protect people from the ignorance and prejudices that may be associated with disability.

**POINT OF INTEREST 4.2** • *Resolution of the Association for Persons with Severe Handicaps on Infant Care*

TASH opposes the withholding of medical treatment and/ or sustenance to infants when the decision is based upon the severity, diagnosis of, or prognosis for mental retardation or any other disability. TASH affirms the right to equal medical treatment for all infants in accordance with the dignity and worth of these individuals, as protected by federal and state laws and regulations. TASH acknowledges the responsibilities of society and state government to share with parents and other family members the support necessary for life-long medical, financial and educational support to persons with disabilities extending to them opportunities offered to all members of society. Furthermore, families and caregivers must be supported so that infants can remain or return to the most natural environment, which is the home.

The rationale for this resolution is as follows:

• The right to life and liberty is guaranteed by our Constitution, Bill of Rights and federal and state laws and regulations.
• The life and liberty of persons with disabilities are threatened by the prejudice which results from the ignorance generated by segregation and separation.
• This prejudice can only be overcome when the next generation of children born without disabilities grows up, plays, goes to school, lives and works with their peers who have disabilities.
• TASH supports the provision of medical treatment and/or sustenance for infants regardless of the severity, diagnosis of or prognosis for disability.

*Source:* Association for Persons with Severe Handicaps (1999, February). TASH resolution on infant care. (Resolution originally adopted in April 1983; amended April 1989 and February 1999. Available: http://www.tash.org/resolutions/R11INFNT.html.

## *Advances in Newborn Intensive Care*

---

*Focus 8*
Identify recent advances in the treatment of high-risk infants in newborn intensive care units.

---

> Bright lights shine day and night; there is a din caused by monitors and high technology machines. Incubators, intravenous tubes, and monitoring equipment abound.... The babies, some of whom look no different from a fetus, lay in isolettes, bassinets, cribs, or on slanted hotbeds warmed by radiant lamps. The smallest babies have arms that are not any bigger than their mother's finger; their heels are as tiny as a pencil eraser. (Cohen, 1990, p. 75)

Advances in medical treatment for infants born prematurely, as well as those with low birthweight and birth anomalies, have resulted in the development of highly specialized hospital settings to treat these newborns comprehensively. Begun in the early 1960s, these settings are known variously as neonatal intensive care units (NICUs), high-risk neonatal centers, special-care nurseries, and perinatal centers. Since their inception, these units have had considerable success in reducing infant mortality, and improving the long-term prognosis for infants born with birth anomalies. Whereas only 10 percent of infants admitted to NICUs weighing less than 1,000 grams survived in the 1960s, about 70 percent survive today. The survival rate for infants weighing between 1,500 and 2,500 grams is more than 90 percent. While the neurological development of low-birthweight babies (LBW) admitted to NICUs has improved as well, a severe disability is six times more likely to occur in a LBW baby than in one who is full-term. Overall, 60 percent of LBW babies have some developmental disability (Bernbaum & Batshaw, 1997).

Hospitals with newborn units are generally organized into three levels of care. Level I hospitals provide treatment for normally developing newborns. In level II hospitals, a newborn intensive care unit is available with a limited range of services. The full range of services, including a staff of neonatologists, and a neonatal transport system, is available in the level III hospital. Infants admitted to level III units have low birthweights, usually under 2,500 grams although some may be as low as 800 grams (under 2 pounds). Many of the infants weighing less than 800 grams will have significant medical problems, including respiratory distress syndrome (underdeveloped lungs), infections, asphyxia (lack of oxygen), hypothermia, heart problems, jaundice, and congenital malformations (Horbar & Lucey, 1995).

Recent advances in neonatal medicine have significantly reduced the incidence of the leading cause of death in preterm infants: respiratory distress syndrome. Preterm infants may be born with an inadequate supply of a natural substance in the lungs—surfactin. The preterm infant with a lack of surfactin is highly susceptible to disease that often results in death. Surfactant-replacement therapy is a process whereby a surfactant is instilled through the trachea to restore the depleted substance in the infant's lungs. This therapy reduced the number of preterm infant deaths from 10,000 per year in the 1970s to about 5,000 per year in the 1980s (Avery & Merritt, 1991).

There are many other advances in the medical care available in newborn intensive care units beyond the use of surfactin. Oxygen therapy involves both mechanical ventilation to breathe for a baby unable to take in air spontaneously, and a plastic hood with oxygen that helps support an infant's breathing. Continuous positive airway pressure (CPAP) prevents the neonate's lungs from totally deflating by maintaining a gas pressure than is greater than atmospheric pressure. Ventricular shunts may be implanted in the infant's head to remove excessive cerebrospinal fluid in the brain and reduce head size. Neonatal surgery can correct many anomalies, such as esophageal atresia, perforations in the gastrointestinal tract, abdominal wall defects, and congenital heart disease.

While there have been concerns about such factors as the costs associated with intensive care, and some of the side effects resulting from the physical environment of the unit (for example, strong lights and high noise levels resulting in some infants having visual and hearing impairments), there can be no doubt as to the growing impact of these units on the lives of high-risk infants. Many infants who virtually had no chance of survival only a few years ago now go on to lead normal healthy lives. Follow-up studies suggest that improved care in newborn intensive care units is contributing to improved long-term developmental outcomes for many children (Bernbaum & Batshaw, 1997; Horbar & Lucey, 1995; Widerstrom et al., 1991).

## Conclusion

This chapter has examined the complex biomedical issues associated with the prevention and treatment of severe disabilities. These issues include genetic engineering, organ transplantation, genetic screening and counseling, abortion, and withholding medical treatment. Bioethical concerns have been addressed in the context of both utilitarian and deontological philosophical positions. Although the prevention of severe disabilities has historically been considered a laudable goal for society, advances in medical science are raising difficult questions about how far society will go. Will genetic engineering continue to focus exclusively on ameliorating genetic deficiencies, or eventually be used to perfect human beings? What will be the impact on people with severe disabilities as the need for organs for transplantation continues to increase? Will geneticists eventually be able to screen for every known human genetic disease, and, if so, will there be more demand for selective abortions? As more and more infants are kept alive through the advances in medical treatment in newborn intensive care units, how will the difficult decisions of resource allocation and selective treatment be made?

## Focus Review

Focus 1: Distinguish between the two philosophical positions of utilitarianism and deontological theories.

- Utilitarianism suggests that ethical decisions be based on the greatest good for the greatest number of people—the end justifies the means. An individual has only those rights granted by the larger society.

- Deontological theorists indicate that it is not the impact on society as a whole that is most important, but the rights of an individual. It is the individual who has basic rights that cannot be abrogated nor curtailed by society.

Focus 2: What is the purpose of genetic engineering, and why are there concerns about its future use with human beings?

- Genetic engineering is concerned with the conquest of the more than 5,000 genetic diseases in human beings. The prevention and treatment of these diseases requires the identification of the faulty gene that causes the disease.
- There are some fears that genetic engineering will result in the remaking of human beings, as well as the elimination of genetic disease.

Focus 3: Identify two bioethical issues associated with the advancement of organ transplantation.

- There is a shortage of organs available for transplantation.
- Most organs used in transplantation must be removed prior to the cessation of heart and breathing functions. Because medical life-support techniques can maintain breathing and heart actions even when the brain is no longer functioning, the question is what constitutes "brain death."

Focus 4: Identify the three major types of genetic screening.

- Prenatal assessment involves the use of amniocentesis, fetoscopy, and ultrasonography. In amniocentesis, a needle is used to withdraw a small amount of fluid from the amniotic sac to access cells in the fetus when there is an increased risk of chromosomal or inborn metabolic error. Fetoscopy also involves inserting a needle into the amniotic sac, but this time with a viewfinder (endoscope) to observe the fetus directly. Ultrasonography, which is now a routine technique in prenatal care, involves the transmission of high-frequency, low-intensity sound waves through the abdomen of the pregnant woman. These sound waves pass through tissue and are then reflected back as two-dimensional visual images on a screen.
- Newborn screening involves testing immediately after birth for "inborn errors of metabolism" and chromosomal abnormalities.
- Carrier screening attempts to identify people of reproductive age who carry abnormal genetic information that could be passed on to their offspring, although they may not have a genetic disease themselves.

Focus 5: What are the responsibilities of genetic counselors, and how do they ensure their neutrality in the decision-making process?

- A genetic counselor has the responsibility to provide the information necessary for the person(s) involved in the screening to make an informed decision.
- Genetics counselors maintain neutrality by applying the principles of informed consent: capacity, information, and voluntariness.

Focus 6: What is selective abortion, and what is its relationship to genetic screening?

- Selective abortion is the process by which a woman may make the decision to terminate a pregnancy.
- Advances in genetic screening now result in a number of chromosomal and metabolic disorders being identified *in utero.* This has placed the parents and the physician in the difficult and complex position of deciding whether to abort a fetus based on information from the genetic tests.

Focus 7: Distinguish between active euthanasia and the withholding of medical treatment (passive euthanasia).

- Active euthanasia is taking a direct action (voluntary or involuntary) designed to end the individual's life. Individuals may voluntarily carry out the act themselves, or have someone else do it for them. Active euthanasia may also be involuntary, where the act is done on their behalf, but not with their knowledge or permission (mercy killing).
- Withholding medical treatment (passive euthanasia) is most often described as allowing the individual to die by taking no direct action (providing a treatment).

Focus 8: Identify recent advances in the treatment of high-risk infants in newborn intensive care units.

- Surfactant-replacement therapy can now restore the depleted substance in the lungs of infants born with respiratory distress syndrome. This therapy has significantly reduced the number of preterm infant deaths.
- Other advances include oxygen therapy (mechanical ventilation and oxygen hoods), continuous positive airway pressure (CPAP) (prevents lung deflation), ventricular shunts (reduces pressure on the brain), and neonatal surgery (corrects many birth anomalies).

## *References*

American Academy of Pediatrics (1992). Infants with anencephaly as organ sources: Ethical considerations. Washington, DC: Author. Available: http://www.aap.org/policy/04790.html.

Association for Persons with Severe Handicaps (1999, February). *TASH resolution on infant care.* Available: http://www.tash.org/resolutions/R11INFNT.html.

Avery, M. E., & Merritt, T. A. (1991). Surfactant-replacement therapy. *The New England Journal of Medicine, 324*(13), 910–911.

Batshaw, M. L., & Cho, M. K. (1997). Ethical choices. In M. L. Batshaw, *Children with disabilities* (4th ed.) (pp. 727–742). Baltimore: Paul H. Brookes.

Beauchamp, T. L., & Childress, J. E. (1994). *Principles of biomedical ethics* (4th edition). Oxford, U.K.: Oxford University Press.

Bernbaum, J. C., & Batshaw, M. L. (1997). Born too soon, born too small. In M. L. Batshaw, *Children with disabilities* (4th edition) (pp. 115–139). Baltimore: Paul H. Brookes.

Boyle, R. J. (2001). Ethics in the neonatal intensive care unit and beyond. *Infants and Young Children, 13*(3), 36–46.

Brock, D. W. (1994). The Human Genome Project and human identity. In R. F. Weir, S. C. Lawrence, & E. Fales, *Genes and human self-knowledge* (pp. 18–33). Iowa City, IA: University of Iowa Press.

Butchvarov, P. (1994). Some concerns about self-knowledge and the Human Genome Project. In R. F. Weir, S. C. Lawrence, & E. Fales, *Genes and human self-knowledge* (pp. 46–48). Iowa City, IA: University of Iowa Press.

Byrnes, P. A., Evers, J. C., & Nilges, R. G. (1993). Anencephaly—Organ transplantation. *Issues in Law and Medicine, 9*(1), 23–33.

Cohen, L. G. (1990). *Before their time: Fetuses and infants at-risk.* AAMR Monographs (Michael J. Begab, Series Ed.). Washington, DC: American Association on Mental Retardation.

Crutcher, D. M. (1990). Quality of life versus quality of life judgments: A parent's perspective. In R. L. Schalock (Eds), *Quality of life: Perspectives and issues* (pp. 17–22). Washington, DC: American Association on Mental Retardation.

Cystic Fibrosis Foundation (2001). Facts about Cystic Fibrosis. Bethesda, MD: Author. Available: http://www.cff.org/facts.htm.

Drew, C. J., & Hardman, M. L. (2000). *Mental retardation: A life cycle approach* (7th ed.). New York: Macmillan.

Duff, R., & Campbell, G. (1973). Moral and ethical dilemmas in the special care nursery. *New England Journal of Medicine, 289,* 890–894.

Fitzgerald, J. (1998). Geneticizing disability: The Human Genome Project and commodification of self. *Issues in Law and Medicine, 14*(2), 147–163.

Fletcher, J. C. (1983). Ethics and trends in applied human genetics. *Birth Defects, 19,* 143–158.

Fox, M. W. (1999). *Beyond evolution.* New York: Lyons.

Glover, N. M., & Glover, S. J. (1996). Ethical and legal issues regarding selective abortion of fetuses with Down syndrome. *Mental Retardation, 32*(4), 207–214.

Hauerwas, S. (1986). Suffering the retarded. Should we prevent retardation? In P. R. Dokecki & R. M. Zaner (Eds.), *Ethics of dealing with persons with severe handicaps* (pp. 53–70). Baltimore: Paul H. Brookes.

Horbar, J. D., & Lucey, J. F. (1995, Spring). Evaluation of neonatal intensive care technologies. *The Future of Children, 5*(1). Available: www.futureofchildren.org/LBW/10LBWHOR.htm.

Human Genome Program (1999). *Human Genome News, 10*(1–2), 1, U.S. Department of Energy.

Human Genome Program (2001). Frequently asked questions. Washington, DC: U.S. Department of Energy Office of Science. Available: http://www.ornl.gov/hgmis/faq/faqs1.html#HGP.

Jamal, N. (1999, October 25). Fragile little lives flourish in the hand of their carers. *The Age.* Available: http://www.theage.com.au/news/19991025/A6637-1999Oct24.html.

Kass, L. R. (1993). Organs for sale? Propriety, property, and the price of progress. In T. A. Shannon (Ed.), *Bioethics* (pp. 468–487). Mahwah, NJ: Paulist.

Kiely, J. L., & Kogan, M. D. (1994). Prenatal care. In *From data to action: CDC's public health surveillance for women, infants, and children. CDC's maternal & child health monograph* (pp. 105–118). Atlanta, GA: Centers for Disease Control.

Kmiec, E. B. (1999). Gene therapy. *American Scientist, 87*(3). Available: http://www.amsci.org:80/amsci/articles/99articles/Kmiec.html.

Lappe, M. (1993). Ethical issues in manipulating the human germ line. In T. A. Shannon (Ed.), *Bioethics* (pp. 123–139). Mahwah, NJ: Paulist.

March of Dimes (2000). On an average day in the United States. Available: http://www.modimes.org/Health Library2/InfantHealthStatistics/avgday.htm.

Meyer, L. H., Peck, C. A., & Brown, L. (1991). Organ transplant unit (Document VI.3). In L. H. Meyer, C. A. Peck, & L. Brown (Eds.), *Critical issues in the lives of people with severe disabilities* (p. 549). Baltimore: Paul H. Brookes.

Morison, R. S. (1973). Implications of prenatal diagnosis for the quality of, and right to human life: Society as a standard. In B. Hilton, D. Callahan, M. Harris, P. Condliffe, & B. Berkley (Eds.), *Ethical issues in human genetics* (pp. 201–211). New York: Plenum.

National Institute of Transplantation (2001). Kidney and kidney/pancrea graft survival data. Los Angeles: Department of Urology and the Division of Nephrology of the University of Southern California School of Medicine. Available: http://www.transplantation.com/kidney.htm.

Neal, B. W. (1990). Ethical aspects in the care of very low birth weight infants. *Pediatrician, 17,* 92–99.

Perry, G. S., Zyrkowski, C. L., Clark, L. D., & Yu, S. (1994). Pregnancy-related nutrition. *From data to action: CDC's public health surveillance for women, infants, and children. CDC's maternal & child health monograph* (pp. 119–128). Atlanta, GA: Centers for Disease Control.

Peushel, S. M. (1991). Ethical considerations relating to prenatal diagnosis to fetuses with Down syndrome. *Mental Retardation, 29,* 185–190.

Pine, M. (1991). Introduction. In *Blazing a genetic trail: A report from the Howard Hughes Medical Institute* (pp. 4–5), Bethesda, MD: Author.

President's Commission for the Study of Ethical Problems in Medicine and Biomedical and Behavioral Research (1983a). *Summing up: Final report on studies of the ethical and legal problems in medicine and biomedical and behavioral research.* Washington, DC: Author.

President's Commission for the Study of Ethical Problems in Medicine and Biomedical and Behavioral Research (1983b). *Splicing life.* Washington, DC: Author.

President's Commission for the Study of Ethical Problems in Medicine and Biomedical and Behavioral Research (1983c). *Defining death.* Washington, DC: Author.

President's Commission for the Study of Ethical Problems in Medicine and Biomedical and Behavioral Research (1983d). *Screening and counseling for genetic conditions.* Washington, DC: Author.

Rachels, J. (1982). Active and passive euthanasia. In T. Beauchamp & L. Walters (Eds.), *Contemporary issues in bioethics* (pp. 313–316). Belmont, CA: Wadsworth.

Ramsey, P. (1973). Screening: An ethicist's view. In B. Hilton, D. Callahan, M. Harris, P. Condliffe, & B. Berkley (Eds.), *Ethical issues in human genetics* (pp. 147–161). New York: Plenum.

Resta, R. G. (2001). Genetic counseling: Coping with the human impact of genetic disease. Access Excellence: The National Health Museum (U.S. Department of Health and Human Services, Public Health Services, National Institutes of Health, National Cancer Institute). Available: http://www.access excellence.org/AE/AEC/CC/counseling_background. html.

*Roe v. Wade.* 410 U.S. 113 (1973).

Silver, T. (1981). Amniocentesis and selective abortion. *Pediatric annals, 10,* 397–400.

Transplant Patient DataSource (2001, February 3). Richmond, VA: United Network for Organ Sharing. Available: www.patients.unos.org/data.htm.

Turnbull, H. R., III. (1977). *Consent handbook.* Washington, DC: American Association on Mental Retardation.

U.S. Congress, Office of Technology Assessment (1987). *Neonatal intensive care for lowbirthweight infants: Costs and effectiveness* (High Technology Case Study 38). Washington, DC: Author.

U.S. Department of Health and Human Services (1999, January). 1997 Report of the OPTN: Waiting List Activity and Donor Procurement, Executive Summary. Rockville, MD, and Richmond, VA: HHS/ HRSA/OSP/DOT and UNOS. Retrieved February 8, 2001. Available: http://www.unos.org/Data/frame _data.asp?SubCat=anrpt.

U.S. Department of Health and Human Services (2001). Understanding gene testing. Washington, DC: Access Excellence: The National Health Museum (U.S. Department of Health and Human Services, Public Health Services, National Institutes of Health, National Cancer Institute). Available: http://www.accessexcellence.org/AE/AEPC/NIH/ index.html.

Veatch, R. M. (2000). *The basics of bioethics.* Upper Saddle River, NJ: Prentice Hall.

Warden S. (1993, January 23). Anatomy of a march. *Washington Post,* A8.

Weaver, K. D. (1997). Genetic screening and the right not to know. *Issues in Law and Medicine, 13*(3), 243–281.

Weir, R. (1984). *Selective nontreatment of handicapped newborns.* New York: Oxford University Press

Widerstrom, A. H., Mowder, B. A., & Sandall, S. R. (1991). *At-risk and handicapped newborns and infants.* Englewood Cliffs, NJ: Prentice Hall.

# 5

# *Multicultural and Diversity Issues*

*Educational and human service programs must be sensitive to the cultural and language needs of people with severe disabilities and their families.*

## WINDOW 5.1 • *Nhia's Story*

Nhia, a 2½-year-old Hmong girl, was the youngest child (of twelve children) in her family. She had a cleft lip and submucous cleft palate, vision impairments, chronic respiratory problems, and profound deafness. Nhia was enrolled in a center-based program, but the early interventionist working with her conducted several initial home visits. These visits typically involved nearly the entire family because the older children often stayed home from school, and extended family members were present as well. A Hmong social worker who served as an interpreter accompanied the early interventionist on each visit.

The family's primary concern was whether Nhia would ever be able to talk. They were informed about the effects of deafness on developing speech and that Nhia's ultimate ability to speak should not be ruled out. In the meantime, the recommendation was to develop her language in school through the use of total communication (i.e., the combination of sign and speech). Nhia's parents and family were receptive to this approach when they understood that it also could facilitate Nhia's learning to read and write and her overall progress in school.

In a subsequent home visit, the early interventionist planned an activity wherein she modeled interacting with Nhia using sign language and speech to teach her common foods that she ate (the first words that her parents wanted her to learn). The interventionist also incorporated a "fun" warm-up activity in which she taught family members how to initialize their respective names by using corresponding alphabet signs. At one point during the session, as the various signs were being demonstrated, Nhia's father and some

of the other adult males abruptly left the room. The social worker also indicated that she needed to leave soon for another appointment. The interventionist, although sensing the tension and apparent embarrassment among some family members, encouraged everyone to continue to follow her modeling of the alphabet signs. She assumed that the *novelty* of using one's hands, face, and body for communication may have been creating discomfort.

When the interventionist later contacted the social worker to determine what had happened in the home visit, she was informed that the family members (and the social worker herself) were uneasy with some of the aspects of signing that involved sustained eye contact and frequent touching of the head and face, which are cultural taboos. Moreover, some of the hand-shapes for the various alphabet signs (particularly the sign for the letter "T"—thumb placed between the curled index and middle fingers) had distinct sexual connotations and/or mimicked obscene gestures.

The early interventionist returned for another home visit shortly thereafter and profusely apologized for her lack of awareness about some of the hand gestures and how she may have inadvertently offended and embarrassed the family. Nhia's parents graciously responded by indicating that it was okay for their daughter to learn and use "those" signs at school, but at home they would use different gestures. The family's relationship with the early interventionist became more endearing over time. However, the mistaken assumption that sign language is "culture free" resulted in a very memorable lesson.

*Source:* Adapted from Chan, S. (1998a). Families with Asian roots. In E. W. Lynch & M. J. Hanson (Eds.), *Developing cross-cultural competence: A guide for working with children and their families* (2nd ed.) (pp. 251–354). Baltimore: Paul H. Brookes.

---

*Vignette 1*
*Mark is a transition coordinator in a diverse urban high school. He is a passionate believer in normalization and self-determination, and is anxious to ensure that the secondary students with severe disabilities in his school district are well prepared for the adult world of*

*work, social relationships, and supported living, and are active participants in community life. He has developed great connections with many of the more innovative adult service agencies and providers and community programs and can be of tremendous help to his students and their families in planning for a smooth transition. He is very frustrated that several of the families of Latino students he works with are planning to have their young adult children live at home and be supported by their families when they finish school. They are among his most skilled and socially appropriate students, and he believes they could be doing so much more with their lives.*

### Vignette 2

*Angie is an early interventionist who has recently moved with her husband to a rural community near a Native American reservation. She has previously lived and worked in predominantly white, middle-class to upper-class suburban neighborhoods. She has always been very well received by families, who have appreciated her warm, outgoing, take-charge personality, her quick grasp of their child's needs and suggestions for ways to facilitate their children's achievement of developmental milestones, and her very reliable punctuality, organization, and record-keeping skills. She is puzzled by how different things are with many of the Native American families she now works with. Some of the families seem to avoid her, being late or not coming for scheduled meetings, or not opening the door when she goes for home visits, even though she can tell they are at home. If they do have a chance to talk, it seems like she does all the talking and they mostly just listen respectfully, but then often don't follow through on her recommendations or even seem overly concerned about the child's disability or the importance of beginning intensive early intervention as early as possible to prevent further delays. Truthfully, she feels that many of the families don't value all of her hard work and just wish she would go away.*

The cultural and linguistic diversity of the United States is increasing rapidly, and the education system in the United States is even more diverse than the population as a whole. This increasing diversity has many benefits but also creates issues, tensions, and multiple opportunities for interactions that are characterized by uncertainty, misunderstanding, or false assumptions among people who may not look, act, talk, or think quite the same way as each other, as illustrated in Window 5.1 and Vignettes 1 and 2. Barrera and Kramer (1997) refer to these misunderstandings and difficulties as "cultural bumps" (p. 229). Bumps can arise during interactions between students, their families, and practitioners who have diverse worldviews, languages, behaviors, skills, or knowledge that are unfamiliar, uncomfortable, or even distasteful to each other. The participants in these interactions can literally "bump up against" one another. "The cognitive and affective dissonance generated by these bumps then inhibits or disrupts desired communication and learning" (p. 229). Preventing bumps when possible, and reestablishing communication and learning as quickly and effectively as possible when bumps have occurred, are critical skills for individuals with severe disabilities, their families and friends, and educators and other service providers as they try to develop and work in partnerships in service provision and support across the age span. This chapter provides an overview of some of the key concepts and definitions and the importance of and need for providing culturally competent services for individuals with severe disabilities and their families. It also describes current trends, approaches, and future directions in more successfully developing and working in partnerships with culturally and linguistically diverse (CLD) individuals with severe disabilities and their families.

# Key Concepts and Definitions

## Context of Increasing Diversity

The population of the United States is increasingly diverse. For example, in the 1970 Census only about 12 percent of the U.S. population was nonwhite. By 2000 nearly 30 percent of the U.S. population was nonwhite (U.S. Census Bureau, Census 2000). Higher birth and immigration rates among nonwhites, and larger numbers of women of childbearing age within these groups, are expected to sustain the trend for the increasing representation of children from what have traditionally been considered "minority" backgrounds in U.S. schools (Hanson, Lynch, & Wayman, 1990). In fact, *minority* has become a misnomer in many parts of the country, where the combined "minority" population represents the majority of individuals in a community or geographic area; "minorities" account for up to 80 percent of enrolled students in some large-city school districts (OSEP/ERIC, 2000).

In 2000, 64 percent of U.S. children ages birth through 18 were white/non-Hispanic; 16 percent were Hispanic; 15 percent were black, non-Hispanic; 4 percent were Asian/Pacific Islander; and 1 percent were Native American/Alaska Native (Federal Interagency Forum on Child and Family Statistics, 2001). Estimates also indicate that there are over 325 languages other than English spoken in the United States, and almost 6 percent of the U.S. population does not speak any English (Sileo, Sileo, & Prater, 1996).

> Currently 15 to 20 percent of students in schools speak a foreign language at home and this percentage is growing at a rapid rate (National Clearinghouse for Bilingual Education, 1998). Most of these students do not speak English as their first language and they are often from cultures that are not well understood in the mainstream American culture. In most cases these students arc also from families that live in poverty. Data from the National Longitudinal Transition Studies (1990) indicates that 47 percent of urban youth with disabilities, mostly from diverse cultures, lived in households with an annual income of less than $12,000. (Avoke & Wood-Garnett, 2001, p. 1)

When quantitative information about diversity is provided, the term *diversity* is often used to refer to cultural, racial, religious, or ethnic group membership as though these are distinct and mutually exclusive categories. "Outmarriage," or marrying someone from a different racial or ethnic group, seems to be increasing among all ethnic groups in the United States (Lynch & Hanson, 1998b), resulting in growing numbers of families and children who are bi- or multiethnic or bi- or multiracial. To put this in perspective, within the broad categories on many application or U.S. Census forms (e.g., African American, White/Nonhispanic), how many people do you personally know whose families have been in the United States for two or more generations and are solely of Irish, Japanese, Ethiopian, or Samoan heritage?

Assumptions are also often made that supposedly distinct group membership is somehow the key predictor of values, beliefs, and behavior for an individual. Thus, it is not uncommon to hear people talk about how all Asians, African Americans, Muslims, or other large and very diverse groups of individuals believe, dress, raise their children, and so on. Although these comments may be made with the best intentions of trying to understand better the diversity within our society, and may be made with admiration or respect for the cultural group being described, broad, unqualified statements like this are still ste-reotypes (Magana, 2000). It may be appropriate and accurate to comment on what many Native Americans traditionally believe, but not to lump everyone together and indicate the "Native American Indian beliefs about disability are…" Lynch further cautions, "Assum-ing that culture-specific information gathered from books, cultural mediators, or language learning applies to all individuals from the cultural group is not only inaccurate but also dangerous; it can lead to stereotyping that diminishes rather than enhances cross-cultural competence. The goal of cultural learning is insight, not stereotype" (1998b, p. 67). It is critical to remember that there is as much diversity within any cultural group as there is be-tween cultural groups (Hanson, 1998a; Lynch, 1998a), and that we must relate to individu-als as unique people, without making culturally based assumptions.

> ### Vignette 3
>
> *Maria is a speech therapist in a city in which many Latino immigrants live. She moved to the United States from Mexico as a young adult and went to college in the United States. Because she is bilingual and understands many of the cultural issues that Latino immigrant families face, her caseload includes many recent immigrants. A couple of days after an IEP meeting she ran into a mother of one of her students who had grown up in the same small town as Maria. The parent was relieved to see her and assumed that because of their common heritage Maria would understand how upset she was with the program being pro-posed by the school for her daughter. She was sure that Maria would understand how inap-propriate she felt it was for school personnel to encourage Connie, her daughter with disabilities, to make all her own decisions, take a sex education/health class, and plan for living in a supported apartment and community employment when she got out of school. These weren't things she wanted the school teaching her daughter! Maria wasn't sure what to say. The mother had just assumed that because they were both women who grew up in the same town and had daughters of similar ages, they would look at things the same way. Ac-tually, Maria talked openly about dating and sex with her daughter, and certainly encour-aged her to plan for her future education, a professional career, and to make her own decisions in life. Her ideas were more like those of her U.S.-born teenage daughter or Anglo colleagues than like those of the mother from her home town.*

Referring to assessment practices, Barrera & Kramer (1997, p. 222) define *diversity* more broadly than group membership, indicating that diversity exists "according to the degree of probability that, 'in interaction with a particular child or family, [the provider] will attribute different meaning or values to behaviors or events than would the family or some-one from that family's environment'" (Barrera, 1996, p. 71). This definition applies to all interactions that professionals may have with family members or individuals with severe disabilities, whether it is about assessment, or developing an IEP, behavior management plan, or transition plans. It is also important to recognize that family members may view or interpret things differently from one another, or view things differently over time. Barrera's definition of diversity is especially useful because it focuses on the level of individual inter-actions, not group "characteristics." While not mentioning them explicitly, it takes into account the many other factors, such as level of acculturation, socioeconomic status, educa-tion, religion, political views, social relationships, recreational interests, or generational membership, that may have just as powerful an effect on the meanings or values attributed to behaviors or events as do cultural, racial, religious, or ethnic group membership.

> **Focus 1**
> Describe the overrepresentation and underrepresentation of children from diverse backgrounds in special education and why there are concerns about it.

## *Diversity and Special Education*

Many students from culturally and linguistically diverse (CLD) backgrounds have been identified as having a disability and are receiving special education services. The Individuals with Disabilities Education Act (IDEA) Amendments of 1997 state that more minority children continue to be served in special education than would be expected from the percentage of minority students in the general school population. The long-term concern that many racial and ethnic groups are "overrepresented" in special education programs has resulted in Congress calling for greater efforts to ensure that culturally and linguistically diverse children be accurately classified and placed within special education. The U.S. Department of Education's (1997) 19th Annual Report to Congress identified at least three problems associated with inappropriate classification and placement of CLD children:

- Being denied access to the general education curriculum
- Being placed in separate programs with more limited curriculum that may impact the student's access to post secondary education and employment opportunities
- Being stigmatized with a misclassification that may negatively impact the student's self-perception, as well as the perceptions of others (OSEP/ERIC, 2000)

In addition to overrepresentation of CLD children in special education, children from some racial and ethnic backgrounds are also more likely to be identified as having certain disabilities. For example, African American and Native American students are overrepresented in programs for students with mental retardation, and European American students are overrepresented in programs for students with learning disabilities (Turnbull & Turnbull, 2001).

Overrepresentation is a concern because it may unnecessarily stigmatize or limit expectations or opportunities for children who are perceived as having a disability only because their cultural or language differences are misunderstood by teachers and other professionals who are predominantly white and middle-class. Overrepresentation often results from the use of referral, assessment, and intervention strategies that are inappropriate or misleading. Teachers, like anyone else, can also be guilty of conscious or unconscious prejudice or bias, which then results in discriminatory attitudes and practices (Grossman, 1998).

The school population has become increasingly diverse, but the same cannot be said of teachers (Thorp, Fynn, Takemoto, & Evans, 1996). The teaching profession continues to be composed primarily of White women of Anglo-European origins. This lack of diversity in the profession means that few teachers have had the opportunity to learn about diverse cultural and linguistic groups through peer or professional relationships, either as they themselves were going through school or in the schools in which they are employed. Yet, the best cultural learning occurs as a result of informal relationships and interaction. Thus, teachers tend to have limited vocabulary and behaviors for interacting with individuals from diverse cultures. Further, too many of us avoid asking questions about cultural experience of others in order to broaden our knowledge base. This avoidance stance has often unwittingly been supported by the "melting pot" view of the United States. This view may deny the role of culture and language in people's lives by suggesting, "We're all people. We're color blind here," and so forth. Unfortunately, taking this position may cause us to avoid the difficult task of acknowledging that there are cultural differences, to set about discovering them, and to learn from the varied cultural perspectives that may be found in the communities where we teach. (Thorp, 1997, p. 262)

Pointing out the difficulties inherent in having education or medical professionals who are less diverse than the communities they serve is not, however, meant to imply that people can receive culturally appropriate services only from members of their own race or culture. As Singh (1995) indicates, having a service provider of the same race as the child or family who is receiving services is no guarantee that a family will receive outstanding, or even better services. "The defining characteristic of effective professionals is not race, but sensitivity, understanding, and compassion. A same-race therapist without these characteristics may well be less effective than someone of another race" (Singh, 1995, p. 10).

There is concern that "underidentification" of students from some CLD backgrounds may also be occurring. One concern relates to the lower than expected numbers of Asian American children who are receiving special education and related services (Byrd, 1999). Parental reluctance to acknowledge the presence of a disability, which can be considered shameful within some Asian cultural groups, and the stereotypic perceptions of some Americans that Asians are a "model minority" who are invariably academically gifted and materially successful, may be contributing factors to the apparent underidentification of Asian students with disabilities (Byrd, 1999). Native Americans with disabilities have also been identified as being underserved, especially in service availability for adults with disabilities (Clay, 1992). "Importantly, the proportion of rehabilitation services provided to Native Americans is substantially lower than the general population. Indeed, Native Americans with disabilities appear to be the least served and most overlooked minority" (Clay, 1992, p. 41). Clay further reports that there are no federally funded independent learning centers (ILC) located on a reservation, even though 46 percent of Native Americans live on reservations or in rural areas. The concern related to underidentification or limited access to services someone is eligible for, but that are not mandated to be provided to all eligible individuals, is that children, youth, or adults with disabilities will not receive the support services they need to learn most effectively and function well within society.

Special education and disability law and policy in the United States are reflective of mainstream cultural values, including individualism, choice, and equity (Kalyanpur & Harry, 1999). Through IDEA 1997 we choose goals and services for an individual child, and yet many cultures deemphasize the individual in favor of the collective good. We emphasize the choice and rights of individuals with disabilities and their parents, and yet many cultures do not encourage children to make their own choices, and believe that professionals should make appropriate educational decisions for their child. We focus on equity, yet many cultures have different beliefs about the opportunities that should be afforded to women versus men and who has the authority to make decisions for an individual. The principle of normalization has been very influential in the development of laws, policy, and services for individuals with severe disabilities, and urges the "use of culturally valued means in order to enable people to live culturally valued lives" (Wolfensberger, 1980, p. 4). "Since the inception of the normalization movement, most professionals have turned to the dominant culture for guidelines regarding what is culturally normative or culturally valued, so that beliefs about what will lead to quality of life have tended to be entrenched in the values of that culture" (Harry, Rueda, & Kalyanpur, 1999, p. 125). Professionals need to remember that individuals with severe disabilities and their families may have different values and "the assumption should not be made that all individuals ought to subscribe to mainstream indicators of quality of life" (Harry et al., 1999, p. 125).

Understandings of disability are themselves very divergent both within and across cultural groups (Hanson, 1998a; Skinner, Rodriquez, & Bailey, 1999; Zuniga, 1998). For example, the birth of a child with a disability may be viewed as a positive sign or gift from God (Skinner et al., 1999), the result of a curse, angry or evil spirits, or a punishment from God (Willis, 1998; Zuniga, 1998), a failure in the mother's dietary or health care practices or some wrongdoing during pregnancy (Chan, 1998a; Sharifzadeh, 1998), or the result of a variety of genetic disorders, diseases, or forms of prenatal or postnatal trauma (Hanson, 1998b). Different individuals within various cultural groups will have different understandings, and these understandings may change over time. Family understandings of the causation and meaning of disability will influence beliefs about what actions should be taken and may also affect family relationships with each other and with the family member with severe disabilities. For example, if the mother's behavior is deemed responsible for the disability, this can strain family relationships and make her acceptance and adjustment more difficult. A belief that disabilities are to be accepted, rather than changed or overcome, may make families more reluctant to undertake corrective surgery or to agree to intensive behavioral therapy or treatment for children with autism. A sense of shame or embarrassment about the child with a severe disability may make inclusion in school or community less acceptable to the family. Point of Interest 5.1 provides some information about how many Native American groups have traditionally viewed disability. How might this relate to Angie's frustration in Vignette 2 that families of some of the infants and toddlers she works with don't seem overly concerned about initiating intensive early intervention to minimize the impact of disability?

## Culture and Key Cultural Dimensions

Culture is a complex, dynamic, and multifaceted concept. Most individuals belong to a number of different microcultures, which have varying levels of influence on them, in different contexts, and over time. For example, a teenager may act completely differently with one group of friends (the "preppies") than with another ("the nerds"), both of which are different from how they act at their part-time job, with their grandmother, or during religious services. If the same teenager becomes a parent, or the parent of a child with disabilities, this may create new microcultural group identifications, and either strengthen or change the ties to previous identifications (Kalyanpur & Harry, 1999). This does not necessarily mean that the teenager is being less genuinely themselves in some situations than others, but may merely reflect the complexity of their individuality and the people and situations that influence them and that they in turn influence over time. "Cultural identity is multifaceted and highly individualized" (Kalyanpur & Harry, 1999, p. 4).

**POINT OF INTEREST 5.1 • *What You Should Know about Native Americans and Disability***

The Native American population includes over 300 tribes. Each has distinct living conditions, languages, environments, and subgroups within itself. There is also significant variation in assimilation among them.

***How do traditional teachings about the causes of disability differ from current medical understanding?***
Overall, Native Americans historically have linked the source of disability to natural causes or a consequence of breaking sacred laws and taboos.

***What is the unifying theme behind traditional Native American views of disability?***
Accidents don't happen, they are caused. The effect of the cause arises from disharmony. The healer and the family goal then is to replace disharmony with harmony. For example, if a woman gives birth to a baby with fetal alcohol syndrome, the mother is responsible not for the actual drinking, but for the disharmony within that caused her to drink. Disharmony is "why." Alcohol is "how." A medicine man would not try to "cure" the child. Rather he would "heal" by helping those involved to regain harmony and spiritual energy.

***How does the concept of spirit influence disability belief?***
A common traditional belief among Native Americans is that humans have three elements: body, mind, and spirit. Most tribes believe the spirit chooses its earthly body, which may be a disabled body. In terms of value, the body is less important than the spirit. A family may reject medical efforts to save a person with critical injuries or with severe deformities, because to save a body may thwart the spirit's attempt to leave the body. The spirit is not "trapped" within a body; it makes the choice. The belief is that when a spirit chooses to live in a body with a disability, this act reflects a strong spirit. This belief in choice extends to all life—the choice of who and what a person is.

***How do Native American beliefs about health and disability affect medical practices?***
Native Americans tend to believe that modern medicine treats only the body, and is a method that does not address the spiritual component. Family-centered medical service providers understand this and encourage necessary ceremonial practices (e.g., marking a hospitalized baby with significant religious symbols and adorning the baby's crib with eagle feathers) to restore harmony.

***How does Native American language reflect disability beliefs?***
Generally speaking, no tribe has a word similar to "disability." However, Native American languages commonly have words or phrases for specific circumstances, such as "crooked back" or "no-eyes."

***Are there any phrases to avoid when talking about disability?***
Virtually all Native American cultures believe thoughts and words have power: Thinking or speaking about something can make it happen. If a person says someone will die or never walk again, and that statement proves true, then the originator of the words bears responsibility. Service providers should refrain from comments such as "will not be able" and other limiting phrases.

***Is the Native American attitude toward disability negative?***
A 1988 study of 170 Native Americans, with various disabilities at three reservations, indicated that they had a positive attitude about living with a disability. On the scale measurement, Native American research participants had an average score of 7.0 (on a 1–10 scale, with 10 being the highest) when indicating their attitude about disability. Traditional Native Americans, in general, typically have a positive, rather than a negative, view of disability. They tend to believe disability happens for a reason and is part of a greater plan. An acquired handicap, caused by self-neglect,

abuse, or disregard for safety elicits more sympathy for the family caring for the person than for the person with the disabling condition.

Information for this fact sheet came from the following sources:

Joe, J. R., & Malach, R. S. (1998). Families with Native American roots. In E. W. Lynch & M. J. Hanson (Eds.), *Developing cross-cultural competence: A guide for working with children and their families* (2nd ed) (pp. 127–164). Baltimore: Brookes.

Locust, C. (1994). *The Piki maker: Disabled American Indians, cultural beliefs, and traditional behaviors.* Tucson: University of Arizona, Native American Research and Training Center.

Hodge, F., & Edmonds, R. (1988). *Socio-cultural aspects of disability: A three-area survey of disabled American Indians.* Tucson: University of Arizona, Native American Research and Training Center.

Locust, C. (1988). *Hopi beliefs about unwellness and handicaps.* Tucson: University of Arizona, Native American Research and Training Center.

Locust, C. (1988). Wounding the spirit: Discrimination and traditional American Indian belief systems. *Harvard Educational Review, 58*(3), 315–330.

Locust, C. (1987). *Yaqui Indian beliefs about health and handicaps.* Tucson: University of Arizona, Native American Research and Training Center.

Locust, C. (1986). *Apache beliefs about unwellness and handicaps.* Tucson: University of Arizona, Native American Research and Training Center.

*Source:* Beach Center on Families and Disabilities, The University of Kansas, Lawrence, KS. Copyright © 1998. Content edited 2000.

Key understandings of culture include the following.

- Culture is composed of the socially generated and socially sanctioned ways of perceiving, believing, evaluating, and behaving shared by members of particular communities and transmitted across generations.
- The aspects of culture most easily perceived (e.g., food, behavior) are only the surface level of culture and are inextricably tied to and generated from deeper values, beliefs, and worldviews, which form culture's primary level.
- Culture functions both to set parameters that both connect and separate people and communities and to transmit from one generation to another ways of perceiving, believing, evaluating, and behaving deemed to be critical to personal and group survival.
- Everyone's ways of perceiving, believing, evaluating, and behaving come from somewhere. That is, everyone participates in one or more cultures, some of which may be identified by ethnic labels, some by other labels, and others that may have no easy labels. (Barrerra & Kramer, 1997, p. 222)

See Point of Interest 5.2 for a brief cultural journey that may help you understand your own cultural background and how it may influence your beliefs and behavior.

An important dimension of culture is the level of acculturation an individual desires or has achieved. *Acculturation* relates to the extent that someone has adopted mainstream cultural views, beliefs, and behavioral patterns (Sturm & Gahagan, 1999). Althen (1988) developed a guide for international visitors to help them understand mainstream American culture and described the predominant ideas, values, and behaviors of Americans as being

**POINT OF INTEREST 5.2 • *A Cultural Journey***

Culture is not just something that someone else has. All of us have a cultural, ethnic, racial, linguistic, and religious (or nonreligious) heritage that influences our current beliefs, values, and behaviors. To learn a little more about your own heritage, take this simple cultural journey.

*Origins*

1. When you think about your roots, what place(s) of origin do you identify for your family?
2. Have you ever heard any stories about how your family or your ancestors came to the place where you grew up or how they came to the United States? Briefly, what was the story?
3. Are there any foods that you or someone else prepares that are traditional for your place of origin or some other aspect of your heritage? What are they? What is their significance?
4. Are there any celebrations, ceremonies, rituals, or holidays that your family continues to celebrate that reflect your place of origin or some other aspect of your heritage? What are they? How are they celebrated?
5. Do you or anyone in your family speak a language other than English because of your origins? If so, what language?
6. Can you think of one piece of advice that has been handed down through your family that reflects the values held by your ancestors? What is it? Does it reflect a cultural, religious, or individual value?

*Beliefs, Biases, and Behaviors*

1. Have you ever heard anyone make a negative comment about people from your place(s) of origin or about another aspect of your heritage? How did you handle it?
2. As you were growing up, do you remember discovering that your family did anything differently from other families because of your culture, religion, or ethnicity? What was it?
3. Have you ever been with someone in a work situation who did something because of his or her culture, religion, or ethnicity that seemed unusual to you? What was it? Why did it seem unusual?
4. Have you ever felt uncomfortable, upset, or surprised by something that you saw when you were traveling in another part of the United States or the world? If so, what was it? How did it make you feel? Pick some descriptive words to explain your feelings. How did you react? In retrospect, how do you wish you would have reacted?
5. Have you ever done anything that you think was culturally inappropriate when you have been in another country or with someone from a different culture? In other words, have you ever done something that you think might have been upsetting or embarrassing to anther person? What was it? What did you try to do to improve the situation?

*Imagine*

1. Imagine that for a week out of this year you will become a member of another cultural or ethnic group. Which group would you choose to be part of for that week? Why?
2. What is one value from that culture or ethnic group that attracts you to it?
3. Is there anything about that culture or ethnic group that concerns or frightens you?
4. Name one concrete way in which you think your life would be different if you were from that ethnic or cultural group.

*Source:* Lynch, E. W. (1998b). Developing cross-cultural competence. In *Developing cross-cultural competence: A guide for working with children and their families* (2nd ed.) (pp. 47–90). Baltimore: Paul H. Brookes.

white and middle class. He also identified several key components of American culture, based on how Americans, in general, see themselves and how foreigners see Americans.

> Predominant American values, according to Althen (1988), include emphases on (1) individualism and privacy; (2) equality; (3) informality; (4) the future, change, and progress; (5) goodness of humanity; (6) time; (7) achievement, action, work, and materialism; and (8) directness and assertiveness. (Hanson, 1998a, p. 19)

Each of these values, which are typically European American, may differ from those held by many other cultural groups, both within the United States and from the countries from which immigrants arrive. See Point of Interest 5.3 for an example of contrasting mainstream U.S. values, and those held by many traditional Asian cultures. Keep in mind that these "contrasts" are generalizations only, and may tell you very little about the actual beliefs and values of a white middle-class American or an individual who is Asian American, African American, and so on.

Acculturation is believed to be influenced by many factors, including place of birth (United States or foreign), educational attainment, proficiency in English, sense of ethnic identification, urban or rural background, residence in immigrant enclaves, and length of time their family has lived in the United States (Pachter, 1994). Although these factors may be influential, "research indicates that acculturation is a selective process" (Sturm & Gahagan, 1999, p. 353), and will play out differently for people with similar mixes of such demographic characteristics. Many recent immigrants to the United States have arrived due to adverse political and/or economic conditions in the regions from which they have emigrated (e.g., Africa, Eastern Europe, Southeast Asia). Immigration under these circumstances can result in tremendous stress, repeated loss experiences, social isolation, and financial hardship (Sturm & Gahagan, 1999). It is important to consider the poverty and trauma that students and their families may have encountered, along with the many obstacles to adjusting successfully to life in a new country. A useful consideration for educators and other service providers is to think whether we are often too critical of families that are struggling to survive intense hardships. A similar consideration is whether we are more supportive and affirming of families that have chosen to assimilate mainstream values, culture, and language as quickly as possible, as compared to families who have chosen to hold on to more traditional cultural values, beliefs, and lifestyle. If so, what impact does this have on our students, and our partnerships with their families?

## *Cultural Competence*

Special educators and other professionals involved with providing services to children with disabilities, or who are at risk for developing disabilities, and their families frequently refer to *cultural competence* as a framework for approaching multicultural interactions.

Cultural competence has several definitions:

- "…the ability of service providers to respond optimally to all children, understanding both the richness and the limitations of the sociocultural contexts in which children and families as well as service providers themselves, may be operating" (Barrera & Kramer, 1997, p. 217)

**POINT OF INTEREST 5.3 • *Contrasting Beliefs, Values, and Practices***

| *Traditional Asian* | *Mainstream Culture* |
|---|---|
| *Civilization* | |
| Agricultural | Industrial |
| • Harmony with nature | • Mastery over nature |
| *Religion* | |
| Polytheistic, spiritualistic | Monotheistic |
| • Humanistic | • Christian |
| *Philosophy* | |
| Heart-oriented | Mind-oriented |
| • Contemplative, circular thinking | • Analytic, linear thinking |
| • Fatalism | • Personal control over environment and one's fate |
| • Stoicism, patience | • Optimism, eagerness to take action |
| • Tradition, living with the past | • Change, future orientation |
| • Being (person orientation) | • Doing (task orientation) |
| • Self-denial, self-discipline | • Self-assertiveness, self-gratification |
| • Spiritualism, detachment | • Materialism |
| *Social Orientation* | |
| Collectivist (we) | Individual (I) |
| • Group welfare, public consciousness | • Self-actualization, privacy |
| • Mutual interdependence, collective | • Individual autonomy, independence, self-reliance |
| • Hierarchy, role rigidity, status defined by ascription (birthright inheritance, family name, age, sex) | • Equality, role flexibility, statues defined by achievement |
| • Conformity | • Challenge or question authority |
| • Cooperation, nonconfrontation, andt reconciliation | • Competition, aggressiveness |
| *Family* | |
| • Family-centered | • Individual-centered |
| • Family as primary unit | • Individual as primary unit |
| • Family solidarity, responsibility, and harmony | • Individual pursuit of happiness, fulfillment, and self-expression |
| • Continued dependence on family is fostered | • Early independence is encouraged |
| • Hierarchical family roles, ascribed status | • Variable roles, achieved status |
| • Parent–child (parental) bond is stressed | • Husband–wife (marital) bond is stressed |
| • Parent provides authority and expects unquestioning obedience, submission to structure | • Parent provides guidance, support, explanations, and encourages curiosity, critical/independent thinking |
| • Family makes decisions for the child | • Child is given many choices |
| • Children are extension of parents | • Children are individuals |
| • Parents ask: "What can you do to help me?" | • Parents ask: "What can I do to help you?" |

- Older children are responsible for the siblings' actions

- Each child is responsible for his or her own actions

*Expression*

Indirect
- Implicit, nonverbal
- Formal
- Goal orientated
- Emotionally controlled
- Self-effacing, modest

Direct
- Explicit, verbal
- Informal
- Spontaneous
- Emotionally expressive
- Self-promoting, egocentric

*Note:* "Traditional Asian" values must be viewed within a historical context. There are obviously significant differences in values among contemporary Asian Americans who represent a highly diverse population. Similarly, "mainstream culture" values should not be equated with "American values" as if they were "homogeneous, clearly defined, static, and synonymous with middle-class, Euro-American attitudes and beliefs. [Moreover,] American values are not necessarily the opposite of Asian values" (Uba, 1994, p. 14). However, the respective values presented above serve to illustrate the distinct historical contrasts between traditional Asian and dominant cultural orientations that continue to be prevalent among various ethnic subgroups.

*Source:* Chan, S. (1998a). Families with Asian roots. In E. W. Lynch & M. J. Hanson (Eds.), *Developing cross-cultural competence: A guide for working with children and their families* (2nd ed.) (pp. 251–354). Baltimore: Paul H. Brookes.

---

- "...the ability to think, feel, and act in ways that acknowledge, respect, and build upon ethnic, [socio]cultural, and linguistic diversity" (Lynch & Hanson, 1993, p. 50)

- "...a program's ability to honor and respect those beliefs, interpersonal styles, attitudes, and behavior, of both the families who are clients and the multi-cultural staff who are providing services. The use of the term 'competence' has gained ascendance in the field because it is felt that competence implies more than beliefs, attitudes and tolerance, though is also includes them. Competence also implies skills which help to translate beliefs, attitudes, and orientation into action and behavior" (Roberts et al., 1990, p. 1).

- "An adequate understanding of and response to cultural parameters as they affect teaching, learning, and interactions with children and families form the bedrock for cultural competency" (Barrera & Kramer, 1997, p. 225).

- "Cultural competence is the skillful, creative, and sometimes intuitive application of knowledge and skills to determine the source of cultural and linguistic dissonance and re-establish the desired communication and learning" (Barrera & Kramer, 1997, p. 225).

Roberts et al. (1990) described several stages, with examples, that health, educational, or service programs may experience as they move toward cultural competence: (1) cultural destructiveness (e.g., requiring Native American children attending U.S. Bureau of Indian

Affairs schools to cut their hair and wear European-American clothing); (2) cultural incapacity (e.g., requiring that signs or forms be completed in English in areas where families speak a variety of languages); (3) cultural blindness (e.g., assuming there are no cultural differences among families who utilize services); (4) cultural precompetence (e.g., conducting workshops for staff on cultural issues); (5) cultural competence (e.g., ensuring that staff is multicultural and materials and services are available in languages needed by constituents); and (6) cultural proficiency (e.g., parents of representative cultures are involved in developing policy, teaching parts of workshops, and working with staff on problem solving and conflict resolution.) If these stages of cultural competence were applied to an individual, rather than a program, what would be some examples that might illustrate each stage? Which stage of cultural competence do you think you are currently in?

Cultural competence is clearly not something you accomplish in a day or two, but is more an ongoing goal for effective service providers and members of a diverse society. The underlying definitions and concepts related to cultural diversity and cultural competence have broad application within society, school and service systems, and special education. The next section of this chapter emphasizes the importance and need for increasing cultural competence for individuals with severe disabilities, their families, friends, and service providers.

## *Importance and Need for Culturally Competent Services for People with Severe Disabilities and Their Families*

Most of the attention paid to providing appropriate educational, health, or social services for people from culturally or linguistically diverse backgrounds has focused on people without disabilities, or with mild-moderate disabilities (e.g., Baca & Cervantes, 1998; Baker & Jones, 1998; Craig, Hull, Haggart, & Perez-Selles, 2000; Grossman, 1998; Hough & Nurss, 1992). As a part of this discussion, there has been considerable controversy about (1) the best way to teach English and academics to English as a Second Language (ESL) or Limited English Proficient (LEP) learners, and (2) the overidentification and representation of CLD students in special education programs. In comparison, very little attention has been directed to the needs of culturally and linguistically diverse individuals with severe disabilities and their families (Harry et al., 1995). Although there is much less chance of identifying someone as having a severe disability, as opposed to a mild disability, based solely on cultural bias, the provision of culturally competent services is equally critical during the communication, assessment, intervention, and collaboration interactions that form the basis of partnerships with CLD students and families. Harry et al. (1995) express concern that inappropriate assessment, placement, and instructional decisions are frequently being made about CLD students with severe disabilities, including placing them in English-only classrooms without ESL instruction or opportunities to interact in their native language. Not suprisingly, this situation may lead to seriously underestimating the abilities of the student and to inappropriate decisions about communication modes and strategies for a "nonverbal" student, who in fact may have substantial language skills in his or her primary language.

> *Focus 2*
> What are some of the factors that may limit the participation of family members from culturally and linguistically diverse backgrounds in the planning and implementation of their child's special education program?

Two areas where the need for culturally competent services for individuals with severe disabilities and their families are particularly evident are improving family participation in the educational process and the selection of appropriate goals and assessment and intervention strategies. Although research studies have had mixed results, greatly complicated by socioeconomic factors, participation of families from CLD backgrounds in educational decision making for their children with disabilities is often reported to be lower than for European American families (Greene, 1996; Kalyanpur & Harry, 1999). Some cultural traditions may find the expectations for parental participation inherent in IDEA 1997 and recommended practices in special education to be in conflict with their own beliefs (Turnbull & Turnbull, 2001). For example, there may be cultural traditions of deferring to authorities or experts (Greene, 1996). Prior negative experiences may also limit the trust for schools or willingness of parents or other family members to participate in educational decision making for their children. For example, a study by Harry, Allen, and McLaughlin (1995) identified five aspects of professional educator behavior that actively deterred African American families from participating and advocating for their children in special education conferences: (1) late notices and inflexible scheduling of conferences, (2) limited time available for conferences, (3) an emphasis on documents rather than participation, (4) the use of jargon, and (5) the structure of power, which usually gave power and authority to professionals, even though this is not the intent of special education law or recommended practices. Many barriers to more active family participation may be primarily logistical, including problems such as conflicting work schedules, transportation and child care problems, or costs (Parette & Petch-Hogan, 2000). Many of these barriers are problematic for too many families, and, unless addressed, significantly limit the extent to which appropriate educational or support services can be developed for individuals with severe disabilities.

The instructional goals for many learners with severe disabilities can be greatly influenced by cultural parameters, partly because many of them are so closely linked to everyday functioning in home and community settings, and within the social as well as academic networks at school. These cultural influences begin during infancy, when parenting and caregiving practices related to feeding, enhancing communication and motor development, and responding to crying are prominent considerations, through the work, social relationship, and living arrangements of adulthood. For example, consider some of the cultural considerations related to independent self-feeding (Sturm & Gahangan, 1999; Wayman, Lynch, & Hanson, 1990) that may influence the development of an IEP goals and intervention plan in this area.

- Developmental norms for appropriate times to wean a child from the breast or bottle or for mothers to discontinue other feeding of a child vary by many months or years across different cultures and may create discrepancies between when interventionists think goals in this area are appropriate and when family members do.

- Different utensils, foods, and mealtime routines may be used, and these may vary from what is available or common in school or community contexts.
- There may be cultural or religious taboos about certain foods or food preparation practices.
- The identity and number of individuals who assist in feeding the child, and need information about recommended practices or instruction, may vary.
- Acceptance of specialized feeding techniques and equipment that might be recommended, for example, for a child with cerebral palsy, may vary.
- Acceptance of nutritional recommendations that differ from traditional cultural practices may vary.

Ignoring any of these factors that have importance or significance to an individual family will clearly undermine the effectiveness of efforts to promote self-feeding skills and may also be highly offensive to the child's family, undermining further opportunities for partnerships.

Similar considerations apply to planning programs for older individuals with severe disabilities, and illustrate the importance and need for increasing the cultural competence of service provision. For example, self-advocacy is often highly valued within mainstream cultural values. See Window 5.2 for an example of how a Lakota woman with developmental disabilities who is living in a group home responded to her own opportunities to participate in the People First self-advocacy group. In what ways did group home staff appropriately support culturally based lifestyle choices for Gloria? What opportunities for developing a deeper understanding of cultural values and differences did interacting with Gloria provide for group home staff? Now read Point of Interest 5.4 for some information on working with Hispanic or Latino families that may have implications for transition planning and adult services for individuals with severe disabilities. Review Vignette 1 at the beginning of this chapter. After reading Point of Interest 5.4, would you have any suggestions for Mark regarding his frustrations with some of his students' families?

Designing appropriate educational and support services for individuals with severe disabilities obviously involves many important cultural considerations. In the next section of this chapter, current trends in providing culturally competent services are described, followed by more specific strategies and approaches for overcoming barriers to family participation and incorporating cultural considerations during interactions with students and their families and throughout the instructional process.

## Current Trends: Providing Culturally Competent Services

### Honoring Differences

As discussed throughout this chapter, there is considerable evidence to support the potential for conflict between professionals and families who come from diverse sociocultural backgrounds. This is particularly true in light of the fact that most educators are from white, middle-class families. Harry (1997) identifies four areas of potential dissonance between professionals and families. These include differing beliefs about groups of people,

*"I'm not Indian anymore."*

When Gloria said this to me, I was standing with a bill in my hand for a pink sweat suit she had charged to the agency, ready to talk to her about who pays for what: however, now I was faced with a far more important issue. Actually, I was shocked, as Gloria had seemed to be very secure in her Indian identity. Thus, I asked her what made her Indian. She quickly told me two things:

*"Wearing dresses. No haircuts."*

She was quite right that she now only occasionally wore the dresses she had worn every day at home on the reservation, opting instead for the pink sweat suit, and that she had asked to get a haircut. We assumed that Gloria had chosen both changes, although she may have stopped wearing dresses and had her hair cut because she wanted to be like the others in her new group. I did not realize that these changes would make her feel less Indian or that, maybe, she had succumbed to subtle pressures we, the staff, were unknowingly exerting.

We had tried to communicate a message of acceptance. For example, we added Native American art as part of the decorations in the group home; tuned radios to the local Indian station; subscribed to the Indian newspaper, *Lakota Times;* showed videotapes that had positive images of Native Americans; added Indian tacos to the menu; and provided transportation to the reservation so Gloria could visit family and participate in pow-wows and ceremonies. These things were helpful; but clearly, there were other features that meant more to Gloria. Over the next several weeks, we continued to talk about what it meant to be Indian, and she added two more behaviors to her list: "talking Indian" and going to church. Eventually, her team found a bilingual friend for her with whom she had pie, coffee, and Lakota conversation once a week (O'Connor, 1993). We also assisted her in attending several different churches, a choice not unusual for Lakota who accept that there are many paths to spirituality not just a single, right one (Powers, 1987).

Gloria and I and several other people attended a Native Americans with Disabilities conference in Albuquerque, New Mexico, where Gloria met some people active in the People First organization. As a result, she founded a local People First group and participated in a self-advocacy training sponsored by the state advocacy office. Gloria eventually stopped attending People First meetings; she discovered that her motivation had been to learn to stand up to racism and prejudice about being Indian, not to be an advocate because she had been labeled as having a disability. According to Strenta and Kleck, "individuals with stigmatizing characteristics often take it for granted that their treatment by others is causally linked to these attributes," (1984, p. 279). In the town where Gloria received services, both her Indian identity and her disability were stigmatizing. Gloria, however, identified herself in the same way other Indians did, as Lakota, not as a person with a disability; therefore, she saw her mistreatment as a consequence of her Indian identity. In Lakota culture, having a disability is not stigmatizing (Ross, 1989); therefore, helping Gloria see her treatment as being due to her disability would have challenged her schema of what it means to have a disability. To provide values-based services to Gloria it is necessary to support her self-identity and her analysis of the reasons for her mistreatment.

Gloria and I continued to talk about being Indian. I explained the concepts of values and value differences. She explained to me what it was like to be hurt and disrespected just because you are Indian. Once she asked me to write a letter to complain about a state employee who had treated her disrespectfully. Together, we wrote a letter to the employee's supervisor and received a typical "he was only doing his job" response that Gloria knew was further proof of how little others understood her value of respect. Another time, we visited a museum that prominently featured Lakota artifacts. Gloria contributed to their fundraising campaign because she believed they were helping people respect Lakota history and culture.

*Source:* Pengra, L. M. (2000). *Your values, my values: Multicultural services in developmental disabilities.* Baltimore: Paul H. Brookes.

The growth in the U.S. Hispanic population has prompted service professionals and educators to examine their service practices for Hispanic families and their children with disabilities. This is particularly critical regarding the need for Hispanic students with disabilities to prepare for adult living. An extensive literature review on the Hispanic population and *transition*—moving from high school to adult living, offers the following tips for working with Hispanic families who have children and youths with disabilities.

• Take time to learn more about your own culture. Compare your cultural values with those of other cultures to increase your cultural self-awareness.

• The more you know about the different values of families from culturally diverse backgrounds, the better you can provide effective services. Read information about Hispanic culture, and spend time with people from that culture to learn more about Hispanic customs, values, and practices. For instance, the cultural values of *familism* (family unity and interdependence), *personalism* (trust in personal relationships rather than institutions), *respeto* (respect for authority), and *simpatia* (tendency to avoid conflict) often influence Hispanic families of many generations. Use these cultural values as guidelines rather than absolute truths. Recognize that cultural values are tendencies and should not be used to stereotype anyone. Remember, Hispanic families vary greatly in the degree to which they have assimilated non-Hispanic, mainstream cultural values, beliefs, and practices. Don't be afraid to ask questions.

• If you need to provide families with information, first ask them how they would like the information. On paper? In a different language? Through video? By phone? In person? If the family did not understand the information after you provided it in their preferred format, try to find out why. Was it: not in their primary language? Filled with too much jargon? In the wrong dialect? Confusing in the way contents were arranged?

• Although many Hispanic families have the support of family members, some do not. Be aware of each family's existing support network.

• To best serve a family, find out what its members need and want. When you have a good idea of what it will take to best meet the family's needs, then see what services you can provide for the family. Custom fitting support to a family's needs is more effective than squeezing a family into available services. If necessary services do not exist, consider using person-centered planning methods, such as Personal Futures Planning or Group Action Planning, to bring together community and natural supports.

• A family's vision may be greatly influenced by information about such options as educational programs and residential settings, employment, or leisure options. To help parents make informed decisions about the future, make sure you provide currently available community resources, as well as current eligibility requirements for getting these services. A question to keep in mind is: How do we make this partnership a "win–win" situation for everyone concerned? Develop collaborative partnerships with schools, adult service agencies, and local community organization to keep families up-to-date on community services.

• Be aware that many Hispanic families may have plans and dreams for their child's future after high school that differ from common, non-Hispanic U.S. expectations. For instance, a Hispanic family may not want their adult child to live away from the family home. Work to achieve the individual's and the family's goals rather than those of the service agency.

• Typically, when people think about planning for life after high school, they think of jobs. A well-rounded life has many other areas to consider, too. Explore, for example, the family's preference about what their son or daughter does or might do for relaxation and recreation.

*Source:* Beach Center on Families and Disabilities, The University of Kansas, Lawrence, KS. Copyright © 1997. Content edited 2000.

the meaning of disability, parenting styles, and educational goal setting. To avoid these potential pitfalls, professionals must move beyond a basic understanding of the need for culturally competent services and become "culturally sensitive," where differences are not only understood but "honored." Roberts et al. (1990) suggest that culturally sensitive programs *honor and respect* differing beliefs, interpersonal styles, attitudes, and behaviors.

The concept of "honoring differences" is fundamental to the basic tenets of the IDEA and the development of effective programs for students with disabilities. Kalyanpur and Harry (1999) suggest that the core values of individualism, equity, and choice are at the heart of the IDEA. Individualism focuses on recognizing and supporting student need no matter how unique or different they are from the norm. Equity ensures that both students and parents are able to participate fully in and benefit from an appropriate educational experience based on nondiscriminatory assessment and the principle of zero rejection. Freedom of choice implies that all people, regardless of the nature or extent of their differences, can aspire to the valued goal of independence and participation in family, school, and community life.

Yet, in spite of the IDEA's core values, special education as a profession has had considerable difficulty in understanding and effectively meeting the needs of parents from culturally diverse backgrounds. Correa, Blanes-Reyes, and Rapport (1996) indicate that "if the educational outcomes of a free appropriate public education are to achieve post-school success in employment, independent living, and/or community participation, the outcomes for minority students with disabilities are not being realized" (p. 535). Students with disabilities from culturally diverse backgrounds are most negatively affected by the lack of cultural competence on the part of both general and special educators, and the limited involvement on the part of families in the IEP process. These problems are exacerbated for families who have a child with severe disabilities (Westling & Fox, 2000). Parents often experience considerable stress and anxiety in raising their child in a world that is all too often ambivalent about the plight of both the child and the family. It is, therefore, incumbent upon professionals working with parents of a child with severe disabilities to become sensitive to family needs, and to take affirmative and direct steps to ensure that diversity is valued within the child's program (O'Shea & Lancaster, 2001).

---

**Focus 3**
What are some important features or strategies that will assist education and other human services programs in honoring cultural-linguistic differences?

---

Barrera (2000) identifies five features that will assist education and other human services programs in honoring cultural-linguistic differences.

• Recognize the pervasive influence of culture and cultural differences. Everyone sees the world through culturally tinted lenses. "The words we use and the categories we tend to perceive are largely the result of the culture(s) in which we participate" (pp. 17–18).

• Increase access between families and services. A major hurdle in serving students with disabilities and their families is access to services by the families and access to the families by professionals. For many families from diverse backgrounds, oral communication has more credibility than written communication. A great deal of importance is placed on face-to-face contacts.

• Recognize the importance of establishing rapport. Rapport is established when one person believes that the other person not only understands his or her point of view but also validates it in some way. Rapport is facilitated by "understanding the stress that often accompanies learning new cultural parameters and language" (p. 20) and by communication that is effective and responsive to individual need. (Strategies for building rapport and communicating effectively are discussed in more depth later in this chapter.)

• Support families' efforts to deal with diverse culture(s) and language(s). Professionals must take the responsibility to identify the role that culture and language play in a particular situation and then provide the necessary support for families. One way to provide this support is through the use of paraprofessionals and volunteers fluent in a family's language and culture.

• Develop *reciprocal* "additive responses" to families and children. Additive responses support the addition of new information or behaviors to existing situations. Professionals "respect the linguistic and behavioral repertoire of the children and their families and seek to expand rather than limit it" (p. 22).

Programs honor differences when they become culturally responsive to the needs of both the students and the families. Point of Interest 5.5 highlights considerations for honoring the linguistic and behavioral patterns of several cultural groups, including Hispanic Americans, African Americans, Asian Americans, and Native Americans. As suggested by Fielder (2000), professionals must be cautious about stereotyping culturally diverse groups. The considerations presented in Point of Interest 5.5 are generalizations, and individual communication patterns may vary from the group representation.

## Increasing the Cultural Competence of Professionals

The provision of culturally competent services is highly dependent on the values, knowledge, and skills of each professional. What professionals know and can do makes the crucial difference in what individuals learn, and professional development begins with a quality preservice program. In the field of education, there is an urgent need for recruitment efforts targeted at attracting professionals from minority backgrounds into teaching (Edmunds, Martinson, & Goldberg, 1990; O'Shea & Lancaster, 2001). O'Shea and Lancaster suggest that "students with cultural and language diversity require teachers, role models, and personnel to address the changing demographics of their special education needs" (p. 57). It is also incumbent upon universities and colleges to recruit faculty from diverse backgrounds. If education is to move beyond a workforce of primarily white female teachers, universities must actively recruit faculty who are more representative of the diversity in schools. Approximately 16 percent of special education faculty members who took positions in higher education in recent years came from culturally diverse backgrounds, whereas 34 percent of the school population are ethnic minority children (Smith, Tyler, Sindelar & Rosenberg, 2001; U.S. Department of Education, 2000).

Correa et al. (1996) recommend every teacher education program in the country be required to include course work and field experiences that will prepare tomorrow's teachers to

**POINT OF INTEREST 5.5** • *Honoring the Linguistic and Behavioral Patterns of Culturally Diverse Families*

| Cultural Group | Verbal Linguistic and Behavioral Patterns | Nonverbal Behaviors |
|---|---|---|
| Hispanic American | (1) May be hesitant to participate in meeting <br> (2) Do not question authority figures <br> (3) Possible language barriers | (1) Physical contact during conversation is acceptable <br> (2) Required distance between people not maintained or expected |
| African American | (1) Direct in stating their opinions <br> (2) Active participation during discussions <br> (3) Feel restricted by turn taking <br> (4) Less likely to verbally reinforce or acknowledge what is said | (1) Much use of body language and gestures <br> (2) Eye contact avoided as sign of respect |
| Asian American | (1) Relatively passive during discussions to avoid attention to self <br> (2) Avoid confrontation in favor of harmony; do not actively assert rights <br> (3) Courteous and respectful to authority <br> (4) Voluntarily expressing opinions or discussing personal matters is avoided | (1) Eye contact avoided with elders and authority figures <br> (2) Comfortable with more distance during conversations <br> (3) Dislike pointing at someone and physical contact |
| Native American | (1) Taking turns and mutual respect emphasized during discussion <br> (2) Cooperation, rather than individualism is stressed <br> (3) Embarrassed by praise or compliments <br> (4) Dislike lots of questions | (1) Prefer a gentle handshake <br> (2) Silence during discussion is acceptable <br> (3) Prefer eye movements and gestures rather than verbal communications |

*Source:* Adapted from Fielder, C. R. (2000). *Making a difference: Advocacy competencies for special education professionals* (p. 146). Boston: Allyn & Bacon. Portions of the above are from Misra, A. (1994). Partnership with multicultural families. In S. K. Alper, P. J. Schloss, and C. N. Schloss (Eds.), *Families of students with disabilities: Consultation and advocacy.* Boston: Allyn & Bacon.

work with children from culturally diverse backgrounds. The authors indicate that culturally responsive education programs are characterized by teachers who have a positive vision of these students. Teachers view students from culturally diverse backgrounds as capable learners, and provide a content-rich curriculum that heightens each child's self-concept and pride in his or her culture. Interactive and experiential teaching techniques are used to promote feelings of responsibility, self-worth, and belonging in the diverse learner (Voltz & Damiano-Lantz, 1993). In addition, instructional materials and the school environment must reflect the backgrounds of culturally diverse students. Student learning is facilitated by the selection of programs, services, and materials that have relevance to each child.

---

*Focus 4*
What are some guidelines that will assist new teachers in developing culturally responsive teaching strategies?

---

Wlodkowski and Ginsberg (1995) developed a framework to assist new teachers in developing strategies that will facilitate culturally responsive teaching and ensure that the classroom is open to cultural diversity.

- *Establish inclusion.* Emphasize the human purpose of what is being learned and its relationship to each student's experiences. Encourage collaboration and cooperation while students assume a hopeful view of all people and their capacity to change.
- *Treat all students equitably.* Constantly review how you treat all students. Invite students to point out behaviors or practices that discriminate.
- *Develop positive attitudes.* Relate teaching and learning activities to each student's background experiences or prior knowledge. Encourage students to make choices in content and assessment methods based on experiences, values, needs and strengths.
- *Enhance meaning.* Provide challenging learning experiences involving higher-order thinking and critical inquiry. Encourage discussion of relevant experiences. Rather than avoiding students' family diversity, for example, incorporate family traditions into classroom dialogue.
- *Rely on competence.* Connect the assessment process to each student's world, frame of reference, and values. By doing so, you recognize home and community backgrounds. Include multiple ways to represent knowledge and skills and allow for attainment of outcomes at different points in time. Encourage self-assessment.

Point of Interest 5.6 provides additional tips to help new teachers value diversity in the classroom. The following section of the chapter provides an overview of some approaches for enhancing the cultural competence of communication and service provision for individuals with severe disabilities and their families.

## Approaches for Enhancing Cultural Competence

### Enhancing Cross-Cultural Communication

Cultures vary in the extent to which communication is explicitly transmitted through words versus the extent to which communication is based on the context of the situation, the relationship between the communicators, and physical cues such as body language and facial expressions (Hall, 1976, 1984; Lynch, 1998b). Anglo-European-American, Swiss, German, and Scandinavian cultures tend to be *low-context* cultural communicators who place emphasis on logical, direct, verbal communication and who want people to get to the point quickly (Hecht, Anderson, & Ribeau, 1989). Individuals from these cultures may be less skilled at reading the gestures, expressions, contextual cues, moods of others, and what has been left unsaid than high-context cultural communicators (Lynch, 1998b). *High-context* cultural communicators rely less on spoken words and more on an understanding achieved

**POINT OF INTEREST 5.6 • *Tips to Ensure New Teachers' Support in Valuing Diversity***

• Teachers can learn as much as they can about their students' diverse families by talking.

• Family structures, values, and child rearing practices vary greatly. Teachers can use cultural differences as strengths rather than work at cross-purposes.

• Instead of lumping groups together, effective teachers recognize that many differences exist within groups of Hispanics, Whites, African Americans, or Asian individuals. Lessons reflect this philosophy.

• Each country, each region, and most importantly, each individual has unique ways of interpreting individual cultural experiences. Teachers recognizing the uniqueness of interpretation experiences plan lessons accordingly.

• Effective teachers actively seek to weed out the stereotypes and prejudices that have been acquired through the teachers' own cultural roots. They try to approach people individually and openly in all home-school encounters.

• Teachers can discuss the negative effects of prejudice and discrimination during lessons.

• Planning ways to include families of linguistically/culturally diverse students in classroom activities can recognize students' use of their native language, while encouraging family members to participate in school activities.

• Teachers can plan how to involve minority parents formally and informally in their children's education by asking families how and when they want to be involved.

• Adjusting instructional approaches and activities to accommodate cultural backgrounds can help teachers adjust to cultural differences and bring schools and families together.

• Teachers can capitalize on celebrations and special traditions. They can familiarize themselves with different cultural, language-based, and religious practices, such as fasting or holiday celebrations, that might affect students' school attendance and participation. They can learn to correctly pronounce students' names in the proper order and how to address students' parents.

• Effective teachers realize the importance of never feeling that they have to apologize for their own culture or ethnicity. As human beings, they recognize that all people have something special to contribute.

• Teachers seek actively to learn about family differences and are sensitive to unique differences. They seek opportunities for students to share information about their home life during social studies, geography, and other classes.

*Source:* O'Shea, D. J., & Lancaster, P. L. (2001). Families of students from diverse backgrounds. In D. J. O'Shea, L. J. O'Shea, R. Algozzine, & D. J. Hammitte (Eds.), *Families and teachers of individuals with disabilities* (p. 66). Boston: Allyn & Bacon.

through joint history, shared experience, and the implicit, rather than the explicit, message (Hecht et al., 1989). "Asian, Native American, Arab, Latino, and African-American cultures are examples of high-context cultures in which meaning does not have to be communicated through words" (Lynch, 1998b, p. 68). Individuals from high-context cultures are more skilled at communicating through nonverbal cues and messages, much like some siblings, married couples, or long-term colleagues or friends are able to do. With few words or the exchange of a look within a certain context, they can still communicate much (Lynch, 1998b). Although we readily recognize that speaking different languages creates communication barriers, the extent to which communicators from high-context and low-context cultures may have difficulties communicating effectively, and without frustration or misunderstandings, can be easily underestimated.

> When families and interventionists differ in the level of context that they use in communication, there may be misunderstandings. On the one hand, lots of talking, clearly specified verbal directions, and detailed demonstrations may seem insensitive and mechanistic to individuals from high-context cultures. They may feel that the talking is proof that the other individual does not truly understand them and cannot, therefore, be of help. On the other hand, members of low-context cultures may be uncomfortable with long pauses and silences, cryptic sentences, and indirect modes of communication such as story-telling. They may feel that these are time wasters or are signs of resistance. These interactions are further complicated by the fact that under pressure or when confronted with a communication style that they do not understand, people rely on patterns of behavior that reflect their own zone of comfort. Thus, low-context communicators talk more, speak more rapidly, and often raise their voices; whereas high-context communicators say less, make less eye contact, and withdraw from interaction. (Lynch, 1998b, p. 69)

Take a moment to review Vignette 2 at the beginning of this chapter. How might the differences between low- and high-context communicators be contributing to the situation described in this vignette? What do you tend to do when you are feeling uncomfortable while communicating with others? Are there instances when you have been a part of, or have witnessed, an interaction between members of different cultures, where communication broke down more as attempts to communicate continued? Did high- or low-context cultural communication patterns play a role in these misunderstandings?

Earlier in this chapter, one of the definitions for cultural competence related to reestablishing communication when "cultural bumps" have gotten in the way. This will usually necessitate that interventionists adapt their style to one that is comfortable for the students and families with whom they work. "It may often mean that interventionists must slow down, listen more than they talk, observe family communication patterns, and consult with cultural guides or mediators to begin to pace their interactions to the family's communication style" (Lynch, 1998b, p. 69). Strategies for meeting families, building rapport, and using cultural or language interpreters or mediators are described below.

---

*Focus 5*
What are some helpful strategies in building rapport with families from CLD backgrounds?

## Strategies for Building Rapport and Communicating Effectively

Several characteristics seem to be shared by individuals who are effective cross-cultural communicators:

- Respects individuals from other cultures
- Makes continued and sincere attempts to understand the world from others' points of view
- Is open to new learning
- Is flexible
- Has a sense of humor
- Tolerates ambiguity well
- Approaches others with a desire to learn (Lynch, 1998b, p. 77)

Although these characteristics are very helpful, what actual strategies can be used to build rapport and communicate more effectively? One of the first steps is to recognize the importance of taking time to meet families respectfully and to establish rapport before beginning to discuss their child's disability and decisions related to their child's disability, assessment, or program development options. This may happen fairly quickly and easily with some families, and may be much more challenging or time consuming with others, especially if an interpreter is needed to deal with language differences. "Taking the time" may be difficult for interventionists who value efficient use of time, but it is useful to question how much is really accomplished if the student and/or the family are not really participating. Lynch & Hanson (1998c) suggest that professionals use some of the following strategies before and during the first meeting with families.

1. Learn about cultural beliefs and practices in the community in which you work.
2. Work with cultural mediators or guides who are knowledgeable about the cultures of the families with whom you work, and with individual and regional variations in cultural identification in your area.
3. In addition to having interpreters present, learn and use words and forms of greeting in the primary language of the family.
4. Use as few written forms as possible when meeting with non-English speaking, or limited-English speaking families, and make sure they are available in the families' primary or native language.

Joe and Malach (1998) provide some additional suggestions for working with families with Native American roots. These suggestions may also be very helpful in working with many families, regardless of cultural heritage.

- When first establishing contact with a family, the interventionist must proceed at a pace that is comfortable for the family. Take some time for "small talk." Ask how they are, comment on the weather, talk about the roads, share an appropriate personal experience (e.g., you were glad to have rain for your own garden), or find things you have in common. This provides an opportunity for the family to get to know you as a person, and it forms a foundation for developing rapport with the family. (Joe & Malach, 1998, p. 153)

- When you need to ask a lot of questions (e.g., when obtaining case history information), first explain to the family that you will be asking them questions, tell them about the types of questions, and inform them as to how the information will help you to serve their child. Tell the family that it is okay for them to ask you questions at any time if they do not understand a question or do not understand why you are asking it. Let them know that it is okay if they need to discuss a question with other family members before they answer it. Ask them to tell you if they want to think about a question or discuss it with other family members before they answer. (Joe & Malach, 1998, p. 154)

One of the advantages in working with cultural mediators or guides is to learn some of the cultural variations in the use of nonverbal language, and the protocol of first meetings or home visits common in different cultural contexts (Lynch, 1998b). For example, a "V" for victory or placing the thumb and forefinger together may be considered a sign of approval in some cultures, vulgar in others (Lynch, 1998b). Direct eye contact is a sign of respect in some cultures, and of disrespect in others (Chan, 1998b; Hanson, 1998b; Joe & Malach, 1998). The level of first-name informality may not be viewed as appropriately respectful for first meetings within some cultures, at least until family members have indicated they wish to be called by their first names (Willis, 1998). Who should be greeted or addressed first in a meeting or other group setting also has numerous cultural variations (Chan, 1998b; Lynch, 1998b; Willis, 1998).

Books and other written sources of information can be useful, as long as individual families are not assumed to "match up" with described common practices and courtesies. Lynch and Hanson (1998a) is a very useful resource, and includes a number of chapters written by individuals from various cultural heritages (e.g., Mokuau & Tauili'ili, 1998; Sharifzadeh, 1998). Resource information can also be accessed over the Internet. See Point of Interest 5.7 for some useful background and strategies for working with many Asian families that was obtained from a Website, including information that might be useful during first meetings with families. "If there is one recommendation that stands out above all others, it is the need to demonstrate respect, all other shortcomings, such as not knowing the culture or language of the family, become secondary" (Malach & Joe, 1998, p. 156).

---

*Focus 6*
What are some important considerations in working with interpreters and families?

---

## Cultural Mediators and Language Interpreters

Hiring bilingual and bicultural staff is often suggested as a way of assuring that families have access to qualified personnel who will understand their language and cultural background (Lynch & Hanson, 1998c). However, because of a shortage of bilingual and bicultural staff, many educational and social service programs rely on interpreters to communicate with families during meetings concerning special education and related services and transition planning for their children with disabilities (Ohtake, Santos, & Fowler,

**POINT OF INTEREST 5.7** • *How to Deliver Services to Asian Families Who Have Children with Disabilities*

Cultural sensitivity starts with understanding your own culture. Once you have developed this awareness, you will be better able to understand the culture of a variety of families living with disability.

Recognize that differences as well as similarities exist among Asian groups. Asians originate from the Far East, Southeast Asia, the Pacific Islands, and Indian subcontinent. This area includes China, India, Philippine Islands, Sri Lanka, Vietnam, Malaysia, Korea, Japan, and Samoa. People from these areas have many diverse religions, including Confucianism, Islam, Christianity, Taoism, Buddhism. Asians' language, reasons for immigration, and experiences in the community upon arrival differ greatly. Yet, shared values and behavior do exist and provide the cornerstone for effective service delivery practices.

*Roles*

Similar to many cultures, many Asians value and respect their elder family members. Elder family members hold a high role of authority within the family. When addressing families, talk to the oldest member first. Besides showing respect, you also may be talking with the family decision maker. If you do not convey respect to elders, your recommendations may be politely ignored by the family. Asians perceive professionals as experts who have solutions to problems. Many Asians typically defer to authority and tend to not challenge professional opinion or practices. They also may avoid asking the service provider questions, so as not to be disrespectful. This is true even when families don't fully understand what the service provider has said.

*Family Interdependence*

In many Asian cultures, family needs are seen as more important than the needs of any one individual family member. Asian parents may not agree with special education goals that focus on developing independence. Independent living for an adult child with disabilities, a common goal for U.S. parents, is not necessarily a goal of Asian families, who may prefer the adult child to live with family members. In Hawaiian culture, several generations often live in one household, where Kupuna (elders) typically care for grandchildren while parents work.

Many Asian families do not want their children encouraged to make decisions. Family and community come first over freedom of choice. Children are not prompted to make decisions for themselves. Older family members oversee decision-making authority.

*Courtesy*

A value on contained emotions makes many Asians consider it inappropriate to discuss family problems with service providers whom the family does not know well. Service providers may mistake this traditional modesty for low self-esteem. Another practice that may confuse service providers involves agreement. When Asians, particularly Indochinese Americans, say "yes," they may mean "Yes, I heard you," but not, "Yes, I agree." If they do agree, they will add, "Yes, I agree." Seeming to agree is an act of courtesy, but does not necessarily mean agreement. Direct eye contact, a practice associated with honesty and respect by mainstream America, is another courtesy issue service providers need to understand: Many Asian cultures view direct eye contact as a rude gesture. Also, service providers' appearance and clothing connote respect toward a family. If you dress casually to put a family at ease or for whatever reason, the family may see your appearance as showing lack of respect, even contempt.

*Disability*

Some Asian families view disability as retribution for previous sins of current and past family, or as a result for a mother's behavior during pregnancy. To them, the child's disability reflects punishment and causes parents shame and isolation. These beliefs can result in families resisting intervention efforts for their young children with disabilities. Then again, other Asian parents may refuse surgery for something like a child's clubfoot because

*(continued)*

**POINT OF INTEREST 5.7 • Continued**

of the traditional belief that a clubfoot signals a blessing for the community. Regarding behavior, many Asians typically believe a child's poor conduct reflects substandard parenting skills. Even if the child displays signs of attention deficit disorder or other disabling conditions that affect behavior, many Asian families will still regard the behavior as their "fault." Well-meaning inclusion efforts can backfire with Asian families. For instance, the Individuals With Disabilities Education Act (IDEA) encourages parent participation in special education, which reflects democratic philosophy and freedom of choice. Many traditional Asian parents perceive professionals rather than themselves as the experts on the child with a disability and therefore find it difficult to accept their role as "equal partners" in educational decision-making.

The information in this fact sheet is to provide guidelines only. As with any form of cultural sensitivity, the more you know about your own culture and the culture in which you are working, the better service you can provide to families from diverse cultures. Information for this fact sheet came from the following source(s):

Char, S. (1998a). Families with Asian roots. In E. W. Lynch & M. J. Hanson (Eds.), *Developing cross-cultural competence: A guide for working with children and their families* (2nd ed.) (pp. 251–354). Baltimore: Brookes.

Harry, B., & Kalyanpur. (1994). Cultural underpinning of special education: Implication for professional interactions with culturally diverse families. *Disability & Society, 9*(2), 14–165.

Mokuau, N., & Tauili'ili, P. (1998). Families with Native Hawaiian and Samoan roots. In E. W. Lynch & M. J. Hanson (Eds.), *Developing cross-cultural competence: A guide for working with children and their families* (2nd ed.) (pp. 40–440). Baltimore: Brookes.

Turnbull, A. P., & Turnbull, H. R. (2000). *Families, professionals and exceptionality: Collaborating for empowerment* (4th ed.). Upper Saddle River, NJ: Merrill/Prentice Hall.

Yee, B. W. K. (1990, Summer). Gender and family issues in minority groups. *Generations*, pp. 342.

2000). *Interpreters* is often used to refer to individuals who translate spoken language, between family and/or community members and program providers, such as school personnel. *Translators* are people who translate written communication or documents, also very useful, as in the case of transition plans, IEPs, or home–school communication. *Mediators* is a broader term, incorporating making two different cultures and/or languages comprehensible to each other, in addition to translating written or spoken language (Barrera, 2000). Mediators or interpreters have a very challenging task, and often have no formal training in special education or related fields, or in how to be an interpreter (Ohtake et al., 2000). For this reason, it is important that special educators and others who work with individuals with severe disabilities learn how to work with untrained interpreters both before, during, and after meetings between family members and service providers. Characteristics of effective interpreters include (1) proficiency in both languages and cultures; (2) an understanding of cross-cultural communication, the role of an interpreter, and the roles of family members and professionals within the professional field in which they are working; and (3) an ability to appreciate and tactfully and sensitively communicate subtle nuances of both cultures (Lynch, 1998b).

Interpreters who do not have these characteristics or abilities may scramble the communication either unintentionally or because they have their own agendas. Particular caution should be taken about using the student, a family member, or a community member known to the family as an interpreter (Lynch, 1998b). As examples of the problems this may create, a student's brother or sister may not wish to share behavioral difficulties that a student is having at school with their parents, a husband or wife may not wish to share a viewpoint they disagree with and would just as soon their partner not hear about, or parents may be embarrassed or reluctant to share private problems in front of a community member they know through a work or church affiliation or whom they do not trust to keep what is said confidential. Confidentiality for interpreters is absolutely key to maintaining trust in relationships with families and students. Some other suggestions for the use of interpreters include the following.

- Introduce yourself and the interpreter, describe your respective roles, and clarify mutual expectations, and the purpose of the encounter.
- During the interaction, address your remarks and questions directly to the family (not the interpreter); look at and listen to family members as they speak and observe their nonverbal communication....
- Use a positive tone of voice and facial expressions that sincerely convey respect and interest in the family. Address the family in a calm, unhurried manner.
- Speak clearly and somewhat more slowly but not more loudly....
- Avoid technical jargon, colloquialisms, idioms, slang, and abstractions.
- Avoid oversimplification and condensing important explanations.
- Give instructions in a clear, logical sequence; emphasize key words or points; and offer reasons for specific recommendations....
- Be patient and be prepared for the additional time that will inevitably be required for careful interpretation. (Lynch, 1998b, pp. 82–83)

Language interpreters are not always enough to assist families in receiving effective and culturally appropriate services for their children with disabilities. For example, Park & Turnbull (2001) conducted in-depth interviews with eight Korean parents of children with disabilities who were receiving special education services in the United States. The majority of parents had sought assistance from Korean American cultural mediators who were proficient in English and Korean, and who were also mothers of children with disabilities. They had met these mediators through sources such as friends or church connections. Because they were both Korean and mothers of children with disabilities, the Korean immigrant parents reported they did not feel a "loss of face" in asking for help in navigating the special education system and understanding their rights (Park & Turnbull, 2001). The satisfaction that parents in this study reported about their interactions with the mediators did not extend to language interpreters. Even though they knew they had a right to have an interpreter present, only one parent made use of an interpreter, and only once, due to dissatisfaction with the process. The parents in this study indicated that they needed more help than direct translation alone provided. Having more appropriately trained interpreters available for families would also be of assistance for both families and school personnel.

Obviously, many families from CLD backgrounds speak only English, or speak English fluently and do not need or want the services of interpreters. Families and family members within various cultures will also have many different communication preferences and styles. Two key points to remember are:

> In communicating with families from culturally/linguistically diverse backgrounds, remember that one approach does not fit all. (Parette & Petch-Hogan, 2000, p. 8)

> Professionals who emphasize information sharing in contrast to information giving and collection help to reduce the impact of parental anxieties associated with parent-professional interactions. (Sileo et al., 1996, p. 151)

## Selected Approaches for Planning and Implementing Culturally Competent Services

Sensitive and effective cross-cultural communication is important across the life span of the individual with severe disabilities, and across the various stages of intervention. Examples from different ages will be used to illustrate approaches that incorporate cross-cultural communication in intervention planning and implementation.

As described in later chapters in this book, a variety of informal assessment procedures are usually used to guide IFSP/IEP goal selection for individuals with severe disabilities. These approaches may include environmental analysis, observations in home, school, and community activities and routines, and teacher and family interviews. Information from informal assessments are used to select goals and instructional strategies. Because informal assessment strategies are so individualized and contextually based, they are not only more appropriate for planning instruction for individuals with severe disabilities, but also have the potential to be more culturally appropriate than most assessment strategies.

One of the most comprehensive and well-validated examples of a commercially available informal assessment and educational program planning approach designed for individuals with moderate and severe disabilities is COACH, *Choosing Outcomes and Accommodations for Children: A Guide to Educational Planning for Students with Disabilities,* 2nd ed. (Giangreco, Cloniger, & Iverson, 1998). The newest edition of COACH has been revised based on research studies, ongoing field tests in schools, and a cross-cultural review of COACH (Dennis & Ginagreco, 1996). There are three major components to COACH, beginning with a family prioritization interview, which is used to identify family-selected learning outcomes for the student. Other components include defining the educational program components, which includes translating family-selected priorities into IEP goals and objectives, and addressing implementation of the program in general education and other integrated settings, including evaluating the impact of the educational experiences (Dennis & Giangreco, 1996).

Steps within the COACH family interview process include introducing the process, asking parents to prioritize valued life outcomes for their child, selecting curriculum areas to explore during the family interview (communication, socialization, personal management, leisure/recreation, selected academics, home, school, community, vocational, and other), indicating how skillful family members believe the student is on a variety of learning outcomes and their perception of whether this is an area where a student "needs work," and rank ordering up to five priorities (see Figure 5.1 for an example of a completed page from the COACH parent

# Socialization

**Step 1.2**

Mark only one box to indicate if the family wants to discuss this set of learning outcomes in:
Step 1 (Family Interview; priority this year?) ☒; Step 2 (Additional Learning Outcomes) ☐; Skip for Now ☐

| # | Learning Outcomes | Step 1.3 Circle Score | Needs Work? | Step 1.4 Rank up to 5 Priorities |
|---|---|---|---|---|
| 13 | Responds to the Presence and Interactions of Others (e.g., peers, family, adults) | E  P  (S) | (N)  Y | |
| 14 | Initiates Social Interactions | E  (P)  S | N  (Y) | 5 |
| 15 | Sustains Social Interactions | E  (P)  S | N  (Y) | 2 |
| 16 | Terminates Social Interactions | E  (P)  S | N  (Y) | |
| 17 | Distinguishes and Interacts Differently with Familiar People, Acquaintances, and Strangers | (E)  P  S | (N)  Y | |
| 18 | Maintains Socially Acceptable Behavior When Alone and with Others | E  P  (S) | N  (Y) | 3 |
| 19 | Accepts Assistance from Others | E  P  (S) | (N)  Y | |
| 20 | Offers Assistance to Others | E  (P)  S | N  (Y) | 4 |
| 21 | Makes Transitions Between Routine Activities | E  P  (S) | (N)  Y | |
| 22 | Adjusts to Unexpected Changes in Routine | E  (P)  S | N  (Y) | |
| 23 | Shares with Others | E  (P)  S | N  (Y) | 1 |
| 24 | Advocates for Self | (E)  P  S | (N)  Y | |
| | | E  P  S | N  Y | |
| | | E  P  S | N  Y | |
| | | E  P  S | N  Y | |
| | | E  P  S | N  Y | |

*Comments:* Understands concept of sharing but sometimes gets into disagreements with others. Happens when child approaches and asks to share but Keisha does not get the message. When child stops asking & tries to take toy, K's response may be aggressive. Kids need to know how to be sure she gets the message.
   K needs to use signs to get others to interact, not just use gestures or objects.

Scoring Key (use scores for Step 1.3 alone or in combination):
   **E** = Early/Emerging Skill (1% – 25%)   **P** = Partial Skill (25% – 80%)   **S** = Skillful (80% – 100%)

---

**FIGURE 5.1  *Socialization Curriculum Area Example from COACH***

*Source:* Giangreco, M. F., Cloninger, C. J., & Iverson, V. S. (1998) *Choosing outcomes and accommodations for children (COACH): A guide to educational planning for students with disabilities (2nd edition).* Baltimore: Paul H. Brookes Publishing.

interview). As you look at the learning outcomes on the socialization curriculum sheet in Figure 5.1, how many of these outcomes do you think are influenced by cultural variables? Think of examples for some of the listed outcomes, and of how they might influence intervention planning. What kinds of information would you want families to share with you to help plan culturally competent interventions in these areas?

Participants in a cross-cultural analysis of COACH made suggestions for conducting the family interview in more culturally sensitive ways (see Point of Interest 5.8). Many of these suggestions are strategies for effective cross-cultural communication.

There are five valued life outcomes in COACH: (1) being *safe* and *healthy*; (2) having a *home,* now and in the future; (3) having meaningful *relationships*; (4) having *choice* and control that match one's age and culture; and (5) participating in meaningful *activities* in various places. The outcomes and questions related to them are purposefully broad, "so families can attach their own meanings to questions" (Giangreco et al., 1998, p. 59). One of the interesting features of COACH is that it begins with very broad values-based outcomes, which students and their families can tailor to many different individual and cultural contexts, and results in very specific plans to guide instruction and the selection of accommodations and supports. COACH can be useful from the preschool years through transition planning to adult services.

Another approach for increasing culturally competent services is based on the self-determination principle, which is highly valued within the field of severe disabilities and within mainstream U.S. culture. Let us briefly examine one definition of self-determination, some cultural and family implications, and how one of the initiatives that grew out of the self-determination and family empowerment perspectives could potentially utilize this initiative to support more culturally competent adult services.

Various approaches and definitions of self-determination exist in the professional literature (Turnbull & Turnbull, 2001; Wehmeyer, Agran, & Hughes, 1998; Wehmeyer & Sands, 1998). "We define *self-determination* as living one's life consistent with one's own values, preferences, strengths, and needs" (Turnbull & Turnbull, 2001, p. 165). While recommending that working toward self-determination begin in early childhood, the adolescent, transition, and adult years are when self-determination is most strongly emphasized, including adolescent participation in decision making about school programs, vocational preparation, and social and leisure activities (Turnbull & Turnbull, 2001).

> What are the cultural implications of self-determination? Some analysts argue that self-determination is a "Western," product-oriented concept that needs modification to better suit families from diverse cultural backgrounds. For instance, Latin American parents often desire their adult children with disabilities to live with them or other family members in adulthood. This is not "wrong"; it is a family characteristic. Service providers can tap into their own flexibility, creativity, and willingness to help families balance between the family's culture and the general culture. One good way to do this is to honor and examine how the family has achieved positive changes in the past. (Beach Center on Families and Disabilities, 1998, p. 2)

How can self-determination potentially contribute to more culturally competent services? One possibility relates to an important program that has grown out of the self-determination movement, the Robert Woods Johnson Foundation funding of initiatives to change state policy regarding the distributions of federal and state Medicaid benefits. This

**POINT OF INTEREST 5.8 • *Participant Suggestions for Conducting Family Interviews in More Culturally Sensitive Ways***

Seek help from "cultural interpreters" before the interview.

- Have someone from the community determine whether the interview protocol "fits" in the community.
- Become aware of the social interaction norms of the community, so that initial impressions will be appropriate.
- Have a community liaison worker who knows the specific cultural patterns of families within that neighborhood make initial contacts and present realistic choices to parents.

Carefully ascertain literacy and language status of family members.

- Adjust the interview style for nonreaders and speakers of other languages.
- Consider that family members may not be literate in their native language or English.
- Advise families who speak another language in the home that they are entitled to the services of an interpreter, rather than just asking if they wish one, since they may decline, thinking that it is too much to ask.
- Be knowledgeable of skills needed by educators to work successfully with interpreters.
- Do not use siblings or other students as interpreters.
- Familiarize the interpreter ahead of time with any documents that must be presented at the conference.
- Team members should address both the parent and the interpreter as they speak, rather than facing only the interpreter.

Involve family members in planning interviews.

- Let families know that their input is important by including them in scheduling a date, time, and location of the interview and determining who should attend.
- Consider meeting with parents at their places of employment during lunch or right after work, at a community center, at another agency location, or in the family home at flexible times so that the parent feels comfortable.

- Be aware that some families may be very uncomfortable with school personnel visiting their homes for various reasons (e.g., their undocumented status, embarrassment about the condition of their homes, previous bad experiences with school personnel).
- Consider whether parents might feel intimidated by too many professionals, and adjust the number as appropriate.
- Allow for inclusion of "significant others" (e.g., extended family).
- Be sensitive to problems that may arise when both parents cannot be present.
- Consider meeting with several families at one time. Family members may feel more comfortable sharing information within a close network of family members and neighbors.
- Plan to involve a team member who knows the family or can establish rapport. If the interviewer is from the same culture, he or she can better individualize the information in terms of use of native language and vocabulary.

Preview the interview with family members.

- Let family members know that they will be respected and that if something annoys them, they can say that.
- Be sensitive to what parents would like you to do. Would they be more comfortable with a social visit, or would they like you to be more businesslike?
- Put yourself in the learner role.... Acknowledge your own ignorance, and ask for ideas or questions the family may have to improve the interview.
- Follow the parents' lead right from the start, and allow them to establish the parameters of the interview.

Be flexible and responsive to the family's interaction style.

- Assess the situation; expect that every situation is going to be different.
- Allow the family to tell stories about the child. Parents need time to think when answering the

*(continued)*

**POINT OF INTEREST 5.8 • Continued**

broad, sweeping questions.... Their answers may not be specific or clear.

• Telling stories is one way they can clarify their thoughts on their priorities for their child. Stories can establish a common understanding of the background, family history, and relationships in order to build trust.

Adapt the time frame to meet the needs of the family.

• Be prepared to spend time with the family before and after the family interview.
• Be sensitive to the need for some families to confer with other family members and think through important educational decisions over time.
• Be aware that in some families it is important to "break bread" with one another and first "connect." It may take months before a family is comfortable with school personnel and willing to divulge the level of information that is requested by the system.

Carefully examine the nature of the questions you ask.

• Confidentiality needs to be highlighted and emphasized as much as possible. Discretion is critical; loss of confidentiality can lead to a failure to work with the team and ultimately, to the child's losing out.

• There are things you ask and things you don't ask.... A family member may be offended if someone were to ask questions without his or her understanding why they wanted to know. It might be a very spiritual or personal subject and may be perceived as having nothing to do with how their child is going to do in school.
• Issues of shame and guilt could arise if the parents feel blamed or if the child's problems are possibly related to parental substance abuse or other behaviors.
• Because some parents who may receive public assistance feel that their lives are constantly being invaded, informing them of the fact that they do not have to answer questions that are too sensitive is critical.
• Ask family members for feedback regarding questions that are not appropriate for future use with other families.
• Continually focus the conversation on what will benefit the child, because across all culture groups, what is most important is the welfare of their children.

*Source:* Dennis, R. E., & Giangreco, M. F. (1996). Creating conversation: Reflections on cultural sensitivity in family interviewing. *Exceptional Children, 63,* 103–116.

policy change allows benefits to go directly to individuals with developmental disabilities and their families, rather than to a service program (Turnbull & Turnbull, 2001). This national movement is currently being implemented in more than half the states in the United States.

Planning principles for this approach include (Nerney, 1998):

• Paying for individual support and companionship to enhance community relationships rather than providing 24-hour supervision
• Paying for food, transportation, and clothing consistent with valued preferences and lifestyle options
• Paying for job coaches to enable individuals to have real jobs that produce significant income (West, Revell, Kregel, & Bricuot, 1999)

- Paying for one-time investments such as a down payment for a home, business-related equipment, and assistive technology
- Having control of the budget so that individuals and their families and friends can participate in hiring and firing support people rather than only having access to agency staff (Nerney, 1998) (Turnbull & Turnbull, 2001, p. 220)

Kalyanpur and Harry (1999) cite a case reported by Shafer and Rangasamy (1995) about the difficulties that can arise if cultural context is not fully considered during high school and transition planning. The example involved White Mountain Apache youth who had been taught to work at fast-food restaurants. The problem was that the nearest fast-food restaurant was 45 miles away! They indicated that it would have been more appropriate as a part of transition planning for these youth to include some skills and activities that were functional and valued within their tribal village or community, facilitating their "partial participation in the spiritual activities of the community, traditional crafts, or engagement in chores around the family compound (wood gathering; chopping, bread making, herding, etc.)" (Shafer & Rangasamy, 1995, p. 65). Sileo et al. (1996) similarly reported that a school-to-community transition program for Alaska Native youth with disabilities consulted with tribal elders about what skills would be important for valued adult roles in the students' villages. Skills such as dog mushing, trapping, mending nets, and beadwork and roles such as berry picking, ice fishing, and basket making were identified as being important because of their connection to both survival and continuation of native culture.

Briefly review the planning principles for the Robert Wood Johnson Foundation initiatives listed above. In what ways could this initiative support the development of culturally competent high school, transition, and adult services for youth and adults who wish to maintain a traditional lifestyle on the White Apache reservation or in a Native village in Western Alaska? What considerations would you need to make to assure that services met the *individual* student's and family's cultural values and not just the traditional values of the cultural *group* to which they belong?

## Future Directions

A significant amount of the growing diversity in the United States is related to immigration patterns, including many of the challenges in trying to communicate with students and parents who speak a different primary language than many service providers. During the next decade it will be important to become more aware and involved in the global provision of services for individuals with severe disabilities. In many instances, other countries have developed policies and programs that can assist us in providing more effective and appropriate services for some of the CLD students and their families with whom we work (Jeisien, 1996). In other instances, we will have the opportunity to share with families and professionals in other countries where the types of opportunities and supports readily available for individuals with severe disabilities in the United States either are not available at all, or are only beginning to be developed (see Window 5.3). Expanding technology, including the development and use of the Internet, can aid these efforts. A Website that provides "a global community of disability-related resources" can be found at http://www.familyvillage.wisc.edu/.

## WINDOW 5.3 • *Thoughts on a Recent Visit to Russia*

I recently had the opportunity of visiting Russia for the purpose of meeting with families of children with Down Syndrome who had made the decision to keep their child at home and raise the child in the community. Most children in Russia who have special needs are institutionalized. Families, for the most part, do not have the financial resources, medical or community support, or educational opportunities for typical children, let alone those who have disabilities or developmental delays. The abortion rate in Russia today is over 80%. Most families have only one child. More than one child is extremely rare because of the costs of raising children and the poverty of the country in general. Many of the mothers we met with said they would like to have more children.

Families treasure their children. I thought it was charming to see mother and child walking hand in hand. The families of children with Down Syndrome we met love their child also. If the mother decides to keep the child with a disability with her, the father often leaves. There is a great social stigma to raising a child with a disability and the economic, medical and educational issues are almost overwhelming. A pediatrician makes less than $80 a month, with most families (mom and dad both working) earning less than that. To compound the financial issues, many people do not receive wages in a timely way.

Medical services for children and the quality of care are very poor. Russian doctors lack technology and information and the availability of medical services to typical Russian families is scarce. We met wonderful, caring professionals who want to help families and are frustrated by the situation there. Doctors from other countries have been offering technical assistance, supplies, and equipment in order to update medical services, and there are pediatric cardiac services in Moscow, but it is beyond the means of almost all of the families outside of Moscow to receive any prenatal care or follow up pediatric care.

We met a pediatrician in a large city many miles from Moscow. She asked me to send her information on premature and low birth weight babies. She told us that in her city no child under the age of 5 would ever be operated on, and under no condition would a child with Down Syndrome or other disabilities ever be considered for surgery. There are wealthy families whose children have had surgeries, but they were taken to London for the operations. One mother asked if we thought her 4 month old daughter would die. She said she could get some medicine through the black market, but she thought the medicine was making her child unable to eat, and she could not get the medical attention her child needed.

If a mom keeps her child with Down Syndrome, she must have someone (usually the child's grandmother) who can help with care giving. People can retire when they are 50 but their pension is only about $12.00 per month. The child who is kept home is not allowed in school. We know of some mothers who have a vision for their child and will teach them skills, but for many families the care means keeping the child inside all day without any education or training. Many times there are no other options except to institutionalize the child.

Most Russian citizens have learned to look to the government for the solution of all their life situations. Today the government is unable to meet even the most basic needs of a Russian family. People have not typically looked to their community for strengths, answers to problems, or to see within their communities the ability and opportunities to meet each other's needs. Because gathering together to address community issues was not allowed, and was severely punished in the past, it is still hard for families to see the value of such an activity. We talked to the families about coming together, seeing each other's strengths, how to team, and how to focus on the children. We also talked about mutual empowerment, and families working with professionals for the benefit of children and looking to their communities for ways to improve the quality of life for their children. Parents cannot imagine that anyone would ever hire their child, so we talked about opportunities to volunteer and the kind of skills one would need to be in public places. The families in Russia face so many obstacles.

We have heard from some families that they are feeling more empowered by coming together, by asking for more services, and not being as afraid to take their children in public. During our visit, one mother asked me what I did when I took Reed outside and people threw rocks at him, called him a fool, and struck me. I cried with her. This question revealed so much about what the parents are facing and how courageous the parents are who have kept their children against all the odds and hardships which exist. We met one mom whose son with Down Syndrome is 13 years old (very rare because most babies die very early). He is reading, very verbal (in Russian of course) and has a lot of social skills. Zinaida, his mother, is amazing. We left many materials with her and asked her to be the leader of a fledgling parent support group. We also met a wonderful father in Moscow who came to every session. He told us that he called his daughter with DS his princess, and that he was committed to her. It probably took all his wages to buy the outfit he had her in, but he wanted us to notice it.

I called the program director in Moscow to see if things have gotten any better in the year since we were there. She said that they were now working with about 200 families out of hundreds more who need help. Just the logistics of getting around in Moscow are hard. Home visiting is almost impossible. My friend said to get anywhere is Moscow, first you take the metro and then you walk 5 miles. The parents in Moscow have a site, equipment, and a dedicated staff. Their program is called "Downside Up." In other places we visited the parents have almost nothing to sustain them but their love for their child. Each place we went we were so impressed with the courage of the families we met. The Moscow program also has access to the Net, and technology from other countries. The director and many staff members are from different countries, and they have status there because of all the international interest in Downside Up.

The parents in Russia had a hard time believing the videos we had taken of our children with Down Syndrome, and when I talked about my son's friends and what he was doing in the community they were really amazed. They also had a hard time relating to his love of life. One mother asked me if her child was a blessing or a curse. I told her that her child was a blessing and an opportunity. I think just as parents have been the reason for change here, they will be in Russia also. And along the way, those professionals who make such a difference will be there, too.

*Source:* Contributed by Karen Hahne of Orem, Utah. Karen is the director of Kids On The Move, which provides Early Intervention and Early Head Start Programs, and is the mother of six children, including Reed Hahne, who has Down syndrome. Karen visited Russia to assist families with children with Down syndrome in the Summer of 2000 and the Spring of 2002.

It is imperative that teacher preparation, research, curriculum, and program development efforts concerning severe disabilities become more attuned to meeting the needs of students and families who are CLD. For example, there is very limited research or professional literature on how the communicative competence of individuals with severe or severe multiple disabilities can best be facilitated when English is not the primary language spoken in the student's home. This leaves many educators, staff development personnel, teachers, families, and other team members taking best guesses in an area (communication) that can have a profound impact on the social, educational, and vocational opportunities available to an individual throughout his or her lifetime. All of the questions and controversies associated with second language learners are compounded with someone who has significant cognitive impairments and may have physical, vision, or hearing impairments as well. Although many teachers and other professionals take for granted the contributions of technology, there is some evidence that some culturally and linguistically diverse families do not want some types of augmentative and assistive communication devices used with their children, finding them more conspicuous and stigmatizing than their child's own efforts to communicate (Harry et al., 1995). It clearly becomes even more complex and challenging for families and teams to make good decisions about communication choices when two or more languages, as well as modes of communication, are involved. Although family values and beliefs may drive the final decision, the fact that we have almost nothing beyond educated guesses to share with families as they try to make the best decisions for their children needs to be changed. A similar lack or sparsity of information about the effectiveness of educational and support strategies exists for many of the important decisions CLD students with severe disabilities, teams, and families need to make on a frequent basis about designing and providing individualized services and supports.

Part of the future direction also depends on all of us being willing to listen and to learn.

> On a deeper level the process of coming to know another culture allows us to gradually become ourselves again. Many of us, not knowing which of our behaviors may be culturally acceptable (or neutral) and which may not, err on the side of caution and move through intercultural situations in a state of semiparalysis, earnestly practicing the greatest possible self-restraint; we do and, are, quite literally, not ourselves. (Storti, 1989, p. 93)

The vast majority of special educators and other individuals who interact with people with severe disabilities and their families grew up as a part of a much less diverse "mainstream" American culture. As university professors doing research and preparing the next generation of teachers and as special educators or other professionals interacting with children and families, we often, and rightfully, have limited confidence in our knowledge and experience base about diversity. We are not sure we are even close to being "culturally competent" and often find it easier to (1) structure the IEP meeting as usual, and just have a district interpreter talk directly to the family, (2) have similar (our) goals for all of our students, or (3) tell our teacher education students to go take a class in that department— they are the experts on culture and diversity in education—and then teach our classes as if understanding "mainstream" values is all our students need to understand as they learn the methods for working with children, families, and community members. Once we begin thinking about culture and the implications for our professional work it becomes clear that this will not meet the needs of either future teachers or the children and families we are committed to serving. A severe disability does not make culturally competent services and interactions any less important. If we are committed to "people first" language, because we believe that the disability does not define the person, or is not the most important thing about the person, then we need to look at people with severe disabilities and their families as they really are. Culture is complex, but it is also pervasive, and to ignore it, to be "color blind," is a serious disservice. We cannot establish true partnerships with students, families, or other educators when we are "not ourselves." The only answer is to take the risks involved in becoming more culturally competent, knowing that we will make mistakes along the way. If enough of us are willing to take the time to learn from each other, and to take the risks, it will make a difference in the lives of the individuals with severe disabilities we work with and their families.

## *Focus Review*

Focus 1: Describe the overrepresentation and underidentification of children from diverse backgrounds in special education, and why there are concerns about it.

- *Overrepresentation* refers to the fact that more minority children are served in special education than would be expected from the percentage of minority children in the general school population.
- *Underidentification* refers to the fact that lower than expected numbers of children from some ethnic backgrounds, e.g., Asian, are receiving special education and related services, based on their representation in the general school population.
- Concerns about overrepresentation include limited access to the general education curriculum, placement in separate programs that may limit postsecondary education and employment opportunities, and the stigma and negative impact on self-perception and the perceptions of others that may occur from misclassification.
- Concerns about underidentification include limited access to services or supports that are needed to learn effectively or to function well within society.

Focus 2: What are some of the factors that may limit the participation of family from culturally and linguistically diverse backgrounds in the planning and implementation of their child's special education program?

- Some cultural traditions believe such decision making should be deferred to authorities or experts.
- Prior negative experiences in schools may limit family members' trust or willingness to participate in educational decision making.
- Late notices, inflexible scheduling, and limited time for conferences or meetings may make participation difficult or unrewarding.
- An emphasis on documents rather than participation may limit participation.
- A structure of power within meetings may give power and authority to professionals, even though this is not the intent of federal law or recommended practices.
- Logistical barriers such as conflicting work schedules, transportation or childcare problems, or cost, may limit paricipation.

Focus 3: What are some important features or strategies that can assist education and other human services programs in honoring cultural-linguistic differences?

- Recognize the pervasive influence of culture and cultural differences.
- Increase access between families and services.
- Recognize the importance of establishing rapport.
- Support families' efforts to deal with diverse culture(s) and language(s).
- Develop *reciprocal* "additive responses" to families and children.

Focus 4: What are some guidelines that will assist new teachers in developing culturally responsive teaching strategies?

- Establish inclusion and a hopeful view of all people and their capacity to change.
- Treat all students equitably, including reviewing your behavior and inviting student feedback about behaviors or practices that discriminate.
- Develop positive attitudes by relating teaching and learning experiences to each student's background experiences or prior knowledge and encouraging student to make educational choices.
- Enhance meaning through the provision of challenging and relevant learning experiences.
- Rely on the competence that students bring to the learning experience and connect the assessment process to each student's world, frame of reference, and values.

Focus 5: What are some helpful strategies in building rapport with families from CLD backgrounds?

- Take time to meet families and establish rapport before beginning to discuss their child's disability and decisions related to the disability. Proceed at a pace that is comfortable for the family.
- Learn about cultural beliefs and practices in the community where you work.
- Work effectively with cultural mediators or guides and interpreters.
- Use as few written forms as possible when meeting with non-English speaking or limited-English speaking families, and make sure forms are available in the families' primary or native language.
- Learn cultural variations in the use of nonverbal language, greetings, and first meetings.

Focus 6: What are some important considerations in working with interpreters and families?

- Introduce yourself and the interpreter and your respective roles.
- Address your remarks and questions directly to the family, not the interpreter.
- Look and listen to family members as they speak and observe their nonverbal communication.
- Speak clearly and somewhat more slowly but not more loudly.
- Be patient and be prepared for the additional time that will be required for careful interpretation.

## References

Althen, G. (1988). *American ways: A guide for foreigners in the United States.* Yarmouth, ME: Intercultural Press.

Avoke, S. K., & Wood-Garnett, S. (2001). *Language minority children and youth in special education.* Available: www.ideapractices.org.

Baca, L. M., & Cervantes, H. T. (1998). *The bilingual special education interface* (3rd ed.). Columbus, OH: Merrill.

Baker, C., & Jones, S. P. (1998). *Encyclopedia of bilingualism and bilingual education.* Philadelphia: Multilingual Matters.

Barrera, I. (1996). Assessment of infants and toddlers from diverse sociocultural backgrounds. In S. Meisels and E. Fenichel (Eds.), *New visions for developmental assessment* (pp. 69–84). Washington, DC: Zero to Three/National Center for Clinical Infant Programs.

Barrera, I. (2000). Honoring differences: Essential features of appropriate ECSE services for young children from diverse sociocultural environments. *Young Exceptional Children, 3*(4), 17–24.

Barrera, I., & Kramer, L. (1997). From monologues to skilled dialogues: Teaching the process of crafting culturally competent early childhood environments. In P. J. Winton, J. A. McCollum, & C. Catlett (Eds.), *Reforming personnel preparation in early intervention: Issues, models, and practical strategies* (pp. 217–251). Baltimore: Paul H. Brookes.

Beach Center on Families and Disabilities (1998). *How to develop self-determination.* Lawrence, KS: Beach Center on Families and Disabilities, University of Kansas. Available: http://www.beachcenter.org.

Byrd, H. B. (1999). Focus on critical issues in the education of Asian and Pacific Islander exceptional learners. *Multiple Voices, 3,* 48–53.

Chan, S. (1998a). Families with Asian roots. In E. W. Lynch & M. J. Hanson (Eds.), *Developing cross-cultural competence: A guide for working with children and their families* (2nd ed.) (pp. 251–354). Baltimore: Paul H. Brookes.

Chan, S. (1998b). Families with Pilipino roots. In E. W. Lynch & M. M. Hanson (Eds.), *Developing cross-cultural competence: A guide for working with children and their families* (2nd ed.) (pp. 355–408). Baltimore: Paul H. Brookes.

Cho, S., Singer, G. H., & Brenner, M. (2000). Adaptation and accommodation to young children with disabilities: A comparison of Korean and Korean-American parents. *Topics in Early Childhood Special Education, 20,* 236–249.

Clay, J. A. (1992). Native American independent living. *Rural Special Education Quarterly, 11,* 41–50.

Correa, V., Blanes-Reyes, M. E., & Rapport, M. J. (1996). Minority issues. In *Improving the implementation of the Individuals with Disabilities Education Act: Making schools work for all America's children* (Supplement) (pp. 535–556). Washington, DC: National Council on Disability.

Craig, S., Hull, K., Haggart, A. G., & Perez-Selles, M. (2000). Promoting cultural competence through teacher assistance teams. *Teaching Exceptional Children, 32*(3), 6–13.

Dennis, R. E., & Giangreco, M. F. (1996). Creating conversation: Reflections on cultural sensitivity in family interviewing. *Exceptional Children, 63,* 103–116.

Edmunds, P., Martinson, S. A., & Goldberg, P. F. (1990). *Demographics and cultural diversity in the 1990s: Implications for services to young children with special needs.* Minneapolis, MN: PACER Center. (ERIC Document Reproduction Service No. ED 325565.)

Federal Interagency Forum on Child and Family Statistics (2001). *America's children: Key national indicators of well-being, 2001.* Federal Interagency Forum on Child and Family Statistics. Washington, DC: U.S. Government Printing Office.

Fielder, C. R. (2000). *Making a difference: Advocacy competencies for special education professionals.* Boston: Allyn & Bacon.

Giangreco, M. G., Cloninger, C. J., & Iverson, V. S. (1998). *Choosing outcomes and accommodations for children: A guide to educational planning for students with disabilities* (2nd ed.). Baltimore: Paul H. Brookes.

Greene, G. (1996). Empowering culturally and linguistically diverse families in the transition planning process. *Journal for Vocational Special Needs Education, 19,* 26–30.

Grossman, H. (1998). *Ending discrimination in special education.* Springfield, IL: Charles Thomas.

Hall, E. T. (1976). *Beyond culture.* Garden City, NY: Anchor Books.

Hall, E. T. (1984). *The dance of life: The other dimension of time.* Garden City, NY: Anchor Books.

Hanson, M. J. (1998a). Ethnic, cultural, and language diversity in intervention settings. In E. W. Lynch & M. J. Hanson (Eds.), *Developing cross-cultural competence: A guide for working with children and their families* (2nd ed.) (pp. 3–22). Baltimore: Paul H. Brookes.

Hanson, M. J. (1998b). Families with Anglo-European roots. In E. W. Lynch & M. J. Hanson (Eds.), *Developing cross-cultural competence: A guide for working with children and their families* (2nd ed.) (pp. 93–126). Baltimore: Paul H. Brookes.

Hanson, M. J., Lynch, E. W., & Wayman, K. L. (1990). Honoring the cultural diversity of families when gathering data. *Topics in Early Childhood Special Education, 10,* 112–131.

Harry, B. (1996). Developing cultural self-awareness: The first step in values clarification for early interventionists. *Topics in Early Childhood Special Education, 12,* 333–350.

Harry, B. (1997). Leaning forward or bending over backwards: Cultural reciprocity in working with families. *Journal of Early Intervention, 21,* 62–72.

Harry, B., Allen, N., & McLaughlin, M. (1995). Communication versus compliance: African-American parents' involvement in special education. *Exceptional Children, 61,* 364–377.

Harry, B., Grenot-Scheyer, M., Smith-Lewis, M., Park, H., Xin, F., & Schwartz, I. (1995). Developing culturally inclusive services for individuals with severe disabilities. *Journal of the Association for Persons with Severe Handicaps, 20,* 9–19.

Harry, B., Rueda, R., & Kalyanpur, M. (1999). Cultural reciprocity in sociocultural perspective: Adapting the normalization principle for family collaboration. *Exceptional Children, 66,* 123–136.

Harry, B., Torguson, C., Katkavich, J., & Guerrero, M. (1993). Crossing social class and cultural barriers in working with families: Implications for teacher training. *Teaching Exceptional Children,* 48–51.

Hecht, M. L., Andersen, P. A., & Ribeau, S. A. (1989). The cultural dimensions of nonverbal communication. In M. K. Asanate & W. B. Gudykunst (Eds.), *Handbook of international and intercultural communication* (pp. 163–185). Beverly Hills, CA: Sage.

Hough, R. A., & Nurss, J. R. (1992). Language and literacy for the limited English proficient (LEP) child. In L. O. Ollila & M. I. Mayfield (Eds.), *Emerging literacy: Preschool, kindergarten, and primary grades* (pp. 253–279). Boston: Allyn & Bacon.

Jesien, G. S. (1996). Future challenges in early intervention. In P. Rosin, G. S. Jesien, A. D. Whitehead, A. L. Begun, L. I. Tuchman, & L. Irwin (Eds.), *Partnerships in family-centered care: A guide to collaborative early intervention* (pp. 249–266). Baltimore: Paul H. Brookes.

Joe, J. R., & Malach, R. S. (1998). Families with Native American roots. In E. W. Lynch & M. J. Hanson (Eds.), *Developing cross-cultural competence: A guide for working with children and their families* (2nd ed.) (pp. 127–164). Baltimore: Paul H. Brookes.

Kalyanpur, M., & Harry, B. (1999). *Culture in special education: Building reciprocal family-professional relationships.* Baltimore: Paul H. Brookes.

Lynch, E. W. (1998a). Conceptual framework: From culture shock to cultural learning. In E. W. Lynch & M. J. Hanson (Eds.), *Developing cross-cultural competence: A guide for working with children and their families* (2nd ed.) (pp. 23–46). Baltimore: Paul H. Brookes.

Lynch, E. W. (1998b). Developing cross-cultural competence. In E. W. Lynch & M. J. Hanson (Eds.), *Developing cross-cultural competence: A guide for working with children and their families* (2nd ed.) (pp. 47–90). Baltimore: Paul H. Brookes.

Lynch, E. W., & Hanson, M. J. (1993). Changing demographics: Implications for training in early intervention. *Infants and Young Children, 6,* 50–55.

Lynch, E. W., & Hanson, M. J. (1998a). *Developing cross-cultural competence: A guide for working with children and their families* (2nd ed.). Baltimore: Paul H. Brookes.

Lynch, E. W., & Hanson, M. J. (1998b). Children of many songs. In E. W. Lynch & M. J. Hanson (Eds.), *Developing cross-cultural competence: A guide for working with children and their families* (2nd ed.) (pp. 483–488). Baltimore: Paul H. Brookes.

Lynch, E. W., & Hanson, M. J. (1998c). Steps in the right direction: Implications for interventionists. In E. W. Lynch & M. J. Hanson, *Developing cross-cultural competence: A guide for working with children and their families* (2nd ed.) (pp. 491–512). Baltimore: Paul H. Brookes.

Magana, S. M. (2000). Mental retardation research methods in Latino communities. *Mental Retardation, 38,* 303–315.

Misra, A. (1994). Partnership with multicultural families. In S. K. Alper, P. J. Schloss, and C. N. Schloss (Eds.), *Families of students with disabilities: Consultation and advocacy* (pp. 143–179). Boston: Allyn & Bacon.

Mokuau, N., & Tauili'ili, P. (1998). Families with Native Hawaiian and Samoan roots. In E. W. Lynch & M. J. Hanson (Eds.), *Developing cross-cultural competence: A guide for working with children and their families* (2nd ed.) (pp. 409–482). Baltimore: Paul H. Brookes.

Nerney, T. (1998). The poverty of human services: An introduction. In T. Nerney & D. Shumway (Eds.), *The importance of income* (pp. 2–14). Concord, NH: Robert Wood Johnson Foundation.

Ohtake, Y., Santos, R. M., & Fowler, S. A. (2000). It's a three-way conversation: Families, service providers, and interpreters working together. *Young Exceptional Children, 4,* 12–18.

OSEP/ERIC. (2000). Improving results for culturally and linguistically diverse students. *Research Connections in Special Education, 7,* 1–2.

O'Shea, D. J., & Lancaster, P. L. (2001). Families of students from diverse backgrounds. In D. J. O'Shea, L. J. O'Shea, R. Algozzine, & D. J. Hammitte (Eds.), *Families and teachers of individuals with disabilities* (pp. 51–76). Boston: Allyn & Bacon.

Pachter, L. M. (1994). Culture and clinical care: Folk illness beliefs and behaviors and their implications for health care dilivery. *Journal of the American Medical Association, 271,* 690–694.

Parette, H. P., & Petch-Hogan, B. (2000). Approaching families: Facilitating culturally/linguistically diverse family involvement. *Teaching Exceptional Children, 33,* 4–10.

Park, J., & Turnbull, A. P. (2001). Cross-cultural competency and special education: Perceptions and experiences of Korean parents of children with special needs. *Education and Training in Mental Retardation and Developmental Disabilities, 36,* 133–147.

Pengra, L. M. (2000). *Your values, my values: Multicultural services in developmental disabilities.* Baltimore: Paul H. Brookes.

Roberts, R. N., Barclay-McLaughlin, G., Cleveland, J., Colston, W., Malach, R. Mulvey, L., Rodriguez, G., Thomas, T., & Yonemitsu, D. (1990). *Developing culturally competent programs for families of children with special needs.* Logan, UT: Utah State University, Early Intervention Research Institute, Developmental Center for Handicapped Persons. (Prepared by Georgetown University Child Development Center, Washington, DC).

Shafer, M. S., & Rangasamy, R. (1995). Transition and Native American youth: A follow-up study of school leavers on the Fort Apache Indian Reservation. *Journal of Rehabilitation, 61,* 60–65.

Sharifzadeh, V. S. (1998). Families with Middle Eastern roots. In E. W. Lynch & M. J. Hanson (Eds.), *Developing cross-cultural competence: A guide for working with children and their families* (2nd ed.) (pp. 441–482). Baltimore: Paul H. Brookes.

Sileo, T. W., Sileo, A. P., & Prater, M. A. (1996). Parent and professional partnerships in special education: Multicultural considerations. *Intervention in School and Community, 31,* 145–153.

Singh, N. N. (1995). In search of unity: Some thoughts on family-professional relationships in service delivery systems. *Journal of Child and Family Studies, 4,* 3–18.

Skinner, D., Rodriguez, P., & Bailey, D. B. (1999). Qualitative analysis of Latino parents' religious interpretations of their child's disability. *Journal of Early Intervention, 22,* 271–285.

Smith, D., Tyler, N., Sindelar, P., & Rosenberg, M. (2001). *The study of leadership personnel with particular attention to the professorate.* Washington, DC: U.S. Department of Education, Office of Special Education Programs.

Storti, C. (1989). *The art of crossing cultures.* Yarmouth, ME: Intercultural Press.

Sturm, L., & Gahagan, S. (1999). Cultural issues in provider-parent relationships. In D. B. Kessler & P. Dawson (Eds.), *Failure to thrive and pediatric undernutrition: A transdisciplinary approach* (pp. 351–374). Baltimore: Paul H. Brookes.

Thorp, E. K. (1997). Increasing opportunities for partnership with culturally and linguistically diverse families. *Intervention in School and Clinic, 32,* 261–269.

Turnbull, A., & Turnbull, R. (2001). *Families, professionals, and exceptionality: Collaborating for empowerment* (4th ed.). Saddle River, NJ: Prentice Hall.

U.S. Census Bureau (2000). Profile of general demographics.

U.S. Department of Education (1997). *19th annual report to Congress on the implementation of the Individuals with Disabilities Education Act.* Washington, DC: Author. Available: http://www.ed.gov/offices/OSERS/OSEP/osep97anlrpt/ED412721.

U.S. Department of Education (2000). *22nd annual report to Congress on the implementation of the Individuals with Disabilities Education Act.* Washington, DC: Author.

Voltz, D. L., & Damiano-Lantz, M. (1993). Developing ownership in learning. *Teaching Exceptional Children, 25,* 18–28.

Wayman, K. I., Lynch, E. W., & Hanson, M. J. (1990). Home-based early childhood services: Cultural sensitivity in a family systems approach. *Topics in Early Childhood Special Education, 10,* 56–75.

Wehmeyer, M. L., Agran, M., & Hughes, C. (1998). *Teaching self-determination to students with disabilities: Basic skills for successful transition.* Baltimore: Paul H. Brookes.

Wehmeyer, M. L., & Sands, D. J. (1998). *Making it happen: Student involvement in education planning, decision-making, and instruction.* Baltimore: Paul H. Brookes.

Westling, D. L., & Fox, L. (2000). *Teaching students with severe disabilities.* Upper Saddle River, NJ: Merrill.

Willis, W. (1998). Families with African American roots. In E. W. Lynch & M. J. Hanson (Eds.), *Developing cross-cultural competence: A guide for working with children and their families* (2nd ed.) (pp. 165–208). Baltimore: Paul H. Brookes.

Wlodkowski, R. J., & Ginsberg, M. B. (1995). *Diversity and motivation: Culturally responsive teaching.* San Francisco: Josey-Bass.

Wolfensberger, W. (1980). The definition of normalization: Update, problems, disagreements, and misunderstandings. In R. J. Flynn & K. E. Nitsch (Eds.), *Normalization, social integration, and community services* (pp. 71–115). Baltimore: University Park.

Zuniga, M. E. (1998). Families with Latino roots. In E. W. Lynch & M. J. Hanson (Eds.), *Developing cross-cultural competence: A guide for working with children and their families* (2nd ed.) (pp. 209–250). Baltimore: Paul H. Brookes.

# 6

# *Assistive Technology*

*Assistive technology devices can help people with severe disabilities increase the control they have over their own lives.*

*Brent, a preschool-aged child who is deaf and blind and has severe physical disabilities, loves to be tickled by his mom and dad but is not able to verbally express a desire to be tick-led. How can Brent communicate this desire? Jacob, a middle school student, has physical disabilities. He has enough control over his arms and hands to write, but the paper on which he is writing constantly slides off of his desk. Can something be done to allow Jacob to write without the paper moving? Karin, a high school student, is blind. She reads and writes Braille, but would like to use a computer to e-mail her friends. Can she access a computer using Braille? Liesl, an adult with severe mental retardation, enjoys watching sit-coms on television but is unable to manipulate the buttons on her television independently, to change the channels. Is there any way to help Liesl engage in this activity independently?*

Brent, Jacob, Karin, and Liesl may all benefit from the use of *assistive technology* (AT). Assistive technology is "any item, piece of equipment, or product system, whether acquired commercially off the shelf, modified, or customized, that is used to increase, maintain, or improve the functional capabilities of a child with disabilities" (Technology Related Assistance for Individuals with Disabilities Act of 1988). Assistive technology might be as simple as a piece of nonslip material, such as Dycem™, under Jacob's paper to keep it stationary, or as complex as a Braille keyboard to allow Karin to use the computer. Regardless of whether it is simple or complex, the use of assistive technology can greatly enhance the participation of an individual with disabilities in the home, school, and community environment.

---

**Focus 1**
Identify the kinds of needs that assistive technology can meet for individuals with severe disabilities. Provide examples of assistive technology that address each of these needs.

---

## Importance and Needs for People with Severe Disabilities

Assistive technology can meet a wide range of needs for individuals with severe disabilities. AT can be categorized into aids for (1) daily living, (2) communication, (3) working, learning, and playing, (4) mobility, and (5) positioning.

### Aids for Daily Living

As humans, we spend a significant amount of time each day participating in activities such as eating, bathing, cooking, dressing, and toileting. Individuals with disabilities may experience numerous challenges as they engage in these tasks. Demchak and Downing (1996) provide a list of assistive technologies that might be included during mealtimes and a rational for their use. This list includes (1) a nonslip placemat to hold a plate or bowl in place, (2) a plate guard to allow an individual to scoop food against it, (3) utensils with built-up handles to provide a better gripping surface, (4) utensils with Velcro cuffs to help an individual to maintain grasp, and (5) two-handed mugs to allow for two-handed grasping. Window 6.1 provides additional examples of assistive technology that may help decrease or eliminate challenges encountered during daily living activities.

**WINDOW 6.1** • *Examples of Assistive Technology That May Help Decrease or Eliminate Challenges Encountered during Daily Living Activities*

Clock/watch with Braille face

Large-print clock/watch

Audible clock/watch

Tactual control on home appliances

Larger numbers/words on home appliances

Knife with cutting guide

Rocking knife

Cooking thermometer with tactual gauge

Spatula with top and bottom blade to grasp items to be turned

Braille or large-print label maker for foods, medicines, etc.

Talking thermometer

Large-button telephone

Talking scale

Talking blood pressure gauge

Magnifying mirror

Label for marking colors, patterns, sizes on clothing items

Needle threader for sewing

Tape measure and ruler with tactual markings

Built-up handles on eating utensils

Built-up sides on plates

Modified handle on toothbrush

Dycem™ (or other nonslip material) to stabilize toys/objects

Magnifier

Bath seat

## Communication Aids

Individuals with disabilities may have difficulty communicating with people in their environment. For example, individuals with cerebral palsy may have difficulty using verbal language because of motor limitations. Furthermore, individuals with cognitive disabilities may have difficulty using and/or understanding language. Communication aids can provide support to assist individuals who experience these difficulties in expressive and receptive communication. Communication aides may be low-tech (e.g., pointing to pictures to indicate choices) or high-tech (e.g., computers with voice output, hearing aids). Cavalier and Brown (1998) discuss how assistive technology enabled Sue, a woman with profound mental retardation and severe cerebral palsy, to exert control over her environment. Prior to the use of assistive technology, Sue spent much of each day in a wheelchair or on a mat in an activity room of a residential facility. Sue was completely dependent on other people to identify her needs and then meet them. Although Sue was able to emit some consistent vocal sounds (e.g., approximations of the words "for," "move," "ray"), this skill was not being used in any functional manner. However, through the use of speech recognition technology and an environmental control unit, Sue learned to control different devices using different vocalizations (e.g., turn on a VCR, activate a vibrating massage pad, turn on a radio). This was possible because the speech recognition technology enabled Sue to operate a computer via her vocalizations and an environmental control unit enabled the computer to control electrical appliances in Sue's environment. This example demonstrates the impact of a high-tech application of assistive technology. However, low-tech strategies can provide an equally impressive impact. Reichle and Johnston (1999) describe a low-tech application of assistive technology to enhance communication. In this study, the authors taught Billy, a 7-year-old boy with a severe intellectual disability, and Jake, an 8-year-old boy with a moderate to severe intellectual disability, to (1) point to a picture symbol representing a desired item when the item was out of reach, and (2) simply take the desired item when it was within reach. The focus on these two behaviors illustrates that assistive technology (e.g., pointing to a symbol representing a desired object) should be used only if it is the most efficient way for the individual to meet his or her needs. If the individual has a socially appropriate, efficient way to meet his or her needs (e.g., taking a desired item when it is within reach), then assistive technology is not necessary. Window 6.2 provides examples of assistive technology that may help decrease or eliminate challenges related to communication.

## *Aids for Working, Learning, and Playing*

Assistive technology can increase, maintain, or improve the ability of an individual with disabilities to work, learn, or play. Lane and Mistrett (1996) discussed the effective use of assistive technology in increasing opportunities for Seth, a 12-month-old child with periventricular leukomalasia, which results in muscle tone abnormalities, developmental delays, and extreme irritability, to play. One example of assistive technology for Seth included a boxtop with three sides secured to a tabletop, to contain toy cars. Seth and his father took turns "crashing" the cars into the sides while Seth's father provided sound effects. As this activity continued, Seth's father added to the play experience by incorporating new props to crash the cars into. Another example of assistive technology that enhanced Seth's ability to play involved the use of a switch that was connected to a battery-operated dinosaur. Every time Seth activated the switch, the dinosaur moved a short distance. Seth's dad pointed the dinosaur toward Seth and, with each activation of the switch, Seth moved the dinosaur closer and closer until he was able to grab it. After grabbing the dinosaur, Seth smiled and looked at his father, seeming to ask him to play the game again.

---

**WINDOW 6.2 • *Examples of Assistive Technology That May Help Decrease or Eliminate Challenges Encountered during Communication***

| | |
|---|---|
| Voice-output communication aid | Telecommunications device for the deaf (TDD) |
| Laptop computer with voice output | Telephone amplifier |
| Nonelectronic communication aid (pictures in a notebook or wallet, etc.) | Visual/vibrating alerting signal (for alarm clock, door bell, baby crying, etc.) |
| Braille writer | Switch (push, lever, joystick, pull) to access computers, etc. |
| Slate and stylus (used to write in Braille) | |
| Hearing aid | Software that "reads" what is on the monitor |

This category also includes assistive technology that replaces, substitutes, or augments missing body parts, such as splints, braces, and artificial limbs. Krebs, Lembeck, and Fishman (1988) examined the effectiveness of using child-sized body-powered hands for twenty-four children ranging in age from 1.8 years to 8.3 years with below-elbow limb deficiencies by asking the children, the children's parents, and clinicians to provide information regarding their reactions to the prosthetic hands. Findings revealed that most of the participants reported an increase in their functional skills (e.g., grasping a toothbrush, catching a ball). Furthermore, several parents reported that their previously shy children became more willing to participate in social activities and interactions as a result of the natural appearance of the prosthetic hand.

Assistive technology that will allow individuals with disabilities to access and use computers may also affect their ability to work, learn, and play. Window 6.3 provides an example of how assistive technology allowed Michael, a 17-year-old with spinal muscular atrophy, to access and use a computer. Window 6.4 provides examples of assistive technologies that aid in working, learning, and playing.

## Mobility Aids

Individuals with severe disabilities may encounter difficulty when trying to go from one place to another. Examples of assistive technologies that aid mobility include wheelchairs, lifts, and walkers. Gilson and Huss (1995) discuss products available that will allow an individual to operate a vehicle independently (i.e., gas pedal, brakes, horn, light dimmer switch) by using the control of one upper extremity. They also provide information on a range of mobility aids that help individuals participate in recreational activities, such as water skis for persons who are unable to stand, sailboats that can be operated from a seated position, and adapted bicycles. Window 6.5 provides examples of mobility aids.

## Positioning Aids

Sometimes, individuals with disabilities will benefit from positioning aids. Positioning aids are modifications to wheelchairs or other seats that provide stability and/or reduce pressure on the skin surface. Radell (1997) provides examples of the use of positioning aids for individuals with physical disabilities. For example, a child's wheelchair may be equipped with cushions, pelvic straps, hip guides, trunk supports, and head supports in order to ensure that the child is positioned appropriately for functional activities.

In summary, a vast array of assistive technologies is available to meet the needs of individuals with disabilities. Furthermore, these technologies span the continuum from no-tech/low-tech to high-tech systems. However, the existence of these technologies alone does not ensure access to assistive technology. Major federal legislation that has increased access to assistive technology is described in the next section.

---

**Focus 2**
Identify and summarize the main points of some of the federal legislation that has served to increase awareness of and access to assistive technology devices and services.

**WINDOW 6.3 •** *Assistive Technology Helps Students Overcome*
*Physical Limitations*

Michael Phillips is a bright, articulate, 17-year-old who is physically challenged with spinal muscular atrophy (SMA), a neuromuscular disorder that attacks the nerves and the muscles they control. A congenital disease, SMA is degenerative, leaving Michael without the ability to control muscle contractions in his arms and legs. As a result, Michael cannot perform simple tasks such as turning a page, using a pen, or typing on a keyboard. Yet, thanks to the use of assistive computer technology, the Tampa, Florida, resident boasts an impressive record of academic achievement and enjoys a variety of extracurricular activities.

In the fall of 1998, Michael entered his senior year at Plant High School in Tampa with a 4.12 grade-point average. He is an editor and columnist of the high school newspaper and writes a regular column on the Internet entitled "Palpatines's Mac World." He has been awarded a Chair scholarship to any public college or university in the state of Florida. Michael is an accomplished photographer and enjoys playing computer games and surfing the net.

*Overcoming Disabilities*
Michael's accomplishments in the face of adversity have caught the attention of local papers, resulting in his selection as a key speaker at a conference in Orlando sponsored by the Assistive Technology Network (ATEN) of Florida, a federally and state-funded organization that, through its educational and training programs, advocates the use of assistive technology for the disabled. The assistive technology that has enabled Michael to overcome his physical disability is called Discover:Kenx, a combination of adaptive computer hardware and software developed by Don Johnston Incorporated (Wauconda, Illinois).

Discover:Kenx allow Michael to bypass the keyboard and access his Macintosh computer with a device called a string switch. The highly sensitive string switch connects to the Discover:Kenx interface, allowing Michael to use the string switch as a mouse that responds to his slightest thumb movement, clicking on keyboard icons displayed on the screen. "When I pull the switch, a menu comes up on the screen and on that menu is everything from the alphabet to mouse controls. It only took me four days to learn how to use Discover:Kenx," explains Michael, who began using the system four years ago.

Don Johnston developed Discover:Kenx so that students like Michael could be included in regular educational classes as mandated by the Americans with Disabilities Act of 1990 and the Individuals with Disabilities Education Act. Currently, all states receive federal funds under the Technology Related Assistance for Individuals with Disabilities Act, which requires states to "purchase and use electronic and information technology that is accessible to individuals with disabilities." It is estimated that, in Florida alone, about 6,000 students have some form of physical disability. According to Bob Keller of Don Johnston, 10,000 students and adults throughout the world are using Discover:Kenx.

*The Right Tools*
Although Discover:Kenx has allowed Michael to overcome physical disabilities that previously would have limited his scholastic achievements, its real value is in the enhanced quality of life that reaches far beyond the classroom. "With my Mac and assistive technology like Discover:Kenx, I can write a column for my school newspaper, get on the Internet, create 3-D artwork and my own Web page, work on Adobe PhotoShop, and last but not least, do my homework," says Michael.

Michael's mother, Karen Moore, shares Michael's enthusiasm for the program. "Discover:Kenx has changed our lives. Before this technology was available to him, his life was passive, watching TV or watching others play video games. He's so bright, wanting to participate but unable to. It was like an opera singer inflicted with laryngitis," Mrs. Moore relates. She first learned about Discover:Kenx through the Florida Diagnostic and Learning Resources System (FDLRS), a federally and state-funded organization that advocates the use of assistive technology throughout

*(continued)*

**WINDOW 6.3 • Continued**

the state. She fought through the bureaucracy of the school district for 3 years until Michael finally received Discover:Kenx from his school in January of 1995. Don Johnston offers a complete line of Kenx products that assist people with physical, visual, or cognitive disabilities and who cannot use a standard keyboard or mouse.

The Discover line of products consists of devices designed to help students and teachers more easily access computers. The series includes Discover:Switch, a large, colorful computer switch; Discover:Board, an oversized, alternate keyboard; and Discover:Kenx, a multi-input product that allows users to access the computer through multiple devices including different types of switches such as the one used by Michael.

What is amazing about these types of products is not necessarily their function, but what they allow otherwise handicapped individuals to accomplish. You'd be amazed how a student can blossom if they are simply provided with the right tools. It's a bit like giving a Cray supercomputer to Einstein—just think what he could accomplish with modern day scientific tools!

*Source:* Assistive technology helps students overcome physical limitations (1998). *T. H. E. Journal, 26*(5), 43.

**WINDOW 6.4 • *Examples of Assistive Technology That May Help Decrease or Eliminate Challenges Encountered during Working/ Learning/Playing***

Books on tape

Books in Braille

Television screen magnifiers

Audiodescriptive narration of television shows and live theater

Tactual lock on locker at a gym

Audible device (beeper) to make a ball (basketball, tennis ball, etc.) project a sound

Large-print/Braille calendar and telephone book

Guide for writing

Large-print checks

Talking calculator

Magnified computer screen

Captioning for television programs

Modifying buttons, switches, levers on toys/ appliances

Adaptive switches to allow access to battery-operated toys, electrical appliances, etc.

Touch window for computer

EyeGaze-operated keyboard

Speech recognition software

Adapted books with page separators to allow for page turning

Modified or alternative keyboard

Word processor/spell checker/proofreading program

Screen reading program

Word prediction software

Splints

Braces

Artificial limb

**WINDOW 6.5 • *Examples of Assistive Technology That May Help Decrease or Eliminate Challenges Encountered during Daily Living Activities***

| | |
|---|---|
| Cane | Power-operated scooter |
| Walking pole/stick | Adapted van or automobile |
| Electronic travel aide (e.g., a laser cane that sends out a signal that is bounced back from objects in the traveler's path) | Assisted driving devices (hand controls, modified steering wheel) |
| | Ramp |
| Crutches | Lifts |
| Walker | |
| Manual or power wheelchair | |

## Federal Legislation and Assistive Technology

Federal legislation has served to increase awareness of and access to assistive technology devices and services. Significant legislation that has affected assistive technology devices and services includes the Rehabilitation Act of 1986, the Technology-Related Assistance for Individuals with Disabilities Act of 1988, the Telecommunications Accessibility Enhancement Act of 1988, the Americans with Disabilities Act of 1990, and the Individuals with Disabilities Education Act (IDEA) Amendments of 1997.

### Rehabilitation Act

The Rehabilitation Act of 1986 was the first significant piece of legislation to address issues related to assistive technology. Section 508 of this act, titled "Electronic Equipment Accessibility Guidelines," was written to ensure that individuals with disabilities could access and manipulate information from electronic equipment so that the results for the individual with disabilities were the same as for any nondisabled user. In 1992, Section 508's focus of the Rehabilitation Act was amended. The title was changed to "Electronic and Information Technology" in order to apply to all types of electronic media. Furthermore, this amendment required that guidelines be established to ensure that individuals with disabilities can produce and access information that is comparable to all technology users (Mondak, 2000).

### Technology Related Assistance Act

Another early piece of federal legislation that addressed the use of assistive technology with individuals with disabilities was the Technology-Related Assistance for Individuals with Disabilities Act of 1988 (Public Law 100-407). This act is often referred to as the

Tech Act (1988). The Tech Act stated that providing assistive technology services and devices enables individuals with disabilities to:

    (a) have greater control over their own lives,
    (b) participate in and contribute more fully to activities in their home, school, and work environments, and in their communities,
    (c) interact to a greater extent with non-disabled individuals, and
    (d) otherwise benefit from opportunities that are taken for granted by individuals who do not have disabilities. (p. 1044)

In addition to Congress's decree regarding the importance of assistive technology for individuals with disabilities, the Tech Act also required states to develop programs that provided technology-related services for individuals with disabilities.

In 1994, Congress amended the Tech Act of 1988. Among other things, the amendment required states to engage in six activities to ensure access to assistive technology devices and services. These activities included examining and, if necessary, modifying existing service delivery systems; developing systems to change funding strategies; increasing collaboration across state agencies; ensuring that state agencies work with the disability community in order to better serve individuals with disabilities; increasing state agencies' work with underrepresented populations or populations that were located in rural areas; and ensuring timely acquisition and delivery of assistive technology devices and services.

## Telecommunications Accessibility Enhancement Act

The Telecommunications Accessibility Enhancement Act of 1988 (P.L. 100-542) required that the federal telecommunications system be fully accessible to hearing- and speech-impaired individuals. Telecommunication devices for the deaf (TDD) are one way to make telecommunication accessible for individuals with speech and/or hearing disabilities. A TDD is a machine that uses typed input and output, usually with a visual text display, to allow individuals to communicate over the telephone. In addition to devices such as the TDD that were developed specifically for individuals with disabilities, some technology that was created for nondisabled users is flexible enough to accommodate the needs of speech- and/or hearing-impaired individuals (e.g., e-mail, FAX).

## Americans with Disabilities Act

The Americans with Disabilities Act of 1990 required that the public and the private sector provide accommodations to persons with disabilities. Title I (Employment) of the Americans with Disabilities Act states that employers with fifteen or more employees (1) cannot discriminate against an individual with a disability in hiring or promotion if the individual is otherwise qualified for the job, (2) can ask about an individual's ability to perform a job but cannot inquire if the individual has a disability or subject him or her to a test that tends to screen out people with disabilities, (3) need to provide reasonable accommodations to individuals with disabilities (e.g., job restructuring, modification of equipment), and (4) do not need to provide accommodations that impose undue hardships on business operations. The provision of reasonable accommodations can often be accomplished through the use of assistive technologies. In many cases, providing reasonable accommodations does not impose undue hardship. Lee's summary of studies conducted in 1986 and 1992 (as cited in Mondak, 2000) revealed that more than half of the accommodations made for employees with disabilities cost nothing and another 15 percent cost less than $500.

### 1997 IDEA Amendments

The Individuals with Disabilities Education Act (IDEA) Amendments of 1997 mandate that Individualized Education Program (IEP) teams consider whether a child requires assistive technology devices and services to receive a free and appropriate public education. The requirement now states that, "in developing each child's IEP, the IEP team shall consider whether the child requires assistive technology devices and services." These amendments focus on "identifying student's assistive technology needs instead of just identifying students who might need assistive technology" (Wehmeyer, 1999, p. 52).

In summary, federal legislation has served to increase awareness of and access to assistive technology devices and services. Although the importance of this legislation cannot be emphasized enough, it is only one step in the process of providing assistive technology that enhances the ability of individuals with disabilities to participate in their home, school, and community environments. Another step involves the identification and functional use of assistive technologies and services that are appropriate for any given individual.

---

**Focus 3**
Identify and provide examples of issues that should be considered when attempting to identify appropriate assistive technology devices and services.

---

## Identification and Functional Use of Assistive Technology Devices and Services

Although assistive technology has enormous potential to enhance the lives of individuals with disabilities, this potential is often not realized. Individuals with disabilities are frequently dissatisfied with their assistive technology and, as a result, discontinue their use (Philips & Zhao, 1993). Studies suggest that assistive technology abandonment rates range from 8 to 75 percent (Tewey, Barnicle, & Perr, 1994). Some of the reasons given for discontinuance of assistive technology include that the assistive technology did not meet an important functional need (Beigel, 2000; Reimer-Reiss & Wacker, 2000), or the consumer of the technology was not involved in the entire process (Reimer-Reiss & Wacker, 2000). Assessment and intervention strategies that meet important functional needs as well as involve the consumer of the technology may serve to decrease the abandonment of assistive technologies.

### Identification of Appropriate AT Devices and Services

In most cases, a team of individuals is required to complete the myriad of activities related to AT assessment, intervention, and follow-up. The members of the team may vary based on the needs of the learner, the age of the individual (e.g., child versus adult), and the service delivery system (e.g., school versus residential). For example, consider Liesl, an adult with severe mental retardation and physical disabilities. Liesl lives in a group home setting and enjoys watching sitcoms on television but is unable to manipulate the buttons on her television independently, to change the channels. Liesl's team is considering the use of an environmental control unit that, when connected to the TV, will enable Liesl to touch a switch with the side of her head when she wants to change channels. Liesl's team consists of Liesl, her caregivers, a speech language pathologist, and an occupational therapist. Liesl's involvement is critical, because she will provide information regarding her preferences and needs. The input of her caregivers is necessary because they will provide information regarding the impact that the use of the environmental control unit will have on the group home routine as well as how it will influence their work responsibilities. The speech language pathologist will assess Liesl's communication needs and determine whether AT could be provided to enhance communicative interactions (e.g., to comment on the show) while she watches television. Finally, the occupational therapist can determine what motor skills are necessary to access the environmental control unit and how to position Leisl to maximize her functional use of the AT.

Regardless of the team's composition, it is important that the team consider a range of issues that may effect AT assessment, intervention, and follow-up. Parette (1997) organizes these issues into five areas: user characteristics, technology features, family concerns, cultural factors, and service system issues. Table 6.1 identifies the specific considerations that should be addressed for each of these issues. Although many of these considerations seem obvious, they are often overlooked when conducting an AT assessment. For example, Parette and Hourcade (1997) surveyed the Part H (of the IDEA) coordinators in thirty-eight states regarding characteristics that are considered in augmentative and alternative communication "high-tech" assistive technology assessment processes. Among other things, they discovered that issues such as (1) the identification of training needs, (2) the extent to which modifications in the home environment will be required, (3) family preferences, and (4) cultural issues were reported as being considered to a great extent by fewer than 50 percent of the respondents.

In summary, assessment strategies that utilize a team approach and focus on the needs of the user of AT as well as individuals who interact with the AT user may increase the likelihood that appropriate AT is identified. However, another important consideration involves ensuring the functional use of the AT.

---

*Focus 4*
Identify the four components of matching theory that may affect the choice of an individual with disabilities to use assistive technology.

---

## Functional Use of AT Devices and Services

One way to increase the functional use of AT devices and services is to increase the likelihood that the AT is efficient and effective for the user. It is often the case that, when presented with AT, the user has a choice to use it or not to use it. Herrnstein (1961) conducted a classic study in which he demonstrated that choice behavior depended on the rate of rein-

**TABLE 6.1** *Domains of Influence to Be Considered by Assistive Technology Team Members*

| Issue Area | Specific Considerations |
|---|---|
| User characteristics | Performance levels (from assessment data) <br> User age <br> Gender <br> Current devices used, past experiences, and preferences <br> Academic and vocational aspirations <br> Desire for independence <br> Training needs and willingness to receive training <br> Changes in user characteristics across time |
| Technology features | Range and availability of devices <br> Potential to enhance user performance levels <br> Real cost <br> Ease of use <br> Comfort <br> Dependability <br> Transportability <br> Longevity and durability <br> Adaptability <br> Comparability with other devices <br> Safety features <br> Availability for hands-on demonstrations <br> Repair considerations |
| Family concerns | Changes in activities, routines, and resources <br> Effect on family interaction patterns <br> Degree of expectations for independence |
| Cultural factors | Compatability of device with cultural values <br> Extent to which device calls attention to the user in social and public settings <br> Extent to which dependence/independence is valued <br> Developmental expectations for the acquisition of skills <br> Perception of disability |
| Service system issues | Cost <br> Community usage of device <br> Protection from theft and damage <br> Training |

*Source:* Parette, H. (1997). Assistive technology devices and services. *Education and Training in Mental Retardation and Developmental Disabilities, 32*(4), 267–280.

forcement for each of the available behaviors. This led to the hypothesis that when individuals have the opportunity to choose between two or more responses, they will select the response that is perceived as most efficient (Mace & Roberts, 1993). An individual's concept of efficiency is affected by at least four components: rate of reinforcement (e.g., Mace,

Neef, Shade, & Mauro, 1994; Horner & Day, 1991), quality of reinforcement (e.g., Mace, Neef, Shade, & Mauro, 1996; Neef et al., 1993), response effort (e.g., Horner & Day, 1991; Mace et al., 1996), and immediacy of reinforcement (e.g., Neef, Mace, & Shade, 1993; Horner & Day, 1991). Mcdowell (1988) discussed how these components interact to affect the probability that an individual will choose one response option over another.

It seems plausible that one or more of the components of response efficiency may influence a learner's choice regarding whether to use AT. The following sections illustrate the potential role of the four components of response efficiency (rate of reinforcement, quality of reinforcement, response effort, and immediacy of reinforcement) in the choice to use AT.

*Rate of Reinforcement.*    Herrnstein (1961) notes that when one behavior is chosen over another, the chosen behavior may receive a higher rate of reinforcement. This component of matching theory has particular significance for the implementation of AT. Consider Julie, a learner who is being taught to point to a picture symbol representing "juice" rather than trantruming when she wants a drink. If all other variables are held constant, matching theory suggests that she must be reinforced more often for using the picture symbol than when she engages in an alternative behavior to achieve the same function. If Julie receives the same rate of reinforcement regardless of whether she tantrums or points to a picture representing the item, there may be little incentive to use the picture symbol to communicate, because the rate of reinforcement is not significantly greater than that for the tantruming response.

*Quality of Reinforcement.*    Mace and Roberts (1993) discuss that when one event is preferred over another, the preferred event has a higher quality of reinforcement. Furthermore, they state that quality of reinforcement can affect choice behavior. When applied to AT, this implies that the reinforcement delivered contingent on the use of a specific assistive technology must be preferred over the reinforcement delivered for not using it. This is illustrated when Jacob, a young man with cerebral palsy, begins to use his new electric wheelchair. After using the new wheelchair for a few weeks, Jacob states that he is disheartened by the wheelchair being so big, because students do not touch him as much as when he was in a nonmotorized chair. In this case, if Jacob does not prefer the way his peers respond to him in his electric wheelchair, the quality of reinforcement received for using it may not provide adequate incentive for its continued use.

*Response Effort.*    The physical effort required to produce a behavior can significantly affect whether a learner will choose to emit that response (Horner & Day, 1991; Mace et al., 1996). The potential effect of response effort can be applied to a variety of situations involving AT. Consider James, who is learning to use his prosthetic hand to engage in activities (e.g., writing) rather than relying on the assistance of caregivers. If all other variables are held constant, matching theory suggests that the effort involved to use the prosthetic hand must be less than the effort involved in procuring a caregiver's attention and having the caregiver provide assistance. If the same response effort is involved regardless of whether he uses his prosthetic hand or obtains the attention and the assistance of his caregivers, there may be little incentive to learn to use the prosthetic hand.

*Immediacy of Reinforcement.*    The latency between the use of AT and the delivery of a reinforcer can influence a learner's choice to use the assistive technology (Horner & Day,

1991; Neef et al., 1993). For example, Alfonso is a young man who is being taught to use adapted utensils when eating, rather than being fed by a caregiver. If all other variables are held constant, matching theory suggests that he must be reinforced more quickly for using the adapted eating utensils than when he is fed by caregivers. If Alfonso receives the same immediacy of reinforcement regardless of whether he uses the adapted utensils or is fed by caregivers, there may be little incentive to use the AT because the immediacy of reinforcement is not significantly greater than waiting to be fed by a caregiver.

***Manipulating the Components of Matching Theory to Increase the Effectiveness of Interventions.***     The components of matching theory may be useful when developing procedures to teach individuals with disabilities to use AT. The procedures can be designed by examining the role of response efficiency for the AT user and/or individuals who interact with the AT user. For example, consider the following scenario, in which the components of matching theory are adjusted to influence choice behavior. In this situation, teachers are considering teaching a preschool learner, Kelly, a more efficient means of acquiring attention. Currently, Kelly requests attention by producing the unintelligible (and sometimes inaudible) utterance /na/. As discussed by Mace and Roberts (1993), the first step involved in incorporating the components of matching theory into a teaching procedure involves collecting information on the efficiency of Kelly's current method of communication. Table 6.2 summarizes information that was collected via direct observation of Kelly in her preschool setting.

After obtaining information regarding the efficiency of the current system, the second step in the process is to formulate a teaching procedure (in this situation, Kelly's teachers are considering teaching her to depress a switch in order to emit a prerecorded message to obtain attention) that competes with the current behavior across the four components of matching theory. Table 6.2 illustrates how the teachers adjusted their teaching procedures. This table reveals that the adjustments result in (1) a higher rate of reinforcement, (2) more immediate reinforcement, (3) lower response effort, and (4) an equal quality of reinforcement for using the switch. These adjustments will increase the probability that Kelly will choose to use the switch over her current method of communication.

In conclusion, it may be feasible to adjust various parameters (e.g., rate of reinforcement, immediacy of reinforcement, response effort, quality of reinforcement) in order to alter an AT user's behavior and/or the behavior of individuals who interact with the AT user. This, in turn, has the potential to increase the overall efficiency and effectiveness of AT interventions. However, to date, interventionists are only able to speculate on the applicability of matching theory to choice behaviors related to the use of AT. This speculation may or may not be accurate. Therefore, empirical investigations are necessary in order to validate the applicability of matching theory to AT.

# Knowledge and Skill Competencies

It is evident that identifying, obtaining, and using assistive technologies and services that are appropriate for any given individual is a challenging and ongoing process. Teachers and related service providers must become competent in assistive technology in order to serve their students and comply with legal mandates. The Knowledge and Skill Subcommittee of the

**TABLE 6.2    *Rate of Reinforcement, Quality of Reinforcement, Response Effort, and Immediacy of Reinforcement for Current Method of Communication and for Teaching Procedures***

| Factor Influencing Efficiency | Current System | Teaching Procedures |
|---|---|---|
| Rate of reinforcement | Kelly's teacher cannot always hear her vocalizations. As a result, she is currently reinforced for only 60% of her requests. | Ensure that the volume of the prerecorded message is audible so that Kelly is reinforced for 90–100% of her requests. |
| Quality of reinforcement | If Kelly's teacher hears and understands her utterance, she receives attention 100% of the time. Therefore, the quality of reinforcement for Kelly's utterances is high. | Provide an equal quality of reinforcement for use of the new behavior as well as the current behavior. |
| Response effort | Kelly often fatigues following repeated vocalizations as a result of the effort required to vocalize with sufficient volume. Therefore, across time, the response effort for Kelly's request for attention increases. | Ensure that response effort for the new behavior requires low effort by appropriate selection and placement of switch. |
| Immediacy of reinforcement | Sometimes it is unclear whether Kelly's vocalizations are intentional or reflexive. Therefore, the teacher's responses are not always immediate (average latency of teacher's responses is 30 seconds) | Ensure that teacher response to the new behavior is immediate so that latency of response is less than that of current behavior. |

Council for Exceptional Children's (CEC) Professional Standards and Practice Standing Committee has written and validated knowledge and skill statements for assistive technology (Lahm & Nickels, 1999). Window 6.6 provides a list of these essential knowledge and skill competencies. This list may serve to assist professionals by guiding them in their quest to become competent in the area of AT.

## Conclusion and Future Directions

In summary, it is difficult to overstate the impact that assistive technology can have on the lives of individuals with severe disabilities. This chapter has provided information regarding ways in which assistive technology can increase, maintain, and/or improve an individual's functional capabilities. Although a significant amount of progress has been made in establishing legislation, policies, and models for providing assistive technology, its impact is not being fully realized. Too often, assistive technology is not provided to individuals who could benefit from it. Furthermore, when assistive technology is provided, technology

# WINDOW 6.6 • *Essential Knowledge and Skills Competencies*

### *Philosophical, Historical, and Legal Foundations of Special Education*

*Knowledge*

1. Legislation and regulations related to technology and their implications for special education.

*Skills*

2. Articulate a philosophy and goals for using technology in special education.
3. Use technology-related terminology appropriately in written and oral communications.

### *Characteristics of Learners*

*Knowledge*

4. Characteristics of exceptional learners that influence the use of technology.
5. Impact of technology on exceptional learners.
6. Impact of technology on exceptional learners with moderate disabilities.

*Skills*

7. Identify the academic and physical demands placed on learners by computer software and related technology materials.

### *Assessment, Diagnosis, and Evaluation*

*Skills*

8. Analyze, summarize, and report student performance data to aid instructional decision making regarding technology.
9. Identify functional needs, screen for functional limitations, and identify if the need for a comprehensive assistive technology evaluation exists.
10. Refer for additional evaluation regarding technology if adequate data are not available for plan development.
11. Recognize the need for further evaluation regarding technology, and refer to other professionals when appropriate.
12. Recognize poor outcomes regarding technology needs, and reevaluate and reinitiate the process as needed.
13. Work with assistive technology team members to identify assistive technologies, both hardware and software, that can help individuals meet the demands placed on them in their environments.
14. Define measurable objectives to monitor progress toward achieving stated goals regarding technology.
15. Observe and measure consumer's performance with assistive technology over a period of initial use.
16. Compare actual performance with anticipated performance and the goals stated in the intervention plan.
17. Interview the consumer, the family, and caregivers to determine if the technology meets their present and future needs.

### *Instructional Content and Practice*

*Knowledge*

18. Procedures for evaluating computer software and other technology materials for their applicability in special education programs.

*Skills*

19. Identify elements of the special education curriculum for which technology applications are appropriate and ways they can be implemented.
20. Design, deliver, and assess student learning activities that integrate computers/technology for a variety of student populations.
21. Design student learning activities that foster equitable, ethical, and legal use of technology by students.
22. Identify and operate software that meets educational objectives for students in multiple educational environments.
23. Use computers to support various stages of the learning process and to facilitate student reporting of educational achievements.
24. Use technology to compensate for learning and performance barriers.
25. Identify and use assistive technologies that can provide access to educational materials that are otherwise inaccessible to some individuals.
26. Use computer-based productivity tools to develop classroom materials.

*(continued)*

**WINDOW 6.6 • Continued**

27. Teach special education students to use productivity software programs to perform tasks such as word processing, database management, graphics production, and telecommunications.
28. Teach special education students to operate equipment and run associated educational programs.
29. Use productivity tools for word processing, database management, and spreadsheet applications.
30. Solicit accurate feedback from end-users and others having experience with technology.
31. Understand proper mechanical and electrical safety practices, or direct their use in the assembly and integration of the technology at a defensible level of competence.

### Planning and Managing the Teaching and Learning Environment

*Skills*
32. Demonstrate the proper care of technology systems and related software; use simple diagnostics to determine problems that arise, and perform routine maintenance.
33. Arrange and manage the classroom environment to facilitate the use of technology.

### Managing Student Behavior and Social Interaction Skills

*Skills*
34. Organize computer activities to promote positive social interaction.

### Communication and Collaborative Partnerships

*Knowledge*
35. Roles that related service providers assume in providing technology services to special education students.

*Skill*
36. Recognize the need (how, when, where) to refer a consumer to another professional regarding technology.

37. Identify assistive technology team members and their roles.
38. Design and implement integrated technology classroom activities that involve teaming and/or small group collaboration.
39. Collaborate with consumer and other team members in planning and implementing the use of assistive and adaptive devices.
40. Participate in collaborative projects and activities involving technology.
41. Demonstrate effective group process skills.
42. Communicate effectively including listening, speaking, and writing on technology issues.
43. Use e-mail and Web browser applications for communication and for research to support instruction.
44. Advise general education teachers about the use of technology systems with special education students who are mainstreamed into their classes.

### Professionalism and Ethical Practices

*Knowledge*
45. Confidentiality of information
46. Limits of expertise—recognize and seek outside expertise.

*Skills*
47. Recognize own skill and knowledge regarding technology and limit individual practice accordingly.
48. Maintain a professional development program to ensure the acquisition of knowledge and skill about new developments in technology as they become available.
49. Identify activities and resources to support professional growth related to technology.
50. Demonstrate knowledge of equity, ethical, legal, and human issues related to technology use in special education.
51. Adhere to copyright laws about duplication and distribution of software and other copyrighted technology materials.

*Source:* Lahm, E., & Nickels, B. (1999). What do you know? *Teaching Exceptional Children, 32*(1), 56–63.

abandonment may occur. The abandonment of assistive technology may be addressed through appropriate assessment and instruction.

---

*Focus 5*
Describe what is meant by "universal design" and discuss how is it different from assistive technology.

---

How do we progress further in our attempts to increase, maintain, and improve upon the functional capabilities of individuals with disabilities? One strategy is *Universal Design*. Universal design is the process of creating mass market products that, from the outset, accommodate the widest spectrum of users, including those with disabilities. Universal design is different from assistive technology, in which the focus is on providing individuals with disabilities with modifications that will allow them access to products or activities (Rose, 2000). Newsworthy 6.1 illustrates the ways in which universal design may affect the lives of individuals with disabilities. The widespread application of universal design could increase the use of mass market products by individuals with disabilities. Furthermore, it could result in a decrease in the number of specialized products that individuals with disabilities must obtain, learn to use, and infuse into their daily lives.

# Focus Review

Focus 1: Identify the kinds of needs that assistive technology can meet for individuals with severe disabilities. Provide examples of assistive technology that address each of these needs.

- Assistive technology can be used to meet daily living needs. Examples include a modified handle on a toothbrush, a magnifier, and an audible clock.
- Assistive technology can be used to address communication needs. Examples include a voice-output communication aid, a nonelectronic communication aid (e.g., pictures in a notebook), a Braille writer, a hearing aid, and a telecommunications device for the deaf (TDD).
- Assistive technology can be used to address needs related to working, learning, and playing. Examples include a book on tape, a talking calculator, speech recognition software, and a splint.
- Assistive technology can address needs related to mobility. Examples include canes, crutches, a wheelchair, and an adapted automobile.
- Assistive technology can be used to meet needs related to positioning. Examples include cushions, hip guides, trunk supports, and head supports.

Focus 2: Identify and summarize the main points of some of the federal legislation that has served to increase awareness of and access to assistive technology devices and services.

- Section 508 of the Rehabilitation Act of 1986 ensured that individuals with disabilities could access and manipulate information from electronic equipment. In 1992, Section 508 was amended in order to apply to all types of electronic media.
- The Technology Related Assistance Act of 1988 (Tech Act) stressed the importance and potential impact of assistive technology for individuals with disabilities and

**NEWSWORTHY 6.1 • *Devices Free Workers from Disabilities***

Jesse Leaman is what you might call a rocket scientist. A University of Maryland astronomy major, he's spending the summer at the Goddard Space Flight Center's high-energy astrophysics lab in Greenbelt, Md., creating simulations of high-orbit satellite missions.

The 22-year-old, who has interned at another NASA facility, the Marshall Space Flight Center in Huntsville, Ala., says none of his work would be possible without a speech-recognition program called Dragon Dictate, which lets users control PCs by voice commands.

The off-the-shelf software is popular with doctors dictating medical notes and office workers with repetitive stress injuries. But Leaman uses it because he is paralyzed from the neck down as a result of a skiing accident in 1996.

"Everything has to be voice-activated if I am to be independent," he says.

Since the landmark passage of the Americans with Disabilities Act (ADA) 10 years ago, those with disabilities have seen tremendous changes. Thanks largely to the proliferation of technology, even those like Leaman with severe disabilities can do things that previously would have been almost impossible.

In 1990 the rallying cry was "assistive technology." The idea was that specialized devices could be used to give people with disabilities greater freedom and independence. But today the move is toward "universal design," emphasizing products with all possible users in mind.

Many innovations that make life easier for everyone began as special accommodations for the disabled: vibrating pagers, curb cuts, telephone dials that light up in the dark and PCs that allow you to increase the letter size on the screen to make things easier to read.

Donna Sorkin, who is profoundly deaf and hears with the aid of a cochlear implant, now can use public telephones because the ADA mandated that in banks of more than four phones, one must have a volume control.

"That's a perfect example of universal design, because there are always times when people with normal hearing are in a noisy place and need a little boost in volume," says Sorkin, executive director of the Alexander Graham Bell Foundation, which works with deaf children.

Electronic books are another example of the convergence of assistive technology and universal design. Audio books are popular with the blind and with commuters but aren't searchable, so finding a particular passage is difficult.

The new digital e-books are searchable, but for the blind, they must be read by a machine that produces synthetic speech, a less than optimal solution.

To combine the best of both, the Digital Audio-based Information Systems (DAISY) Consortium was formed to create a standard for what it calls digital talking books. They are human-read books that include "a table of contents on steroids," says George Kerscher of Recording for the Blind & Dyslexic, the nation's education library for people who can't read the printed word.

"Using a DAISY-compliant playback device, you can jump to any heading or page in the book," Kerscher says.

Users can watch words go by as the books talk—useful for people learning English as a second language, new readers, and those with dyslexia or similar problems. The text also can be output as Braille.

By having accessibility standards in place before e-books take off, developers hope all digital books and reading devices will contain features that will make them useful for everyone.

Standards-setting bodies like the eBook Forum are important because it's easy for technologies to be inaccessible if no one is paying attention. That's what happened with the Web.

Initially, it could be used by those with visual or other physical disabilities because most pages had simple text and layouts that make navigation with "talking" browsers easy. But then came images, frames and sound, which turned the Web into a black hole for people with visual problems.

To keep that from happening again, the Web's standards-setting body, the World Wide

Web Consortium, has created an initiative to make the Web accessible, which in some cases is as simple as making sure a descriptive "alternative" text block is attached to an audio or video clip.

"If you don't have captions, you just lost everyone who can't hear it, whether they're deaf or just don't have their speakers turned on," project director Judy Brewer says.

Not getting the full impact of the latest Britney Spears fan page isn't a major loss, but leaving those descriptions out can have major implications for some users. Web-based grocery delivery services are an excellent example. For people in wheelchairs, those with speech difficulties and the deaf, being able to shop online is a major boon.

Which makes it all the more frustrating for those left out, says Jackie Brand of San Rafael, Calif., who founded the Alliance for Technology Access. Grocery sites "just don't quite work if you don't have vision," so the sight-impaired have to hire someone to go online and read screens for them.

Then there are the crossover projects, which with little tweaking turn from cool toys to indispensable tools. Among the techies at Netscape, Mark Stern's Wyndtell communications device looks like just another two-way pager. But it is an integral part of his workday, says the director of application architecture and design, who is deaf.

The Wyndtell, from Wynd Communications, can send and receive text messages and send a text message as a fax. Users also can type notes and have them sent as a text page.

"I sometimes think of it as a Swiss Army knife, with many different tools to contact different people using different methods of communication," Stern says.

"That way, I am in control and can choose how I want to communicate. It's very empowering."

*Source:* Weise, E. (2000, July 25). Devices free workers from disabilities. *USA Today.* [on-line serial]. Available: www.usatoday.com/life/cyber/tech/review/crh333.htm.

required all states to develop programs that provided assistive technology-related services for individuals with disabilities. An amendment to the Tech Act in 1994 required states to engage in six explicit activities to ensure access to assistive technology devices and services.

- The Telecommunications Accessibility Enhancement Act of 1988 required that the federal telecommunications system be fully accessible to hearing- and speech-impaired individuals.
- The Americans with Disabilities Act of 1990 required that the public and private sector provide accommodations to persons with disabilities.
- The Individuals with Disabilities Education Act (IDEA) amendments of 1997 mandated that Individualized Education Program (IEP) teams consider whether a child requires assistive technology devices and services to receive a free and appropriate public education.

Focus 3: Identify and provide examples of issues that should be considered when attempting to identify appropriate assistive technology devices and services.

- User characteristics such as user age, gender, and desire for independence should be considered.
- Technology features such as the potential to enhance user performance levels, ease of use, transportability, and comparability with other devices should be considered.

- Family concerns such as the effect on family interaction patterns and degree of expectations for independence should be considered.
- Cultural factors such as compatibility of the device with cultural values, extent to which the device calls attention to the user in social and public settings, and the developmental expectations for the acquisition of skills should be considered.
- Service system issues such as cost, protection from theft and damage, and training should be considered.

Focus 4: Identify the four components of matching theory that may affect the choice of an individual with disabilities to use assistive technology.

- Rate of reinforcement
- Quality of reinforcement
- Response effort
- Immediacy of reinforcement

Focus 5: Describe what is meant by universal design and discuss how is it different from assistive technology.

- Universal design refers to the process of creating mass market products that, from the outset, accommodate the widest spectrum of users, including those with disabilities. Universal design is different from assistive technology, in which the focus is on providing individuals with disabilities with modifications that will allow them to access products or activities.

*References*

Assistive technology helps students overcome physical limitations (1998, December). *T.H.E. Journal, 26*(5), 43.

Biegel, A. (2000). Assistive technology assessment: More than the device. *Intervention in School and Clinic, 35*(4), 237–243.

Cavalier, A., & Brown, C. (1998). From passivity to participation: The transformational possibilities of speech-recognition technology. *Teaching Exceptional Children, 30*(6), 60–65.

Demchak, M., & Downing, J. (1996). The preschool child. In J. Downing (Ed.), *Including students with severe and multiple disabilities in typical classrooms* (pp. 63–82). Baltimore: Paul H. Brookes.

Gilson, B., & Huss, D. (1995). Mobility: Getting where you want to go. In K. Flippo, K. Inge, & M. Barcus (Eds.), *Assistive technology: A resource for school, work, and community* (pp. 87–103). Baltimore: Paul H. Brookes.

Herrnstein, R. J. (1961). Relative and absolute strength of response as a function of frequency of reinforce-

ment. *Journal of the Experimental Analysis of Behavior, 4,* 266–267.

Horner, R., & Day, H. M. (1991). The effects of response efficiency on functionally equivalent competing behaviors. *Journal of Applied Behavior Analysis, 24,* 719–732.

Krebs, D., Lembeck, W., & Fishman, S. (1988). Acceptability of the NYU number 1 child-sized body-powered hand. *Archives of Physical and Medical Rehabilitation, 69,* 137–141.

Lahm, E., & Nickels, B. (1999). What do you know? *Teaching Exceptional Children, 32*(1), 56–63.

Lane, S., & Mistrett, S. (1996). Play and assistive technology issues for infants and young children with disabilities: A preliminary examination. *Focus on Autism & Other Developmental Disabilities, 11*(2), 96–104.

Lee, B. (1993). *Reasonable accommodation under the Americans with Disabilities Act.* Horsham, PA: LRP Publications.

Mace, F., Neef, N., Shade, D., & Mauro, B. (1994). Limited matching on concurrent-schedule reinforcement of academic behavior. *Journal of Applied Behavior Analysis, 27*(4), 585–596.

Mace, F., Neef, N., Shade, D., & Mauro, B. (1996). Effects of problem difficulty and reinforcer quality on time allocated to concurrent arithmetic problems. *Journal of Applied Behavior Analysis, 29*(1), 11–24.

Mace, F., & Roberts, M. (1993). Factors affecting the selection of behavioral treatments. In J. Reichle & D. Wacker (Eds.), *Communicative approaches to the management of challenging behavior.* Baltimore: Paul H. Brookes.

McDowell, J. (1988). Matching theory in natural human environments. *Behavior Analyst, 11,* 95–109.

Mondak, P. (2000). The Americans with disabilities act and information technology access. *Focus on Autism & Other Developmental Disabilities, 15*(1), 43–51.

Neef, N. A., Mace, R. C., & Shade, D. (1993). Impulsivity in students with serious emotional disturbance: The interactive effects of reinforcer rate, delay and quality. *Journal of Applied Behavior Analysis, 26*(1), 37–52.

Parette, H. (1997). Assistive technology devices and services. *Education and Training in Mental Retardation and Developmental Disabilities, 32*(4), 267–280.

Parette, H., & Hourcade, J. (1997). Family issues and assistive technology needs: A sampling of state practices. *Journal of Special Education Technology, 13,* 27–43.

Philips, B., & Zhao, H. (1993). Predictors of assistive technology abandonment. *Assistive Technology, 5*(1), 36–45.

Radell, U. (1997). Augmentative and alternative communication assessment strategies: Seating and positioning. In S. Glennen & D. DeCoste (Eds.), *Handbook of augmentative and alternative communication* (pp. 193–241). San Diego, CA: Singular.

Reichle, J., & Johnston, S. (1999). Teaching the conditional use of communicative requests to two school-aged children with severe developmental disabilities. *Language, Speech, and Hearing Services in the Schools, 30*(4), 324–334.

Riemer-Reiss, M., & Wacker, R. (2000). Factors associated with assistive technology discontinuance among individuals with disabilities. *Journal of Rehabilitation, 66*(3), 44–50.

Rose, D. (2000). Universal design for learning. *Journal of Special Education Technology, 15*(1), 67–70.

Tewey, B. P., Barnicle, K., & Perr, A. (1994). The wrong stuff. *Mainstream, 19*(2), 19–23.

Wehmeyer, M. (1999). Assistive technology and students with mental retardation: Utilization and barriers. *Journal of Special Education Technology, 14*(1), 48–58.

Weise, E. (2000, July 25). Devices free workers from disabilities. *USA Today* [on-line serial]. Available:. www.usatoday.com/life/cyber/tech/review/crh333. htm.

# 7

## *Positive Behavioral Support*

*Focusing on why a student engages in problem behavior allows teachers to be more effective in developing behavioral support programs.*

*Amber displayed self-injury as early as 13 months of age.... She would hit the bridge of her nose with her full milk bottle, leaving it red and swollen. By two years of age, Amber was banging her head so hard that she caused large, swollen red patches on her forehead.... With serious injuries mounting up, she began to target her hits at her shunt implant, a behavior we and her neurologist considered life-threatening due to the danger of dislodging or damaging the shunt....I was now sleeping with my arms wrapped tight around her all night to prevent nightly head banging episodes.... I was desperate. Not only were her self-injurious behaviors dangerous to her health, they were interfering with her educational goals and threatened her quality of life. (VanDuser & Phelan, 1993, pp. 77–78)*

Persons with severe disabilities sometimes exhibit serious problem behaviors such as self-injury, aggression toward others, and property destruction. Amber's severe self-injurious behavior and the desperation of her grandmother as she attempted to care for her illustrate the substantial impact that such behaviors can have on individuals and their caregivers and families. This chapter will provide information about the prevalence and impact of such behaviors, provide an overview of the conceptual foundations of positive behavioral supports, and describe the assessment and programmatic strategies that can be used to support individuals engaging in such behaviors.

## Prevalence of Severe Problem Behaviors

> **Focus 1**
> What are some of the effects that engaging in problem behaviors can have on individuals with severe disabilities and their families?

Research has been conducted with different groups of people in various settings to attempt to determine how often problem behaviors are exhibited by children and adults with severe disabilities. Differences in the types of participants, definitions of behaviors, and other methods used in this research make it difficult to draw hard-and-fast conclusions. However, the results of some of the larger and more carefully conducted of these investigations provide some reasonable estimates. Studies in California and the northwest of England, primarily involving adults, found that 6 to 14 percent of persons exhibited one or more types of self-injury, aggression, or property destruction (Borthwick-Duffy, 1994; Emerson, 1995; Qureshi; 1994). Horner, Diemer, and Brazeau (1992) surveyed 162 teachers of 1,535 school-aged students with severe disabilities in the state of Oregon. The teachers reported that 12 percent, or 184 of the students, exhibited significant problem behaviors, with 59 percent of that subgroup exhibiting multiple types of behaviors (e.g., self-injury and aggression). In addition, research has found that the greater the impairment, the more likely is the occurrence of problem behaviors in individuals with severe disabilities (Emerson, 1995).

A number of studies have demonstrated a relationship between problem behaviors and such things as where people live and the severity of their disabilities. Children and adults living in more restrictive living arrangements such as large institutional settings and group homes are more likely to exhibit such behaviors in comparison with those living in less restrictive settings such as parental homes or semi-independent apartment living (Borthwick-Duffy, 1994; Bruininks, Olson, Larson, & Lakin, 1994). This type of finding is usually interpreted to indicate the end result of a process in which persons exhibiting more severe problem behaviors are admitted and readmitted to more restrictive settings (Emerson, 1995).

## *Life Impact*

As exemplified in the vignette about Amber, severe problem behaviors can have a variety of negative physical, social, educational, and economic consequences. Self-injurious and aggressive behaviors of children and adults with severe disabilities can result in significant pain, injury, and emotional stress, both for the persons themselves and for the families and staff providing support to them (Bromley & Emerson, 1995). Participation in schools, work environments, residential programs, and other community settings may be jeopardized, and as mentioned above, there may be increased risk for readmission to public residential facilities (Borthwick-Duffy, Eyman, & White, 1987; Jacobson, 1982; Schroeder, Rojahn, & Oldenquist, 1991). Providing necessary staffing, programmatic, and medical support results in greatly increased costs. A study by the National Institutes of Health in 1991 found that the annual cost of services for people with mental retardation in the United States who exhibit self-injury, aggression, or property destruction exceeds $3.5 *billion* per year (NIH, 1991). Along with the additional costs, a major concern is that such behaviors may place persons with severe disabilities at greater risk for abusive treatment by support staff (Rusch, Hall, & Griffin, 1986).

## *A Shift in Perspective on Providing Behavioral Support*

Given the challenges posed by severe problem behaviors, it is not surprising that professionals such as teachers and school personnel consistently identify help in managing such behaviors as their primary technical assistance need (Horner et al., 1992; Reichle, 1990). For many years school- and community-based intervention strategies have predominantly revolved around reinforcement of appropriate behaviors, punishment of problem behaviors, and exclusion strategies (Repp & Singh, 1990). More recently, concern with the lack of effectiveness and the reactive and restrictive aspects of such procedures has led to a more positively oriented and comprehensive approach (Horner et al., 1990; Meyer & Evans, 1989). This approach includes, in part, an emphasis on early intervention and prevention, access to appropriate normalized activities and lifestyle, provision of good instruction on adaptive skills, interventions involving multiple components, and an emphasis on careful functional assessment as a basis for selecting and implementing intervention and support strategies (Dunlap et al., 1993; Neef & Iwata, 1994). Together these components have frequently come to be referred to as positive behavioral support (PBS; Carr et al., 1999; Koegel, Koegel, & Dunlap, 1996). Describing this approach and its key components will be the focus of the remainder of this chapter.

## Key Concepts and Definitions

> *Focus 2*
> What are the critical features of current approaches to positive behavioral support (PBS)?

### Whose Problem Is It Anyway?

It is interesting to examine the different terms that have been used to describe problem behaviors in clinical practice and research literature over the years. For example, such behaviors used to frequently be labeled as "maladaptive." However, in more recent times it has become clear that such troubling behaviors may indeed be very adaptive for the persons exhibiting them, as they may result in achievement of various desired outcomes (e.g., getting out of an undesired situation, gaining social attention/interaction). Currently, a range of terms is used, including difficult behaviors (Lovett, 1996), destructive behaviors (Thompson & Gray, 1994), and challenging behaviors (Emerson, 1995). This chapter employs the term problem behavior, as an indication that a wide range of behaviors may be considered a problem by various people, given a particular situation or context.

This leads to an issue that has frequently been examined from conceptual and philosophical points of view, that is, *who* decides what is a problem behavior, and therefore in need of intervention and support? Clearly there are some behaviors, such as the severe self-injury exhibited by Amber (described above), that create such potential or actual physical danger or damage to individuals or the environment that it is clear they need to be addressed to maintain health and safety. However, there may be a broad range of other behaviors that fall into more of a "gray area," with different persons in an individual's life (parents, teachers) having different perspectives on the need for intervention (Kazdin, 2001). For example, a student who frequently rocks while sitting in a chair, or emits loud vocalizations in regular classroom settings, may not be physically hurting anyone, but his or her behavior may have other potential negative effects on social interactions or academic learning that would be of concern. Most researchers and clinicians have recommended that decisions about the need for intervention and support be made by groups of relevant persons, which should include the individual with severe disabilities to the greatest extent possible (Sprague, 1994).

***Severity of Behavior versus Intensity of Intervention.***     It is typically recommended that the intrusiveness or aversiveness of potential interventions be matched to the severity of the behavior, and that interventions follow a least-to-most hierarchy in terms of intrusiveness or aversiveness (Bailey, Wolery, & Sugai, 1988; Kazdin, 2001). That is, more extreme interventions such as physical restraint or corporal punishment should only be considered in situations involving truly dangerous self-injurious or aggressive behavior, and only after less intrusive or restrictive interventions have been competently and exhaustively attempted. In addition, any more intrusive or aversive interventions must be carried out in the context of strategies designed to develop and positively reinforce alternative appropriate behaviors (Alberto & Troutman, 1999; Lovaas & Favell, 1987; Van Houten et al.,

1988). In making such decisions it is critical that team members such as parents and family members, researchers, and clinicians become knowledgeable about the rules and regulations that govern the use of intervention procedures at federal, state, and local levels.

## What's in a Name? Positive Behavioral Support

Like terms for problem behavior, labels for strategies for coping with such behaviors have changed over the years. In the past, terms such as *behavior modification* and *behavior management* were frequently used in the literature and in practice. As mentioned above, in more recent years terms such as *nonaversive behavioral support, comprehensive behavioral support,* and *positive behavioral support* have become more common (Horner et al., 1990; Meyer & Evans, 1989; O'Neill, Vaughn, & Dunlap, 1998; Repp & Singh, 1990). More than just different labels for the same thing, these new terms reflect true changes in perspectives and approaches for supporting children and adults exhibiting problem behaviors. As opposed to identifying interventions to do *to* people, such terms denote a broader, more collaborative approach to working *with* individuals to try to understand and meet their needs.

## Current Definitions and Features of Positive Behavioral Support

Window 7.1 presents several basic descriptions or definitions of positive behavioral support. These and other authors have elaborated on the critical common themes or features of this approach.

***A Broadened Perspective on Outcomes of Behavioral Support.***    A primary goal of behavior modification and management procedures has been the reduction in the frequency, intensity, and/or duration of targeted problem behaviors (Kazdin, 2001). Although

**WINDOW 7.1 • *Sample Definitions of Positive Behavioral Support (PBS)***

- "Positive behavioral support refers to the broad enterprise of helping people develop and engage in adaptive, socially desirable behaviors and overcome destructive and stigmatizing responding" (Koegel, Koegel, & Dunlap, 1996, p. xiii).
- "Positive behavior support is a values-driven approach to solving problems that educators can use effectively across a variety of settings" (Bambara & Knoster, 1998, p. 1).
- "The goal of PBS is to apply behavioral principles in the community in order to reduce problem behaviors and build appropriate behaviors that result in durable change and a rich lifestyle" (Carr et al., 1999, p. 3).
- "A positive behavioral supports approach emphasizes the use of a collaborative problem-solving process to develop individualized interventions that stress prevention of problem behaviors through the provision of effective educational programming" (Janney & Snell, 2000, p. 2).

change in problem behavior is a critical outcome, proponents of PBS have in addition emphasized the need to look at the broader impact of behavioral support in terms of changes in educational, residential, vocational, and social outcomes (Horner et al., 1990; Sugai et al., 2000). That is, is the person more physically and socially integrated in their school, work, home, and community settings? Do they appear to be getting more enjoyment and satisfaction out of their day-to-day lives?

***Functional Assessment: Support Based on a Thorough Understanding of a Person's Situation.***    One of the most significant components of PBS is the refocusing of attention on understanding the full range of setting, antecedent, and consequence variables that are related to a person's problem behaviors (Iwata et al., 1994; Repp & Horner, 1999). Recent years have seen a literal explosion of writing, research, and materials in the area of functional assessment (Johnston & O'Neill, 2001; Witt, Daly, & Noell, 2000). This resurgence is exemplified by the inclusion of language in the reauthorized Individuals with Disabilities Education Act (IDEA) that specifically requires functional behavioral assessments in particular situations. The basic theme is that we have no business intervening significantly in someone's life unless we first have as clear an understanding as possible of the range of things that may be positively and negatively influencing their behavior (Janney & Meyer, 2000; O'Neill et al., 1997). For example, individuals who have difficulty communicating in conventional ways may engage in problem behavior to express what they want and need; that is, the behavior may serve a communicative function or purpose (Durand, 1990). Based on such assessment information, support plans that make sense can then be developed and implemented (Bambara & Knoster, 1999).

***A Focus on Preventive and Educative Supports.***    Previous research on and application of behavior interventions have been characterized as overly reactive, with an emphasis on negative consequences (i.e., punishment) when problem behaviors occurred (Carr et al., 1999; Horner et al., 1990). Although both positive and negative consequences have a significant role to play, PBS places a heavy emphasis on strategies to prevent the occurrence of problem behaviors and to teach and promote adaptive behaviors that can serve as positive alternatives for a person. Prevention may focus on changes in medical supports, such as treatment for allergies or changes in medication levels, and educational and activity variables, such as changes in curriculum or instructional strategies, or job requirements (Luiselli & Cameron, 1998). In the area of positive alternative behaviors the greatest emphasis has been on teaching communicative skills and behaviors (e.g., use of speech, signing, electronic devices) to allow persons to indicate what they need and want, instead of engaging in problem behaviors to achieve such outcomes (Carr et al., 1994; Reichle & Wacker, 1993).

***Comprehensive Multielement Support Plans.***    Applied behavior analysis has always emphasized the importance of the context in which behavior occurs, including the broader and more specific environmental events preceding behavior, and the events or consequences that follow it (Baer, Wolf, & Risley, 1968). Positive behavioral support has built on this approach and added a values-based component with regard to looking at the places people live, what they spend their time doing, and their social relationships, and how those things can affect a person's behavior. The variables that affect problem behaviors can range from very specific, such as the type of job task assigned in a work setting, to very broad, such as the mix of roommate temperaments and personalities in a home setting. The field has been moving away from what we might call the "magic bullet" approach, where parents and support providers attempt to identify a single technique or strategy that will make the difference or solve a problem. Instead, there has been increased recognition of the fact that situations involving lengthy and complex histories of problem behaviors will require a comprehensive multielement approach (Repp & Horner, 1999). That is, along with the preventive, educative, and consequence components described above, support providers may need to also understand and address broader physical/medical and lifestyle issues in home, school, work, and other community settings in order to eliminate the conditions that contribute to problem behavior (Meyer & Evans, 1989).

***Evaluation of Support Outcomes.***    Applied behavior analysis has a lengthy history of emphasizing concrete and objective methods of measuring changes in behavior related to support and intervention (Baer, Wolf, & Risley, 1968, 1987). This continues to be a critical component of PBS. It is important to have data and information that can allow judgments about the effectiveness of support and guide decisions about changes that may be needed to maximize its impact. However, as mentioned above, PBS includes evaluation of a range of outcomes including, but not limited to, changes in problem behavior. These include effects on a person's living, work, and leisure activities, and their overall happiness and satisfaction (Wolf, 1978).

## *Models and Strategies for Conducting Functional Assessments and Providing Comprehensive Positive Behavioral Support*

---

**Focus 3**
What are the main components of a comprehensive behavioral support plan?

---

PBS has developed to the point where there are substantial similarities across different authors' models for conducting assessments and providing support. The main components common to these models are described below.

### *Initial Lifestyle Assessment and Planning*

Either before or as part of a comprehensive functional assessment, many authors and practitioners have recommended that consideration be given to assessment and planning concerning broader lifestyle issues and concerns (Janney & Snell, 2000; O'Neill et al., 1997). What are the goals of the person with regard to school, work, and community outcomes and activities? How are those goals going to be met, and what kinds of supports will be necessary to do so? This type of planning will typically require input from parents, family members, friends, neighbors, support staff, and other community members (Mount and Zwernik, 1988). Such groups can meet with the individual in question, usually with a group leader to facilitate the process, and identify relevant goals and strategies for achieving them. In some cases this type of planning will identify lifestyle factors that, when changed, will create positive effects with regard to problem behaviors, thus decreasing the need for more focused and elaborate assessment and intervention strategies (Kincaid, 1996; Risley, 1996). Examples of this type of lifestyle planning are presented in Chapters 10 and 11.

***Example of Behavioral Support: Marco.*** Marco is a 16-year-old who has been labeled as having severe mental retardation and autism. He communicates mainly via gestures, a few formal signs, and picture arrays to which he can point to indicate wants and needs. Marco is currently living at home with his parents and two younger siblings, and attends his local high school. He spends about half of his time working on his IEP goals in regular education classes, and the other half in various school jobs and community-based instructional activities. His family and teachers are concerned about his screaming, self-injury, and aggressive behavior (hitting and/or kicking others). They conducted two meetings following the Big Picture Planning process delineated by McDonnell, Mathot-Buckner, & Ferguson (1996). This allowed them to identify Marco's current situation and future preferences with regard to living situation, possible work activities, social relationships, transportation and community access, and resource management. This served as the foundation for identifying a range of IEP goals and objectives that could be pursued in both school and community settings. Based on this information and additional functional assessment activities (see below), a variety of support and intervention strategies were implemented for Marco.

## Functional Assessment and Analysis

As described above, there has been a tremendous resurgence of interest in strategies for conducting functional assessments of problem behaviors as a basis for developing and implementing support plans (Repp & Horner, 1999). Conceptual and technological development of such strategies has been the focus of literally hundreds of workshops, journal articles, books, manuals, CD-ROMs, and other materials (Johnston & O'Neill, 2001). Although approaches may differ with regard to specific details and methods, there is general agreement on the main critical components of the process. These include gathering relevant information via a variety of means, developing hypotheses about the variables influencing the behaviors and the functions or purposes they serve, and using these hypotheses as a basis for the development and implementation of support plan strategies (Foster-Johnson & Dunlap, 1993).

Although speakers and authors may sometimes use the terms functional assessment and functional analysis relatively interchangeably, there has been a developing consensus on the need to differentiate between these procedures. *Functional assessment* is now considered to be a broader, more inclusive term that refers to a range of activities in which someone may engage to gather information to improve the effectiveness and efficiency of a behavior support plan (O'Neill et al., 1997). These activities might include interviewing people, having them complete rating scales, checklists, or questionnaires, or conducting systematic observations in particular situations. *Functional analysis* is a subset of these procedures that comes under the broader functional assessment umbrella. A functional analysis entails conducting controlled systematic presentations of environmental events (antecedents and/or consequences for problem behaviors) and collecting data to determine their effects on problem behaviors. These presentations are usually carried out in the context of a structured experimental design, in order to allow for clear conclusions about the relationships among environmental events and the problem behaviors (Iwata, Vollmer, & Zarcone, 1990; Wacker et al., 1999).

***Functional Assessment Outcomes.***    O'Neill et al. (1997) identified five major outcomes of the assessment process. These are (1) identification of the full range of problem behaviors of concern, and how they may be related to or interact with one another; (2) identification of the broader setting events and more immediate antecedent events leading to problem behaviors; (3) identification of the outcomes or consequences that appear to be reinforcing and maintaining the behaviors; (4) synthesis of this information into succinct summary statements or hypotheses; and (5) some level of systematic observational data that can confirm or disconfirm the hypotheses. Again, the main idea is that with this information in hand, support providers and caregivers can choose strategies that will be logically related to *why* the behaviors are occurring, or the functions they are serving for the individual.

***Functional Assessment Methods.***    Functional assessment methods are generally classified into three main categories. *Indirect* or *informant assessments* involve gathering information from relevant persons (parents, teachers, the "target person" him/herself) via interviews, rating scales, checklists, and/or questionnaires. Table 7.1 presents a list and description of commonly used tools of this type and sample items or questions from each. Although research has indicated that such instruments and procedures can provide valid and important information, it has also indicated that they may also provide information that is less trustworthy and helpful (Johnston & O'Neill, 2001). The basic message is that this type of data gathering can be critical, but should rarely be relied upon as the sole source of information in the assessment process. These approaches can help in developing initial hypotheses about behavior, which can then be validated via additional procedures. It is critical that the child or adult who is the focus of the assessment be a part of this process, if it makes sense. If she or he has the social and communicative skills to participate in an interview type of interaction with an appropriate person, this input would be very important to paint a complete picture of the situation.

Systematic observation strategies involve recording structured data on the occurrence of behavior and related environmental events during routines and activities in typical settings such as classrooms and homes. A wide range of procedures for collecting such data has been described in the applied behavior analysis literature (Lalli & Goh, 1993). These include such things as antecedent-behavior-consequence (A-B-C) recording, interval recording, scatterplot recording, and other formats, such as the Functional Assessment Observation form (Lalli & Goh, 1993; O'Neill et al., 1997). Figure 7.1 presents an example of an A-B-C type of format in which different antecedents, behaviors, and consequences can be noted during ongoing time periods. Each behavior episode and its related

**TABLE 7.1**  *Tools and Instruments That Have Been Used for Indirect/Informant Functional Assessment*

| Tool/Instrument | Description | Sample Items |
|---|---|---|
| Motivation Assessment Scale (MAS) (Durand & Crimmins, 1992) | Sixteen-item rating scale focusing on functions of an individual's behavior (attention, escape from undesired activities, obtaining tangibles, and sensory stimulation); used primarily with individuals with more severe developmental disabilities | 2. Does the behavior occur following a request to perform a difficult task?<br>4. Does the behavior occur whenever you stop attending to this person? |
| Problem Behavior Questionnaire (PBQ) (Lewis, Scott, & Sugai, 1994) | Fifteen-item rating scale focusing on functions of behavior in classroom settings (peer and teacher attention, escape from undesired activities); used primarily with students in regular education classroom settings | 4. When the problem behavior occurs do peers verbally respond or laugh at the student?<br>13. Will the student stop doing the problem behavior if you stop making requests or end an academic activity? |
| Functional Analysis Screening Tool (FAST) (Iwata, 1994) | Twenty-seven-item yes–no response scale focusing on functions of behavior; used primarily with individuals with more severe developmental disabilities | 4. The behavior often occurs when the person has not received much attention.<br>10. The behavior often occurs when you inform the person that s/he cannot have a certain item or engage in a particular activity. |
| Student-Assisted Functional Assessment Interview (Kern, Dunlap, Clarke, & Childs, 1994) | Fifty-two-item guideline for interviewing students to identify instructional and curricular variables that may influence problem behaviors in classroom settings | 1. When do you think you have the fewest problems with your behavior in school?<br>7. If you had the chance, what activities would you like to do that you don't have the opportunity to do now? |
| Functional Assessment Interview Form (FAI) (O'Neill et al., 1997) | Twenty-nine-section interview format to identify a range of physical, setting, antecedent, and consequence variables that may influence problem behavior | A2. Which of the behaviors described above are likely to occur together in some way (i.e., a chain or a sequence)?<br>C4. What *activities* are most and least likely to produce the behaviors? |

169

**FIGURE 7.1**   *Example of an Antecedent-Behavior-Consequence Format for Observational Data Collection*

| Time | Antecedents | | | Behavior(s) | | | Consequences/Responses | | | | Potential Function(s) | | | | |
|---|---|---|---|---|---|---|---|---|---|---|---|---|---|---|---|
| | Work Request | Alone/No Attention | Crowded/Noisy | Scream | Hit/Kick | Head Hit | Ignore | Redirect | Time-Out | Reprimand | Get Attention | Self-Stimulation | Escape Requests/Situation | Get Item/Activity | Other |
| 9:00–9:30 | 1 2 | | | 1 2 | | | 1 2 | | | | | | 1 2 | | |
| 9:30–10:00 | | | | | | | | | | | | | | | |
| 10:00–10:30 | | 3 4 | | | | 3 4 | | 3 4 | | | | 3 4 | | | |
| 10:30–11:00 | | | 5 | | 5 | | 5 | | | | | | 5 | | |

antecedents (what happens before the behavior), consequences (what happens after the be-havior), and functions (why the behavior occurs, or motivation) are noted by a different number. These data collection formats share common strategies in that they typically in-volve recording (i.e., marking on a data sheet) the occurrence of relevant antecedents to the problem behaviors, the behaviors themselves, and the consequences or results that follow them. These data can then be analyzed to identify consistent relationships among problem behaviors and categories of environmental events (Repp, 1999). This information is used to help decide on the accuracy and validity of hypotheses initially developed from indirect assessments.

The third major category is *experimental functional analysis,* which was described above (Iwata, Vollmer, Zarcone, & Rodgers, 1993). In this procedure environmental events are presented or withdrawn during relatively short sessions (10 to 15 minutes) to assess their influence on behavior. These might include obtaining desired items or activities, es-caping from aversive situations (e.g., work requests), or obtaining social interaction. During these sessions observational data are collected on the frequency of problem behav-iors in the different conditions. For example, antecedent events may be manipulated, such as the presentation of particular tasks or activities such as listening to music or doing a math worksheet. Alternatively, different social responses (e.g., social attention) can also be provided when the person engages in a problem behavior, to assess whether it increases the likelihood that the behavior will occur. Typically, these kinds of manipulations are systematically controlled in order to develop the best possible explanation of what variables are contributing to the occurrence of a problem behavior and why a person is engaging in it. These types of functional analyses have been used both to help develop and to validate hypotheses about the functions or purposes of problem behaviors (Wacker et al., 1999).

***Is There a Best Approach?***   There has been considerable debate about the most effective and efficient methods for conducting functional assessments. As mentioned above, indirect assessments may not always provide valid information. Some authors have contended that the experimental functional analysis approach provides the most precise and reliable data (Iwata et al., 1990). Others have expressed concerns about these approaches, such as safety problems and the need for trained personnel and resources to be able to carry them out effectively (Sturmey, 1995). To help respond to these concerns there is a substantial need for further research on the comparative validity of different assessment methods (Cunningham & O'Neill, 2000). In addition, recently enacted legal requirements have resulted in increasing logistical demands for assessment services in educational and other service settings (Sugai et al., 2000). This has created a substantial challenge for service providers as they attempt to identify and implement procedures that will be effective but can also be done within the time and resource constraints present in schools and other service settings (Drasgow, Yell, Bradley, & Shriner, 1999). Until further research and practice produce additional data-based guidance, the best approach is likely to be one that is individualized to particular situations, begins with less time- and resource-intensive strategies, and moves on to more demanding procedures as needed (Horner & Carr, 1997; Johnston & O'Neill, 2001).

***Final Hypotheses/Summary Statements.***   As described above, the final outcome of the assessment process should be one or more hypotheses that characterize the range of situations and functions concerning an individual's behavior. Table 7.2 presents examples of such hypotheses or summary statements that include broader setting events, more immediate antecedent factors, the different types of behaviors of concern, and the functions or purposes they appear to serve in those situations (O'Neill et al., 1997). Note that there are multiple statements for some persons, illustrating the fact that certain behaviors may occur in one situation for one reason, but similar or other behaviors may occur in other situations for other reasons. It is critical to make sure that the full range of situations is identified so that they can all be taken into consideration in designing and implementing support strategies. For example, with Marco, situations involving task or activity demands, peer interactions, and the desire to control conversations were all problematic and involved multiple types of problem behaviors and motivations.

***Functional Assessment as an Ongoing Process.***   It is important to keep in mind that functional assessment is not something that occurs once and never has to be repeated. Like all people, individuals with severe disabilities may experience changes over time with regard to their situations, preferences, and behavior. Therefore, various aspects of the assessment process may need to be revisited periodically to ensure that assessment outcomes and support strategies continue to be relevant and up to date (O'Neill et al., 1997).

**TABLE 7.2   *Examples of Hypotheses/Summary Statements Concerning Problem Behaviors***

| Student | Behaviors | Hypotheses/Summary Statements |
|---|---|---|
| Monique | Cursing, property destruction, aggression | When Monique has not had much sleep, and is asked to do a nonpreferred activity in her work setting, she will curse, tear up her work materials, and hit her job coach in order to escape the task demands. |
| Jackie | Spitting, hitting | When Jackie wants to maintain access to the cassette player at the end of an activity, she will spit at and/or hit the teacher in order to maintain access to the music. |
| Randy | Rocking, drumming | In situations with low levels of activity or attention, Randy will rock back and forth and "drum" on things in order to obtain internal stimulation. |
| Marco | Screaming, self-injury, aggression | When Marco's medication levels are low, and he is asked to do independent seatwork, he is likely to begin screaming and/or hitting himself to get teacher attention. |
| | | When Marco has fought with his siblings at home, and is teased by his co-workers, he will curse at and/or hit them in order to stop the aversive teasing. |
| | | When Marco wants to control the conversation during break time at work, he will scream at and/or hit his co-workers to try to get them to talk about what he wants to. |

## Developing and Implementing Assessment-Based Comprehensive Behavior Support Plans

A critical issue that has arisen in the field is that practitioners may be able to carry out an effective behavioral assessment, but often struggle with how to use that information to bridge the gap to developing and implementing a plan. Although a variety of frameworks have been developed to help practitioners move through this process (Bambara & Knoster, 1998; Witt et al., 2000), they are all based on several basic principles (O'Neill et al., 1997).

***Plans Must Be Based on Assessment Results.***   The whole point of functional assessment is to allow us to understand the things that influence a person's problem behavior so that we can make a difference. Consequently, the hypotheses or summary statements must be incorporated into the plan and guide the selection of strategies that are used with the individual.

***Behavior Support Plans Typically Should Focus on Our Behavior.***   Parents, teachers, and other caregivers may often want a consultant or expert to do something to or with a child or adult that results in stopping the occurrence of the problem behavior. However, in most cases behavior support plans will mainly describe the changes that parents, teachers, and others must make in the environment or their own behavior to reduce the likelihood of problem behavior. Behavior support is about what *we* do differently to construct an environment that supports appropriate behavior and allows a person to be more successful. This does not mean that support shouldn't involve things that might have a more direct effect on an individual (e.g., counseling, medication). However, even these kinds of strategies will require support by a variety of other persons to be effective (e.g., driving the person to a therapy appointment or offering reminders to take medication).

***Plans Should Be Technically Sound.***     Behavior plans must be based on empirically established principles and procedures of applied behavior analysis (Baer, 1991; Horner, 1991). However, they must be comprehensive with regard to including strategies that aim at proactively *preventing* behaviors, as well as *reacting* to them when they occur. Proactive strategies can help make the behaviors irrelevant. For example, if the aversive work demands that have been contributing to a person's behavior can be removed or modified to be less aversive, then there will be no need for the person to engage in the behaviors. On the reactive side, it is important that, to the extent possible, teachers or caregivers do not reinforce the individual when she or he engages in problem behaviors (Lerman, Iwata, & Wallace, 1999).

***Plans Should Fit the Settings Where They Will Need to Be Implemented.***     In recent years, increasing attention has been paid to the factors that might influence whether support providers will implement the strategies called for in a plan. This can be thought of as the "goodness of fit" of a plan for parents or teachers. It is important to determine whether support providers have the values, skills, and resources to carry out the necessary strategies effectively (Albin, Lucyshyn, Horner, & Flannery, 1996). This highlights the need for all relevant persons to be involved in the assessment and plan development process. This allows parents, teachers, and others to provide input on what they think is most important and "do-able" within given settings and situations.

## The Competing Behavior Perspective

Based on previous work by Billingsley and Neel (1985) and Horner and Billingsley (1988), O'Neill et al. (1997) described a competing behavior model for laying out assessment results and guiding intervention and program development. This model involves delineating a given hypothesis/summary statement describing a problem behavior, and then doing two things: (1) identifying the *desired behavior* that a person should be exhibiting in a given situation (completing work, attending to the teacher), and (2) identifying at least one *appropriate alternative behavior* that the person could perform that would produce the same outcome as the problem behavior (asking for attention or a break from an activity). These behaviors have been referred to as "functional equivalents" to problem behaviors (Carr, 1988). The task of the group planning support is then to identify factors in a multitude of areas that will make the desired and alternative behaviors more likely to occur, and the problem behaviors less likely to occur. As described above, strategies need to be considered in four areas: broader setting events, more immediate antecedent events, teaching and/or prompting skills/behaviors, and consequences for appropriate and problem behaviors (Bambara & Knoster, 1998).

***Setting Event Interventions.*** In some respects the evaluation and management of broader setting events is still a technology in its infancy. There are good conceptual frameworks for how such events influence the likelihood of problem behaviors, and some examples of how interventions in such areas might be successful (Horner, Day, & Day, 1997). Horner, Vaughn, Day, and Ard (1996) delineated proactive and reactive strategies for dealing with influential setting events. These general strategies are outlined in Table 7.3, and specific examples for Marco are presented in Table 7.4. There is a great need for ongoing research in these areas to develop more effective assessment and intervention practices.

***More Immediate Antecedent Event Strategies.*** There is quite a range of strategies that fall into this more proactive category, some of which have received substantial empirical support (see examples for Marco in Table 7.4). For example, offering choices can help to mitigate problem behaviors in situations involving less preferred activities (Dunlap et al., 1994; Vaughn & Horner, 1997). Several studies have been done on behavioral momentum or high-probability request sequences, in which people are asked to respond to multi-

**TABLE 7.3**  *Proactive and Reactive Strategies for Dealing with Influential Setting Events*

| Strategy | Examples |
| --- | --- |
| Minimizing the likelihood of setting events (proactive) | Preventing the occurrence of problematic events, such as managing peer conflict at home or on the playground; ensuring adequate rest/sleep; treating and resolving medical problems (e.g., ear infections); adjusting levels of psychoactive medications |
| Neutralizing the effects of setting events (reactive) | Mitigating the influence of events that have already occurred, such as allowing a student a "cool-down" period (e.g., take a walk, listen to music) after a playground or bus altercation; providing medication to a student who is ill |
| Withholding stimuli that set off problem behaviors (reactive) | Minimizing or eliminating (at least temporarily) events that frequently lead to problem behaviors, such as not engaging in a demanding academic or work activity when someone is in an agitated state |
| Increase prompts for desired behavior (reactive) | Increasing prompts and reminders for appropriate alternative behaviors (e.g., signing to ask for a break) when it is known that that a person is in a problematic state |
| Increase value and quantity of reinforcers for desired behaviors (reactive) | Increasing the quantity and quality of rewards or reinforcement that will be made available for the occurrence of appropriate behaviors, such as letting a student know he can have 15 minutes of free time with the computer when usually he only gets 10 minutes of free time without the computer |

*Source:* Adapted from Horner, R. H., Vaughn, B. J., Day, H. M., & Ard, W. R. (1996). The relationship between setting events and problem behavior: Expanding our understanding of behavioral support. In L. K. Koegel, R. L. Koegel, & G. Dunlap (Eds.), *Positive behavioral support: Including people with difficult behavior in the community* (pp. 381–402). Baltimore: Paul H. Brookes.

**TABLE 7.4** *Summary of Behavioral Support Strategies for Marco*

*Setting Event Strategies*
• Increased doctor visits to check medication levels

*Antecedent Strategies*
• Preemptive/noncontingent social attention
• Proactive prompting to engage in appropriate social interactive behaviors

*Teaching/Promoting Alternative Behaviors*
• Teach hand-waving to recruit attention
• Sign "Stop" and walk away from teasing
• Use picture book to initiate social interactions

*Consequence Strategies*
• Honoring communicative responses
• Responses to social initiations/interactions
• Ignore/move away from inappropriate behavior
• Block and sit alone for aggressive behavior

*Crisis Management*
• Not applicable

*Data Collection/Evaluation*
• Ongoing A-B-C data collection
• Weekly meetings to review data and make programming decisions

ple requests to which they are likely to respond and get reinforced before being asked to do a task or activity that has been more problematic (Davis & Brady, 1993; Plaud & Gaither, 1996). There is a wide range of potential curricular and instructional modifications that fit into this category as well. Changes in task length, difficulty, content, and other variables can have positive effects on problem behaviors (Dunlap & Kern, 1993; Munk & Karsh, 1999). Several studies in recent years have examined the effects of providing access to preemptive or "noncontingent" reinforcement; that is, individuals are provided with periodic social attention or breaks from task demands in order to prevent the occurrence of problem behaviors to achieve those outcomes (Tucker, Sigafoos, & Bushell, 1998). Over time the schedules of reinforcement can be extended so it does not need to be so frequently provided. Lastly, two straightforward approaches include (1) simply to remove, if possible, the problematic stimuli that are setting off the problem behaviors (e.g., changing IEP goals to eliminate a problematic task/activity), and (2) to make sure to prompt appropriate alternative behaviors *before* the problem behaviors occur.

***Teaching/Prompting Appropriate Alternative Behaviors.*** This approach has received a great deal of attention from researchers and practitioners (Carr et al., 1994). The main focus for persons with severe disabilities has been on teaching social communicative behaviors that can replace and serve the same function as problem behaviors; this is known as functional communication training (Durand, 1990; see examples for Marco in Table 7.4). For example, an individual might be taught to use verbal phrases ("Please talk to me"), signs or gestures, or other alternative communication methods to request attention, a break, help with a task, or a desired item or activity. These responses are taught with typical modeling and prompting strategies. Initial reinforcement by honoring the requests is critical, as is trying to ensure that there is minimal or no reinforcement for problem behaviors (O'Neill & Sweetland-Baker, 2001). Over time, delays can be implemented so that requests don't have to honored by caregivers so quickly or frequently.

***Acceptable Consequences for Appropriate and Problem Behaviors.***    Although there has been less emphasis in recent years on reactive consequence strategies, they are still a critical component of a comprehensive plan (see examples for Marco in Table 7.4). Reinforcement for appropriate behaviors should be programmed in both more natural (e.g., responding to communicative requests) and more structured ways (e.g., point/token systems) as needed (Williams, Williams, & McLaughlin, 1989). As mentioned, research has demonstrated that reinforcement for problem behaviors must be minimized or prevented in order for other strategies to be maximally effective (Hagopian et al., 1998). Finally, appropriate, acceptable consequences for punishment and reduction of problem behavior should be considered (Iwata, 1988). These might include procedures such as reprimands, response cost, and time-out from reinforcement (O'Brien, 1989). There has been a massive volume of discussion and debate on this topic (Cipani, 1989; Harris & Handleman, 1990; Meyer & Evans, 1989; Repp & Singh, 1990). For example, Amber, who is mentioned in the initial vignette of this chapter, underwent a contingent electric shock program to suppress her severe self-injurious behavior; this program was very controversial among those providing support to her (VanDuser & Phelan, 1993). Support providers need to ensure that in making decisions about potentially intrusive and aversive procedures they are following (1) best practice guidelines for selecting and implementing such interventions (Lovaas & Favell, 1987; Van Houten et al., 1988), (2) full input from individuals with severe disabilities and their families and caregivers, and (3) all applicable legal guidelines and restrictions at local and state levels (Christian, Luce, & Larsson, 1992).

***Crisis/Emergency Support.***    Again, although most emphasis should be on proactive and educative procedures, even with appropriate positive strategies in place some individuals will sometimes exhibit behavior of such intensity or severity that it will be necessary to intervene in very intrusive ways, such as brief physical restraint (Carr et al., 1994; Walker, Colvin, & Ramsey, 1995). It is critical that such procedures be implemented only by support persons who have been thoroughly trained in their use, and that they are carried out in accord with all applicable legal and regulatory guidelines. It is very important that everyone involved keep in mind that the sole purpose of such procedures is the protection of the individual and others around him or her. These *are not* procedures that should be expected to bring about any positive behavior change (Carr et al., 1994; LaVigna & Donnellan, 1986).

***Data Collection/Evaluation.***    A long-standing hallmark of applied behavior analysis is ongoing collection of data or information that allows for decision making about the success of support plans (Brown & Snell, 2000; Westling & Fox, 2000; Young, West, & Mac-Farlane, 1994). There needs to be some type of ongoing data collection and review so that support providers can decide whether to maintain, modify, or terminate a support plan or one or more of its components (see examples for Marco in Table 7.4). It is very important that those persons responsible for collecting data (support staff, parents) are involved in regularly reviewing the summarized data and contributing to the decision-making process.

# Future Directions in Behavioral Support

> **Focus 4**
> What are two of the important future directions for positive behavioral support?

## Early Intervention and Lifestyle Factors as Interventions and Outcomes

It has become clear that broader lifestyle variables such as activity patterns and social relationships can be related to the likelihood of problem behaviors. Further empirical research and evaluation of clinical applications are needed to understand the impact of lifestyle issues as both interventions and outcomes (Risley, 1996). Ideally, such work will facilitate greater preventive efforts so that development of problem behaviors can be avoided, rather than dealing with them after they begin to occur (Dunlap & Fox, 1996; McGee & Daly, 1999; Reeve & Carr, 2000).

## Broader Perspectives on Implementing Behavioral Support

In recent years researchers and practitioners have begun to develop and implement broader system-wide approaches to behavioral support. For example, Sugai, Horner, and their colleagues (Sugai et al., 2000) have been running a federally funded national center on Positive Behavioral Interventions and Supports. The main focus of this center is to provide information, training, technical assistance, and research on school-wide systems for supporting the full range of students presenting behavioral challenges in the schools, including students with severe disabilities and those labeled as having emotional/behavioral disorders. Often referred to as *effective behavioral support* (EBS), this approach emphasizes the need for considering multiple systems within a school (school-wide, specific settings [playground, cafeteria], classroom, individual assessment-based programs) and how they need to be structured to support the full range of more and less behaviorally challenging students in school settings (Lewis & Sugai, 1999; Sugai & Horner, 1999). Demonstrations of the effectiveness of these comprehensive approaches are beginning to accumulate in the literature (Scott, 2001; Taylor-Greene et al., 1997), and provide important direction for future research and application.

## Continued Development of Functional Assessment Technology

As mentioned above, there are still a number of challenges that remain with regard to identifying the most effective and efficient functional assessment strategies in school, home, and community settings. Fortunately, this is an area receiving considerable attention from both researchers and practitioners (Neef & Iwata, 1994; Scotti & Kennedy, 2000). Down the road, support providers should expect to see fairly concrete recommendations concerning which types of assessment procedures will be effective and most easily carried out with which kinds of individuals and situations (Cunningham & O'Neill, 2000). In addition, new technology should become available to facilitate the functional assessment process in terms of both training and implementation (Liaupsin, Scott, & Nelson, 2001).

### Research into Practice: Where the Rubber Meets the Road

Recent years have seen a growing consensus concerning the development of a valid and effective set of principles and procedures comprising positive behavioral support (Carr et al., 1999; Koegel et al., 1996; Scotti & Meyer, 1999). However, a sizable gap still remains between the cutting edge in research and practice and what is actually available to many individuals with disabilities and their families (Schwartz, 1997). This problem is part of the larger issue of a lack of resources and services for individuals with developmental disabilities and their families (Davis, Abeson, & Lloyd, 1998; Lakin, 1998). However, short of a massive infusion of money and other resources, there are still a variety of avenues for attacking this problem. Better information can be disseminated to the general public concerning what they should expect with regard to competent behavioral services (Van Houten et al., 1988). Information on appropriate behavioral assessment and support services needs to be more effectively included in pre- and inservice training for a range of relevant professionals such as teachers and school psychologists (O'Neill, Johnson, Kiefer-O'Donnell, & McDonnell, 2001; Reichle et al., 1996; Vollmer & Northup, 1997). Finally, more training and information can be made available to parents and families to allow them to work effectively with professionals as they collaborate to support their children in home, school, and community settings (Fox, Vaughn, Dunlap, & Bucy, 1997; Vaughn et al., 1997).

## Conclusion

The development of the approach known as positive behavioral support represents a unique integration of philosophical values and the empirically based procedures of the science of applied behavior analysis (Durand, 1987; Sugai et al., 2000). This combination should allow researchers and practitioners to pursue important, socially valid goals for individuals with severe disabilities and their families, and do so from a solid grounding of effective principles and procedures.

## Focus Review

Focus 1: What are some of the impacts that engaging in problems behaviors can have on individuals with severe disabilities and their families?

- Admission and readmission to more restrictive settings
- Limited participation in home, work, and community settings
- Pain and injury to individuals and their caregivers

- Increased costs for medical and staffing support
- Increased risk for abusive treatment

Focus 2: What are the critical features of current approaches to positive behavioral support (PBS)?

- A broadened perspective on outcomes
- Functional assessment and understanding as a basis for support plans
- Focus on preventive/educative supports
- Comprehensive multielement support plans
- Evaluation of support outcomes

Focus 3: What are the main components of a comprehensive behavioral support plan?

- Setting event interventions
- Immediate antecedent interventions
- Teaching/prompting appropriate alternative behaviors
- Acceptable consequences for appropriate and problem behaviors
- Crisis/emergency support procedures
- Data collection and evaluation

Focus 4: What are two of the important future directions for positive behavioral support?

- Early intervention and lifestyle factors as interventions and outcomes
- Broader perspectives on implementing behavioral support
- Continued development of functional assessment technology
- Decreasing the gap between research and practice

## References

Alberto, P. A., & Troutman, A. C. (1999). *Applied behavior analysis for teachers* (5th ed.). Columbus, OH: Merrill.

Albin, R. W., Lucyshyn, J. M., Horner, R. H., & Flannery, K. B. (1996). Contextual fit for behavior support plans: A model for "goodness of fit." In L. K. Koegel, R. L. Koegel, & G. Dunlap (Eds.), *Positive behavioral support: Including people with difficult behavior in the community* (pp. 81–98). Baltimore: Paul H. Brookes.

Baer, D. M. (1991). The future of applied behavior analysis for people with severe disabilities: Commentary II. In L. H. Meyer, C. A. Peck, & L. Brown (Eds.), *Critical issues in the lives of people with severe disabilities* (pp. 613–615). Baltimore: Paul H. Brookes.

Baer, D. M., Wolf, M. M., & Risley, T. R. (1968). Some current dimensions of applied behavior analysis. *Journal of Applied Behavior Analysis, 1,* 91–97.

Baer, D. M., Wolf, M. M., & Risley, T. R. (1987). Some still-current dimensions of applied behavior analysis. *Journal of Applied Behavior Analysis, 20,* 313–327.

Bailey, D. B., Wolery, M., & Sugai, G. (1988). *Effective teaching: Principles and procedures of applied behavior analysis for exceptional students.* Boston: Allyn & Bacon.

Bambara, L. M., & Knoster, T. (1998). *Designing positive behavior support plans.* Washington, DC: American Association on Mental Retardation.

Billingsley, F. F., & Neel, R. S. (1985). Competing behaviors and their effects on skill generalization and maintenance. *Analysis and Intervention in Developmental Disabilities, 5,* 357–372.

Borthwick-Duffy, S. A. (1994). Prevalence of destructive behaviors: A study of aggression, self-injury, and property destruction. In T. Thompson & D. B. Gray, (Eds.), *Destructive behavior in developmen-*

*tal disabilities: Diagnosis and treatment* (pp. 3–23). Thousand Oaks, CA: Sage.

Borthwick-Duffy, S. A., Eyman, R. K., & White, J. F. (1987). Client characteristics and residential placement patterns. *American Journal of Mental Deficiency, 92,* 24–30.

Bromley, J., & Emerson, E. (1995). Beliefs and emotional reactions of care staff working with people with challenging behavior. *Journal of Intellectual Disability Research, 39,* 341–352.

Brown, F., & Snell, M. E. (2000). Measurement, analysis, and evaluation. In M. E. Snell & F. Brown (Eds.), *Instruction of students with severe disabilities* (5th ed.) (pp. 173–206). Columbus, OH: Merrill.

Bruininks, R. H., Olson, K. M., Larson, S. A., & Lakin, K. C. (1994). Challenging behaviors among persons with mental retardation in residential settings: Implications for policy, research, and practice. In T. Thompson & D. B. Gray, (Eds.), *Destructive behavior in developmental disabilities: Diagnosis and treatment* (pp. 24–48). Thousand Oaks, CA: Sage.

Carr, E. G. (1988). Functional equivalence as a mechanism of response generalization. In R. H. Horner, G. Dunlap, & R. L. Koegel (Eds.), *Generalization and maintenance: Life-style changes in applied settings* (pp. 221–241). Baltimore: Paul H. Brookes.

Carr, E. G., Horner, R. H., Turnbull, A. P., Marquis, J. G., McLaughlin, D. M., McAtee, M. L., Smith, C. E., Ryan, K. A., Ruef, M. B., & Doolabh, A. (1999). *Positive behavior support for people with developmental disabilities: A research synthesis.* Washington, DC: American Association on Mental Retardation.

Carr, E. G., Levin, L., McConnachie, G., Carlson, J. I., Kemp, D. C., & Smith, C. E. (1994). *Communication-based intervention for problem behavior: A user's guide for producing positive change.* Baltimore: Paul H. Brookes.

Christian, W. P., Luce, S. C., & Larsson, E. V. (1992). Peer review and human rights committees. In J. K. Luiselli, J. L. Matson, & N. N. Singh (Eds.), *Self-injurious behavior: Analysis, assessment, and treatment* (pp. 352–366). New York: Springer-Verlag.

Cipani, E. (Ed.) (1989). *The treatment of severe behavior disorders: Behavior analysis approaches.* Washington, DC: American Association on Mental Retardation.

Cunningham, E., & O'Neill, R. E. (2000). A comparison of results of functional assessment and analysis procedures with young children with autism. *Education and Training in Mental Retardation and Developmental Disabilities, 35,* 406–414.

Davis, C. A., & Brady, M. P. (1993). Expanding the utility of behavioral momentum with young children: Where we've been, where we need to go. *Journal of Early Intervention, 17,* 211–223.

Davis, S., Abeson, A., & Lloyd, J. C. (1998). The list grows on and on. *TASH Newsletter, 24,* 17–19.

Drasgow, E., Yell, M. L., Bradley, R., & Shriner, J. G. (1999). The IDEA amendments of 1997: A schoolwide model for conducting functional behavioral assessments and developing behavior intervention plans. *Education and Treatment of Children, 22,* 244–266.

Dunlap, G., dePerczel, M., Clarke, S., Wilson, D., Wright, S., White, R., & Gomez, A. (1994). Choice making and proactive behavioral support for students with emotional and behavioral challenges. *Journal of Applied Behavior Analysis, 27,* 505–518.

Dunlap, G., & Fox, L. (1996). Early intervention and serious problem behaviors: A comprehensive approach. In L. K. Koegel, R. L. Koegel, & G. Dunlap (Eds.), *Positive behavioral support: Including people with difficult behavior in the community* (pp. 31–50). Baltimore: Paul H. Brookes.

Dunlap, G., & Kern, L. (1993). Assessment and intervention for children within the instructional curriculum. In J. Reichle & D. P. Wacker (Eds.), *Communicative alternatives to challenging behaviors: Integrating functional assessment and intervention strategies* (pp. 177–208). Baltimore: Paul H. Brookes.

Dunlap, G., Kern, L., dePerczel, M., Clarke, S., Wilson, D., Childs, K. E., White, R., & Falk, G. (1993). Functional analysis of classroom variables for students with emotional and behavioral disorders. *Behavioral Disorders, 18,* 275–291.

Durand, V. M. (1987). "Look Homeward Angel": A call to return to our (functional) roots. *The Behavior Analyst, 10,* 299–302.

Durand, V. M. (1990). *Severe behavior problems: A functional communication training approach.* New York: Guilford.

Durand, V. M., & Crimmins, D. (1992). *The Motivation Assessment Scale Administration Guide.* Topeka, KS: Monaco & Associates.

Emerson, E. (1995). *Challenging behaviour: Analysis and intervention in people with learning difficulties.* Cambridge, UK: Cambridge University Press.

Foster-Johnson, L., & Dunlap, G. (1993). Using functional assessment to develop effective, individualized interventions for challenging behaviors. *Teaching Exceptional Children, 25,* 44–50.

Fox, L., Vaughn, B. J., Dunlap, G., & Bucy, M. (1997). Parent-professional partnership in behavioral support: A qualitative analysis of one family's experience. *Journal of the Association for Persons with Severe Handicaps, 22,* 198–207.

Hagopian, L. P., Fisher, W. W., Sullivan, M. T., Acquisto, J., & LeBlanc, L. (1998). Effectiveness of functional communication training with and without extinction and punishment: A summary of 21 inpatient cases. *Journal of Applied Behavior Analysis, 31,* 221–229.

Harris, S. L., & Handleman, J. S. (1990). *Aversive and nonaversive interventions: Controlling life-threatening behavior by the developmentally disabled.* New York: Springer.

Horner, R. H. (1991). The future of applied behavior analysis for people with developmental disabilities: Commentary I. In L. H. Meyer, C. A. Peck, & L. Brown (Eds.), *Critical issues in the lives of people with severe disabilities* (pp. 607–611). Baltimore: Paul H. Brookes.

Horner, R. H., & Billingsley, F. F. (1988). The effect of competing behavior on the generalization and maintenance of adaptive behavior in applied settings. In R. H. Horner, G. Dunlap, & R. L. Koegel (Eds.), *Generalization and maintenance: Lifestyle changes in applied settings* (pp. 197–220). Baltimore: Paul H. Brookes.

Horner, R. H., & Carr, E. G. (1997). Behavioral support for students with severe disabilities: Functional assessment and comprehensive interventions. *Journal of Special Education, 31,* 84–104.

Horner, R. H., Day, H. M., & Day, J. R. (1997). Using neutralizing routines to reduce problem behaviors. *Journal of Applied Behavior Analysis, 30,* 601–614.

Horner, R. H., Diemer, S., & Brazeau, K. C. (1992). Educational support for students with severe problem behaviors in Oregon: A descriptive analysis from the 1987–1988 school year. *Journal of the Association for Persons with Severe Handicaps, 17,* 154–169.

Horner, R. H., Dunlap, G., Koegel, R. L., Carr, E. G., Sailor, W., Anderson, J., Albin, R. W., & O'Neill, R. E. (1990). Toward a technology of "nonaversive" behavioral support. *Journal of the Association for Persons with Severe Handicaps, 15,* 125–132.

Horner, R. H., Vaughn, B. J., Day, H. M., & Ard, W. R. (1996). The relationship between setting events and problem behavior: Expanding our understanding of behavioral support. In L. K. Koegel, R. L. Koegel, & G. Dunlap (Eds.), *Positive behavioral support: Including people with difficult behavior in the community* (pp. 381–402). Baltimore: Paul H. Brookes.

Iwata, B. A. (1988). The development and adoption of controversial default technologies. *The Behavior Analyst, 11,* 149–157.

Iwata, B. A. (1994). The FAST: Functional Assessment Screening Tool. Unpublished instrument. Gainesville, FL: Center for the Study of Self-Injury, University of Florida.

Iwata, B. A., Dorsey, M. F., Slifer, K. J., Bauman, K. E., & Richman, G. S. (1994). Toward a functional analysis of self-injury. *Journal of Applied Behavior Analysis, 27,* 197–209. (Reprinted from *Analysis and Intervention in Developmental Disabilities, 2,* 3–20, 1982.)

Iwata, B. A., Vollmer, T. R., & Zarcone, J. R. (1990). The experimental (functional) analysis of behavior disorders: Methodology, applications, and limitations. In A. C. Repp & N. N. Singh (Eds.), *Perspectives on the use of nonaversive and aversive interventions for persons with developmental disabilities* (pp. 301–330). Sycamore, IL: Sycamore.

Iwata, B. A., Vollmer, T. R., Zarcone, J. R., & Rodgers, T. A. (1993). Treatment classification and selection based on behavioral function. In R. Van Houten & S. Axelrod (Eds.), *Behavior analysis and treatment* (pp. 101–125). New York: Plenum.

Jacobson, J. W. (1982). Problem behavior and psychiatric impairment within a developmentally disabled population I: Behavior frequency. *Applied Research in Mental Retardation, 3,* 121–139.

Janney, R., & Snell, M. E. (2000). *Behavioral support.* Baltimore: Paul H. Brookes.

Johnston, S., & O'Neill, R. E. (2001). Searching for effectiveness and efficiency in conducting functional assessments: A review and proposed process for teachers and other practitioners. *Focus on Autism and Developmental Disabilities, 16,* 205–214.

Kazdin, A. E. (2001). *Behavior modification in applied settings* (6th ed.). Belmont, CA: Wadsworth.

Kern, L., Dunlap, G., Clarke, S., & Childs, K. (1995). Student-assisted functional assessment interview. *Diagnostique, 19,* 29–39.

Kincaid, D. (1996). Person centered planning. In L. K. Koegel, R. L. Koegel, & G. Dunlap (Eds.), *Positive behavioral support: Including people with difficult behavior in the community* (pp. 439–465). Baltimore: Paul H. Brookes.

Koegel, L. K., Koegel, R. L., & Dunlap, G. (Eds.) (1996). *Positive behavioral support: Including people with difficult behavior in the community.* Baltimore: Paul H. Brookes.

Lakin, K. C. (1998). On the outside looking in: Attending to waiting lists in systems of services for people with developmental disabilities. *Mental Retardation, 36,* 157–162.

Lalli, J. S., and Goh, H. (1993). Naturalistic observations in community settings. In J. Reichle & D. P.

Wacker (Eds.), *Communicative alternatives to challenging behavior: Integrating functional assessment intervention strategies* (pp. 11–39). Baltimore, MD: Paul H. Brookes.

LaVigna, G. W., & Donnellan, A. M. (1986). *Alternatives to punishment: Solving behavior problems with non-aversive strategies.* New York: Irvington.

Lerman, D. C., Iwata, B. A., & Wallace, M. D. (1999). Side effects of extinction: Prevalence of bursting and aggression during the treatment of self-injurious behavior. *Journal of Applied Behavior Analysis, 32,* 1–8.

Lewis, T. J., Scott, T., & Sugai, G. (1994). The Problem Behavior Questionnaire: A teacher based instrument to develop functional hypotheses of problem behavior in general education classrooms. *Diagnostique, 19,* 103–115.

Lewis, T. J., & Sugai, G. (1999). Effective behavior support: A systems approach to proactive schoolwide management. *Focus on Exceptional Children, 31,* 1–24.

Liaupsin, C. J., Scott, T. M., & Nelson, C. M. (2001). *Functional behavioral assessment: An interactive training module.* Longmont, CO: Sopris West.

Lovaas, O. I., & Favell, J. E. (1987). Protection for clients undergoing aversive/ restrictive interventions. *Education and Treatment of Children, 10,* 311–325.

Lovett, H. (1996). *Learning to listen: Positive approaches and people with difficult behavior.* Baltimore: Paul H. Brookes.

Luiselli, J. K., & Cameron, M. J. (Eds.) (1998). *Antecedent control: Innovative approaches to behavioral support.* Baltimore: Paul H. Brookes.

McDonnell, J. J., Mathot-Buckner, C., & Ferguson, B. (1996). *Transition programs for students with moderate/severe disabilities.* Pacific Grove, CA: Brooks/Cole.

McGee, G., & Daly, T. (1999). Prevention of problem behaviors in preschool children. In A. C. Repp & R. H. Horner (Eds.), *Functional analysis of problem behavior: From effective assessment to effective intervention* (pp. 171–196). Belmont, CA: Wadsworth.

Meyer, L. H., & Evans, I. M. (1989). *Nonaversive intervention for behavior problems: A manual for home and community.* Baltimore: Paul H. Brookes.

Mount, B., & Zwernik, K. (1988). *It's never too early, it's never too late: A booklet about personal futures planning.* Minneapolis: Metropolitan Council on Developmental Disabilities.

Munk, D. D., & Karsh, K. G. (1999). Antecedent curriculum and instructional variables as classwide interventions for preventing or reducing problem behaviors. In A. C. Repp & R. H. Horner (Eds.), *Functional analysis of problem behavior: From effective assessment to effective intervention* (pp. 259–276). Belmont, CA: Wadsworth.

National Institutes of Health (NIH) (1991). *Treatment of destructive behaviors in persons with developmental disabilities.* Washington, DC: Author.

Neef, N. A., & Iwata, B. A. (1994). Special issue on functional analysis approaches to behaviors assessment and treatment. *Journal of Applied Behavior Analysis, 27,* 197–418.

O'Brien, F. (1989). Punishment for people with developmental disabilities. In E. Cipani (Ed.), *The treatment of severe behavior disorders: Behavior analysis approaches* (pp. 37–58). Washington, DC: American Association on Mental Retardation.

O'Neill, R. E., Horner, R. H., Albin, R. W., Sprague, J. R., Storey, K., & Newton, J. S. (1997). *Functional assessment and program development for problem behavior: A practical handbook* (2nd ed.). Belmont, CA: Wadsworth.

O'Neill, R. E., Johnson, J. W., Kiefer-O'Donnell, R., & McDonnell, J. J. (2001). Preparing teachers and consultants for the challenge of severe problem behavior. *Journal of Positive Behavior Interventions, 3,* 101–108.

O'Neill, R. E., & Sweetland-Baker, M. (2001). An assessment of stimulus generalization and contingency effects in functional communication training with two students with autism. *Journal of Autism and Developmental Disorders, 31,* 235–240.

O'Neill, R. E., Vaughn, B., & Dunlap, G. (1998). Comprehensive behavioral support: Assessment issues and strategies. In A. M. Wetherby, S. F. Warren, & J. Reichle (Eds.), *Transitions in prelinguistic communication* (pp. 313–341). Baltimore: Paul H. Brookes.

Plaud, J. J., & Gaither, G. A. (1996). Behavioral momentum: Implications and development from reinforcement theories. *Behavior Modification, 20,* 183–201.

Qureshi, H. (1994). The size of the problem. In E. Emerson, P. McGill, & J. Mansell (Eds.), *Severe learning disabilities and challenging behaviours: Designing high quality services* (pp. 17–36). London: Chapman & Hall.

Reeve, C. E., & Carr, E. G. (2000). Prevention of severe behavior problems in children with developmental disorders. *Journal of Positive Behavior Interventions, 2,* 144–160.

Reichle, J. (1990). *National working conference on positive approaches to the management of excess behavior: Final report and recommendations.* Minneapolis: Institute on Community Integration, University of Minnesota.

Reichle, J., McEvoy, M., Davis, C., Rogers, E., Feeley, K., Johnston, S., & Wolff, K. (1996). Coordinating preservice and in-service training of early interventionists to serve preschoolers who engage in challenging behavior. In L. K. Koegel, R. L. Koegel, & G. Dunlap (Eds.), *Positive behavioral support: Including people with difficult behavior in the community* (pp. 227–259). Baltimore: Paul H. Brookes.

Reichle, J., & Wacker, D. P. (Eds.) (1993). *Communicative alternatives to challenging behaviors: Integrating functional assessment and intervention strategies.* Baltimore: Paul H. Brookes.

Repp, A. C. (1999). Naturalistic functional assessment with regular and special education students in classroom settings. In A. C. Repp & R. H. Horner (Eds.), *Functional analysis of problem behavior: From effective assessment to effective intervention* (pp. 238–258). Belmont, CA: Wadsworth.

Repp, A. C., & Horner, R. H. (Eds.). (1999). *Functional analysis of problem behavior: From effective assessment to effective intervention.* Belmont, CA: Wadsworth.

Repp, A. C., & Singh, N. N. (1990). *Perspectives on the use of nonaversive and aversive interventions for people with developmental disabilities.* Sycamore, IL: Sycamore.

Risley, T. R. (1996). Get a life! Positive behavioral intervention for challenging behavior through life arrangement and life coaching. In L. K. Koegel, R. L. Koegel, & G. Dunlap (Eds.), *Positive behavioral support: Including people with difficult behavior in the community* (pp. 425–437). Baltimore: Paul H. Brookes.

Rusch, R. G., Hall, J. C., & Griffin, H. C. (1986). Abuse provoking characteristics of institutionalized mentally retarded individuals. *American Journal of Mental Deficiency, 90,* 618–624.

Schroeder, S. R., Rojahn, J., & Oldenquist, A. (1991). Treatment of destructive behavior among people with mental retardation and development disabilities: Overview of the problem. In *Treatment of destructive behaviors in persons with developmental disabilities* (pp. 125–171). Washington, DC: National Institutes of Health.

Schwartz, I. S. (1997). It is just a matter of priorities: A response to Vaughn et al. and Fox et al. *Journal of the Association for Persons with Severe Handicaps, 22,* 213–214.

Scott, T. M. (2001). A schoolwide example of positive behavioral support. *Journal of Positive Behavior Interventions, 3,* 88–94.

Scotti, J. R., & Kennedy, C. H. (2000). Introduction to issues in the application of functional assessment. *Journal of the Association for Persons with Severe Handicaps, 25,* 195–196.

Scotti, J. R., & Meyer, L. H. (1999). *Behavioral intervention: Principles, models, and practices.* Baltimore: Paul H. Brookes.

Sprague, R. L. (1994). Ethics of treatment evaluation: Balancing efficacy against other considerations. In T. Thompson & D. B. Gray, (Eds.), *Destructive behavior in developmental disabilities: Diagnosis and treatment* (pp. 293–311). Thousand Oaks, CA: Sage.

Sturmey, P. (1995). Analog baselines: A critical review of the methodology. *Research in Developmental Disabilities, 16,* 269–284.

Sugai, G., & Horner, R. H. (1999). Discipline and behavioral support: Preferred processes and practices. *Effective School Practices, 17,* 10–22.

Sugai, G., Horner, R. H., Dunlap, G., Hieneman, M., Lewis, T. J., Nelson, C. M., Scott, T. M., Liaupsin, C., Sailor, W., Turnbull, A. P., Turnbull, R., Wickham, D., Wilcox, B., & Ruef, M. (2000). Applying positive behavior support and functional assessment in schools. *Journal of Positive Behavior Interventions, 2,* 131–143.

Taylor-Greene, S, Brown, D., Nelson, L., Longton, J., Gassman, T., Cohen, J., Swartz, J., Horner, R. H., Sugai, G., & Hall, S. (1997). School-wide behavioral support: Starting the year off right. *Journal of Behavioral Education, 7,* 99–112.

Thompson, T., & Gray, D. B. (Eds.) (1994). *Destructive behavior in developmental disabilities: Diagnosis and treatment.* Thousand Oaks, CA: Sage.

Tucker, M., Sigafoos, J., and Bushell, H. (1998). Use of noncontingent reinforcement in the treatment of challenging behavior: A review and clinical guide. *Behavior Modification, 22,* 529–547.

VanDuser, N., & Phelan, S. (1993). Aversives and the controversy: A view from the parents' perspective. *Child and Adolescent Mental Health Care, 3,* 77–93.

Van Houten, R., Axelrod, S., Bailey, J. S., Favell, J. E., Foxx, R. M., Iwata, B. A., Lovaas, O. I. (1988). The right to effective behavioral treatment. *The Behavior Analyst, 11,* 111–114.

Vaughn, B. J., Dunlap, G., Fox, L., Clarke, S., & Bucy, M. (1997). Parent-professional partnership in behavioral support: A case study of community-based intervention. *Journal of the Association for Persons with Severe Handicaps, 22,* 186–197.

Vaughn, B., & Horner, R. H. (1997). Identifying instructional tasks that occasion problem behaviors and assessing the effects of student versus teacher choice among these tasks. *Journal of Applied Behavior Analysis, 30,* 299–312.

Vollmer, T. R., & Northup, J. (1997). Applied behavior analysis and school psychology: An introduction to the mini-series. *School Psychology Quarterly, 12,* 1–3.

Wacker, D. P., Cooper, L. J., Peck, S. M., Derby, K. M., & Berg, W. K. (1999). Community-based functional assessment. In A. C. Repp & R. H. Horner (Eds.), *Functional analysis of problem behavior: From effective assessment to effective support* (pp. 32–56). Belmont, CA: Wadsworth.

Walker, H. M., Colvin, G., & Ramsey, E. (1995). *Antisocial behavior in school: Strategies and best practices.* Pacific Grove, CA: Brooks/Cole.

Westling, D. L., & Fox, L. (2000). *Teaching students with severe disabilities* (2nd ed.). Columbus, OH: Merrill.

Williams, B. F., Williams, R. L., & McLaughlin, T. F. (1989). The use of token economies with individuals who have developmental disabilities. In E. Cipani, (Ed.), *The treatment of severe behavior disorders: Behavior analysis approaches* (pp. 3–18). Washington, DC: American Association on Mental Retardation.

Witt, J. C., Daly, E. M., & Noell, G. (2000). *Functional assessments: A step-by-step guide to solving academic and behavior problems.* Longmont, CO: Sopris West.

Wolf, M. M. (1978). Social validity: The case for subjective measurement or how applied behavior analysis is finding its heart. *Journal of Applied Behavior Analysis, 11,* 203–214.

Young, K. R., West, R. P., & MacFarlane, C. A. (1994). Program development, evaluation, and data-based decision-making. In E. C. Cipani & F. Spooner (Eds.), *Curricular and instructional approaches for persons with developmental disabilities* (pp. 50–80). Boston: Allyn & Bacon.

# 8

## *Early Intervention Programs for Infants and Toddlers with Disabilities and Their Families*

*Newborns with disabilities present a number of unique challenges to new parents. Early intervention services can help parents and families adjust to these demands.*

**WINDOW 8.1 • *Letter from Rachel's Mother***

August 1994

Dear Family and Friends,

We appreciate all the help and kindness you have given to us through this difficult and challenging time of our lives. Since many of you have inquired concerning our family and/or the twins, the following is a brief summary of some of the events that have occurred in the last 3 years.

On August 20, 1989 an ultrasound examination revealed that one of the twins we were expecting had hydrocephalus (water on the brain). Due to premature labor I was confined to bed until they were delivered.... Sarah was healthy with a normal head measurement of 13" while Rachel's head had expanded to 16½". They were nearly 6 pounds each. Rachel had other "mid line" abnormalities; a cleft palate, a life threatening bowel deformity (discovered later), missing nails on her fifth fingers. The doctors and nurses did not expect her to live. Supposing that I might never see her again I asked that her incubator be brought to me before they took her in the ambulance to Primary Children's Hospital. When Dave [her father] reached down to stroke her tiny little hand she grasped his finger with all her strength and seemed to be pleading for help to keep her alive.

The day after she was born, Rachel had a shunt (tube) surgically implanted between her scalp and skull to drain excessive brain fluid into her body. This operation was not healing properly and so within her first 2 weeks she had 3 shunt surgeries. She was almost entirely covered with tubes, tape, wires, and bandages. An IV needle was in her vein, a respirator was down her throat to help her breath, and a feeding tube was through her nose going into her stomach. She had patches over her eyes to protect them from the light therapy for her liver.

Rachel came home on the 21st of December and was back at Primary's with shunt problems on Christmas Day. She came home again then returned to the hospital one week later on New Year's night by Life Flight Helicopter when her

oxygen saturation had dropped to 50% (80% is serious).... I was trying to heal from my c-section surgery and to take care of the other newborn at home besides visiting the hospital when possible to see Rachel. The three older children (Linda in kindergarten, Andrea in 5th and Steven in 7th) were each trying to establish his or her individual importance, each feeling set aside with the focus on the new babies. Then at 5 weeks old, my "healthy" twin, Sarah, stopped breathing during an apnea spell.... They took her in the ambulance to University Hospital.... We brought Sarah home a few days later attached to an apnea/respiration/ heartbeat monitor. Rachel came home with an oxygen tank and still needed feeding through the tube down her nose because she has brain damage from the hydrocephalus and does not swallow. Keeping track of feedings, changings, medicines and heart/breathing monitors 24 hours per day, day after day, was incredibly overwhelming for two parents....

I feel sad that no one in my immediate family lives here in Utah because I believe it would be a great help. And unfortunately it's not possible to move there because there is no FHP insurance in their state. Neighbors and friends offer to help with the healthy twin but are concerned and overwhelmed with the responsibility of caring for a medically fragile child. Many are aware of the numerous hospitalizations and paramedic visits in our home. Anyone taking care of Rachel requires special training.

Understandably, neighbors, friends and family were concerned about Rachel dying if they were to take care of her. Taking care of someone in this condition for an extended period of time is extremely tense and stressful on the entire family. Respite care is critical in these circumstances to let the family get even one good night's sleep.... On Saturday, April 2, Dave made the third trip in a week back to the Medical Center when Rachel's fever reached 104.2 degrees F. The doctor on call noted severe respiratory distress and sent her to Primary Children's Hospital....

She's back home now but the challenge never ceases. The other children are handling it pretty well but it's difficult to balance each child's needs. When Rachel was first born we didn't know whether she would be blind or deaf, whether she would ever be able to walk, talk, learn to eat by herself, or live. We were told she may not ever smile. Now at 2½ years old, she cannot crawl, walk, talk, or eat. She still is fed through the gastronomy tube. But we know she can hear somewhat and she has some eyesight. She reaches for things. She's learned to clap her hands and roll over. And yes, she definitely has learned to smile.

Thanks for your care and concern,

Kendra Burton

Salt Lake City, Utah

The time between the birth of a baby and that child's third birthday is an exciting and challenging time for any family. Both the child and its family undergo rapid developmental changes. Typically developing children begin this period as newborns who are totally dependent on others to meet their nutritional and self-care needs, are unable to hold up their heads without support, and who communicate with others through (1) subtle changes in body tone and movement, (2) the use of eye contact and facial expressions, and (3) frequent and not so subtle cries. Three years later these tiny babies have become active preschoolers who are able to speak in short sentences, using hundreds of different words, who run and jump with ease, eat meals with their families, are toilet trained, and are rapidly learning about shapes, colors, letters, and numbers (Allen & Marotz, 1994).

Family members also undergo rapid developmental change during this time with their young children. If it is the first child in the family, parent(s) will experience one of the major adjustments and transitions of adult life (Cowan & Cowan, 1995; Hamner & Turner, 2001). Becoming parents produces an overnight change from being largely autonomous individuals who have significant freedom in structuring their own routines and activities to assuming 24-hour-a-day responsibility for another human being. To make this transition even more challenging, becoming a parent is a responsibility that in all likelihood will last for at least eighteen years, with a life-long continuation of the strong emotional attachment. If the parent(s) of a newborn have already had a child, the lifestyle and personal growth changes may be somewhat less dramatic. However, a return to the intensive caretaking and nurturing needs of infants and toddlers, and the adjustment to a new set of relationships within the family, are always a major event.

The rapid developmental growth of the child and family members precipitated by the birth of an infant creates a challenging set of adjustments for any family, ones that are unique to nurturing a child of this age (Hamner & Turner, 2001). Some formerly satisfying relationships and activities often must take a lesser role in family members' lives in order to meet these new demands. The happiness and well-being of various family members is often intertwined at this time to a degree that may not be repeated at later stages of family life. For families that meet most of the challenges of these early years successfully, the rapid growth and increased responsiveness and competence of the typically developing child often seem like more than adequate rewards for the expended energy and numerous adjustments.

For adults who are asked to meet too many challenges with too few resources and supports, the results can be much less satisfactory for all concerned (Hanson & Lynch, 1992; LeLaurin, 1992). Sometimes overwhelming problems on the part of the parent(s) (e.g., substance abuse, mental health problems, mental retardation, poverty, homelessness, family violence) may prevent or interfere with a parent's ability to nurture and care for a young child effectively. When this occurs, it often has negative impacts not only on the child's health, emotional well-being, and learning (Brookes-Gunn & Duncan, 1997; English, 1998; Feldman, 1997; Sherman, 1997), but also on the way the parent(s) feel about themselves as individuals and as parents (Bromwich, 1997). Very few adults will not experience considerable unhappiness and lowered self-esteem if they are unable to meet their child's needs adequately.

Infants and toddlers with developmental delays or severe disabilities present some unique challenges and adjustments for parents and other caregivers and family members. The parent has to make many emotional adjustments in accepting the child's disability and learning to interact with a group of professionals who wish to help in meeting the child's special needs (Begun, 1996; Turnbull & Turnbull, 2001). The child's health, behavioral, or other caregiving needs may be very intensive, and his or her rate of growth and development may be much slower or different than that which occurs for typically developing children (Blasco, 2001; Kohrman, 1990; Zotkiewicz, 1996). Even under the best of circumstances, the combined impact of increased caregiving demands and less rapid or "satisfactory" progress on the part of the child can seriously affect a parent(s) ability to meet the always significant challenges of early parenthood.

When considering the many additional challenges and adjustments faced by the families of a young child with severe disabilities, it is sometimes too easy to lose sight of the fact that these are first of all families, with many of the same joys, dreams, problems, and issues as any other family. Similarly, an infant or toddler with severe disabilities is first of all a young child, with many of the same sources of enjoyment, frustration, and need as any other child of the same age. As with any young child, her closest and most important ties are to her family, and her relationship with her family is much more influential than her relationship with service providers. It is for this reason that early intervention programs have been developed to support not only the health and developmental progress of the infant or toddler with disabilities, but the family that is so important to them as well. Sometimes the services will assist families in more quickly or more fully reestablishing a satisfying family relationship or in supporting the child in reaching his optimal potential. Sometimes the services may be critical to preserving the family unit, or to the child being able to live at home as a part of his family. Regardless of the specific goal or type of services provided as a part of early intervention programs, these services need to be based not only on the unique and constantly evolving strengths, needs, and preferences of the infant or toddler with disabilities, but on the inevitably related, unique, and constantly changing strengths, needs, and preferences of that child's family as well.

This chapter provides an overview of the types of services that have historically been available to infants and toddlers with disabilities and their families, and of the current trends, expected outcomes, organization, effective practices, and future directions for family-centered early intervention for infants and toddlers and their families.

---

**Focus 1**
What types of services were made available in the past to infants and toddlers with disabilities and their families?

---

# Historical Overview of Early Intervention Services

The current availability of a variety of health, social service, educational, and family support services designed to meet the needs of infants and toddlers with disabilities and their families is a very recent development. The number of children with severe disabilities who survive early infancy is increasing, due to the many advances in treating premature infants as well as those with life-threatening illnesses or birth defects (Horbar & Lucey, 1995). Fifty years ago families had very limited service choices available to them if they had a baby with a recognizable condition or syndrome that might result in severe disabilities. This section describes the changes in typical early intervention services from those formerly provided to institutionalized infants and toddlers, to current family-centered and family-directed early intervention models.

## Institutionalization

As recently as the 1950s, virtually all families were advised to place a family member with severe disabilities in a state institution at birth or at the time the extent of the disabilities was recognized. If the diagnosis of a physical condition associated with disability (e.g., Down syndrome) was made at the time the child was born, the parents were frequently advised to decide to institutionalize the child before they had a chance to build a relationship or grow attached to the child through holding him in the hospital and taking him home to be a part of the family (Harbin, 1993). In some instances families were encouraged to act as though the child had died, sparing any other children knowledge of their child with disabilities, not visiting the child with disabilities in the institution, and basically getting on with what professionals perceived to be more productive and positive aspects of their lives.

Sometimes the presence of a severe disability would not be recognized until persistent patterns of seriously delayed development could be observed in the young child. For children with severe disabilities, this identification would usually occur during the infant or toddler years. Commonly, professional advice at the time would again center on institutionalization, based on the rationale of what would be most beneficial for other family members. The role of staff in the institution was to replace or substitute for the parents as caregivers (Harbin, 1993), making sure that the child's physical needs were attended to, and that there was a safe, protective environment to shelter the child from harm.

Not all families followed professional recommendations to institutionalize their child. In the face of the identification of the disability, the advice to institutionalize the child, and an almost complete lack of services in the community for either the child or their family, some families still chose to take the child home to raise in the best way they knew how (Featherstone, 1980). In some instances the decision concerning institutionalization was postponed to a later time. In other families there was a definite intent to have the child with severe disabilities live within the family throughout his or her life.

## *Child-Centered Early Intervention*

In the late 1950s and early 1960s, professionals working with young children and their families began to pay closer attention to earlier research on the impact of a stimulating and responsive environment on the learning of young children, including those with disabilities. When a child with severe disabilities was born or identified, parents began to be encouraged to take the child home, to love him or her, and to access available services that would assist them in stimulating their child's development, and in helping them deal with the emotional impact of having a child with disabilities (Harbin, 1993). During this same decade, powerful parent advocacy organizations were formed, including the Association for Retarded Citizens, the National Association for Down Syndrome, and the National Society for Autistic Children. Parent groups and a variety of public and private agencies offered an increasing number of programs and services, including infant stimulation programs, occupational, physical, and speech therapy services, family counseling, and respite care (Turnbull & Turnbull, 2001). Professionals concentrated their efforts on working directly with the child. Parents were encouraged to observe and carry over therapy or stimulation activities with the child at home (Harbin, 1993).

By the 1970s, both the learning potential of children with severe disabilities and the importance of parent involvement in facilitating the child's learning were more widely recognized by service providers in a variety of professions. Federal legislation such as Public Law 94-142 (1975) and federally funded model demonstration projects funded through the Handicapped Children's Early Education Program (HCEEP) were also requiring more extensive parental involvement and decision making. Professionals began to view parents as important teachers of their young children with disabilities. Parent training programs, designed to have professionals teach parents to teach their own child, were among the most widely utilized intervention strategies (Baker, Brightman, Blacher, Heifetz, Hinshaw, & Murphy, 1989; Baldwin, Fredericks, & Brodsky, 1973; Lillie & Trohanis, 1976).

During the 1970s a number of curriculum materials were produced by federally funded model demonstration projects that were designed to assist parents in fulfilling this teaching role. Several of these curriculum or training guides, and other publications written at the same time, were designed specifically for use by parents of infants and toddlers, including those with moderate to severe disabilities. Many of these curricula and teaching tools, or their later editions, are still in widespread use in early intervention programs today. These curricula include the *Portage Guide to Early Education* (Bluma, Shearer, Frohman, & Hilliard, 1976), *Teaching the Infant with Down Syndrome* (Hanson, 1987), *Hawaii Early Learning Profile* (HELP) (Furuno, O'Reilly, Hosaka, Inatsuka, Allman, & Zeisloft, 1985), *The Carolina Curriculum for Infants and Toddlers with Special Needs* (Johnson-Martin, Jens, Attermeier, & Hackett, 2nd ed., 1991), and *Handling the Young Cerebral Palsied Child at Home* (Finnie, 1975).

In spite of the many advances in providing programs during the 1970s and early 1980s, early intervention services continued to be fragmented or simply unavailable for many infants and toddlers with severe disabilities and their families (McDonnell & Hardman, 1988). This is not surprising considering that federal legislation did not require states to provide any special services to meet the needs of infants and toddlers with disabilities. However, during the 1980s and early 1990s, changing perceptions and policies about the relationship between professionals and families of individuals with disabilities combined with the 1986 passage of Public Law 99-457 to bring about major changes in the structure of early intervention programs and services.

## *Family-Focused to Family-Centered Early Intervention*

Many parent training programs have reported success in teaching parents to use a variety of prescribed intervention strategies, and positive child outcomes have been reported for programs in which parents had primary responsibility for direct intervention (Bailey & Simeonsson, 1988; Benson & Turnbull, 1986; Guralnick & Bricker, 1987; Hanson & Schwarz, 1978; Shearer & Shearer, 1976). In spite of these positive outcomes, families and interventionists began to express reservations about using parent training as the dominant early intervention model. For one thing, less positive parent training outcomes were reported for many families, particularly those in which the parent(s)' socioeconomic status or educational level were low or the families were experiencing financial, marital, or health crisis (Bailey & Simeonsson, 1988; Benson & Turnbull, 1986; Bromwich, 1997). Additional concerns related to the many families who (1) dropped out of the programs (Stile, Cole, & Garner, 1979), (2) did not use the intervention techniques effectively with their young children (Bailey & Simeonsson, 1988; Bromwich, 1987), and/or (3) had parent(s) who simply preferred to be a parent, not their child's teacher (Benson & Turnbull, 1986; McDonnell & Hardman, 1988). Even for families that had been very successful in learning to use the prescribed intervention techniques, there was little evidence to suggest that families chose to continue in a "formal" teaching role for any length of time (Bailey & Simeonsson, 1988; Benson & Turnbull, 1986; McDonnell & Hardman, 1988), although many of the techniques may have been maintained or generalized to facilitate the child's development and learning in a more natural or incidental way within daily family routines (Baker, Heifetz, & Murphy, 1980; Benson & Turnbull, 1986). In summary, teaching parents to carry out intervention with their infants and toddlers had many positive outcomes within some families. However, because of the many families who did not elect to adopt a "teaching" role, or who were unsuccessful in being effective in this role, training parents to be a primary interventionist or teacher for their child has evolved into being one of many options rather than the primary focus for early intervention programs.

Family advocacy, family systems theory (see Chapter 3), and research on families also changed perceptions about how early intervention programs should be structured. While the needs of the child with disabilities continued to be an important intervention focus, service providers began to realize how inseparable these needs were from those faced by other family members and the family unit as a whole. Families and interventionists also became increasingly concerned about the deficit focus of both child- and family-focused intervention (Dunst, Trivette, & Deal, 1988; Summers, Behr, & Turnbull, 1989; Turnbull & Turnbull, 1986). It almost seemed as if the purpose of early intervention could be condensed to answering one question: "What is lacking/needed/wrong with this child and/or family and how do *we* get *them* to fix it?" To move away from a deficit focus, interventionists began to place more emphasis on acknowledging the strengths and individuality of families, and on using the families, rather than professional perceptions and insights, as a basis for determining program goals and needed supports and services. The emphasis on "enabling and empowering" families became a new, and well-articulated model for early intervention services, family-centered early intervention (c.f. Dunst et al., 1988; McGonigel, Kaufmann, & Johnson, 1991).

One way of identifying major paradigm shifts in service programs is to identify the forces that most significantly drive service delivery. Table 8.1 describes four major paradigms that could be used by early intervention programs. At the time Public Law 99-457 was passed in 1986, many early intervention programs were making a transition from being child-centered to being family-focused. Changes from P.L. 99-457 in the 1991 (P.L. 102-119) and 1997 (P.L. 105-17) Reauthorizations of the Individuals with Disabilities Education Act mirrored the shift from family-focused to family-centered services. Major federal legislation affecting the provision of early intervention services is described in the next section of this chapter.

## Current Trends: Federal Legislation and Early Intervention

Although the 1975 passage of the Education of the Handicapped Act (EHA) (P.L. 94-142) had created incentive grants to encourage states to provide preschool special education programs, similar comprehensive federal incentives to provide services to infants and toddlers with disabilities did not occur until more than a decade later, with the 1986 passage of an amended EHA, P.L. 99-457. As discussed in Chapter 3, P.L. 99-457 is the most significant federal legislation to date in terms of its impact on early intervention services for infants and toddlers with developmental delays or disabilities and their families. The 1986 passage of P.L. 99-457 not only extended the Part B full service mandate to preschoolers with disabilities (Section 619), it also established a new program for infants, toddlers, and their families, The Infant and Toddlers with Disabilities Program (Part H). States were not required to par-

**TABLE 8.1** *The Driving Forces of Service Delivery*

| Approach | Description |
| --- | --- |
| System-centered | The needs of, or benefits to, the service system drive the delivery of services. |
| Child-centered | The strengths and needs of the child drive the delivery of services. |
| Family-focused | The strengths and needs of the family, as determined by providers, drive the delivery of services. |
| Family-centered | The priorities and choices of the family drive the delivery of services. |

*Source:* McGonigel, M. J. (1992). Moving from family-focused to family-centered early intervention: The journey continues. Workshop presented at the University of Utah Summer Institute II, Salt Lake City. Adapted from Edelman, L. (1990). *Recognizing the driving focus of service delivery.* Baltimore: Kennedy Krieger Institute.

ticipate in Part H, but they were eligible for federal funds if they chose to do so and agreed to meet federal implementation requirements after an initial five-year planning period.

As you will recall, in 1990 the title of EHA was changed to the Individuals with Disabilities Act (IDEA, P.L. 101-476). Amendments to the IDEA were passed in 1991 (P.L. 102-119) and 1997 (P.L.105-17), including several affecting the Infant and Toddler Program. (The Infant and Toddler Program is contained within Part C, rather than Part H, in the most recent reauthorization of the IDEA). Although the legislative changes reflected in P.L. 99-457, 101-476, 102-119, and 105-17 represent a major policy shift in favor of more active federal involvement in early childhood special education and early intervention, they fall short of mandating the availability of early intervention services for eligible infants, toddlers, and their families, an end desired by most involved families, advocates, and professionals.

---

**Focus 2**
How are early intervention services currently defined in Part C of the 1997 Reauthorization of the IDEA (P.L. 105-17)?

---

## Early Intervention as Defined by P.L. 105-17, Part C

Several major components of Part C differentiate it from the Part B (preschool and school age) requirements of the IDEA. These components include the following:

**1.** *Eligibility.* Participating states are required to provide services to infants and toddlers who are developmentally delayed or who have a diagnosed physical or mental condition with a high probability of resulting in developmental delay (e.g., cerebral palsy, Down syndrome). States determine their own definition for developmental delay, and may choose also to define and provide services to a third group of infants and toddlers, those who are at risk for future developmental delays. Regardless of how a state chooses to define developmental delay, establishing eligibility for Part C early intervention programs is noncategorical in nature. Parents will know whether their child is currently developmentally delayed, but states do not determine that a child has "severe disabilities" or "behavior disorders" or "profound mental retardation" in order to make the child and family eligible for early intervention services.

**2.** *Individual Family Service Plan (IFSP).* IFSPs are a required written document developed for every eligible child and his or her family. The IFSP is very important because it reflects the outcomes, plan of action, services, and evaluation strategies that families and multidisciplinary early intervention team members agree upon as defining the individualized early intervention most important for that child and family. Key components of the IFSP include:

- A statement of the child's present developmental status (based on appropriate assessment of cognitive, communication, social/emotional, and adaptive development)
- A statement of the family's resources, priorities, and concerns related to enhancing the development of the child

- A statement of the major outcomes expected to be achieved for the child and family, including criteria, procedures, and timelines used to determine the degree of progress toward these outcomes
- A list of specific early intervention services and supports needed, and plan for service coordination, including the frequency, intensity, and method of service delivery
- A statement of the natural environments in which services will be provided, including justification, if necessary, for any services that will not be provided in the natural environment
- The projected dates for beginning services and the anticipated duration of service provision
- The name of a qualified, appropriate service coordinator who will be responsible for coordinating services and implementing the plan
- Transition plans to support the child and family as they move on to preschool or other appropriate services
- Provisions for ongoing review, evaluation, and revision of the IFSP Early Intervention Program, 1999, Section 303.344

**3.** *Service coordination.* Service coordination was called case management in the original Infants and Toddlers with Disabilities Program (P.L. 99-457, 1987). Not too surprisingly, many families were not enthusiastic about the idea of being a "case" that someone would "manage" (Dunst, 1991). Consequently, in the 1991 Amendments the language was changed from "case management" to "service coordinator." The identification of a service coordinator is a required part of the IFSP. The rules and regulations for Part C describe service coordination as "an active, on-going process that involves assisting parents of eligible children in gaining access to early intervention services and other services identified in the individualized family service plan" (Section 303.23). Specific service coordination activities include:

- Coordinating the performance of evaluations and assessments
- Facilitating and participating in the development, review, and evaluation of individualized family service plans
- Assisting families in identifying available service providers
- Coordinating and monitoring the delivery of available services
- Informing families of the availability of advocacy services
- Coordinating with medical and health providers
- Facilitating the development of a transition plan to preschool services, if appropriate

Service coordinators must be qualified to carry out these responsibilities. Often service coordinators are early interventionists from a variety of professions, or parents or paraprofessionals who have been specially trained for a service coordination role. Survey results have found that parents consider strong skills in building rapport, gathering and synthesizing information and resources, and a positive and concerned attitude to be important characteristics of service coordinators (Dinnebeil & Rule, 1994).

**4.** *Broadened range of services.* Early intervention services that may be provided under Part C include a broader range of services than the special education and related services that might be included on an IEP for a preschooler with disabilities. Early intervention services are identified and provided on an individual child and family basis, in order to achieve desired outcomes specified in the IFSP. The menu of early intervention services included in Part C, Section 632 are

- Family training, counseling, and home visits
- Special instruction
- Speech-language pathology and audiology services
- Occupational therapy
- Physical therapy
- Psychological services
- Service coordination services
- Medical services only for diagnostic or evaluation purposes
- Early identification, screening, and assessment services
- Health services necessary to enable the infant or toddler to benefit from the other early intervention services
- Social work services
- Vision services
- Assistive technology devices and assistive technology services
- Transportation and related costs that are necessary to enable an infant or toddler and the infant's or toddler's family to receive early intervention services

Very few early intervention programs have a large and diverse enough staff to be able to provide this wide an array of services on their own. Interagency coordination is often needed to implement IFSPs successfully. This is one of the reasons for the service coordination requirement in Part C of the IDEA.

**5.** *Interagency coordinating council.* Each state that participates in the Part C Infant and Toddler Program is required to select a lead agency and form an interagency coordinating council (ICC). The lead agency is responsible for administration of Part C programs within its state, with the advice and assistance of the state ICC. Different states selected different agencies to fill the lead agency role, including Education, Health, Mental Health, and Social Services. Federal regulations require membership on state-level interagency coordinating councils to include parents of infants and toddlers with developmental delays or disabilities, service providers, a state legislator, representatives from early intervention and preschool service providers, health insurance, Head Start, and child care agencies, and representatives from higher education (P.L. 105-17, Part C, Section 641).

## Family-Centered Early Intervention

Family-centered early intervention embraces a positive and holistic view of families, including families with an infant or toddler with severe disabilities or delays. The philosophy and practice of family-centered early intervention is consistent with federal legislation, but in many ways goes much farther in the attempt to empower families. Parent advocacy and educational groups and professionals from a variety of disciplines have participated in developing the key concepts and practices related to family-centered early intervention. While often regarded as "best practice" for early intervention programs or services at this time, family-centered early intervention did not develop until the late 1980s and early

1990s. There is very strong professional and family philosophical support for family-centered early intervention. However, widespread use of high-quality family-centered early intervention practices and efficacy research on family-centered early intervention are still in the early stages of development (Bruder, 2000; Krauss, 1997). Brinker (1992) captured this gap between philosophical commitment and legislative support and actual practice and research in early intervention.

> If we accept that our knowledge about how to apply child development research to early intervention is in its infancy, then our knowledge about the application of family systems research is probably in the second trimester of our grandmother's pregnancy. (p. 315)

## A Philosophy of Enabling and Empowering Families

The philosophy of *enabling* and *empowering* families (Dunst et al., 1988) is central to family-centered early intervention as well as increasingly accepted as a basis for a variety of professional-family partnerships. McGonigel (1991) defined these terms in relation to early intervention in the following manner:

> *Enabling* families means creating opportunities and means for families to apply their present abilities and competencies and to acquire new ones as necessary to meet their needs and the needs of their children (Dunst et al., 1988). *Empowerment* is both a process and an outcome that takes different forms in different families (Rappaport, 1984). Empowering families in early intervention does not mean giving or bestowing power on families—the power is theirs by right. Rather, it means interacting with families in such a way that they maintain or acquire a sense of control over their family life and attribute positive changes that result from early intervention to their own strengths, abilities, and actions. (Dunst et al., 1998, p. 8)

A focus on enabling and empowering families creates a very different role for early interventionists than the previously common role of an expert who focuses on child-centered intervention. Window 8.2 summarizes the rationale and principles of family-centered early intervention as they relate to development of IFSPs. Although these principles are not unique to families that have an infant or toddler with severe disabilities or developmental delays, their very responsiveness to individual child and family needs is likely to be beneficial to families who may be facing some unique challenges that are not readily addressed by signing up for a prepackaged set of services or programs.

> **Focus 3**
> What are the major goals or expected outcomes of early intervention for infants and toddlers with severe disabilities and their families?

## Expected Outcomes of Early Intervention

As mentioned earlier, the empowerment of families is both an end goal and a means for reaching other goals or expected outcomes of early intervention programs for infants and

## WINDOW 8.2 • *Principles Underlying the IFSP Process*

- Infants and toddlers are uniquely dependent on their families for their survival and nurturance. This dependence necessitates a family-centered approach to early intervention.
- States and programs should define "family" in a way that reflects the diversity of family patterns and structures.
- Each family has its own structure, roles, values, beliefs, and coping styles. Respect for and acceptance of this diversity is a cornerstone of family-centered early intervention.
- Early intervention systems and strategies must honor the racial, ethnic, cultural, and socioeconomic diversity of families.
- Respect for family autonomy, independence, and decision making means that families must be able to choose the level and nature of early intervention's involvement in their lives.
- Family/professional collaboration and partnerships are the keys to family-centered early intervention and to successful implementation of the IFSP process.

- An enabling approach to working with families requires that professionals reexamine their traditional roles and practices and develop new practices when necessary—practices that promote mutual respect and partnerships.
- Early intervention services should be flexible, accessible, and responsive to family-identified needs.
- Early intervention services should be provided according to the normalization principle—that is, families should have access to services that are provided in as normal a fashion and environment as possible and that promote the integration of the child and family within the community.
- No one agency or discipline can meet the diverse and complex needs of infants and toddlers with special needs and their families. Therefore, a team approach to planning and implementing the IFSP is necessary.

*Source:* McGonigel, M. J. (1991). Philosophy and conceptual framework. In M. J. McGonigel, R. K. Kaufmann, & B. H. Johnson (Eds.), *Guidelines and recommended practices for the Individualized Family Service Plan* (2nd ed.) (pp. 9). Bethesda, MD: Association for the Care of Children's Health.

toddlers with disabilities and their families. Some additional expected outcomes for early intervention programs and their importance for children with severe disabilities are described briefly below.

**1.** *Mutually enjoyable family relationships that include the child with disabilities are established and maintained.* An important outcome for early intervention is the establishment of enjoyable and reciprocal family relationships that include the young child with disabilities (Bromwich, 1997; Hanson & Lynch, 1995). Infants with significant disabilities may have a number of atypical behaviors that can discourage the attempts of already stressed parents in establishing a satisfying relationship. For example, they may (1) sound different when they cry, cry more frequently, and be more difficult to soothe; (2) stiffen and pull away when being held, rather than molding to the caregiver's body; (3) avert their gaze when caregivers attempt to establish eye contact; and (4) smile later, or less often, or in response to different stimuli than other children (Calhoun, Rose, & Pendergast, 1991; Cicchetti & Beeghly, 1990; Fraiberg, 1974; McCollum, 1987; McCollum & Hemmeter,

1997). Early intervention can assist families in understanding these behaviors help parents learn to read their infants' cues and signals, and adapt their own behavior to allow a more satisfying, reciprocal relationship to develop (Bromwich, 1997; Hanson & Lynch, 1995; Hedlund, 1989; Rose, Calhoun, & Ladage, 1989). As an infant develops, early intervention can also support family relationships by helping families cope with new challenges, such as teaching the infant to play, or to eat with the family, and to understand the importance of making time for other relationships within the family.

**2.** *The family unit as a whole is strengthened and individual family members have their critical needs met.* Central to the idea of family-centered early intervention is the recognition that the well-being of various family members is interrelated, and that strengthening the family unit as a whole, and the individual members within it, will also benefit the child with severe disabilities. An example of support or intervention that may strengthen the family and benefit the infant or toddler is assisting a family in arranging quality day care so that a parent who has been a full-time caregiver can return to work that he or she enjoys. Having a parent return to fulfilling work may have the added benefits of continuing medical insurance coverage, providing some caregiving respite for the parent, and increasing the family's income. With high-quality child care, the infant may also benefit from opportunities to interact with typically developing children, and to experience and learn to be a part of a new set of relationships, activities, and routines (O'Brien, 1997).

**3.** *The child's health is maintained or improved.* The physical health of a child has a profound impact on his or her learning and development, relationships with family and friends, and overall quality of life. If a child is in constant pain or discomfort, suffers from frequent fatigue or exhaustion, or spends large amounts of time hospitalized, on life-support equipment, or receiving medical treatments, it may leave little room for the child to invest energy in new learning or for the child and family just to relax and have fun together. Many children with developmental delays or conditions that may result in severe disabilities have additional health problems. For example, about 40 to 50 percent of children born with Down syndrome also have heart defects (Spiker & Hopmann, 1997). Also, premature infants or other individuals who have needed ventilator therapy may develop bronchopulmonary dysplasia (BDP), a chronic lung disorder that can result from scarring of the lungs. Children with BDP may require continued use of oxygen for long periods of time, may have a number of nutritional and feeding difficulties (McCamman & Rues, 1990), and are at higher risk for serious—and potentially fatal—respiratory infections, and for delays in motor skills and speech development, apparently due to difficulty in coordinating oral–motor function with the increased difficulty in breathing (McNab & Blackman, 1998). Many infants with BDP develop pneumonia or bronchitis before their first birthday. Rehospitalization will be required for many of them. For many infants and toddlers with severe disabilities, good health cannot be taken for granted. Achieving the best possible health outcomes is an important function of early intervention, one that will support the success of all other goals.

**4.** *Secondary disabilities are prevented.* Many young children with severe developmental delays have multiple disabilities and/or delayed development in a number of different performance areas. For example, a young child with severe cerebral palsy may have mild to moderate cognitive impairments, severe physical impairments, and be very delayed in the development of communication skills, due to the impact of the physical disabilities on the ability to control the muscles needed for speech, facial expressions, and gestures. Additionally, the limitations in the motor and communication areas will very likely lead to delays or deficits in adaptive and social interaction skills. The physical limitations alone may keep the child from being able to move, to explore and interact with the physical environment, and to develop the typical communication patterns and methods that foster satisfying personal relationships with family and friends. These difficulties, in turn, may hamper optimal cognitive development, and the development of the motivation to be an active learner and to optimize any potential for controlled, purposeful movement.

Although none of these impairments or difficulties can be completely prevented, a failure to intervene early can result in permanent physical impairments, such as contractures, chronic shortening of spastic muscles that results in the abnormal positioning of joints (Pellegrino, 1998). With early and ongoing physical therapy, many of the undesirable outcomes of untreated cerebral palsy can be prevented. Early intervention can also help caregivers to facilitate the developmental potential of the child, and to adapt or support the child's physical and social environment in ways that will allow them to have contingent and fulfilling interactions.

**5.** *The child's learning and development are enhanced.* Research has demonstrated that systematic and early intervention can improve the developmental, educational, and social outcomes for young children with disabilities (see Guralnick [1997] for a series of chapters that provide comprehensive reviews of existing research on early intervention). Because learning and performance builds on previous learning and performance, earlier attainment of various critical skills can create the opportunity for future learning and more proficient performance at many levels and in many contexts. The transactional model of child development (Sameroff & Chandler, 1975) describes how an interactive sequence of child–caregiver–environmental interactions continually modify or affect each contributor to the interactions, influencing future interactions and learning in either a facilitative or hindering fashion. The Down Syndrome Infant–Parent Program provides an example of how early intervention can influence developmental outcomes for children. This home-based early intervention program was a federal model demonstration project that operated in the mid-1970s at the University of Oregon (Hanson, 1987; Hanson & Schwarz, 1978). The project compared the age at which the projects' parent-taught infants with Down syndrome, normal children, and children with Down syndrome who were raised at home but did not participate in early intervention attained a number of key early developmental milestones. Point of Interest 8.1 displays some of the results of the study. Although there is obviously considerable variation for all three groups of children, the children with Down syndrome who were in early intervention attained the milestones at ages more like the normally developing children than the children with Down syndrome who had not participated in early intervention. It is important to note that this program and the reported data are based on a small number of infants ($n = 9$–12) and are not necessarily representative of what would be achieved for a larger number of children and families. During a follow-up on the children at 8–10 years of age, the children who had participated in the early intervention project showed a large range of abilities, with individual children performing anywhere from the normal range on cogni-

**POINT OF INTEREST 8.1** • *Comparative Ages at Which Infants and Young Children Attained Developmental Milestones*

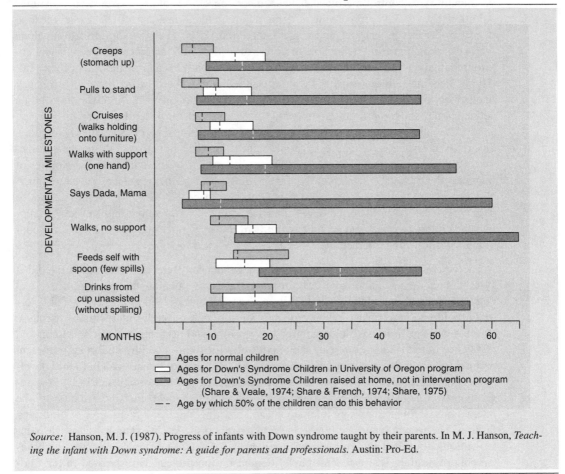

*Source:* Hanson, M. J. (1987). Progress of infants with Down syndrome taught by their parents. In M. J. Hanson, *Teaching the infant with Down syndrome: A guide for parents and professionals.* Austin: Pro-Ed.

tive and academic measures to being considered severely delayed. However, as Hanson (1987) notes, "The most striking finding in a follow-up observation is that these children are *all* accepted and complete members of their families and that their parents are *all* confident and caring parents" (p. 30).

**6.** *The independence and inclusion of the child and family are facilitated.* The infant and toddler years may seem early to be concerned about independence, particularly for a child with severe developmental delays or disabilities. However, it is in these years that parents and children not only develop an intimate relationship but also begin to reassert their individuality and independence (Hamner & Turner, 2001; Ramey & Ramey, 1999). If either the child with severe disabilities or the family is denied the opportunity to begin this process during the infant and toddler years, they miss an important chance to build a foundation for later independence and inclusion within the society at large.

Taking a baby or toddler along on parent ventures into the community is often a challenging and time-consuming enterprise at best. Parents of young children with severe disabilities may find this task even more difficult. They may have concerns about how they will feel and respond to comments or reactions from other people about their childs' appearance, behavior, or specialized equipment (Calhoun, Rose, & Armstrong, 1989; Turnbull & Turnbull, 2001). They may also have concerns about physical and architectural barriers, or exposing their child to illnesses, cigarette smoke, or other potential health threats. Early intervention can play an important role in supporting families in overcoming these barriers to joint family participation in the community. It can also support childcare providers, family friends, or community members who can include the young infant or toddler with disabilities in activities that will allow them to interact on a frequent basis with typically developing children of similar ages (Hanson & Bruder, 2001; O'Brien, 1997). This provides the child with disabilities with a wider and more enjoyable base of experience, and an opportunity to learn to respond to the challenges of the world outside the home and family.

## Structure and Organization: Implementing Family-Centered Early Intervention

Families and early interventionists work in partnership to develop an IFSP that can guide early intervention during a period of the child's infant or toddler years. While IFSPs must be reevaluated at least every six months, they are designed to be a fluid document, reflecting the rapid and often unpredictable changes that occur with very young children and their families. Any part of the IFSP can be updated or altered when the family–early intervention team believe that such changes can better characterize current needs. Examples of changes that might be desirable before it is time to write a new IFSP are adding new outcome statements and changing the methods for meeting or evaluating outcomes if previous methods have been unsuccessful or are disliked. Four important components of IFSP development include (1) conducting a family-directed assessment, (2) developing outcome statements and identifying the needed supports and services to achieve the outcomes, (3) identifying the service coordinator and service coordination plan, and (4) planning for any forthcoming transitions.

---

*Focus 4*
Describe family-directed assessment and Individualized Family Service Plans and discuss how they are used to achieve the goals of family-centered early intervention.

---

### Family-Directed Assessment and Selecting Intervention Goals

Professionals from a variety of disciplines have often been used to conducting test-based standardized or curriculum-based assessments in their area of expertise and summarizing and sharing the results and their recommendations with families and other team members.

Numerous concerns have been raised about the meaningfulness of such test results for intervention planning, particularly when they are used to assess the performance of very young children, or individuals with severe disabilities, and are done in isolation of professionals with other types of expertise or the family who are so important to the child (Barrera, 1994; Greenspan & Meisels, 1994).

Public Law 99-457 (1986) introduced a new component to early intervention assessment, that of "family assessment," in which, with a family's permission, their strengths and needs in relation to the child with disabilities would be assessed by professionals as a key to planning intervention. While acknowledging the importance of the family to the young child with disabilities, this approach had the potential to be intrusive to the family, creating a situation in which a family might feel that they needed to complete an endless series of interviews and checklists in order to obtain early intervention services for their child. To counter these possible misuses of family assessment, the 1991 reauthorization of the IDEA changed the language to a "family-directed assessment." Family-directed assessment can address issues related to both the child and family and is used for purposes of IFSP development, implementation, and evaluation. "A family's agenda—its priorities for how early intervention will be involved in family life—shapes the entire family-centered IFSP process" (McGonigel, 1991, p. 17). One of the primary purposes of family-directed assessment is to identify family concerns, priorities, and resources. Several principles have been described for identifying family concerns, priorities, and resources and can assist professionals in working in partnership with families in this identification process.

- The inclusion of family information in the IFSP is voluntary on the part of families.
- The identification of family concerns, priorities, and resources is based on an individual family's determination of which aspects of family life are relevant to the child's development.
- A family need or concern exists only if the family perceives that the need or concern exists.
- Families have a broad array of formal and informal options to choose from in determining how they will identify their concerns, priorities, and resources.
- Family confidences are respected, and family-shared information is not discussed casually among staff.
- The process of identifying family concerns, priorities, and resources leads to the development of IFSP outcomes, strategies, and activities that help families achieve the things they want from early intervention for their children and themselves. (Kaufmann & McGonigel, 1991, p. 50)

Families also play an important role in directing and shaping assessment related to their child with developmental delays or disabilities. This can occur through sharing information about their child's current level of performance, including strengths and needs, by making suggestions on how to get optimal performance from their child, or by sharing information on the relevant people, places, and routines in the child's life, as well as their vision for the child's future. Family priorities for the child and the family may be very different from priorities generated by a group of professionals, who tend to focus on achieving physical health for the child and maximizing developmental progress. Window 8.3

## WINDOW 8.3 • *Typical Family Priorities*

*For our child we want*

independence

personal happiness

feelings of accomplishment

respect

ability to walk

ability to communicate

good friends

understanding that he/she is loved

employment

skills to feed him/herself

skills to dress him/herself

comfortable enough to sleep through the night

skills to drive car

the experience of having a loving relationship
with a member of the opposite sex

to know and love God

*For our family we want*

social outings (especially restaurants)

sleep-filled nights

enjoyment of an evening out (as a couple)

normal sibling relationships

relatives and friends to understand the nature of
our child's disabilities

help with planning some adaptations to our home

*Source:* Hunt, M., Cornelius, P., Leventhal, P., Miller, P., Murray, T., & Stoner, G. (1990). *Into our lives.* Akron, OH: Children's Hospital Medical Center.

includes some typical family priorities. Although the individual expression of the achievements may be very different in form from person to person, very few parents do not want the majority of these outcomes for their children and family. Clearly, some of these priorities (e.g., skills to drive a car, employment) are very long range for infants or toddlers with disabilities. However, many of them (e.g., ability to walk and communicate, understanding that he or she is loved, personal happiness, feelings of accomplishment, skills to feed and dress oneself, being comfortable enough to sleep through the night) are very much the focus of early intervention. All of the priorities listed in the section of Window 8.3 that address what parents want for their family are outcomes that can be important to address as early as when an infant with severe disabilities is coming home from the hospital.

The overriding intent of family-directed assessment is to gather and share information that will assist families and early interventionists in developing an effective and supportive Individualized Family Service Plan. A multidisciplinary team of skilled professionals cannot effectively design either an assessment plan or an IFSP without the active participation of the family on some level. As Hunt et al. (1990) indicated to family members, "Your identification of resources, strengths, and concerns becomes the foundation of your individual plan—-and no one knows these better than you do" (p. 3).

Important priorities for the child or family that have been identified through family-directed assessment are developed into goal or outcome statements on the IFSP. An outcome statement may focus on a desired end for either the child with disabilities or some other member of their family. The emphasis in the wording of the goal or outcome statement is one that reflects the family's way of expressing the outcome and is free of professional terminology and jargon. The resources and supports for achieving the goal or outcome statement are included, as are the criteria by which attainment of the goal will be judged. An example of an IFSP for a young child with severe disabilities and their family is provided in Figure 8.1.

## Effective Practices in Family-Centered Early Intervention

> ### Focus 5
> Describe the role of natural supports, natural environments, transition planning, and interagency coordination and collaboration via service coordination in family-centered early intervention.

### Natural Supports and Natural Environments

Natural supports and natural contexts or environments are critical to family-centered early intervention. The concept of natural supports was introduced in Chapters 2 and 3. At the early intervention age level, natural supports are identified as part of the family-centered assessment process, and are often called "informal supports" because they are based on a family's network of friends and the services and settings available to all community members. These natural or informal supports or resources are identified as strengths on the IFSP, and linked to individual goal or outcome statements as a primary and preferred means of achieving the outcome. Although professional services and supports are valued, and often incorporated, strengthening the use of natural supports is one of the primary mechanisms for empowering families. Early intervention research results tend to support this preference for informal supports, demonstrating a pattern that "informal rather than formal support showed the strongest relationship to any number of outcomes, perhaps because, as evidence indicates, social support exchanges among personal network members are characterized by psychological closeness and mutual caring that appears to influence the degree to which support has positive effects" (Dunst, Trivette, & Jodry, 1997, p. 517).

A reliance on *natural environments* is not only consistent with recommended practices, it is also tied directly to the requirements for provision of early intervention services under federal regulations for the Part C Infant and Toddler Program. *Natural environments* are "settings that are natural or normal for the child's age peers who have no disabilities" (34 CFR Part 303.18), and include family, child care, and community settings and routines. National surveys of more than 3,000 parents of infants, toddlers, and preschoolers identified twenty-two categories of activities that provide sources of learning opportunities for young children within natural environments (Dunst, Hamby, Trivette, Raab, & Bruder, 2000). About half of these opportunities were identified within home and family activity categories, and the other half within community activity categories. Examples of home and family categories and activities include family routines (e.g., chores, errands), parenting routines (e.g., child's bathtime, meal times), child routines (e.g., washing hands, picking up toys), literacy activities (e.g., bedtime stories, looking at books), physical play (e.g., rough-housing, ball games), and entertainment activities (e.g., dancing, singing, watching

**FIGURE 8.1**  *Individualized Family Service Plan*

Western Carolina Center
Family, Infant and Preschool Program
Individualized Family Support Plan

| Background Information: | Family Member's Name: | Relationship to Child: |
|---|---|---|
| Child's Name:  Tammy Natasha | Sandy | Mom |
| Family's Name: Shook | Woody | Dad |
| No OPD 0 2:    0000 | Amy | Sister |
| Date of Birth:    8-19-88 Age: 12 mos | | |
| County:        Cook | | |

Family Support Plan Team

| Name | Title | Agency | Date |
|---|---|---|---|
| Sandy Shook | Parent | | 10-12-89 |
| Woody Shook | Parent | | 10-12-89 |
| Patricia N. Dill  RN | Case coordinator | Family, Infant and Preschool Program | 10-12-89 |
| Jim Given, MD | Pediatrician | Family, Infant and Preschool Program | 10-12-89 |
| Mary Lou O'Keefe | Physical therapist | Family, Infant and Preschool Program | 10-12-89 |
| Pam C. Brede  oe - SLP | Speech language therapist | Family, Infant and Preschool Program | 10-12-89 |
| Laurel Hensley | Social worker | Family, Infant and Preschool Program | 10-12-89 |
| Donald Whisit | Staff psychologist | Family, Infant and Preschool Program | 10-12-89 |
| Lynda Patch | Teacher | Family, Infant and Preschool Program | 10-12-89 |
| Marilyn Yakinovich | Family resource specialist | Family, Infant and Preschool Program | 10-12-89 |

Team Review Dates

| 0 Months | 3 Months | 6 Months | 9 Months |
|---|---|---|---|

Griffiths Scale of Mental Development          Child's Functioning Level

| Domain | CA | Age Level/Range | Domain | CA | Age Level/Range | Domain | CA | Age Level/Range |
|---|---|---|---|---|---|---|---|---|
| Locomotor | 12 mos | 2.7 mos | Eye/Hand | 12 mos | 2.3 mos | Gen. quot. | | 24.5 |
| Personal/Social | 12 mos | 2.3 mos | Performance | 12 mos | 2.7 mos | Mental age | 12 mos | 2.9 mos |
| Hear/Speech | 12 mos | 4.6 mos | | | | | | |

| Child's Strengths | Family's Strengths |
|---|---|
| Vocalizes and makes sound imitations<br>Sleeps through the night<br>Enjoys being held<br>More alert to surroundings | Love one another<br>Have good coping skills for dealing with stress<br>Commitment to getting treatments for Tammy<br>Take preventive measures with the children<br>Advocate for children's needs |

| Formal Resources and Support Services | Dates Started | Ended | Informal Resources and Support Services | Dates Started | Ended |
|---|---|---|---|---|---|
| Cook Co. DSS | 8-88 | | Maternal grandparents | | |
| Cook Co. Mental Health | 2-90 | | Pastor | | |
| Cook Co. Cluster | 7-89 | | Contribution fund from church | | |
| FIPP Home-based serv. | 6-89 | | Friends Gail | | |
| Social Security | 7-89 | | Tim | | |
| Cook Co. Health Dept. | 8-88 | | Cousins Michele & Albert | | |
| Private pediatricians | 8-88 | | | | |
| Private PT | 7-89 | | | | |

*(continued)*

**FIGURE 8.1** **Continued**

Child's Name: __Tammy__ OPDO: __2-0000__ Family's Name: __Shook__ FIPP Staff Member: __P. Bell__ IFSP#: __1__ Page#: __1__

| Date / # | Need/Project Outcome Statement | Source of Support/Resource | Course of Action | Family's Evaluation Date | Rating |
|---|---|---|---|---|---|
| 06-12-89 / 1 | Parents will obtain information about FIPP in order to decide which resources are going to best meet their needs. | Parents–ability to process information and choose resources<br><br>Case coord.–information on FIPP<br><br>Social worker–information on FIPP | Case coord. & social worker will provide information about FIPP during home visit. Parents will review information, ask questions and decide if they wish to access FIPP resources. If FIPP resources are not chosen, other alternative resources will be explored. | 07-12-89<br>08-08-89 | 4<br>7 |
| 06-22-89 / 2 | Parents will obtain information on available financial resources in order to meet expenses related to Tammy's care. | Parents–ability to gather information<br><br>Case coord.–information<br><br>Social security–information | Case coord. will share information about community financial resources during weekly home visit. Parents will contact social security and social services for eligibility information and gather family financial records. | 07-12-89<br>08-07-89 | 3<br>6 |
| 07-12-89 / 3 | Parents will obtain information on available physical therapists in order to obtain service for Tammy. | Parents–ability to process information & schedule appointment with PT<br><br>Case coord.–information<br><br>PT–consultation | Case coord. will share names of PTs in the area during weekly home visit. Parents will contact PTs to ask about availability and schedule a consultation with PT of choice. | 07-19-89<br>08-07-89<br>08-28-89 | 4<br>6<br>7 |
| 07-19-89 / 4 | Woody will obtain counseling in order to learn ways to control his anger. | Woody–ability to schedule appointment and utilize counseling<br>Family members–support & encouragement<br>Case coord.–information & support<br>DSS caseworker–information & support | DSS caseworker & case coord. will provide information to Woody on available counseling services during weekly home visit. Woody will make an appointment & attend counseling sessions. Family will give support & encouragement. | 08-07-89<br>09-20-89<br>10-23-89<br>on hold | 2<br>4<br>5 |
| 08-01-89 / 5 | Parents will participate in PT sessions in order to learn handling techniques for Tammy. | Parents–abilities to utilize PT suggestions & provide feedback on usefulness of techniques<br><br>PT–evaluation of Tammy & information on handling techniques | Parents will schedule PT evaluation & share information about Tammy with PT. PT will evaluate Tammy's motor development & demonstrate handling techniques during weekly PT sessions held at local recreation department. | 08-28-89<br>09-20-89<br>ongoing | 4<br>7 |
| 08-21-89 / 6 | Parents will identify their goals and priorities for Tammy in order to prepare for assessment and intervention planning day at FIPP. | Parents–ability to identify goals<br><br>Case coord.–developmental screening of Tammy & provide information about assessment procedures | Case coord. will administer Griffiths during weekly home visit & discuss results with parents. Parents & case coord. will discuss family's goals & priorities for Tammy and decide on objectives for the assessment & IPD. | 09-20-89<br>10-01-89 | 3<br>7 |

Family's Evaluations:
1 .... Situation changed, no longer a need
2 .... Situation unchanged, still a need, goal or project
3 .... Implementation begun; still a need, goal or project
4 .... Outcome partially attained or accomplished
5 .... Outcome accomplished or attained, but not to the family's satisfaction
6 .... Outcome mostly accomplished or attained to the family's satisfaction
7 .... Outcome completely accomplished or attained to the family's satisfaction

**FIGURE 8.1  Continued**

Child's Name: __Tammy__  OPDO: __2-0000__  Family's Name: __Shook__  FIPP Staff Member: __P. Bell__  IFSP#: __1__  Page#: __2__

| Date / # | Need/Project Outcome Statement | Source of Support/Resource | Course of Action | Family's Evaluation Date | Rating |
|---|---|---|---|---|---|
| 09-20-89 / 7 | Parents will use firm, deep pressure during physical contact with Tammy in order to increase her tolerance for touch. | Parents–ability to use PT techniques<br><br>PT–consultation on handling techniques<br><br>Case coord.–support & feed-back | Parents will schedule & participate in weekly PT sessions with Tammy. PT will demonstrate handling techniques. Case coord. will assist family in incorporating techniques into daily routines & give feedback on use of techniques. | 09-27-89<br>10-05-89<br>ongoing | 4<br>7 |
| 09-20-89 / 8 | Parents will obtain as much information as possible about Tammy's medical history in order to have a better understanding of events that occurred during her hospitalization. | Parents–skill in generating questions<br><br>Case coord.–medical information<br><br>Family physician–information & consultation<br><br>FIPP physician–consultation | Case coord. will obtain medical records and schedule meeting with FIPP physician. Parents will identify their questions and consult with physicians. Family physician & FIPP physician will interpret records & answer questions. | 10-12-89<br>11-06-89<br>12-18-89 | 4<br>4<br>6 |
| 09-20-89 / 9 | Tammy will consistently hold her head up in order to work toward sitting independently. | Parents–abilities to use techniques to promote head control<br><br>PT–consultation on techniques to promote head control<br><br>Case coord.–support & information | Parents will attend PT consultation weekly and use suggested techniques with Tammy. PT will evaluate Tammy's motor abilities and suggest techniques for promoting head control. Case coord. will provide support to family in using techniques during weekly home visits. | 10-12-89<br>11-06-89<br>12-11-89<br>See goal #18 | 3<br>4<br>4 |
| 10-12-89 / 10 | Parents will take Tammy for an eye examination in order to determine her visual abilities. | Parents–abilities to schedule exam & understand results<br><br>Private physician–information<br><br>Eye doctor–evaluation & information<br><br>Case coord.–support & information | Parents will obtain names of eye doctors from private physician and schedule eye evaluation. Parents will take Tammy for eye exam & consult with doctor. Case coord. will provide support & information related to eye evaluation during weekly home visits. | 10-12-89<br>11-06-89 | 3<br>6 |
| 10-12-89 / 11 | Tammy will use her hands to bring toys to her mouth in order to explore and become aware of her surroundings. | Case coord.–information<br><br>Parents–abilities to use suggested techniques to promote hand use | Case coord. will demostrate techniques for promoting hand use during weekly home visits. Parents will use techniques in daily routines with Tammy. | 10-12-89<br>11-06-89<br>12-11-89<br>See goal #19 | 3<br>3<br>3 |
| 10-12-89 / 12 | Tammy will tolerate being in water in order to make bathtime more relaxing. | Parents–skills in using sug-gested techniques for bathtime<br><br>Case coord.–bathchair, information on use of chair & feedback on use of techniques | Case coord. will provide a bathchair on loan & demonstrate use during weekly home visits. Parents will use chair & other techniques such as keeping Tammy wrapped in towel until placed in the tub, gently placing her in warm water, having the bathroom warm, using gentle but firm motions & holding Tammy firmly. | 11-13-89<br>12-11-89<br>01-22-90 | 4<br>4<br>7 |

Family's Evaluations:
1 . . . . Situation changed, no longer a need
2 . . . . Situation unchanged, still a need, goal or project
3 . . . . Implementation begun; still a need, goal or project
4 . . . . Outcome partially attained or accomplished
5 . . . . Outcome accomplished or attained, but not to the family's satisfaction
6 . . . . Outcome mostly accomplished or attained to the family's satisfaction
7 . . . . Outcome completely accomplished or attained to the family's satisfaction

*(continued)*

# FIGURE 8.1 Continued

Child's Name: __Tammy__ OPDO: __2-0000__ Family's Name: __Shook__ FIPP Staff Member: __P. Bell__ IFSP#: __1__ Page#: __3__

| Date / # | Need/Project Outcome Statement | Source of Support/Resource | Course of Action | Family's Evaluation Date | Rating |
|---|---|---|---|---|---|
| 10-17-89 / 13 | Parents will obtain information on respite options in order to make decisions on the best respite resources for their family. | Case coord.–information on formal respite programs–feedback & support / Parents–ability to identify people they know for child care / Grandmother–support & feedback | Case coord. will provide information on respite programs during weekly home visits. Parents will identify people they know (with Grandmother's help) who might provide respite. Parents will decide which options to pursue for respite. | 10-30-89 / 11-06-89 / 12-11-89 | 3 / 6 / 7 |
| 10-17-89 / 14 | Parents will gather information on preschool programs in their community in order to decide if attending preschool will further promote Tammy's development. | Case coord.–information on local preschools & feedback / DSS–information on preschools / Parents–ability to gather information & select services | Case coord. will provide information on available preschools & assist family in knowing what to look for in selecting a program, during weekly home visits. Will provide support to family as they consider programs. Parents will contact DSS for information on local programs and contact programs they choose to visit. | 10-30-89 / 11-13-89 / 12-11-89 / See goal #17 | 4 / 4 / 6 |
| 11-06-89 / 15 | Parents will obtain a second neurological consultation in order to better understand the reasons for Tammy's delays. | Parents–ability to access community resources / Physician–referral to neurologist / Neurologist–evaluation of Tammy & interpretation of results / Case coord.–emotional support & feedback | Parents will ask private physician for names of neurologists, schedule a neurological & ask their questions concerning Tammy's delays. Case coord. will assist the parents in listing their questions for the neurologist & provide emotional support during weekly home visits. | 12-18-89 / 01-06-90 / 01-22-90 | 3 / 3 / 3 |
| 12-11-89 / 16 | Woody will obtain information on local literacy programs in order to decide on enrolling in a program. | Woody–ability to get information & decide on enrolling / Family–support & encouragement to Woody / Case coord.–medical information / Community college–information on enrollment | Case coord. will provide information on literacy programs during weekly home visits. Woody will contact community college for information. Other family members will provide encouragement to Woody in learning to read. | 01-22-90 / 02-28-90 / on hold | 4 / 4 |
| 12-11-89 / 17 | Parents will complete application papers for Family Place in order for Tammy to be enrolled in the preschool program. | Parents–ability to complete application & provide information on their goals for Tammy / Family Place staff–information on application process / Case coord.–support & feedback for family | Parents will make appointment & meet with Family Place staff to complete application process & share their goals for Tammy. Case coord. will provide support to family in completing application process. Family Place staff will meet with Tammy's parents & keep them informed on enrollment process. | 01-16-90 / 01-22-90 / on hold | 3 / 6 |
| 12-11-89 / 18 | Tammy will consistently hold her head up for 30 seconds during playtime in order to develop skills for sitting independently. | Case coord.–support & information / Parents–ability to use suggested techniques to promote head control / PT–techniques for head control | Parents will take Tammy to weekly PT sessions & use suggested techniques with Tammy during playtimes. PT will demonstrate techniques during weekly sessions. Case coord. will provide feedback on use of techniques during weekly home visits. | 01-22-90 / 02-28-90 | 3 / 4 |

Family's Evaluations:
1 . . . . Situation changed, no longer a need
2 . . . . Situation unchanged, still a need, goal or project
3 . . . . Implementation begun; still a need, goal or project
4 . . . . Outcome partially attained or accomplished
5 . . . . Outcome accomplished or attained, but not to the family's satisfaction
6 . . . . Outcome mostly accomplished or attained to the family's satisfaction
7 . . . . Outcome completely accomplished or attained to the family's satisfaction

# FIGURE 8.1    Continued

Child's Name: __Tammy__  OPDO: __2-0000__  Family's Name: __Shook__  FIPP Staff Member: __P. Bell__  IFSP#: __1__  Page#: __4__

| Date / # | Need/Project Outcome Statement | Source of Support/Resource | Course of Action | Family's Evaluation Date | Family's Evaluation Rating |
|---|---|---|---|---|---|
| 12-11-89 / 19 | Tammy will use her hands to bring her 6 oz. bottle with handles to her mouth in order to become more aware of hand use. | Case coord.–information<br><br>Parents–ability to teach Tammy to hold her bottle | Case coord. will demonstrate ways to encourage Tammy to hold bottle during weekly home visits. Parents will talk to Tammy about what they are doing as they place the bottle in her hands and use prompts to encourage her to hold it. | 01-22-90<br>02-28-90 | 3<br>6 |
| 12-11-89 / 20 | Parents will explore financial resources in order for Amy to be able to attend Family Place. | Case coord.–information on resources<br><br>DSS & Family Place–information on financial resources<br><br>Parents–ability to access community resources | Case coord. will provide information on possible financial resources during weekly home visits. Parents will contact DSS & Family Place to inquire about other possible financial resources for funding daycare for Amy and pursue options they think are appropriate. | 01-16-90<br>01-22-90<br>02-28-90 | 3<br>4<br>7 |
| 01-16-90 / 21 | Parents will consult with physician in order to determine if Tammy may receive immunizations. | Case coord.–information on immunizations<br><br>Parents–ability to access & share information with physician<br><br>Physician–information & recommendations on immunization | Case coord. will share information about importance of immunizations with parents during weekly home visits. Parents will consult with private physician about immunizations for Tammy & their plans to enroll her in daycare. If immunizations are not advised, parents will obtain statement from physician for Family Place. | 01-22-90<br>02-28-90 | 3<br>3 |
| 01-22-90 / 22 | Parents will gather information on housing options in Cook County in order to consider the possibilities of buying a house. | Case coord.–information & emotional support<br><br>DSS, Housing Authority, & FHA–information on housing options<br><br>Parents–ability to gather information & consider options | Case coord. will provide information on local housing agencies & provide emotional support during weekly home visits. Parents will contact local DSS, Housing Authority & FHA to gather information on options & provide information on their financial status. | 02-28-90 | 4 |
| 01-22-90 / 23 | Tammy will eat 2 or 3 mashed table foods in order to adjust to more texture in her food. | Case coord.–demonstration of ways to add texture to food & feeding techniques<br><br>Parents & grandparents–abilities to teach Tammy to eat table foods | Case coord. will provide information on adding texture & suggestions on foods to try (bananas, cooked carrots, scrambled eggs, etc.) during weekly home visits. Parents & grandparents will give Tammy 1 or 2 bites of mashed foods as she will tolerate. | 02-28-90 | 5 |
| 01-22-90 / 24 | Parents will obtain a third neurological consultation in order to get another opinion on the reasons for Tammy's delays. | Parents–abilities to access community health resources<br><br>Case coord.–emotional support & feedback<br><br>Neurologist–evaluation of Tammy & interpretation of results | Parents will select a neurologist from previously recommended list, make appointment & ask questions at neurological. Case coord. will assist family in reviewing their question list & provide emotional support during weekly home visits. | 02-28-90 | 3 |

Family's Evaluations:
1 . . . . Situation changed, no longer a need
2 . . . . Situation unchanged, still a need, goal or project
3 . . . . Implementation begun; still a need, goal or project
4 . . . . Outcome partially attained or accomplished
5 . . . . Outcome accomplished or attained, but not to the family's satisfaction
6 . . . . Outcome mostly accomplished or attained to the family's satisfaction
7 . . . . Outcome completely accomplished or attained to the family's satisfaction

*(continued)*

**FIGURE 8.1  Continued**

| Child's Name: _____Tammy_____ | OPD 0: _0000_ | Matrix#: __1__ |

| IFSP Goal # / Date Started | Objectives | Routines | | | | | | Date Attained |
|---|---|---|---|---|---|---|---|---|
| | | Mealtimes | Dressing & Diapering | Bathtime | Independent Playtime | Playtime with Others | | |
| #9 / 09-20-89 | Tammy will consistently hold her head up in order to work toward independent sitting. | X | X | X | | | | See #18 |
| #11 / 10-12-89 | Tammy will use her hands to bring toys to her mouth in order to explore and become more aware of her surroundings. | | | | X | X | | See #19 |
| #12 / 10-12-89 | Tammy will  tolerate being in water in order to make bathtime more relaxing. (Use bathchair for support and put Tammy in the water slowly.) | | | X | | | | 1-22-90 |
| #18 / 12-11-89 | Tammy will consistently hold her head up for 30 seconds during playtime in order to work toward independent sitting. | | | | | X | | 2-28-90 |
| #19 / 12-11-89 | Tammy will use her hands to bring her 6 oz. bottle with handles to her mouth in order to become more aware of her hand use. | X | | | | | | 3-28-90 |
| #23 / 01-22-90 | Tammy will eat 2 or 3 mashed table foods in order to adjust to more texture in her food (start with 1 or 2 bites of the food). | X | | | | | | 2-28-90 |
| | | | | | | | | |

*Source:* These IFSP forms are reprinted with permission of Dunst, C. J., & Deal, A. G., Family, Infant, & Preschool Program, Western Carolina Center, Morganton, NC.

TV). Examples of community categories and activities include family outings (e.g., eating out, visiting friends), play activities (e.g., outdoor playgrounds, child play groups), recreational activities (e.g., swimming, recreation centers), church/religious activities (e.g., Sunday school), and sports (e.g., soccer, T-ball). While the specific activities will vary from child to child, and from family to family, there are many rich and varied learning opportunities for young children within natural environments (Dunst et al., 2000), including for young children with disabilities.

Public Law 105-17 (1997) strengthened the natural environments provision that had been included in earlier Infant and Toddler Program legislation, not only continuing to require a statement in the IFSP of natural environments in which services can appropriately be provided, but also requiring teams to justify on the IFSP any services that are not provided in natural environments. On p. 210, Figure 8.1 included a goals by routines matrix, which identified which child-focused goals could be incorporated within which daily routine. This is one way of looking at how intervention can be included in natural contexts and specified in the IFSP. Recently, Cripe & Venn (1997) developed the "Family-Guided Routines" process for choosing natural environments and intervention strategies within family-centered early intervention. The process has six overall steps:

> Step 1: Identify the general schedule of the day, including typical routines.
> Step 2: Select preferred daily routines.
> Step 3: Build upon natural strategies used by care providers.
> Step 4: Implement and discuss plans with service providers.
> Step 5: Teach new strategies and model when appropriate.
> Step 6: Monitor progress, revise, adjust, and gather feedback. (Cripe & Venn, 1997)

An overview of considerations in planning family-guided routines based intervention is given in Figure 8.2.

## Transition Planning

Transitions are often a stressful time for individuals with disabilities and their families (Turnbull & Turnbull, 2001). Recognizing the need for support of families and children during transitions, Part C requires a transition plan to be developed as children receiving early intervention services approach their third birthday, or move between early intervention programs. The goals of transition include uninterrupted provision of necessary services, and supporting children, families, and service providers. Most children in early intervention will transition to preschool special education programs when they turn 3. Preschool special education programs are often administered by different agencies than early intervention programs, are classroom-based, and may have different eligibility criteria. Many children beginning to attend preschool at age 3 will be expected to ride a school bus with other preschoolers, and the family-centered nature of early intervention is often replaced by more typical parent–teacher–child relationships. These differences between early intervention and preschool programs can create many adjustments for the parent and child (Rosenkoetter, Hains, & Fowler, 1994). These adjustments and stresses may be more intense when the child entering preschool has severe disabilities. Many families will want the preschooler included in a high-quality early childhood program in which most of the children are typically developing, while still having their child's individual educational, health, and related service needs met by specially trained personnel. The extent to which both inclusion and intensive educational support needs are met in the same classroom is very variable at this time in preschool programs around the country. Some families also report frustration with decreased communication with service providers once their child begins attending a preschool classroom (Hadden & Fowler, 1997).

Transition plans may also be developed as children move from a hospital to home setting, between communities, or when children and families make other shifts during the

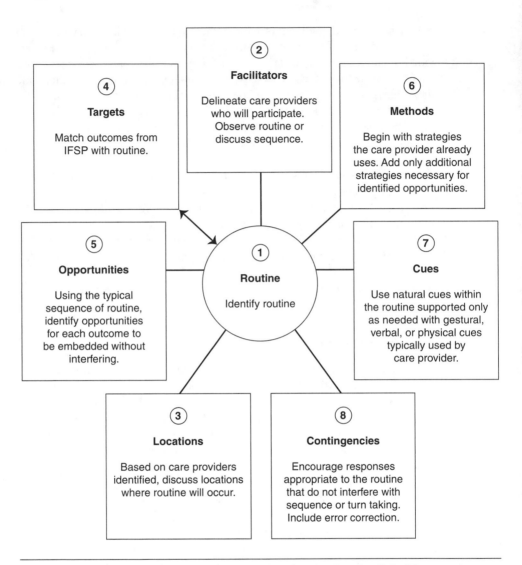

**FIGURE 8.2** *FACETS Project: Considerations for Planning Routine-Based Intervention.*

FACETS is a joint project of Kansas University Affiliated Program and Florida State University.

infant or toddler years. Part C requires IFSPs to include "steps to be taken to support the transition of the toddler with a disability to preschool or other appropriate services." These steps usually include educating parents about available preschool options and the changes and expectations that occur when their child begins preschool, visiting preschool programs and teaming with preschool staff to develop the final IFSP and the first preschool IEP, and sharing information or providing support that will enhance the effectiveness of the transition in meeting child, family, and interventionist's needs.

Sharon is three months away from her third birthday. Sharon has Down syndrome and a mild hearing impairment. She lives with her mother and her 10-year-old brother. Her parents are divorced but she usually sees her father several times a week. Her father has remarried and Sharon has a 4-year-old stepsister. Sharon and her brother stay with their father, stepmother, and stepsister every other weekend. They also visit for late afternoon play and dinner at least one evening during the week. Sharon's mother works full-time as an administrative assistant at the local community college. Sharon attends a childcare center while her mother works. There are ten other children in her toddler group and there are two caregivers assigned to the group at any one time.

Sharon has been walking for over a year. She likes to play outdoors with the other children in her childcare center, and is particularly fond of playing in the sandbox, climbing on the toddler size jungle gym, and going down the small slide. She can feed herself well and likes most foods, especially macaroni and cheese, ice cream, and chocolate chip cookies. Sharon can put on and take off her coat and hat by herself, but usually needs help with other clothing. Sharon is not toilet trained. She has not shown much interest in this, even though some of the other children in her class are using potty chairs and wearing training pants or underpants. Sharon enjoys baths and likes to have her hair fixed, although she has a hard time sitting still if her mother wants to do anything more than put a bow in it. Sharon knows about fifty different words and says them clearly enough that people who know her can usually understand what she is saying. She usually uses one word at a time, and will try to repeat things she has heard other people say. Sharon loves to play with her parents and older brother, and she tries to copy everything her stepsister does. They are inclined to fight over toys or because of her stepsister trying to tell Sharon what to do. Sharon likes to play around the other children in her childcare class and enjoys most of the same activities they do. Sometimes she gets frustrated because she can't talk as well or use her hands as skillfully as many of the other children. This can make it hard to play some of their games or to do art activities.

Sharon goes to Sunday school, goes shopping, and goes out to restaurants with both her mom's and dad's families. She also likes to go to the park or to her cousin's house to play.

Sharon's mother and father have been pleased with the early interventionists they have worked with since Sharon was two weeks old. The early intervention program staff have included both of Sharon's parents and their families and have also been available to provide training or support to teachers at the childcare center that Sharon attends. Although Sharon's parents really want to help her learn as much as she can, they also feel that not everything can revolve around doing teaching or intervention with her. The interventionists have helped them see how to include "teaching" within the other things Sharon does on a regular basis, and in particular in the things she really enjoys, like play and meal times.

Sharon's family is concerned as they approach the transition to preschool special education programs. They are a little worried that the school district will want Sharon to attend a class that has been specially designed for preschoolers with developmental delays or disabilities rather than a regular preschool classroom. The fact that Sharon is not talking much and is not toilet trained is also raising some new issues at her childcare center. The staff there feel that she is not ready to be moved into the 3-year-old class until she is toilet trained. In this and in other areas she is more like the 2-year-olds, and she might benefit from an extra year in that class. Sharon's family and early intervention team plan to begin working on the transition to preschool and the 3-year-old class within the next two weeks. They want to have time to prepare and support the childcare and preschool staff, but still ensure that Sharon can receive the specialized services she needs while participating in preschool and childcare programs with children of her own age. Her family feels that the extent to which Sharon has been actively included in family, childcare, and community activities up to this point in her life will help her make whatever adjustments will be necessary to continue to be included in school and community life as she gets older.

## Service Coordination

Early intervention as defined by Part C has been described as a linking mechanism rather than a separate program. The reason for this rests in the fact that one of the primary purposes of early intervention is to identify and coordinate formal and informal resources and supports to meet needs and priorities identified by the family. Rather than funding a new program to meet all of the needs, the Infant and Toddler Program develops, links, and supplements existing resources. The degree of reliance on informal or natural supports and interagency cooperation has many advantages but can also create a significant challenge in attempting to keep all of the resources and services coordinated and functioning effectively to meet the child and family needs. Recognizing this challenge, Part C requires the identification of a service coordinator who is responsible for seven major service coordination activities, including: coordinating evaluations and assessment; facilitating the development, review, and evaluation of the IFSP; assisting families in the identification of service providers; coordinating and monitoring the delivery of services; informing families of the availability of advocacy services; coordinating medical and health care; and facilitating the transition plan to preschool services. The service coordinator is identified as a part of IFSP development and is recorded on the document itself. The IFSP should also show the services and informal supports that will be utilized for IFSP implementation.

## Changing Needs: Birth to Three

The most critical feature of family-centered early intervention is that it meets the individual and changing needs of infants or toddlers with disabilities and their families. While the individual nature of early intervention limits the usefulness of generalizations across children and families, some similarities occur often. One of these similarities is the changing focus and form of early intervention as the child with developmental delays or disabilities matures through early infancy, being an older baby or young toddler, and being an almost 3-year-old, ready to move on to preschool experiences. The priorities and roles of families and interventionists change along with the developing child. Figure 8.3 summarizes some of the common concerns, goals, and priorities for the child and family at 2 months after birth, 1½ years, and 2½ years. Common intervention strategies or interventionist roles are also summarized in the figure.

# Future Directions in Early Intervention

Future directions in early intervention include ongoing research and program improvement efforts related to the prevention of developmental disabilities, potential treatment of some neurodevelopmental disorders, and effective early intervention service provision for children and families.

## Prevention and Treatment of Developmental Disabilities

Great progress has been made during the last decade in understanding the early development of the human brain, and how this affects learning, development, and growth throughout the lifespan. Many of these advances have been made possible through improved

**FIGURE 8.3** *Common Concerns and Changing Needs in Early Intervention*

| Child's Age: | Two Months | One and a Half Years | Two and a Half Years |
|---|---|---|---|
| Major concerns | • Understanding and accepting child's developmental delay or disability<br>• Explaining disability to family and friends<br>• Resolving or planning for ongoing health care needs of child<br>• Establishing workable family routines that meet the child's needs<br>• Establishing a satisfying, reciprocal relationship with infant | • Helping child maximize developmental progress<br>• Being able to communicate with child, and have child communicate with others<br>• Having some relief from constant caregiving demands<br>• Having time to play and have fun with child, other family members, and friends<br>• Overcoming any barriers to community participation for child or family | • Discipline-related issues<br>• Explaining child's disability and special needs to school and community members<br>• Child's readiness for classroom program and peer relationships<br>• Obtaining desired preschool program placement and special services<br>• Changing nature of services from family-centered to child-centered |
| Goals for child | • Regulation of feeding, sleeping, and elimination patterns<br>• Responding to caregiver and self comforting and consoling<br>• Interacting with caregiver(s) through making eye contact, vocalizing, smiling, and responsive body movements<br>• Showing interest in sounds, objects, people, and activities in the environment. | • Communicating through gestures and single words<br>• Walking<br>• Feeding self at meals<br>• Enjoying playing with simple toys<br>• Playing simple games with caregivers, and imitating caregiver actions | • Following routines and directions<br>• Understanding and using simple phrases and sentences to communicate<br>• Playing alone for brief periods of time<br>• Showing interest and enjoyment in other children and ability to play with them for a brief time<br>• Toilet training |
| Common roles for interventionist | • Supporting parent(s) in developing a positive, enjoyable relationship with child<br>• Helping parent(s) link with services and agencies that can support meeting their own or the child's needs<br>• Supporting parents in finding out about, trying out, and choosing caregiving strategies and routines that work for their family<br>• Support to families in linking with other parents of children with disabilities or other sources of understanding and emotional support | • Providing caregivers with ideas on how to facilitate the child's development across a variety of developmental areas and within natural play and caregiving routines<br>• Working with family members to integrate and coordinate input from a variety of service providers with other family priorities and demands | • Providing support for family in assuming more of service coordination role<br>• Collaborating with early intervention team, preschool team, and family in planning for transition to preschool<br>• Facilitating intervention on goals that will help child as preschooler |
| Common intervention strategies | • Listening very carefully to parents' concerns, priorities, and requests for assistance<br>• Helping families to be aware of available options and to feel comfortable with the choices and decisions they make<br>• Focusing on short-term, high-priority concerns, and refocusing intervention as often as needed to respond to rapidly changing infant and family needs | • Working with family members on developing and trying intervention strategies that are designed to teach the child skills that have been identified as a priority goal by parents as a part of IFSP<br>• Working with family members on integrating intervention strategies across different developmental goals, as they would naturally occur within play or caregiving routines<br>• Supporting families in identifying supports or services that will allow the child's needs to be met while other family members have time to pursue other needs or goals | • Developing transition plan with family and preschool team<br>• Involving child in frequent activities with typical peers of similar ages<br>• Identifying ways to increase child's independence<br>• Using modeling and expansion of child's communication to increase the flexibility and effectiveness of the child's communication with others |

technology, which because it is noninvasive allows for study of the human brain during pregnancy and early childhood (Shore, 1997). For example, magnetic resonance imaging (MRI) has provided much more detailed images of the brain than was previously possible, and positron emission tomography (PET) scans allow neuroscientists not only to view the fine structures of the brain, but to see the level of activity that is taking place in different parts of the brain, and as the individual responds to changes in their environment (Shore, 1997). These techniques have led researchers to conclude that the brain is most active during the first three years of life, especially during the early months, and that the synapses are actually "hard-wired" during this period (Ramey & Ramey, 1999), when early childhood experiences "exert a dramatic and precise impact, physically determining how the intricate neural circuits of the brain are wired (Newsweek, Feb. 19, 1996)" (Begley, 1997, p. 30). Research has also demonstrated that certain windows exist for optimal learning and possible recovery from brain damage or deprivation (Shore, 1997). Ongoing research not only highlights the critical importance of early intervention, but also may lead to treatment for a variety of developmental disabilities (Blasco & Pearson, 2001).

Improvements in medical technology and treatment have led to both increases in the number of children surviving with severe disabilities, and in the prevention and/or treatment for other disabilities. One of the primary causes of this "good news–bad news" situation is the increased survival of extreme-low-birth-weight (ELBW) infants, defined as infants weighing less than 1,000 grams at birth. Of surviving ELBW infants, major neurodevelopmental deficits (cerebral palsy, mental retardation, blindness, deafness, multiple disabilities) occur in approximately 20 to 25 percent of the children, more minor problems occur in close to 50 percent (e.g., learning disability, ADHD), and the remaining 25 percent are typically developing (Blasco, 2001). The increasing incidence of shaken baby syndrome (SBS) is another cause of severe and multiple disabilities. Although children are vulnerable to SBS through age 5, they are particularly likely to suffer permanent brain damage or death between 2–4 months of age. The 75 percent of children who survive with SBS may experience blindness caused by bleeding around the brain and eyes, or other disabilities resulting from brain damage, including mental retardation, to paralysis (Poussaint & Linn, 1997). Some other highlights of prevention, treatment, and research efforts that are likely to affect the number of children with severe disabilities in the future, and how well we are able to assist them in meeting their potential, include the following:

- The cause of 75 percent of birth defects is unknown, yet very limited federal funds are devoted to research in this area.
- The risks of neural tube defects such as spina bifida can be reduced by two-thirds if women take folic acid before and during pregnancy.
- At-risk babies whose mothers received magnesium sulfate appeared to be protected from cerebral palsy caused by oxygen deprivation.
- Prevention of cerebral palsy can also be helped through reductions in lead poisoning and head injuries. (Riccitiello & Adler, 1997)

## *Future Trends in Early Intervention Services*

In the last forty years the quality and availability of services for infants and toddlers with severe disabilities and their families has improved dramatically. Research studies that have examined the effectiveness of early intervention for these infants and toddlers have often focused on developmental outcomes for the child or a reduction of later intervention costs. Although there are a number of other meaningful outcomes to be examined, past research has been supportive of the effectiveness of early intervention, including for children with autism or Down syndrome (Dawson & Osterling, 1997; Spiker & Hopmann, 1997; Strain, Wolery, & Izeman, 1998). For example, the combination of not institutionalizing infants with Down syndrome and the availability of early intervention for many of these children has been sufficiently successful that Down syndrome is now viewed as a condition most likely to result in moderate delays or impairments, rather than severe-profound impairments as was the prognosis a generation ago. In an extensive review of existing research, Spiker & Hopmann (1997) concluded that recent longitudinal research demonstrates highly variable outcomes for individuals with Down syndrome, but that "at the very least, researchers acknowledge the presence of a progressive decline in the rate of development for children with Down syndrome and expect that participation in early intervention will slow the decline" (p. 274). A select group of early intervention programs for children with autism have also attained very positive results when the intervention has (1) begun at an early age, (2) included highly supportive teaching environments and generalization strategies within predictable routines, (3) been intensive in nature (multiple hours per day, year round, home and center), (4) involved parents in carrying out intervention in the home, (5) had a curriculum that emphasized attending to the environment, ability to imitate others, comprehension and use of language, appropriate toy play, and social interaction, (6) used a functional approach to problem behaviors, and (7) carefully prepared children for the transition from preschool (Dawson & Osterling, 1997). In fact, some of the children in programs that met these criteria seemed to show near "recovery" by the time the children were ready to enter school, with many children showing a gain of about 20 points in IQ testing, and placement in inclusive classrooms when they entered school.

The intensity of the intervention, the degree of family involvement in intervention, and the comprehensiveness of the provided services have been several of the key variables associated with positive early intervention outcomes in the more child-centered early intervention on which most currently referenced efficacy research is based. Intensity, comprehensiveness, and family involvement are conceptualized differently in family-centered early intervention. Although the policy, family, and professional support are strong for family-centered early intervention, we are not yet certain whether it will yield similar child outcomes or what all of the potential benefits will be. We are also still developing only a beginning understanding about what kinds of programmatic variables make family-centered early intervention most likely to be a success. Guidelines provided to interventionists at this point are often based on values or philosophical positions and may not be empirically validated for large numbers of children and families. Future directions for early intervention will include developing this understanding of the parameters of how to make family-centered early intervention work.

Several of the variables associated with successful early intervention outcomes in the past (i.e., intensity of services, comprehensiveness of services) may require an expanded funding base for either early intervention or for the community programs (e.g., child care, preventive health care) to which early intervention can link. Although the concept of linking existing services and building on informal or natural supports has many strengths, in a number of communities needed services or supports are still not available or can be readily developed on existing resource bases. Examples of needed services for which funding is currently tenuous or missing in many communities include supported child care (extra staff or training available to meet the needs of children with disabilities), and a cadre of respite care providers trained to care appropriately for technologically dependent children. To really take advantage of the potential of early intervention it may be necessary not only to pass federal legislation mandating the availability of early intervention services but also to increase funding to the agencies and services with which early intervention needs to link as well. As a society, can we afford an intensive early intervention program for children with autism that results in regular class placement for many of its graduates, or in early intervention services that provide sufficient family and community health support to maintain a technologically dependent child at home? Although there are no easy answers to questions such as this, as one examines the alternative costs to society of not intervening, another reasonable question is whether we can afford not to.

Meisels (1992) ties together many of the issues in building on the demonstrated successes and difficulties of previous early intervention models or paradigms as we seek to enhance the effectiveness of more family-centered early intervention:

> As we review the efforts of the past, and as we anticipate the needs of the future, we can see distinct need for a better match between the child and family's lived context and the context of early intervention, with particular attention paid to the manner in which services are delivered. It is essential that we shift the way that systems and structures are organized so that they work more effectively for families. No longer can we consider the child as isolated from his or her family. No longer should we attend to the needs of parents without also recognizing that they must know how to respond to the changing needs of their children. No longer is it appropriate to follow the dictates of a theoretical view of intervention without questioning its relevance to a particular child and family's social and community situation. Rather, we must foster highly individualized programs of intervention that consider the needs of children and families in tandem, and that seek to address these needs through theoretically-driven and empirically-substantiated models that are consistent with the family's world.
>
> Instead of searching "out there" for the "best" intervention or assessment model overall, we must pay systematic attention to the child and family in context. As we learn to appreciate and intervene with their context, we will become more successful in enhancing development and strengthening families. (pp. 5–6)

## Focus Review

Focus 1: What types of services were made available in the past to infants and toddlers with disabilities and their families?

- Institutionalization was recommended to families of infants and toddlers with severe disabilities through the 1950s.
- Child-centered early intervention services became increasingly available between the late 1950s and the mid-1980s. These services were initially developed and operated by parent advocacy groups and by private and public agencies and focused on enhancing the child's skill development and preventing secondary disabilities.

**POINT AND COUNTERPOINT 8.1** • *Family-Centered Care: Is It Always in the Child's Best Interests?*

Kylie is a 9-month-old baby with cerebral palsy and a controlled seizure disorder. She was born two-and-a-half months prematurely and had anoxia (oxygen deprivation) at birth, as well as seizures and symptoms associated with cocaine withdrawal. Kylie has very limited voluntary control or movement of her arms and legs and is unable to hold up her head independently. The rigidity of her body makes her difficult to carry or hold. She is alert and responsive to interactions, but tends to be irritable and hard to soothe. Kylie has serious feeding difficulties and dislikes being fed.

Marcy is Kylie's mother. Marcy was 15 when Kylie was born and is now 16 years old. She is no longer dating Kylie's father and he has no contact with the baby. Marcy became addicted to cocaine when she was 14. She has been treated at substance abuse centers on several occasions but has been unable to stay "clean" for more than a few weeks at a time. Marcy tried living with her mother after Kylie was born but couldn't take her mother's interference in her life, particularly her constant criticism of the men Marcy was seeing and of her suspected return to cocaine usage. Marcy is currently estranged from her mother and receiving public assistance. She has a steady boyfriend who usually stays with her, a man named Michael who is ten years older than herself, and who is also a user. Michael doesn't pay much attention to Kylie one way or another, although he does find her crying very irritating and asks Marcy to put her in her crib in the other room if Marcy is unable to quiet her quickly.

Kylie is being seen by a pediatrician, occupational therapist, and physical therapist at a public health agency that provides early intervention services to children with developmental delays. The physical therapist is her service coordinator, and she makes home visits twice a week. Kylie's pediatrician is very concerned about her minimal weight gain, or failure to thrive, and seriously doubts that Marcy is following through on the admittedly very time-consuming procedures that he and the occupational therapist are recom-

mending to improve her nutritional and health status. Her physical therapist is also very concerned about lack of follow-through on the range of motion exercises she asks Marcy to do with Kylie twice a day. If these exercises are not carried out on a regular basis, muscle contractures will permanently limit Kylie's movement.

The early intervention team who work with Kylie and Marcy are uncertain how to proceed. The have very genuine concerns about Kylie's welfare, and suspect that she is left to lie around much of the time, without the attention to her special needs that will assure her health and development. On the other hand, Marcy does bring her to the clinic, is home when the therapist comes for home visits, gives Kylie the medication needed to control her seizures, and talks about her love and concern for Kylie. There are no signs that Michael or Marcy has ever abused Kylie. The team feels that if Kylie were a typically developing child who did not require so much extra time and attention, her physical needs could be adequately met within her current home environment.

*Point*

Although Marcy may have good intentions, she is currently unable to meet Kylie's basic health and developmental needs on her own. Marcy obviously loves Kylie, but if Kylie continues in her care at this time she may suffer damage that will permanently limit her development and well-being, such as through the development of muscle contractures or through an extended period of malnutrition. Kylie must receive the care she needs now. The early intervention team should contact child protective services and push for the addition of home care services or the temporary removal of Kylie from her home. They have tried to reach Marcy about the importance of the feeding and therapy procedures. She is too young and has too many problems of her own to respond as needed at this time. If Marcy is unable to get her life turned around within a reasonable period of time, child protective services should seek to

**POINT OF INTEREST 8.1 • Continued**

terminate her parental rights. Although Marcy has rights, Kylie should also have the right to grow up in a family that can not only love her but also take care of her.

*Counterpoint*
The early intervention team should continue working with Marcy, using a family-centered approach that responds to the concerns, priorities, and needs she identifies. Although Kylie's needs are not being adequately met in many ways, it is important for her sake to keep the family intact and to support Marcy in doing her best with her child. If child protective services is contacted, Marcy may lose all trust in professionals and simply not take Kylie in for any type of treatment. Look what happened when her mother tried to "interfere": Marcy cut her off both from herself and from her granddaughter. However inadequate the current situation is, it is better than having Marcy take off with Kylie, with both of them receiving no support at all.

- Federally funded model development projects increased the quality, comprehensiveness, and availability of early intervention services.
- Parents played prominent roles in early intervention services, including as teachers for their child with disabilities.

Focus 2: How are early intervention services currently defined in Part C of the 1997 Reauthorization of the IDEA (P.L. 105-17)?

- Eligibility is based on the determination of developmental delay or the existence of a diagnosed physical or mental condition with a high probability of resulting in developmental delay. States have the option of defining and providing services to children who are at risk of developmental delay.
- Individualized Family Service Plans (IFSPs) are developed for every eligible child and family. Required components of the IFSP include a statement of the child's present level of development; a family-directed assessment of the resources, priorities, and concerns of the family; major desired outcomes or goals for the child and family; and the identification of a service coordinator and the early intervention services necessary to meet the unique needs of the child and family.
- States participating in the Part C Early Intervention Program must identify a lead agency and form an Interagency Coordinating Council.

Focus 3: What are the major expected outcomes of early intervention for infants and toddlers with severe disabilities and their families?

- Mutually enjoyable family relationships that include the child with disabilities are established and maintained.
- The family unit as a whole is strengthened and individual family members have their critical needs met.
- The child's health is maintained or improved.

- Secondary disabilities are prevented.
- The child's learning and development are enhanced.
- The independence and inclusion of the child and family are facilitated.

Focus 4: Describe family-directed assessment, Individualized Family Service Plans, service coordination, and transition planning, and discuss how they are used to achieve the goals of family-centered early intervention.

- Family-directed assessment involves family members in directing and/or shaping the process of gathering and sharing information that will assist the family and early intervention team in developing and implementing an effective and supportive Individualized Family Service Plan (IFSP).
- Individualized Family Service Plans (IFSPs) are the required written documents used to define the goals, plan of action, services, and evaluation strategies that family members and multidisciplinary early intervention team members agree upon as defining the early intervention most important for an individual child and family.
- Service coordination services are designed to assist families of infants and toddlers with developmental delays in accessing and benefitting from a variety of services and supports identified within a child and family's IFSP. Regulations require the identification of a service coordinator on every IFSP.
- Transition planning is a required component of IFSPs as children receiving early intervention services approach their third birthday. IFSPs must include the "steps to be taken to support the transition" to preschool special education.
- One of the goals of early intervention is to enable and empower families in meeting the needs of family members, including those of the infant or toddler with developmental delays. Family-directed assessment uses methods that are meaningful to the family to gather and share information about child and family strengths, needs, supports, and priorities. This information is used to assist in the development of the IFSP, which includes family priorities for goals, the natural contexts in which intervention will occur, and the supports and services that will best assist a family in achieving the identified goals or outcomes. Service coordination services are provided to help tie together the formal and informal supports and services that are used to implement an IFSP. Transition planning assists families in preparing for the next phase in their child's and their family's life.

Focus 5: Describe the role of natural supports, natural environments, and interagency coordination and collaboration via service coordination in family-centered early intervention.

- Natural or informal supports are identified as strengths on a child and family's IFSP, and are linked to individual goals or outcome statements as a primary or preferred means of achieving many outcomes.
- Natural contexts refer to the settings and routines that typically developing children of similar ages participate in within family, child care, and community settings. These natural environments or contexts must be identified as a part of the IFSP, and teams must justify any service provision outside of natural environments.

- Interagency coordination and collaboration are required to make early intervention successful. One of the primary purposes of early intervention is to identify and coordinate formal and informal resources, services, and supports, in order to meet the needs and priorities identified by the family. The requirements to include service coordination and Interagency Coordinating Councils (ICCs) as a part of early intervention reflect how critical this type of coordination and collaboration are to successful intervention.

## References

Allen, K. E., & Marotz, L. (1994). *Developmental profiles: Pre-birth through eight* (2nd ed.). Albany, NY: Delmar.

Bailey, D. B., & Simeonsson, R. J. (1988). Home-based early intervention. In S. L. Odom & M. B. Karnes (Eds.), *Early intervention for infants and children with handicaps: An empirical base* (pp. 199–215). Baltimore: Paul H. Brookes.

Baker, B. L., Brightman, A. J., Blacher, J. B., Heifetz, L. J., Hinshaw, S. P., & Murphy, D. M. (1989). *Steps to independence: A skills training guide for parents and teachers of children with special needs* (2nd ed.). Baltimore: Paul H. Brookes.

Baker, B. L., Heifetz, L. J., & Murphy, D. M. (1980). Behavioral training for parents of mentally retarded children: One-year follow-up. *American Journal of Mental Deficiency, 85*(1), 31–38.

Baldwin, V. L., Fredericks, H. D., & Brodsky, G. (1973). *Isn't it time he outgrew this? or a training program for parents of retarded children.* Springfield, IL: Charles C. Thomas.

Barrera, I. (1994). Thoughts on the assessment of young children whose sociocultural background is unfamiliar to the assessor. *Zero to Three, 14*(6), 9–13.

Begley, S. (1997). How to build a baby's brain. *Newsweek Special Edition: Your child from Birth to Age Three,* Spring/Summer, 28–32.

Begun, A. L. (1996). Family systems and family-centered care. In P. Rosin, G. S. Jesien, A. D. Whitehead, A. L. Begun, L. I. Tuchman, & L. Irwin (Eds.), *Partnerships in family-centered care: A guide to collaborative early intervention* (pp. 33–64). Baltimore: Paul H. Brookes.

Benson, H. A., & Turnbull, A. P. (1986). Approaching families from an individualized perspective. In R. H. Horner, L. H. Meyer, & H. D. Fredericks (Eds.), *Education of learners with severe handicaps: Exemplary service strategies* (pp. 127–157). Baltimore: Paul H. Brookes.

Blasco, P. A. (2001). Medical considerations. In P. M. Blasco (Ed.), *Early intervention services for infants, toddlers, and their families* (pp. 213–258). Boston: Allyn & Bacon.

Blasco, P. M., & Pearson, J. (2001). Living in our world: The first year. In P. M. Blasco (Ed.), *Early intervention services for infants, toddlers, and their families* (pp. 63–96). Boston: Allyn & Bacon.

Bluma, S. M., Shearer, M. S., Frohman, A. H., & Hilliard, J. M. (1976). *Portage guide to early education.* Portage, WI: CESA 5.

Brinker, R. P. (1992). Family involvement in early intervention: Accepting the unchangeable, changing the changeable, and knowing the difference. *Topics in Early Childhood Special Education, 12,* 307–332.

Bromwich, R. (1978). *Working with parents and infants: An interactional approach.* Austin, TX: PRO-ED.

Bromwich, R. (1997). *Working with families and their infants at risk: A perspective after 20 years of experience.* Austin, TX: Pro-Ed.

Brooks-Gunn, J., & Duncan, G. (1997). The effects of poverty on children. *The Future of Children, 7,* 55–71.

Bruder, M. B. (2000). Family-centered early intervention: Clarifying our values for the new millennium. *Topics in Early Childhood Special Education, 20,* 105–115.

Calhoun, M. L., Rose, T. L., & Armstrong, C. (1989). Getting an early start on community participation. *Teaching Exceptional Children, 21*(4), 51–53.

Calhoun, M. L., Rose, T. L., & Prendergast, D. E. (1991). *Charlotte Circle intervention guide for parent–child interactions.* Tucson, AZ: Communication Skill Builders.

Cicchetti, D., & Beeghly, M. (1990). An organizational approach to the study of Down syndrome: Contributions to an integrative theory of development. In D. Cicchetti & M. Beeghly (Eds.), *Children with Down syndrome: A developmental perspective* (pp. 29–62). Cambridge, England: Cambridge University Press.

Cowan, C., & Cowan, P. (1995). Intervention to ease the transition to parenthood: Why they are needed and what they can do. *Family Relations, 44,* 412–423.

Cripe, J. W., & Venn, M. L. (1997). Family-guided routines for early intervention services. *Young Exceptional Children, 1*(1) 18–26.

Dawson, G., & Osterling. J. (1997). Early intervention in autism. In M. Guralnick (Ed.), *The effectiveness of early intervention* (pp. 307–326). Baltimore: Paul H. Brookes.

Dinnebeil, L. A., & Rule, S. (1994). Variables that influence collaboration between parents and service coordinators. *Journal of Early Intervention, 18,* 349–361.

Dunst, C. J. (1991). Implementation of the Individualized Family Service Plan. In M. J. McGonigel, R. K. Kaufmann, & B. H. Johnson (Eds.), *Guidelines and recommended practices for the Individualized Family Service Plan* (2nd ed.) (pp. 67–78). Bethesda, MD: Association for the Care of Children's Health.

Dunst, C. J., Hamby, D., Trivette, C. M., Raab, M., & Bruder, M. B. (2000). Everyday family and community life and children's naturally occurring learning opportunities. *Journal of Early Intervention, 23,* 151–164.

Dunst, C. J., Trivette, C. M., & Deal, A. G. (1988). *Enabling and empowering families: Principles and guidelines for practice.* Cambridge, MA: Brookline.

Dunst, C. J., Trivette, C. M., & Jodry, W. (1997). Influences of social support on children with disabilities and their families. In M. Guralnick (Ed.), *The effectiveness of early intervention* (pp. 499–522). Baltimore: Paul H. Brookes.

English, D. J. (1998). The extent and consequences of child maltreatment. *The Future of Children, 8,* 39–53.

Featherstone, H. (1980). *A difference in the family: Living with a disabled child.* New York: Penguin.

Feldman, M. A. (1997). The effectiveness of early intervention for children of parents with mental retardation. In M. L. Guralnick (Ed.), *The effectiveness of early intervention* (pp. 171–191). Baltimore: Paul H. Brookes.

Finnie, N. R. (1975). *Handling the young cerebral palsied child at home.* New York: Dutton.

Fraiberg, S. (1974). Blind infants and their mothers: An examination of the sign system. In M. Lewis & L. A. Rosenblum (Eds.), *The origins of behavior: Vol. I, The effect of the infant on its caregiver* (pp. 215–232). New York: Wiley.

Furuno, S., O'Reilly, K. A., Hosaka, C. M., Inatsuka, T. T., Allman, T. L., & Zeisloft, B. (1985). *Hawaii Early Learning Profile (HELP): Activity guide.* Palo Alto, CA: VORT Corporation.

Greenspan, S., & Meisels, S. (Eds.) (1994). Toward a new vision for the developmental assessment of infants and young children. *Zero to Three, 14*(6), 1–8.

Guralnick, M. (Ed.) (1997). *The effectiveness of early intervention.* Baltimore: Paul H. Brookes.

Guralnick, M. J., & Bricker, D. (1987). The effectiveness of early intervention for children with cognitive and general developmental delays. In M. J. Guralnick & F. C. Bennett (Eds.), *The effectiveness of early intervention for at-risk and handicapped children* (pp. 115–174). Orlando, FL: Academic.

Hadden, S., & Fowler, S. (1997). Preschool: A new beginning for children and parents. *Teaching Exceptional Children, 21,* 51–53.

Hamner, T. J., & Turner, P. H. (2001). *Parenting in contemporary society* (4th ed.). Boston: Allyn & Bacon.

Hanson, M. J. (1987). *Teaching the infant with Down Syndrome: A guide for parents and professionals* (2nd ed.). Austin, TX: Pro-Ed.

Hanson, M. J., & Bruder, M. B. (2001). Early intervention: Promises to keep. *Infants and Young Children, 13,* 47–58.

Hanson, M. J., & Lynch, E. W. (1992). Family diversity: Implications for policy and practice. *Topics in Early Childhood Special Education, 12*(3), 283–306.

Hanson, M. J., & Lynch, E. W. (1995). *Early intervention: Implementing child and family services for infants and toddlers who are at-risk or disabled.* (2nd ed.) Austin: Pro-Ed.

Hanson, M. J., & Schwarz, R. H. (1978). Results of a longitudinal intervention program for Down's syndrome infants and their families. *Education and Training of the Mentally Retarded, 13,* 403–407.

Harbin, G. L. (1993). Family issues of children with disabilities: How research and theory have modified practice in intervention. In N. J. Anastasiow & S. Harel (Eds.), *At-risk infants: Interventions, families, and research* (pp. 101–114). Baltimore: Paul H. Brookes.

Hedlund, R. (1989). Fostering positive interactions between parents and infants. *Teaching Exceptional Children, 21*(4), 45–48.

Horbar, J. D., & Lucey, J. F. (1995). Evaluation of neonatal intensive care technology. *The Future of Children, 5,* 139–161.

Hunt, M., Cornelius, P., Leventhal, P., Miller, P., Murray, T., & Stoner, G. (1990). *Into our lives.* Akron, OH: Children's Hospital Medical Center.

Johnson-Martin, N. M., Jens, K. G., Attermeier, S. M., & Hacker, B. J. (1991). *The Carolina Curriculum for Infants and Toddlers with Special Needs* (2nd ed.). Baltimore: Paul H. Brookes.

Kaufmann, R. K., & McGonigel, M. J. (1991). Identifying family concerns, priorities, and resources. In M. J. McGonigel, R. K. Kaufmann, & B. H. Johnson (Eds.), *Guidelines and recommended practices for the Individualized Family Service Plan* (2nd ed.)

(pp. 47–56). Bethesda, MD: Association for the Care of Children's Health.

Kohrman, A. F. (1990). Bringing home a medically complex baby: Psychological issues for families, caretakers, and professionals. *Zero to Three, 11*(2), 36–41.

Krauss, M. W. (1997). Two generations of family research in early intervention. In M. Guralnick (Ed.), *The effectiveness of early intervention* (pp. 611–624). Baltimore: Paul H. Brookes.

LeLaurin, K. (1992). Infant and toddler models of service delivery: Are they detrimental for some children and families? *Topics in Early Childhood Special Education, 12*(1), 82–104.

Lillie, D. L., Trohanis, P. L., & Goin, K. W. (Eds.). (1976). *Teaching parents to teach.* New York: Walker.

McCamman, S., & Rues, J. (1990). Nutrition monitoring and supplementation. In J. C. Graff, M. M. Ault, D. Guess, M. Taylor, & B. Thompson (Eds.), *Health care for students with disabilities: An illustrated medical guide for the classroom* (pp. 79–118). Baltimore: Paul H. Brookes.

McCollum, J. A. (1987). Looking patterns of retarded and non-retarded babies in play and instructional situations. *American Journal of Mental Deficiency, 91,* 516–522.

McCollum, J. A., & Hemmeter, M. L. (1997). Parent-child interaction intervention when children have disabilities. In M. Guralnick (Ed.), *The effectiveness of early intervention* (pp. 549–576). Baltimore: Paul H. Brookes.

McDonnell, A., & Hardman, M. (1988). A synthesis of "best practice" guidelines for early childhood services. *Journal of the Division for Early Childhood, 12*(4), 328–341.

McGonigel, M. J. (1991). Philosophy and conceptual framework. In M. J. McGonigel, R. K. Kaufmann, & B. H. Johnson (Eds.), *Guidelines and recommended practices for the Individualized Family Service Plan* (2nd ed.) (pp. 7–14). Bethesda, MD: Association for the Care of Children's Health.

McGonigel, M. J., Kaufmann, R. K., & Johnson, B. H. (Eds.) (1991). *Guidelines and recommended practices for the Individualized Family Service Plan* (2nd ed.). Bethesda, MD: Association for the Care of Children's Health.

McNab, T. C., & Blackman, J. A. (1998). Medical complications of the critically ill newborn: A review for early intervention professionals. *Topics in Early Childhood Special Education, 18,* 197–205.

Meisels, S. J. (1992). Early intervention: A matter of context. *Zero to Three. 12*(3), 1–6.

O'Brien, M. (1997). *Inclusive child care for infants and toddlers: Meeting individual and special needs.* Baltimore: Paul H. Brookes.

Pellegrino, L. (1998). In J. P. Dormans & L. Pellegrino (Eds.), *Caring for children with cerebral palsy: A team approach* (pp. 71–98). Baltimore: Paul H. Brookes.

Poussaint, A. F., & Linn, S. (1997). Fragile: Handle with care. *Newsweek Special Edition: Your Child from Birth to Three,* Spring/Summer, 33.

Ramey, C. T., & Ramey, S. L. (1999). *Right from birth: Building your child's foundation for life—birth to 18 months.* New York: Goddard.

Rappaport, J. (1984). Studies in empowerment: Introduction to the issues. In J. Rappaport, C. Swift, & R. Hess (Eds.), *Studies in empowerment: Steps toward understanding and action* (pp. 1–37). New York: Haworth.

Riccitiello, R., & Adler, J. (1997). "Your baby has a problem." *Newsweek Special Edition: Your Child from Birth to Age Three,* Spring/Summer, 46–50.

Rose, T. L., Calhoun, M. L., & Ladage, L. (1989). Helping young children respond to caregivers. *Teaching Exceptional Children, 21*(4), 48–51.

Rosenkoetter, E. S., Hains, A. H., & Fowler, S. A. (1994). *Bridging early services for children with special needs and their families: A practical guide for transition planning.* Baltimore: Paul H. Brookes.

Sameroff, A. J., & Chandler, M. J. (1975). Reproductive risk and the continuum of caretaking causality. In F. D. Horowitz (Ed.), *Review of child development research* (Vol. 4, pp. 187–244). Chicago: University of Chicago Press.

Shearer, D. E., & Shearer, M. S. (1976). The Portage Project: A model for early childhood intervention. In T. D. Tjossem (Ed.), *Intervention strategies for high risk infants and young children* (pp. 335–350). Baltimore: University Park Press.

Sherman, A. (1997). *Poverty matters.* Washington, DC: Children's Defense Fund.

Shore, R. (1997). *Rethinking the brain: New insights into early development.* New York: Families and Work Institute.

Spiker, D., & Hopmann, M. R. (1997). The effectiveness of early intervention for children with Down syndrome. In M. Guralnick (Ed.), *The effectiveness of early intervention* (pp. 271–306). Baltimore: Paul H. Brookes.

Stile, S., Cole, J., & Garner, A. (1979). Maximizing parental involvement in programs for exceptional children: Strategies for education and related service personnel. *Journal of the Division for Early Childhood, 1,* 68–82.

Strain, P. S., Wolery, M., & Izeman, S. (1998). Considerations for administrators in the design of service options for young children with autism and their families. *Young Exceptional Children, 1*(2) 8–16.

Early Intervention Programs for Infants and Toddlers with Disabilities and Their Families **225**

Summers, J. A., Behr, S. K., & Turnbull, A. P. (1989). Positive adaptation and coping strength of families who have children with disabilities. In G. H. Singer & L. K. Irvin (Eds.), *Support for caregiving families: Enabling positive adaptation to disabilities* (pp. 27–40). Baltimore: Paul H. Brookes.

Turnbull, A. P., & Turnbull, H. R. (1986). Stepping back from early intervention: An ethical perspective. *Journal of the Division for Early Childhood, 10*(2), 106–117.

Turnbull, A. P., & Turnbull, H. R. (2001). *Families, professionals, and exceptionality: Collaborating for empowerment* (4th ed.). Upper Saddle River, NJ: Prentice-Hall.

Zotkiewicz, T. T. (1996). Home at last. In J. Zaichkin, *Newborn intensive care: What every parent needs to know* (pp. 305–342). Petaluma, CA: NICULink.

# 9

# *Programs for Preschool Children*

*Like their peers, young children with severe disabilities learn important cognitive, social, communication, and self-help skills through play.*

## WINDOW 9.1 • *Beginning Preschool*

As my daughter's third birthday approached, I lived in dread, not wishing to leave the familiar, comfortable environment of her infant program. The infant program had become home away from home for me. It was supportive and intimate. I had made some lifelong friendships, as well as having established a comfortable routine in our lives. I saw making the transition to a preschool program in the school district as an extremely traumatic experience, second only to learning of Amy's diagnosis.

What were my fears? First, I was concerned that my husband and I, along with professionals, would be deciding the future of our child. How could we play God? Would our decisions be the right ones? Second, I feared loss of control, as I would be surrendering my child to strangers—first to the school district's intake assessment team and then to the preschool teacher. The feeling of being at the mercy of professionals was overwhelming. In addition, I had more information to absorb and a new system with which to become familiar. Finally, I feared the "label" that would be attached to my child and feared that this label would lower the world's expectations of her.

The first week Amy attended her new preschool was wonderful, as I was in the classroom with her every day. Then came the reality of being in the classroom only one day a week. That change was most difficult, as I was going through separation anxiety. I was convinced that the staff was incompetent, and I had made the worst decision possible. However, the staff sensed my anxieties and were extremely patient and cooperative. We have now established a pattern of mutual support and partnership. I feel fortunate, as my daughter has done remarkably well in the preschool.

Patti Wood, parent

*Source:* Hanline, M. F., & Knowlton, A. (1988). A collaborative model for providing support to parents during their child's transition from infant intervention to preschool special education public school programs. *Journal of the Division for Early Childhood, 12,* 116–125.

Three- through 5-year-olds are known for their active, energetic, enthusiastic, and noisy exploration of the world around them. Though often shy or in need of adult assistance or reassurance, preschoolers enjoy enlarging their world to include regular classmates and playmates and building relationships with adults beyond their immediate family and caregivers (Allen & Marotz, 1994). As with younger children, this age is characterized by rapid physical and developmental growth. Preschoolers not only learn many new skills, they also become much more sophisticated in both applying skills and learning new ones. Preschoolers are absorbed with play and with becoming more independent in daily routines. Play and daily routines are the natural contexts for learning for children of this age (Gestwicki, 1995; Hamner & Turner, 2001). As they approach school age, children become increasingly interested in the wider world, in the relationships between people and events, and in the mystery of books and reading (Allen & Martoz, 1994). Most preschoolers are very social and want to be included in everything that their family, classmates, and friends do. The majority of preschool-age children in the United States attend preschool or child care programs for at least part of the day, regardless of whether they have a mother who works outside the home (Hofferth, 1996). However, preschoolers also continue to spend many of their waking hours at home with family members. If families have developed close relationships while the child was an infant and toddler, the preschool years are often a very enjoyable time for both parents and children.

For the parents of a child with severe developmental delays or disabilities, the preschool years may present new challenges. The gap between what their child and what typically developing children of the same age can do is noticeably widening. Having their child receive preschool special education services in a classroom that includes typically developing age peers may accentuate this realization, particularly if the child has been at home or in a mixed-age family child care program up to this point in time. There may also be the adjustment to meeting and conversing with the parents of typically developing children who are their child's classmates. The public school years begin to seem much closer, with all of the attendant concerns about whether their child will be accepted by other children, where will they attend school, and how productive and enjoyable the whole school experience will be for their child. For some families, getting their child ready for school becomes a focus. Other families may struggle with the realization that their child will not be "ready" to blend into a kindergarten classroom, no matter how hard they, the child, and their child's preschool teachers work. Although it was clearly not the intent of federal legislation, most families realize that the decisions that they and school district teams make about their child's initial school placement may have substantial impact not only on the type of curricular goals that are emphasized for their child (e.g., academic or adaptive), but also on the amount of time their child will be educated with peers without disabilities.

Even though the preschool years introduce a new set of concerns and stresses for families of young children with severe developmental delays, there is often diminished program support for other family members. Whereas early intervention has become increasingly family-centered, preschool programs continue to be primarily child-focused and to be offered in center-based settings. However positive the parent–teacher–team relationship may be, the increased focus on the child may make parents feel less supported and as though the family issues and contexts are treated as less central or less well understood. This chapter provides an overview of the types of preschool services that have historically been provided, and of the current trends, expected outcomes, organization, effective practices, and future directions for preschool programs for young children with severe developmental delays and their families.

---

*Focus 1*
What types of services were made available in the past to preschoolers with developmental disabilities and their families?

---

# Historical Overview of Preschool Services

## Types of Services and Service Delivery Models

The history of preschool programs for children with severe developmental delays is similar to that described for infants and toddlers and their families in Chapter 8. Until the last forty or fifty years, most individuals with severe disabilities, including preschool-age children, were either living in institutions or at home with their families (Harbin, 1993). If children lived at home they were usually without the benefit of either specialized services or access to public education or community programs. From the late 1950s through the mid-1980s there were growing opportunities for children with disabilities to attend preschool special education programs or to access other specialized services. However, these opportunities were not consistently available, and generally appear to have been less available to young children with severe disabilities and their families (Demchak & Drinkwater, 1992; Hanline, 1993; Thompson et al., 1993). Many preschoolers with severe disabilities were not able to attend preschool programs that would provide appropriate special education and related services until after Public Law 99-457 was passed in 1986, requiring all school districts to provide services for all eligible preschool-age children by 1991.

Preschool special education programs have traditionally been organized as center-based, home-based, or combined home- and center-based programs (see Thurman & Widerstrom, 1990, for a thorough description and numerous examples of traditional early childhood intervention models). Center-based preschool programs usually provide IEP-based special instruction and related services within a variety of preschool classroom activities and routines. Part of this intervention might be planned to ensure many practice opportunities, and part of it might include providing just one or two opportunities for a child to use a specific targeted skill throughout the entire class activity. Window 9.2 provides an example of how IEP goals might be infused within preschool activities and routines.

Preschool classes may be part-day or full-day and may meet every day or only a few times during a week. Examples of early center-based model demonstration projects that have enrolled preschool children with severe disabilities include the Infant, Toddler, and Pre-school Research and Intervention Program (Bricker & Bricker, 1973, 1976), The Down Syndrome Program at the Experimental Education Unit at the University of Washington (Hayden & Haring, 1976; Hayden & Dmitriev, 1975), and The Teaching Research Infant and Child Center Data-based Classroom for the Moderately and Severely Handicapped (Fredericks et al., 1977). More recent center-based models enrolling preschool children with severe disabilities include the Social Integration Program (Rule et al., 1987), which served children enrolled in community day care centers, The Circle of Inclusion Project (Thompson et al., 1993), and the CHIME Institute model for preschool inclusion (Cavallaro & Haney, 1999). Some advantages for center-based programs include the opportunity for the child with disabilities to interact with other children of the same age, the provision of some respite or child care help for the child's family, the opportunity for specially trained professionals to work directly with the child and to team with each other on intervention issues, and the opportunity the child receives to become competent in the many skills needed to learn successfully and to get along with others in a classroom environment before beginning kindergarten.

Home-based programs for preschoolers with disabilities have usually concentrated on teaching other family members to carry out intervention within the child's home, either in teaching sessions or within the context of daily family routines. Figure 9.1 provides an example of how intervention for Joshua's IEP goals could be infused in his family's typical activities and routines. Given an option, many families choose to have preschool-age children spend most of their time at home with their family, and home-based programs support these families if they choose to be the primary interventionist(s) for their child at this age.

Home-based programs may also be more appropriate for children with very fragile or failing health, when exposure to infectious diseases carried by other children could be a threat. Prior to federally mandated preschool special education programs, home-based programs were also sometimes favored because they could be less expensive to operate, particularly in rural areas or for children with low-incidence disabling conditions (Bailey & Simeonsson, 1988). An example of a home-based model program that included some preschool-age children with severe disabilities is the Portage Project, which was originally developed in rural Wisconsin (Shearer & Shearer, 1976). Not all home-based programs have concentrated on teaching family members to be interventionists for their child. Some programs have introduced interveners into the home to provide support for the child and family (Alsop, Blaha, & Kloos, 2000). Although many people favor home-based over center-based programs for infants and toddlers, some preschool classroom experience is generally favored for 3-, 4-, and 5-year-olds, unless individual family preferences or other extenuating circumstances prevent this from being a desirable option.

Many preschool programs combine center- and home-based components—for example, having children attend classes three or four days a week and having staff do home visits or parent education groups an additional one or two days. Prior to the implementation of P.L. 99-457, preschool programs generally made commitments to the funding

## WINDOW 9.2 • *Joshua's Day at Preschool*

Joshua is a 3-year-old child with severe and multiple disabilities. He lives with his mother and father, and will have a new brother or sister in a few months. His mother stays home with Joshua when he is not attending preschool. Joshua attends a community preschool program located in his local elementary school. Joshua's family and preschool team (which includes his parents, the community preschool teacher, a preschool special education consulting teacher, an instructional aide, a physical therapist, a speech-language pathologist, and an occupational therapist) have identified high-priority goals on Joshua's IEP. These goals include:

1. Maintaining head control, or keeping his head erect when properly positioned
2. Supported sitting, or maintaining his balance when supported at hips and trunk by an adult or an adaptive chair
3. Purposefully reaching for objects or people when in a prone position
4. Using adaptive switches to activate toys and media

5. Playing functionally with three or more toys, i.e., playing with them in their usual or intended fashion; toys must be selected so that batting, pushing, or tapping motions are all that is needed for play
6. Responding to peer initiations through eye contact, facial expression, and/or vocalization
7. Using lip closure to pull food off a spoon when eating snacks and meals
8. Using a purposeful reach to request desired objects, activities, and interactions with people.

The matrix below lists Joshua's preschool class schedule down the left side of the matrix. A short description of Joshua's IEP goals are listed across the top. Checks are used to indicate for which IEP goals intervention can most naturally be included in the context of each of the daily preschool activities. The abbreviations in the last column show the physical therapist's recommendations for positioning Joshua during each activity.

| Goals | head control | supported sitting | purposeful reach, prone | uses switch to activate | funct, use 3+ toys | responds to peers | pulls food off spoon | uses reach to request | Recommended Position |
|---|---|---|---|---|---|---|---|---|---|
| 9:00 – **Arrival** (Coats off, diaper change, free play) | ✔ | ✔ | | | | ✔ | | ✔ | WC |
| 9:15 – **Circle** (Finger plays, weather, show and tell) | ✔ | ✔ | | | | ✔ | | | SS |
| 9:30 – **Manipulative Toys or Block Area** | ✔ | ✔ | ✔ | ✔ | ✔ | ✔ | | ✔ | SS PB |
| 9:50 – **Science or Social Studies Activities** (Preacademic skills and stories) | ✔ | | | | ✔ | ✔ | | ✔ | WC |
| 10:10 – **Outdoor Play** (Gross motor activities) | ✔ | | | | ✔ | ✔ | | ✔ | PS or M |
| 10:30 – **Imaginative Play** (Diaper change included) | ✔ | | ✔ | ✔ | ✔ | ✔ | | ✔ | PB |
| 11:00 – **Snack** | ✔ | | | | | ✔ | ✔ | ✔ | WC |
| 11:20 – **Art or Music** | ✔ | (✔) | | (✔) | | ✔ | | ✔ | WC or SS |
| 11:50 – **Closing Circle** | ✔ | ✔ | | | | ✔ | | | SS → WC |
| 11:50 – **Bus to Go Home** | | | | | | | | | |

*Positioning Abbreviations*

PS  - Prone Stander
PB  - Prone on Bolster
WC  - Wheel Chair
SS  - Adult Supported Sitting
M   - Mat (range of motion)

**FIGURE 9.1** *A Day at Home for Joshua*

| | Head Control | Supported Sitting | Purposeful Reach, Prone | Uses Switch to Activate | Functional Use, 3+ Toys | Responds to Peers | Pulls Food off Spoon | Uses Reach to Request | Recommended Position |
|---|---|---|---|---|---|---|---|---|---|
| 7:00 – Wake-up cuddle, diaper change | ✔ | ✔ | ✔ | | | | | | |
| 7:20 – Breakfast, watch Mom clean up kitchen | ✔ | | | | | | ✔ | ✔ | WC |
| 8:00 – Get ready for school, play with Mom | ✔ | ✔ | ✔ | | ✔ | | | | |
| 8:40 – Bus arrives | | | | | | | | | WC |
| 12:15 – Diaper change, lunch | ✔ | | | | | | ✔ | ✔ | WC |
| 12:45 – Story or singing | | | | | | | | (✔) | |
| 1:00 – Nap | | | | | | | | | |
| 3:30 – Diaper change, range of motion | ✔ | ✔ | | | | | | (✔) | M |
| 4:00 – Snack | ✔ | | | | | | ✔ | ✔ | WC |
| 4:30 – Play w/Mom (or have friend over) | ✔ | ✔ | ✔ | ✔ | ✔ | (✔) | | | SS, PB |
| 5:00 – Play by self, watch Mom cook dinner | ✔ | ✔ | ✔ | | ✔ | | | | SS or PB |
| 5:30 – Sit w/Dad while he watches the news | ✔ | ✔ | | | (✔) | | | (✔) | SS PB |
| 6:00 – Diaper change, dinner | ✔ | | | | | | ✔ | ✔ | WC |
| 6:45 – Bath | ✔ | ✔ | | | ✔ | | | ✔ | |
| 7:15 – Play with Mom or Dad, diaper change | ✔ | | | | | | ✔ | ✔ | SS PB |
| 7:45 – Story, singing | | | | | | | | (✔) | |
| 8:00 – Bedtime | | | | | | | | | |

*Positioning Abbreviations*

PS  - Prone Stander          WC - Wheel Chair                    M - Mat (range of motion)
PB  - Prone on Bolstera      SS  - Adult Supported Sitting

agency outlining the range and types of service delivery options they would provide. With the 1986 passage of P.L. 99-457, the IEP became the document that legally determined the amount and type of services the individual child would receive. Changing philosophies about family-centered early intervention and the importance of inclusive preschool and early childhood programs have expanded and modified the ways service delivery models are conceptualized.

## Philosophical and Curricular Models

Several different philosophical and curricular models have defined the ways in which preschool special education programs have approached intervention for children and families. These models have included the developmental, behavioral, cognitive, and functional/ecological curricular approaches (Hanson & Lynch, 1995). Interventionists often blend these models to varying degrees at the program implementation level. Bailey and Wolery (1992) summarized the assumptions of three of these perspectives as they are related to children, the nature of learning and development, and assessment and intervention (see Table 9.1). The ecological model has gained increasing favor in recent years (Bailey & Wolery, 1992), and is particularly valid and useful for children with severe and/or multiple delays or disabilities (Hanson & Lynch, 1995). The ecological model is holistic, blends many of the strengths of the other perspectives, and is applicable to children with widely varying abilities, interests, and family and cultural backgrounds.

In the past, children with severe and profound disabilities have been most likely to attend preschool programs that (1) used a developmental or functional curricular orientation as the basis for selecting intervention goals, and (2) emphasized the use of behavioral teaching strategies for intervention. For recent reviews of model evaluation reports and preschool research studies, see Barnett, Bell, and Carey (1999) and Guralnick (2001). As with model programs for infants and toddlers with disabilities and their families, many of these projects were originally funded through the federal government's Handicapped Children's Early Education Program (HCEEP). The HCEEP projects have been highly successful in many regards, with nearly 80 percent of the almost 600 funded demonstration projects continuing after federal funding ended (Bailey & Wolery, 1992). As a group, these programs and similar projects were successful in demonstrating that educational gains can be made by young children with severe and profound developmental disabilities if they have access to effective instruction or intervention, although they are likely to be proportionally smaller than the gains demonstrated by children with more mild to moderate developmental delays (Guralnick, 1991).

## Models of Integration and Inclusion

The Infant, Toddler, and Pre-school Research and Intervention Program (Bricker & Bricker, 1973) was among the first programs to systematically integrate preschool children with disabilities with their typically developing peers. In the broadest sense, any program that actively mixes children with and without disabilities can be considered integrated (Odom & McEvoy, 1988). A variety of different approaches have been utilized to achieve integration or inclusion, including *reverse mainstream, integrated,* and *fully mainstreamed*

**TABLE 9.1** *Three Theoretical Perspectives and Their Implications*

| *Theoretical Perspective* | *Basic Assumptions about the Nature of Children* | *Basic Assumptions about Learning and Development* | *Assessment Implications* | *Intervention Implications* |
|---|---|---|---|---|
| Developmental | Children are born with an intrinsic motivation to explore and master the environment. Skills emerge in a relatively predictable sequence. | Development is primarily a result of physical maturation. Competence is gained through self-initiated exploration and play. | Document the extent to which the child has attained specific developmental milestones. | Arrange the environment and provide materials that are highly interesting to children and are most likely to facilitate competence in developmentally appropriate skills. |
| Behavioral | Children are born with the capacity to learn. The skills that a child displays emerge as a result of experiences with the environment. Biological and physiological processes also are acknowledged as important. | Antecedents and consequences serve to shape behavior. Children learn behaviors through repeated reinforcing interactions with the environment. | Identify the functional skills needed by the child to increase the likelihood of success in current and future environments. | Provide experiences and supports that promote success: Identify and use effective reinforcers to ensure rapid and efficient learning. |
| Ecological | Children influence and are influenced by the environment. Children inevitably are a part of a family system. Likewise, families are embedded within larger neighborhood, community, and institutional systems. | Development results from the complex interactions or transactions between children and the environment over time. Development cannot be examined in isolation, but rather must be examined over time and in the context of systems within which children and families function. | Determine the child's skills, the characteristics of the caregiving environment, and the family's needs, resources, expectations, and aspirations. | Provide services that support families and children in ways that are congruent with their ecology and are consistent with expressed family goals. |

*Source:* D. B. Bailey, Jr., & Wolery, M. (1992). *Teaching infants and preschoolers with disabilities* (2nd ed.) New York: Macmillan.

234

*or inclusive* preschool programs. These terms have been used in a variety of ways and to describe a wide range of organizational and teaching practices (Odom & McEvoy, 1988). For purposes of this chapter, a common definition of each is included. Reverse mainstream preschool programs have usually been designed to meet the needs of children with disabilities and have "recruited" typically developing children to attend and serve as role models, peer interventionists, and/or playmates for the children with disabilities (Striefel, Killoran, & Quintero, 1991). In reverse mainstream preschool programs the group of children is usually quite heterogeneous, and often more than 50 percent of the enrolled children have developmental delays (Odom & McEvoy, 1988). The definition of integrated preschools, as distinct from reverse mainstream or inclusive programs, is probably the most ambiguous. Integrated preschools can be used to refer to a variety of arrangements that have resulted in part-time integration in a regular preschool class and part-time participation in special class or pull-out services. An example of an integrated preschool program is one where children with moderate to severe developmental delays attend a special education preschool class adjacent to a Head Start classroom. The children with severe disabilities join the Head Start class for opening and closing circle, outdoor play, snack, music, and art, but also receive special instruction and individual therapy in the special preschool program.

Fully mainstreamed or inclusive preschool programs are those that were designed to meet the needs of either typically developing children or *all* children, including those with developmental delays. These programs strive to meet the needs of the child with developmental delays within the "regular" or general early childhood program, although this may involve the provision of substantial adaptation, individualized intervention, and/or support. In an inclusive preschool program the child with developmental delays does not usually spend parts of the classroom experience segregated from typically developing children. Children with developmental delays are substantially "outnumbered" in fully mainstreamed or inclusive preschool programs by typically developing children. The number of children with developmental delays in inclusive preschool programs is expected to represent natural proportions, or the incidence of developmental delays in society as a whole.

Traditionally, children were believed to receive more intensive and specialized intervention in reverse mainstream or integrated programs than would occur in fully mainstreamed programs (Striefel et al., 1991). However, it is perfectly possible to offer the same variety and intensity of services in an inclusive class as in a completely separate special class setting, although the manner in which such services are delivered may vary. Conversely, grouping children with severe and profound disabilities in a separate classroom does not assure a high quality or intensity of specialized instruction and therapy services; it only assures that children are isolated from the positive outcomes of being jointly educated with their typically developing peers. In fact, recent research suggests that "When general early education quality indicators…are used to assess quality, inclusive preschool programs receive comparable or higher mean ratings in comparison to traditional special education programs (LaParo, Sexton, & Snyder, 1998) or regular early childhood education programs (Buysse, Wesley, Bryant, & Gardner, 1999)" (Odom, 2000, p. 21).

Children with multiple or severe and profound disabilities have usually been the least likely to be included in integrated or inclusive preschool programs (Demchak & Drinkwater, 1992; Hanline, 1993). Summarizing the results of a recent study in California, Cavallaro, Ballard-Rosa, and Lynch (1998) reported that "Services for preschoolers tend to fall into two configurations: children with mild disabilities who are frequently fully included and children with severe disabilities and low incidence disabilities who are more often partially included or placed in special day classes only" (p. 169). Although it has not been customary to include children with the most intensive needs in general early childhood programs, the foundation for this tradition is not rooted in unfavorable research results or in an individual assessment of children's educational or support needs (Demchak & Drinkwater, 1992; Strain, 1990; Strain, McGee, & Kohler, 2001). In fact, "there may be good reasons for including children with severe disabilities in general preschool settings. Hundert and colleagues (1998) found that children with severe disabilities who participate in inclusive settings appear to score higher on standardized measures of development than comparable children enrolled in traditional special education settings" (Odom, 2000, p. 21).

In a recent national study, Odom et al. (1999) used a variety of qualitative and quantitative research methods to investigate and describe a national sample of inclusive preschool programs. They used a two-dimensional model to describe current variations in inclusive models. The first dimension, the organizational context of classroom settings, identified the range of agencies that are administering inclusive classrooms, and included community-based child care, Head Start, public school early childhood education, and dual enrollment (special education and general education) programs. The second dimension, the models of organizational service delivery, examined the variation in how special education and related services that were tied to IEP objectives were delivered. These models included team teaching between early childhood special educators and early childhood educators, and an itinerant teaching collaborative/consultative model in which the special educator and related service providers worked with early childhood educators to assist them in implementing individualized services for children with disabilities within the general education classroom curriculum and activities, rather than directly teaching the children themselves. Issues related to educating preschool children with severe disabilities in inclusive settings will be discussed in a later section of this chapter.

## The Influence of Federal Legislation on Preschool Programs

During the last thirty years federal legislation has had a substantial impact on the availability and quality of preschool services for young children who are at risk or have disabilities (Bailey, 2000; Hebbler, Smith, & Black, 1991; Zigler & Styfco, 2000). As discussed in Chapter 3, P.L. 99-457, Section 619, has had the greatest impact on preschool special education services, by extending the mandate to provide appropriate special education and related services to all eligible 3- to 5-year-olds. The earlier Education of the Handicapped Act (P.L. 94-142) paved the way for this mandate through the establishment of Preschool Incentive Grants for the purpose of encouraging states to establish preschool programs for children with disabilities. As with programs for infants and toddlers and their families, an early positive influence was P.L. 90-538, the Handicapped Children's Early Education Assistance Act. This act established the Handicapped Children's Early Education Program (HCEEP), which stimulated the development of model programs, curricula, and assessments, as well as evaluation and research and the continuation and expansion of model programs to additional young children with disabilities and their families. The reader is encouraged to review information in Chapter 3 on Preschool Incentive Grants and the

P.L. 99-457 requirements for preschool special education services. This chapter will briefly discuss Head Start legislation, which has also had a significant impact on preschool programs for children with disabilities.

***Head Start Legislation and Regulations.***     "The major significance of the original Head Start legislation was not the substance of the law but what it represented. It was the first indication of legislative concern for early education for children with special needs and the beginning of a national expansion and consolidation of early intervention efforts" (Noonan & McCormick, 1993, p. 8). No specific mention of children with disabilities was made in the original 1966 Head Start legislation. However, following the 1972 passage of P.L. 92-424 (the Economic Opportunity amendments), Head Start programs were required to ensure that at least 10 percent of the enrollment opportunities were reserved for children with disabilities. Comparatively few children with severe disabilities were enrolled in Head Start as the result of this act. Most of the openings were used to enroll children with mild–moderate disabilities. Nevertheless, the role of Head Start in providing integration and inclusion opportunities for young children with developmental delays or disabilities has been an important one, and one that is likely to continue to be of importance in the future.

In January 1993 new Head Start Disability Regulations were released. The regulations require Head Start programs to (1) develop a disabilities service plan to meet the special needs of children with disabilities and their families, (2) designate a coordinator of services for children with disabilities, and (3) arrange or provide necessary special education and related services for eligible children with disabilities, unless these services are already being provided by another agency. Interagency cooperation is specifically encouraged as a part of the regulations, and Head Start programs are reminded of relevant state and federal regulations or standards governing services provided to 3- through 5-year-olds with disabilities and their families. Two components of the regulations are likely to make enrollment in Head Start programs more available to children with severe or profound disabilities, when an IEP team has determined that this is the most appropriate placement for the child.

Among other things, the regulation…:

- ….States that a grantee "must not deny placement on the basis of a disability or its severity to any child when:

  1) The parents wish to enroll the child,
  2) The child meets the Head Start age and income eligibility criteria,
  3) Head Start is an appropriate placement according to the child's IEP, and
  4) The program has space to enroll more children, even though the program has made 10 percent of its enrollment opportunities available to children with disabilities."

- Indicates enrollment cannot be denied because of staff attitudes, and/or apprehension, inaccessibility of facilities, need to access additional resources to serve a specific child, unfamiliarity with a disabling condition or special equipment, such as a prosthesis, or need for personalized special services, such as feeding or suctioning, and assistance with toileting, including catheterization, diapering, and toilet training. (Walsh, 1993, p. 3)

*Gearing up for the Federal Preschool Special Education Mandate.*    During the 1990s preschool personnel in many school districts and states concentrated on beginning or expanding programs in order to implement the 1991 federal mandate for preschool special education services. Some of the challenges that school districts and state offices of education faced during this time included: (1) providing for increasing numbers of children, (2) hiring qualified preschool special education teachers and related service providers, (3) considering how to offer preschoolers opportunities to be educated in the "least restrictive environment" when many districts educate only a limited number of typically developing preschoolers, if any, (4) locating classroom space and funds for personnel, transportation, and other costs, which are only partially covered by new federal funds, (5) developing procedures for transitioning children into preschool from early intervention and for transitioning children into school programs as they reach kindergarten or school age, (6) establishing child find and eligibility procedures, which differ from those previously used for special education, and (7) examining due process procedures used with preschoolers and their families to assure that they meet all of the requirements of the IDEA. Given these many challenges it is not surprising that in many parts of the country extensive efforts have been directed to getting universal preschool programs for children with developmental delays in place and to assuring that they are in compliance with the requirements of the IDEA. The next decade should be an exciting time for preschool programs. Now that programs are established there will be an opportunity to devote more time and resources to focusing on providing an enjoyable and effective experience for children and their families. The next section of this chapter will examine the educational needs of preschool children and the goals of preschool services, as well as the characteristics of programs which implement recommended practices for preschoolers with developmental delays and their families.

# Current Trends and Issues in Meeting the Educational Needs of Preschoolers with Severe Disabilities

Preschool children with severe developmental delays or disabilities have many of the same educational needs as typically developing children of the same age. These educational needs include developmentally appropriate learning experiences, inclusion in learning and social environments that value and respect individuality and diversity, and comprehensive and individually appropriate educational intervention.

> **Focus 2**
> What is developmentally appropriate practice and how does it apply to preschool children with severe disabilities?

## Developmentally Appropriate Learning Experiences

Like other preschoolers, children with severe developmental delays or disabilities need to have access to high-quality, developmentally appropriate learning experiences. In order to assist early childhood educators in planning and providing these learning experiences, The National Association for the Education of Young Children (NAEYC) developed a paper defining and describing *developmentally appropriate practice (DAP)* (Bredekamp, 1986), which has since been revised and used as the basis for a position paper and guidelines and recommendations for assessment, curriculum, professional preparation, and program ac-creditation efforts (e.g., Bredekamp, 1987; Bredekamp & Copple, 1997; Bredekamp & Rosegrant, 1992; International Reading Association (IRA) and the National Association for the Education of Young Children (NAEYC), 1998; NAEYC, 1997; NAEYC and the National Association of Early Childhood Specialists in State Departments of Education (NAECS/SDE), 1991). The NAEYC is the largest national organization for early child-hood professionals and other interested individuals dedicated to the education of children between the ages of birth and 8 years. Through its policy, advocacy, and informational ac-tivities NAEYC has had a substantial influence on the way childcare and educational ser-vices for young children are conceptualized and implemented in the United States. Within the NAEYC position paper, developmentally appropriate practice guidelines are used to define appropriate learning environments and experiences for young children as distinct from those provided to older children. These distinctions include (1) a need for many learning activities that are initiated and directed by the child and supported by the teacher, and (2) an emphasis on learning through play, exploration, social interaction, and inquiry, rather than structured, directive teaching to specific academic goals (Bredekamp, 1987; Bredekamp & Copple, 1997; Carta et al., 1991; NAEYC & NAECS/SDE, 1991; Neuman, Copple, & Bredekamp, 2000; Wolery, Holcombe, Venn, & Werts, 1992).

Developmentally appropriate practice has sometimes been misinterpreted to stipu-late the use of learning environments, expectations, and practices that are based strictly on the child's achievement of "normal" developmental milestones (Kostelnick, 1992)—that is, if you act like a 2-year-old, your learning environment should be structured in ways that are congruent to those that would facilitate learning for a 2-year-old. This misinterpreta-tion of developmentally appropriate practice conflicts with recommendations for age-appropriate practice in special education and would be especially restrictive when applied to children with severe disabilities whose developmental skill level, by definition, is signif-icantly delayed from their typically developing chronological age peers. *Age appropriate-ness* deliberately emphasizes an individual's chronological age over his or her "mental age" or developmental level. This perspective values the idea that a 4-year-old is first of all a 4-year-old, regardless of the presence or absence of disabilities, and should be treated as such, including being involved with the same kinds of instructional opportunities, materi-als, patterns of interaction, and social and instructional groupings as are typically develop-ing peers of the same chronological age (McDonnell & Hardman, 1988).

Although age appropriateness and an interpretation of developmentally appropriate practice that ties such practice exclusively to normal development may appear to be in conflict, there are many ways to create learning experiences for young children that are *both* developmentally appropriate and age appropriate. For example, Mark is a 5-year-old child with limited gross and fine motor movement and control. His cognitive development is similar to a typically developing 11-month-old. Mark is learning to use adaptive switches to activate toys and a radio or tape player. Mark enjoys listening to music and toys that make noise and move simultaneously. Mark would enjoy the lullabies and bat-tery-operated lamb and giraffe toys that might usually be purchased for an 11-month-old.

However, he also enjoys Raffi songs and songs from the Disney movies, as well as automated race tracks and battery-operated dinosaurs and robots. The latter selection of music and toys would also interest other children his age, and could provide some familiar and pleasurable experiences for Mark to enjoy in classroom and play settings with typically developing peers.

The applicability of DAP to young children with disabilities sparked a lively debate in early childhood special education and early childhood education journals and professional forums (e.g., Carta et al., 1991; Johnson & Johnson, 1992; Kostelnik, 1992; Mallory, 1992; NAEYC & NAECS/SDE, 1991; Wolery, Strain, & Bailey, 1992; Wolery et al., 1993). One of the primary concerns expressed by many special educators was that whereas empirical research supported the effectiveness of intensive, focused and/or directive intervention for young children with disabilities, there is only very limited research to support the effectiveness of DAP for young children with disabilities or developmental delays. In a research review on DAP and the efficacy of early intervention with children with disabilities, Carta et al. (1991) comment, "In summary, these studies have not provided convincing evidence that teacher-directed instruction is harmful, nor have they substantiated that adherence to developmentally appropriate practice (e.g., child-directed and nonacademic in focus) leads to better outcomes for average children, or more importantly, *for children who are at risk or who have disabilities*" (p. 10). Additionally, "The studies cited above, as well as many others, provide empirical support for the effectiveness of structured interventions for young children with special needs, and demonstrate that failure to intervene places children at relatively greater risk for developmental decline and restricted educational opportunities (Guralnick & Bennet, 1987)" (Carta et al. (1991), p. 11–12).

Both DAP and recommended practice recommendations in early childhood special education are evolving (Bredekamp & Copple, 1997; Sandall, McLean, & Smith, 2000b), and are being heavily influenced by one another through an unprecedented amount of professional dialogue and collaboration. In the most recent position statement and guidelines on developmentally appropriate practice (Bredekamp & Copple, 1997), explanations and examples are provided to illustrate that a variety and range of practices can be developmentally appropriate, that rather than "polarizing into *either/or* choices" it may be more "fruitfully seen as *both/ands*" (p. 23). Several of the provided examples include:

- Children construct their own understanding of concepts **and** they benefit from instruction by more competent peers and adults.
- Children benefit from predictable structure and orderly routine in the learning environment **and** from the teacher's flexibility and spontaneity in responding to their emerging ideas, needs, and interests.
- Children benefit from opportunities to make meaningful choices about what they will do and learn **and** from having a clear understanding of the boundaries within which choices are permissible.
- Children benefit from situations that challenge them to work at the edge of their developing capacities **and** from ample opportunities to practice newly acquired skills and to acquire the disposition to persist.
- Children benefit from engaging in self-initiated, spontaneous play **and** from teacher-planned and -structured activities, projects, and experiences. (Bredekamp & Copple, 1997, p. 23)

**POINT OF INTEREST 9.1**

Read the following examples of "widely held expectations" for preschool children from the most influential professional organization for educators of young children.

*A Sample Set of "Widely Held Expectations"*

- For 3-year-olds:
  - Runs at an even pace, turns and stops well
  - Builds block towers, easily does puzzles with whole objects, pours liquids with some spills
  - Shows a steady increase in vocabulary, ranging from 2,000 to 4,000 words
  - Uses simple sentences of at least three words to express needs
  - Asks many who, what, where, and why questions

- For 4-year-olds:
  - Develops sufficient timing to jump rope or play games requiring quick reactions
  - Draws combinations of simple shapes, draws person with at least four parts
  - Expands vocabulary from 4,000 to 6,000 words, shows more attention to abstract uses
  - Usually speaks in five- to six-word sentences
  - Can retell a four- or five-step directive or the sequence in a story
  - Skips unevenly

- For 5-year-olds:
  - Walks backward quickly, skips and runs with agility and speed
  - Hits nail with hammer head, uses scissors and screwdrivers unassisted
  - Prints letters crudely but most are recognizable by an adult
  - Employs a vocabulary of 5,000 to 8,000 words, with frequent plays on words
  - Enjoys repeating stories, poems, and songs; enjoys acting out plays or stories

*Consider this:*

1. How many of these expectations seem realistic and/or functional for a preschool-age child with severe or profound disabilities?
2. In what ways would the inclusion of one or more children with severe or profound disabilities in a preschool educational program assist typically developing children in meeting these goals?
3. What might be some of the potential advantages and disadvantages for a preschool-age child with severe or profound disabilities in attending an inclusive preschool program with broad and high expectations for all children? What could teachers and parents do to help the child benefit from the advantages and to minimize any potential disadvantages?

*Note:* The "widely held expectations" are included in the document for illustrative purposes only and are not a part of the official position statement on developmentally appropriate practice. Further, it is not implied in this document that these expectations are appropriate for all preschool age children.

Adapted from: Bredekamp, S., & Copple, C. (Eds.) (1997). *Developmentally appropriate practice in early childhood programs*, (rev. ed.). Washington, DC: National Association for the Education of Young Children.

## Inclusive Learning Environments

A second educational need that preschoolers with severe developmental delays share with typically developing peers is the opportunity to learn and develop friendships in inclusive educational, home, and community settings. The underlying rationale for inclusion was presented in Chapter 2 and applies to preschool-age children. Many people feel that pre-school is a very important time to implement inclusive programs, because it is the time that many children first learn to participate in classroom activities and to interact with a number of similar-age peers. If children always attend programs that include children with develop-mental delays or disabilities, then there is essentially no need to "change attitudes" or "teach acceptance" or get children "ready" to be mainstreamed because inclusion will simply seem natural to the children. Although there are methodological flaws in many re-search studies, and variability in research results, "several recent reviews of the research on [preschool] mainstreaming all have concluded that mainstreaming can be implemented successfully and almost always results in positive outcomes" (Bailey & Wolery, 1992, p. 50). The vast majority of studies indicate that the developmental outcomes of integrated and inclusive programs are at least as positive as those for special segregated or traditional early childhood special education programs for children with disabilities (Buysse & Bailey, 1993; Lamorey & Bricker, 1993; Odom, 2000; Odom & Diamond, 1998), and some studies suggest that integrated or inclusive programs are more successful in facilitating the frequency and competence of social, communicative, and play behavior on the part of chil-dren with developmental delays (e.g., Guralnick, Connor, Hammond, Gottman, & Kinnish, 1996; Hundert et al., 1998; Jenkins, Odom, & Speltz, 1989; Levine & Antia, 1997). It is important to note that studies have not documented negative outcomes for either develop-mentally delayed or typically developing children who have been enrolled in integrated or inclusive preschool programs (Bailey & McWilliam, 1990). In fact, a number of studies have documented positive developmental and attitudinal outcomes for preschoolers with-out disabilities (Guralnick, 1990; Hanline, 1993; McLean & Hanline, 1990; Peck, Carlson, & Helmstetter, 1992). For recent reviews of the outcomes of integrated and/or inclusive preschool programs, see Barnett et al., (1999), Guralnick (2001), Odom (2000), and Odom and Bailey (2001).

---

*Focus 3*
What policy statements have been made about preschoolers with developmental delays and inclusion? How well do these statements correspond to federal regulations related to educating children with disabilities in the least restrictive environment?

---

An example of the strong philosophical support for inclusive early childhood pro-grams is provided by the Position Statement on Inclusion of the Division for Early Child-hood of the Council for Exceptional Children (DEC) (see Window 9.4, page 245). Originally adopted by DEC in 1993, it was reaffirmed and updated by DEC in 2000, and has also been endorsed by the NAEYC (the early childhood professional organization whose membership is primarily general early childhood educators) in 1994 and 1998. This statement makes no exceptions to the recommendation for full inclusion for children with severe or profound disabilities.

The reality of opportunities for inclusion for young children with severe and pro-found disabilities continues to be quite different; they are often excluded. One of the rea-sons for this gap between philosophical position and day-to-day reality is that inclusion in generic or mainstream early childhood programs is not required by federal regulations

## WINDOW 9.3 • *April's Preschool*

April is a 4-year-old child with autism who attends A Place for Children, a "regular" preschool/child care program associated with the child development training program at the local community college. She lives with her mother and 8-year-old brother. Her parents are divorced and April's father lives out of state. She and her brother visit him for a month every summer. Her mother is employed full-time and April is enrolled in the full-day program at her preschool. Three other children with developmental delays are enrolled in other classrooms at April's preschool program, and her school district pays for a teaching assistant to be on-site at the facility five hours a day to support the children, including carrying out individualized instruction within the various preschool activities. The teaching assistant is in April's class more than the other children's. April is the only one of the four children with severe developmental delays. The teaching assistant is supervised by an itinerant special education preschool teacher. A communication disorders specialist is also a part of April's preschool IEP team, as are the teacher and assistant teacher of the preschool program and April's parents.

April has moderate developmental delays in gross and fine motor skills, and severe developmental delays in cognitive, social, communication, and self-help skills. April is very physically active and has high rates of stereotypic behaviors such as hand flapping, jumping in place, and grimacing. She is interested in other children, and is affectionate with familiar adults and her older brother. April uses a few word approximations appropriately, and on occasion will spontaneously imitate the actions of other children and adults. She is not toilet trained and dislikes washing and grooming activities. April eats well and is able to dress and undress herself with some assistance. April likes to play with Legos and puzzles and hugs dolls and stuffed animals. She loves to swing and climb on playground equipment. April does not play games or engage in imaginative play at this time, although she seems to enjoy watching other children involved in these play activities.

April will usually follow simple directions from familiar adults if they first use her name.

April's preschool class has twenty children, and is staffed by one teacher, one assistant teacher, and one to three students in training, in addition to the part-time help from the special education teaching assistant. April is included in the ongoing preschool activities throughout the day. Except for snack and outdoor play times, there are usually two or three activities going on simultaneously in the preschool class. Children are allowed to choose which activity they will join, and most activities are planned to facilitate many opportunities for child initiation and interaction with each other and with the activity materials. If left to her own devices, April has a tendency to wander between activities at a very frequent rate, sometimes observing briefly before moving on, but often seeming to be very restless, and more interested in humming, hand flapping, and jumping in place than the very creative high-interest activities that are characteristic of the program she attends. The adults in April's preschool have learned to encourage April to make a choice and then ask her to sit down near the center of the action. If she begins to engage in stereotypic activities they quickly redirect her to an activity that is more socially appropriate and more likely to be a learning experience for her. They work with the preschool special education teacher, the teaching assistant, and the communication disorders specialist to make sure that many teaching and practice opportunities on the skills on April's IEP are included throughout April's day. Because April is primarily working on communication, cognitive, and social goals, it is easy for the early childhood educators to see how to include these within preschool activities; they are used to facilitating learning in these areas for other children throughout a variety of activities, although the other children are at a more sophisticated developmental level.

The other children in April's class have mixed reactions to her, just as they do to each other. Many of them have noticed that April often

*(continued)*

**WINDOW 9.3 • Continued**

behaves differently than other children in the class and have expressed curiosity about this. Some of the children ignore April, some are sometimes irritated by her humming or jumping, and others have shown interest in playing with April or in helping her learn to do things that they can do. The teachers have encouraged other children who have shown an interest in being April's friend or helping her learn things, but are always careful to insist that she be treated as another 4-year-old who is a part of their class. Some of the strategies her teachers have found most successful in helping the children relate to April are helping to interpret what she is saying, showing them how to help April play or communicate, and making suggestions on how they can include April in their play and learning activities. The teachers have been pleased to see that a number of the children have become very good at understanding and helping April, and that several children consider her to be a good friend.

During the last month that April has been in preschool she has been invited to play at another child's house and has also been invited to a birthday party. April's mother can see that April looks forward to preschool and seeing the other children, even though she isn't able to tell her mom much about what goes on during the day. April's teacher has started taking at least one instant photograph of April every day and writing a brief note on the back to tell what April is doing and who she is with. This has helped April and her mother be able to talk about her classmates and what happened in preschool that day.

governing the education of preschoolers with disabilities in the least restrictive environment. Although children are to be educated "to the maximum extent possible" with children without disabilities, as with other special education programs, intensive needs are often used to justify a special, segregated program placement. An additional challenge is faced by school districts in attempting to offer inclusive programs for preschoolers with developmental delays. Many school districts administer or have access to only a few preschool classes or programs for typically developing 3-, 4-, 5-year-olds. Districts need to expand their overall efforts to educate preschoolers or develop contractual arrangements with private preschool and child care providers if they are to be able to educate preschool children in inclusive programs with natural proportions of children with and without developmental delays. At this time, federal regulations allow and in some ways encourage such arrangements, but there are some financial disincentives for districts in pursuing either of these options. An additional factor that may be limiting the inclusion opportunities for many preschool children with severe disabilities is the number of inclusive programs in which children are being enrolled without benefit of systematic support from special educators and/or related service providers (McDonnell, Brownell, & Wolery, 1997; Wolery 1994). Although some children with mild-moderate disabilities may do fairly well in inclusive settings, even without added program support, this is unlikely to be the case for most children with severe or multiple disabilities. General education preschool teachers have generally expressed favorable attitudes about inclusion (Odom & Bailey, 2001) and seem eager to receive more support from special educators who are actively involved in their classrooms (McDonnell, Brownell, & Wolery, 2001).

## WINDOW 9.4 • *Position on Inclusion*

*Division for Early Childhood of the Council for Exceptional Children*

Adopted April 1993

Revised December 1993

Reaffirmed 1996

Updated 2000

Inclusion, as a value, supports the right of all children, regardless of abilities, to participate actively in natural settings within their communities. Natural settings are those in which the child would spend time had he or she not had a disability. These settings include, but are not limited to home, preschool, nursery schools, Head Start programs, kindergartens, neighborhood school classrooms, child care, places of worship, recreational (such as community playgrounds and community events) and other settings that all children and families enjoy.

DEC supports and advocates that young children and their families have full and successful access to health, social, educational, and other support services that promote full participation in family and community life. DEC values the cultural, economic, and educational diversity of families and supports a family-guided process for identifying a program of service.

As young children participate in group settings (such as preschool, play groups, child care, kindergarten) their active participation should be guided by developmentally and individually appropriate curriculum. Access to and participation in the age appropriate general curriculum becomes central to the identification and provision of specialized support services.

To implement inclusive practices DEC supports: (a) the continued development, implementation, evaluation, and dissemination of full inclusion supports, services, and systems that are of high quality for all children; (b) the development of preservice and inservice training programs that prepare families, service providers, and administrators to develop and work within inclusive settings; (c) collaboration among key stakeholders to implement flexible fiscal and administrative procedures in support of inclusion; (d) research that contributes to our knowledge of recommended practice; and (e) the restructuring and unification of social, educational, health, and intervention supports and services to make them more responsive to the needs of all children and families. Ultimately, the implementation of inclusive practice must lead to optimal developmental benefit for each individual child and family.

**Endorsed by NAEYC—April 1994, April 1998**

### Comprehensive and Individually Appropriate Interventions

A third educational need for preschoolers with severe developmental delays is for comprehensive and individually appropriate intervention. Although all children might in fact benefit from access to intensive and individualized intervention, most children will learn successfully and develop from a broad range of planned and unplanned learning activities, even if that learning and development are not at an optimal level. Because they experience so many more difficulties in both learning and applying new skills in a variety of meaningful contexts, it is critically important to facilitate the development of children with severe disabilities during the preschool years. Effectively facilitating this development requires the use of intervention strategies that have been demonstrated to be effective with learners with significant learning impairments. It also requires the frequent rather than sporadic or occasional use of these strategies. For example, for a preschool-age child with severe developmental delays, a teacher might try to plan for ten to twenty practice trials per day for each specific learning objective or IEP goal. (For goals such as handwashing this would obviously be less often!). Some of the components of effective intervention for preschoolers with severe developmental delays include (1) the use of ecologically or environmentally based assessment, (2) family and team selection of priority IEP goals, (3) careful specification of intervention steps and strategies for meeting these IEP goals, (4) teaching within the context of natural caregiving, preschool, play, and family routines and activities, (5) using strategies that are not only effective in teaching new skills or behaviors, but that will help the child generalize and maintain use of those skills, and (6) monitoring the effectiveness of intervention strategies by assessing the child's performance in natural settings, how family members and peers perceive the child's progress, and the changes that have occurred in the child or family's life as a result of intervention. Several of these components will be described in this chapter. Complete descriptions of effective naturalistic intervention strategies for young children with severe developmental delays can be found in Bailey and Wolery (1992) and in Noonan and McCormick (1993). Research studies that demonstrate the effectiveness of naturalistic intervention strategies for preschool children who are enrolled in inclusive, developmentally appropriate preschool classrooms include Fox and Hanline (1993) and Malmskog and McDonnell (1999).

## *Interventions for Young Children with Challenging Behaviors*

Some preschool-age children with disabilities have challenging behaviors that may interfere with their learning, social relationships, and opportunities to participate in a variety of activities and settings, or may be destructive or harmful to property, themselves, or others. The IDEA '97 regulations regarding functional assessment of problem behaviors, as described in Chapter 7, also apply to preschool-age children with disabilities. However, many behaviors that are "challenging" may also be common among typically developing children during the toddler and preschool years. For example, toddlers frequently have tantrums, refuse to share toys, and bite, kick, hit, or pull hair on occasion when they are frustrated or angry. It is also common for preschoolers to yell and be disruptive when they are angry or frustrated, to make up stories and insist they are the truth, and to use name calling and taunts to exclude other children from play or to get their way (Allen & Marotz, 1994). With appropriate guidance most young children will mature out of these developmental phases (e.g., the "terrible twos"), and therefore it is important to understand many of the difficult behaviors of young children with or without disabilities as a normal part of growing up. At the same time, early and effective intervention is important for children with genuine emotional or behavioral disorders, or who have persistent challenging behaviors that do not respond to the usual parental, teacher, or caregiver guidance strategies. The Division for Early Childhood of the Council for Exceptional Children (DEC) has developed a position statement on interventions for challenging behaviors for young children that has also been endorsed by NAEYC (see Window 9.5). The position statement attempts to balance an understanding of young children's needs and development, the critical role of

**WINDOW 9.5 • *Position Statement on Interventions for Challenging Behavior***

Adopted April 1998

**Many young children engage in challenging behavior in the course of early development. The majority of these children respond to developmentally appropriate management techniques.**

Every parent, including parents of young children with disabilities, wants his or her child to attend schools, child-care centers, or community-based programs that are nurturing and safe. Many young children engage in challenging behavior at various times during their early development. Typically, this behavior is short-term and decreases with age and use of appropriate guidance strategies. However, for some children these incidences of challenging behavior may become more consistent despite increased adult vigilance and use of appropriate guidance strategies. For these children, the challenging behavior may result in injury to themselves or others, cause damage to the physical environment, interfere with the acquisition of new skills, and/or socially isolate the child (Doss & Reichle, 1991). Additional intervention efforts may by required for these children.

**DEC believes strongly that many types of services and intervention strategies are available to address challenging behavior.**

Given the developmental nature of most challenging behavior, we believe that there is a vast array of supplemental services that can be added to the home and education environment to increase the likelihood that children will learn appropriate behavior. A variety of intervention strategies can be implemented with either formal or informal support. Services and strategies could include, but are not limited to: (a) designing environments and activities to prevent challenging behavior and to help all children develop appropriate behavior; (b) utilizing effective behavioral interventions that are positive and address both form and function of a young child's challenging behavior; (c) adopting curricular modification and accommodation strategies designed to help young children learn behaviors appropriate to their settings; and (d) providing external consultation and technical assistance or additional staff support. In addition, all professionals who work with children in implementing IEPs or IFSPs must have opportunities to acquire knowledge and skills necessary for effective implementation of prevention and intervention programs.

**DEC believes strongly that families play a critical role in designing and carrying out effective interventions for challenging behavior.**

Given the family-focused nature of early childhood education, we acknowledge the critical role that families play in addressing challenging behavior. Often times, challenging behavior occurs across places, people and time, thus families are critical members of the intervention team. A coordinated effort between family members and professionals is needed to assure that interventions are effective and efficient and address both child and family needs and strengths. All decisions regarding the identification of a challenging behavior, possible interventions, placement, and ongoing evaluation must be made in accordance with the family through the IEP, IFSP, or other team decision-making processes.

Endorsed by NAEYC

families in guiding or intervening with young children who are experiencing behavioral difficulties, and the need for early and effective intervention for challenging behavior.

*Focus 4*
Describe the expected outcomes of preschool programs for children with disabilities.

## Expected Outcomes for Preschool Services

The expected outcomes or goals for preschool services include many similarities to the early intervention goals discussed in Chapter 8. Four goals are often stressed by families and educational programs during the preschool years.

   **1.** *Maximizing the child's development in a variety of important developmental areas.* The goal of maximizing development includes meeting specific high-priority goals identified as a part of the child's IEP as well as creating learning environments that will facilitate learning and growth in many other important skills and activities. For most preschool children, some of the important curriculum areas in which to facilitate development include social, communication, motor, cognitive, emerging literacy and mathematics, self-care, play, and personal management. The learning and development that takes place in the preschool years creates a critical foundation for the school years. For preschoolers with severe developmental delays, part of maximizing development is the identification of effective alternatives for the behaviors or functions of behavior that child is unable to perform in the usual way. Some examples of alternatives or functional equivalents (Noonan & McCormick, 1993) that might be used by preschool children include (a) indicating words or ideas by pointing to a photo on a communication board, rather than talking, (b) pushing a switch to activate toys, rather than grasping and moving the usual on/off switches, or (c) using a wheelchair to get places instead of walking.

   **2.** *Developing the child's social interaction and classroom participation skills.* Many children have limited experiences with peers prior to entering preschool, and any experiences they have had have often been limited to a few familiar siblings, cousins, and neighbors, and/or other children attending the same family or infant/toddler center child care program. Even if a child has regularly attended a center-based child care program, he or she will face substantial adjustments to larger preschool classes, which usually contain more frequent structured activities and higher performance expectations than are found in toddler classes. One of the most important developmental tasks for preschool-age children is learning to establish successful relationships with peers, including learning to play together, share, stick up for yourself, communicate thoughts and feelings, and make and keep friends. These skills not only are important to being successful in school, but also form the basis of the child and adult friendships that are such an important contributor to an individual's enjoyment and quality of life. In addition to developing social skills and relationships with peers, preschool-age children need to learn to follow adult directions and classroom rules and routines, to ask for assistance appropriately, and to complete activities and tasks as requested by teachers without constant adult supervision or attention. The acquisition of such social and task-related skills may be even more important to kindergarten teachers than the child's academic preparedness or skill level, and has resulted in their inclusion in the development of transition preparation, kindergarten entry level, and "survival skills" curricula for preschoolers with developmental delays (Johnson, Gallagher, Cook, & Wong, 1995; McCormick & Kawate, 1982; Rous, Hemmeter, & Schuster, 1994; Rule, Fiechtl, & Innocenti, 1990).

   **3.** *Preparing the child for inclusive school placement and providing support for the transition to kindergarten or elementary school.* Maximizing the child's skill development, learning and practicing social skills with typically developing peers, and success-fully adjusting to classroom patterns and expectations are important ways to prepare children for inclusive school placement. Additionally, it is important for the preschool team and the child's family to work collaboratively with the elementary school staff who will be responsible for educating the child when he or she enters kindergarten or first grade. Together, the family, preschool team, and elementary team can plan for the pre-school–kindergarten transition and assure that the child, the family, and the school staff have received the preparation and support necessary to make the transition as smooth and successful as possible for all concerned (Rosenkoetter, Hains, & Fowler, 1994).

**4.** *Increasing community participation through support to family members and other caregivers.* One of the goals of preschool services takes place primarily outside pre-school classrooms. As the child with developmental delays gets older, families are often very anxious to return to employment, social, and recreational activities in which they have participated before the child was born. As the child with developmental delays be-comes older, it is also important for the child to extend his or her experiences and social networks beyond the immediate family and preschool. Although some families may wish to wait, and many families will have begun the process during the infant/toddler years, preschool is a good time to support families in identifying and extending alternative care-givers so that family members have more flexibility to pursue their own interests. Simi-larly, these years are a very good time to identify community or neighborhood activities or relationships that their preschooler might enjoy. Examples of such activities might in-clude swim or dance lessons, playing with neighborhood friends, joining a neighborhood soccer team, community outings with Grandma, attending a community child care or pre-school program, or eating in a restaurant once a week as a family. Dunst (2001) indicates that child participation in community learning activities is so valuable that it should be considered an intervention "in and of themselves" (p. 309). Similar to the role of early in-terventionists, preschool team members can be an important source of information and ideas on what is available in the community and who to call to make arrangements. They can also help families work with community program staff in identifying ways to include the child.

# Structure/Organization of Preschool Programs

## Recommended Practices for Preschool Programs

The identification of recommended practices for preschool programs serving children with disabilities has been an important area for professional and advocacy attention (e.g., DeStefano, Howe, Horn, & Smith, 1991; Hanson & Lynch, 1995; McDonnell & Hardman, 1988). In 1993 the Division for Early Childhood of the Council for Exceptional Children (DEC) formed a task force to develop recommended practices for early childhood special education (DEC Task Force on Recommended Practices, 1993). With the intent of incorpo-rating new knowledge, more effectively translating research into practice, and identifying the systems needed to support the adoption and ongoing use of the recommended practices (Sandall & Smith, 2000), DEC recently published new recommended practices (Sandall, McLean, Santos, & Smith, 2000a). Recommended practices for preschool programs have been organized in a variety of different ways and continue to evolve at a rapid pace. Window 9.6 provides an overview of the five direct service strands or areas in which the DEC 2000 recommended practices have been organized. Listed below each area are the major themes or descriptors that have been used to organize the specific practices. Because there are more than 130 recommended practices within the direct service strands, specific practices have not been included in this chapter. It will be interesting to see how preschool programs incorporate the philosophy and practices of family-centered intervention so that it can be combined with providing effective intervention within inclusive, developmentally appropriate early childhood programs.

**WINDOW 9.6 • *DEC Recommended Practices 2000: Direct Service Strands for Practices and Themes/Organizers for Practices within Strands***

- Strand 1: Assessment
  - Professionals and families collaborate in planning and implementing assessment.
  - Assessment is individualized and appropriate for the child and family.
  - Assessment provides useful information for intervention.
  - Professionals share information in respectful and useful ways.
  - Professionals meet legal and procedural requirements *and* meet recommended practice guidelines.

- Strand 2: Child-focused Interventions
  - Adults design environments to promote children's safety, active engagement, learning, participation, and membership.
  - Adults individualize and adapt practices for each child based on ongoing data to meet children's changing needs.
  - Adults use systematic procedures within and across environments, activities, and routines to promote children's learning and participation.

- Strand 3: Family-Based Practices
  - Families and professionals share responsibility and work collaboratively

  - Practices strengthen family functioning.
  - Practices are individualized and flexible.
  - Practices are strengths- and assets-based.

- Strand 4: Interdisciplinary Models
  - Teams including family members make decisions and work together.
  - Professionals cross disciplinary boundaries.
  - Intervention is focused on function, not services.
  - Regular caregivers and regular routines provide the most appropriate opportunities for children's learning and receiving most other interventions.

- Strand 5: Technology Applications
  - Professionals utilize technology in intervention programs for children.
  - Families and professionals collaborate in planning and implementing the use of assistive technology.
  - Families and professionals use technology to access information and support.
  - Training and technical support programs are available to support technology applications.

*Source:* Adapted from: Sandall, S., McLean, M. E., & Smith, B. J. (2000). *DEC recommended practices in early intervention/early childhood special education.* Longmont, CO: Sopris West.

## *Effective Practices for Preschool Programs: Developing and Implementing IEPs for Preschoolers*

The Individualized Education Program (IEP) is intended to guide the collaborative planning and implementation of special education and related services for preschoolers with developmental delays, including those with severe disabilities. IEPs for preschoolers have the same required components as IEPs written for older students. However, because of the uniqueness of the preschool years, these IEP components are often developed and implemented quite differently than they might be for an older child.

## *Team Membership and Collaboration*

IFSP development for infants and toddlers is generally conceptualized as family-centered or family-driven, with the child's family and the selected service coordinator having the strongest or most prominent influence on team decisions or actions. Early intervention service coordinators are often not special educators, nor are special educators required members of early intervention teams. In contrast, regulations regarding the makeup of IEP teams for preschoolers with developmental delays are essentially the same as those for school-age children. A preschool special education teacher usually serves in the service coordinator role, although a formal identification of a service coordinator is not required as it is for early intervention services. Parents are very important team members, although they do not usually have as prominent a role in team decisions and actions as is true in early intervention programs. In addition to a preschool special education teacher and family members, a general education early educator or preschool teacher, a school district administrator or designated representative, and relevant related service providers, such as a speech-language pathologist, occupational therapist, or physical therapist, are all key members of preschool IEP teams. Because children transition into preschool at around age 3 and move into school services at around age 5, IEP development teams also commonly include one or more team members from a transition program. Many preschoolers are involved in child care or community recreation programs, or spend significant amounts of time with neighborhood friends or extended-family members. These other caregivers can be an invaluable part of a preschool team. For some children, additional collaboration with community health care or social service providers may also be important.

Collaborative teaming among family members and caregivers, early educators, early childhood special educators and related servers, transition program professionals, and other community members or agencies presents some obvious challenges. It is virtually impossible to collect all of these team members for regular meetings or planning sessions, and too many individuals would be involved to give everyone a chance to communicate effectively anyway. Transdisciplinary teaming can provide the flexibility in team roles and communication strategies to be able to ensure opportunities for information sharing, brainstorming, collaborative problem solving, and team implementation and evaluation of the IEP without requiring *all* team members to be physically present for each interaction. Family and other team members can all select the types of decisions or actions in which they would most like to be direct participants, and those for which they would primarily like to be informed about how things are going on a less frequent or direct basis.

## Ecologically Based Curriculum and IEP Development for Preschool Children

As mentioned earlier in the chapter, ecologically based, naturalistic, or functional curricular models are usually favored for preschoolers, particularly for those with severe developmental delays (Bricker & Waddell, 1996; Hanson & Lynch, 1995; McLean, McNay, & Kottwitz, 1995; McNay, Kottwitz, Simmons, & McLean, 1995; Noonan & McCormick, 1993). (For the purposes of this chapter, the terms *ecologically based, environmentally based, functional,* and *naturalistic curricula* will be used interchangeably). The use of ecologically based curriculum influences the IEP development process, including the way assessment activities are conducted, the types of goals that are selected, and the way that intervention is implemented and evaluated. The ecologically based curriculum approach emphasizes the importance of teaching functional skills that will increase participation in the natural contexts in which the child is currently involved, and in those in which he or she is likely to participate in the future (Bricker, Pretti-Frontczak, & McComas, 1998; McDonnell & Hardman, 1988; Noonan & McCormick, 1993; Vincent et al., 1980). Natural contexts and the child and family preferences are important considerations in the planning and implementation of all phases of the intervention process. The rationales for teaching young children within natural play and care giving routines include the following:

- The child learns where and when to use the targeted skills as part of the learning process. Integration of skill performance is more likely.
- Communication among team members is increased, as is the role of parents and caregivers in facilitating the child's learning.
- More learning opportunities are available to the child.
- Children participating in inclusive child care or preschool programs or in community activities and settings have an opportunity to learn from more competent peer models.
- The purpose for learning is more obvious to the child, and the learning experiences tend to be more enjoyable. Motivation may be increased, and reinforcement is more likely to be intrinsic. Maintenance of learning is therefore more likely.
- Learning in natural contexts increases the range of people, materials, activities, and events with which the child interacts. The child is more likely to generalize concepts and responses being learned.
- Teaching in natural contexts provides a useful reality check for teachers, families, and other team members about how useful learning targets on the IEP really are. If it isn't useful in the child's daily routines, why are we teaching it?

Ecologically based assessments are used more extensively than formalized testing in ecologically based curriculum models. Observing the child in natural contexts and talking with individuals who spend significant amounts of time with the child on a regular basis are important sources of information for selecting IEP and other intervention goals. Assessment strategies that simulate natural contexts may also be used in order to facilitate team observation and collaboration and to gather information about the child's performance across a number of different developmental areas within a condensed time period. An example of a detailed and well-designed assessment strategy that simulates natural contexts for the purpose of observing the child's performance is transdisciplinary play-based assessment (TPBA) (Linder, 1993). Another child-guided assessment approach that is designed for learners with severe multiple disabilities was developed by Dr. van Dijk and some of his colleagues in the Netherlands. This assessment approach follows the child's lead as it looks at some of the underlying processes of learning, including biobehavioral states, orienting responses, anticipation and routine learning, and the expression and use of these processes within social interaction (Nelson, van Dijk, McDonnell, & Thompson, in press).

An example of an environmentally based curriculum for preschoolers is one that is part of a cross-age ecological curriculum produced by several grant projects in the School and Community Integration Program (SCIP) in the Department of Special Education at the University of Utah (McDonnell et al., 1994). The SCIP curriculum framework and IEP development process is similar across the preschool, early elementary, upper elementary, intermediate school, secondary school, and early adult (19–21) age levels. The curricular framework at each age level is organized around naturally occurring routines in which typically developing individuals of that age often participate on a daily or weekly basis (see Figure 9.2 for sample pages from the preschool curricular framework). Contexts are used as an organizer and include the time of day (e.g., morning, evening) and the location of the routines (e.g., home, preschool/daycare, community). Within each context common routines are listed, as are activities that might occur as a part of that routine. Broad skill areas, including specific skills that an individual would need to perform to complete activities or routines, are also included within the curricular framework.

Curriculum catalogs have been developed at each level to assist family members and transdisciplinary teams in identifying priority IEP goals (see Figure 9.2 for sample pages from the Preschool Curriculum Catalog). The Preschool Activities Curriculum Catalog organizes preschool activities within leisure/play, personal management, and social relationships domains. For each domain, activities are organized by the location in which they occur, specifically within home or home-based child care settings, school and/or center-based child care settings, or the community. The Preschool Skills Curriculum Catalog organizes generic skills or skill groups within six skill areas: social/communication, motor, mobility, self-help, cognitive/preacademic, and play. Both the activities and skill groups are still very broad and need to be identified much more specifically before they can serve as a complete IEP goal or objective. Parent IEP Preparation worksheets are included within the Preschool Curriculum Catalogs to assist parents in prioritizing goals and providing the rest of the IEP team with critical information about how the goals fits into the child's daily life (see Figure 9.3).

The SCIP/Utah Statewide Preschool Inservice Network (U-SPIN) IEP development process (McDonnell, Berki, Hoagland, & Kiefer-O'Donnell, 1992) uses the curricular framework and curriculum catalogs as a key part of individual, ecologically based curriculum development. The process begins with preassessment planning, during which individual peer and family referenced routines are generated and analyzed to select high-priority routines for increased child participation or performance. The chosen routines, current assessment information, progress in past interventions, and team concerns and priorities serve as the basis for selecting additional assessment strategies and participants. Functional and ecologically based assessment strategies are emphasized. After assessment

**FIGURE 9.2    *Sample Pages from SCIP Curricular Framework and Activity and Skill Curriculum Catalogs for Preschoolers***

CONTEXT: EVENING: HOME

| ROUTINES | ACTIVITIES | SKILLS |
|---|---|---|
| Has dinner 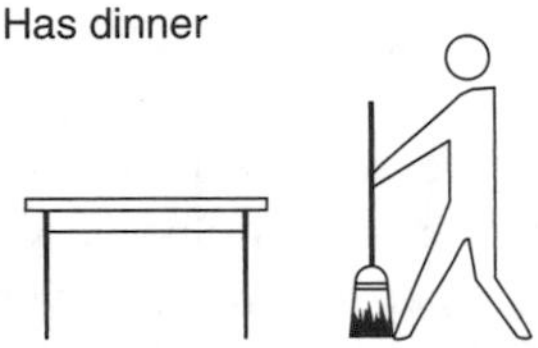 | Helps prepare<br>Gets self to table<br>Eats meal<br>Helps clean up<br>Other: (See Activities Catalog)<br>_____ | Social/Communication<br>Motor<br>Mobility<br>Self-Help<br>Self-Management<br>Cognitive/Pre-Academics<br>Play |
| Free time  | Plays with friends, siblings<br>Plays with toys, games<br>Other: (See Activities Catalog)<br>_____<br>_____ | |
| Personal care  | Toileting<br>Bath<br>Grooming<br>Other: (See Activities Catalog)<br>_____ | |
| Prepares for bed 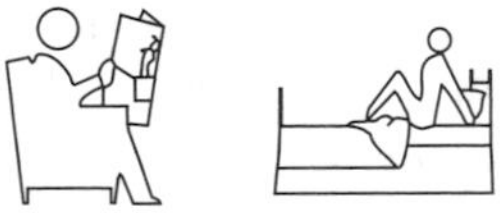 | Dressing/Undressing<br>Grooming<br>Listen to stories<br>Other: (See Activities Catalog)<br>_____ | |
| Ends Day 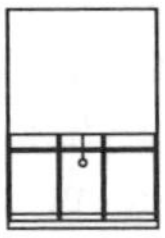 | Goes to bed | |

*(continued)*

**FIGURE 9.2** *Continued*

| Curricular Domain | I. LEISURE/PLAY | | |
|---|---|---|---|
| ENVIRONMENTAL CONTEXT | HOME AND/OR HOME-BASED CHILDCARE | SCHOOL AND/OR CENTER-BASED CHILDCARE | COMMUNITY |
| Activities | Have friends over<br>Participate in play group<br>Interactive games (tag, ring around the rosy)<br><br>INDOOR<br>Record player<br>Tape recorder<br>Radio<br>TV, VCR, DVD<br>Home video, computer game<br>Hand-held video game<br>Books<br>Board games<br>Card games<br>Musical instruments<br>Drawing, painting, coloring<br>Playdoh, clay<br><br>PRESCHOOL AGE TOYS<br><br>Dress ups<br>Child size kitchen<br>Tool bench<br>Action figures<br>Dolls<br>Construction (legos, blocks)<br>Puppets<br>Battery operated toys<br>Car, road sets<br>Puzzles<br><br>OUTDOOR<br><br>Swing set, jungle gym<br>Tricycles, big wheels<br>Hopscotch<br>Water play (pool, slide, sprinkler)<br>Sand play<br>Ball activities | Participate in whole school activities (assemblies, carnivals)<br>Interactive games<br>Library, story time<br><br>INDOOR<br>Record player<br>Tape recorder<br>Radio<br>TV, VCR<br>Video, computer games<br>Card games<br>Musical instruments<br>Drawing, painting, coloring<br>Playdoh, clay<br><br>PRESCHOOL AGE TOYS<br><br>Dress ups<br>Child size kitchen<br>Tool bench<br>Action figures<br>Dolls<br>Construction (legos, blocks)<br>Puppets<br>Battery operated toys<br>Car, road sets<br>Puzzles<br><br>OUTDOOR<br><br>Swing set, jungle gym<br>Tricycles, big wheels<br>Hopscotch<br>Sand play<br>Ball activities | ORGANIZED ACTIVITIES<br>Attending religious group activities<br>Team sports<br>Lessons (dance, swimming)<br><br>INFORMAL ACTIVITIES<br>Playing at friend's house<br>Playing at park, playground<br>Swimming<br>Skating<br>Going for walks<br>Library<br>Movies |

*(continued)*

**FIGURE 9.2    *Continued***

| SKILL AREA | SOCIAL/ COMMUNICATION | MOTOR | MOBILITY |
|---|---|---|---|
| Skills/Skill Group | Attends to environment<br>Expresses needs, desires, and refusals<br>Responds to communication<br>Initiates communcative Interactions<br>Uses new word/ symbols and word/symbol combinations in communication<br>Follows directions<br>Behaves appropriately for setting<br>Maintains social interactions<br><br><u>Other</u> | Range of motion<br>Head control<br>Righting, protective reactions<br>Sitting, trunk control<br>Standing<br>Lifting/carrying<br><br><u>Use of Hands</u><br>Pushing, pulling<br>Reaching<br>Grasping, releasing<br>Twisting, turning manipulations<br>Coordinated use of two hands<br><br><u>Other</u> | Moves to people or activities within same room<br>Moves to people or activities beyond immediate room<br>Moves to people or activities, outdoors<br>Opens/closes doors<br>Goes up/down stairs<br>Maneuvers curbs/ barriers<br>Moves safely with supervision, in community setting<br><br><u>Other</u> |

activities have been completed, the results are shared with all team members. Parents and other preschool team members then use the routines-based curricular framework and curriculum catalogs to select priority IEP goals. During the IEP meeting, parent and preschool team goals are listed and collaborative negotiation is used to (1) select the highest-priority goals, (2) examine the possibilities for integrating goals across curricular areas, and (3) infuse goals into peer and family routines. Examples of IEP goals and objectives for a child with severe developmental delays that might result from the use of this IEP process are provided in Table 9.2.

---

*Focus 5*
How do interventionists implement ecologically based curriculum for preschool children with developmental delays?

---

## *Implementing Intervention in Natural Routines and Activities*

Much of the planning for implementing intervention in natural routines and activities has already occurred by the time the IEP is written if assessment activities, goal selection and

**FIGURE 9.3**   *Parent IEP Preparation Worksheet for Activities*

1. Choose 3–7 activities you feel are most important for your child to learn during the next school year. Activities are listed on the pink stages in the Curriculum Catalog. You may select activities within home, school and/or community environments.
2. Write the activities in the space provided. Write the activity you think is most important on line 1, the next most important activity on line 2, etc.

3. If you have ideas about where your child can practice or use the activity, answer the other questions about the selected activities. An example has been included at the top of the chart.

| *Activity* | *When?* | *Where?* | *With Whom?* | *Other* |
|---|---|---|---|---|
| Example: Tricycle, bike | After preschool | In front of the house At park with family In front of friend's house | Brother Kid across street | Training wheels |
| 1. | | | | |
| 2. | | | | |
| 3. | | | | |
| 4. | | | | |
| 5. | | | | |
| 6. | | | | |
| 7. | | | | |

Please remember to bring these worksheets with you to your child's IEP meeting.

Date: _____

Time _____

Place: _____

development, and the infusion of goals in natural routines have been conducted in ways that are consistent with an ecologically based curriculum model. However, it is still necessary for families and team members to collaborate on ways to assure that focused intervention on IEP goals can be integrated within these natural routines. One way to assure that quality planning and evaluation strategies have been developed is through the development of individual program or intervention plans for each IEP goal. The development of specific intervention plans that pay careful attention to the use of response prompting and fading procedures, reinforcement strategies, and corrections is particularly important for children with severe developmental delays, due to their significant learning difficulties. An example of a simple plan that has been developed for a preschool IEP goal is included in Figure 9.4.

**TABLE 9.2**  *Examples of Jason's IEP Goals and Objectives*

| Annual Goal | Short-Term Objectives |
|---|---|
| **1.** Jason will respond socially to others by establishing and maintaining eye contact when he is spoken to, 90% of opportunities during 1 day/week probe for 6 consecutive weeks. | **A.** Given a verbal cue (name and/or "look") and a physical prompt, Jason will respond by making eye contact within 5 seconds and maintaining it for at least 3 seconds, in at least 3 different preschool activities, for 3 consecutive days.<br>**B.** Same as A but with verbal cue only.<br>**C.** In a variety of activities in preschool, the community, or at home, when Jason is spoken to (by name), he will respond by making eye contact within 5 seconds and maintaining it for at least 3 seconds, at least 9/10 opportunities during a 1-week probe for 6 consecutive weeks. |
| **2.** Jason will spontaneously express his wants and needs by signing "eat" and "drink" to request items, at least once per snack or meal during 1 day/week probes for 6 consecutive weeks. | **A.** When given the verbal cue, "Do you want (eat) / (drink)?," in presence of desired items, Jason will imitate a model of the sign with 90% accuracy for 3 days.<br>**B.** When given a verbal cue that does not contain a model (e.g., "What do you want?"), Jason will use the appropriate sign to make a request when presented with one preferred and two nonpreferred items with 90% accuracy for 3 days.<br>**C.** During times when food is available (lunch, snack, etc.) and visible to Jason, he will independently use the appropriate sign to make a request at least twice per day for 6 consecutive weeks, during 1-week probe.<br>**D.** During times when food/drink is not immediately available, at home or in community settings, Jason will initiate signing his requests for food and drink at least once/snack or meal during 1 day/week probes for 6 consecutive weeks. |
| **3.** Jason will independently use adaptive switches to activate battery operated recreational activities and will maintain appropriate involvement for at least 5 minutes, 80% of activity opportunities for 4 weeks. | **A.** When presented with switches that activate simple, battery operated toys (e.g., car, radio), Jason will independently activate one and maintain involvement for at least 10 seconds with an adult in his immediate presence, 90%+ of opportunities for 3 consecutive sessions.<br>**B.** Same as A but for 3 minutes.<br>**C.** Same as A but with adult anywhere in room, for 5 minutes.<br>**D.** Given free play (at preschool, day care, home, or friend's house) and access to switches that activate simple, battery-operated toys, Jason will use the activity and maintain appropriate involvement with it for at least 5 minutes with no more than 1 verbal reminder from an adult or peer, at least 80% of activity periods for 4 weeks. |

**FIGURE 9.4**   *Sample Intervention Plan for Preschool IEP Goal*

Date begun: 4/1/92

Infant/Child: Sarah B.

Date completed: _____

Objective: Turn-taking     Interventionist: Casey Kealoha

Conditons: When an adult or child begins a game and pauses, or passes the material/toy to Sarah.

Response: Sarah will take a turn by playing for a few moments, and pausing or passing the material/toy back to the adult or child.

Criterion: Plays for 10-60 seconds; pauses or passes material/toy 3 of 4 times.

| Intervention Context | Prompting/Facilitation Techniques | Consequences |
|---|---|---|
| *Setting(s):*<br>• In the morning at the sitter's<br>• After school with her brother<br>• After dinner with Mom, Dad or Grandpa<br><br>*Routine(s)/Activity(ies):*<br>• Clapping games, rocking or "dancing" to music, playing with toys that shake<br><br>*Skill Sequence(s):*<br>1. Vocalizes to request attention<br>2. Turn-taking<br>3. Request "more"<br><br>Occasions for incidental Intervention:<br>n/a | *Positioning and Handling; Special Equipment/Materials:*<br>• Supported sitting in high chair, propped against couch or in corner of couch, or on someone's lap; a table top (lap tray or high chair tray) will help her to manipulate and shake toys.<br><br>*Environmental Modifications:* n/a<br><br>*Prompting/Facilitation:*<br>• Start a turn-taking game and play for about 30 seconds.<br>• Then implement time delay: Physically assist Sarah to take her turn 2 times. For all additional turns, wait 4 seconds. If Sarah takes her turn within the 4-second delay, reinforce. If Sarah does not take her turn within 4 seconds, implement correction 1. | *Reinforcement:*<br>• Verbally praise Sarah, laugh and show lots of excitement as she takes her turn.<br>• Immediately take a turn when Sarah stops (play for about 30 seconds).<br><br>*Corrections:*<br>1. (If Sarah waits beyond the 4-second delay) Physically assist Sarah to take her turn.<br>2. (If Sarah starts doing something else) Start the turn-taking game again. If she doesn't attend and does something else again, stop the intervention and try again later. |

*Source:* Noonan, J. J., & McCormick, M J. (1993). *Early intervention in natural environments: Methods and procedures.* Pacific Grove, CA: Brooks/Cole.

The collection and monitoring of instructional and performance data is also very important to assure that intervention is being carried out as intended, and that intervention changes are made promptly unless the child is making regular progress toward meeting the intervention goal. Data collection within natural routines is a challenge for most preschool teachers, and may be viewed as an unwarranted intrusion in home and community settings. This is one of the many reasons why it is important to include family members and other caregivers as part of the intervention team, so that they can make informed decisions about if and how they would like to participate in evaluation efforts.

Although individual intervention plans may be developed for specific IEP goals, intervention on different goals is usually integrated within the same activity period or natural context. For example, if Jason is about to eat snack with his preschool classmates, he will be expected to use his wheelchair to transition to the snack activity, to sign "eat" and "drink" to request snack items, to sign "more" if he wants seconds on something, and to make eye contact when someone is talking to him. This same type of integration of intervention across goals would ideally occur throughout the routines in Jason's day.

## Transition Planning and Preschool IEPs

Preschool programs usually serve children in the limited age range between 3 and 5 years. Sometimes children with developmental delays will continue in a preschool program for the remainder of the school year in which they turn 6. In these instances, or in districts that do not have kindergarten, children may transition directly between preschool special education services and first grade. Most children enter preschool around their third birthday, and begin kindergarten two years later. Consequently, preschool programs are continuously involved in assisting children and families in making transitions between programs. The inclusion of steps and services to support transition are a part of IFSPs and IEPs as children and families prepare to transition from early intervention to preschool programs, and again as the child enters kindergarten or first grade.

Although transitions are a natural part of life, even planned and positive transitions are often difficult due to the many adjustments. Families of individuals with disabilities have identified major service transitions as one of the more stressful and repetitious events they experience. Window 9.1 provides one parent's reaction to the early intervention–preschool transition. Though generally stressful, transitions are also often a time of opportunity and growth. The role of program personnel during the transitions at either end of the preschool years is primarily to provide support and to facilitate a smooth adjustment on the part of the child, family, and individuals in the new program(s) who will be involved with the child. Conn-Powers, Ross-Allen, and Holburn (1990) summarized the goals for a preschool–elementary transition as follows.

### Goals of a Successful Transition
1. To promote the speedy adjustment of the child and family to the new educational setting.
2. To enhance the child's independent and successful participation in the new educational setting.

3. To insure the uninterrupted provision of appropriate services in the least restrictive school setting.
4. To support and empower the family as an equal partner in the transition process.
5. To promote collaboration among all constituents in the transition process.
6. To increase the satisfaction of all constituents with
   a. the outcomes of the transition process, and
   b. the transition process itself, including their participation,
7. To increase the likelihood that the child is placed and maintained in the regular kindergarten setting and elementary school mainstream. (p. 94)

These goals also apply, with minor modifications, to the early intervention to preschool transition. Table 9.3 provides examples of some of the common concerns and transition-related child goals associated with the two preschool program transitions.

A number of model demonstration projects, school districts, and other program planners or providers have identified recommended steps or processes for preschool program

**TABLE 9.3**   *Common Concerns and Intervention Strategies during Preschool Transitions*

| *Transition* | *Early Intervention to Preschool* | *Preschool to Elementary School (K or 1)* |
|---|---|---|
| Common concerns | • Child's readiness for classroom program, peer relationships, and bus transportation<br>• Changing nature of services from family-centered to child-centered<br>• Safety of child with active peers and in playground and bus settings<br>• Obtaining desired preschool placement and special services<br>• Whether child's individual health and caregiving needs will be met in group setting | • Child's readiness for more structured school programs and full-day program (when applicable)<br>• Whether child will be disruptive, ignored, or rejected in "regular" elementary classes and by typical peers<br>• Obtaining desired school placement and special services<br>• Safety of child in less closely supervised school settings |
| Common child goals related to transition | • Follows directions, rules, and routines<br>• Communicates with familiar adults and peers<br>• Toilet training<br>• Is socially appropriate with peers in a variety of play and preschool activities<br>• Transitions between activities at appropriate time<br>• Occupies self and sustains attention during caregiving, preschool group, and play activities | • Completes seat work independently<br>• Pays attention and participates without disruption in large and small group activities and instruction<br>• Locates and manages own belongings<br>• Is socially appropriate with peers in a variety of classroom and school activities<br>• Takes care of own toileting, eating, grooming, and dressing needs as required in school setting<br>• Demonstrates early academic or "readiness" skills |

transitions (e.g., Bennett, Raab, & Nelson, 1991; Hains, Rosenkoetter, & Fowler, 1991; Noonan & McCormick, 1993; Ross-Allen, Conn-Powers, & Fox, 1991; Rous & Hallam, 1998; Rous et al., 1994). Some of the steps or activities that are recommended by many of these programs include the following.

1. Collaborative teaming among the family, sending program, and receiving program staff in developing a written transition plan that identifies steps or actions to be taken, who will do them, and when
2. Staff and family visits to the receiving program to (a) identify the environmental performance demands, (b) determine important skills to teach the child, and/or (c) identify supports or adaptations to be made in the environment to support the child's success
3. Receiving program staff observations of the child in the current environment, and suggestions on what they believe would (a) be most helpful to teach the child, or (b) be important areas on which to provide training or support to receiving staff
4. Family education and support made available in a variety of ways and throughout the transition process
5. Child visit(s) to the receiving program environment shortly before the transition takes place

It is important to note that transitions are not a one-time meeting with follow-up phone calls. To be effective, transition planning and support must begin well before the program change and continue support and evaluation of the transition for a period after the change has occurred. It is also important that transition planning occur at both the individual child and family level and at the system level, including local community planning and state systems change (Brown, 1996; Rosenkoetter et al., 2001; Ross-Allen et al., 1991). Some Web sites on early childhood transitions include:

- FACTS/LRE Project: Family and Child Transitions in to Least Restrictive Environments (http://facts.crc.uiuc.edu/)
- National TEEM Outreach: A Systematic Planning and Collaborative Decision-Making Process for the Transition of Young Children with Disabilities and Their Families into Kindergarten and Other General Education Settings (http://www.uvm.edu/%7euapvt/programs/teem/purpose.html)
- Project STEPS (Sequenced Transition to Education in the Public Schools) National Outreach Project (http://www.ihddi.uky.edu/projects/steps/steps.html)

## Future Directions for Preschool Programs

The passage of Public Law 99-457 mandated the provision of preschool special education and related services to all eligible children with disabilities. As a result of this mandate there has been a substantial growth in the number of children receiving services, as well as in the comprehensiveness and quality of the services themselves. Although legislation can assure

**POINT AND COUNTERPOINT 9.1 • *How Important Is Inclusion for a Preschool Child with Profound Disabilities?***

Shannon is a 4-year-old child with multiple and profound disabilities. She is the third child in a warm and loving family. Shannon was a very healthy and bright child until shortly after her first birthday. At this time she developed a number of disturbing behavior patterns, including repetitive body rocking, hand wringing, humming, and hair pulling. Even more disturbing, she seemed to be moving backward rather than learning new skills. For example, her walking gait became more awkward and her increasingly skillful use of toys and other objects became more and more primitive. Formerly a very social child, she would now often ignore or avert her gaze when someone spoke to her. She quit calling her mother and father "Mama" and "Dada," and meaningful, back-and-forth gestural or vocal communication became less and less frequent. Shannon's family consulted with medical experts, who initially believed she might have autism. After additional tests and observation Shannon was diagnosed as having Rhett syndrome, a rare degenerative neurological disease.

Shannon and her family participated in an early intervention program. Shannon's goals focused on trying to maintain and improve the quality and usefulness of her existing skills (e.g., walking, some use of her hands, some social responsiveness, an apparent enjoyment of noise, motion, light, and sound) and on including Shannon as a part of her family and community. After the family had a chance to grieve over the changes in Shannon's life and their own, they resumed their many activities and interests. They also became actively involved in advocacy activities intended to improve the lives of individuals with disabilities.

While she was a toddler Shannon stayed with a babysitter three afternoons a week. Shannon did not show a lot of reaction to being around other children or to new and stimulating situations. However, her babysitter did notice that she would walk over to other children, and stand by them and rock. Sometimes Shannon would put her face close to the other children's

and breathe in and out quickly and loudly. These were the same patterns that her family observed at home. Although it was difficult to say for sure, her family interpreted these behaviors as Shannon's attempts to be near and to interact with others. If she didn't enjoy others, why didn't she just stay still or walk away from them?

When Shannon was old enough to begin preschool, her family wanted to enroll her in the Jefferson County Community Preschool, which was located at the elementary school her brother and sister attended. Two other children receiving special education services already attended this preschool. Both were children with mild–moderate developmental delays. The school district placement committee was puzzled both by Shannon's parents' plans to enroll her in Community Preschool, and by their assumption that she could receive all needed special education and related services within that setting. The district placement committee recommended enrolling Shannon in the Mountain View Preschool Program. It was only a half-hour bus ride for Shannon to go to this special education preschool, and because it was located in an elementary school with several special classes it had all of the specialists Shannon would need, right in the building. Some of the children in the special education preschool went into the kindergarten class for about half an hour two or three times a week, and if her parents felt it would make a difference to Shannon, this could also be arranged for her.

*Point:*

The district special education placement team do not believe that Shannon's parents are making the decision that will be in Shannon's best interest. Although they do have district children with developmental delays attending "regular" preschool programs, these are almost entirely children with mild–moderate delays who can really benefit not only from regular contact with preschool children without disabilities, but also from the preschool curriculum. Although these children receive speech therapy and special instruction, it is on an

*(continued)*

**POINT AND COUNTERPOINT 9.1 • Continued**

itinerant basis only, and this would not be sufficient for a child like Shannon. Shannon needs intensive daily instruction and also needs to be seen
by a physical therapist at least twice a week. The
staff at Jefferson County Community Preschool
also cannot be expected to change Shannon's dia-
per, feed her lunch and snacks, and lead her by the
hand to every new group activity. Besides, what's
the point? She doesn't imitate or play with the
other children, and her cognitive level is much
like that of a 3-month-old. What will she get out
of the early literacy, Spanish, Children Around
the World, and Nature and Science programs that
are implemented so well in the community preschool? It just isn't fair to Shannon, the community preschool teachers, or the many children with
mild–moderate disabilities who still aren't integrated into regular preschool programs to try to
attempt something like this. Maybe sometime in
the future there will be enough community preschool placements, and enough specialized support resources to make something like this work.

*Counterpoint:*

Regardless of her abilities or disabilities, Shannon's family believes that she has a basic right to
be included within her family and community
and to attend the same school as her brother and
sister. Maybe Shannon doesn't play or imitate
children in the usual way, but she does seem to
show an interest in her peers in the best way she
knows how. Even if she doesn't learn the same
things as the other children, all of her educational
goals can readily be incorporated within the ongoing preschool activities and she'll probably
enjoy it at least as much as she would the more
structured and less play-oriented special education classroom. Who's to say what really goes on
in Shannon's mind, what she is learning, aware
of, or enjoys? Can a more clear benefit for Shannon really be predicted if she attends the special
education preschool? What exactly is a clear educational benefit anyway for a child like Shannon with a degenerative condition? Does she
have to make as much progress as the children
without disabilities to be viewed as "able to benefit" from the Jefferson County program, and if
so, how do we justify making these opportunities
available to children with mild–moderate disabilities? If the specialists and resources to support a
child like Shannon are not currently available in
the Jefferson County preschool, is there any
reason why they can't be? Let's face it, it does
cost more to support and educate a child like
Shannon wherever she attends school. It just isn't
at all clear that bussing her to a special program
will make it any less so.

some things and the federal government still needs to play a strong role in preschool special
education, at this point much of any continued striving toward excellence may need to come
from families and leadership and interagency collaboration at the state and local levels
(Hebbler et al., 1991; Smith, 2000). Some of the greatest challenges for preschool programs
in the next decade will include removing or overcoming the barriers to full inclusion for all
preschool children with developmental delays, developing a firmer understanding of how to
make programs both developmentally appropriate and effective for learners with intensive
needs, and developing a stronger sense of how preschool programs can maintain the strong
family–professional partnerships developed in early intervention through a more family-
centered approach. Meeting these challenges effectively will require a redefinition of the
early childhood professions as well as a redefinition of professional relationships with families and other caregivers. The editors' introduction to a chapter on reaching the potentials

of children with special needs in a recent NAEYC publication talks about this redefinition of the professions, as well as the inclusion of all children:

> Both political and pedagogical trends are causing the fields of early childhood education and early childhood special education to converge. From a political perspective national laws now ensure access to services for children with disabilities. Due to the recent passage of the landmark civil rights legislation, the Americans with Disabilities Act (ADA), all early childhood programs must be prepared to serve children with special needs. Full implementation of the ADA, coupled with the Individuals with Disabilities Education Act, means the full inclusion of children with disabilities will become a reality, thus bringing early childhood education and early childhood special education closer together than ever before. Work remains to be done to expand the knowledge base but the foundation is well laid. As Safford (1989) points out, "The fields of early childhood education and special education have a great deal in common because of their stress on children as individuals, and their recognition of every child's right to an education that is appropriate to individual and developmental needs" (p. xi). (Bredekamp & Rosegrant, 1992, p. 92).

Preschool children with severe disabilities are clearly a part of this inclusive future, as conceptualized by early childhood educators, as well as by early childhood special educators, related professions, and the children's families.

## Focus Review

Focus 1: What types of services have been made available to preschoolers with disabilities and their families?

- If preschoolers with severe disabilities received any services prior to the late 1950s or early 1960s, they were usually provided within institutions.
- Home-based or classroom-based programs for preschoolers became increasingly available from the late 1950s through the 1980s. However, preschool services were not available for all children with disabilities and their families, and services such as transportation were frequently not provided.
- Since 1991 states have been required to provide preschool special education and related services for all eligible 3- to 5-year-olds.

Focus 2: What is developmentally appropriate practice and how does it apply to preschool children with severe disabilities?

- Developmentally appropriate practice (DAP) guidelines are used to define appropriate learning environments and experiences for young children (birth–age 8) as distinct from those provided to upper elementary, intermediate, and secondary students. These distinctions include (a) a need for learning activities that are initiated and directed by the child and supported by the teacher, and (b) an emphasis on learning through play, exploration, social interaction, and inquiry, rather than through directive teaching to specific goals.

- Many early childhood special educators believe that developmentally appropriate practice provides an environment that is necessary and desirable for young children with severe disabilities but that it is "not sufficient" to meet all of their educational needs. They favor implementing intensive individualized intervention within developmentally appropriate settings and doing frequent evaluation to determine whether this intervention is being effective or needs to be modified.

Focus 3: What policy or position statements have been made about preschoolers with developmental delays and inclusion? How well do these statements correspond to federal regulations related to educating preschoolers with disabilities in the least restrictive environment?

- The Division for Early Childhood of the Council for Exceptional Children has issued a position statement in favor of supported inclusion for all young children. This position has been endorsed by the National Association for the Education of Young Children.
- The federal regulations require preschoolers with disabilities to be educated in the least restrictive environment (LRE) or to the maximum extent possible with their peers without disabilities. Because this is open to interpretation, at this time the LRE requirement in effect allows IEP teams and school districts to choose to serve preschool children with disabilities in special school settings or in elementary schools that do not have classes for typically developing preschoolers.

Focus 4: Describe the major goals of preschool programs for children with disabilities.

- Four goals are often stressed by families and educational programs during the preschool years. These goals include (a) maximizing the child's development in a variety of important developmental areas, (b) developing the child's social interaction and classroom participation skills, (c) preparing the child for inclusive school placements and providing support for the transition to kindergarten or elementary school, and (d) increasing community participation through support to family members and other caregivers.

Focus 5: How do interventionists implement ecologically based curriculum for preschool children with developmental delays?

- Interventionists implement ecologically based curriculum in the natural play and caregiving routines and activities in which preschoolers participate in home, preschool/child care, and community settings.
- Family, caregivers, and preschool team members collaborate in assessment and IEP development activities. IEP goals are selected to support the child's performance and participation in valued natural routines. Once priority IEP goals have been developed, the team can collaborate to infuse goal-based intervention into relevant natural settings. One way of carefully planning for quality individualized intervention is to

record the methods for carrying out and evaluating intervention in natural settings in an individual intervention plan.

## *References*

Allen, K. A., & Martoz, L. (1994). *Developmental profiles: Birth to six* (2nd ed.). Albany, NY: Delmar.

Alsop, L., Blaha, R., & Kloos, E. (2000). *The intervener in early intervention and educational settings for children and youth with deafblindness.* Monmouth, OR: National Technical Assistance Consortium for Children and Young Adults Who Are Deaf-Blind.

Bailey, D. B., Jr. (2000). The federal role in early intervention: Prospects for the future. *Topics in Early Childhood Special Education, 20,* 71–78.

Bailey, D. B., Jr., & McWilliam, R. A. (1990). Normalizing early intervention. *Topics in Early Childhood Special Education, 10*(2), 33–47.

Bailey, D. B., Jr., & Simeonsson, R. J. (1988). Home-based early intervention. In S. L. Odom & M. B. Karnes (Eds.), *Early intervention for infants and children with handicaps: An empirical base* (pp. 199–216). Baltimore: Paul H. Brookes.

Bailey, D. B., Jr., & Wolery, M. (1992). *Teaching infants and preschoolers with disabilities* (2nd ed.). New York: Macmillan.

Barnett, D. W., Bell, S. H., & Carey, K. T. (1999). *Designing preschool interventions: A practitioner's guide.* New York: Guilford.

Bennett, T., Raab, M., & Nelson, D. (1991). The transition process for toddlers with special needs and their families. *Zero to Three, 11,* 17–21.

Bredekamp, S. (1986). *Developmentally appropriate practice.* Washington, DC: National Association for the Education of Young Children.

Bredekamp, S. (1987). *Developmentally appropriate practice in early childhood programs serving children from birth through age 8: Expanded edition.* Washington, DC: National Association for the Education of Young Children.

Bredekamp, S., & Copple, C. (Eds.) (1997). *Developmentally appropriate practice in early childhood programs* (rev. ed). Washington, DC: National Association for the Education of Young Children.

Bredekamp, S., & Rosegrant, T. (1992). *Reaching potentials: Appropriate curriculum and assessment for young children* (Vol. 1). Washington, DC: National Association for the Education of Young Children.

Bricker, D. D., & Bricker, W. A. (1973). Infant, toddler, and preschool research and intervention project report: Year III. *IMRID Behavior Science Mono-*graph (No. 23). Nashville, TN: Institute on Mental Retardation and Intellectual Development, George Peabody College.

Bricker, W. A., & Bricker, D. D. (1976). The infant, toddler, and preschool research and intervention project. In T. D. Tjossem (Ed.), *Intervention strategies with high risk infants and young children.* Baltimore: University Park Press.

Bricker, D., Pretti-Frontczak, K., & McComas, N. (1998). *An activity-based approach to early intervention* (2nd ed.). Baltimore: Paul H. Brookes.

Bricker, D. B., & Waddell, M. (1996). *Assessment, evaluation, and programming system for infants and children: AEPS Curriculum for three to six years.* Baltimore: Paul H. Brookes.

Brown, W. H. (1996). Project BLEND: An inclusive model of early intervention services. *Journal of Early Intervention, 20,* 364–375.

Buysse, V., & Bailey, D. B. (1993). Behavioral and developmental outcomes in young children with disabilities in integrated and segregated settings: A review of comparative studies. *Journal of Special Education, 26,* 434–461.

Buysse, V., Wesley, P. W., Bryant, D. M., & Gardner, D. (1999). Quality of early childhood programs in inclusive and noninclusive settings. *Exceptional Children, 65,* 301–314.

Carta, J. J., Schwarz, I. S., Atwater, J. B., & McConnell, S. R. (1991). Developmentally appropriate practice: Appraising its usefulness for young children with disabilities. *Topics in Early Childhood Special Education, 11*(1), 1–20.

Cavallaro, C. C., Ballard-Rosa, M., & Lynch, E. W. (1998). A preliminary study of inclusive special education services for infants, toddlers, and preschool-age children in California. *Topics in Early Childhood Special Education, 18,* 169–182.

Cavallaro, C. C., & Haney, M. (1999). *Preschool inclusion.* Baltimore: Paul H. Brookes.

Conn-Powers, M. C., Ross-Allen, J., & Holburn, S. (1990). Transition of young children into the elementary education mainstream. *Topics in Early Childhood Special Education, 9*(4), 91–105.

Demchak, M., & Drinkwater, S. (1992). Preschoolers with severe disabilities: The case against segregation. *Topics in Early Childhood Special Education, 11*(4), 70–83.

DeStefano, D. M., Howe, A. G., Horn, E. M., & Smith, B. A. (1991). *Best practices: Evaluating early childhood special education programs.* Tucson, AZ: Communication Skill Builders.

Division for Early Childhood Task Force on Recommended Practices (Eds.) (1993). *DEC recommended practices: Indicators of quality in programs for infants and young children with special needs and their families.* Reston, VA: Council for Exceptional Children.

Doss, L. S., & Reichle, J. (1991). Replacing excess behavior with an initial communicative repertoire. In J. Reichle, J. York, & J. Sigafoos (Eds.), *Implementing augmentative and alternative communication: Strategies for learners with severe disabilities.* Baltimore: Paul H. Brookes.

Dunst, C. J. (2001). Participation of young children with disabilities in community learning activities. In M. J. Guralnick (Ed.), *Early childhood inclusion: Focus on change* (pp. 307–336). Baltimore: Paul H. Brookes.

Fox, L., & Hanline, M. F. (1993). A preliminary evaluation of learning within developmentally appropriate early childhood settings. *Topics in Early Childhood Special Education, 13,* 308–327.

Fredericks, H. D., Baldwin, V. L., Moore, W., Furey, V., Grove, D., Riggs, C., Moore, B., Gage, M. A., Levak, L., Alrick, G., Wadlow, M., Fruin, C., Makohon, L., Lyons, B., Samples, B., Jordan, E., Moses, C., & Rogers, G. (1977). *A data-based classroom for the moderately and severely handicapped* (2nd ed.). Monmouth, OR: Instructional Development Corporation.

Gestwicki, C. (1995). *Developmentally appropriate practice: Curriculum and development in early education.* Albany, NY: Delmar.

Guralnick, M. J. (1990). Major accomplishments and future directions in early childhood mainstreaming. *Topics in Early Childhood Special Education, 10,* 1–17.

Guralnick, M. J. (2001). A framework for change in early childhood inclusion. In M. J. Guralnick (Ed.), *Early childhood inclusion: Focus on change* (pp. 3–36). Baltimore: Paul H. Brookes.

Guralnick, M. J., & Bennett, F. C. (Eds.). (1987). *The effectiveness of early intervention for at-risk and handicapped children.* New York: Academic Press.

Guralnick, M. J., Connor, R. T., Hammond, M. A., Gottman, J. M., & Kinnish, K. (1996). Immediate effects of mainstreamed settings on the social interaction and social integration of preschool children. *American Journal on Mental Retardation, 100,* 359–377.

Hains, A. H., Rosenkoetter, S. E., & Fowler, S. A. (1991). Transition planning with families in early intervention programs. *Infants and Young Children, 3*(4), 38–47.

Hamner, T. J., & Turner, P. H. (2001). *Parenting in contemporary society* (4th ed.). Boston: Allyn & Bacon.

Hanline, M. F. (1993). Inclusion of preschoolers with profound disabilities: An analysis of children's interactions. *Journal of the Association for Persons with Severe Handicaps, 18*(1), 28–35.

Hanline, M. F., & Knowlton, A. (1988). A collaborative model for providing support to parents during their child's transition from infant intervention to preschool special education public school programs. *Journal of the Division for Early Childhood, 12*(2), 116–125.

Hanson, M. J., & Lynch, E. W. (1995). *Early intervention: Implementing child and family services for infants and toddlers who are at-risk or disabled* (2nd ed.). Austin, TX: Pro-Ed.

Harbin, G. L. (1993). Family issues of children with disabilities: How research and theory have modified practice in early intervention. In N. J. Anastasiow & S. Harel (Eds.), *At-risk infants: Interventions, families, and research* (pp. 101–114). Baltimore: Paul H. Brookes.

Hayden, A. H., & Dmitriev, V. (1975). The multi-disciplinary preschool program for Down's syndrome children at the University of Washington Model Preschool Center. In B. Z. Friedlander, G. M. Sterritt, & G. E. Kirk (Eds.), *Exceptional infant: Assessment and Intervention* (Vol. 3). New York: Brunner/Mazel.

Hayden, A. H., & Haring, N. G. (1976). Early intervention for high risk infants and young children: Programs for Down's syndrome children. In T. D. Tjossem (Ed.), *Intervention strategies for high risk infants and young children.* Baltimore: University Park Press.

Hebbler, K. M., Smith, B. J., & Black, T. L. (1991). Federal early childhood special education policy: A model for the improvement of services for children with disabilities. *Exceptional Children, 58*(2), 104–114.

Hofferth, S. L. (1996). Child care in the United States today. *The Future of Children, 6,* 41–61.

Hundert, J., Mahoney, B., Mundy, F., & Vernon, M. L. (1998). A descriptive analysis of developmental and social gains of children with severe disabilities in segregated and inclusive preschools in southern Ontario. *Early Childhood Research Quarterly, 13,* 49–65.

International Reading Association (IRA) and the National Association for the Education of Young Children (NAEYC) (1998). Learning to read and write: Developmentally appropriate practices for young children: A joint position statement of the IRA and NAEYC. *Young Children, 30*–46.

Jenkins, J. R., Odom, S. L., & Speltz, M. C. (1989). Effects of social integration of preschool children with handicaps. *Exceptional Children, 55,* 420–428.

Johnson, J. E., & Johnson, K. M. (1992). Clarifying the developmental perspective in response to Carta, Schwartz, Atwater, and McConnell. *Topics in Early Childhood Special Education, 12*(4), 439–457.

Johnson, L. J., Gallagher, R. J., Cook, M., & Wong, P. (1995). Critical skills for kindergarten: Perceptions from kindergarten teachers. *Journal of Early Intervention, 19,* 315–349.

Kostelnik, M. J. (1992). Myths associated with developmentally appropriate programs. *Young Children, 47*(4), 17–23.

Lamorey, S., & Bricker, D. D. (1993). Integrated programs: Effects on young children and their parents. In C. Peck, S. Odom, & D. Bricker (Eds.), *Integrating young children with disabilities into community-based programs: From research to implementation* (pp. 249–269). Baltimore: Paul H. Brookes.

LaParo, K. M., Sexton, D., & Snyder. P. (1998). Program quality characteristics in segregated and inclusive early childhood settings. *Early Childhood Research Quarterly, 13,* 151–168.

Levine, J. M., & Antia, S. D. (1997). The effects of partner hearing status on social and cognitive play. *Journal of Early Intervention, 21,* 21–35.

Linder, T. W. (1993). *Transdisciplinary play-based assessment: A functional approach to working with young children* (rev. ed). Baltimore: Paul H. Brookes.

Mallory, B. (1992). Is it always appropriate to be developmental?: Convergent models for early intervention practice. *Topics in Early Childhood Special Education, 11*(4), 1–12.

Malmskog, S., & McDonnell, A.. (1999). Teacher-mediated facilitation of engagement for preschool children with developmental delays in inclusive developmentally appropriate classrooms. *Topics in Early Childhood Special Education, 19,* 203–216.

McCormick, L., & Kawate, J. (1982). Kindergarten survival skills: New directions for preschool special education. *Education and Training of the Mentally Retarded, 17,* 247–252.

McDonnell, A., Berki, P., Hoagland, V., & Kiefer-O'Donnell, M. (1992). *Transdisciplinary team IEP development for preschoolers with disabilities: A peer and family-referenced approach.* Salt Lake City: University of Utah, Department of Special Education, Utah Statewide Preschool Inservice Network.

McDonnell, A., Brownell, K., & Wolery, M. (1997). Teaching experience and specialist support: A survey of preschool teachers in NAEYC-accredited programs. *Topics in Early Childhood Special Education, 17,* 263–285.

McDonnell, A., Brownell, K., & Wolery, M. (2001). Teacher's views concerning individualized intervention and support roles within developmentally appropriate preschool programs. *Journal of Early Intervention, 24,* 67–83.

McDonnell, A., & Hardman, M. (1988). A synthesis of "best practice" guidelines for early childhood services. *Journal of the Division for Early Childhood, 12*(4), 328–341.

McDonnell, J., McDonnell, A., Mathot-Buckner, C., Thorson, N., Berki, P., Hightower, J., & Kiefer-O'Donnell, R. (1994). *The School and Community Integration Program Cross-Age Curriculum for Students with Severe Disabilities.* Salt Lake City, UT: Department of Special Education.

McLean, M., & Hanline, M. F. (1990). Providing early intervention services in integrated environments: Challenges and opportunities for the future. *Topics in Early Childhood Special Education, 10,* 62–77.

McLean, L., McNay, V. J., & Kottwitz, E. (1995). *Preparing children to learn: A family-centered approach to functional skills assessment manual.* Tucson, AZ: Communication Skill Builders.

McNay, V. J., Kottwitz, E., Simmons, S., & McLean, L. (1995). *Preparing children to learn: A family-centered approach to functional skills assessment curriculum.* Tucson, AZ: Communication Skill Builders.

National Association for the Education of Young Children (1997). *NAEYC guidelines for early childhood professional preparation programs: Associate, Baccalaureate, and Advanced Levels.* Washington, DC: NAEYC.

National Association for the Education of Young Children and the National Association of Early Childhood Specialists in State Departments of Education (1991). Guidelines for appropriate curriculum content in programs serving children ages 3 through 8: A position statement. *Young Children, 46,* 21–38.

Nelson, C., van Dijk, J., McDonnell, A., & Thompson, K. (in press). A framework for understanding young children with severe multiple disabilities: The van Dijk approach to assessment. *The Journal of the Association for Persons with Severe Handicaps.*

Neuman, S. B., Copple, C., & Bredekamp, S. (2000). *Learning to read and write: Developmentally appropriate practices for young children.* Washington, DC: National Association for the Education of Young Children.

Noonan, M. J., & McCormick, L. (1993). *Early intervention in natural environments: Methods and procedures.* Pacific Grove, CA: Brooks/Cole.

Odom, S. L. (2000). Preschool inclusion: What we know and where we go from here. *Topics in Early Childhood Special Education, 20,* 20–27.

Odom, S. L., & Bailey, D. B. (2001). Inclusive preschool programs: Classroom ecology and child outcomes. In M. J. Guralnick (Ed.), *Early childhood inclusion: Focus on change* (pp. 253–276). Baltimore: Paul H. Brookes.

Odom, S. L., & Diamond, K. A. (1998). Inclusion in young children with special needs in early childhood education: The research base. *Early Childhood Research Quarterly, 13,* 3–25.

Odom, S. L., Horn, E., Marquart, J. M., Hanson, M., Wolfberg, P., Beckman, P., Lieber, J., Li, Shouming, Schwartz, I., Janko, S., & Sandall, S. (1999). On the forms of inclusion: Organizational context and individualized service models. *Journal of Early Intervention, 22,* 185–199.

Odom, S. L., & McEvoy, M. A. (1988). Integration of young children with handicaps and normally developing children. In S. L. Odom & M. B. Karnes (Eds.), *Early intervention for infants and children with handicaps: An empirical base* (pp. 241–268). Baltimore: Paul H. Brookes.

Peck, C. A., Carlson, P., & Helmstetter, E. (1992). Parent and teacher perceptions of outcomes for typically developing children enrolled in integrated early childhood programs: A statewide survey. *Journal of Early Intervention, 16,* 53–63.

Rosenkoetter, S. E., Whaley, K. T., Hains, A. H., & Pierce, L. (2001). The evolution of transition policy for young children with special needs and their families: Past, present, and future. *Topics in Early Childhood Special Education, 21,* 3–15.

Ross-Allen, J., Conn-Powers, M., & Fox, W. (1991). *TEEM: A manual to support the transition of young children with special needs and their families from preschool into kindergarten and other regular education environments.* Burlington: University of Vermont, Center for Developmental Disabilities, The University Affiliated Program of Vermont.

Rous, B., & Hallam, R. A. (1998). Easing the transition to kindergarten: Assessment of social, behavioral, and functional skills in young children with disabilities. *Young Exceptional Children, 1*(4), 17–27.

Rous, B., Hemmeter, M. L., & Schuster, J. (1994). Sequenced transition to education in the public schools: A systems approach to transition planning. *Topics in Early Childhood Special Education, 14,* 374–393.

Rule, S., Fiechtl, B. J., & Innocenti, M. (1990). Preparation for transition to mainstreamed post-preschool environment: Development of a survival skills curriculum. *Topics in Early Childhood Special Education, 9*(4), 78–90.

Rule, S., Stowitschek, J. J., Innocenti, M., Striefel, S., Killoran, J., Swezey, K., & Boswell, C. (1987). The Social Integration Program: An analysis of the effects of mainstreaming handicapped children into daycare centers. *Education and Treatment of Children, 10*(2), 175–192.

Safford, P. L. (1989). *Integrated teaching in early childhood: Starting in the mainstream.* White Plains, NY: Longman.

Sandall, S., & Smith, B. J. (2000). Introduction to the DEC recommended practices. In S. Sandall, M. E. McLean, & B. J. Smith (Eds.), *DEC recommended practices in Early Intervention/Early Childhood Special Education* (pp. 1–4). Longmont, CO: Sopris West.

Sandall, S., McLean, M. E., Santos, R. M., & Smith, B. J. (2000a). DEC's new recommended practices: The context for change. In S. Sandall, M. E. McLean, & B. J. Smith (Eds.), *DEC recommended practices in early intervention/early childhood special education* (pp. 5–13). Longmont, CO: Sopris West.

Sandall, S., McLean, M. E., Smith, B. J. (2000b). *DEC recommended practices in early intervention/early childhood special education.* Longmont, CO: Sopris West.

Shearer, D. E., & Shearer, M. S. (1976). The Portage Project: A model for early childhood intervention. In T. D. Tjossem (Ed.), *Intervention strategies for high risk infants and young children.* Baltimore: University Park Press.

Smith, B. J. (2000). The federal role in early childhood special education policy in the next century: The responsibility of the individual. *Topics in Early Childhood Special Education, 20,* 7–13.

Strain, P. S. (1990). LRE for preschool children with handicaps: What we know, what we should be doing. *Journal of Early Intervention, 14*(4), 291–296.

Strain, P. S., McGee, G. G., & Kohler, F. W. (2001). Inclusion of children with autism in early intervention environments: An examination of the rationale, myths, and procedures. In M. J. Guralnick (Ed.), *Early childhood inclusion: Focus on change* (pp. 337–364). Baltimore: Paul H. Brookes.

Striefel, S., Killoran, J., & Quintero, M. (1991). *Functional integration for success: Preschool Intervention.* Austin, TX: Pro-Ed.

Thompson, B., Wickham, D., Wegner, J., Ault, M. M., Shanks, P., & Reinertson, B. (1993). *Handbook for the inclusion of young children with severe disabilities: Strategies for implementing exemplary full inclusion programs.* Lawrence, KS: Learner Managed Designs.

Thurman, S. K., & Widerstrom, A. H. (1990). *Infants and young children: A developmental and ecological approach* (2nd ed.). Baltimore: Paul H. Brookes.

Vincent, L. J., Salisbury, C., Walter, G., Brown, P., Gruenewald, L., & Powers, M. (1980). Program evaluation and curriculum development in early childhood/special education: Criteria of the next environment. In W. Sailor, B. Wilcox, & L. Brown (Eds.), *Methods of instruction for severely handicapped students* (pp. 303–328). Baltimore: Paul H. Brookes.

Walsh, S. (1993). Head Start disability regulations released. *DEC Communicator, 19*(3), 3.

Wolery, M., Holcombe, A., Venn, M. A., & Werts, M. G. (1992, December). *Finding the balance: Developmentally appropriate practice and instruction of young children with special needs.* Preconference workshop presented at the International Early Childhood Conference on Children with Special Needs, Washington, DC.

Wolery, M., Martin, C. G., Schroeder, C., Huffman, K., Venn, M. L., Holcombe, A., Brookfield, J., & Fleming, L. A. (1994). Employment of educators in preschool mainstreaming: A survey of general educators. *Journal of Early Intervention, 18,* 64–77.

Wolery, M., Strain, P. S., & Bailey, D. B., Jr. (1992). Reaching potentials of children with special needs. In S. Bredekamp & Teresa Rosegrant (Eds.), *Reaching potentials: Appropriate curriculum and assessment for young children, Vol. I* (pp. 92–112). Washington, DC: National Association for the Education of Young Children.

Zigler, E., & Styfca, S. (2000). Pioneering steps (and fumbles) in developing a federal preschool intervention. *Topics in Early Childhood Special Education, 20,* 67–70.

# 10

# *Elementary Programs*

*Peers without disabilities play an important role in supporting the inclusion of students with severe disabilities in general education classes.*

## WINDOW 10.1 • *A New Day for the Fifth Grade*

As students in Ms. Nelson's fifth-grade class begin a second day's work on team projects in science, their teacher temporarily interrupts them to introduce two new pupils in the class.

"Girls and boys, I would like you to stop your work for a moment. We have two new students in our class I would like to introduce."

One girl, Joanne, has just moved into the community from the Philippines. She lived there for two years. Before that, she lived in California, where she attended a school on a military base. She has recently returned to the States with her parents because of the closure of the island military base.

"I would like to introduce Joanne Wilson. She just moved back to the United States from the Philippines. Her parents were stationed there. I bet she has quite a bit to tell us about living and going to school there. Marsha, will you move those books on the empty desk next to you? Joanne will join in with your team, and work with you on the science project."

Students in Marsha's group are excited about having the new student be part of their team. As Joanne takes her seat, her teammates simultaneously begin to ask her questions about her experiences in the Philippines.

"All right children, settle down for a moment. We have another new student to introduce." The second girl is also new to the school. Unlike Joanne, Jennifer has lived in town all her life. Actually, she has lived a block from school for the past four years. She has always attended a special school for children with severe disabilities.

"Class, this is Jennifer McCarthy. As you can see, she uses a wheelchair to move through school. Jennifer had been attending Middleton School, across town, but will now be going to our school. We'll have to make sure to keep the aisles clear so that Jennifer can get in and out. Tom, can you help her back by you? Her aide will be here soon to help her with her math."

Within several minutes, the period ends and it's time for lunch. The special education aide has not yet arrived, so Tom helps Jennifer out of class and to the gym for lunch. He pushes her to an open table, where Ms. Nelson asks if she'll be okay until the aide comes with her lunch. Jennifer nods, indicating "yes," and Tom and his teacher leave. Joanne has taken a seat at another table with a number of other classmates, and is already busy with lunch. Girls from Marsha's group have joined her and have begun to ask about living in the Philippines.

After about ten minutes, Jennifer's aide arrives with lunch, apologizing for her tardiness. She gives Jennifer her lunch and begins her own meal, as Jennifer does the same. The meal proceeds quietly, until both are done. The aide, knowing that Jennifer has not yet completed her math assignment, wheels Jennifer to her homeroom, where they spend the remainder of lunch period doing addition problems.

Many of our best childhood memories date from the time spent in elementary school. For most children, life in elementary school is fun, challenging, and rewarding. It is there that future computer specialists, bank managers, and electricians develop the essentials of living. Students learn to multiply fractions, write poems, use maps, and problem-solve with computers. Equally important, they become sympathetic counselors for a buddy who failed the spelling quiz, and adept at the art of negotiation while preventing a fight on the playground. Through elementary schools, young children begin to experience an exciting new life—one that takes them a step beyond the family activities and relationships and the play routines of preschool. The educational experiences that children have during this period of their lives profoundly affect their perceptions of themselves and other people. These experiences also lay the foundation for children's future success in school and ultimately adulthood.

The task of providing an effective education to elementary students has become much more complex as the character of our communities has changed (Baca & Cervantes, 1998). The demands placed on elementary schools have also increased as parents and policy makers have called for higher educational standards for all children. The result is that elementary schools have been compelled in recent years to evaluate their mission, organization, and operation (Darling-Hammond, 1997; National Research Council, 1997).

The same challenges hold true for elementary school programs for children with severe disabilities. These programs must prepare their young students to face the hurdles of everyday life and ultimately the challenges they will face as they transition from school to work and community living. The organization of elementary school programs for students with severe disabilities has changed dramatically in the last three decades in order to meet these challenges. This chapter discusses the historical development of elementary programs, the structure of these programs today, effective curriculum and instructional practices, and future directions.

## The History of Elementary Programs

The contemporary history of the education of students with severe disabilities has been driven by the Individuals with Disabilities Education Act (IDEA) and its predecessor, the Education of All Handicapped Children's Act (EHA). Prior to 1975, school districts were not required to provide educational services to children with disabilities. In most parts of the country, the only option available to parents of children with severe disabilities was institutionalization (see Chapter 2). Those parents who decided to keep their children at home were often criticized by their families, medical professionals, and other community members. Gradually, these parents banned together at the local level to establish school programs for their children. These programs were often supported by nonprofit organizations and advocacy groups. Classes were located in places such as church basements and community centers. The curriculum focused on teaching students daily living, communication, motor, and preacademic skills. Teachers had little training and few resources to meet the needs of students. Obviously, all of this changed when the EHA took effect. Today, the IDEA guides the design and implementation of educational programs for elementary-age students with severe disabilities. IDEA'97 included a number of new requirements that affect directly the nature of educational programs for this group of students. The development of elementary school programs for students with severe disabilities has also been affected in recent years by several educational reform initiatives. Perhaps two of the most influential of these initiatives are the Regular Education Initiative (REI) and the inclusion movement.

### Influence of IDEA '97

> **Focus 1**
> What are the legal foundations for including children with severe disabilities in general education curriculum?

As discussed in Chapter 3, IDEA '97 is the statutory framework for educational services for children with disabilities. The key elements of IDEA include the requirements that school districts provide students with a *free appropriate public education* (FAPE), in the *least restrictive environment* (LRE), and that the student's educational program be driven by an Individualized Education Program (IEP). However, in 1997 Congress adopted several amendments to the IDEA that have the potential to change dramatically the focus of educational programs for students with disabilities, including children with severe disabilities. These amendments require that (1) IEPs address how students will be involved in and progress in the general education curriculum, (2) general educators participate in the development of student IEPs if the student is going to be included in general education classes, and (3) students with disabilities participate to the extent appropriate in state- and district-wide assessments of student achievement. For example, Section 300.346 (4) states: "The regular education teacher of a child with a disability, as a member of the IEP team, must, to the extent appropriate, participate in the development, review, and revision of the child's IEP." The statute goes on to say in Section 300.347 (a)(2)(i):

> The IEP for each child with a disability must include—
>
> > (2) A statement of measurable annual goals, including benchmarks or short-term objectives, related to—
> > > (i) Meeting the child's needs that result from the child's disability to enable the child to be involved in and progress in the general education curriculum (i.e., the same curriculum as for nondisabled children).

Section 300.138 of the IDEA requires that state educational agencies develop procedures to ensure that:

> (a) Children with disabilities are included in general State and district-wide assessment programs, with appropriate accommodations and modifications in administration, if necessary;
> (b) As appropriate, the State of LEA—
> > (1) Develops guidelines for the participation of children with disabilities in alternative assessments for those children who cannot participate in State and district-wide assessment.

Although the impact of these amendments on special education programs is not yet fully understood, it is clear that Congress intended that students with disabilities participate in the general education curriculum and that, whenever possible, they should be held to the same performance standards as their peers without disabilities. Furthermore, students' IEPs and the special education services they receive should be structured to maximize the success of students in the general education curriculum. Finally, Congress recognized that the success of students with disabilities in the general education curriculum would require strong partnerships among general and special education professionals.

## *Influence of the Regular Education Initiative and the Inclusion Movement*

In many respects, the emphasis in IDEA '97 on the participation of students with disabilities in the general education curriculum reflects the evolution of an ongoing public dialog about the inclusion of children with disabilities in the general education system. This dialog occurred simultaneously with the general education reform movement. This movement began during the 1980s because of growing concerns that the United States was being displaced by other industrialized nations as the major player in the world economy. One of the reasons cited for this decline was the ineffectiveness of public schools in preparing students to compete in the global market place (Murphy, 1991). In response, a number of prestigious commissions and organizations called for a complete restructuring of the public school system (Carnegie Forum, 1986; Education Commission of the States, 1983; National Commission on Excellence in Education, 1983; National Governors' Association, 1986). Given the significant federal investment in special education programs, it is not surprising that proposals intended to improve the effectiveness of these programs also emerged.

One of the most controversial proposals was the Regular Education Initiative (REI) (Lloyd, Singh, & Repp, 1990). Essentially, the REI proposed a merger of general and special education and the elimination of a separate system of special education. The primary argument in favor of the REI was that special education programs were not adequately preparing youth with disabilities to assume productive roles in the community after leaving school (Lipsky & Gartner, 1990). Indeed, national studies examining the postschool outcomes of students with disabilities painted a bleak picture of unemployment, isolation, and dependence on social service programs (Wagner, 1989) (see Chapter 11 for a more detailed discussion of this research). Proponents of the REI suggested that changing these outcomes would require that students with disabilities have equal access to the new curriculum and instructional approaches being developed and implemented in the schools for students without disabilities. Furthermore, they argued that the participation of students with disabilities in the restructured schools could be accomplished only if the resources directed to the separate system of special education were reallocated to improve the quality of education for all students. Although there was strong opposition to the REI (Kauffman, 1990), it prompted significant interest in the development of curriculum, instructional, and classroom organizational strategies that could support the full participation of children with disabilities in general education classes and the general education curriculum (Lipsky & Gartner, 1997; Thousand, Villa, & Nevin, 1994).

Whereas the REI focused primarily on programs serving students with mild disabilities, there was growing interest among parents, advocates, and researchers in expanding the opportunities for students with severe disabilities to be educated alongside their peers without disabilities in typical schools and classrooms (Meyer, Peck, & Brown, 1991; National Association of State Boards of Education, 1992). Thus, the inclusion movement, and the idea of inclusive education, emerged as a driving force behind the development of service programs for students with severe disabilities. Although the development of inclusive educational programs is based on the principle that these students should have equal access to the general education program (Laski, 1991; Nisbet, Jorgensen, & Powers, 1994), a growing research base suggested that inclusive programs also had many positive educational and social outcomes for students with and without disabilities (Giangreco & Putnam, 1991; Halvorsen & Sailor, 1990; Snell, 1990). Proponents of inclusive education also argued that the significant investments that federal, state, and local educational agencies had made in reforming the general education system created the conditions necessary to support the increased participation of students with severe disabilities in general education classes. They pointed to the growing support for the development and adoption of curriculum and instructional approaches by general educators that could accommodate the full range of students in a school, including children with disabilities and other special needs (Cohen, McLaughlin, & Talbert, 1993; Darling-Hammond, 1996; Lee, Bryk, & Smith, 1993; Murphy, 1991; Sizer, 1992). For example, Darling-Hammond (1996) stated:

> If we want all students to actually learn in the way that new standards suggest and today's complex society demands, we will need to develop teaching that goes far beyond dispensing information, giving a test, and giving a grade. We will need to understand how to teach in ways that respond to students' diverse approaches to learning, that are structured to take advantage of students' unique starting points, and that carefully scaffold work aimed at more proficient performances. (p. 7)

In summary, educational programs for students with severe disabilities have changed dramatically over the last three decades. Legislation, research, and advocacy have allowed children to move out of church basements into typical schools and classrooms; to move from social isolation to participation in their school, neighborhood, and community; and from separate, specialized curriculum to equal access to the curriculum that is provided to all students in schools.

# Structure of Elementary Programs

Elementary schools are typically structured to serve students in kindergarten through sixth grade. Children are assigned to grade-level classes based on their chronological age. For example, kindergarten classes have children who are 6 years old whereas sixth-grade classes have children who are 12 years old. In contrast, special education programs for children with severe disabilities often serve students across the entire age range from 6 to 12 years old. In addition, the IDEA mandates that school districts provide a continuum of educational placements for students with disabilities. In this section we describe the range of educational settings available to students with severe disabilities and discuss inclusive education as an alternative structure to the continuum.

## The "Continuum" of Educational Services

Table 10.1 describes the various settings in which students with severe disabilities may receive special education services. These placement alternatives range from full-time regular class placement to public institutions. In the typical school district, however, most students are served in one of five placement alternatives. Under the IDEA, decisions about a student's educational placement must be driven by the IEP. In addition, students must be educated in the least restrictive environment (LRE) and receive their education with peers without disabilities to the maximum extent appropriate.

---

**Focus 2**
Where do the majority of students with severe disabilities receive their educational service?

**TABLE 10.1**   *The Continuum of Educational Placements*

| Placement Alternative | Description |
| --- | --- |
| Public institution | Student receives special education services while living in a public institution. |
| Residential school | Student receives special education services while living in a private residential school for children with disabilities. |
| Homebound instruction | Student receives special education services in his or her own home. |
| Special school | Student receives special education services in a separate school for children with disabilities. |
| Special class placement | Student receives special education services in a self-contained class located in a typical school building. |
| Part-time special class placement | Student receives special education services in both self-contained special education and general education classes in a typical school building. |
| Regular class placement with resource support | Student receives special education services in a general education class. |
| Full-time regular class placement | Student is placed in a typical general education class and does not receive special education services. |

National data on the number of children with severe disabilities placed in the various service options are not readily available. However, the U.S. Department of Education gathers data from state educational agencies on the number of children in each disability category defined in the IDEA who are served outside regular classrooms, in separate school facilities, in residential facilities, and in home/hospital settings. Window 10.2 presents the percentage of children nationally with mental retardation, multiple disabilities, autism, and deaf-blindness between the ages of 6 and 11 served in these various settings (U.S. Department of Education, 2000). A close examination of the information presented in Window 10.2 indicates that the vast majority of students with these classifications receive special education services outside regular classrooms for 60 percent or more of the school day. A significant number of children receive special education services in separate school facilities, residential programs, or home/hospital settings.

• *Homebound service programs.* In this placement alternative, students are provided special education services in their own homes. These programs typically serve children whose medical or educational needs are so intense that they cannot be provided in a school setting. An itinerant teacher, and/or a paraprofessional who is supervised by a licensed teacher, will go to the child's home to provide instruction and other educational services. The number of hours of service that students are provided is based on the goals and objec-

**WINDOW 10.2** • *Percentage of Students Served in Various Educational Placements*

| Student Group | Outside Regular Class | | | Separate Facility | Residential Facility | Home/Hospital Setting |
|---|---|---|---|---|---|---|
| | <21% | 21–60% | >60% | | | |
| Students with mental retardation | 12.6 | 29.6 | 51.7 | 5.2 | .6 | .4 |
| Students with multiple disabilities | 10.0 | 17.3 | 45.1 | 22.3 | 2.9 | 2.5 |
| Students with deaf-blindness | 13.6 | 11.3 | 39.0 | 19.9 | 14.8 | 1.5 |
| Students with autism | 18.3 | 12.7 | 39.0 | 14.6 | 1.8 | .5 |

*Source:* U.S. Department of Education (2000). *22nd Annual Report to Congress on the implementation of the Individuals with Disabilities Education Act.* Washington, DC: U. S. Government Printing Office.

tives included in their IEP. School staff will often provide training to parents and other family members to implement instructional programs and provide other supports.

• *Special schools.* Some school districts have separate schools for students with disabilities. Children who attend these schools are usually bussed from their home to school each day. Most of these schools serve children from age 6 through 22.

• *Special class placements.* In this alternative, students with severe disabilities are placed in a special class in a typical school. These special classes may be located in students' neighborhood schools, or they may be "clustered" together in a single school. There is great variability in the age range of students served in these classes. In some school districts, classes located in elementary schools serve only elementary-age students. In other districts, however, classes located in elementary schools may serve students up to age 22.

• *Part-time class placement.* In these programs, students spend part of their school day in a special class and part of the day in general education classes. Typically, students are included in general education classes for instruction in areas such as music and art, and for nonacademic activities such as recess, lunch, and assemblies. Instruction in core academic domains (e.g., reading, math) is often conducted in the special education classroom.

• *Regular class placement with resource support.* Students in these programs are enrolled in a general education class. Special education services to meet IEP goals may be provided within the general education class, or students may be "pulled out" of the general education class for brief periods to receive these services.

At this point, no research has compared directly the relative effectiveness of the various placement alternatives included in the continuum in promoting student educational achievement (Harrower, 1999; Hunt & Goetz, 1997). However, there is significant variability from one state to another in the educational placements of students with severe disabilities (U.S. Department of Education, 2000). For example, in the 22nd Annual Report to Congress on the Implementation of IDEA, the U.S. Department of Education reported that the percentage of students with multiple disabilities who are served outside of general education for less than 21 percent of the school day ranges from a high of 75 percent in Vermont to a low of 0 percent in Delaware. At this point, it seems that placement decisions for students with disabilities, especially for those with severe disabilities, are based more on financial, political, social, and cultural factors than on students' educational needs (Danielson & Bellamy, 1989).

Although no research has compared the effectiveness of various educational placements for students with severe disabilities, research has consistently demonstrated that even students with the most significant disabilities can learn a variety of skills in general education classes and that students benefit socially from their interactions with peers without disabilities (Harrower, 1999; Hunt & Goetz, 1997). In addition, there is a growing body of research suggesting that students with severe disabilities can be provided effective instruction in general education classes (Hollowood, Salisbury, Rainforth, & Palombaro, 1995; Logan, Bakemen, & Keefe, 1997; McDonnell, Thorson, & McQuivey, 1998; McDonnell, Thorson, McQuivey, & Kiefer-O'Donnell, 1997) and that the quality of instruction provided to students in general and special education classrooms is not markedly different (Logan & Keefe, 1997).

## Inclusive Educational Programs

The growing body of research demonstrating that the educational and social needs of students with severe disabilities can be met within general education classes has prompted parent, advocacy, and professional groups to call for the development and expansion of inclusive educational programs for these students (The ARC, 1998; National Association of State Boards of Education, 1992; The Association of Persons with Severe Handicaps, 2000). See Point-of-Interest 10.1.

McDonnell, Mathot-Buckner, Mendell, Thorson, and Allen (2000) have argued that effective inclusive education programs have several critical features:

**1.** *The student attends his or her neighborhood school.* Students should attend the school that they would attend if they had not been identified as needing specialized services. If a school district gives parents a "choice" of which school their child will attend, then this policy should apply to all children including those with disabilities and other special needs. Attendance at the neighborhood school allows students the opportunity to develop relationships with same-age peers that are necessary for successful participation in the general education class and the community.

**2.** *The student is placed in age-appropriate grade-level or subject-area classes.* The educational placement of students should be based on their chronological age rather than their developmental age. It is unlikely that students can or will develop strong social relationships with significantly younger or older peers. It is also important that students be assigned to the general educator's class roster. The general educator must view the student as

**POINT OF INTEREST 10.1 • *TASH Resolution on Inclusive Education***

TASH, an international advocacy association of people with disabilities, their family members, other advocates and people who work in the disability field, affirms that a definition of inclusion begins with the educational and moral imperatives that students with disabilities belong in general education classrooms and that they receive the supports and services necessary to benefit from their education in general education settings. Inclusive education is based upon current understandings about how children and young people are educated, and embraces an acceptance of all children into the school community as active, fully participating members. A commitment to inclusive education views diversity and the norm assures effective teaching and necessary supports to each in the general educations setting.

Local, state, provincial, regional and federal governments, as well as all related organizations, stand accountable for the development and maintenance of educational opportunities for all students that are inclusive and ultimately effective. The United States government must be urged to vigorously enforce, at all levels, legislation already enacted that assures quality, inclusive educational practices.

*Source:* The Association for Persons with Severe Handicaps (2000). *TASH resolution on inclusive education.* Online: www.tash.org/resolutions/R33INCED.html.

a full member of the class rather than a "visitor." Teachers are more likely to look for solutions to a student's educational or social difficulties if the student is on their caseload.

**3.** *The number of students with disabilities or other special needs in general education classes does not exceed the natural proportions of these groups of people in the general population.* Teachers who have a large number of students with disabilities or special needs will have a more difficult time making the accommodations necessary to ensure their success than if they have only one or two students in their classes. By making class assignments based on natural proportions, teachers will be better able to provide the level of support necessary to ensure the students' success in the class.

**4.** *The student is provided the instructional support necessary to participate successfully in the general education curriculum.* Schools that practice effective inclusive education allocate the available staff, material, and fiscal resources to ensure that each student receives the support necessary to be successful in the general education class. Special education services are provided within the general education class and are used to supplement the curriculum and instructional activities used by the general education teacher.

**5.** *The student is provided the support necessary to promote his or her acceptance as a full member of the school community.* In addition to receiving educational support, students must be provided with the support necessary to ensure that they are accepted as part of the school community. Although this sometimes means developing interventions directed at the student, often it means developing school-wide programs that increase the sensitivity of peers to the needs of students and create opportunities for peers to develop positive relationships with students with disabilities or other special needs.

# Effective Practices

## Student and Family-Centered Planning

The idea of student- and family-centered planning for elementary students with severe disabilities is based on the principle that educational programs must be tailored to students' unique needs and circumstances. Furthermore, students (and their families) should control the ultimate outcomes of education. This approach requires that decisions about the focus of students' educational programs are driven by their personal values, beliefs, and preferences. Several models for carrying out this type of planning have been described in the literature, including lifestyle planning (O'Brien, 1987), the McGill Action Planning System (MAPS) (Vandercook, York, & Forest, 1989), personal futures planning (Mount & Zwernick, 1988), TEAMS (Campbell, Campbell, & Brady, 1998), and Big Picture Planning (McDonnell, Mathot-Buckner, & Ferguson, 1996). The key feature of all of these models is that the planning process is directed by students and their families. The process is focused on broad quality-of-life outcomes such as students' participation in family, school, and community life; their satisfaction with friendships and social relationships; and their ability to make choices for themselves. Planning also considers the long-term hopes and dreams of students by addressing issues such as the kinds of jobs they want, where they want to live, marriage, and financial security. The planning process culminates by identifying the activities and resources that will be necessary for students to achieve these outcomes. An example of this type of student-centered plan, called the Big Picture Plan (McDonnell et al., 1994), is presented in Figure 10.1.

> **Focus 3**
> Who should be involved in the development of future plans for students with severe disabilities?

Typically, plans like the Big Picture are developed before the student's IEP meeting. The meetings may involve a number of individuals, including the student, his parents, siblings, teachers, and other community members. The intent is to involve the individuals who are the most important in the student's life and who can help him to achieve his desired educational outcomes. The plan then serves as a reference point in the development of future IEPs for the student. Each goal and objective included in a student's IEP is evaluated in terms of its contribution to the outcomes included in the Big Picture Plan. Although student-centered planning is extremely useful, it can also be time consuming to implement each year. McDonnell et al. (1994) have recommended that student-centered planning be conducted in conjunction with major transitions in students' lives. For example, for elementary-age students they recommend that the Big Picture planning process be implemented when students enter kindergarten, when they move from primary to intermediate grades, and when they transition from elementary to middle/junior high school.

## Curriculum and Instruction Referenced to Home, School, and Community

There is broad consensus that curriculum for students with severe disabilities be designed to promote their full participation at home, in school, and the community (Browder, 2001;

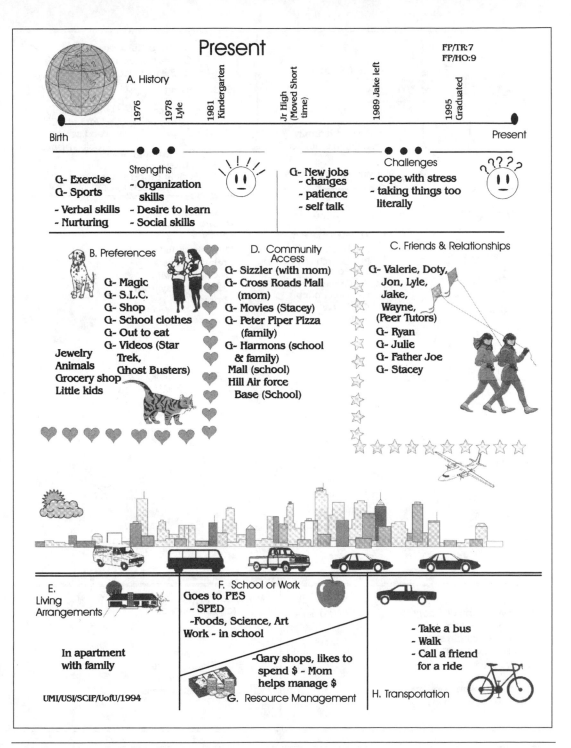

**Present**

A. History

1976 · 1978 Lyle · 1981 Kindergarten · Jr High (Moved Short time) · 1989 Jake left · 1995 Graduated

Birth — Present

**Strengths**

- Q- Exercise
- Q- Sports
- Verbal skills
- Nurturing
- Organization skills
- Desire to learn
- Social skills

**Challenges**

- Q- New jobs
- changes
- patience
- self talk
- cope with stress
- taking things too literally

**B. Preferences**

- Q- Magic
- Q- S.L.C.
- Q- Shop
- Q- School clothes
- Q- Out to eat
- Q- Videos (Star Trek, Ghost Busters)

Jewelry
Animals
Grocery shop
Little kids

**D. Community Access**

- Q- Sizzler (with mom)
- Q- Cross Roads Mall (mom)
- Q- Movies (Stacey)
- Q- Peter Piper Pizza (family)
- Q- Harmons (school & family)
- Mall (school)
- Hill Air force Base (School)

**C. Friends & Relationships**

- Q- Valerie, Doty, Jon, Lyle, Jake, Wayne, (Peer Tutors)
- Q- Ryan
- Q- Julie
- Q- Father Joe
- Q- Stacey

**E. Living Arrangements**

In apartment
with family

UMI/USI/SCIP/UofU/1994

**F. School or Work**

Goes to PES
- SPED
-Foods, Science, Art
Work - in school

-Gary shops, likes to spend $ - Mom helps manage $

**G.** Resource Management

**H. Transportation**

- Take a bus
- Walk
- Call a friend for a ride

---

**FIGURE 10.1** *Big Picture Planning Forms*

*(continued)*

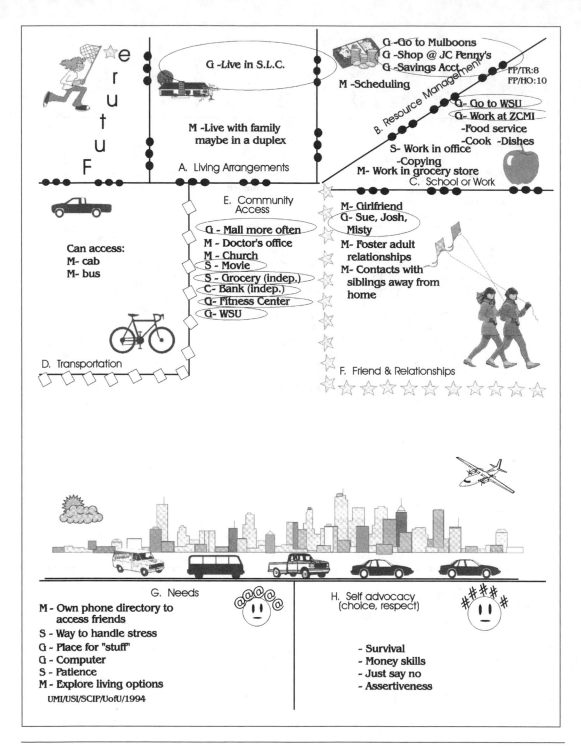

Future

G -Live in S.L.C.

M -Live with family
maybe in a duplex

A. Living Arrangements

G –Go to Mulboons
G –Shop @ JC Penny's
G –Savings Acct
M -Scheduling

FP/TR:8
FP/HO:10

B. Resource Management

G- Go to WSU
G- Work at ZCMI
-Food service
-Cook  -Dishes
S- Work in office
-Copying
M- Work in grocery store

C. School or Work

E. Community Access

G - Mall more often
M - Doctor's office
M - Church
S - Movie
S - Grocery (indep.)
C- Bank (indep.)
G- Fitness Center
G- WSU

Can access:
M- cab
M- bus

D. Transportation

M- Girlfriend
G- Sue, Josh, Misty
M- Foster adult relationships
M- Contacts with siblings away from home

F. Friend & Relationships

G. Needs

M - Own phone directory to access friends
S - Way to handle stress
G - Place for "stuff"
G - Computer
S - Patience
M - Explore living options

UMI/USI/SCIP/UofU/1994

H. Self advocacy
(choice, respect)

- Survival
- Money skills
- Just say no
- Assertiveness

FIGURE 10.1    Continued

284

| A. PRIORITIES | B. SOLUTIONS | C. RESOURCES (available, *possible, needed?) | | | | |
|---|---|---|---|---|---|---|
| | | PHYSICAL | PEOPLE | COMMUNITY | SOCIAL/ EDUCATIONAL | FINANCIAL |
| E/11/F. Friends (includes self advocacy community access) | 1. Play football w/ Joey's city rec. team. | 1. ∅ | Joey *Coach Brown | City teams | ∅ | $10.00 fee |
| | 2. Choose fun night activity 1x month, invite friend. | 2. pic phone book? | Joey tutors* | Movies restaurants sports events | ∅ | allowance |
| | 3. picture address book w/ school friends | 3. pictures book | Mom friends tutors teacher | ∅ | teacher* train phone/ book use | ∅ |
| | 4. part. in church youth group | 4. Way to after school activities? | Ms. Smith Steven* | Church scout gc | ∅ | ∅ |
| | 5. regular scouts | 5. uniform* way to scouts (after school)? | scout? master other scouts | Scout* groups | ∅ | ? |
| | 6. Neighborhood party for all kids. | 6. Where to have it park* | Sue Joeys mom Joey | city rec games equip | ∅ | 100.00 aprox |
| B. Work/School —Build spaceships (includes more reg classes) | 1. take science class | 1. Adapt* curric. | reg* ed teacher Sp Ed teacher tutor | ∅ | school inservice teacher | Lab fee $5.00 |
| | 2. take shop class | 2. " | " | " | " | " |
| | 3. Computer lab | 3. Adapt* curric. | Reg Ed T * Sp Ed T tutor | ∅ | school * Inservice | ∅ |
| | 4. Write to NASA | 4. strat. for letter writing ? | Sp Ed* Teach Grandpa | ∅ | teach* stat. | stamps |

D. IN THE SOLUTIONS AND RESOURCES COLUMNS, CIRCLE THE MOST PROMISING OPTIONS AND NUMBER THOSE IN ORDER OF LIKELY SUCCESS. THE OPTIONS INDICATED AS "1s" WILL BE THE FIRST TO BE TARGETED FOR ACTION. COMPLETE OPPOSITE SIDE OF FORM USING THIS INFORMATION.

FIGURE 10.1   Continued

**PART 2—BIG PICTURE ACTION PLAN**

| A. PRIORITIES | B. SOLUTIONS | C. TARGETED RESOURCE(S) | | | |
|---|---|---|---|---|---|
| IN ORDER FROM SIDE 1 | ABBREVIATED FROM SIDE 1 IN PRIORITY SEQUENCE | WHO | WHAT | WHEN | FOLLOW-UP |
| FRIENDS | 2. CHOOSE FRI* ACTIVITY | Mun Matt | Plan Date call friend Go on Activity | By Sept 15 ↓ | |
| | 3. PICT. ADDRESS* BOOK | Teacher | take pictures get phone #s assemble book begin training | By 7/30/98 By 10/15/98 | |
| | 1. Play Football city rec | Mom Joey coach Brown | get registered arrange trans. talk to rec committee | By 7/99 7/99 5/99 | |
| Work/School | 1. Take science* class | reg/sp ed teachers | schedule/ inservice T Adapt curric. get tutor | By 1/99 ongoing By 1/99 | |
| | 2. Take shop* class | " | " | By 3/99 | |
| | 4. write letters to* NASA | SLP/ grandpa | Develop strat. teach strat. (send to grandpa) Begin writing letters | B 12/98 B 1/98 | |

***INCLUDE IMMEDIATE AND LONG TERM SOLUTIONS. STAR (*) IMMEDIATE SOLUTIONS.**

## FIGURE 10.1  Continued

*Source:* McDonnell, J., McDonnell, A., Mathot-Buckner, C., Thorson, N., Berki, P., Hightower, J., & Kiefer-O'Donnell, R. (1994). *The School and Community Integration Program Cross-Age Curriculum for Students with Severe Disabilities.* Salt Lake City, UT: Department of Special Education, University of Utah.

Snell & Brown, 2000; Westling & Fox, 2001). Curricula based on this philosophy are referred to as "ecological" curricula (Browder, 2001; McDonnell et al., 1996; Westling & Fox, 2001). In this section we discuss ecological curriculum models and how the new emphasis on inclusive education and student participation in the general education curriculum may influence the content of educational programs in the future.

***Ecological Curricula.***    A number of ecological curriculum models have been proposed over the last two decades (e.g., Ford et al., 1989; Giangreco, Cloninger, & Iverson, 1998; McDonnell et al., 1994; Neel & Billingsley, 1989; Wilcox & Bellamy, 1987). At the elementary level, the content of these ecological curricula are focused on the routines, activities, and skills necessary for children between 6 and 12 years old to participate fully in home, school, and community life. The instructional targets included in these curricula are organized in broad curriculum domains such as community living, leisure/recreation, personal management, and work. The instructional targets typically include things such as preparing a snack, using the library, going out to recess, doing after-school chores, and making purchases at grocery stores. Figure 10.2 presents an example of an ecological curriculum for elementary students that was developed by McDonnell et al. (1994).

Another key feature of ecological curriculum is that functional academic and developmental skills are selected and taught to improve student performance of daily routines and activities. For example, playing a board game such as Monopoly with peers requires students to have a variety of reading, math, communication, and fine motor skills. Similarly, going to lunch with the sixth-grade class in the cafeteria requires students to have a number of reading, math, communication, social, and self-help skills. Within an ecological curriculum approach, instruction on functional academic and developmental skills is designed to improve students' performance of the routines and activities that support full participation in home, school, and community life.

The process of developing IEPs through these curriculum models typically begins with a careful analysis of the routines and activities that a student will need to do each day to be successful at home, in school, and in the community. Then, the student's ability to complete these important routines and activities is assessed. IEP goals and objectives are structured to teach the skills and develop the personal supports that will be necessary for them to complete these routines and activities as independently as possible. An example of IEP goals and objectives developed from an ecological curriculum is presented in Figure 10.3.

---

*Focus 4*
What is the purpose of an activity/skill scheduling matrix?

---

Research indicates that students are more likely to learn to use academic and developmental skills, and generalize those skills to untrained situations, when they are provided instruction on these skills within daily routines and activities (McDonnell, 1996; Mulligan, et al., 1980; Neef, Iwata, & Page, 1980; Winterling, Dunlap, & O'Neill, 1987). For example, teaching a student how to transfer from a wheelchair to a regular chair could be done during transitions from one instructional activity to another in his general education class, at lunch, and when going to the library. A student could be provided instruction on writing

**FIGURE 10.2** *SCIP Curriculum Software*

|  | Routine/Activity Inventory–Upper Elementary | | |
|--|--|--|--|
| Routine | Does your student do this? | Would you want/expect a sibling or same-age peer to do this? | How often does this occur? Does it change on days off? | What skills could the person develop that would offer the most opportunity for increased presence, choice, respect, and participation? |
| | | *Context: Day/Home* | | |
| Does chores | ___ Yard care    Yes ___ No ___<br>___ Babysitting    Yes ___ No ___<br>___ Paper route    Yes ___ No ___<br>___ Budget allowance    Yes ___ No ___<br>___ Takes out garbage    Yes ___ No ___<br>___ Cleans room    Yes ___ No ___<br>___ Feeds pets    Yes ___ No ___<br>___ OTHER ACTIVITIES    Yes ___ No ___<br>___ Milks cows    Yes ___ No ___<br>___ Moves water lines    Yes ___ No ___ | | | |
| Has snack | ___ Prepares snack    Yes ___ No ___<br>___ Eats snacks    Yes ___ No ___<br>___ OTHER ACTIVITIES    Yes ___ No ___ | | | |
| Free time at home | ___ Plays with friends    Yes ___ No ___<br>___ Watches TV    Yes ___ No ___<br>___ Plays video games    Yes ___ No ___<br>___ OTHER ACTIVITIES    Yes ___ No ___ | | | |

*Source:* McDonnell, J., McDonnell, A., Mathot-Buckner, C., Thorson, N., Berki, P., Hightower, J., & Kiefer-O'Donnell, R. (1994). *The School and Community Integration Program Cross-Age Curriculum for Students with Severe Disabilities.* Salt Lake City, UT: Department of Special Education, University of Utah.

FIGURE 10.3   *Illustrative IEP Goals and Objectives for an Elementary-Age Student*

| Annual Goal | Short-Term Objectives |
|---|---|
| **1.** While in her third-grade class, the lunch room, the library, or on the playground, Patrice will independently move her wheelchair a distance of 30 feet on two consecutive weekly probes. | **1.1.** While in her third-grade class, the lunch room, the library, or on the playground, Patrice will independently move her wheel chair a distance of 10 feet on two consecutive weekly probes. |
| | **1.2.** While in her third-grade class, the lunch room, the library, or on the playground, Patrice will independently move her wheel chair a distance of 20 feet on two consecutive weekly probes. |
| **2.** During Math in her third-grade class, Patrice will use a calculator to add money values up to 10 dollars with 90% accuracy on two consecutive instructional sessions. | **2.1.** When given a worksheet of 20 problems, Patrice will add money values up to 10 dollars with 90% accuracy on two consecutive instructional sessions. |
| | **2.2.** When given sample of savings account ledger pages from First Interstate Bank, Patrice will add money values up to 10 dollars with 90% accuracy on two consecutive instructional sessions. |
| | **2.3** When given printed problems during Math relays, Patrice will add money values up to 10 dollars with 90% accuracy across two consecutive sessions. |

his first name during opening circle and when completing in-class reading and math assignments. Providing instruction to students within daily routines and activities begins with developing an activity/skill matrix (Downing, 1996; Giangreco et al., 1998). First, the teacher conducts a routine/activity analysis to identify the natural times during the day when students must, or could, use the skills targeted for instruction. Then the teacher develops an activity/skill matrix to schedule when and where instruction on specific skills will occur. Finally, the teacher develops written instructional procedures that can be used to teach the skill across all routines and activities. Figure 10.4 presents an example of an activity/skill matrix for a student enrolled in a third-grade class.

***Participation in the General Education Curriculum.***   As discussed earlier in this chapter, IDEA '97 strongly encourages the participation of all students with disabilities in the general education curriculum. The focus on the development of inclusive educational programs for students with severe disabilities has also increased interest in developing curriculum and instructional strategies that will allow students to participate meaningfully in

FIGURE 10.4  *Illustrative Activity/Skill Matrix for Morgan, a Third Grader*

| Activities \ Skills | Care of Belongings | Wheelchair Transitions | Reading Sight Words | Calculator Addition | Initiates Greetings | Asks for Assistance | Puts on/ Takes off Jacket | Washes Hands |
|---|---|---|---|---|---|---|---|---|
| Arrival from playground | X | X | | | X | X | X | X |
| Opening Review | | X | X | | X | X | | |
| Math | X | X | | X | | X | | |
| Recess | X | X | | | | X | X | X |
| Reading | X | X | X | | X | X | | |
| Lunch/Recess | X | X | | | X | X | X | X |
| Language Arts | X | X | X | | X | X | | |
| Partner Reading | X | X | X | | X | X | | |
| Recess | X | X | | | X | X | X | X |
| Social Studies/Science | X | X | X | X | X | X | | |
| Art/Music | X | X | X | | X | X | | |
| Closing Circle | X | X | X | | X | X | | |
| Go To Bus | X | X | | | X | X | X | X |

the general education curriculum (Ford, Davern, & Schnorr, 2001). In spite of the growing support for including students with severe disabilities in the general education curriculum, it is clear that much more research is needed to develop validated practices that can be easily implemented by general and special educators (Harrower, 1999; McDonnell, 1998; Nietupski, Hamre-Nietupski, Curtin, & Shrikanth, 1997; Wolery & Schuster, 1997). At this point, three strategies appear to hold some promise for addressing this complex problem successfully. These include developing and implementing curriculum and instructional adaptations, cooperative learning, and multilevel curricula.

*Curriculum and Instructional Adaptations.*   Perhaps the least intrusive approach to supporting the participation of students in the general education curriculum is to develop curriculum and instructional adaptations. In this approach, the way that information is presented or evaluation is conducted is changed but the content of the curriculum is not modified. Deschenes, Ebeling, and Sprague (1994) describe a seven-step process for accomplishing this outcome (Figure 10.5). The first four steps of the process are focused on defining the teacher's goals for all of the students in the class and the specific activities that will be used to present the information to students. These steps are designed to define the "what" and "how" of the lesson. The last three steps focus on identifying, developing, and evaluating the curriculum and instructional adaptations. Deschenes et al. (1994) identify nine different ways that a lesson can be adapted to meet the needs of a student (Figure 10.6). These adaptations range from altering the materials to modifying the evaluation strategies used by the teacher to assess student learning.

*Cooperative Learning.*   The concept of "cooperative learning" has been defined as "the instructional use of small groups so that students work together to maximize their own and each other's learning" (Johnson, Johnson, & Holubec, 1993, p. 6). A number of cooperative learning models have been described in the literature, including Student Team Learning (Slavin, 1983, 1990), Learning Together (Johnson et al., 1993), Numbered Heads Together (Kagan, 1990), and Complex Instruction (Cohen, 1991). Although these various models are based on different theoretical frameworks, they all share a number of common structural elements. Key among them are that (1) students are assigned heterogeneously to groups for instruction, (2) instructional activities are designed specifically to encourage groups to work together in completing assignments, (3) students are taught a process for organizing the completion of assigned academic tasks by establishing clear work goals, developing specific work plans, and defining the work roles for each student in the group, (4) students are taught the social skills necessary to support one another constructively and to resolve differences in completing assignments, and (5) students are assessed individually to ensure that they have mastered targeted skills. Table 10.2 compares cooperative learning and traditional small-group instruction formats.

In cooperative learning, students work together to formulate the expected outcomes of their efforts, divide work responsibilities, plan how work will be completed, and allocate resources. For example, in a sixth-grade social studies class the goal of a cooperative learning group may be to understand the impact of the westward migration of the pioneers on Native American cultures. One student might investigate how various tribes responded to the pioneers, another might research the treaties that were developed between the tribes and

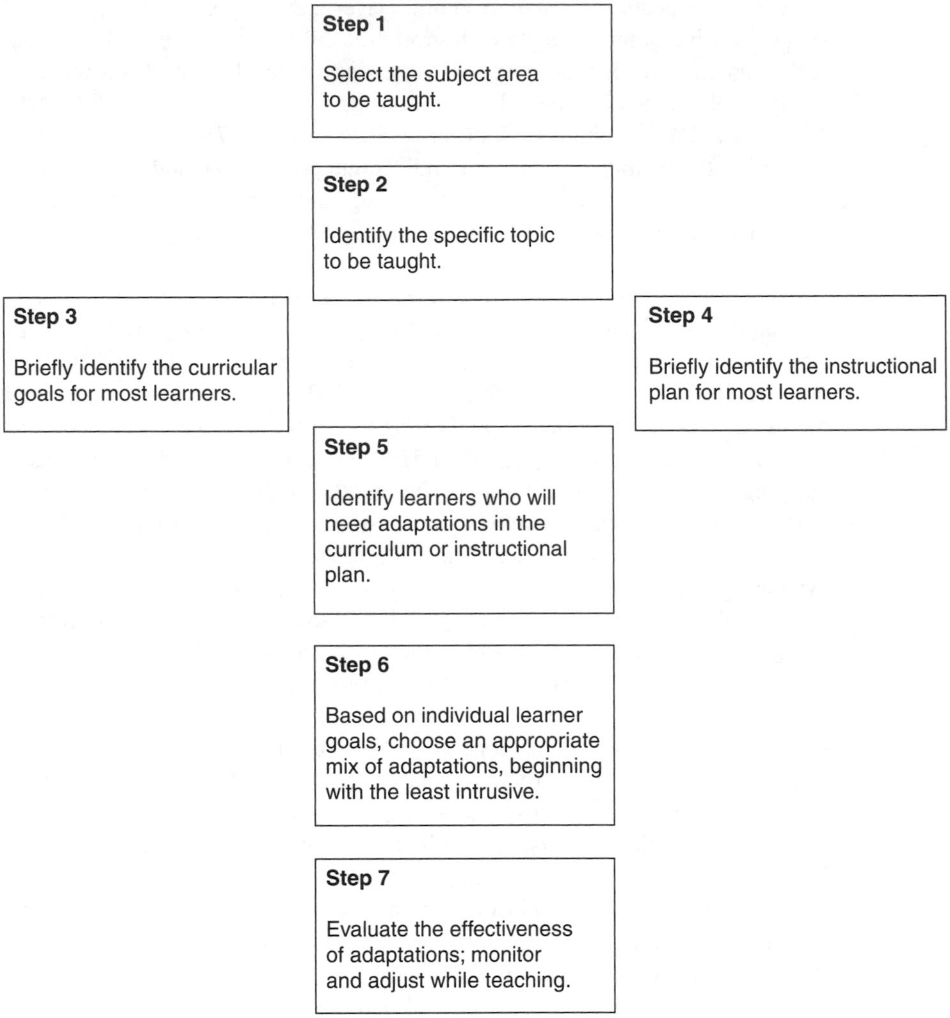

**Step 1**

Select the subject area
to be taught.

**Step 2**

Identify the specific topic
to be taught.

**Step 3**

Briefly identify the curricular
goals for most learners.

**Step 4**

Briefly identify the instructional
plan for most learners.

**Step 5**

Identify learners who will
need adaptations in the
curriculum or instructional
plan.

**Step 6**

Based on individual learner
goals, choose an appropriate
mix of adaptations, beginning
with the least intrusive.

**Step 7**

Evaluate the effectiveness
of adaptations; monitor
and adjust while teaching.

**FIGURE 10.5   *A Process for Developing Curriculum and Instructional Adaptations***

*Source:* Deschenes, C., Ebeling, D. G., & Sprague, J. (1994). *Adapting curriculum and instruction in inclusive classrooms: A teacher's desk reference.* Bloomington, IN: Center for School and Community Integration, Indiana University.

the federal government, another might examine how the reservation system was developed, and so on. Students with severe disabilities can be included in cooperative learning groups because the group members' roles vary and are tailored to their specific strengths. In the example, a student might help make a map showing the most common westward routes or participate in a skit reenacting an important meeting between the pioneers and the Indians. Instruction on the student's IEP goals and objectives would be embedded within these in-

**FIGURE 10.6**   *Possible Curriculum and Instructional Adaptations*

| Size | Time | Level of Support |
|---|---|---|
| Adapt the number of items that the learner is expected to learn or complete. | Adapt the time allotted and allowed for learning, task completion, or testing. | Increase the amount of personal assistance with a specific learner. |
| *For example:* | *For example:* | *For example:* |
| Reduce the number of social studies terms a learner must learn at any one time. | Individualize a timeline for completing a task; pace learning differently (increase or decrease) for some learners. | Assign peer buddies, teaching assistants, peer tutors, or cross-age tutors. |

| Input | Difficulty | Output |
|---|---|---|
| Adapt the way instruction is delivered to the learner. | Adapt the skill level, problem type, or the rules on how the learner may approach the work. | Adapt how the student can respond to instruction. |
| *For example:* | | *For example:* |
| Use different visual aids, plan more concrete examples, provide hands-on activities, place students in cooperative groups. | *For example:* | Instead of answering questions in writing, allow a verbal response, use a communication book for some students, allow students to show knowledge with hands-on materials. |
| | Allow the use of a calculator to figure math problems; simplify task directions; change rules to accommodate learner needs. | |

| Participation | Alternative Goals | Substitute Curriculum |
|---|---|---|
| Adapt the extent to which a learner is actively involved in the task. | Adapt the goals or outcome expectations while using the same materials. | Provide different instruction and materials to meet a student's individual goals. |
| *For example:* | *For example:* | *For example:* |
| In geography, have a student hold the globe, while others point out locations. | In social studies, expect a student to be able to locate just the states while others learn to locate capitals as well. | During a language test, one student is learning computer skills in the computer lab. |

*Source:* Deschenes, C., Ebeling, D. G., & Sprague, J. (1994). *Adapting curriculum and instruction in inclusive classrooms: A teacher's desk reference.* Bloomington, IN: Center for School and Community Integration, Indiana University.

TABLE 10.2   *Differences between Cooperative Learning and Traditional
Small Group Formats*

| Cooperative Learning | Traditional Small Group Formats |
| --- | --- |
| Promotes interdependence of group members. | Promotes individual performance. |
| Individual and group accountability. | Individual accountability. |
| Group members share leadership for setting goals and completing activities. | Teacher sets goals and structures instructional activities. |
| Teacher observes and provides feedback on collaborative process and work tasks. | Teacher directs group activities. |

structional activities. So a student might practice her printing skills in making the map or work on specific language skills in the skit.

There is a robust research base on the relative effects of cooperative and competitive models of teaching (Johnson et al., 1993; Slavin, 1996). Studies have consistently indi-

## WINDOW 10.3 • *Cooperating to Write a Newspaper*

One more week and school will be out for the summer! And language class has a new project. Students, as part of cooperative learning teams, will each develop a school newspaper article, interviewing students in different grade levels. Jennifer's group has chosen the fourth-grade classes, while Joanne's team will report on the activities of the third grade. The purpose of the interviews is to find out what plans students have for the summer. Each team is to plan the project together, including (1) identification of who will be interviewed (four students from each of the three classes in a grade), (2) arrange, schedule, and conduct the interviews, (3) write the articles, (4) draw, take, or collect pictures, and (5) print and reproduce the newspaper for the class. Jennifer's team has a total of four members on it. Her skills do not include being able to write or speak orally. She can use her communication board to ask basic questions, uses a tape recorder independently, and gets around the school by herself. All the children will have different duties, based on both individual and group agreement. Roles that the team have jointly decided for Jennifer include:

1. Taking a written message down to each fourth-grade teacher to request a time and volunteers for the interview.
2. Initiating the interview with her tape recorder, playing a premade tape for the student about the newspaper article.
3. Recording the interview with her tape recorder.
4. Together with other team members, choosing segments of the interview to write and pictures to include.
5. Printing the complete article and newspaper from the computer.
6. Jointly distributing the completed newspaper.

The activity proceeded as planned, without many glitches. The tape recorder batteries did run out in the middle of the second interview, so it had to be started over. Students from the fourth-grade class asked if they could have their tapes to play for their parents. All in all, it was a good way to end the school year and jump into summer.

cated that cooperative learning is equal, or superior, to competitive learning models in promoting academic achievement of students without disabilities and those who are at risk of school failure. These results hold across student age, ability level, type of instructional tasks (e.g., recall of factual information, problem solving), and subject areas (Bossert, 1989; Slavin, 1996, Qin, Johnson, & Johnson, 1995). Equally important, the positive effects of cooperative learning models on the social interactions of students and the development of self-concept are also very powerful (Johnson et al., 1993; Slavin, 1996).

Similar results have been reported in studies examining the effects of cooperative learning on students with more significant disabilities (Dugan et al., 1995; Eichenger, 1990; Hunt, Staub, Morgen, & Goetz, 1994). Dugan et al. (1995) reported the results of a study examining the impact of a cooperative learning strategy on the academic performance of two students with autism and their nondisabled peers during social studies in a typical fourth-grade class. The researchers compared the effect of traditional lecture formats and cooperative learning on student performance on weekly pre/post-unit tests, academic engagement during instructional activities, and the duration of social interactions between the students with disabilities and their peers. The results showed substantial increases for students with and without disabilities on all measures when the classroom teacher employed the cooperative learning strategy.

*Multielement Curriculum.*   In this curriculum approach, students with severe disabilities are provided instruction on different skills from the same curriculum domain in which their peers are receiving instruction (Giangreco & Putnam, 1991). For example, a student with limited reading skills might be taught to read sight words while his peers are being taught to identify the mains points of a story. Or, a student might be taught how to use a calculator to add money values while the other students in the class are being taught to divide.

The primary evidence supporting the effectiveness of parallel instruction in inclusive programs comes from a small number of case studies that have described the process professionals go through to develop such programs and their immediate effect on educational and social outcomes (Farlow, 1996; Ferguson, Meyer, Jeanchild, Juniper, & Zingo, 1992; Jorgensen, 1996; York & Vandercook, 1991). Additional evidence comes from studies that have evaluated the effect of planning systems such as COACH—Choosing Options and Accommodations for Children (Giangreco, 1996; Giangreco, Edelman, Dennis, & Cloninger, 1995), which have found that these formats not only lead to improved educational outcomes for students but can be implemented successfully by general and special educators in typical classrooms.

One criticism of multilevel curriculum is that students without disabilities may develop negative attitudes about students with severe disabilities because they are not working on the same skills. To date, however, no research suggests that this occurs. An alternative perspective is that multilevel curriculum provides students with opportunities for individualized instruction in general education classes rather than being "pulled out." Thus, students are provided with opportunities to learn important communication, social, and behavioral skills that will enhance their acceptance by their peers.

---

*Focus 5*
What strategies can teachers use to support the development of friendships and natural supports between students and their peers without disabilities?

## Promoting Friendships and Natural Supports

Elementary programs should be designed to encourage the development of friendships among students with and without disabilities. These relationships will promote the development of a strong social network of friends and neighbors that enable students to participate fully in home, school, and community life. A number of different approaches have been recommended in the literature to achieve this outcome for students, including the development of natural supports (Nisbet, 1992), circles of friends (Forest & Lusthaus, 1989), and peer buddies (Mathot-Buckner, McConnell, Anderson, Baker, & Cano, 1994). The implementation of these strategies may initially be directed at meeting the needs of students with severe disabilities, but they have also been shown to be very effective in addressing the educational needs of students without disabilities. From a practical standpoint, the full potential of these strategies will be realized only if they are put into place for all students in the class—not just for students with severe disabilities.

***Natural Supports.*** Nisbet (1992) suggests that "The concept of natural supports is based on the understanding that relying on typical people and environments enhances the potential for inclusion more effectively than relying on specialized services and personnel" (p. 5). The idea of natural supports is to build on what already exists in the classroom and school rather than create new support structures (Jorgensen, 1996). For example, if the teacher uses a partner or team structure, then a student with severe disabilities can simply be assigned a partner or to a team. Or, if the teacher uses cooperative learning groups, students can be assigned to participate as a member of a group for instructional activities.

The development of natural supports for a student should be linked to an analysis of the instructional and social activities of the general education class. The first step is to summarize the typical routines that students are required to complete each day in the class. Next, the teacher identifies the supports that occur naturally for all students as they complete those routines. Finally, the teacher ensures that these supports are made available to the student and are implemented consistently across the school day.

***Circles of Friends.*** Perske (1988) describes a circle of friends as a formalized process in which the teacher asks a group of students without disabilities to provide social support for a peer with disabilities (see Window 10.4). This strategy is designed to involve peers in the lives of students with disabilities, at home, school, and in the community (Forest & Lusthaus, 1989; Vandercook et al., 1989). Ideally, the members of the circle encourage and support the participation of the students with disabilities in their personal network of friends. By doing so, the natural supports available to the student in the school are dramatically expanded.

While the objective is for a student's circle of friends to provide direct support in the general education class, the teacher encourages the circle to come up with new ways to promote the student's participation in the instructional and social activities of the general education class. This is accomplished by having the circle meet regularly with the teacher to discuss how things are going, issues that may have developed either in or out of school, and/or to identify ways to improve the student's participation in school and after-school activities. For example, the group may meet with the special education teacher to identify the type of words and phrases that a student should have on his touch talker.

## WINDOW 10.4 • *The Beginning of a New Circle of Friends*

Both Joanne and Jennifer are new students in the fifth-grade homeroom. It is mid-afternoon of their first day at the new school, and time for recess. The special education aide has break now, so Tom and Maria, two students in the homeroom, volunteer to help Jennifer outside to the playground. Halfway down the hall, Jennifer begins to wheel her chair—slowly, but by herself. Tom lights up. "Hey, I didn't know that you could do that. Why didn't you tell me before?"

Jennifer first smiles, and then, lets out a full laugh. The two other fifth graders join in. They continue slowly outside, where Tom leaves to play softball. Joanne, the other new student, has been invited to join an impromptu soccer game, serving, because of her height, as goalie. Maria, not wanting to leave Jennifer simply sitting by herself during recess, asks, "Do you want to play jump rope?"

Again, Jennifer smiles, and looks toward the group of girls next to the building who have already begun to play jump rope. Maria understands, and helps Jennifer over a curb, as the two girls move on to the game. Once there, Maria asks, "Do you know how to twirl?"

Jennifer shakes her head, "no," so Maria places the end of the rope in her hand, and holding it together, says, "Okay, hold it like this, and go round this way," guiding her movements with her hand.

Soon, Jennifer gets the hang of it, and Maria is able to let go. It's her turn to jump, so she leaves Jennifer's side, and begins her routine. She is able to jump longer than any of the other girls. As she spins around to complete a maneuver, she faces Jennifer as she jumps. Seeing her twirl, Maria sticks out her tongue and both girls laugh. Unfortunately, the twirling stops, ending Maria's turn. It doesn't really matter, because a new game will start again tomorrow, and Maria usually wins anyway.

In a moment Ms. Nelson calls to the students to return to class, and Maria and Jennifer come in together. As they enter the room, Ms. Nelson asks the classmates to take out their library books and use the remaining time to read silently. Marsha, who had been playing soccer with Joanne, asks her teacher if she could lend her one of her books to read. Ms. Nelson approves, and the girls go to the reading corner of the room to choose among Marsha's three books.

*Peer Buddies.*    Peer buddies are students in the class who are either assigned by the teacher or volunteer to be helpers for a peer with disabilities (Mathot-Buckner et al., 1994). Buddies are placed in proximity to the student with disabilities and are often given specific roles to help support the student's instructional or social needs. For example, a buddy may assist a student on and off the bus, to "hang out" in the halls before and after classes, or tell the student what page he is supposed to be completing. Buddies may meet periodically with the teacher for training and direction on strategies that will assist them to provide more effective support to the student with disabilities.

### Promoting Choice and Autonomy

Learning how to make choices and to control one's daily activities are two of the most important skills that elementary-age students need to learn. Children have to make a number of choices each day, ranging from what kind of snack they will have after school to what they will do during recess. To be sure, the range of choices that are available to children are often controlled by their parents, teachers, and caregivers. However, as children become older the adults in their lives expect and encourage them to make more and more of these choices on their own. This occurs because we understand that the quality of life that children will have as adults will be limited if they do not have these skills. The ability to make choices and to control daily activities is no less important for students with severe disabilities.

Promoting choice and autonomy begins with the type of student- and family-centered planning described earlier. However, students will not become skillful at making choices unless they are provided instruction and support in practicing these skills every day. Teachers must organize students' schedule and design instruction so that students are provided frequent opportunities to make choices. For example, does the student have the opportunity to choose the activities that he does when he completes an assignment early? These choices might include looking at a favorite picture book, listening to a tape, or using the classroom computer. Similarly, is instruction designed to encourage choice making and self-directed learning? Students can be provided instruction on how to organize their work, and opportunities to make specific choices can be built into instructional activities and tasks (e.g., choosing the materials for a collage or selecting which Website to research).

## Transdisciplinary Teaming

Students with severe disabilities often have a variety of academic, communication, motor, and behavioral needs. Meeting these needs adequately requires the expertise of various professionals, including communication specialists, occupational therapists, physical therapists, behavior specialists, and adaptive physical educators. The practical question for schools is how to organize these professional resources so that the needs of students can be met in an effective and efficient manner.

Three staffing structures have been used to orchestrate the delivery of related services to students. These include the multidisciplinary, interdisciplinary, and transdisciplinary team models (Rainforth & York-Barr, 1997). See Window 10.5 for a description of each model. There is a growing consensus among professionals that the transdisciplinary collaborative team model is the most appropriate for students with severe disabilities (Blasco, 1999; Lehr & Brown, 1996; Rainforth & York-Barr, 1997; Orelove & Sobsey, 1996; Snell & Brown, 2000; Westling & Fox, 2001). In the transdisciplinary collaborative team model, instructional and therapy strategies are integrated to focus on a common set of skills and activities for each student. In addition, instructional and therapy goals are implemented concurrently by all the individuals who work directly with the student. This approach increases the likelihood that the student's educational needs are addressed throughout the day by all of the individuals who interact with him or her.

Despite the advantages of a transdisciplinary model, its successful implementation may at times be difficult because of the philosophical orientation of some professional staff. All too often, classroom teachers and related service staff feel that only they are qualified to meet a student's needs in a particular area of development. For example, classroom teachers may feel that they must assume sole responsibility for teaching basic academic skills. Similarly, language specialists may feel that they must be responsible for a student's communication programs, and physical therapists feel they must assume responsibility for programming

**WINDOW 10.5 • *Staffing Models***

| Model | Description |
|---|---|
| Multidisciplinary | Professional staff members recognize the important contribution that other specializations make to the educational program of each child. However, assessment, IEP development, design and implementations of instruction/therapy, and evaluation are completed independently by each professional. |
| Interdisciplinary | Professional staff members not only recognize the contributions of other staff members but also acknowledge the impact that other specializations may have on his or her area of service delivery. Assessment and IEP development are usually completed jointly by all staff members. In addition, specialists share information with one another in order to integrate services for the student more fully. However, delivery of service is done independently. |
| Transdisciplinary | Professional staff members are committed to working collaboratively across disciplinary lines. All aspects of students' educational programs are implemented jointly. Specialists train each other to integrate instructional and therapy strategies into their practice. |

focused on increasing a student's range of motion. Such attitudes can create artificial divisions across disciplines and inhibit efforts to focus each professional's expertise on achieving functional performance for students in home, work, and community settings. Orelove and Sobsey (1996) describe several strategies that have been used successfully to overcome or avoid the barriers to developing and implementing transdisciplinary models in classrooms for students with developmental disabilities. These strategies are:

1. Keep the interests of the student first. Focus on what is best for the student rather than what particular staff members want or know best.
2. Develop student goals and standards for evaluating student progress collaboratively.
3. Employ a common, data-based system for monitoring student progress.
4. Consult regularly with staff concerning student progress and focus interactions on solving instructional problems.
5. Meet regularly on an informal and formal basis to evaluate the educational programs of all students.
6. Maintain an attitude of openness toward other disciplines' philosophies and practices.

## *Future Directions and Issues*

Research, legislation, and advocacy have dramatically changed elementary programs for students with severe disabilities. As a result, students are able to access more educational services and have more opportunities to participate in home, school, and community life.

Elementary programs for this group of students will undoubtedly continue to evolve. Although many factors will influence this process, three issues in particular seem especially important at this time. First, there is a need to ensure that the future development of elementary programs for students with severe disabilities is linked directly to the ongoing efforts to reform the general education system. Second, there is a need to examine how the pedagogical innovations being developed in general and special education can be integrated in order to ensure every student's participation in the general education curriculum. Finally, achieving the intended outcomes of inclusive educational programs for this group of students requires an examination of the roles of general and special education professionals in elementary schools.

## Linkages with Ongoing School Reform Initiatives

As discussed earlier, public education has gone through several waves of reform since the 1980s. These reforms have resulted in a rethinking of curriculum in many different discipline areas (Pugach & Warger, 1996), the development of new guidelines and standards for the preparation of teachers (National Commission on Teaching and America's Future, 1996), and the development of high-stakes testing programs to increase accountability for public schools (National Research Council, 1997). Given the potential impact of these reforms on the structure and organization of schools, it is surprising how little input into the process students with disabilities, parents, advocates, and special education professionals have had (Lipsky & Gartner, 1997; Pugach & Warger, 1996). In addition, even when special education professionals have been asked to participate in reform efforts, the focus has been primarily on students with mild disabilities. The needs of students with severe disabilities in educational reform have essentially been ignored. It seems unlikely that continued progress will be made toward the development of inclusive educational programs and the participation of these students in the general education curriculum unless their needs are included in the ongoing national dialog about educational reform.

Although the impact that special education professionals can have on the national debate is limited, they can have tremendous impact on how reform efforts are implemented at the local level. Special educators, especially teachers of students with severe disabilities, must become actively involved in school committees charged with curriculum, instructional, and program organization issues. They must ensure that, when schools begin the process of reform to improve education for all students, *all* includes children with severe disabilities. Of course, this means that special educators must become informed about the issues that students without disabilities and general educators face and become actively involved in linking the needs of students with and without disabilities to local efforts to improve the effectiveness of education.

## Integrating General and Special Education Pedagogy

A number of factors inhibit the full participation of students with severe disabilities in typical schools and classrooms, but perhaps the biggest is the fundamental differences between the models of education used in general and special education programs. Traditionally, general educators have adopted a curriculum-centered approach to instruction (Darling-Hammond, 1996; Lee et al., 1993). In this approach, the teacher presents the same curriculum content to all students and uses instructional methods that are geared to the common needs of students enrolled in the class. If a student's performance is consistently below expectations, he or she is placed in other classes with peers who have similar skills and abilities. The teacher is not responsible for modifying the curriculum or instruction to accommodate the needs of the students.

In contrast, special education professionals are expected to take a student-centered approach to the design and implementation of instruction. This approach is based on the theories of applied behavior analysis (c.f. Gardner et al., 1994), which maintains that teaching is effective only when curriculum content and instructional procedures are continuously tailored to the individual needs of the student. If the student does not learn, the teacher must modify the curriculum and/or the instructional procedures to assure the student's success.

Although it is easy to "blame" general educators for resisting the adoption of instructional methods and strategies that can accommodate the individualized needs of all students, special educators have also been unwilling to grapple with this thorny problem. In 1992, Fantuzzo and Atkins noted the pressing need for special educators to "develop more adaptive and effective strategies to promote academic and social competency, and develop strategies that teachers and school personnel *can* and *will* actually use" (p. 37; italics in original). Further, they observed that "there is no rigorous behavior-analytic technology that reflects an appreciation for the factors involved in entering complex school systems" (p. 38).

Our inability to build theoretical and applied bridges between the context of typical classrooms and a student-centered approach to instruction has frequently resulted in the implementation of instructional activities for students with severe disabilities in general education classes that are separate from or only tangentially related to those provided to all students. In many inclusive classrooms, the solution to providing effective instruction is to maintain a "special education program" in the general education classroom. In addition, often little effort is given to the implementation of strategies that are more conducive to a student-centered approach for all students. This situation only further reinforces the disciplinary biases of both general and special education professionals, and does little to foster the development of a technology of instruction that will promote the long-term success of inclusion.

A new way of thinking is needed about the challenges posed in integrating effective instruction in typical classrooms. Rather than developing instructional programs that create a "boy in the bubble" approach to teaching these students, we need to begin to view student learning as the product of the entire classroom system. Clearly, additional research is needed to develop new instructional approaches that integrate the most effective instructional strategies and methods from both general and special education.

## *Redefining the Roles of Special and General Educators*

The increased emphasis in recent years on inclusive education for elementary students with severe disabilities necessitates a rethinking of the traditional roles of general and special education teachers in the school. General educators will need to assume more responsibility for the design, implementation, and evaluation of students' educational programs. Special educators will need to learn how to work more effectively as collaborators in support of students' participation in general education classes. It seems unlikely that goals of inclusive education can be achieved unless new staffing models are developed and validated. Additional research is also needed on how to install these new staffing models in schools and how to support teachers and administrators in the change process.

## Focus Review

Focus 1: What are the legal foundations for including children with severe disabilities in the general education curriculum?

- IDEA '97 requires:
  - That students' IEPs address how they will participate in the general education curriculum
  - That general educators participate in the development and revision of students' IEPs when they are placed in a general education class

Focus 2: Where do the majority of students with severe disabilities receive their educational services?

- The vast majority of students receive special education services outside of regular classrooms for 60 percent or more of the school day or in separate special education facilities.

Focus 3: Who should be involved in the development of future plans for students with severe disabilities?

- The student, his or her parents, siblings, family members, friends, and other community members. The planning team should include any individual who can play a role in helping the student to achieve his or her expected educational outcomes.

Focus 4: What is the purpose of an activity/skill scheduling matrix?

- The matrix identifies when functional academic and developmental skills will be taught to students during the school day.
- It provides a structure to ensure that students will receive adequate levels of instruction on important functional academic and developmental skills.

Focus 5: What strategies can teachers use to support the development of friendships and natural supports between students and their peers without disabilities?

- Build on the natural support systems already in place in the school and classroom.
- Promote the development of "circles of friends" for the student.
- Implement structured peer buddy programs in the school and classroom.

# References

ARC—A National Organization on Mental Retardation (1998). *The education of students with mental retardation: Preparation for life in the community.* Online: www.thearc.org/welcome.htm.

Association for Persons with Severe Handicaps (2000). *TASH resolution on inclusive education.* Online: www.tash.org/resolutions/R33INCED.html.

Baca, L. M., & Cervantes, H. T. (1998). *The bilingual special education interface.* Upper Saddle River, NJ: Merrill.

Blasco, P. M. (1999). Collaboration and teams. In D. K. Lowman, & S. M. Murphy (Eds.), *The educators guide to feeding children with disabilities* (pp. 13–34). Baltimore: Paul H. Brookes.

Bossert, S. (1989). Cooperative activities in the classroom. In E. Rothkopf (Ed.), *Review of Research in Education* (Vol. 15, pp. 225–238). Washington, DC: American Educational Research Association.

Browder, D. M. (2001). *Curriculum and assessment for students with moderate and severe disabilities.* New York: Guilford.

Campbell, P. C., Campbell, C. R., & Brady, M. P. (1998). Team Environmental Assessment Mapping System: A method for selecting curriculum goals for students with disabilities. *Education and Treatment in Mental Retardation and Developmental Disabilities, 33,* 264–272.

Carnegie Forum on Education and the Economy. (1986). *A nation prepared: Teachers for the 21st century.* Washington, DC: Author.

Cohen, D. K., McLaughlin, M. W., & Talbert, J. E. (Eds.) (1993). *Teaching for understanding: challenges for policy and practice.* San Francisco: Jossey-Bass.

Cohen, E. (1991). Strategies for creating a multi-ability classroom. *Cooperative Learning, 12,* 4–8.

Danielson, L. C., & Bellamy, G. T. (1989). State variation in placement of children with handicaps in segregated environments. *Exceptional Children, 55,* 448–455.

Darling-Hammond, L. (1996). The right to learn and the advancement of teaching: Research, policy, and practice for democratic education. *Educational Researcher, 25,* 5–18.

Darling-Hammond, L. (1997). *The right to learn: A blueprint for creating schools that work.* San Francisco: Jossey-Bass.

Deschenes, C., Ebeling, D. G., & Sprague, J. (1994). *Adapting curriculum and instruction in inclusive classrooms: A teacher's desk reference.* Bloomington, IN: Center for School and Community Integration, Indiana University.

Downing, J. E. (1996). *Including students with severe and multiple disabilities in typical classrooms: Practical strategies for teachers.* Baltimore: Paul H. Brookes.

Dugan, E., Kamps, D., Leonard, B., Watkins, N., Rheinberger, A., & Stackaus, J. (1995). Effects of cooperative learning groups during social studies for students with autism and fourth-grade peers. *Journal of Applied Behavior Analysis, 28,* 175–188.

Education Commission of the States (1983). *Action for excellence.* Denver: Author.

Eichenger, J. (1990). Goal structure effects on social interaction: Nondisabled and disabled elementary students. *Exceptional Children, 56,* 408–416.

Fantuzzo, J., & Atkins, M. (1992). Applied behavior analysis for educators: Teacher centered and classroom based. *Journal of Applied Behavior Analysis, 25,* 37–42.

Farlow, L. (1996). A quartet of success stories: How to make inclusion work. *Educational Leadership, 53,* 51–55.

*Federal Register* (March 12, 1999). *34 CFR Parts 100 and 303: Assistance to states for the education of children with disabilities and the Early Intervention Program for Infants and Toddlers with Disabilities; Final regulations.* Washington, DC: U.S. Government Printing Office.

Ferguson, D. L., Meyer, G., Jeanchild, L., Juniper, L., & Zingo, J. (1992). Figuring out what to do with the grownups: How teachers make inclusion "work" for students with disabilities. *Journal of the Association for Persons with Severe Handicaps, 17,* 218–227.

Ford, A., Davern, L., & Schnorr, R. (2001). Learners with significant disabilities: Curricular relevance in era of standards-based reform. *Remedial and Special Education, 22,* 214–222.

Ford, A., Schnorr, R., Meyer, L., Davern, L., Black, J., & smpsey, P. (1989). *Syracuse community-referenced curriculum guide for students with moderate and severe disabilities.* Baltimore: Paul H. Brookes.

Forest, M., & Lusthaus, E. (1989). Promoting educational quality for all students: Circles and MAPS. In S. Stainback, W. Stainback, M. Forest (Eds.), *Education for all students the mainstream of regular education* (pp. 43–58). Baltimore: Paul H. Brookes.

Gardner, R., Sainato, D. M., Cooper, J. O., Heron, T. E., Heward, W. L., Eshlemann, J., Grossi, T. A. (1994). *Behavior analysis in education: Focus on measurably superior instruction.* Pacific Grove, CA: Brooks/Cole.

Giangreco, M. F., Cloninger, C. J., & Iverson, V. S. (1998). *Choosing outcomes and accommodations for children: A guide to educational planning for students with disabilities* (2nd ed.). Baltimore: Paul H. Brookes.

Giangreco, M. F., Edelman, S. W., Dennis, R. E., & Cloninger, C. J. (1995). Use and impact of COACH with students who are deaf-blind. *Journal of The Association for Persons with Severe Handicaps, 20,* 121–135.

Giangreco, M. F., & Putnam, J. (1991). Supporting the education of students with severe disabilities in regular education environments. In L. H. Meyer, C. A. Peck, & L. Brown (Eds.)., *Critical issues in the lives of people with severe disabilities* (pp. 245–270). Baltimore: Paul H. Brookes.

Halvorsen, A. T., & Sailor, W. (1990). Integration of students with severe and profound disabilities. In R. Gaylord-Ross (Ed.), *Issues and research in special education* (pp. 110–172). New York: Teachers College Press.

Harrower, J. (1999). Educational inclusion of children with severe disabilities. *Journal of Positive Behavioral Interventions, 1,* 215–230.

Hollowood, T. M., Salisbury, C. L., Rainforth, B., & Palombaro, M. M. (1995). Use of instruction time in classrooms serving students with and without severe disabilities. *Exceptional Children, 61,* 242–254.

Hunt, P., & Goetz, L. (1997). Research on inclusive educational programs, practices, and outcomes for students with severe disabilities. *Journal of Special Education, 31,* 3–29.

Hunt, P., Staub, D., Morgen, A., & Goetz, L. (1994). Achievement by all students within the context of cooperative learning groups. *Journal of the Association for Persons with Severe Handicaps, 19,* 290–301.

Johnson, D. W., Johnson, R. T., & Holubec, E. J. (1993). *Circles of learning: Cooperation in the classroom* (4th ed.). Edina, MI: Interaction.

Jorgensen, C. M., (1996). Designing inclusive curricula right from the start: Practical strategies and examples for the high school classroom. In S. Stainback & W. Stainback (Eds.), *Inclusion: A guide for educators* (pp. 221–236). Baltimore: Paul H. Brookes.

Kagan, S. (1990). A structural approach to cooperative learning. *Educational Leadership, 47,* 12–15.

Kauffman, J. M. (1990). Restructuring in socialpolitical context: Reservations about the effects of current reform proposals on students with disabilities. In J. W. Lloyd, N. N. Singh, & A. C. Repp (Eds.), *The regular education initiative: Alternate perspectives on concepts, issues, and models* (pp. 57–66). Sycamore, IL: Sycamore.

Laski, F. J. (1991). Achieving integration during the Section Revolution. In L. H. Meyer, C. A. Peck, & L. Brown (Eds.), *Critical issues in the lives of people with severe disabilities* (pp. 399–408). Baltimore: Paul H. Brookes.

Lee, V. E., Bryk, A. S., & Smith, J. B. (1993). The organization of effective secondary schools. In L. Darling-Hammond (ed.), *Review of research in education* (pp. 171–268). Washington, DC: American Education Research Association.

Lehr, D. H., & Brown, F. (1996). *People with disabilities who challenge the system.* Baltimore: Paul H. Brookes.

Lipsky, D. K., & Gartner, A. (1990). Restructuring for quality. In J. W. Lloyd, N. N. Singh, & A. C. Repp (Eds.), *The regular education initiative: Alternate perspectives on concepts, issues, and models* (pp. 43–56). Sycamore, IL: Sycamore.

Lipsky, D. K., & Gartner, A. (1997). *Inclusion and school reform: Transforming America's classrooms.* Baltimore: Paul H. Brookes.

Lloyd, J. W., Singh, N. N., & Repp, A. C. (1990). *The regular education initiative: Alternate perspectives on concepts, issues, and models.* Sycamore, IL: Sycamore.

Logan, K. R., Bakeman, R., & Keefe, E. B. (1997). Effects of instructional variables on engaged behavior of students with disabilities in general education classrooms. *Exceptional Children, 63,* 481–498.

Logan, K. R., & Keefe, E. B. (1997). A comparison of instructional context, teacher behavior, and engaged behavior for students with severe disabilities and general education and self-contained elementary classrooms. *Journal of the Association for Persons with Severe Handicaps, 22,* 16–27.

Mathot-Buckner, C., McConnell, T., Anderson, M., Baker, G., & Cano, G. (1994). *Peer tutor and social sponsor manual.* Salt Lake City, UT: School and Community Inclusion Program, Department of Special Education, University of Utah.

McDonnell, A. (1996). The acquisition, transfer, and generalization of requests by young children with severe disabilities. *Education and Training in Mental Retardation and Developmental Disabilities, 31,* 213–234.

McDonnell, J. (1998). Instruction for students with severe disabilities in general education settings. *Education and Training in Mental Retardation and Developmental Disabilities, 33,* 199–215.

McDonnell, J., Mathot-Buckner, C., & Ferguson, B. (1996). *Transition programs for students with moderate/severe disabilities.* Pacific Grove, CA: Brooks/Cole.

McDonnell, J., Mathot-Buckner, C., Mendel, J., Thorson, N., & Allen, C. (2000). *Developing schools that support inclusive education: A guide for inclusion planning teams.* Salt Lake City, UT: School and Community Inclusion Programs, Department of Special Education, University of Utah.

McDonnell, J., McDonnell, A., Mathot-Buckner, C., Thorson, N., Berki, P., Hightower, J., & Kiefer-O'Donnell, R. (1994). *The School and Community Integration Program Cross-Age Curriculum for Students with Severe Disabilities.* Salt Lake City, UT: Department of Special Education, University of Utah.

McDonnell, J., Thorson, N. & McQuivey, C. (1998). The instructional characteristics of inclusive classes for elementary students with severe disabilities: An exploratory study. *Journal of Behavioral Education, 8,* 415–438.

McDonnell, J., Thorson, N., & McQuivey, C. (2000). A comparison of the instructional contexts of students with severe disabilities and their peers in general education classes. *Journal of the Association for Persons with Severe Handicaps, 25,* 54–58.

McDonnell, J., Thorson, N., McQuivey, C., & Kiefer-O'Donnell, R. (1997). The academic engaged time of students with low incidence disabilities in general education classes. *Mental Retardation, 35,* 18–26.

Meyer, L. H., Peck, C. A., & Brown, L. (1991). *Critical issues in the lives of people with severe disabilities.* Baltimore: Paul H. Brookes.

Mount, B., & Zwernick, K. (1988). *It's never too early, it's never too late. A booklet about personal futures planning.* Minneapolis, MN: Metropolitan Council.

Mulligan, M., Lacy, L., & Guess, D. (1982). Effects of massed, distributed, and spaced trials sequencing on severe handicapped students' performance. *Journal of the Association for the Severely Handicapped, 7,* 48–61.

Murphy, J. (1991). *Restructuring schools: Capturing and assessing the phenomena.* New York: Teachers College Press.

National Association of State Boards of Education (1992, October). *Winners all: A call for inclusive schools.* Alexandria, VA: Author.

National Commission on Excellence in Education (1983). *A nation at risk: The imperative of educational reform.* Washington, DC: U.S. Government Printing Office.

National Commission on Teaching and America's Future (1996). *What matters most: Teaching for America's future.* New York: Author.

National Governors' Association (1986). *Time for results.* Washington, DC: Author.

National Research Council (1997). *Educating one and all.* Washington, DC: National Academy Press.

Neef, N. A., Iwata, B. A., & Page, T. J. (1980). The effects of interpersonal training versus high density reinforcement on spelling acquisition and retention. *Journal of Applied Behavior Analysis, 13,* 153–158.

Neel, R. S., & Billingsely, F. F. (1989). *IMPACT: A functional curriculum handbook for students with moderate and severe disabilities.* Baltimore: Paul H. Brooks.

Nietupski, J., Hamre-Nietupski, S., Curtin, S., & Shrikanth, K. (1997). A review of curricular research in severe disabilities from 1976 to 1995 in six selected journals. *Journal of Special Education, 31,* 36–55.

Nisbet, J. (1992). *Natural supports in school, at work, and in the community for people with severe disabilities.* Baltimore: Paul H. Brookes.

Nisbet, J. A., Jorgensen, C., & Powers, S. (1994). Systems change directed at inclusive education. In V. J. Bradley, J. W. Ashbaugh, & B. C. Blaney (Eds.), *Creating individual supports for people with developmental disabilities: A mandate for change at many levels* (pp. 213–236). Baltimore: Paul H. Brookes.

O'Brien, J. (1987). A guide to life-style planning: Using the Activities Catalog to integrate services and natural support systems. In B. Wilcox & G. T. Bellamy (Eds.), *A comprehensive guide to the Activities Catalog: An alternative curriculum for youth and adults with severe disabilities* (pp. 175–189. Baltimore: Paul H. Brookes.

Orelove, F. P., & Sobsey, D. (1996). *Educating children with multiple disabilities: A transdisciplinary approach* (3rd ed.). Baltimore: Paul H. Brookes.

Perske, R. (1988). *Circles of friends: People with disabilities and their friends enrich the lives of one another.* Nashville, TN: Abingdon Press.

Pugach, M. C., & Warger, C. L. (1996). *Curriculum trends, special education, and reform: Refocusing the conversation.* New York: Teachers College Press.

Qin, A., Johnson, D. W., & Johnson, R. T. (1995). Cooperative versus competitive efforts and problem solving. *Review in Educational Research, 65,* 129–144.

Rainforth, B., & York-Barr, J. (1997). *Collaborative teams for students with severe disabilities.* Baltimore: Paul H. Brookes.

Slavin, R. E. (1983). *Cooperative learning.* New York: Longman.

Slavin, R. E. (1990). *Cooperative learning: Theory, research, and practice.* Englewood Cliffs, NJ: Prentice Hall.

Slavin, R. E. (1996). *Education for all: Contexts of learning.* Lisse, France: Swets & Keitlinger.

Sizer, T. (1992). *Horace's school: Redesigning the American high school.* Boston: Houghton-Mifflin.

Snell, M. E. (1990). Schools are for all kids: The importance of integration for students with severe disabilities and their peers. In J. W. Lloyd, N. H. Singh, and A. C. Repp (Eds.), *The regular education initiative: Alternative perspectives on concepts, issues, and models* (pp. 133–148). Sycamore IL: Sycamore.

Snell, M. E., & Brown, F. (2000). *Instruction of students with severe disabilities (6th ed.).* New York: Merrill.

Thousand, J. S., Villa, R. A., & Nevin, A. I. (1994). *Creativity and collaborative learning: A practical guide to empowering students and teachers.* Baltimore: Paul H. Brookes.

U.S. Department of Education (2000). *22nd annual report to Congress on the implementation of the Individuals with Disabilities Education Act.* Washington: DC: U.S. Government Printing Office.

Vandercook, T., York, J., & Forest, M. (1989). The McGill Action Planning System (MAPS): A strategy for building the vision. *Journal of the Association for Persons with Severe Handicaps, 14,* 205–215.

Wagner, M. (1989). *Youth with disabilities during transition: An overview of descriptive findings from the National Longitudinal Transition Study.* Menlo Park, CA: SRI International.

Westling, D. L., & Fox, L. (2001). *Teaching students with severe disabilities (2nd ed.).* New York: Merrill.

Wilcox, B., & Bellamy, G. T. (1987). *A comprehensive guide to the Activities Catalog.* Baltimore: Paul H. Brookes.

Winterling, V., Dunlap, G., & O'Neill, R. E. (1987). The influence of task variation on the aberrant behaviors of autistic students. *Education and Treatment of Children, 10,* 105–119.

Wolery, M., & Schuster, J. W. (1997). Instructional methods with students who have significant disabilities. *Journal of Special Education, 31,* 61–80.

York, J., & Vandercook, T. (1990). Strategies for achieving an integrated education for middle school students with severe disabilities. *Remedial and Special Education, 11,* 6–16.

# 11

# *Secondary Programs*

*Preparation for adulthood and community life is the primary focus of secondary programs for students with severe disabilities.*

## WINDOW 11.1 • *Meet Wendy!*

Wendy is 20 years old and has severe mental retardation. She attends a post-high school program located at the local community college. Last spring, Wendy and the other members of her Individualized Education Program (IEP) team met to discuss her program for her last year of school. Based on that meeting they developed an IEP/Transition plan for her that focused on getting a job in a local pet store, learning how to ride the bus to and from work and the community college, attending art classes at the community college with her friends, going to the community recreation center to go swimming and ice skating with her friends, and assuming more responsibility at home. Wendy and her parents have decided that she will live at home for at least a couple of years after she graduates.

Wendy works at the pet store about three hours a day in the morning. Dave, one of the paraprofessionals from the post-high school program, meets her at a bus stop near the pet store and then they walk to her job. Dave trained her to do her job and now provides support to make sure she gets it done right. Wendy has learned to do the job well enough now that Dave is starting to leave her alone for longer and longer periods of time. Dave expects that soon he will only need to observe Wendy doing her job every other day and hopes to fade his support to just once a week. After work, Wendy and Dave take the bus to the community college. Wendy meets Michelle and Erin for lunch at the student center. Michelle and Erin went to high school with Wendy and are attending the community college too. Michelle is studying to be a graphic artist and Erin wants to be a chef. After lunch, Wendy meets her teacher Connie at her office in the Student Services Building. Wendy and Connie review her performance at work that day and her schedule for tomorrow. Wendy meets her friend Susan at the Student Services Building to go to their Hand Building Ceramics class. After her class, Dave meets Wendy at the bus stop and takes the bus with her to a stop near her house.

Like many of her peers, Wendy is spending her time preparing for her transition to adulthood. Her post-high school program has been focused on developing the employment, personal management, and leisure skills that she will need to work and live in the community. The program is also designed to help Wendy develop friendships and other social relationships that will support her participation in the community. Finally, the program is designed to assist Wendy and her parents to get access to community service programs that will allow Wendy to meet her postschool goals.

---

For most of us, the period between our teens and our mid-twenties is a time of intense preparation for adulthood (Arnett, 2000; Levinson, 1986). We are focused on establishing our own identities, setting long-term goals, learning to make our own decisions and accepting responsibility for our choices, building personal and social relationships, and becoming financially independent from our parents and families. Achieving these outcomes is a cumulative process that is facilitated through the exploration and evaluation of different directions and opportunities. However a number of factors, especially the type and quality of the education that we receive, can have a significant impact on our ultimate success or failure in making this transition.

Adolescents and young adults with severe disabilities face the same challenges in their transition to adulthood as their peers without disabilities. Research has consistently shown that the educational opportunities that secondary-age students receive have a significant impact on their postschool adjustment (Benz, Lindstrom, & Yovanoff, 2000; Blackorby & Wagner, 1996; Phelps & Hanley-Maxwell, 1997; Wehman & Revell, 1997). These findings highlight the importance of middle/junior high school, high school, and post-high school programs in supporting the transition of students with disabilities from school to community life. This chapter examines the role of secondary programs in this process. The history of secondary education for students with severe disabilities over the last three decades and how federal legislation has impacted the evolution of these programs is reviewed. Program practices that are predictive of successful postschool adjustment by students with severe disabilities are outlined. Finally, issues that may impact the effectiveness of secondary programs in the future are discussed.

## The History of Secondary Programs

The passage of the Education of All Handicapped Children Act (EHA) (now known as the Individuals with Disabilities Education Act, IDEA), created the first real opportunities for many adolescents and young adults with severe disabilities to receive comprehensive educational services. Unfortunately, at the time the law was enacted, few models were available to guide the development of programs for this group of students (Wilcox & Bellamy, 1982). In most cases, local education agencies simply extended elementary programs for older students. Instruction was often guided by the student's "developmental age" and focused on teaching basic academic, communication, motor, and self-help skills, rather than the knowledge and skills that he would need to be successful in the community after leaving school (Bellamy, Wilcox, Rose, & McDonnell, 1985). Pressure to address the specific needs of adolescents and young adults with severe disabilities in preparing for adulthood grew as the number of secondary-age students being served by public schools increased during the 1980s (McDonnell, Wilcox, & Boles, 1986). In addition, follow-up studies began to paint a bleak picture of the postschool adjustment of students with disabilities once they entered community life (Hasazi, Gordon, & Roe, 1985; Hasazi, Johnson, Hasazi, & Gordon, 1989; Wagner, 1989; Wehman, Kregel, & Seyfarth, 1985b). It was within this context that the idea of "transition" to work and community life began to emerge as an underlying principle of secondary education for students with disabilities (Halpern, 1985; Hardman & McDonnell, 1987; McDonnell, Hardman, & Hightower, 1989; Wehman, Kregel, & Barcus, 1985; Wilcox, McDonnell, Bellamy, & Rose, 1988).

In 1984, the Office of Special Education and Rehabilitative Services (OSERS) proposed a transition model that was intended to provide a policy framework for improving the postschool employment outcomes of students with disabilities (Will, 1983). The OSERS model emphasized the need to develop formal linkages or "bridges" between high school and post-secondary education programs, employers, vocational rehabilitation agencies, and mental retardation/developmental disabilities agencies to support students' successful transition to community life (Figure 11.1). In the OSERS model, high school programs were responsible for developing the knowledge and skills that students would need to function successfully in the workplace. Adult service agencies for people with disabilities (i.e., state vocational rehabilitation and mental retardation/developmental disabilities agencies) would provide the supports necessary to ensure that individuals were successful in the workplace after school. Students could transition into employment via three different

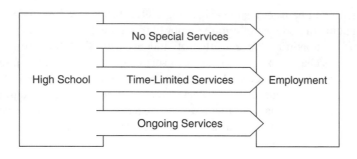

**FIGURE 11.1**  *OSERS Transition Model*

*Source:* Will, M. (1983). *OSERS programming for the transition of youth with disabilities: Bridges from school to working life.* Washington, DC: U.S. Department of Education, Office of Special Education and Rehabilitative Services.

"bridges:" (1) transition to employment with no specialized services, (2) transition to employment with time-limited services, or (3) transition to employment with ongoing services and supports. These alternative bridges were designed to accommodate the diverse needs of students with disabilities. The services provided by school and adult service agencies would be coordinated through a formal transition plan designed to meet the unique needs of each student.

The OSERS model had a significant effect on the design of secondary education for students with disabilities. However, a number of researchers also recognized the need to expand the concept of transition beyond employment, to include other aspects of community life (Halpern, 1985; Wehman, Moon, Everson, Wood, & Barcus, 1988; Wilcox & Bellamy, 1987). These authors believed that a successful adjustment to community life required students not only to be effective employees but to live as independently as possible, to use community resources (i.e., banks, stores, restaurants), and to develop stable and satisfying personal social relationships. This view of transition services provided the basis for over a decade of federal, state, and local reform initiatives designed to improve the effectiveness of secondary programs for students with disabilities (c.f. Rusch & Chadsey, 1998).

> *Focus 1*
> What should be the expected outcomes of secondary programs for students with severe disabilities?

Perhaps the most significant impact of the OSERS transition initiative was how the field of special education defined the expected outcomes of schooling for students with severe disabilities. Traditionally, programs were evaluated in terms of the number of basic academic, communication, motor, and self-help skills that students learned. The transition initiative focused programs instead on promoting students' adjustment to life in the community after school. The concern of students, parents, and educators shifted from "How many skills has the student learned?" to "Is the student (or will the student be) successful in home, work, and community settings after graduation?" For example, in 1994 the Council for Exceptional Children, Division for Career Development and Transition defined the expected outcomes of transition in this way:

> Transition refers to a change in status from behaving primarily as a student to assuming emergent adult roles in the community. These roles include employment, participating in post-secondary education, maintaining a home, becoming appropriately involved in the community, and experiencing satisfactory personal and social relationships. (Halpern, 1994, p. 116)

## *The Influence of Federal Legislation on Secondary Programs*

As discussed in Chapter 3, federal legislation has had a tremendous impact on the rights of people with disabilities in our society and on the range of services and supports that they receive to participate fully in our communities. The current structure and organization of educational programs for adolescents and young adults with severe disabilities are influenced primarily by the Individuals with Disabilities Education Act of 1997 (IDEA '97). However, several other federal laws have been designed to ensure that the transition mandates in IDEA '97 are coordinated at the federal and state levels with other employment programs and the reform of general secondary education. These include the Rehabilitation Act Amendments of 1992 and 1998, the Ticket to Work and Work Incentives Improvement Act of 1999, and the School to Work Opportunities Act of 1994.

---

**Focus 2**
How does IDEA '97 define "transition services"?

---

### *Individuals with Disabilities Education Act*

In 1990, a decade of research and model development efforts culminated with the inclusion of specific amendments in the IDEA (Public Law 101-476) designed to improve postschool outcomes for students with disabilities. Through these amendments, Congress directed state and local educational agencies to provide students with a set of "transition services" designed to promote their successful movement from school to adult life. The transition mandates in the IDEA were further refined in amendments adopted by Congress in 1997. IDEA '97 makes clear that Congress intended for state and local education agencies not only to provide "transition services" to students but to structure those services in ways that increased the likelihood that students would be able to achieve their own postschool goals. Transition services are defined in Section 602 of IDEA '97 as:

> coordinated set of activities for a student with a disability that—
>
> > (A) is designed within an outcome-oriented process, that promotes movement from school to postschool activities, including postsecondary education, vocational

training, integrated employment (including supported employment), continuing
and adult education, adult services, independent living, or community participation;

(B)  is based on the student's needs, taking into account the student's preferences and
interests; and

(C)  includes instruction, related services, community experiences, the development of
employment and other postschool objectives, and, when appropriate, acquisition
of daily living skills and functional vocational evaluation. [Sec. 602, (30)]

It is also evident in IDEA '97 that Congress viewed transition from school to community life as a cumulative process that begins early in a student's educational career and
continues until he or she leaves school. In addition, Congress emphasized the need for
local education agencies to work collaboratively with post-secondary education agencies
and other human service providers to ensure that each student receives access to the training and supports he or she needs to be successful after school. These elements of the transition process are outlined in the sections of IDEA '97 that address the statement of needed
transition services and the development of IEPs:

(vii)  (I)  beginning at age 14, and updated annually, a statement of the transition service
needs of the child…that focuses on the child's course of study (such as participation in advanced-placement courses or a vocational education program);

(II)  beginning at age 16 (or younger, if determined by the IEP Team), a statement of needed transition services for the child, including, when appropriate a statement of the interagency responsibilities or any needed linkages.
[Sec. 614(d)(A)(vii)]

## Vocational Rehabilitation Act Amendments of 1992 and 1998

In 1992, Congress made significant changes to the Vocational Rehabilitation Act (Public
Law 102-569) that enhanced the access of adolescents and young adults with severe disabilities to employment services that would allow them to obtain a paid job. These amendments required that states develop a plan for providing supported employment services to
adults with disabilities (see Chapter 12 for a more detailed description of supported employment programs). The inclusion of supported employment in the act created the first
opportunity for many adults with severe disabilities to get real jobs in the community.
These amendments also emphasized the need for supported employment programs to
obtain jobs for individuals with severe disabilities that reflected their capabilities and interests, paid at least the minimum wage, and created regular and frequent interactions with
co-workers who were not disabled. Finally, the 1992 amendments required that states develop policies that would encourage state and community rehabilitation agencies to be
active partners in the transition of students with disabilities from school to work, including
the provision of rehabilitation service before graduation when appropriate, and the participation of rehabilitation caseworkers in transition planning for individual students.

The 1998 amendments of the Vocational Rehabilitation Act reinforced the significant changes enacted by Congress in 1992 and increase the ability of states and local communities to respond to the unique employment needs of adults with disabilities. These
amendments were included as part of the Workforce Investment Act (WIA) of 1998

(P.L. 105-220). The WIA consolidated a number of federal employment programs and created several block grant programs that gave states and local communities increased flexibility to design systems that met the unique employment training needs of their consumers. A critical aspect of the 1998 amendments to the Rehabilitation Act is the presumption of eligibility for individuals with the most severe disabilities for vocational rehabilitation services. Previously, many of these individuals were excluded from supported employment and other vocational programs because of the severity of their disabilities. The 1998 amendments also require vocational rehabilitation agencies to develop individual programs of employment that will provide adults with severe disabilities with opportunities to obtain a paid job.

## The Ticket to Work and Work Incentives Improvement Act of 1999

The "Ticket to Work" act was intended to remove several of the major barriers to employment for people with disabilities. One of these was the possible loss of Medicaid benefits for people with severe disabilities when they became employed. As discussed in Chapter 3, the Medicaid program provides publically funded health care for a significant number of individuals with severe disabilities. Historically, individuals who received Medicaid benefits lost their health care benefits if they earned too much money. This situation created a significant disincentive to employment for many people with severe disabilities, because the jobs they could get often did not provide health care benefits or did not pay enough to allow them to purchase private medical insurance (Braddock, Hemp, Parish, & Rizzolo, 2000). Thus, many individuals with severe disabilities were forced to choose between their jobs and critical health care benefits. The "Ticket to Work" act took a significant step toward removing this disincentive by providing federal grants to states to provide Medicaid benefits to some individuals with disabilities who went to work. The "Ticket to Work" act also provides grants to states to provide other critical services that have historically been barriers to successful long-term employment for people with severe disabilities, including a lack of supported living and personal assistance programs.

## The School-to-Work Opportunity Act (STWOA) of 1994

The School-to-Work Act is intended to provide all students in the public schools with education and training to prepare them for their first jobs in high-skill, high-wage careers and for further education following high school. The act also seeks to strengthen the linkages between secondary and post-secondary education. Although the STWOA is focused on all students, individuals with disabilities are specifically identified as a target population. The provisions of STOWA are consistent with the transition mandates in IDEA '97 and create opportunities for students with disabilities to access employment training activities provided by school districts to students without disabilities, such as technical preparation programs, career academies, and apprenticeship programs. The act emphasizes the need for schools to examine ways to integrate academic and vocational learning and provide experiences that are tailored to the unique needs of the student.

## Structure of Secondary Programs

Although the administrative organization of secondary programs for students with severe disabilities may vary slightly across school districts, they are usually designed to provide services to students in three distinct age groups. Middle school or junior high school programs typically serve students between the ages of 11 or 12 and 14 or 15 years old. High school programs serve students between the ages of 15 or 16 through age 18. Post-high school programs typically serve students 19 years of age and older. These age levels not only provide convenient administrative divisions for school districts, they also recognize the dramatic differences in the educational and social needs of these three groups of students (Arnett, 2000; Braddock & McPartland, 1993; Clark & Clark, 1994; Levinson, 1986). Table 11.1 summarizes the recommendations of researchers about the expected outcomes of educational programs for students at each of these age levels.

Although the long-term goals of middle/junior high school, high school, and post-high school programs are the same, the content of the educational program at each age level should change in order to gradually build the skills and supports necessary to promote the student's successful adjustment to community life (Halpern, 1994; McDonnell, Mathot-Buckner, & Ferguson, 1996; Wehman, 1996). During the middle school years, emphasis is placed on developing basic skills and social relationships with peers. The educa-

**TABLE 11.1** *Educational Outcomes for Secondary Programs*

| Middle School | High School | Post-High School |
|---|---|---|
| Build basic academic, communication, social, and self-management skills through participation in the general education curriculum. | Build basic academic, communication, social, and self-management skills through participation in the general education curriculum. | Identify employment and living options. |
| Establish performance of age-appropriate leisure and personal management activities through participation in typical school routines. | Explore employment, leisure, and living options available to adults without disabilities through community-based instruction. | Establish performance of employment, leisure, and personal management activities and routines. |
| Promote the development of friendships and other social relationships with peers without disabilities. | Promote the development of friendships and other social relationships with peers without disabilities. | Promote the development of friendships and other social relationships with peers without disabilities. |
| Encourage and support participation in school and community social activities and organizations. | Encourage participation in social activities available through work and other community organizations. | Encourage participation in school and community social activities and organizations. |
| | | Establish linkages with community-based employment, residential, and leisure service agencies. |

tional program should emphasize the development of students' social identities and the skills necessary to establish and maintain friendships. During high school, the emphasis is placed on exploration of adult life and making choices about working and living in the community after school. Students should be provided opportunities to learn about the range of employment and living options available to adults in their community. High school students also must develop the skills necessary to begin to use the resources of the community and to manage the demands of daily living. Finally, post-high school programs should be focused on achieving specific employment and living outcomes for students. These outcomes include obtaining paid employment, developing a cohesive network of friends, and establishing the student's reliable performance of the daily routines that will make up his life in the community after he leaves school.

# Effective Practices

Research over the last decade has identified a number of practices that are associated with the successful postschool adjustment of students with severe disabilities (Benz, Yovanoff, & Doren, 1997; Blackorby & Wagner, 1996; Heal & Rusch, 1995; Phelps & Hanley-Maxwell, 1997; Wehman & Revell, 1997). These practices include (1) inclusive education, (2) curriculum and instruction that is referenced to the demands of adulthood, (3) person-centered transition planning, (4) securing paid employment for students prior to their leaving school, and (5) the development of natural supports.

> ***Focus 3***
> What educational practices are associated with improved postschool outcomes for students with severe disabilities?

## Inclusive Education

Research has shown that educating students with severe disabilities with their peers without disabilities is one of the most important things that secondary programs can do to facilitate their successful transition to community life (McDonnell et al., 1996; Wehman & Revell, 1997). Including students with severe disabilities in general education settings gives them the opportunities to develop the communication and social skills that are necessary to interact successfully with their peers without disabilities (Hunt & Goetz, 1997; Giangreco & Putnam, 1992). In addition, inclusive educational programs create the conditions necessary for students to develop a network of friendships and other social relationships that can support their adjustment to community life. Inclusive educational programs also allow students without disabilities to develop more positive attitudes about people with disabilities, learn how to support persons with disabilities appropriately in school, work, and neighborhood settings, and establish meaningful friendships with people with disabilities (Hunt & Goetz, 1997; Giangreco & Putnam, 1992). Successfully promoting the inclusion of adolescents and young adults with severe disabilities will require that secondary programs serve students in their neighborhood schools (the schools they would attend if they were not disabled), promote the development of friendships between students and their peers without disabilities, and include students in the general education curriculum and general education classes.

***Neighborhood Schools.***    It is frequently recommended that students with severe disabilities be educated in the school they would attend if they were not disabled, as opposed to bussing students to centralized, self-contained programs located on regular school campuses (Lipsky & Gartner, 1997; McDonnell et al., 1996; Snell & Brown, 2000; Westling & Fox, 2000). Neighborhood school models have at least two potential advantages over centralized programs for secondary-age students. First, they allow secondary schools to focus instructional resources on teaching students to complete the activities, and use the community resources, that are available in the neighborhoods or communities in which they live. Instruction can be designed not only to build students' future competence for adult living but also improve the quality of their lives and their participation inclusion in the community while they are in school. Second, and perhaps more important, students are more likely to develop and maintain friendships and other social relationships with peers without disabilities if they have the opportunity to interact with them during *and* after school hours. When students with severe disabilities do not attend their neighborhood schools, the opportunity for their social relationships to extend beyond the walls of the school building are drastically diminished (McDonnell, Hardman, Hightower, & O'Donnell, 1991). This occurs because the students or their friends must often travel considerable distances to see each other. The result is that the student's social network may be intact only from 8:00 a.m. to 3:00 p.m.

---

*Focus 4*
What strategies can teachers use to promote friendships between students with severe disabilities and their peers without disabilities?

---

***Promoting Friendships.***    Secondary programs also should be designed to actively encourage the development of friendships between students and their peers without disabilities. To accomplish this aim, teachers should implement strategies that support students' participation in extracurricular activities sponsored by the school and promote their interactions with peers without disabilities after school hours (Harrower, 1999; Hunt & Goetz, 1997; Staub, Peck, Gallucci, & Schwartz, 2000). An underlying theme of inclusion efforts in secondary programs should be to assist students to learn how to adjust their social behavior and interactions with peers to the various contexts in which they will ultimately be expected to perform as adults.

There are a growing number of strategies available to practitioners to achieve these outcomes for students (Giangreco, 1997, 1998; Snell & Janney, 2000). These include (1) circles of friends that encourage the development of friendships between students with severe disabilities and a small group of peers without disabilities who share common interests, (2) buddy programs that encourage peers without disabilities to provide support to students with severe disabilities in specific situations, such as opening their lockers or getting their wheelchair into an elevator, and (3) peer tutoring programs that are designed to have peers without disabilities provide students with support in learning important skills in school and community settings. These strategies create systematic opportunities for stu-

dents with and without disabilities to interact with one another and promote the development of natural supports necessary for students' participation in the typical school and
community activities.

***Inclusion in General Education Classes.***     Research also suggests that students with
severe disabilities benefit educationally and socially from being included in general education classes and from participating in the general education curriculum (Harrower, 1999;
Hunt & Goetz, 1997). Postschool adjustment to employment also appears to be improved
if students participate in general vocational education classes, especially during the last
two years of high school (Benz et al., 2000; Phelps & Hanley-Maxwell, 1997; Wehman &
Revell, 1997). Although it is clear that there are advantages to placing secondary students
with severe disabilities in content-area classes, it is also clear that the typical curricular and
instructional practices of many secondary teachers are not currently compatible with the
intense and individualized educational needs of this group of students (Darling-Hammond,
1996; Lee, Byrk, & Smith, 1993; McDonnell, 1998; Reynolds, Wang, & Walberg, 1997).
However, a growing number of demonstrations suggest that this situation can be changed
and that secondary teachers will adopt more student-centered approaches to curriculum
and instruction if they are provided adequate training and support (Fisher, Sax, & Pumpian, 1999; Jorgensen, 1998). Some of the most promising practices for supporting the inclusion of students in subject-area classes include (1) layered or differentiated curricula,
(2) cooperative learning, which allows students to participate as part of a heterogeneous
student group in a content-area class (e.g., participating as a member of a "team" in a home
economics class in preparing meals), (3) adapted instruction in which a student works on
different skills within the same content area (e.g., the student learns to type her name, address, and telephone number during a computer class), and (4) embedded instruction designed to allow students to receive instruction on basic skills within the ongoing activities
of the general education class (Harrower, 1999; Hunt & Goetz, 1998; McDonnell, 1998).

## Curriculum and Instruction Referenced to the Demands
## of Adulthood

Educational programs of secondary students with severe disabilities should be designed to
improve the quality of their lives before and after they leave school. To accomplish this goal,
curriculum and instruction should be anchored to the demands of adulthood and community
living, provide instruction in natural performance settings, and promote autonomy and control (Billingsley & Albertson, 1999; Eisenman, 2000; McDonnell et al., 1996; Phelps &
Hanley-Maxwell, 1997; Rosenthal-Malek & Bloom, 1998; Wehman & Revell, 1997).

***Curricula Anchored to the Demands of Adult Living.***     Curriculum for students with
severe disabilities should be designed to ensure that they leave school with the ability to live
as independently as possible in the community. The most widely recommended approach
for achieving these outcomes are activity-based curricula that are referenced to typical
home, school, work, and community environments (McDonnell et al., 1996; Snell &
Brown, 2000; Wehman & Kregel, 1997; Westling & Fox, 2000). These curricula differ from
traditional academic and developmental curricula in several ways. First, the instructional

units in these curricula are "activities" rather than isolated skills. An activity is a chain of behavior that, if performed under natural circumstances, results in a functional outcome for the individual (Wilcox & Bellamy, 1987). The outcome, or effect, is the same whether or not the individual performing the activity is disabled. Examples of activities that occur in community settings include riding the bus to work, shopping for groceries, using an automated teller machine, or going to a movie. Activities can also be defined in ways that they focus on improving students' participation in school settings, such as attending a keyboarding class, using the school store, or participating in assemblies. These curricula also include activities that adults must complete to be successful at home, such as washing dishes, watching a television program, or cooking dinner.

---

*Focus 5*
What are the differences between traditional developmental and academic curricula and activity-based curricula?

---

Second, the overall structures of activity-based curricula reflect typical adult roles. Activities are organized into curriculum domains such as Employment, Leisure/Recreation, Personal Management, Domestic Skills, Community Skills, and Self-Management/Home Living (e.g., Falvey, 1989; Ford et al., 1989; McDonnell et al., 1996; Wehman & Kregel, 1997; Wilcox & Bellamy, 1987). These broad domains are then used as the framework to develop students' Individualized Education Programs (IEPs).

Finally, the activities that are included in the curricula are determined by the specific opportunities available in the communities where students live. The curricula content is based on a "cataloging" of the employment, leisure/recreation, and personal management activities completed by other adults in the community. The intent is to focus students' educational programs on the specific demands they will face once they leave school. An example of an activity-based curriculum structure developed by McDonnell et al. (1994) is presented in Figure 11.2.

***Instruction in Natural Performance Settings.***    Research on the extent to which students with severe disabilities generalize skills learned in schools to home, work, and community settings has raised serious questions about the effectiveness of traditional classroom-based instruction (Horner, McDonnell, & Bellamy, 1986; Rosenthal-Malek & Bloom, 1998). This research has shown that students with severe disabilities have great difficulty applying skills learned in the classroom in the settings where they are actually used. For example, students who learned to count money at school are often unable to count money when they are in stores, restaurants, and theaters. The research also suggests that it is unlikely that students will successfully apply skills under natural performance conditions unless they are directly taught to do so. It seems clear that facilitating the successful transition of students from school to community life will require secondary programs to provide instruction in a variety of home, school, and community environments.

***Autonomy and Control.***    Living and working successfully in the community requires students to regulate and control their own behavior. Consequently, secondary programs

**FIGURE 11.2** *Example of an Activity-Based Curriculum Structure*

| Context: Morning at Home | | |
|---|---|---|
| *Routines* | *Activities* | *Skills* |
| Initiates daily schedule | Gets up on time<br>Toileting<br>Showering/bathing<br>Grooming<br>Dressing<br>Other (See Activities Catalog)<br>_____<br>_____ | Motor<br>Mobility<br>Self-help<br>Social/Communication<br>Self-Management/<br>  Self-Regulation |
| Has Breakfast | Sets table<br>Prepares food<br>Eats<br>Talks with family or roommates<br>Clears dishes<br>Washes dishes<br>Wipes counter<br>Other (Activities Catalog)<br>_____<br>_____ | |
| Completes household chores | Makes bed<br>Empties garbage<br>Feeds pet<br>Prepares lunch<br>Other (Activities Catalog)<br>_____<br>_____ | |

*Source:* McDonnell, J., McDonnell, A., Mathot-Buckner, C., Thorson, N., Berki, P., Hightower, J., & Kiefer-O'Donnell, R. (1994). *The School and Community Integration Program Cross-Age Curriculum for Students with Severe Disabilities.* Salt Lake City, UT: Department of Special Education, University of Utah.

must be designed not only to teach students the work, personal management, and leisure activities necessary to achieve their postschool goals, but also to teach students how to make choices and decisions based on their own preferences, to act upon those choices and decisions, to evaluate the effects of their choices and decisions, and to develop solutions when problems arise. In recent years, these outcomes have been synthesized into a single concept referred to as "self-determination" (Wehmeyer, Agran, & Hughes, 1998). The ultimate goal of teaching self-determination skills is to give students the knowledge and experiences necessary to influence the direction of their lives. In order to achieve these outcomes, self-determination must be an underlying consideration in the design of students' educational programs. The IEP team must actively identify the opportunities that students have to make their own choices and regulate their own behavior, and teachers must develop instructional procedures that will teach students these skills directly within the context of daily activities.

## Person-Centered Transition Planning

Federal law now requires that school districts conduct formal transition planning for all students with disabilities. These planning efforts should be person-centered and focused on achieving students' postschool goals. The development of a formal transition plan is done as part of the Individualized Educational Program (IEP). The transition plan should assist students to: (1) identify clear postschool goals, (2) develop the knowledge and skills that will be necessary to achieve those goals, (3) identify the services and resources that are necessary to support adjustment to community life, and (4) establish linkages with postschool service providers. A sample transition planning format is presented in Figure 11.3.

At a minimum, the IEP/Transition planning team should include the student, parent, teacher, adult services case manager(s) (e.g., vocational rehabilitation, mental retardation/developmental disabilities), and representatives from local community service programs. In addition, the transition planning team may be expanded to include friends, co-workers, or neighbors who provide support to the student in home, school, work, or other community settings. Successful implementation of the transition plan will typically require interagency cooperation to ensure that students access needed support services when they leave school. The transition plan for students with severe disabilities should address all areas of adult living, including friendships and social supports, employment, living arrangements, leisure/recreation activities, ongoing medical support, and transportation.

## Securing Paid Employment

Research suggests that students' transition to employment is enhanced if they receive ongoing community-based job training during high school and obtain a paid job before graduation (Benz et al., 1997; McDonnell et al., 1996; Phelps & Hanley-Maxwell, 1997; Wehman & Revell, 1997). McDonnell et al. (1996) have suggested that these outcomes can be achieved through a differentiated employment curriculum for students that, first, emphasizes sampling a range of job opportunities available in the local community during high school and, then, provides specific training during the last two years of school focused on a job that matches their interests and abilities.

Job sampling begins during high school and is designed to placed students in a number of nonpaid jobs in local businesses and industries. These placements should be structured to (1) expose students to the range of career options available in the local community, (2) train students to complete general work skills (use of tools and equipment, staying ontask, soliciting assistance from supervisors and co-workers, etc.), and (3) provide instruction to students on key work-related skills (transportation and mobility skills, personal hygiene and dressing skills, self-management skills, etc.). Although the development of work and work-related

**FIGURE 11.3**   *Illustrative Transition Planning Form in the Area of Employment*

---

Student: Robert Brown                                                    Date: January 20, 2000

Graduation Date: June, 2001

IEP/Transition Planning Team Members: Robert Brown (student), Mrs. Brown (parent), Jill Green (Teacher), Mike Weatherby (Vocational Education), Dick Rose (Rehabilitation), Susan Marr (MR/DD)

| Transition Planning Area: Employment |
| --- |
| Student Preferences and Desired Postschool Goals: Robert would like to work in a grocery store as a produce stocker. |
| Present Levels of Performance: Robert has held several work experience placements in local grocery stores (See attached work placement summaries). He requires a self-management checklist using symbols to complete assigned work tasks. His rate of task completion is below the expected employer levels. |
| Need Transition Services: Robert will require job placement, training and follow-along services from an employment specialist. In addition, he needs bus training to get to his job. |

| Annual Goal: Robert will work Monday through Friday from 1:00 to 4:00 pm at Smith's Food Center as a produce stocker completing all assigned tasks without assistance from the employment specialist on ten consecutive weekly performance probes. |
| --- |

Short-Term Objectives:

1. When given his bus pass, Robert will independently take the number 5 outbound bus to Smith's Food Center on 5 consecutive daily performance probes.
2. When given his bus pass, Robert will independently take the 11 inbound bus to the Mill Hollow bus stop on 5 consecutive daily performance probes.
3. When given a self-management checklist using symbols, Robert will initiate all assigned tasks without prompts from the employment specialist on 5 consecutive daily performance probes.
4. During break, Robert will purchase a drink and snack from the deli without prompts from the employment specialist on 5 consecutive daily performance probes.

| Related Activities | Person | Completion Date |
| --- | --- | --- |
| 1. Place Robert on the MR/DD supported employment waiting list. | Susan Marr | May 1, 2000 |
| 2. Obtain a monthly bus pass. | Mrs. Brown | February 1, 2000 |
| 3. Schedule Robert for employee orientation training. | | February 15, 2000 |

skills is an important outcome of job sampling, another important purpose is to conduct a comprehensive assessment of students' performance across different types of jobs. The focus is on determining students' strengths and weakness in completing the assigned job tasks and necessary work-related skills, their level of satisfaction with various jobs, and the level of support and assistance that they may need to be successful in the job. Following each employment training placement, teachers summarize students' performance across a number of factors (Figure 11.4). This procedure provides a cumulative record of the student's performance in different types of jobs. This information is used during the IEP/Transition planning meeting to help define students' postschool employment goals and to identify the level of support and assistance that will be necessary for them to achieve these goals.

The second phase of employment preparation is specific job training and placement. The primary outcomes of this phase are to (1) identify a job in the community that matches the students' interests and needs, (2) train students to complete assigned job tasks to employer standards, (3) develop friendships and other social relationships between students and their co-workers, and (4) resolve logistical issues that might interfere with the students' ongoing success in their job. In order to be effective, job training and placement efforts must begin at least two years before students with severe disabilities leave school.

---

**Focus 6**
What are natural supports?

---

**FIGURE 11.4**   *Illustrative Summary Form for a Nonpaid Work Experience Placement*

---

Student:  Robert Brown               Date:  April 22, 1999

Job Site:  Dan's Market              Assigned Tasks:  Stocking shelves and produce bins

Level of support:  Daily monitoring          Placement Period:  January 15, 1999–March 20, 1999
                   and follow-along

1. **Level of task completion:** Robert completed all assignments with 100% accuracy. He maintained 100% accuracy on four consecutive weekly performance probes.
2. **Quality of work:** Robert's average weekly supervisor rating on work quality during the placement period was 4.2 on five point scale (1 = poor; 5 = excellent).
3. **Rate of task completion:** Robert's rate of task completion was below his supervisor's expectations. Robert is occasionally distracted by customers and co-workers. He will require training to increase on-task levels in the next placement.
4. Work related skills and activities:
   (a) Self-management: Robert will use a self-management checklist with symbols independently.
   (b) Transportation: Robert rode the bus to Dan's Market with the employment specialist.
   (c) Social/Interpersonal Skills: Robert is very friendly and appropriate with customers and co-workers.
   (d) Other: Robert requires assistance in planning his break-time activities.

---

### Developing Natural Supports

> The concept of natural supports is based on the understanding that relying on typical people and environments enhances the potential for inclusion more effectively than relying on specialized services and personnel. Though apparently simple, this concept forces a reconceptualization of service delivery models and options and at the same time forces us to disassemble some of our thinking. (Nisbet, 1992, p. 5)

The idea of natural supports has significant implications for how secondary programs go about facilitating the transition of students from school to community life (McDonnell et al., 1996; Wehman & Revell, 1997). Instead of defining students' postschool options based on the specialized service programs that are available in the local community, secondary programs must look first at building relationships between students and other community members that will create the opportunities for them to achieve their postschool goals. It is clear that employment, residential, and other community services programs will play an important role in helping students with severe disabilities to be fully included as adults in the community. However, these service programs should be used to supplement rather than supplant the support that is available to students through their networks of family members and friends.

On paper, the steps of developing natural supports for students' home, school, work, and other community settings are relatively straightforward. They include (1) identifying when students will need assistance or support in activities, (2) identifying individuals within the environments who are able and willing to provide support to students to complete activities, (3) providing information and training to these individuals as necessary in order for them to provide assistance or support to students, and (4) maintaining collaborative relationships with the individuals in order to address students' future needs (Hagner, Butterworth, & Keith, 1995; Hughes & Carter, 2000). The problem is that facilitating the development of natural supports takes a significant amount of time and energy (Hagner et al., 1995; Walker, 1999). This reality highlights the need for secondary programs to incorporate the development of natural supports into the ongoing transition planning and training process.

## Future Directions and Issues

The structure of secondary programs for students with severe disabilities has changed dramatically over the last three decades. The combination of changing societal perspectives about people with disabilities, research, and legislation has improved the ability of secondary programs to prepare students for their transition to adulthood and community life. However, debates about how secondary programs should be designed continue today. Some of the most controversial issues facing the field include the amount of control that adolescents and young adults should have over their educational programs, the full inclusion of students in the general secondary curriculum, and the structure of post-high school programs for students between the ages of 19 and 22.

### Student Control

One of the most controversial amendments of IDEA '97 was the transfer of rights to students when they reached the age of majority [Section 615(10)(m)]. Put simply, Congress gave students control over their educational programs when they legally become adults under state law. Furthermore, all of the rights in IDEA '97 that are given to parents (e.g., informed consent for assessment, eligibility, placement) are transferred to the student under this provision. Congress qualified the statute to exclude students who are determined to be incompetent under state law. In most states, this includes individuals who have moderate to profound mental retardation. However, the determination of incompetence in most states must be established by the courts, and parents or other family can retain control over students' educational programs only if they establish partial or full guardianship of the student. Obviously, this amendment raises a number of critical questions for adolescents and young adults with severe disabilities, their families, and school personnel. For example, how do students and families balance the concepts of empowerment, self-determination, and guardianship within the transition planning process? Should school personnel advocate for students or their families when disagreements arise about postschool goals? What responsibilities do school personnel have to assist students and their families in making these crucial decisions?

There is general agreement that strong parent and professional partnerships will be critical in addressing these issues for students with severe disabilities (Algozzine, O'Shea, & Algozzine, 2001; Berry & Hardman, 1998; Turnbull & Turnbull, 1997). These partnerships must focus on helping students and parents access information in a timely fashion so that they can make informed decisions and on helping students and families access advising and counseling resources that can assist them as they deal with the stresses associated with their changing relationships. However, additional research is needed in order to develop comprehensive models that can help secondary programs grapple with these complex issues.

## Inclusion in the General Secondary Curriculum

During the last two decades, there has been strong support for including students with severe disabilities in general education classes (Giangreco & Putnam, 1992; Hunt & Goetz, 1997; McDonnell et al., 1996; Wilcox & Bellamy, 1982). As a result, the educational programs of many high school students are designed to support their participation in at least some general education classes and community-based instruction on employment, personal management, and leisure activities (Agran, Snow, & Swaner, 1999). This practice is based on research that shows that both inclusion in general education classes and instruction in community settings are strongly associated with improved postschool outcomes for young adults with disabilities (Benz et al., 2000; Blackorby & Wagner, 1996; Phelps & Hanley-Maxwell, 1997). It has generally been recommended that the proportion of time that students spend in general education classes decrease as students get older, and the amount of instruction they receive in community settings should increase, in order to focus their educational programs on specific postschool employment and community living goals (Hughes & Carter, 2000; McDonnell et al., 1996; Wehman & Revell, 1997). It is the responsibility of students, their parents, and the other members of the IEP team to decide what mix of general education classes and community-based instruction is the most appropriate for students as they age.

The 1997 amendments to the IDEA reinforced the need for students with disabilities, including those with severe disabilities, to access the general education curriculum whenever possible. For example, the law requires that each student's IEP include "(ii) a statement of measurable annual goals, including benchmarks or short-term objectives related to—(I) meeting the child's needs that result from the child's disabilities to enable the child to be involved in and progress in the general curriculum" [Sec. 614(d)(1)(A)(ii)]. In addition, the law requires that students with disabilities be included in general state and district-wide assessment programs as appropriate. The language of the IDEA '97 clearly indicates that Congress believed that students with disabilities benefit from participating in the general education curriculum and that they should be held to the same standards as their peers without disabilities whenever possible.

Research on the positive benefits of inclusive education, and the clear preference in the law for students with disabilities to participate in the general education curriculum, has prompted some advocates to call for full inclusion of secondary students with severe disabilities in the general education curriculum (Fisher et al., 2000; Jorgensen, 1998; Tashie, Jorgensen, Shapiro-Barnard, Martin, & Schuh, 1996). They suggest that students with severe disabilities should be included in general education classes throughout the day and that instruction in community settings should occur as part of general education classes for all students or should occur after school hours. Their position is based on the beliefs that students should have equal access to the same content and educational experiences as their peers without disabilities and that instructional practices that separate students from their peers during the school day are inherently exclusionary. For example, Tashie et al. (1996) state that instruction in community settings "erects barriers to full academic and social inclusion, and gives mixed messages to students and communities alike" (p. 20).

Unfortunately, there is no research demonstrating the effect of full inclusion on the postschool adjustment of students with severe disabilities. Based on this, other authors have suggested that there is a need to continue to seek balance between students' inclusion in subject-area classes and instruction in community settings based on their individual needs (Agran et al., 1997; Billingsley & Albertson, 2000; McDonnell, 1997; Wehman & Revell, 1997). In making this recommendation these authors point to the research on the difficulty that students with severe disabilities have in generalizing skills learned in the classroom to natural performance settings and the demonstrated effect of community-based instruction on the postschool adjustment of this group of students. These authors also point out that the proponents of full inclusion ignore the concerns of a growing number of general educators and educational psychologists who have argued that the curriculum and instructional approaches used in most secondary schools is not adequate to prepare students without disabilities to meet the demands of adulthood and community living (Berryman, 1993; Brophy, 1997; Darling-Hammond, 1996; Resnick & Wirt, 1996). Traditional curriculum and instruction approaches have been criticized for emphasizing rote memorization of content rather than requiring students to apply their knowledge and skills in real-life contexts or situations. They suggest that successful employment and citizenship require that students be able to integrate knowledge and skills from many different subject areas, work successfully with peers, and independently manage their own performance. For example, Brophy (1997) argues that instruction should be designed to "emphasize developing student expertise within an application context and with emphasis on conceptual understanding of content and self regulated use of skills" (p. 221). Berryman (1993) characterizes the weaknesses in current instructional practices as the "transfer problem." She observes that "research, extensive and spanning decades, shows that individuals do not *predictably* transfer knowledge in any of three situations where transfer should occur. They do not predictably transfer school knowledge to everyday practice.... They do not predictably transfer everyday practice to school endeavors, even when the former seems clearly relevant to the latter. They do not predictably transfer their learning across school subjects" (pp. 371–372). Brophy's and Berryman's concerns are echoed by curriculum reformers in a number of curriculum areas including science (Schukar, 1997; Yager, 1987), social studies (Alleman & Brophy, 1994; Wade & Saxe, 1996), and vocational education (Hamilton & Hamilton, 1997).

It is clear that there are significant benefits for including adolescents and young adults in the general education curriculum and subject-area classes. However, it is also clear that there are important benefits for providing students with severe disabilities instruction in community settings. At this point, it seems an "either/or" approach to designing students' educational programs is unwise. Additional research is needed to understand the impact of full inclusion in subject-area classes on the postschool adjustment of adolescents and young adult students with severe disabilities.

## The Structure of Post-High School Programs

A significant issue facing the field is the development of appropriate and effective programs for students between the ages of 19 and 22 (Certo, Pumpian, Fisher, Storey, & Smalley, 1997; Kiernan, Schalock, Butterworth, & Mank, 1997; McDonnell, Ferguson, & Mathot-Buckner, 1992; Wehman & Revell, 1997). Typically, young adults with severe disabilities are served on high school campuses. This service delivery pattern prevents students with severe disabilities from accessing age-appropriate educational programs that match their unique needs. Beyond this, serving older students on regular high school campuses creates a number of logistical problems for secondary programs in preparing students' for their transition to work and community life. These include, for example, the incongruence of traditional school schedules with the demands of many entry-level jobs, inflexible staffing patterns, and inadequately trained staff (McDonnell et al., 1992). Another significant barrier is the lack of coordination and collaboration between secondary programs and vocational rehabilitation and mental retardation/developmental disabilities agencies. Under the current service structure, none of these agencies has the resources or capacity to provide all of the services that are necessary to support students' transition from school to community life. One approach to addressing this problem is to develop service delivery models that allow the resources of these three agencies to be pooled to meet the needs of students immediately before and after their transition into the community (Certo et al., 1997; McDonnell et al., 1996). Certo et al. (1997) have suggested that this service integration approach requires these agencies to:

> ...change how business is conducted, negotiating new service roles, resulting in accommodations such as decreased paper work requirements, provision of new services, or expansion of potential providers. For service integration to be effective, each system must assume full responsibility for the complete service outcome, and jointly assist each other to achieve that outcome. (p. 75)

To meet the diverse needs of young adults with disabilities, post-high school programs must be designed to provide students with multiple service options. A number of possible alternatives exist, ranging from community-based employment and residential living programs that are similar to those currently provided to adults with disabilities, to inclusive programs located on community college or university campuses (Certo et al., 1997; McDonnell et al., 1996). Developing new service delivery models for this group of students presents significant policy and technical challenges to the field. However, it is unlikely that substantial progress in improving the effectiveness of secondary programs in meeting the transition needs of students with severe disabilities can occur without addressing this issue.

## Focus Review

Focus 1: What should be the expected outcomes of secondary programs for students with severe disabilities?

- Become productive members of the community.
- Live as independently as possible.
- Use community resources (e.g., banks, stores, restaurants).
- Develop stable and satisfying personal social relationships.

Focus 2: How does IDEA '97 define "transition services"?

- It focuses students' educational programs on achieving specific postschool goals that reflect their needs and interests and includes instruction and other services necessary to achieve their goals.

Focus 3: What educational practices are associated with improved postschool outcomes for students with severe disabilities?

- Inclusive education
- Curriculum that is referenced to the demands of adulthood
- Person-centered transition planning
- Securing paid employment before leaving school
- The development of natural supports

Focus 4: What strategies can teachers use to promote friendships between students with severe disabilities and their peers without disabilities?

- The use of circles of friends, buddy programs, and peer tutoring programs

Focus 5: What are the differences between traditional developmental and academic curricula and activity-based curricula?

- The primary instructional targets are "activities" that reflect typical performance in home, school, work, and community settings. The activities are organized into demands that reflect typical adult performance. The activities included in the curriculum are typically drawn from the community in which students live.

Focus 6: What are natural supports?

- Building a network of family, friends, and other community members to support students' participation in home, school, work, and community activities.

## References

Agran, M., Snow, K., & Swaner, J. (1999). A survey of secondary level teachers' opinion on community-based instruction and inclusive education. *Journal of the Association for Persons with Severe Handicaps, 24,* 58–62.

Algozzine, K., & O'Shea, D. J., & Algozzine, R. (2001). Working with families of adolescents. In D. J. O'Shea, L. R. O'Shea, R. Algozzine, and D. J. Hammitte (Eds.), *Families and teachers of individuals with disabilities: Collaborative orientations and responsive practices* (pp. 179–204). Boston: Allyn & Bacon.

Alleman, J., & Brophy, J. (1994). Taking advantage of out-of-school opportunities for meaningful social students learning. *Social Studies, 85,* 262–267.

Arnett, J. J. (2000). Emerging adulthood: A theory of development from the late teens through the twenties. *American Psychologist, 55,*469–480.

Bellamy, G. T., Wilcox, B., Rose, H., & McDonnell, J. (1985). Education and career preparation for youth with disabilities. *Journal of Adolescent Health Care, 6,* 125–135.

Benz, M. R., Lindstrom, L., & Yovanoff, P. (2000). Improving graduation and employment outcomes of students with disabilities: Predictive factors and student perspectives. *Exceptional Children, 66,* 509–529.

Benz, M. R., Yovanoff, P., & Doren, B. (1997). School-to-work components that predict postschool success for students with and without disabilities. *Exceptional Children, 63,* 151–165.

Berry, J. O., & Hardman, M. L. (1998). *Lifespan perspectives on the family and disability.* Boston: Allyn & Bacon.

Berryman, S. E. (1993). Learning for the workplace. In L. Darling-Hammond (Ed.), *Review of research in education* (pp. 341–404). Washington, DC: American Educational Research Association.

Billingsley, F. F., & Albertson, L. R. (1999). Finding a future for functional skills. *Journal of the Association for Persons with Severe Handicaps, 24,* 298–302.

Blackorby, J., & Wagner, M. (1996). Longitudinal postschool outcomes of youth with disabilities: Findings from the National Longitudinal Transition Study. *Exceptional Children, 62,* 399–413.

Braddock, D., Hemp, R., Parish, S., & Rizzolo, M. C. (2000). *The state of the states in developmental disabilities.* Chicago, IL: Department of Disability and Human Development at the University of Illinois at Chicago.

Braddock, J. H., & McPartland, J. M. (1993). Education of early adolescents. In L. Darling-Hammond (Ed.), *Review of research in education* (pp. 135–170). Washington, DC: American Educational Research Association.

Brophy, J. (1997). Effective teaching. In H. J. Walberg and G. D. Haertel (Eds.), *Psychology and educational practice* (pp. 212–232). Berkeley, CA: McCutchan.

Certo, N., Pumpian, I., Fisher, D., Storey, K., & Smalley, K. (1997). Focusing on the point of transition: A service integration model. *Education and Treatment of Children, 20,* 68–84.

Clark, S. N., & Clark, D. C. (1994). *Restructuring the middle level school: Implications for school leaders.* Albany, NY: State University of New York Press.

Darling-Hammond, L. (1996). The right to learn and the advancement of teaching: Research, policy, and practice for democratic education. *Educational Researcher, 25,* 5–18.

Eisenman, L. T. (2000). Characteristics and effects of integrated academic and occupational curriculum for students with disabilities: A literature review. *Career Development for Exceptional Individuals, 23,* 105–119.

Falvey, M. A. (1989). *Community-based curriculum: Instructional strategies for students with severe handicaps.* Baltimore: Paul H. Brookes.

Fisher, D., Sax, C., & Pumpian, I. (1999). *Inclusive high schools: Learning from contemporary classrooms.* Baltimore: Paul H. Brookes.

Ford, A., Schnorr, R., Meyer, L., Davern, L., Black, J., & Dempsey, P. (1989). *Syracuse community-referenced curriculum guide for students with moderate and severe disabilities.* Baltimore: Paul H. Brookes.

Giangreco, M. F. (1997). *Quick-guides to inclusion: Ideas for education students with disabilities.* Baltimore: Paul H. Brookes.

Giangreco, M. F. (1998). *Quick-guides to inclusion 2: Ideas for education students with disabilities.* Baltimore: Paul H. Brookes.

Giangreco, M. F., & Putnam, J. W. (1992). Supporting the education of students with severe disabilities in regular education environments. In L. H. Meyer, C. A. Peck, & L. Brown (Eds.), *Critical issues in the lives of people with severe disabilities* (pp. 245–270). Baltimore: Paul H. Brookes.

Hagner, D., Butterworth, J., & Keith, G., (1995). Strategies and barriers in facilitating natural supports for employment of adults with severe disabilities. *Journal of the Association for Persons with Severe Handicaps, 20,* 110–120.

Halpern, A. S. (1985). Transition: A look at the foundations. *Exceptional Children, 51,* 479–502.

Halpern. A. S. (1994). The transition of youth with disabilities to adult life: A position statement of the Division on Career Development and Transition, The Council for Exceptional Children. *Career Development of Exceptional Individuals, 17,* 202–211.

Hamilton, S. F., & Hamilton, M. A.(1997). When is learning work-based? *Phi Delta Kappan, 78,* 676–681.

Hardman, M., & McDonnell, J. (1987). Implementing federal transition initiatives for youths with severe handicaps: The Utah Community-Based Transition Project. *Exceptional Children, 52,* 493–499.

Harrower, J. K. (1999). Educational inclusion of children with severe disabilities. *Journal of Positive Behavioral Interventions, 1,* 215–230.

Hasazi, S., Johnson, R. E., Hasazi, J., Gordon, L. R., & Hull, M. (1989). Employment of youth with and without handicaps following school: Outcomes and correlates. *Journal of Special Education, 23,* 243–255.

Hasazi, S. B., Gordon, L. R., & Roe, C. A. (1985). Factors associated with the employment status of handicapped youth exiting high school from 1975 to 1983. *Exceptional Children, 51,* 455–469.

Heal, L. W., & Rusch, F. R. (1995). Predicting employment for students who leave special education high school programs. *Exceptional Children, 61,* 472–487.

Horner, R. H., McDonnell, J. J., & Bellamy, G. T. (1986). Teaching generalized skills: General case instruction in simulation and community settings. In R. H. Horner, L. H. Meyer, and H. D. Fredericks (Eds.), *Education of learners with severe handicaps: Exemplary service strategies* (pp. 289–214). Baltimore: Paul H. Brookes.

Hughes, C., & Carter, E. W. (2000). *The transition handbook: Strategies high school teachers use that work!* Baltimore: Paul H. Brookes.

Hunt, P., & Goetz, L. (1997). Research on inclusive education programs, practices, and outcomes for students with severe disabilities. *Journal of Special Education, 31,* 3–29.

Jorgensen, C. M. (1998). *Restructuring high schools for all students: Taking inclusion to the next level.* Baltimore: Paul H. Brookes.

Kiernan, W. E., Schalock, R. L., Butterworth, J., & Mank, D. (1997). The next steps. In W. E. Kiernan and R. L. Schalock (Eds.), *Integrated employment: Current status and future directions* (pp. 133–144). Washington, DC: American Association on Mental Retardation.

Lee, V. E., Bryk, A. S., & Smith, J. A. (1993). The organization of effective secondary schools. In L. Darling-Hammond (Ed.), *Review of research in education* (pp. 171–268). Washington, DC: American Educational Research Association.

Levinson, D. J. (1986). A conception of adult development. *American Psychologist, 41,* 3–13.

Lipsky, D. K., & Gartner, A. (1997). *Inclusion and school reform: Transforming America's classrooms.* Baltimore: Paul H. Brookes.

McDonnell, J. (1997, February). Participation in content-area classes and community-based instruction in secondary schools: Isn't it about achieving a balance? *TASH Newsletter, 23,* 23–24, 29.

McDonnell, J. (1998). Instruction for students with severe disabilities in general education settings. *Education and Training in Mental Retardation and Developmental Disabilities, 33,* 199–215.

McDonnell, J., Ferguson, B., & Mathot-Buckner, C. (1992). Transition from school to work for students with severe disabilities. In F. R. Rusch, L. Destefano, J. Chadsey-Rusch, L. A. Phelps, and E. Symanski (Eds.), *Transition from school-to-work for youth and adults with disabilities* (pp.33–50). Sycamore, IL: Sycamore.

McDonnell, J., Hardman, M., & Hightower, J. (1989). Employment preparation for high school students with severe handicaps. *Mental Retardation, 27,* 396–404.

McDonnell, J., Hardman, M. L., Hightower, J., & Kiefer-O'Donnell, R. (1991). Variables associated with in-school and after-school integration of secondary students with severe disabilities. *Education and Training in Mental Retardation, 26,* 243–258.

McDonnell, J., Mathot-Buckner, C., & Ferguson, B. (1996). *Transition Programs for Students with Moderate/Severe Disabilities.* Pacific Grove, CA: Brooks/Cole.

McDonnell, J., McDonnell, A., Mathot-Buckner, C., Thorson, N., Berki, P., Hightower, J., & Kiefer-O'Donnell, R. (1994). *The School and Community Integration Program Cross-Age Curriculum for Students with Severe Disabilities.* Salt Lake City, UT: Department of Special Education, University of Utah.

McDonnell, J., Wilcox, B., & Boles, S. M. (1986). Do we know enough to plan for transition? A national survey of state agencies responsible for service to persons with severe handicaps. *Journal of the Association for Persons with Severe Handicaps, 11*(1), 53–60.

Nisbet, J. (1992). *Natural supports in school, at work and in the community for people with severe disabilities.* Baltimore: Paul H. Brookes.

Phelps, L. A., & Hanley-Maxwell, C. (1997). School-to-work transitions for youth with disabilities: A review of outcomes and practices. *Review of Educational Research, 67,* 197–226.

Resnick, L. B., & Wirt, J. G. (1996). *Linking school and work: Roles for standards and assessment.* San Francisco: Jossey-Bass.

Reynolds, M. C., Wang, M. C., & Walberg, H. J. (1997). Categorical programs. In H. J. Walberg and G. D. Haertel (Eds.), *Psychology and educational practice* (pp. 408–429). Berkeley, CA: McCutchan.

Rosenthal-Malek, A., & Bloom, A. (1998). Beyond acquisition: Teaching generalization for students with developmental disabilities. In A. Hilton & R. Ringlaben (Eds.), *Best and promising practices in developmental disabilities* (pp. 139–155). Austin, TX: Pro-Ed.

Rusch, F. R., & Chadsey, J. G. (1998). *Beyond high school: Transition from school to work.* New York: Wadsworth.

Schukar, R. (1997). Enhancing the middle school curriculum through service learning. *Theory into Practice, 36,* 176–183.

Snell, M. E., & Brown, F. (2000). *Instruction of students with severe disabilities* (5th ed.). Upper Saddle River, NJ: Merrill.

Snell, M. E., & Janney, R. (2000). *Social relationships and peer support.* Baltimore: Paul H. Brookes.

Staub, D., Peck, C. A., Gallucci, C., & Schwartz, I. (2000). Peer relationships. In M. E. Snell and F. Brown (Eds.), *Instruction of students with severe disabilities* (5th ed.) (pp. 381–408). Upper Saddle River, NJ: Merrill.

Tashie, C., Jorgensen, C., Shapiro-Barnard, S., Martin, J., & Schuh, M. (1996, February). High school inclusion strategies and barriers. *JASH Newsletter, 22,* 19–22.

Turnbull, A. P., & Turnbull III, H. R. (1997). *Families, professionals, and exceptionality: A special partnership.* Upper Saddle River, NJ: Merrill.

Wade, R. C., Saxe, D. W. (1996). Community service learning in social studies: Historical roots, empirical evidence, and critical issues. *Theory and Research in Social Education, 24,* 331–359.

Wagner, M. (1989). *Youth with disabilities during transition: An overview of descriptive findings from the National Longitudinal Transition Study.* Menlo Park, CA: SRI International.

Walker, P. (1999). From community presence to sense of place: Community experiences of adults with developmental disabilities. *Journal of the Association for Persons with Severe Handicaps, 24,* 23–32.

Wehman, P. (1996). *Life beyond the classroom: Transition strategies for young people with disabilities* (2nd ed.). Baltimore: Paul H. Brookes.

Wehman, P., & Kregel, J. (1997). *Functional curriculum for elementary, middle, and secondary age students with special needs.* Austin, TX: Pro-Ed.

Wehman, P., Kregel, J., & Barcus, J. M. (1985a). From school to work: A vocational transition model for handicapped students. *Exceptional Children, 52,* 25–37.

Wehman, P., Kregel, J., & Seyfarth, J. (1985b). Transition from school to work for individuals with severe handicaps: A follow-up study. *Rehabilitation Counseling Bulletin, 29,* 90–99.

Wehman, P., Moon, M. S., Everson, J. M., Wood, W., & Barcus, J. M. (1988). *Transition from school to work: New challenges for youth with severe disabilities.* Baltimore: Paul H. Brookes.

Wehman, P., & Revell, G. W. (1997). Transition into supported employment for young adults with severe disabilities: Current practices and future directions. *Journal of Vocational Rehabilitation, 8,* 65–74.

Wehmeyer, M. L., Agran, M., & Hughes, C. (1998). *Teaching self-determination to students with disabilities: Basic skills for successful transition.* Baltimore: Paul H. Brookes.

Westling, D. L., & Fox, L. (2000). *Teaching students with severe disabilities* (2nd ed.). Upper Saddle River, NJ: Merrill.

Wilcox, B., & Bellamy, G. T. (1982). *Design of high school programs for severely handicapped students.* Baltimore: Paul H. Brookes.

Wilcox, B., & Bellamy, G. T. (1987). *A comprehensive guide to the Activities Catalog.* Baltimore: Paul H. Brookes.

Wilcox, B., McDonnell, J., Bellamy, G. T., & Rose, H. (1988). Preparing for supported employment: The role of secondary special education. In G. T. Bellamy, L. E. Rhodes, D. M. Mank, & J. M. Albin (Eds.), *Supported employment: A community implementation guide* (pp. 183–208). Baltimore: Paul H. Brookes.

Will, M. (1983). *OSERS programming for the transition of youth with disabilities: Bridges from school to working life.* Washington, DC: U.S. Department of Education, Office of Special Education and Rehabilitative Services.

Yager, R. (1987). Assess all three domains of science. *The Science Teacher, 54,* 33–37.

# 12

## *Employment and Residential Programs for Adults*

*With proper training and support, adults with severe disabilities can successfully work and live in the community.*

## WINDOW 12.1 • *Meet Robyn!*

Robyn is 38 years old and has moderate mental retardation. She has been working in a fast-food restaurant for the last several years. She has become good friends with Beth, who also works at the restaurant. They spend their breaks and lunches together, talking or reading magazines. Three days a week, after work, they go to the community recreation center to exercise or swim.

A local employment service program found Robyn's job for her. The program also provided her with a job coach who helped her to learn to complete her assignments and now checks in with her each week to make sure she is doing okay. Robyn's employer is very happy with her work and has gradually increased the number of jobs that she does and the hours that she works.

Robyn lives with her friend Vivian in an apartment complex close to her job. She and Vivian have divided up the household chores and plan their weekly menus together. Robyn and

Vivian get assistance from a residential service program that hires staff to assist them in paying their bills and managing their money. The staff also assists them in developing a schedule of activities for the week. Initially, the staff helped Robyn and Vivian to complete basic household chores, do their laundry, and prepare meals. Now they are nearly independent in completing these tasks, and the staff simply checks in with them once a day to make sure everything is going well. Robyn and Vivian have hosted several parties at their apartment for their friends from the apartment complex and their jobs.

Robyn also has a boyfriend named Bill. They see each other several times a week. Sometimes they go out and other times they just stay at home and watch television or listen to music. The staff of the residential program have also helped Robyn get involved in a church and participate in activities sponsored by the young women's group.

Most adults with severe disabilities require ongoing support to live successfully in the community. Ideally, most of this support is provided by friends, family, co-workers, and neighbors (Butterworth, Hagner, Kiernan, & Schalock, 1996; Walker, 1999). These sources of support provide the best framework for designing a lifestyle that can meet each individual's needs. However, many people with severe disabilities also require support from community service agencies to obtain meaningful employment and to develop appropriate living options. This chapter examines the roles of employment and residential service programs in supporting persons with severe disabilities in the community.

## History of Employment and Residential Programs

The current system of community-based employment and residential programs evolved over the last several decades because of the downsizing and closure of public institutions for people with disabilities (see Chapter 2). The deinstitutionalization movement sought to create alternative service programs that would allow individuals to live successfully in the mainstream of community life (Nirje, 1969; Wolfensberger, 1972). The result was the development of a "continuum" of employment and residential service programs that are supported by a combination of federal and state funding (Taylor, 1988). The continuum was structured to teach people with disabilities increasingly more complex skills and to move them incrementally toward integrated employment and independent community living. Service programs at the first level in the continuum were designed to serve people with the most significant disabilities. Individuals "graduated" to the next program in the continuum as they learned more skills and became more independent. The continuum is based on the assumption that people will eventually acquire enough skills that they will no longer need support from publically funded programs.

Although the continuum of service has allowed many people with disabilities to move out of institutional settings (Anderson, Lakin, Mangan, & Prouty, 1998), it has been less successful in achieving a quality of life for people with disabilities that is comparable to that of other community members (Braddock, Hemp, Parish, & Rizzolo, 2000; Lakin, 1998; Mank, Cioffi, & Yovanoff, 1998; Wehman, West, & Kregel, 1999). The ineffectiveness of the continuum has prompted advocates, researchers, and policy makers to call for a complete restructuring of the current employment and residential service systems (ARC, 1995; Bradley, Ashbaugh, & Blaney, 1994; Meyer, Peck, & Brown, 1991; Taylor, 1988; Wehman et al., 1999). They believe that, instead of people with severe disabilities having to "earn" their participation in community life by moving through a continuum of services, they should be empowered to develop personalized systems of support that will allow them to control their own lives and achieve their own dreams. Gerry and Mirsky (1992) suggest that future federal and state policies underlying community-based service programs should be driven by five principles:

1. Service programs should be based on the needs and wishes of individuals with disabilities and, as appropriate, their families.
2. Service programs must empower people with disabilities and be flexible enough to reflect their differing and changing needs.
3. Every person with disabilities must have a real opportunity to engage in productive employment.
4. Public and private collaborations must be fostered to ensure that people with disabilities have the opportunities and choices that are to be available to all other Americans.
5. Social inclusion of people with disabilities in their neighborhoods and communities must be a major focus of the overall effort.

## *Structure of Employment Programs*

Meaningful employment is a critical aspect of life for most adults (Syzmanski, Ryan, Merz, Trevino, & Johnson-Rodriguez, 1998). Work is one of the ways that people define themselves in society, generate the resources necessary to control their own lives and support their personal choices, and develop social connections with other community members. The importance of work in shaping the quality of life of people with disabilities is widely acknowledged (Kiernan & Schalock, 1997; Syzmanski & Parker, 1998; Wehman et al., 1999) and has prompted the development of an elaborate system of employment service programs designed to ensure that they can obtain paid employment. As discussed above, the current system of employment programs is based on the concept of a *continuum of services.* This section describes the common employment service programs included in the continuum and their effectiveness in meeting the needs of individuals with severe

**POINT OF INTEREST 12.1** • *What Is the Quality of Life of Adults with Disabilities Living in the Community?*

The 1998 National Organization on Disability (N.O.D.), in cooperation with Louis Harris & Associates, conducted a national survey of adults with disabilities living in the community. The survey found that:

- Only 29 percent of persons with disabilities between 18 and 64 work full- or part-time, compared to 79 percent of people without disabilities. The rate of employment for people with severe disabilities is substantially lower.
- Thirty-four percent of adults with disabilities live in households with total incomes of $15,000 or less, compared to only 12 percent of those without disabilities.
- Only 67 percent of adults with disabilities socialize with close friends, relatives or neighbors at least once a week, compared to 84 percent of people without disabilities.
- Thirty-three percent of adults with disabilities go to a restaurant at least once a week, compared to 60 percent of adults without disabilities.

*Source:* National Organization on Disabilities (1998). *Survey program on participation and attitudes.* Available: www.nod.org/pressurvey.html.

disabilities. In addition, supported employment is discussed as an alternative to traditional employment service programs for this group of people.

## The Continuum of Employment Services

The employment service system for adults with disabilities in most states includes four types of programs: day treatment, work activity centers, sheltered work programs, and transitional employment training programs (Table 12.1). In most communities, these programs are operated by nonprofit organizations created to provide services to adults with disabilities. These nonprofit organizations contract with state agencies (i.e., Rehabilitative Services and/or the MR/DD agency) to provide day treatment and employment services. Frequently, nonprofit agencies are organized to provide all four program alternatives to participants under a single administrative umbrella.

The focus of most day treatment programs is on teaching basic personal care, communication, motor, and academic skills to program participants. Although day treatment programs are considered to be part of the overall community employment service system, they place little emphasis on development of work or work-related skills. These programs do not typically provide significant amounts of paid work to participants.

The primary focus of habilitation efforts in most work activity centers is to provide "therapeutic" activities designed to increase the individual's capacity for employment. Training usually centers on basic developmental skills and prevocational skills. Typically, participants are also provided some paid work. The work that participants complete in most work activity centers is made available through contracts with local businesses and industries. For example, a work activity center may contract with the local Chamber of

**TABLE 12.1** *Continuum of Employment Services*

| Program | Description |
| --- | --- |
| Day treatment | Serves persons with disabilities in a separate facility. Programs focus on developing basic academic and developmental skills. Little emphasis is placed on directly teaching work or work-related skills. |
| Work activity centers | Serves persons with disabilities in a separate facility. Programs focus on "therapeutic" activities designed to increase work capacity. Participants are provided a limited amount of paid work. |
| Sheltered workshops | Serves persons with disabilities in a separate facility. Programs focus on "prerequisite" work and work-related skills necessary for competitive employment. Participants are provided some paid work. |
| Transitional employment training | Serves persons with disabilities in community employment settings. Programs focus on training the participant in a specific set of job skills and placement in a competitive job. The program provides time-limited follow-up once the individual finds a job. |

Commerce to collate and mail its monthly newsletter, or contract with a national airline to place dinnerware, napkins, and salt and pepper in hermetically sealed packages for passengers. These contracts are used as a vehicle to teach skills considered to be important for competitive employment, such as staying on task, basic industrial processes such as assembly and collation, and interaction with co-workers and supervisors.

Sheltered work programs are structured to develop the work and work-related skills necessary for people to obtain a job in community businesses and industries. A second focus of shelter workshop programs is to provide paid work to participants. Typically, the paid work made available to program participants is derived from contracts with local businesses and industries.

Transitional employment training programs are structured to provide work training in community businesses and industries to program participants. Individuals are placed in a community business or industry to learn the skills necessary to obtain a specific type of job. For example, an individual might be placed in a restaurant to learn the skills necessary to become a dish washer. Upon graduation from the program, the agency assists the individual to obtain a dish washing job in another restaurant. Transition employment training programs also provide time-limited follow-along to participants until they have made a successful adjustment to their job. Ultimately, however, support to the participants is eliminated and the individual is expected to work independently.

---

**Focus 1**
What are the primary problems with the traditional continuum of employment services for people with severe disabilities?

Although the continuum of employment services is designed to allow individuals with disabilities to move into competitive employment, research suggests that this outcome is rarely achieved for individuals with severe disabilities. In spite of the significant federal investments in the expansion of integrated employment options for persons with severe disabilities, it has been estimated that there are still between 800,000 and 1 million people who are served in separate day programs nationally (Mank, Buckley, Cioffi, & Dean, 1996; Mank, Cioffi, & Youanoff, 1998; Wehman et al., 1999). Furthermore, research suggests that individuals with severe disabilities are the least likely to gain access to programs that will allow them to obtain employment in integrated community settings (Kregel & Wehman, 1997; McGaughey, Kiernan, McNally, Gilmore, & Keith, 1995). In addition to failing to move people to community employment, these programs have also been ineffective in producing meaningful employment outcomes for program participants. Research suggests that the wages of individuals served in work activity centers and sheltered workshop programs are significantly below the poverty line and provide virtually no opportunities to interact or develop ongoing relationships with persons without disabilities (Wehman et al., 1999).

## *Supported Employment*

The ineffectiveness of the continuum of services led to a number of federal initiatives designed to develop alternative employment programs that would create opportunities for people with severe disabilities to obtain paid jobs in typical businesses and industries (Schalock & Kiernan, 1997). These alternative programs were collectively referred to as supported employment (Bellamy, Rhodes, Mank, & Albin, 1988). The development and implementation of supported employment during the 1980s was provided through two federal laws, the Developmental Disabilities Assistance and Bill of Rights Act of 1984 (P.L. 98-527) and the Rehabilitation Act Amendments of 1986 (P.L. 99-506). The Developmental Disabilities Act described supported employment and directed State Developmental Disability Councils to address supported employment as a priority area through their discretionary grant programs. The Rehabilitation Act Amendments provided the first statutory definition of supported employment programs and provided a funding structure to allow states to establish it as an approved rehabilitation service. The 1986 Rehabilitation Act Amendments defined supported employment as:

> …competitive work in integrated work settings for individuals with the most severe disabilities (i)(I) for whom competitive employment has not traditionally occurred; or (II) for whom competitive employment has been interrupted or intermittent as a result of severe disabilities; and (ii) who because of the nature and severity of their disability, need ongoing support services to preform such work. (29 USC).

The 1994 Rehabilitation Act Amendments clarify the meaning of support employment:

> (34) The term "supported employment services" means ongoing support services and other appropriate services needed to support and maintain an individual with the most severe disability in supported employment, that (a) are provided singly or in combination and are organized and made available in such a way as to assist an eligible individual in entering or

maintaining integrated, competitive employment; (b) are based on a determination of the needs of an eligible individual, as specified in an individualized written rehabilitation program. (706 USC)

---

**Focus 2**
What are the characteristics of supported employment programs?

---

As the federal law suggests, supported employment differs markedly from traditional vocational employment programs for people with disabilities. These programs have four defining characteristics (Hanley-Maxwell, Syzmanski, & Owens-Johnson, 1998; Kiernan & Schalock, 1997; Wehman, West, & Kregel, 1999):

**1.** *Supported employment is paid employment.* Supported employment is intended to be paid employment rather than a training program. Supported employment is focused on obtaining positions for people that provide high wages, job security, job advancement, and acceptance by co-workers without disabilities. This stands in sharp contrast to traditional employment programs for persons with severe disabilities, which emphasize the development of the prerequisite skills assumed to be necessary for competitive employment.

**2.** *Continuous versus time-limited support.* Traditional competitive employment services for persons with disabilities have been structured to provide time-limited support to program participants. In contrast, supported employment acknowledges the ongoing support needs of persons with severe disabilities in the job site. This support may range from monthly telephone contacts with the employer to make sure the person is succeeding to day-to-day supervision on the job site.

**3.** *Inclusive versus segregated service delivery.* A critical feature of supported employment is its emphasis on the inclusion of persons with disabilities in typical businesses and industries. Supported employment assumes that the opportunity to interact with people without disabilities is an important outcome of work. These interactions create opportunities to develop social relationships with peers that will support not only individuals' job performance but also their participation in other aspects of community life.

**4.** *Flexibility.* Supported employment is not a single program; rather it is an assortment of assessment, training, monitoring, and supports strategies that can be used to help people succeed in their jobs. Program providers are encouraged to design services so that they are tailored to unique needs of the individual.

***Types of Supported Employment Programs.*** To date, the most extensively used supported employment programs have been individual supported jobs, enclaves, and work crews (Hanley-Maxwell et al., 1998; Kiernan & Schalock, 1997). Table 12.2 summarizes the primary characteristics of each model.

The individual supported job model is structured to place a single individual with disabilities in a community employment site. The person is provided support in the work setting by an "employment specialist." The specialist usually works for a nonprofit service agency that contracts with state agencies to provide employment services to persons with

**TABLE 12.2** *Features of Three Supported Employment Models*

| Model | Number of Workers with Disabilities | Type of Support |
|---|---|---|
| Individual supported jobs | 1 | An employment specialist provides training and ongoing support. Support is gradually faded across time. The specialist is hired by an employment service program. |
| Enclave | 2–8 | Continuous training and ongoing support is provided by a specialist. The specialist may be hired by the host company. |
| Work crew | 2–8 | Continuous training and ongoing support is provided by a specialist. The specialist is employed by an employment service program. |

disabilities. The responsibility of the support specialist is to assist the individual to identify and obtain an appropriate job, assist the person in learning to do the job successfully, either through direct training or by helping the employer to carry out training activities, monitor the individual's job performance, provide the necessary ongoing supports to ensure that the person continues to perform the job well, and promote the individual's inclusion in the social networks of the workplace (Unger, Parent, Gibson, & Kane-Johnson, 1997).

Enclaves are structured to provide support to a small group of persons with disabilities in a single community employment site. For example, a supported employment program might obtain jobs for several people in a hospital. These individuals might all work in the same area (e.g., the laundry) or in different areas of the hospital (e.g., the laundry, the kitchen, the shipping/receiving department). Program participants would receive training and ongoing support from an employment specialist. Typically, these specialists work for the nonprofit agency providing employment services, but in some cases the host businesses hire their own employment specialists to provide support to employees with disabilities.

Work crews are structured to provide employment opportunities to a small group of persons with disabilities. Unlike enclaves, in which participants work in a single business, crews are designed to procure work contracts with different businesses or individual community members. For example, a work crew might complete landscaping services for businesses or community members in the summer and snow removal services in the winter. Work crew participants also receive training and ongoing support from an employment specialist who supervises the crew. The participants typically work for a nonprofit employment program rather than for the businesses or individuals with whom the work crew has contracts.

***Effectiveness of Supported Employment Programs.*** Research reports have indicated that supported employment allows persons with severe disabilities to work in a wide range of jobs (Morgan, Ellerd, Jensen, & Taylor, 2000), to earn significant wages and other benefits (Mank et al., 1998; Rusch, Heal, & Cimera, 1997), and to develop social relationships with peers without disabilities (Kregel & Wehman, 1997). Research studies comparing the relative effectiveness of supported employment programs and segregated programs have consistently found that supported employment programs produce superior employment outcomes for participants (McGaughey et al., 1995; Reid, Green, & Parsons, 1998; Thompson, Powers, & Houchard, 1992). In addition, supported employment has proven to be as cost-effective as the segregated day treatment and sheltered employment programs currently provided by many states to persons with severe disabilities (Cimera, 1998).

Although individual placements, enclaves, and work crews have been used effectively to support the employment of persons with disabilities, nationally the trend has been toward the use of individual supported jobs (West, Revell, & Wehman, 1992). In 1988, 52 percent of people enrolled in supported employment programs were served through individual supported job models. In 1990 this number had grown to 71 percent. At this point, individual supported jobs appear to offer the best possible outcomes for persons with severe disabilities as well as the flexibility necessary to meet the diverse needs and preferences of this group of people.

---

**Focus 3**
What are some of the current barriers to the full implementation of supported employment for people with severe disabilities?

---

***Barriers to Full Implementation of Supported Employment.***    In spite of its effectiveness, support employment has yet to achieve its full potential for people with severe disabilities (Mank, 1994; Wehman et al., 1999). Supported employment programs were initially designed to provide opportunities for individuals with the most severe disabilities to obtain paid employment in typical businesses and industries (Bellamy, Rhodes, Mank, & Albin, 1998; Rusch, 1990; Wehman, 1981). In addition, the Vocational Rehabilitation Act Amendments of 1994 mandate that the services provided by state rehabilitation agencies must be provided first to individuals with the most severe disabilities. In spite of this, it has been estimated that fewer than 7 percent of the individuals who are enrolled in supported employment programs nationally have severe or profound disabilities (Mank, 1994; Kregel & Wehman, 1997).

A second issue is that supported employment is viewed in many states as an "add-on" program rather than as a replacement to segregated employment service programs for people with severe disabilities (Kiernan, Gilmore, & Butterworth, 1997). For example, McGaughey et al. (1995) found in a national survey of employment program providers that while these agencies were expanding supported employment programs, they were also simultaneously expanding the number of people they served in segregated day treatment and sheltered workshop programs. This trend continues because of conflicting federal and state funding structures, which create significant disincentives for employment service providers to phase out segregated programs in favor of integrated options such as supported employment (West, Johnson, Cone, Hernandez, & Revell, 1998; West, Revell, Kregel, & Bricout, 1999).

Finally, a significant number of individuals with severe disabilities nationally simply cannot access supported employment programs. In fact, the available data suggest that growing numbers of individuals are placed on "waiting lists" for supported employment and other integrated employment programs each year (Braddock et al., 2000; Lakin, 1998;

Wehman & Revell, 1999). Unlike educational service programs that are mandated through a single federal law (i.e., the Individuals with Disabilities Education Act), there is no mandate for supported employment services for people with severe disabilities. Consequently, the expansion of supported employment programs is often subject to the politics underlying state and local budget processes.

It is clear that supported employment programs have the potential to substantially improve the quality of life of many people with severe disabilities. However, achieving the promise of supported employment, and other integrated employment options, will require continued efforts to refine the current employment system. This will require a combination of research designed to improve the quality and cost-effectiveness of supported employment programs, restructuring of the current funding mechanisms to eliminate the disincentives to the expansion of supported employment programs, and the development of federal legislation that will encourage states to phase out segregated service programs.

# Structure of Residential Programs

Residential programs are a critical component of the community service system for adults with severe disabilities. Perhaps no other element of our lives is more important to our feelings of security, happiness, and well-being than our home. The 1970s witnessed a significant increase in the number and types of community-based residential alternatives developed for persons with disabilities. As large institutions began to reduce their populations, states were forced to develop community-based alternatives. These programs ranged from large congregate care facilities to personal care in the individual's home. Like employment programs, the system of residential service programs is also based on the concept of a *continuum of service* (Nisbet, Clark, & Covert, 1991; Taylor, 1988).

Although the types of program alternatives included in the current continuum of residential services are quite diverse, the capacity of these programs to provide living arrangements that approximate the opportunities available to community members without disabilities is questionable. Consumers, researchers, and policy makers have argued that residential programs need to be restructured so that they are sensitive to the needs and preferences of people with severe disabilities (Knoll & Wheeler, 2000; O'Brien, 1994; Racino, Walker, O'Conner, & Taylor, 1993). These alternatives are generally referred to as *supported living programs*. The following sections describe the current continuum of residential services and supported living alternatives.

## The Continuum of Residential Services

The continuum of community-based residential services in most states comprises six program alternatives (Taylor, Biklen, & Knoll, 1987). These are nursing home programs, intermediate care facilities for the mentally retarded (ICF/MRs), group homes, foster care, and supervised apartment programs (Table 12.3).

Nursing home programs are typically focused on long-term medical support and personal care rather than training and support for community living. Taylor et al. (1987) suggest that nursing home programs represent a "transinstitutionalization" of persons with

**TABLE 12.3** *Continuum of Residential Services*

| Program | Description |
| --- | --- |
| Nursing home programs | Congregate care facility designed to provide 24-hour medical care. Little emphasis is placed on providing training that would lead to independent living. |
| Intermediate care facilities for the mentally retarded | Designed to provide 24-hour care to program participants. The size of the facilities varies significantly, from small group homes to large institutions. These programs provide "active treatment" based on an individualized assessment of the participant's habilitative needs. |
| Group homes | Designed to provide habilitative programming that will lead to independent living. The size ranges from small community residences to large congregate care facilities. |
| Foster care | Provides services to individuals in their own home or in the home of another family. These programs provide basic room and board; however, some specialized foster care programs may also provide habilitative programming. |
| Supervised apartments | Designed to provide participants with training that will lead to independent living. Participants live in their own residences. Staff are located nearby to provide necessary training and support. |

disabilities. In other words, individuals are transferred from large public institutions to private institutions. Braddock et al. (2000) estimated that in 1998 over 35,000 people with mental retardation and developmental disabilities were still living in nursing home programs nationally.

Intermediate care facilities for the mentally retarded (ICF/MR) are funded under Title XIX of the Social Security Act (see Chapter 3). ICF/MRs range from small group homes to large private and public institutions. The purpose of the ICF/MR program is to fund residential living and other services for people identified as mentally retarded who need twenty-four-hour care. In order to receive reimbursements under the program, states must provide "active treatment" that includes an individual written plan of care, interdisciplinary evaluations, and an annual review. Braddock et al. (2000) estimated that, in 1998, 44,000 people with mental retardation and developmental disabilities lived in ICF/MR programs nationally. The average annual nationwide cost of serving an individual in publically operated ICF/MRs was $76,115.

Group home programs include both private and public facilities that vary significantly in size. Group homes are typically organized to provide personal care and habilitation programming designed to increase the participant's independence. Most group homes provide training and support in the areas of personal care, maintaining a household, conducting personal business, and leisure/recreational activities.

Foster care providers offer services in their own homes to one or more people with disabilities. The basic support provided to program participants is room, board, and minimal supervision. However, in recent years, some states have developed specialized foster care programs that are designed to provide participants with training and support to promote their independence at home and in the community.

Finally, supervised apartment programs are designed to provide training and support to allow participants to move eventually into their own residence. In these programs, participants share living quarters and program staff members are located nearby. Staff provide support to the participants in carrying out activities of daily living and making decisions regarding their personal finances, assist in transportation, and serve as advocates as necessary.

Braddock et al. (2000) estimated that in 1998 approximately 110,000 people with mental retardation and developmental disabilities lived in group homes across the country. Seventy-three percent of these individuals lived in settings that supported from one to six people. The remainder lived in group homes that supported from seven to fifteen people. During the same year, approximately 26,000 individuals were living in foster care programs and 20,616 were living in apartment programs. Nationally, the average per-person cost of group homes, foster care, and apartment programs serving from one to six people is approximately $40,000 annually. The average per-person cost of large group homes, foster care, and apartment programs serving from seven to fifteen people is over $33,000 annually.

Research has shown clearly that small community-based residential programs produce better outcomes for people with severe disabilities than institutions (Burchard, Hasazi, Gordon, & Roe, 1991; Conroy, 1996; Nisbet et al., 1991; Stancliffe, 1997; Tossebro, 1995). However, the quality of life experienced by persons with severe disabilities in community-based programs can vary significantly (Nisbet et al., 1991). The success or failure of persons with severe disabilities to adjust to community life appears to be affected more by the philosophical orientation and organizational structure of the residential program than the individual's functioning level. Unfortunately, residential programs are often structured to provide a "service" to program participants rather than to create a "home." Consequently, advocates and researchers have recently begun to promote the development of supported living alternatives for persons with severe disabilities.

> *Focus 4*
> What is supported living?

## Supported Living

Many advocates and professionals have embraced the concept of supported living as the basic framework for the design and implementation of residential programs for adults with severe disabilities (Knoll & Wheeler, 2000; Racino & Taylor, 1993; O'Brien, 1994; Walker, 1999). The term *supported living* is used to describe living arrangements that (1) are similar in character and structure to the residential options of persons without disabilities living within a particular community and (2) provide the ongoing support necessary to allow a person with disabilities to be successful in the living option that he or she has selected. Bellamy and Horner (1987) state that: "Supported living is defined as persons with disabilities living where and with whom they want, for as long as they want, with the ongoing support needed to sustain that choice" (p. 506).

Supported living has several critical characteristics that differentiate it from traditional residential programs (Boles, Horner, & Bellamy, 1988; Knoll & Wheeler, 2000; O'Brien, 1994):

1. *An emphasis on living, not programming.* Supported living is not conceptualized as a training program. Rather, it is intended to provide individuals with disabilities the support necessary to allow them to live successfully in the same arrangements as people without disabilities. This may include living with their families, with friends, or on their own. The focus is on supporting the individuals' choices about where and how they want to live rather than preparing for independent living.

2. *Accountability for lifestyle outcomes.* In contrast to traditional residential programs, which emphasize a readiness approach to the design of service support (see Chapter 2), supported living focuses on achieving significant lifestyle outcomes for program participants. Emphasis is placed on the current quality of life of the persons receiving service rather than on some future quality of life implied by skill development. Such lifestyle outcomes include but are not limited to interaction with community members without disabilities, inclusion in the social networks of the neighborhood and community, use of community resources, and empowerment in making lifestyle choices.

3. *Diversity of residential options.* A critical principle of supported living is that people with severe disabilities choose where and how they want to live. Traditionally, the living options available to persons with severe disabilities have been defined by the range of services present in the local community. Supported living is structured to promote personal choice and preference in selecting a living alternative.

4. *Individually determined support.* The level of support required by persons with severe disabilities to live successfully in the community varies significantly. If persons with severe disabilities are going to have real choices, then service programs must be flexible enough to accommodate the unique needs of program participants. Supported living is structured to identify and deliver the level of support necessary to ensure each person's participation in the community throughout his or her lifetime.

5. *Broad technology of residential support.* The notion of supporting a person in his or her residence, as opposed to training for independent living, requires the use of a broad range of technology. Successfully supporting individuals with severe disabilities in their own homes will require the expertise of a number of disciplines, including applied behavior analysis, social work, nutrition, physical and occupational therapy, speech and communication therapy, and medicine. Professionals with knowledge in each of these areas must work as a transdisciplinary team to meet the unique needs of each person.

***Types of Supported Living Alternatives.***    A number of supported living options have been reported in the literature (Boles et al., 1988; Klien, 1992; Nisbet et al., 1991; Taylor et al., 1987). These alternatives include individuals living in their own homes, living in apartments or houses alone or with other persons with disabilities, and living in apartments or houses with other persons without disabilities. Although the settings in which people live are quite diverse, all of these alternatives have several common structural features.

These features include a philosophical assumption that the setting is the person's home rather than a service program, consumer and family involvement in planning and quality assurance, the availability of paid staff necessary to meet the needs of each person within his or her home, and the use of systematic strategies to connect the individual to the social networks of the neighborhood and community.

*Effectiveness of Supported Living.*   Research indicates that supported living can enhance the quality of life of people with disabilities in a number of ways, including promoting interaction with community members, use of community resources, and control over daily activities and lifestyle choices (Knoll & Wheeler, 2000; Nisbet et al., 1991). Comparative studies have found that individuals living in supported living programs have more access to the community, more social interactions, and more opportunities to make their own choices than people who live in traditional group home or apartment programs (Howe, Horner, & Newton, 1998; Newton, Horner, Ard, LeBaron, & Sappington, 1994; Stancliffe, 1997).

The number of people with disabilities living in supported living programs has increased dramatically over the last several years. For example, Braddock et al. (2000) reported that 32,945 people resided in supported living programs nationally in 1993. By 1998 this number had grown to over 82,000 people. This represents nearly a 250 percent increase in the number of people in supported living programs in just five years. Nationally, the average per-person cost of supported living programs in 1998 was $14,396. According to the data reported by Braddock et al. (2000), supported living programs had the lowest per-person costs of all community-based residential options.

*Barriers to Supported Living.*   Although the number of people with disabilities served in supported living programs has increased dramatically in recent years, many individuals who are eligible for these programs simply cannot access them (Braddock et al., 2000; Lakin, 1998). The expansion of supported living programs is hindered by the fact that there is no mandate for states to provide these services to people with severe disabilities, and there is a lack of adequate funding. One of the most difficult problems facing the field is the fact that a significant proportion of the federal and state funds available to pay for services for people with disabilities is still spent on public institutions (Braddock et al., 2000). For example, Braddock et al. (2000) reported that during the 1998 fiscal year the federal government spent 28 percent ($7.1 billion) of the available funds to support approximately 52,000 people living in public institutions. Nationally, the average daily costs of care for each person living in public institutions increased 153 percent between 1977 and 1998.

Clearly, the continued funding of public institutions greatly limits the ability of state and federal agencies to significantly expand supported living options for individuals with severe disabilities. In response, a number of advocacy and professional organizations have called for the elimination of federal support for institutions and the development of a cohesive and flexible system of community-based alternatives (ARC, 1995; Meyer et al., 1982).

## Future Directions

There have been dramatic improvements in employment and residential programs for people with severe disabilities since the 1960s. However, in spite of this progress, these in-

**POINT OF INTEREST 12.2 • *TASH Deinstitutionalization Policy***

The Association for Persons with Severe Handicaps (TASH) believes that a mutual consideration for both quality services and quality of life is necessary, and that this mutual consideration cannot be achieved in environments that segregate persons with disabilities from the community. Thus, TASH calls for the termination of services, activities, and environments that: (1) remove children from their homes and neighborhoods, and citizens from their home communities; (2) require that persons with disabilities live under circumstances that would not be considered acceptable for persons within that same age range were they not disabled, including institutions and large-scale group homes and ICF/MRs; (3) rely exclusively on paid care givers and other professionalized relationships to the detriment of more normalized social support networks, family systems, peer relationships, and friendships; and (4) stigmatize persons with disabilities by portraying them as individuals in need of help, care, and sympathy rather than dignity, respect, mutual companionship, and enjoyment.

*Source:* Meyer, L. H., Peck, C. A., & Brown, L. A. (1991). *Critical issues in the lives of people with severe disabilities.* Baltimore: Paul H. Brookes.

dividuals face a significant number of challenges to achieving full acceptance and participation in community life. Perhaps one of the most significant issues is the level of control that individuals with severe disabilities have over the services and supports they receive from state and federal agencies. A second related problem is the need to develop a technology that can allow program providers to reliably establish the natural supports necessary for people with severe disabilities to live and work in the community. It is likely that these two issues will significantly influence the organization and structure of employment and residential service programs for people with severe disabilities over the next decade.

## *Consumer Control*

Developing employment and residential service programs that will empower people with severe disabilities to make their own choices about their lives is one of the most significant challenges currently facing the field. Although research has repeatedly shown that this group of individuals is capable of working and living in the community with support, the range of options available to them is often limited by the structure and organization of local service providers rather than by their own desires and preferences (Knoll & Wheeler, 2000; Keirnan et al., 1997; Walker, 1999; Wehman et al., 1999). It is becoming increasingly clear that developing responsive service systems will require that individuals be given the power to purchase the services and supports necessary to meet their unique needs.

The use of vouchers or direct cash payments to providers that are controlled by the individual is one of the strategies that has been proposed to accomplish this goal (Kiernan et al., 1997; Knoll & Wheeler, 2000; Wehman, Revell, Kregel & Bricout, 1999). Under this kind of a system, people with disabilities could pick and choose from the array of services options available in the local community or hire people to provide personal supports tailored to their needs. One recent example of this kind of approach is outlined in Public Law

**POINT OF INTEREST 12.3  •  *The ARC's Position on Community Living***

- All people with mental retardation, children and adults, have a right to live in their local community with non-disabled citizens and be fully included;
- All children need a home with a family who provides an atmosphere of love, affection, security and comfort;
- Some adults may choose to stay in their parents' home and the parents may support that choice while other adults may want to have a place of their own, with supports if necessary;
- People with mental retardation should have opportunities to live in homes similar to those individuals without disabilities, including that of owning their own home;
- Supports and services must meet the needs of the individual and be of high quality;

- Funding for supports and services must follow individuals and not be tied to a facility or location;
- All persons with mental retardation have value wherever they live;
- Large congregate facilities (institutions) are no longer necessary or appropriate for anyone, regardless of the type or severity of their disabilities;
- Carefully planned individualized supports and services must be provided during the closing of institutions and the shifting of public funding to the community;
- Families should not be criticized for using institutional placements when this was the only option offered.

*Source:* ARC (1995). *Where people live.* Available: www.thearc.org/posits/reslive.html.

106-170, the Ticket-to-Work and Work Incentives Improvement Act (TWWIIA) of 1999 (see Chapter 3). Over the next several years, the TWWIIA creates a nationwide voucher program that allows beneficiaries of the Social Security Disability Insurance (SSDI) and Supplemental Security Income (SSI) programs to obtain employment, rehabilitation, and other services from providers of their own choice to assist them to get jobs or increase their earnings (Levine, 2000). Although it is too early to assess the full impact of the TWWIIA and other similar legislation, such programs hold promise for people with severe disabilities to increase the control that they have over where they work and where they live.

## Natural Supports

To some extent, all of us rely on others for assistance to succeed in our jobs and to live successfully in the community. This support can range from getting advice from a co-worker on how to complete a job assignment to getting help from your friends to move into a new apartment or house. This simple but powerful idea has been championed in recent years as a key element of employment and residential service programs for people with severe disabilities (Knoll & Wheeler, 2000; Wehman et al., 1999). It has been strongly argued that the primary role of service providers is to assist people to develop and maintain these natural sources of support (Brook, Wehman, Inge, & Parent, 1995; Unger et al., 1997; Walker, 1999). Traditional training and follow-along services are used only when natural supports are not feasible or reliable. For example, an employment specialist might teach a co-worker or supervisor to implement the instructional strategies that would help a colleague with severe disabilities to learn a job assignment (e.g., Lee et at., 1995). Or a residential support specialist might seek out ways to support people with severe disabilities as they participate in neighborhood activities at the recreational center and make connections with neighbors in completing these activities (e.g., Walker, 1999).

Initial research on natural supports suggests that it is an effective and positive strategy for developing the capacity of people with severe disabilities to live and work in the community (Lee, Storey, Anderson, Goetz, & Zivolich, 1997; Mank, Cioffi, & Yovanoff, 1997). Further, individuals with disabilities are more likely to become part of the natural social networks of the workplace and neighborhood when they receive assistance from friends and colleagues rather than from paid support staff (Chadsey & Sheldon, 1998; Walker, 1999). However, additional research is necessary to understand the cultural and social factors that influence the development of natural supports and to validate strategies that service providers can use to help people with severe disabilities develop and maintain these supports (Butterworth et al., 2000).

## *Conclusion*

Employment and residential service programs can play a significant role in enhancing the quality of life of adults with severe disabilities. Technological advancements have created real opportunities for these individuals to become full participants in community life. The challenge currently facing advocates and professionals is to restructure the adult service system so that it is more responsive to the needs and preferences of the people it serves. Supported employment and supported living programs are critical first steps in achieving this goal. In the future, the role of adult service programs must be designed to supplement rather than supplant the natural supports available to persons with severe disabilities from friends, family, co-workers, and neighbors.

## *Focus Review*

Focus 1: What are the primary problems with the traditional continuum of employment services for people with severe disabilities?

- Traditional employment service programs have not promoted paid, inclusive employment for people with severe disabilities.
- Traditional employment service programs have not improved the wages or work skills of people with severe disabilities.

Focus 2: What are the characteristics of supported employment programs?

- Supported employment is paid employment rather than job training.
- Supported employment provides ongoing support as necessary to meet the individual's needs.
- Supported employment recognizes the opportunity to interact with peers without disabilities as a critical outcome of employment.
- Supported employment is flexible; services are tailored around the needs of the individual.

Focus 3: What are some of the current barriers to the full implementation of supported employment for people with severe disabilities?

- Individuals with severe disabilities have not been able to access supported employment programs. Fewer than 7 percent of the people receiving supported employment services nationally have severe or profound disabilities.
- Supported employment is viewed by many state agencies as an "add-on" rather than as an alternative to segregated employment programs. Current federal funding structures prevent states from spending federal dollars on supported employment programs rather than segregated programs.
- Many states have significant waiting lists for supported employment programs.

Focus 4: What is supported living?

- Living arrangements that (1) are similar in character and structure to the residential options of persons without disabilities living within a particular community and (2) provide the ongoing support necessary to allow a person with disabilities to be successful in the living option that he or she has selected.

## *References*

Anderson, L. L., Lakin, K. C., Mangan, T. W., & Prouty, R. W. (1998). State institutions: Thirty years of depopulation and closure. *Mental Retardation, 36,* 431–443.

ARC (1995). *Where people live.* Arlington, TX: Author. Available: http://www.thearc.org/posits/reslive.html.

Bellamy, G. T., Horner, R. H. (1987). Beyond high school: Residential and employment options after graduation. In M. E. Snell (Ed.), *Systematic instruction of persons with severe handicaps* (pp. 491–510). Columbus, OH: Charles E. Merrill.

Bellamy, G. T., Rhodes, L. E., Mank, D. M., & Albin, J. M. (1988). *Supported employment: A community implementation guide.* Baltimore: Paul H. Brookes.

Boles, S., Horner, R. H., & Bellamy, G. T. (1988). Implementing transition: Programs for supported living. In B. L. Ludlow, A. P. Turnbull, & R. Luckason (Eds.), *Transition to adult life for people with mental retardation—Principles and practices* (pp. 85–100). Baltimore: Paul H. Brookes.

Braddock, D., Hemp, R., Parish, S., & Rizzolo, M. C. (2000). *The state of the states in developmental disabilities: 2000 study summary.* Chicago: Department of Disability and Human Development, College of Health and Human Development Sciences, University of Illinois at Chicago.

Bradley, V. J., Ashbaugh, J. W., & Blaney, B. C. (1994). *Creating individual supports for people with developmental disabilities: A mandate for change at many levels.* Baltimore: Paul H. Brookes.

Brooke, V., Wehman, P., Inge, K., & Parent, W. (1995). Toward a consumer-driven approach of supported employment. *Education and Training in Mental Retardation and Developmental Disabilities, 30,* 308–320.

Burchard, S. N., Hasazi, J. E., Gordon, L. R., & Roe, J. (1991). An examination of lifestyle and adjustment in three community residential alternatives. *Research in Developmental Disabilities, 12,* 127–142.

Butterworth, J., Hagner, D., Helm, D. T., & Whelley, T. A. (2000). Workplace culture, social interactions and supports for transition-age young adults. *Mental Retardation, 38,* 342–353.

Butterworth, J., Hagner, D., Kiernan, W., & Schalock, R. (1996). Natural supports in the workplace: Defining an agenda for research and practice. *Journal of the Association for Persons with Severe Handicaps, 21,* 103–113.

Chadsey, J. G., & Shelden, D. (1998). Moving toward social inclusion in employment and postsecondary school settings. In F. R. Rusch & J. G. Chadsey (Eds.), *Beyond high school: Transition from school to work* (pp. 406–438). Belmont, CA: Wadsworth.

Cimera, R. E. (1998). Are individuals with severe mental retardation and multiple disabilities cost-efficient to serve via supported employment programs? *Mental Retardation, 36,* 280–292.

Conroy, J. W. (1996). The small ICF/MR program: Dimensions of quality and cost. *Mental Retardation, 34,*13–26.

Gerry, M. H., & Mirsky, A. J. (1992). Guiding principles for public policy on natural supports. In J. Nisbet (Ed.), *Natural supports in school, at work, and in the community for people with severe disabilities* (pp. 341–346). Baltimore: Paul H. Brookes.

Hanley-Maxwell, C., Syzmanski, E. M., & Owens-Johnson, L. (1998). School-to-adult life transition and supported employment. In R. M. Parker & E. M. Syzmanski (Eds.), *Rehabilitation counseling: Basic and beyond* (pp. 143–180). Austin, TX: Pro-Ed.

Howe, J., Horner, R. H., & Newton, J. S. (1998). Comparison of supported living and traditional residential services in the state of Oregon. *Mental Retardation, 36,* 1–11.

Kiernan, W. E., Gilmore, D., & Butterworth, J. (1997). Provider perspectives and challenges in integrated employment. In W. E. Kiernan & R. L. Schalock (Eds.), *Integrated employment: Current status and future directions* (pp. 17–30). Washington, DC: American Association on Mental Retardation.

Kiernan, W. E., & Schalock, R. L. (1997). *Integrated employment: Current status and future directions.* Washington, DC: American Association on Mental Retardation.

Klien, J. (1992). Get me the hell out of here: Supporting people with disabilities to live in their own homes. In J. Nisbet (Ed.), *Natural supports in school, at work, and in the community for people with severe disabilities* (pp. 277–340). Baltimore: Paul H. Brookes.

Knoll, J. A., & Wheeler, C. B. (2000). My home: Development skills and supports for adult living. In R. W. Flexer, T. J. Simmons, P. Luft, & R. M. Baer (Eds.), *Transition planning for secondary students with disabilities* (pp. 499–540). Upper Saddle River, NJ: Merrill.

Kregel, J., & Wehman, J. (1997). Supported employment: A decade of employment outcomes for individuals with significant disabilities. In W. E. Kiernan & R. L. Schalock (Eds.), *Integrated employment: Current status and future directions* (pp. 31–48). Washington, DC: American Association on Mental Retardation.

Lakin, K. C. (1998). On the outside looking in: Attending to waiting lists in systems of services for people with developmental disabilities. *Mental Retardation, 36,* 157–162.

Lee, M., Storey, K., Anderson, J. L., Goetz, L., & Zivolich, S. (1997). The effect of mentoring versus job coach instruction on integration in supported employment settings. *Journal of the Association for Persons with Severe Disabilities, 22,* 151–158.

Levine, L. (August 15, 2000). *The employment of people with disabilities in the 1990s.* Washington, DC: Congressional Research Service, The Library of Congress.

Mank, D. (1994). The underachievement of supported employment: A call for reinvestment. *Journal of Disability Policy Studies, 5,* 1–24.

Mank, D., Buckley, J., Cioffi, A., & Dean, J. (1996). Do social systems really change? Retrospective interviews with state-supported employment systems-change project directors. *Focus on Autism and Other Developmental Disabilities, 11,* 243–250.

Mank, D., Cioffi, A., & Yovanoff, P. (1997). Patterns of support for employees with severe disabilities. *Mental Retardation, 35,* 433–447.

Mank, D., Cioffi, A., & Yovanoff, P. (1998). Employment outcomes for people with severe disabilities: Opportunities for improvement. *Mental Retardation, 36,* 205–216.

McGaughey, M. J., Kiernan, W. E., McNally, L. C., Gilmore, D. S., & Keith, G. R. (1995). Beyond the workshop: National trends in integrated and segregated day and employment services. *Journal of the Association for Persons with Severe Handicaps, 20,* 270–285.

Meyer, L. H., Peck, C. A., & Brown, L. (1991). *Critical issues in the lives of people with severe disabilities.* Baltimore: Paul H. Brookes.

Morgan, R. L., Ellerd, D. A., Jensen, K., & Taylor, M. J. (2000). A survey of community placements: Where are youth and adults with disabilities working? *Career Development for Exceptional Individuals, 23,* 73–86.

National Organization on Disabilities (1998). *Survey Program on Participation and Attitudes.* Available: www.nod.org/pressurvey.html.

Newton, J. S., Horner, R. H., Ard, W. R., Jr., LeBaron, N., & Sappington, G. (1994). A conceptual model for improving the life of individuals with mental retardation. *Mental Retardation, 32,* 393–402.

Nirje, B. (1969). The normalization principle and its human management implications. In R. Kugel & W. Wolfensberger (Eds.), *Changing patterns in residential services for the mentally retarded* (pp. 231–240). Washington, DC: President's Committee on Mental Retardation.

Nisbet, J., Clark, M., & Covert, S. (1991). Living it up! An analysis of research on community living. In L. H. Meyer, C. A. Peck, & L. Brown (Eds.), *Critical issues in the lives of people with severe disabilities* (pp. 115–144). Baltimore: Paul H. Brookes.

O'Brien, J. (1994). Down stairs that are never your own: Supporting people with developmental disabilities in their own homes. *Mental Retardation, 32,* 1–6.

Racino, J. A., & Taylor, S. J. (1993). "People first": Approaches to housing and support. In J. A. Racino, P. Walker, S. O'Conner, & S. J. Taylor (Eds.), *Housing, support, and community: Choices and strategies for adults with disabilities* (pp. 33–56). Baltimore: Paul H. Brookes.

Racino, J. A., Walker, P., O'Connor, S., & Taylor, S. J. (1993). *Housing, support, and community: Choices and strategies for adults with disabilities.* Baltimore: Paul H. Brookes.

Reid, D. H., Green, C. W., & Parson, M. B. (1998). A comparison of supported work versus center-based program services on selected outcomes for individuals with multiple severe disabilities. *Journal of the Association for Persons with Severe Disabilities, 23,* 69–76,

Rusch, F. R. (1990). *Supported employment: Models, methods, and issues.* Sycamore, IL: Sycamore Publishing Company.

Rusch, F. R., Heal, L. W., & Cimera, R. E. (1997). Predicting the earnings of supported employees with mental retardation: A longitudinal study. *American Journal on Mental Retardation, 101,* 630–644.

Schalock, R. L., & Kiernan, W. E. (1997). How we got to where we are. In W. E. Kiernan & R. L. Schalock (Eds.), *Integrated employment: Current status and future directions* (pp. 5–16). Washington, DC: American Association on Mental Retardation.

Stancliffe, R. J. (1997). Community living-unit size, staff presence, and resident's choice-making. *Mental Retardation, 35,* 1–9.

Syzmanski, E. M., & Parker, R. M. (1998). *Work and disability: Issues and strategies in career development and job placement.* Austin, TX: Pro-Ed.

Syzmanski, E. M., Ryan, C., Merz, M. A., Trevino, B., & Johnston-Rodriguez, S. (1998). Psychosocial and economic aspects of work: Implications for people with disabilities. In E. M. Syzmanski & R. M. Parker (Eds.), *Work and disability: Issues and strategies in career development and job placement* (pp. 9–38). Austin, TX: Pro-Ed.

Taylor, S. J. (1988). Caught in the continuum: A critical analysis of the principle of the least restrictive environment. *Journal of the Association for Persons with Severe Handicaps, 13,* 41–53.

Taylor, S. J., Biklen, D., & Knoll, J. (1987). *Community integration for people with severe disabilities.* Baltimore: Paul H. Brookes.

Thompson, L., Powers, G., & Houchard, B. (1992). The wage effects of supported employment. *Journal of the Association for Persons with Severe Handicaps, 17,* 87–94.

Tossebro, J. (1995). Impact of size revisited: Relation of number of residents to self-determination and deprivation. *American Journal on Mental Retardation, 100,* 59–67.

Unger, D. D., Parent, W. S., Gibson, K. E., Kane-Johnston, K. (1997). Maximizing community and workplace supports: Defining the role of the employment specialist. In P. Wehman & J. Kregel (Eds.), *More than a job: Securing satisfying careers for people with disabilities* (pp. 183–224). Baltimore: Paul H. Brookes.

Walker, P. (1999). From community presence to sense of place: Community experiences of adults with developmental disabilities. *Journal of the Association for Persons with Severe Handicaps, 24,* 23–32.

Wehman, P. (1981). *Competitive employment: New horizons for severely disabled individuals.* Baltimore: Paul H. Brookes.

Wehman, P., West, M., Kregel, J. (1999). Supported employment program development and research needs: Looking ahead to the year 2000. *Education and Training in Mental Retardation and Developmental Disabilities, 34,* 3–19.

West, M., Johnson, A., Cone, A., Hernandez, A., & Revell, G. (1998). Extended employment support: Analysis of implementation and funding issues. *Educational and Training in Mental Retardation and Developmental Disabilities, 1998,* 357–366.

West, M., Revell, G., Kregel, J., & Bricout, J. (1999). The Medicaid Home and Community-Based Waiver and supported employment. *American Journal on Mental Retardation, 104,* 78–87.

West, M., Revell, W. G., & Wehman, P. (1992). Achievement and challenges I: A five-year report on consumer and system outcomes from the Supported Employment initiative. *Journal of the Association for Persons with Severe Handicaps, 17,* 227–235.

Wolfensberger, W. (1972). *Normalization: The principle of normalization in human services.* Washington, DC: National Institute on Mental Retardation.

# 13

## *Programs for Older Adults*

*Advances in medical science have dramatically increased the life spans of individuals with severe disabilities. Supporting people with severe disabilities during retirement has become a significant issue for human service programs.*

## WINDOW 13.1 • *Meet Robert!*

Robert is a 64-year-old man who has moderate mental retardation and is legally blind and deaf. During the last several years he has been having problems with his blood pressure and must eat a restricted diet. Robert works in a sheltered workshop and lives in a group home with six other men, who range in age from 23 to 45.

Robert's mother and father both died recently. He has had problems adjusting to this loss. He would spend holidays at their house, and they would come to visit him at his home once a month or so. He still has contact with two of his brothers who live in another part of the state, but he only sees them once or twice a year. Staff at the workshop and the group home say that he has been depressed but seems to be working through his grief. The staff in the workshop and group home have been trying to keep him involved in lots of activities to keep his spirit up, but they also admit that they aren't really sure how to help him deal with his loss.

Robert still likes to work, but he gets tired easily and needs to take more frequent breaks. Staff at the workshop and group home have discussed the possibility of reducing Robert's work schedule to let him become more involved in other activities or spend more time at home. These agencies recognize that it is probably getting to be time for Robert to retire. They are exploring alternatives such as the community senior center. Unfortunately, the volunteers and professional staff at the senior center have never worked with people with mental retardation before, and they are not sure that they can meet his needs. Although the Developmental Disabilities Act and the Older Americans Act mandate that the state Mental Retardation/Developmental Disabilities Agency and the Area Aging Agencies work together to meet the needs of older adults like Robert, it is unclear at this point who has primary responsibility for providing him services and other supports.

Advances in medical technology and social support have significantly increased the average life span of Americans (U.S. Bureau of the Census, 2000). For example, by the year 2050, the average life expectancy for men will be 75 and for women it will be 81 (U.S. Bureau of Census, 1995). The increased life span of Americans has occurred simultaneously with growth in the proportion of elderly individuals in the general population. The U.S. Bureau of the Census (1995) reported that the number of individuals in our country who are 65 or over has increased by a factor of 11 over the last century. Consequently, the elderly, who comprised only 1 in every 25 Americans in 1900, comprised 1 in 8 in 1994. By 2050, as many as 1 in 5 Americans could be elderly.

The increasing number of elderly persons in our society creates significant demands on the social and health service systems. The U.S. Senate Special Committee on Aging (1991) reported that in 1989 there were approximately 6.9 million elderly individuals who required long-term care. This number is expected to increase to 18 million by the year 2040. The "graying" of American society has focused attention on the needs of aging and elderly people. State and federal governments face significant challenges in developing health and social service programs that can adequately meet the needs of this group of citizens.

Researchers have documented similar demographic trends for persons with disabilities (Janicki, 1996). For example, in 1993 the mean age at death for persons with mental retardation was 66.2 years, up from 18.5 years in the 1930s and 59.1 years in the 1970s. It is projected that there will be approximately 1 million adults with mental retardation and other developmental disabilities over age 60 by 2030 (Heller & Factor, 2001). The growth in the number of older adults in the system is likely to have a significant impact on the structure and organization of the community service system. It is estimated that currently 20 percent or more of the long-term care resources now being consumed by people with developmental disabilities nationally can be attributed to the increases in their life expectancy since 1970 (Braddock, 1999). This chapter examines some of the issues surrounding the development of service programs for older adults with disabilities.

## *Historical Overview of Services for Older Adults*

The first efforts to address the special needs of older adults with mental retardation and other developmental disabilities occurred in 1987, when Congress amended the Developmental Disabilities Act (P.L. 100-146) (see Chapter 3) and the Older Americans Act (P.L. 100-175). The Developmental Disabilities Act amendments focused on the appointment of an administrator of the agency serving elderly people in each state to the Developmental Disabilities Council and required councils to consider aging-related issues in developing their state plans. These amendments also created incentives for training and education for professionals working with persons with disabilities in the areas of gerontology and geriatric services.

> **Focus 1**
> What support programs are mandated under the Older Americans Act for older adults with disabilities?

Congress passed the Older Americans Act in 1965 with the intent to create a national network of services for the aging. This law created the federal Administration on Aging and authorized grants to states to develop Area Agencies on Aging to coordinate community planning and service programs for older adults. These funds were intended to help states to develop social service programs, nutrition programs, and senior centers at the local level. The law also authorized funds for research, model demonstration, and training projects in the field of aging. The 1987 amendments to the Older Americans Act encouraged Area Agencies to design services to ensure that older adults with disabilities had access to the full range of programs available to their peers without disabilities, and to promote their inclusion in the mainstream of society. Congress made additional amendments in the law in 1992, designed to expand the responsibilities of Area Agencies on Aging to include outreach and service delivery to older adults with developmental disabilities and their aging caregivers. States and Area Agencies on Aging are now required to:

- Cooperatively plan, develop, and provide services for older persons with disabilities in conjunction with state and local disabilities agencies
- Provide assistance to aging caregivers to support older adults with disabilities
- Link the long-term care ombudsman program in the Older Americans Act, which is designated to facilitate coordination of aging services in a state, to the advocacy and protection programs authorized under the Developmental Disabilities Act

Despite the intent of these laws, research suggests that cooperation between the Mental Retardation/Developmental Disabilities Agencies and Area Agencies on Aging at the state level is limited (Ansello & Coogle, 2000; Coogle, Ansello, Wood, & Cotter, 1995; Hacker, McCallion, & Janicki, 2000; May & Marozas, 1994; McCallion & Janicki, 1997). For example, May & Marozas (1994) surveyed 221 senior citizen centers in New York State and found that only 14 percent of these agencies indicated that they were serving individuals with disabilities. However, 44 percent of the agencies reported that there was a significant need to develop community services for senior citizens with disabilities.

Although the significant growth in the number of aging and elderly persons with developmental disabilities was projected several decades ago, efforts to develop appropriate service programs for this group of people have not kept pace (Braddock, Hemp, Parish, & Rizzolo, 2000). Because of this, most older adults with disabilities either live with family members or are served in existing employment and residential service programs (Braddock et al., 2000). As a result, the evolution of services for older adults with severe disabilities reflects the changes that have occurred in the community services systems for adults with disabilities. These include (1) a shift from institutional to community-based services, (2) an emphasis on inclusive rather than segregated service programs, (3) an emphasis on developing individualized approaches to supporting people at home, at work, and in the community, and (4) increased consumer control over service programs (see Chapter 12).

Changes in the structure and organization of the community service system over the last several decades have undoubtedly benefitted older adults with severe disabilities. However, several authors have suggested that many employment and residential programs for adults with disabilities are ill-equipped to meet the unique, age-related health and psychological needs of the elderly (Force & O'Malley, 1999; Lavin & Doka, 1999; Udell, 1999). This situation has prompted a number of advocacy groups and researchers to call for the development of service programs that are tailored to the unique needs of older adults with disabilities and are structured to help them cope with the inevitable transitions that occur with aging (see Point of Interest 13.1).

---

*Focus 2*
What factors currently shape the development of service programs for older persons with disabilities?

---

## The Structure of Services for the Aging and Elderly

Although our knowledge about the characteristics and needs of older persons with disabilities is growing, information on how best to organize service programs for this group of people is extremely limited. Discussions about the structure of service programs for older persons with disabilities have focused on two main questions (Blaney, 1994; Janicki & Dalton, 1999; Kultgen, Harlan-Simmons, & Todd, 2000; Mahon & Mactavish, 2000; Palley & Van Hollen, 2000). First, should these programs be designed to serve only people identified as elderly, or should they be designed to provide services for younger persons as well? Second, should programs be designed to meet the needs of persons with disabilities, or should they be designed to serve all elderly individuals? These two factors have driven the develop-

**POINT OF INTEREST 13.1 • *The ARC Position on Aging***

The ARC believes:

- Aging people with mental retardation should be included in their communities.
- Services should be available to all older adults with or without disabilities.

Thus, people with mental retardation who are growing older should:

- be afforded the same rights, dignity, respect and opportunities as other older people in their community;
- receive supports to live, learn, work, play and retire where they prefer, based on their interests and values;
- be provided access to pension plans that include the same provisions for payment and other financial supports as afforded other older citizens who worked and retire;
- be free from discrimination in housing, health care, aging services, transportation, and other services available to older Americans;
- with their families be assisted in planning for the time when family members and friends are no longer able to provide support;
- have access to affordable housing that is barrier-free and enables them to continue to live wherever they may choose.

Further, The ARC believes that as the Older Americans Act and related legislation is periodically amended, the law should include distinct reference to eligibility and inclusion of older adults with mental retardation in all aging network services and activities. Federal and state supports for research into areas of aging among people with mental retardation should also receive vigorous support.

*Source:* The ARC (1997). *Aging.* Available: www.thearc.org/posits/agingpost.html.

---

ment of the existing array of service alternatives currently available for older persons with disabilities (Lavin & Doka, 1999). The matrix presented in Table 13.1 illustrates the interactions between these two factors. As indicated in Table 13.1, there are age-specific and age-general community-based programs, as well as age-specific and age-general institutional programs. Nationally, there are examples of employment, residential, and retirement programs that fit into each cell of the matrix (Davies, Davies, & Sheridan, 2000; Janicki & Dalton, 1999; Lavin & Doka, 1999).

## Age-Segregated or Age-Integrated Programs

A critical decision facing state agencies in the design of service programs for older persons is whether these programs should be age-segregated or age-integrated (Blaney, 1994; Seltzer & Krauss, 1987). The development of age-segregated programs is based on the assumption that the needs of older people with disabilities are quite different from younger individuals. In fact, research suggests that although there are often significant differences in the service needs of older and younger persons with severe disabilities, the needs of older persons with and without disabilities in areas such as later-life planning, dealing with chronic health problems, accessing long-term care, and dealing with death and other personal losses are surprisingly similar (Kapell et al., 1998; Lavin & Doka, 1999; Service, Lavoie, & Herihy, 1999; Smith, Tobin, & Fullmer, 1995). In particular, older adults need

**TABLE 13.1**    *Services for Older Adults with Disabilities*

| Factors | Community-Based | Institutional |
|---|---|---|
| Age-integrated | Persons with disabilities are served with persons who are younger in natural work, home, and community settings. | Persons with disabilities are served with persons who are younger in large congregate care facilities. |
| | Examples: supported employment, supported living | Examples: state institutions, intermediate care facilities for the mentally retarded, group homes, day treatment programs |
| Age-segregated | Persons with disabilities are served with other aging or elderly individuals in natural work, home, and community settings. | Persons with disabilities are served with other aging or elderly individuals in large congregate care facilities. |
| | Examples: generic senior centers, sheltered housing for the elderly, continuum-of-care communities | Examples: Nursing homes |

access to more intense medical support and care. As individuals with disabilities grow older, they are more likely to need immediate access to health facilities and/or ongoing nursing care. In response to this need, some states have developed community-based day and residential programs that include medical support as an integral part of the services provided to participants (Davies et al., 2000; Seltzer & Krauss, 1987). In addition, older persons face a unique set of issues as they age, such as the death of friends and family members, and the frustration and depression associated with the loss of mental and physical abilities. Such events can have a substantial impact on the quality of life experienced by older adults. Service programs must be structured in ways to assist elderly persons with severe disabilities to deal with the emotional and psychological stresses associated with these transitions (Service et al., 1999).

Age-integrated programs are the alternative approach to the provision of service support to older persons with disabilities. Research suggests that there are advantages to designing service programs that allow older persons to be part of age-integrated social networks (Hauber & Short-DeGraff, 1990). The interactions that these individuals have with younger peers are associated with higher levels of satisfaction with quality of life, the development of multidimensional social networks that support participation in the community, enhanced self-concept, and improved self-confidence. Younger individuals also benefit from such relationships by developing a better understanding of the needs of older people. In addition, they may receive guidance in coping with their daily lives through the life experiences of older persons in their social network.

Promoting personal choice has become a critical issue in the development of aging services for people with and without disabilities. Older adults with disabilities must have the same opportunities as their peers without disabilities to choose the type of retirement option that best meets their needs. Ultimately, this choice must be based on personal preferences of the individual, the level of natural support available from their social network, and the service options available within their community (Bigby, 2000; Kultgen et al., 2000; Nisbet, 1992). The opportunity to make such choices will allow older individuals with disabilities to age with dignity (Thurman, 1986).

### Community-Based or Institutional Programs

The majority of elderly people without disabilities prefer retirement options that allow their continued participation in the community and view institutionalization as a dreaded last resort (Ansello, 1988; Blaney, 1994; Kultgen et al., 2000). Improvements in home health care as well as other social support programs (e.g., personal assistance, chore services, meals on wheels) allow an increasing number of elderly people to remain in their own homes. In addition, programs such as housing co-ops, accessory apartments within homes, sheltered housing, and continuum-of-care communities have provided elderly persons with viable alternatives to institutionalization in many states. Increasingly, the aging services network has begun to recognize the need to devise programs that will allow service to be brought to individuals and fitted to their individual needs rather than individuals being brought to the service (Davies et al., 2000). Such service alternatives allow elderly people to maintain critical relationships with families, friends, and neighbors.

This trend in aging services is consistent with the expanding emphasis in the service system on supported education, employment, and living options with disabilities. Although this concept has not been applied extensively to older persons with disabilities, it is consistent with the need to continue to foster the community participation of persons with disabilities across the age range. Given that research has consistently shown that community-based alternatives are superior to institutional programs in promoting personal development and overall quality of life (Conroy & Elks, 1999; Lynch, Kellow, & Willson, 1997; Stancliffe & Abery, 1997), the development of community-based service options for older persons with disabilities is necessary.

---

**Focus 3**
Describe some of the barriers to the development of effective service programs for older persons with disabilities.

---

## Future Directions

Although there is a general consensus about the need to develop appropriate service alternatives for older adults with disabilities, a number of policy, administrative, and financial barriers hinder the development of effective programs (Janicki & Ansello, 2000; Lavin & Doka, 1999; Parkinson & Howard, 1996). Some of these barriers include (1) the absence of a common definition of the term *elderly* for persons with disabilities, (2) a lack of support for aging caregivers of adults with disabilities, (3) limited funding for community service programs for adults with disabilities, (4) a lack of consensus over what constitutes age-appropriate services for older persons with disabilities, and (5) limited coordination between aging and disability service agencies.

## Definition of Elderly for Persons with Disabilities

A significant barrier to addressing the needs of older adults with disabilities is the lack of clarity over who should be considered elderly. Perhaps the most widely accepted standard in determining whether one is "elderly" in our society is chronological age. Most Americans accept age 65 as the universal standard for designating someone as elderly. This standard has emerged primarily because that is when most Americans become eligible for full benefits provided by publically funded retirement, pension, and medical care programs for the elderly. This age standard was selected by Congress when the average life span of most Americans was much shorter. The intent of these programs was to provide support to persons who, because of diminishing health or functioning level, could not realistically support themselves. Recently, political support for increasing the age of eligibility for such services has grown because of the rise in the average life span of Americans and the enormous costs of programs for the elderly.

Most authors have argued that the age standard for determining when a person with disabilities is elderly must be lowered, because they experience declines in functioning level and health much earlier than their peers without disabilities (Janicki & Dalton, 1999; Lifshitz, 1998; Shultz, Aman, & Rojahn, 1998). As a result, support has grown for chronological age standards that identify people with disabilities between 55 and 64 years as "aging" and persons over age 65 as "elderly" (Jacobson, Sutton, & Janicki, 1985; Seltzer & Krauss, 1987). However, these definitions have not been incorporated into legislation that governs the aging or mental retardation/developmental disabilities service systems. The result is that older adults with disabilities who have significant health or psychological needs may not be able to access generic aging services because they are too "young."

## Aging Caregivers and Wait Lists

Nationally, it has been estimated that 60 percent of individuals with mental retardation and developmental disabilities currently live at home (Braddock et al., 2000). Recent analyses also show that as many as 25 percent of these individuals live with care providers who are 60 or older, and that the average age of the family member with a disability is 38 years (Fujiura, 1998). These data suggest that there will be a growing demand in the next decade for residential and other service programs for adults with disabilities whose aging caregivers are no longer able to provide them with support. Meeting the needs of these individuals is likely to be complicated by the significant waiting lists for employment and residential service programs that exist in many states. For example, current estimates suggest that there are as many as 83,000 individuals on formal waiting lists for residential programs across the country (Braddock et al., 2000). The combined effect of these two trends suggests that many mid-aged and older adults with disabilities whose parents or older family members can no longer care for them may not be able to access the services and supports they will need to live successfully in the community. As Braddock et al. (2000) point out:

> The likelihood of older persons with developmental disabilities living into their own retirement and outliving their family caregivers has increased substantially in recent years. This has stimulated a growing demand for additional services and supports. The need to provide these services is frequently unanticipated by federal, state, and local agencies, often result-

ing in a crisis situation for families. It is an unfortunate reality that many family caregivers must die before the disabled relative for whom they are caring can receive services from the publicly-financed system. (pp. 41–42)

It seems clear that addressing this growing need will require a comprehensive examination of the current federal and state funding structures for community service programs for adults with disabilities.

## Age-Appropriate Services

For most people, retirement represents a significant transition in their lives (McPherson, 1990; Thurman, 1986). Time previously allocated to their job or career and raising a family is shifted toward other interests. Like their peers without disabilities, the needs and desires of older people with severe disabilities are extremely diverse and uniquely individual (Browder & Cooper, 1994). This issue is made more complex by the incongruence between the traditional programmatic focus of the aging and developmental disabilities service agencies (Lavin & Doka, 1999) and a lack of systematic later-life planning for older adults (Heller, Miller, Hsieh, & Sterns, 2000; Mahon & Goatcher, 1999). The current set of employment and residential service programs included in the developmental disability system is designed to promote continuous growth of the individual toward independence, whereas the aging system is focused more on maximizing the quality of life of individuals as their skills decline.

Throughout this text we have argued that people with severe disabilities should have the opportunity to achieve certain outcomes, including productivity, independence and autonomy, access to community resources, and participation in a network of friends and acquaintances. We have also stressed that these outcomes remain stable across age levels and service programs. What changes is the way in which personal and service supports are organized to allow each individual to achieve these outcomes. Although much more research is needed, it is clear that service programs must be developed that can address the unique age-related challenges with which older adults with disabilities deal on a day-to-day basis. Without this focus, these individuals are caught in a system that seeks to "habilitate" them rather than let them age with dignity. What is needed is a consensus about the mission and purpose of service programs for this population. Cotten and Spirrison (1986) attempted to articulate the mission of such programs in their Bill of Rights for Elderly Persons with Mental Retardation (Window 13.2). The challenge facing both aging and disability service networks is how to develop program models that ensure these rights are realized and protected.

## Collaboration between Aging and Disability Agencies

As suggested earlier, a significant barrier to meeting the needs of older adults with disabilities is the lack of coordination between those agencies responsible for supporting elderly people in our communities and those agencies responsible for supporting persons with disabilities (Ansello & Coogle, 2000; Hacker et al., 2000; Lavin & Doka, 1999; Parkinson & Howard, 1996). In the current political and economic context, neither the aging nor developmental disability service systems have the resources necessary to meet the needs of

## WINDOW 13.2 • *A Bill of Rights for the Elderly Person with Mental Retardation*

1. The right to an adequate standard of living, economic security, and productive work.
2. The right to humane services designed to help them reach their fullest potential.
3. The right to live as interdependently as they are able in the community of their choice, in as normal a manner as possible.
4. The right to an array of services that is generally available to other elderly groups.
5. The right to choose to retire. In addition, the opportunity to retire "to something," rather than "from something."
6. The right to participate as a member of the community, having reciprocal interdependence.
7. The right to be considered a person and not merely "elderly" or "retarded."
8. The right to protected, personal well-being, and to a qualified guardian when required.
9. The right to be involved in setting one's goals and making one's decisions. The right to fail if necessary.
10. The right to a positive future, and having enough involvement with life to prevent a pre-occupation with death.
11. The right to be romantic, not asexual.
12. The right to sufficient activity and attention to permit continued integrity of self, individual identity, and purpose.
13. The right to an interesting environment and life style, with availability of sufficient mobility to provide a variety of surroundings.
14. The right to live and die with dignity.

*Source:* Cotten, P. D., & Spirrison, C. L. (1986). The elderly mentally retarded developmentally disabled population: A challenge for the service delivery system. In S. J. Brody & B. E. Rugg (Eds.), *Aging and Rehabilitation* (pp. 159–187). New York: Springer.

older adults with disabilities. It is clear that meeting these needs will require high levels of cooperation between these programs at the state and local levels. Parkinson & Howard (1996) suggest that such collaboration is not only desirable but is possible in a number of areas, including the development of cohesive systems of long-term care, access to adequate and affordable health care, employment opportunities for older workers, affordable housing options, ombudsman services for institutionalized older persons, developing adequate income maintenance programs, fostering informal support systems for family, friends, and neighbors, and protective and legal services. However, additional research will be needed to develop and validate service programs that support a collaborative and holistic approach to meeting the unique needs of this group of people.

## Conclusion

Although there is a paucity of research on the nature of service alternatives for aging and elderly persons with disabilities, it does appear that many of these individuals do live successfully in the community. However, the availability of specific age-related service options for older persons is extremely limited. In addition, the use of generic senior service programs to meet some of their support needs appears to be feasible. Several studies have pointed out the critical need to develop service options that will accommodate the diverse needs of older persons with disabilities.

# Focus Review

Focus 1: What support programs are mandated under the Older Americans Act for older adults with disabilities?

- Cooperatively plan, develop, and provide services for older persons with disabilities in conjunction with state and local disabilities agencies
- Target informal aging care givers for assistance in supporting older adults with disabilities
- Link the long-term care ombudsman program in the Older Americans Act, which is designated to facilitate coordination of aging services in a state, to the advocacy and protection programs authorized under the Developmental Disabilities Act

Focus 2: What factors currently shape the development of service programs for older persons with disabilities?

- Programs can be structured as age-segregated or age-integrated. Age-segregated programs have historically been more sensitive to the unique physical and psychological needs of older persons. Age-integrated programs foster the development of heterogeneous social networks that promote a high overall quality of life.
- Programs are provided in either institutional or community settings. Research strongly supports the superiority of community-based service alternatives for older persons with disabilities.

Focus 3: Describe the barriers to the development of effective service programs for older persons with disabilities.

- The absence of a common definition of the term *elderly* for persons with disabilities
- Limited support for aging caregivers of older adults with disabilities
- Limited funding for community service programs for adults with disabilities
- A lack of consensus over what constitutes age-appropriate services for older persons with disabilities
- Limited coordination between aging and disability service agencies

# References

Ansello, E. F. (1988). The intersecting of aging and disabilities. *Educational Gerontology, 14*, 351–364.

Ansello, E. F., & Coogle, C. L. (2000). Building intersystem cooperation: Partners III Integrated Model. In M. P. Janicki & E. F. Ansello (Eds.), *Community supports for aging adults with lifelong disabilities* (pp. 457–476). Baltimore: Paul H. Brookes.

ARC (1997). *Aging.* Available: www.thearc.org/posits/agingpost.html.

Bigby, C. (2000). Informal support networks of older adults. In M. P. Janicki & E. F. Ansello (Eds.), *Community supports for aging adults with lifelong disabilities* (pp. 55–70). Baltimore: Paul H. Brookes.

Blaney, B. C. (1994). Adulthood or oldness: In search of a vision. In V. J. Bradley, J. W. Ashbaugh, & B. C. Blancy (Eds.), *Creating individual supports for people with developmental disabilities: A mandate for change at many levels* (pp. 141–152). Baltimore: Paul H. Brookes.

Braddock, D. (1999). Aging and developmental disabilities: Demographic and policy issues affecting American families. *Mental Retardation, 37,* 155–161.

Braddock, D., Hemp, R., Parish, S., & Rizzolo, M. C. (2000). *The state of the states in developmental disabilities: 2000 study summary.* Chicago: Department of Disability and Human Development, University of Illinois at Chicago.

Browder, D. M., & Cooper, K. J. (1994). Inclusion of older adults with mental retardation in leisure opportunities. *Mental Retardation, 32,* 91–99.

Conroy, J. W., & Elks, M. A. (1999). Tracking qualities of life during deinstitutionalization: A covariance study. *Education and Training in Mental Retardation and Developmental Disabilities, 34,* 212–222.

Coogle, C. L., Ansello, E. F., Wood, J. B., & Cotter, J. J. (1995). Partners II—serving older persons with developmental disabilities: Obstacles and inducements to collaboration among agencies. *Journal of Applied Gerontology, 14,* 275–288.

Cotten, P. D., & Spirrison, C. L. (1986). The elderly mentally retarded developmentally disabled population: A challenge for the service delivery system. In S. J. Brody & B. E. Rugg (Eds.), *Aging and Rehabilitation* (pp. 159–187). New York: Springer.

Davies, D. L., Davies, R. J., & Sheridan, P. (2000). Housing and living supports: An asset management challenge. In M. P. Janicki & E. F. Ansello (Eds.), *Community supports for aging adults with lifelong disabilities* (pp. 257–270). Baltimore: Paul H. Brookes.

Force, L. T., & O'Malley, M. (1999). Adult day services. In M. P. Janicki and A. J. Dalton (Eds.), *Dementia, aging, and intellectual disabilities* (pp. 294–315). Philadelphia: Brunner/Mazel.

Fujiura, G. T. (1998). Demography of family households. *American Journal on Mental Retardation, 103,* 225–235.

Hacker, K. S., McCallion, P., & Janicki, M. P. (2000). Outreach and assistance using area agencies on aging. In M. P. Janicki & E. F. Ansello (Eds.), *Community supports for aging adults with lifelong disabilities* (pp. 439–456). Baltimore: Paul H. Brookes.

Hauber, E. A., & Short-DeGraff, M. A. (1990). Intergenerational programing for an increasingly age-segregated society. *Activities, Adaptation, and Aging, 14,* 35–49.

Heller, T., & Factor, A. (2001). *Older adults with mental retardation and their aging family caregivers.* Available: www.uic.edu/orgs/rrtcamr/OlderAdults.html.

Heller, T., Miller, A. B., Hsieh, K., & Sterns, H. (2000). Later-life planning: Promoting knowledge of op-

tions and choice making. *Mental Retardation, 38,* 395–406.

Jacobsen, J. W., Sutton, M. S., & Janicki, M. P. (1985). Demography and characteristics of aging and aged mentally retarded persons. In M. P. Janicki & Wisniewski (Eds.), *Aging and developmental disabilities: Issues and approaches* (pp. 115–142). Baltimore: Paul H. Brookes.

Janicki, M. P. (1996). Longevity increasing among older adults with intellectual disability. *Aging, Health, and Society, 2,* 2.

Janicki, M. P., & Ansello, E. F. (2000). Supports for community living: Evolution of an aging with lifelong disabilities movement. In M. P. Janicki & E. F. Ansello (Eds.), *Community supports for aging adults with lifelong disabilities* (pp. 529–548). Baltimore: Paul H. Brookes.

Janicki, M. P., & Dalton, A. J. (1999). *Dementia, aging, and intellectual disabilities: A handbook.* Philadelphia: Brunner/Mazel.

Kapell, D., Nightingale, B., Rodriquez, A., Lee, J. H., Zigman, W. B., & Schupf, N. (1998). Prevalence of chronic mental conditions in adults with mental retardation: Comparison with the general population. *Mental Retardation, 36,* 269–279.

Kultgen, P., Harlan-Simmons, J. E., & Todd, J. (2000). Community membership. In M. P. Janicki, & E. F. Ansello (Eds.), *Community supports of aging adults with lifelong disabilities* (pp. 153–166). Baltimore: Paul H. Brookes.

Lavin, C., & Doka, K. J. (1999). *Older adults with developmental disabilities.* Amityville, NY: Baywood.

Lifshitz, H. (1998). Instrumental enrichment: A tool for enhancement of cognitive ability in adult and elderly people with mental retardation. *Education and Training in Mental Retardation and Developmental Disabilities, 33,* 34–41.

Lynch, P. S., Kellow, T., & Willson, V. L. (1997). The impact of deinstitutionalization on the adaptive behavior of adults with mental retardation: A meta-analysis. *Education and Training in Mental Retardation and Developmental Disabilities, 32,* 255–261.

Mahon, M. J., & Goatcher, S. (1999). Later-life planning for older adults with mental retardation: A field experiment. *Mental Retardation, 37,* 371–382.

Mahon, M. J., & Mactavish, J. B. (2000). A sense of belonging: Older adults' perspectives on social integration. In M. P. Janicki & E. F. Ansello (Eds.), *Community supports for aging adults with lifelong disabilities* (pp. 41–54). Baltimore: Paul H. Brookes.

May, D. C., & Marozas, D. S. (1994). Are elderly people with mental retardation being included in community senior citizen centers? *Education and Train-*

ing in *Mental Retardation and Developmental Disabilities, 29,* 229–235.

McCallion, P., & Janicki, M. P. (1997). Area agencies on aging: Meeting the needs of persons with developmental disabilities and their aging families. *Journal of Applied Gerontology, 16,* 270–284.

McPherson, B. D. (1990). *Aging as a social process: An introduction to individual and population aging* (2nd ed.). Toronto: Butterworths.

Nisbet, J. (1992). *Natural supports in school, at work, and in the community for people with severe disabilities,* Baltimore: Paul H. Brookes.

Palley, H. A., & Van Hollen, V. (2000). Long-term care for people with disabilities: A critical analysis. *Health & Social Work, 25,* 181–189.

Parkinson, C. B., & Howard, M. (1996). Older persons with mental retardation/developmental disabilities. *Journal of Gerontological Social Work, 25,* 91–103.

Seltzer, M. M., & Krauss, M. W. (1987). *Aging and mental retardation: extending the continuum.* Washington, DC: American Association on Mental Retardation.

Service, K. P., Lavoie, D., & Herlihy, J. E. (1999). Coping with losses, death, and grieving. In M. P. Janicki & A. J. Dalton (Eds.), *Dementia, aging, and intellectual disabilities* (pp. 330–358). Philadelphia: Brunner/Mazel.

Shultz, J. M., Aman, M. G., & Rojahn, J. (1998). Psychometric evaluation of a measure of cognitive decline in elderly people with mental retardation. *Research in Developmental Disabilities, 19,* 63–71.

Smith, G. C., Tobin, S. S., & Fullmer, E. M. (1995). Elderly mothers caring at home for offspring with mental retardation: A model of permanency planning. *American Journal on Mental Retardation, 99,* 487–499.

Stancliffe, R. J., & Abery, B. H. (1997). Longitudinal study of deinstitutionalization and the exercise of choice. *Mental Retardation, 35,* 159–169.

Thurman, E. (1986). Maintaining dignity in later years. In J. A. Summers (Ed.), *The right to grow up: An introduction to adults with developmental disabilities* (pp. 91–118). Baltimore: Paul H. Brookes.

Udell, L. (1999). Supports in small group home settings. In M. P. Janicki and A. J. Dalton (Eds.), *Dementia, aging, and intellectual disabilities* (pp. 316–329). Philadelphia: Brunner/Mazel.

U.S. Bureau of the Census (1995). *Statistical brief: Sixty-five plus in the United States.* Washington, DC: Economics and Statistics Administration, U.S. Department of Commerce.

U.S. Bureau of the Census (2000). *Aging in the United States—Past, present, and future.* Washington, DC: Economic and Statistics Administration, U.S. Department of Commerce.

U.S. Senate Special Committee on Aging, American Association of Retired Persons, Federal Council on the Aging, and U.S. Administration on Aging (1991). *Aging American: Trends and projections.* Washington, DC: Author.

# Author Index

# Subject Index